Lecture Notes in Artificial Intelligence 13405

Subseries of Lecture Notes in Computer Science

More information about this subseries at https://link.springer.com/bookseries/1244

Mark T. Keane · Nirmalie Wiratunga (Eds.)

Case-Based Reasoning Research and Development

30th International Conference, ICCBR 2022 Nancy, France, September 12–15, 2022 Proceedings

Editors
Mark T. Keane
University College Dublin
Dublin, Ireland

Nirmalie Wiratunga
The Robert Gordon University
Aberdeen, UK

ISSN 0302-9743 ISSN 1611-3349 (electronic)
Lecture Notes in Artificial Intelligence
ISBN 978-3-031-14922-1 ISBN 978-3-031-14923-8 (eBook)
https://doi.org/10.1007/978-3-031-14923-8

LNCS Sublibrary: SL7 – Artificial Intelligence

This Springer imprint is published by the registered company Springer Nature Switzerland AG
The registered company address is: Gewerbestrasse 11, 6330 Cham, Switzerland

Preface

This volume contains the papers presented at the 30th International Conference on Case-Based Reasoning (ICCBR 2022), which was held during September 12–15, 2022, at LORIA in Nancy, France. ICCBR is the premier annual meeting of the Case-Based Reasoning (CBR) research community. The theme of ICCBR 2022 was "Global Challenges for CBR", aiming to consider how CBR can and might contribute to challenges in sustainability, climate change, and global health. Specifically, we posed the question "What can CBR do to meet these challenges?", encouraging submissions from our invited speakers, researchers, policy makers, or practitioners in the CBR community that are tackling these global challenges.

Previous ICCBRs, including the merged European Workshops and Conferences on CBR, were as follows: Otzenhausen, Germany (1993); Chantilly, France (1994); Sesimbra, Portugal (1995); Lausanne, Switzerland (1996); Providence, USA (1997); Dublin, Ireland (1998); Seeon Monastery, Germany (1999); Trento, Italy (2000); Vancouver, Canada (2001); Aberdeen, UK (2002); Trondheim, Norway (2003); Madrid, Spain (2004); Chicago, USA (2005); Fethiye, Turkey (2006); Belfast, UK (2007); Trier, Germany (2008); Seattle, USA (2009); Alessandria, Italy (2010); Greenwich, UK (2011); Lyon, France (2012); Saratoga Springs, USA (2013); Cork, Ireland (2014); Frankfurt, Germany (2015); Atlanta, USA (2016); Trondheim, Norway (2017); Stockholm, Sweden (2018); Otzenhausen, Germany (2019); Salamanca, Spain (2020); and Salamanca, Spain (2021).

Notably, this year's conference marked the 30th anniversary of CBR conferences, since the First European Workshop on Case-Based Reasoning (EWCBR-93) held in Otzenhausen, Germany. Indeed, by an odd bookending coincidence, one of the current Chairs (MK) was also an invited speaker at this very first conference in 1993.

Of course, 2020 and 2021 were exceptionally difficult and shocking years due to the COVID-19 pandemic, and during both of these years the conference was held virtually. Sadly, after two attempts, the community did not get to actually meet in Spain in the end. The Program Chairs (Ian Watson and Rosina Weber in 2020; Antonio Sánchez-Ruiz and Micheal Floyd in 2021) and Local Organizers (Juan Manuel Corchado and Fernando de al Prieta) for both of these conferences deserve our heartfelt thanks, for keeping the flame burning during these two difficult years. So, it was with great relief that the community returned to a face-to-face conference in 2022.

ICCBR 2022 received 68 submissions from authors in 15 countries, spanning Europe, North America, and Asia. Most papers were reviewed by three Program Committee members, with tied decisions being resolved by additional reviewing. Of the 68 submissions, 16 (23%) were selected for oral presentations, with a further 10 (15%) being accepted as posters.

The pre-events for ICCBR 2022 began on Sunday, September 11 with an enlightening visit to the "École de Nancy" museum. After this visit, there was the first meeting of participants in the Doctoral Consortium (DC), who met their mentors for the first time and prepared for their upcoming presentations. The DC is designed to provide opportunities for PhD students to share and obtain feedback on their research and career objectives with senior CBR researchers and peers. In the evening, the conference attendees had a meal together and viewed a sound and light show in the Place Stanislas. The pre-conference events continued on Monday, September 12 with the Doctoral Consortium proper and several Workshops covering breaking topics in CBR. These events gave rise to lively presentations and discussions on key current advances in CBR.

The first full day of the conference kicked off, on Tuesday, September 13, 2022 with an invited talk from Prof Xiaohong Gao of Middlesex University London (UK) on explainable AI for medical image applications, addressing the global challenges in health. This invited talk was followed by the first two technical sessions on "Explainability in CBR" and "Representation & Similarity", after which the poster session began with a Poster Gong Show of rapid two-minute presentations followed by poster-board discussions involving all the attendees.

The second day kicked off with more technical sessions on "Applications" and "CBR & ML", with the second invited talk after lunch being given on explainable AI by Prof Cynthia Rudin of Duke University (USA), the 2022 recipient of the AAAI's Squirrel AI Award for Artificial Intelligence for the Benefit of Humanity. This wonderful presentation was followed by a trip to the historic centre of Nancy and the Gala Dinner.

The third and final day of the conference began with the last invited talk from Prof Sutanu Chakraborti of the Indian Institute of Technology Madras (India) on more cognitively appealing paradigms for CBR. This talk was followed by the final technical session on "Graphs & Optimisation", before a community meeting and lunch. The Local Chairs – Emmanuel Nauer and Nicolas Lasolle – along with the highly efficient Local Organizing Committee were roundly thanked for their efforts in staging the conference, as were the Chairs of the Doctoral Consortium (Kerstin Bach and Stelios Kapetanakis), Workshop (Pascal Reuss and Jakob Schoenborn) and Poster (Jean Lieber) Tracks whose contributions were lauded.

As Program Chairs we relied heavily on the Advisory Committee for advice and a wise sounding board for many of the key decisions we had to make: our thanks to Belén Díaz-Agudo, David W. Aha, Isabelle Bichindaritz, David Leake, Mirjam Minor, Barry Smyth, and Rosina Weber. We would also like to thank the Program Committee and additional reviewers for handling the large reviewing load, and their thoughtful assessments of the submissions and willingness to help.

Lastly, we would like to mark and dedicate this year's conference to Prof Cynthia Marling, who passed away on September 7, 2021 in San Diego (USA). Cindy was a Program Co-chair for ICCBR 2019, she was a passionate advocate for the CBR community and a welcoming mentor to early-stage researchers in the area. We will all miss her this year. May she rest in peace.

September 2022

Mark T. Keane
Nirmalie Wiratunga

Organization

Program Chairs

Mark T. Keane	University College Dublin, Ireland
Nirmalie Wiratunga	The Robert Gordon University, UK

Local Chairs

Emmanuel Nauer	Université de Lorraine, LORIA, France
Nicolas Lasolle	Université de Lorraine, LORIA, France

Workshop Chairs

Pascal Reuss	University of Hildesheim, Germany
Jakob Schoenborn	University of Hildesheim, Germany

Doctoral Consortium Chairs

Stelios Kapetanakis	University of Brighton, UK
Kersten Bach	Norwegian University of Science and Technology, Norway

Poster Chair

Jean Lieber	Université de Lorraine, LORIA, France

Advisory Committee

Belén Díaz Agudo	Complutense University of Madrid, Spain
David Aha	Naval Research Laboratory, USA
Isabelle Bichindaritz	State University of New York at Oswego, USA
David Leake	Indiana University, USA
Mirjam Minor	Goethe University Frankfurt, Germany
Barry Smyth	University College Dublin, Ireland
Rosina Weber	Drexel University, USA

Program Committee

Klaus-Dieter Althoff	DFKI/University of Hildesheim, Germany
Kerstin Bach	Norwegian University of Science and Technology, Norway
Ralph Bergmann	University of Trier, Germany
Hayley Borck	SIFT, USA
Derek Bridge	University College Cork, Ireland
Sutanu Chakraborti	Indian Institute of Technology Madras, India
Alexandra Coman	Capital One, USA
Sarah Jane Delany	Technological University Dublin, Ireland
Viktor Eisenstadt	University of Hildesheim, Germany
Michael Floyd	Knexus Research, USA
Ashok Goel	Georgia Institute of Technology, USA
Odd Erik Gundersen	Norwegian University of Science and Technology, Norway
Stelios Kapetanakis	University of Brighton, UK
Joseph Kendall-Morwick	Missouri Western State University, USA
Luc Lamontagne	Laval University, Canada
Jean Lieber	Université de Lorraine, LORIA, France
Stewart Massie	The Robert Gordon University, UK
Stefania Montani	Universitá del Piemonte Orientale, Italy
Santiago Ontañón	Drexel University, USA
Enric Plaza	IIIA-CSIC, Spain
Luigi Portinale	Università del Piemonte Orientale, Italy
Juan A. Recio-Garcia	Universidad Complutense de Madrid, Spain
Antonio A. Sánchez-Ruiz	Universidad Complutense de Madrid, Spain
Frode Sørmo	Amazon, UK
Anjana Wijekoon	The Robert Gordon University, UK
David Wilson	University of North Carolina at Charlotte, USA

Local Committee

Marie Baron	Université de Lorraine, France
Nathalie Bussy	CNRS, France
Mariana Diaz	CNRS, France
Nathalie Fritz	Université de Lorraine, France
Delphine Hubert	Université de Lorraine, France
Jennifer Masoni	CNRS, France
David Maze	Inria, France
Anne-Marie Messaoudi	Université de Lorraine, France
Agnès Vidard	Inria, France
Lydie Weiss	Inria, France

Additional Reviewers

Bayrak, Betül
Delaney, Eoin
Erduran, Ömer Ibrahim
Goel, Prateek
Hoffmann, Maximilian
Johs, Adam
Malburg, Lukas
Marin Veites, Paola
Martin, Kyle
Mathew, Ditty
Mauri, Marcel
Miclet, Laurent
Murena, Pierre-Alexandre
Nkisi-Orji, Ikechukwu
P., Deepak
Parsodkar, Adwait
Wen, Ximing
Zeyen, Christian

Invited Talks

Seeing Through Black Boxes with Human Vision: Deep Learning and Explainable AI in Medical Image Applications

Xiaohong Gao

Middlesex University, London, UK

Abstract. Artificial Intelligence (AI), particularly deep learning technology, has impacted the world significantly over the last 10 years, from personal smart phone apps to driverless cars, benefiting society immensely. Whilst AI continues to improve the quality of human life, its opaque nature has cast doubt upon its acceptance in the medical domain due to deeper layers associated with unsupervised unknown learning. This presentation will review the current state-of-the-art progress in deep learning techniques towards developing transparent, robust and performant systems with case studies carried out in my research group. These studies include the application of methodologies of case-based reasoning (CBR), vision attention model (vision transformer) and colour appearance model (CIECAM) in medical image applications such as 3D brain CT images for detection of Alzheimer's disease, ultrasonic video images for heart diseases and COVID-19 x-ray images. The presentation will also demonstrate our recent progress in early detection of oesophageal cancers from gastrointestinal endoscopy videos. In this case, it will be seen how AI could tackle the challenge of the difficulty in human vision and perception in identifying inconspicuous changes of skin appearance in the presence of artefacts during real-time clinical situations while patients are undergoing endoscopic observation. Evaluation in a clinical setting will be discussed, leading to increasing clinicians' confidence in AI and facilitating adoption.

Case-Based Reasoning for Clinical Decisions That Are Computer-Aided, Not Automated

Cynthia Rudin

Duke University, Durham, NC, USA

Abstract. Let us consider a difficult computer vision challenge. Would you want an algorithm to determine whether you should get a biopsy, based on an x-ray? That's usually a decision made by a radiologist, based on years of training. We know that algorithms haven't worked perfectly for a multitude of other computer vision applications, and biopsy decisions are harder than just about any other application of computer vision that we typically consider. The interesting question is whether it is possible that an algorithm could be a true partner to a physician, rather than making the decision on its own. To do this, at the very least, we would need an interpretable neural network that is as accurate as its black box counterparts. In this talk, I will discuss a case-based reasoning approach to interpretable neural networks, where parts of images are compared to other parts of prototypical images for each class. This technique is strictly better than saliency maps, because it shows more than where the network is looking; it also shows how it reasons, based on past cases. Papers focussed on:

References

1. Chen, C., Li, O., Tao, D., Barnett, A., Rudin, C., Su, J.K.: This looks like that: deep learning for interpretable image recognition. Adv. Neural Inform. Process. Syst. **32** (2019)
2. Barnett, A.J., et al.: A case-based interpretable deep learning model for classification of mass lesions in digital mammography. Nature Mach. Intell. **3**(12), 1061–1070 (2021)
3. Kim, B., Rudin, C. and Shah, J.A.: The Bayesian case model: A generative approach for case-based reasoning and prototype classification. Adv. Neural Inf. Process. Syst. **27** (2014). [on tabular rather than image data]

Towards More Cognitively Appealing Paradigms in Case-Based Reasoning

Sutanu Chakraborti

Indian Institute of Technology Madras, Chennai, India

Abstract. While the roots of case-based reasoning (CBR) can be traced to models of human experiential problem solving as outlined in the theory of Dynamic Memory proposed by Roger Schank, CBR as applied in practice has often strayed from its cognitive foundations. This talk attempts to make a case for revisiting the cognitive roots of CBR. In particular, we present a novel biologically inspired paradigm called Holographic CBR that allows cases to proactively interact with other cases in the course of problem solving and maintenance. We show how top-down and bottom-up approaches can be flexibly integrated, cases can be generalized in the course of failure driven reminding, and knowledge can be distributed across local containers in each case. We also explore connections of this work to the seminal work "Thinking, Fast and Slow" by Daniel Kahneman and its implications in the context of CBR. Though the Holographic paradigm was explored in the CBR context, we believe it has the potential to impact other areas in Artificial Intelligence as well.

Contents

Explainability in CBR

Using Case-Based Reasoning for Capturing Expert Knowledge on Explanation Methods

Jesus M. Darias, Marta Caro-Martínez(✉), Belén Díaz-Agudo, and Juan A. Recio-Garcia

Department of Software Engineering and Artificial Intelligence, Instituto de Tecnologías del Conocimiento, Universidad Complutense de Madrid, Madrid, Spain
{jdarias,martcaro,belend,jareciog}@ucm.es

Abstract. Model-agnostic methods in eXplainable Artificial Intelligence (XAI) propose isolating the explanation system from the AI model architecture, typically Machine Learning or black-box models. Existing XAI libraries offer a good number of explanation methods, that are reusable for different domains and models, with different choices of parameters. However, it is not clear what would be a good explainer for a given situation, domain, AI model, and user preferences. The choice of a proper explanation method is a complex decision-making process itself. In this paper, we propose applying Case-Based Reasoning (CBR) to support this task by capturing the user preferences about explanation results into a case base. Then, we define the corresponding CBR process to help retrieve a suitable explainer from a catalogue made of existing XAI libraries. Our hypothesis is that CBR helps the task of learning from the explanation experiences and will help to retrieve explainers for other similar scenarios.

Keywords: XAI · Model agnostic models · Explanation experiences

1 Introduction

Increasing understanding has become a requirement to trust in AI models applied to real-world tasks. Some ML models are considered intrinsically interpretable due to their simple structure, such as short decision trees, simple nearest neighbors, or sparse linear models. However, there is typically a black box nature and a lack of transparency associated with the best-performing models. This issue has triggered a new huge body of work on Explainable Artificial Intelligence (XAI), a research field that holds substantial promise for improving trust and transparency of AI-ML-based systems [11,13,22]. Methods for machine learning (ML) interpretability can be classified according to various criteria. Model-specific explanations are limited to specific model classes while model-agnostic methods can be used on any ML model and are applied after the model has been

M. T. Keane and N. Wiratunga (Eds.): ICCBR 2022, LNAI 13405, pp. 3–17, 2022.
https://doi.org/10.1007/978-3-031-14923-8_1

trained (post hoc). Note that post hoc methods can also be applied to intrinsically interpretable models [14]. These model agnostic methods usually work by analyzing feature input and output pairs. By definition, these methods cannot have access to model internals such as weights or structural information. The main advantage of model-agnostic (post hoc) explanation methods is flexibility and re-usability, although some authors consider this type of explanation as limited *justifications* because they are not linked to the real reasoning process occurring in the ML model [2]. Another criterion is categorizing explainers as local or global. Local means that the method is applicable to explain an individual prediction, while global means that it is used for understanding the whole model learned from a certain dataset.

The background context of the research conducted in this paper is the *iSee project*[1] that aims to provide a unifying platform where personalized explanations are created by reasoning with Explanation Experiences using CBR. This is a very challenging, long-term goal as we want to capture complete user-centered explanation experiences on complex explanation strategies. We aim to be able to recommend what explanation strategy better suits an explanation situation. The contribution of this paper is the first step toward this long-term goal: we aim to capture user opinions on the preferred XAI method of a given AI model and domain. To do so, we have conducted an online experiment with several users to elicit a case base capturing their preferences regarding the explanation of several real use cases on explaining AI models. Moreover, we define the corresponding CBR system that exploits this knowledge to help users with the task of selecting an XAI method suitable for a concrete explanation scenario. The query describing the situation includes knowledge about the user expertise, the AI model and task, the data model, and the domain.

This paper runs as follows: Sect. 2 presents the background of this work. Section 3 describes examples of ML models and explanations with basic explainers to get a case base that captures real user preferences on explanations. Then, Sect. 4 describes the associated CBR system that exploits this knowledge. Section 5 presents the evaluation results and Sect. 6 concludes the paper and opens lines of future work.

2 Background

There are several reusable model-agnostic methods that can be used on any ML model and are applied after the model has been trained (post hoc). Some relevant well-known examples are: Local Interpretable Model-Agnostic Explanations (LIME) [17], Anchors [18], Shapley Additive Explanations (SHAP) [12], Partial Dependence Plots (PDPs) [6], Accumulated Local Effects (ALE) [1] and counterfactual explanations [20]. An example of work that reviews different explanation techniques is the taxonomy proposed by Arya et al. [3]. In this work, the authors also propose Explainability 360, an open-source Python toolkit to implement explanation algorithms and metrics to measure them. Both resources, the taxonomy and the toolkit can help users to decide what the best implementation

[1] http://isee4xai.com.

is to explain a specific model. In our previous work [4] we have reviewed some selected XAI libraries (Interpret, Alibi, Aix360, Dalex, and Dice) and provide examples of different model-agnostic explanations. Our work in this paper proposes using CBR to retrieve the best explainer because, even if these methods are reusable, the choice of the most suitable explanation method for a given model is a complex task where expertise is a major requirement. Moreover, one of the most original aspects of our work is that the selected explanation strategy is obtained according to users' opinions, which can enhance the performance of the CBR system since an explanation's effectiveness depends on users' opinions directly.

There are other approaches in the CBR literature related to XAI. Some relevant early works can be found in the review by Leake and McSherry [9]. In the work by Sørmo et al. [19], authors present a framework for explanation in CBR focused on explanation goals, whereas the publication by Doyle et al. [5] develops the idea of explanation utility, a metric that may be different to the similarity metric used for nearest neighbor retrieval. Recently, there is a relevant body of work on CBR to explain other black-box models, the so-called *CBR Twins*. In the paper by Keane et al. [8], the authors propose a theoretical analysis of a post-hoc explanation-by-example approach that relies on the twinning of artificial neural networks with CBR systems. The work by Li et al. [10] combines the strength of deep learning and the interpretability of case-based reasoning to make an interpretable deep neural network. The paper by Gates et al. [7] investigates whether CBR competence can be used to predict confidence in the outputs of a black box system when the black box and CBR systems are provided with the same training data. In the publication by Weber et al. [21], the authors demonstrate how CBR can be used for an XAI approach to justify solutions produced by an opaque learning method, particularly in the context of unstructured textual data. Additionally, CBR has been proven as a suitable strategy to select the most suitable explanation method for a given model outcome. This way, our previous work has analysed its applicability to select explanation methods for image classification tasks [16] and to configure these explanation methods with an optimal setup [15].

3 Case-Based Elicitation

The first contribution of this paper is the elicitation of a case base capturing user preferences on the explanation of existing ML models. To acquire this knowledge we have generated several use cases reproducing real XAI scenarios where, given an ML task, several alternative explanation methods are applied. Then users are asked to select the best explanation according to their expertise and expectations. This section describes the structure of the cases and the elicitation process to collect user knowledge on selecting a proper explanation method.

3.1 Case Structure

Each case is structured as a tuple $\langle D, S, R \rangle$ containing: (1) a description D of the ML model to be explained; (2) a solution S, that describes the explanation method (or explainer); and (3) a result R, which is the opinion (score) of the users about how good the solution is for this specific description. The case description D includes:

Domain: the domain is the situation where the AI model and the explanation system are applied. We have defined some domains: Medicine, Economics, Social, Security, Entertainment, and Image Recognition, although our model is extensible to others.

DataType: the type of data that the *Explainer* accepts as input. It can be text, images, or tabular data.

TrainingData: if the training data of the model is available to feed the explainer methods.

AITask: the artificial intelligence task we want to make interpretable for users. In the examples, we have only used classification and regression tasks, although it is extensible to other AI tasks such as computer vision, information retrieval, robot control, natural language processing, etc.

ModelBackend: the library or technology used to implement the AI model: python libraries *Sklearn*, *Torch* and *TensorFlow*.

ModelType: The AI model we use to carry out the *AITask*, for example, an artificial neural network (ANN), random forest (RF), support vector machine (SVM), and so on.

DomainKnowledgeLevel: the level of knowledge of the target user about the *AITask*, and the *Domain*. It can be low or expert.

MLKnowledge: if the user has some knowledge of machine learning. This is a yes or no attribute.

ExplanationScope: if the target explanations are global, explaining the whole AI model, or local, explaining a single prediction.

According to all these features, we have an *explainer* as a solution S, which will fit the problem described and will be able to generate explanations. The third component in the case structure is the result R, a score that represents the users' opinions about this solution through a 7-point Likert scale. In Table 1, we show an example of a case where we can see its description, its solution, and its user score.

3.2 Case Base Acquisition

We have elicited a case base with real user input. We elaborated a series of use cases where an AI model was applied to solve an AI task. For each case, the user rates different explanations generated by several alternative explainers. One of the advantages of using use cases is that the users do not need to interact directly with the system and worry about aspects such as parameter configuration. In addition, we provide users with the background needed about the case and the description of the explainers being applied. The purpose of each use case is to ask the user about their degree of satisfaction with the explanations proposed using a Likert scale (from 1 to 7).

Table 1. Example of the structure of a case in our case base. This case is related to use case 3, described in Sect. 3.

	Domain	Economics
Description	DataType	Tabular
	TrainingData	Yes
	AITask	Regression
	ModelBackend	Sklearn
	ModelType	RF
	DomainKnowledgeLevel	Low
	MLKnowledge	Yes
	ExplanationScope	Global
Solution		Tabular/Importance
UserScore		6

Additionally, for each use case, two questions were included to do basic profiling of the user where we represent their knowledge in the specific domain and their expertise in machine learning. With this information, each user's answer to a specific explanation is represented as a case. This way, the description of the use case is associated with the explanation method (as its solution) and the scores given by the users are the result of the case. Next, we describe the use cases presented to the participants according to the case structure described in the previous section.

Use case 1: cervical cancer prediction[2]**.** The *Domain* of this use case is Medicine, one of the most critical domains to apply AI prediction tasks and where explanation systems are required. In questionnaire 1, we have random forest and neural networks as the *ModelType* to classify (*AITask*) the high risk of having cervical cancer. These models consider features, represented as tabular data (*DataType*), like the age of the individuals, sexual partners, and the number of pregnancies, among others. We have some explanation methods to justify the model behaviors (i.e., different *Solutions*): some models with global scope (*ExplanationScope*), like Variable Importance and Accumulated Local Effects, and some local models (*ExplanationScope*) like LIME, SHAP, Anchors, and DiCE.

Use case 2: depression screening[3]**.** The second use case is a problem of the psychology field (Medicine *Domain*). In this problem, we try to explain why a machine learning model (*ModelType*) predicts depression in students (classification *AItask*). The models use tabular data (*DataType*) collected through a questionnaire. We have also some explanation methods (*Solutions*) to understand this task: Variable Importance, Accumulated Local Effects

[2] https://forms.gle/ctJZx53wRhTb7hMf8.

[3] https://forms.gle/2jYBkWgNcWjNKRLs6.

(global *ExplanationScope*), LIME, SHAP, and Anchors (local *ExplanationScope*).

Use case 3: cost prediction[4]**.** It predicts the price per square meter of apartments in Poland. We can consider the *Domain* of this case as Economics. The main goal is the prediction of product prices. Both employers and consumers need to know how artificial intelligence works to avoid mistakes in prediction. In the cases related to this questionnaire, we use random forest (*AI Task*) to solve this regression problem (*AITask*) that considers tabular data (*DataType*) describing attributes about the apartment: surface, floor, location, and others. We have proposed some explanation methods (*Solutions*) to try to understand the random forest working: Variable Importance, Accumulated Local Effects (global *ExplanationScope*), LIME, and SHAP (local *ExplanationScope*).

Use case 4: income prediction[5]**.** The *AITask* to solve is a classification to predict if a person earns more than 50K dollars a year. We use ML models (*ModelType*) that use *TrainingData*, using variable importance, Accumulated Local Effects (global *ExplanationScope*), LIME, SHAP or public DiCE (local *ExplanationScope*), as the proposed explanation methods (*Solutions*). If the machine learning model does not use *TrainingData*, we have proposed to use private DiCE, which is also local. The *Domain* of this problem was labeled as Economics.

Use case 5: fraud detection[6]**.** We show the results of some explanation methods when applying a ML model (*ModelType*) to classify (*AITask*) if a transaction was fraudulent. The model is trained using tabular data (*DataType*). We have different *Solutions* to explain these machine learning models: variable importance, Accumulated Local Effects (global *ExplanationScope*), LIME, SHAP, and Anchors (local *ExplanationScope*). The *Domain* of these cases is set to Security. The main goal of this domain is fighting against vulnerabilities in critical systems.

Use case 6: social problems identification[7]**.** This questionnaire is related to Social *Domain*. Artificial intelligence can be applied to solve and detect very important social problems, for instance, alcohol consumption in young people, or discrimination based on race or sex. To make the artificial intelligence model transparent is necessary to understand how to fight against all these problems. Variable importance, Accumulated Local Effects (global *ExplanationScope*), LIME and SHAP (local *ExplanationScope*) are the explanation methods (*Solutions*) proposed in this questionnaire. They try to explain the behavior of machine learning models (*ModelType*) applied to a regression problem that tries to predict the final grades of Portuguese students (*AITask*). Tabular *DataType* as the student's school, her age, study time, etc are used by the machine learning methods.

---

[4] https://forms.gle/Kc91FWF9gKgg5yfS6.
[5] https://forms.gle/KHXTGbJydXHAHH2p6.
[6] https://forms.gle/mFe9ccVhZiLEjk4u6.
[7] https://forms.gle/mFe9ccVhZiLEjk4u6.

Use case 7: text classification[8]**.** This model classifies a newsgroup post in a topic (*AITask*). The machine learning model (*ModelType*) only uses the text (*DataType*) from the post to classify it in religion, autos, baseball, among other topics. Therefore, the *Domain* of this problem is Entertainment. Although this is a domain not as critical as some of the previous ones, explanations in the entertainment industry have many advantages, for example, increasing the user's acceptance and satisfaction, or even persuading users to consume new products. The *Solution* we have for this use case is LIME (local *ExplanationScope*).

Use cases 8, 9, 10: image recognition[9,10,11]**.** These three questionnaires are included in the *Domain* Image Recognition. This domain is specific for understanding the prediction of the objects that appear in images. In these questionnaires we have toy examples related to the classification (*AITask*) of images (*DataType*) using machine learning (*ModelType*). In the questionnaire 8, we present several *Solutions* for image classifications of animals: LIME and Anchors (local *ExplanationScope*). In the questionnaire 9, we have Anchors and Counterfactuals (local *ExplanationScope*) to classify black and white images of clothes. Finally, in the last questionnaire, we have Counterfactuals as the *Solution* to explain black and white images of handwritten digits classification.

Figure 1 shows a screenshot of one of the use cases created to collect user preferences regarding the explanation methods. Next, we detail the CBR process that exploits this knowledge to propose the most suitable XAI method for a given explanation scenario.

4 CBR Process

One of the most important aspects of a CBR system is how similar cases are retrieved. In our system, the proposed retrieval function can be decomposed into two steps: filtering and sorting. Given a case description D, the filtering step takes into account certain attributes that allow identifying the explanation methods that are compatible with that case. Namely, these attributes are *DataType, TrainingData, AITask, ModelBackend, ModelType* and *ExplanationScope.* This filter guarantees that all the retrieved explainers are valid solutions. For example, suppose we have a random forest regressor that works with tabular data, and we want an explanation for an instance. Just by using the *DataType* attribute, only the tabular explainers are retrieved. Since the *AITask* is regression, explainers that only work with classification, such as counterfactuals, will be discarded. Finally, since we want explanations for an instance, the *ExplanationScope* will be local, and thus the final retrieved explainers will be *Tabular/LIME* and *Tabular/SHAP*.

[8] https://forms.gle/KitNg2FnkTbuL3KR6.
[9] https://forms.gle/MCtagTCMB9jiFdgk6.
[10] https://forms.gle/YHYga6d9eqLVFvsh7.
[11] https://forms.gle/tZxzH8ZyY3VejhVv7.

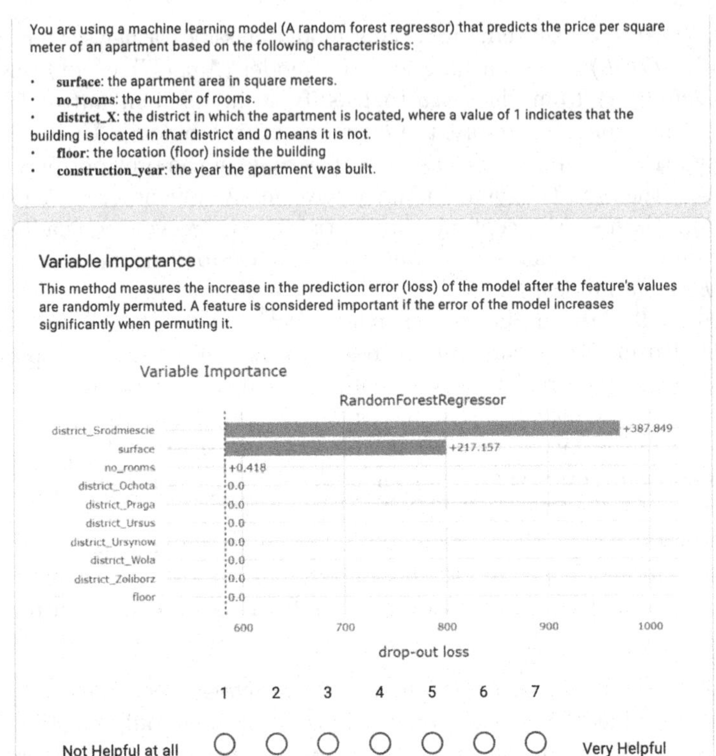

Fig. 1. Screenshot of use case 3. It describes to the user the AI task and proposes several alternative explanation methods to understand the corresponding model.

During the initial filtering, we use the case description attributes so only the compatible explainers are returned. The solutions of these compatible cases contain different potential explainers to solve (explain) the query. We denote the set of cases sharing the same explainer as a solution with $\mathcal{C}^S$. At this point, some solutions (explanation methods) may be more suitable than others for a particular query. For this reason, the sorting phase arranges the cases in ($\mathcal{C}^S$) according to the following similarity metric:

$$sim(q,c) = \frac{1}{W} \sum_{a \in SimAttr} w_a \cdot equal(q(a), c(a))$$

where *SimAttr* represents the following attributes of the case description: *Domain*, *DomainKnowledgeLevel*, *MLKnowledge*, *AItask*, *ModelBackend*, and *ModelType*. The values $w_a \in [0..1]$ are weights that have been computed to obtain the minimum error using a greedy optimization method, and $W = \sum w_a$.

Once the similarity values are calculated for all the cases in $\mathcal{C}^S$, the score (R) of the k most similar cases to the query are averaged to obtain the *Mean Estimated Explanation Utility Score*. This score represents the expected user

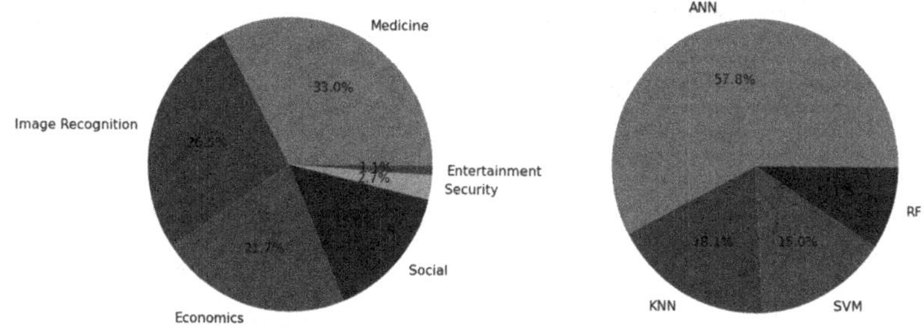

Fig. 2. Stratified analysis of cases per domain (left) and ML model (right).

satisfaction for that explainer. The same process applies for the rest of the compatible solutions: all cases with that explainer as *Solution* are retrieved creating the $\mathcal{C}^S$ set, their similarity values are calculated, and then the scores of the most similar cases are aggregated to determine the estimated utility value. We do not apply a filter considering a minimum number of agreeing with reviews to include a case because doing the mean we are taking into account all the opinions, and not only the majority opinion. Lastly, the explainers are ranked according to the expected score to be proposed to the user.

5 Evaluation and Discussion

The case base includes a total of 746 cases, where users evaluated the explanations for the domain models using 11 different explanation methods from some libraries. 30 different users participated by filling in the questionnaires with different skills in machine learning. Particularly, only 10.7% of cases referred to a user with no previous knowledge of machine learning. Although with a greater amount of responses we could get better results, we think this amount is enough to consider the system trustworthy.

The stratified analysis of the cases regarding the application domain and ML model is shown in Fig. 2. The domains with the most cases are Medicine and Image recognition. There is a greater number of cases for these domains because there were more use cases associated with them. Regarding the distribution of models, there is a majority of cases applied to artificial neural networks (ANN).

The analysis of cases for each explainer and datatype is presented in Fig. 3. Regarding the explainers, all the solutions are guaranteed to be valid methods for their case descriptions thanks to the filtering step of the retrieval phase that was applied when elaborating the questionnaires to evaluate the use cases. As expected, global methods, that can be applied in almost any case involving tabular data (ALE and Feature Importance), have more cases than most of the local explainers. Although logical, it is important to note that the number of cases per explainer is directly proportional to the number of cases of the data type such explainer uses. It is also worth noting that there are few cases representative of the text data type, mainly because we only used one method

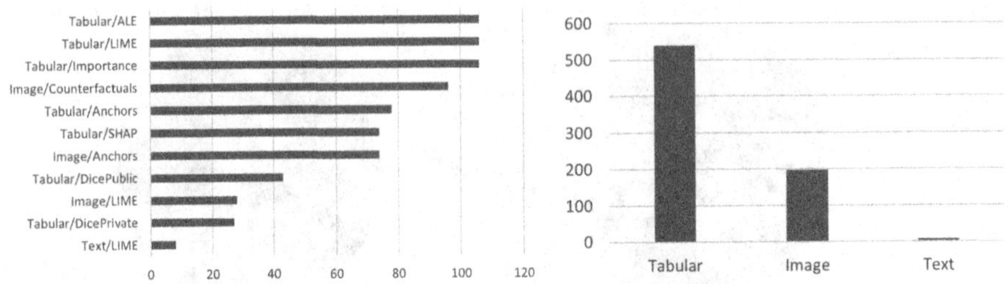

Fig. 3. Stratified analysis of the number of cases per explainer (left) and data type (right).

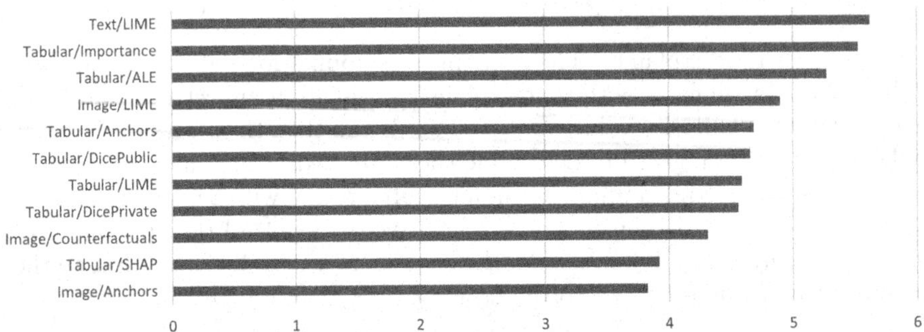

Fig. 4. Average user score by explainer.

to generate explanations (LIME), but also because the Entertainment domain, where this type of explainer was used, did not count with enough cases.

In Fig. 4, we present the average user score of each explainer method. It is worth emphasizing that the scores assigned by the user go from 1 to 7. Although LIME for text data has the higher score, this result is not reliable since the number of cases where this explainer was used is too little. However, the tabular global methods, ALE, and Variable Importance, were the next best-rated explainers with an average score of 5.53 and 5.27, respectively. This does not mean that users disliked local explainers. In fact, most of the local explainers have an average score above the neutral mark of 4. However, explainers such as SHAP for tabular data and Anchors for images did not receive good ratings in general.

The same pattern is identified upon analyzing the mean scores per explainer grouping by the different domains in Table 2. Again, the global methods ALE and Variable Importance are the preferred ones by the users in most of the domains. However, there is an exception where ALE is the worst-rated explainer in the Security domain. One possible explanation for this is that in the only model explained in this domain the meaning of the features was not provided because of data privacy reasons. The low score given by the users may imply that this method is not particularly helpful when the intrinsic meaning of the

Table 2. Mean score per explainer by domain.

Domain	Solution	UserScore
Social	Tabular/ALE	6.07
	Tabular/Importance	5.89
	Tabular/LIME	5.25
	Tabular/SHAP	4.50
Security	Tabular/Importance	4.80
	Tabular/Anchors	3.60
	Tabular/LIME	3.40
	Tabular/ALE	3.20
Medicine	Tabular/Importance	5.34
	Tabular/LIME	4.89
	Tabular/ALE	4.82
	Tabular/Anchors	4.56
	Tabular/DicePublic	3.93
	Tabular/SHAP	3.56
Image recognition	Image/LIME	4.89
	Image/Counterfactuals	4.31
	Image/Anchors	3.82
Entertainment	Text/LIME	5.62
Economics	Tabular/ALE	5.59
	Tabular/Importance	5.59
	Tabular/Anchors	5.07
	Tabular/DicePublic	5.07
	Tabular/DicePrivate	4.55
	Tabular/LIME	3.59

attributes is unknown. Nevertheless, this is one of the domains with the lowest number of cases in the case base, so the standard deviation is considerably higher. Regarding the local tabular methods, LIME, DiCE (counterfactuals), and Anchors were preferred over SHAP in all the domains. As for the image explainers, LIME was the better-rated explainer, followed by image counterfactuals. Anchors for images did not prove to be helpful for the users and its average score fell below the neutral mark of 4.

A similar outcome is obtained when grouping by the AI Task, as shown in Table 3. However, it is worth noting that the same explainers obtained a considerably higher score when used for regression tasks than for classification. One reason for this may be that the regression models proposed in the questionnaires are easier to interpret than the classification ones since the value of a feature is proportional to the predicted value, while classification models work with prob-

Table 3. Mean user score per explainer by AI task.

AITask	Solution	UserScore
Regression	Tabular/ALE	6.07
	Tabular/Importance	5.89
	Tabular/LIME	5.25
	Tabular/SHAP	4.50
Classification	Text/LIME	5.62
	Tabular/Importance	5.39
	Tabular/ALE	4.98
	Image/LIME	4.89
	Tabular/Anchors	4.67
	Tabular/DicePublic	4.65
	Tabular/DicePrivate	4.55
	Tabular/LIME	4.34
	Image/Counterfactuals	4.31
	Image/Anchors	3.82
	Tabular/SHAP	3.56

abilities. However, it is worth pointing out that the sample size was not large enough as only two of the models presented in the questionnaires were regressors.

In Fig. 5, we analyze the mean score given to the explainers depending on the previous domain knowledge of the users. One of the main aspects is that expert users in the proposed domains tend to evaluate the explainers more positively. Although there seems to be a greater disparity for image explainers, it is important to highlight that only one user claimed not to have knowledge in the Image Recognition domain, so it would be incorrect to make interpretations about the suitability of this explainer solely for expert users. However, in domains involving tabular data, the number of users with little knowledge about the domain is more similar to the number of expert users. Thus, the results obtained are more reliable and although the score distance between these types of users is lower, users with low domain knowledge give lower scores to the proposed explanations.

Lastly, we have used cross-validation to evaluate the performance of the CBR system. From the original case base, 15% of the cases were used as the test set, and the rest represented the case base used by the CBR system. Since each case from the test set was composed of the case description, solution, and user score (from 1 to 7), we calculated the predicted score of that explainer by feeding the case description to the retrieval function. This process was repeated using all the cases to obtain the mean error. In Fig. 6, the absolute error distribution is displayed. The mean absolute error was 1.03 with a standard deviation of 0.83.

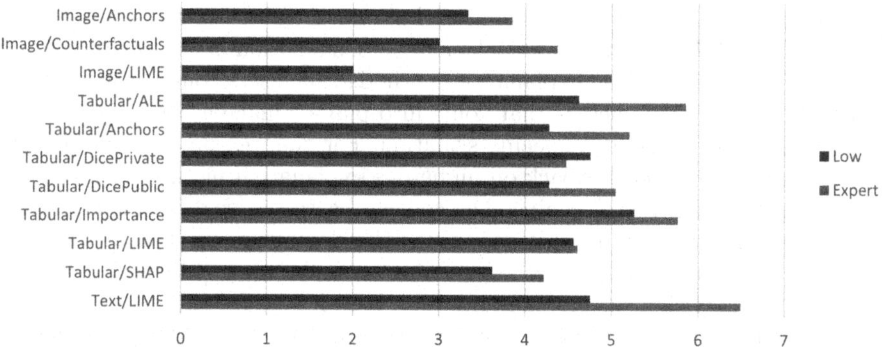

Fig. 5. Mean user score per explainer according to the users' knowledge of the domain.

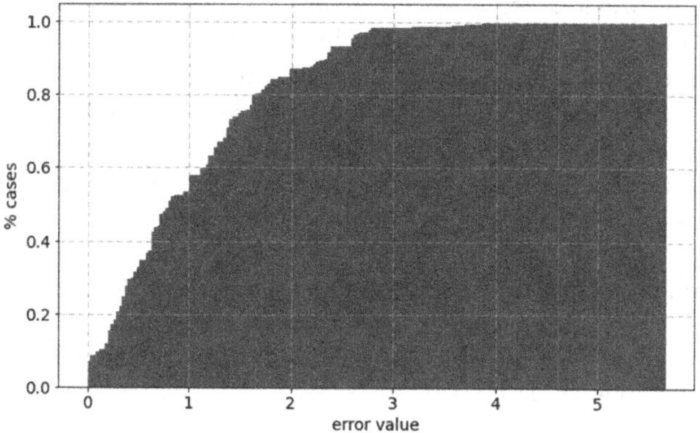

Fig. 6. Cumulative histogram displaying the absolute error distribution of the CBR system. The y-axis represents the percentage of cases (value 1.0 is equal to 100%) having the error value represented by the x-axis.

6 Conclusions

When it comes to interpretability, one of the limitations of an AI engineer is selecting a method to explain the behavior of a particular model, identifying which of those tools produce the most meaningful explanations for users. This is a clear example of a user-centered task, where we propose applying CBR to capture and reuse the expert's knowledge.

In this paper, we have built a simple CBR system that aims to recommend the most suitable explanation method for ML models from different domains and users. By specifying the intrinsic characteristics of the model such as the data type it works with, the task it achieves, and the ML architecture that was used to build it, the compatible explainers are easily filtered in the retrieval phase of our CBR system. Nonetheless, the fact that an explainer method is compatible with a certain model does not mean it will yield good results.

In our previous work [4] we concluded that one of the greatest disadvantages of the available XAI libraries was the lack of personalization of the explanations. However, by identifying the explanation methods that users consider helpful, it is easier to identify the factors that come into play to make a certain explanation better than others in a specific situation. For this reason, we collected a case base gathering user feedback on numerous explanation methods applied to ML models from different domains. The collected cases let us conclude valuable insight regarding preferred explainers given the domain or AI task. However, we are aware that CBR systems are live systems and that XAI is a research field in continuous change, therefore our case base has to be updated with new explainers adapted to new problems and solutions as they arise. This paper is the first step in a very challenging, long-term goal as we want to capture complete user-centered explanation experiences on complex and combined explanation strategies. We are defining an ontology to help with the knowledge-intensive representation of previous experiences, different types of users and explanation needs, characterization of the data, the black-box model, and the contextual properties of the application domain and task. In future work, we will use this ontology to improve user modelling and to provide personalized explanations that suit the needs of the person receiving them, by modelling user intentions and needs. In this way, it will be possible to merge the already existing explainability methods with a user-oriented approach.

Acknowledgements. This research is a result of the Horizon 2020 Future and Emerging Technologies (FET) programme of the European Union through the iSee project (CHIST-ERA-19-XAI-008, PCI2020-120720-2) funded by MCIN/AEI and European Union "NextGenerationEU"/PRTR".

References

1. Apley, D.W., Zhu, J.: Visualizing the effects of predictor variables in black box supervised learning models. J. Roy. Stat. Soc. **82**(4), 1059–1086 (2020)
2. Arrieta, A.B., et al.: Explainable Artificial Intelligence (XAI): concepts, taxonomies, opportunities and challenges toward responsible AI. Inf. Fusion **58**, 82–115 (2020)
3. Arya, V., et al.: AI explainability 360: an extensible toolkit for understanding data and machine learning models. J. Mach. Learn. Res. **21**(130), 1–6 (2020)
4. Darias, J.M., et al.: A systematic review on model-agnostic XAI libraries, vol. 3017, pp. 28–39 (2021)
5. Doyle, D., Cunningham, P., Bridge, D., Rahman, Y.: Explanation oriented retrieval. In: Funk, P., González Calero, P.A. (eds.) ECCBR 2004. LNCS (LNAI), vol. 3155, pp. 157–168. Springer, Heidelberg (2004). https://doi.org/10.1007/978-3-540-28631-8_13
6. Friedman, J.H.: Greedy function approximation: a gradient boosting machine. Ann. Stat. 1189–1232 (2001)
7. Gates, L., Kisby, C., Leake, D.: CBR confidence as a basis for confidence in black box systems. In: Bach, K., Marling, C. (eds.) ICCBR 2019. LNCS (LNAI), vol. 11680, pp. 95–109. Springer, Cham (2019). https://doi.org/10.1007/978-3-030-29249-2_7

8. Keane, M.T., Kenny, E.M.: How case-based reasoning explains neural networks: a theoretical analysis of XAI using *post-hoc* explanation-by-example from a survey of ANN-CBR twin-systems. In: Bach, K., Marling, C. (eds.) ICCBR 2019. LNCS (LNAI), vol. 11680, pp. 155–171. Springer, Cham (2019). https://doi.org/10.1007/978-3-030-29249-2_11
9. Leake, D., Mcsherry, D.: Introduction to the special issue on explanation in case-based reasoning. Artif. Intell. Rev. **24**(2), 103 (2005)
10. Li, O., et al.: Deep learning for case-based reasoning through prototypes: a neural network that explains its predictions. In: AAAI Conference on AI, vol. 32 (2018)
11. Lipton, Z.C.: The mythos of model interpretability: in machine learning, the concept of interpretability is both important and slippery. Queue **16**(3), 31–57 (2018)
12. Lundberg, S.M., Lee, S.I.: A unified approach to interpreting model predictions. In: Advances in Neural Information Processing Systems 30 (2017)
13. Miller, T.: Explanation in artificial intelligence: insights from the social sciences. Artif. Intell. **267**, 1–38 (2019)
14. Molnar, C.: Interpretable Machine Learning, 2 edn. (2022). https://christophm.github.io/interpretable-ml-book
15. Recio-García, J.A., Díaz-Agudo, B., Pino-Castilla, V.: CBR-LIME: a case-based reasoning approach to provide specific local interpretable model-agnostic explanations. In: Watson, I., Weber, R. (eds.) ICCBR 2020. LNCS (LNAI), vol. 12311, pp. 179–194. Springer, Cham (2020). https://doi.org/10.1007/978-3-030-58342-2_12
16. Recio-García, J.A., Parejas-Llanovarced, H., Orozco-del-Castillo, M.G., Brito-Borges, E.E.: A case-based approach for the selection of explanation algorithms in image classification. In: Sánchez-Ruiz, A.A., Floyd, M.W. (eds.) ICCBR 2021. LNCS (LNAI), vol. 12877, pp. 186–200. Springer, Cham (2021). https://doi.org/10.1007/978-3-030-86957-1_13
17. Ribeiro, M.T., et al.: "Why should i trust you?" Explaining the predictions of any classifier. In: ACM SIGKDD, pp. 1135–1144 (2016)
18. Ribeiro, M.T., et al.: Anchors: high-precision model-agnostic explanations. In: AAAI conference on AI, vol. 32 (2018)
19. Sørmo, F., et al.: Explanation in case-based reasoning-perspectives and goals. Artif. Intell. Rev. **24**(2), 109–143 (2005)
20. Verma, S., et al.: Counterfactual explanations for machine learning: a review. arXiv preprint arXiv:2010.10596 (2020)
21. Weber, R.O., Johs, A.J., Li, J., Huang, K.: Investigating textual case-based XAI. In: Cox, M.T., Funk, P., Begum, S. (eds.) ICCBR 2018. LNCS (LNAI), vol. 11156, pp. 431–447. Springer, Cham (2018). https://doi.org/10.1007/978-3-030-01081-2_29
22. Weld, D.S., Bansal, G.: The challenge of crafting intelligible intelligence. Commun. ACM **62**(6), 70–79 (2019)

A Few Good Counterfactuals: Generating Interpretable, Plausible and Diverse Counterfactual Explanations

Barry Smyth[1,2(✉)] and Mark T. Keane[1,2,3]

[1] School of Computer Science, University College Dublin, Dublin, Ireland
{barry.smyth,mark.keane}@ucd.ie

[2] Insight SFI Research Centre for Data Analytics, University College Dublin, Dublin, Ireland

[3] VistaMilk SFI Research Centre, University College Dublin, Dublin, Ireland

Abstract. Counterfactual explanations are an important solution to the Explainable AI (XAI) problem, but good, "native" counterfactuals can be hard to come by. Hence, the popular methods generate synthetic counterfactuals using "blind" perturbation, by manipulating feature values to elicit a class change. However, this strategy has other problems, notably a tendency to generate invalid data points that are *out-of-distribution* or that involve feature-values that do not naturally occur in a given domain. Instance-guided and case-based methods address these problems by grounding counterfactual generation in the dataset or case base, producing synthetic counterfactuals from naturally-occurring features, and guaranteeing the reuse of valid feature values. Several instance-guided methods have been proposed, but they too have their shortcomings. Some only approximate grounding in the dataset, or do not readily generalise to multi-class settings, or are limited in their ability to generate alternative counterfactuals. This paper extends recent case-based approaches by presenting a novel, general-purpose, case-based solution for counterfactual generation to address these shortcomings. We report a series of experiments to systematically explore parametric variations on common datasets, to establish the conditions for optimal performance, beyond the state-of-the-art in instance-guided methods for counterfactual XAI.

1 Introduction

Imagine your research paper has been reviewed by an AI that provides post-hoc explanations for its decisions. It might explain a rejection using a counterfactual statement: "*if the paper was written more clearly and the evaluation used more datasets, then it would have been accepted*". This proposes an alternative outcome (acceptance) if two aspects of the paper had been different (clearer writing *and* a stronger evaluation). This explanation is just one of many possible counterfactuals for explaining the rejection. For example, another might emphasise different aspects of the paper (perhaps related work and technical detail, for example): "*if the paper had included a better treatment of related work and*

M. T. Keane and N. Wiratunga (Eds.): ICCBR 2022, LNAI 13405, pp. 18–32, 2022.
https://doi.org/10.1007/978-3-031-14923-8_2

provided a clearer technical account of the main algorithm, then it would have been accepted". While we hope that neither of these options will be applied to the present work, they show how useful counterfactuals can be in providing a causal focus for how an alternative outcome *could* be achieved [3,29], rather than merely explaining why a particular outcome *was* achieved [10,22,23]. Accordingly, in recent years, there has been an explosion of research on how counterfactuals can be used in Explainable AI (XAI [1,20,36]) and algorithmic recourse [19].

From a machine learning perspective, every dataset will have some existing counterfactuals (what we call *native counterfactuals*), typically the *nearest unlike neighbours* (NUNs) of a target query to be explained [6,10,28]. However, not every NUN makes for a *good* counterfactual; for instance, it is generally agreed that *sparse* NUNs make better counterfactuals, because good native counterfactuals have few feature-differences between the query-instance and its explanatory counter-instance. However, [21] showed that 95% of datasets examined had $<1\%$ of natives with ≤ 2 differences (a common sparsity threshold). Hence, the most popular solutions to counterfactual generation have opted to generate synthetic counterfactuals, by perturbing query-instances using a loss function that balances proximity to the query against proximity to the decision boundary for the counterfactual class, using a scaled L1-norm distance-metric [37]. However, these proximity-driven, optimisation approaches have a tendency to generate invalid data-points, synthetic counterfactual-instances that may be out-of-distribution and/or involve feature-values that do not naturally occur [8,9,26,37].

For these reasons, many researchers have argued that counterfactual generation needs to be, somehow, grounded in the dataset of known instances [8,21,26,32]. Such *instance-guided methods* attempt to generate synthetic counterfactuals to handle a wide-range of target queries while being faithful to characteristics of the dataset [21,32]. However, current methods are *incomplete*, because they fail to identify good valid counterfactuals, and *inefficient*, because the counterfactuals they can generate are not guaranteed to be the best that could be generated, as determined by quality metrics (see below). The present paper advances a novel case-based method, using an elegant algorithm, that generates synthetic counterfactuals by directly adapting instances (native counterfactuals) in the dataset, using actual feature-values, to provide diverse, high-quality counterfactual explanations for a wide variety of target queries. In the remainder of this paper, we first set the scene for the current work by defining the properties of good counterfactual explanations and situate it relative to prior work. Then, we go on to present the details of the current novel algorithm and report several extensive experiments to test it against the current state-of-the-art.

2 Related Work

As AI systems become more widespread, the need for fairness [35], transparency [25], and explainability is increasingly important [1,17,24,31]; indeed, some governmental regulations (such as GDPR) now call for mandatory explanations for AI-based decisions [16]. At the same time, machine learning approaches that have proven to be so effective in real-world tasks (e.g. deep neural networks), appear to be among the most difficult to explain [18]. One approach to this problem is to cast such black-box models as white-box ones and then to use the latter to explain the former; for example, using post-hoc feature-based (e.g., as in LIME [34]) or example-based explanations (e.g., as in twin-systems [15,22,23]). Counterfacutal explanations are another post-hoc explanation strategy, one that is arguably better than example-based explanations [29], as they inform the user about the features that need to change in order to alter an automated decision (hence, their use in algorithmic recourse [19]). Furthermore, psychologically, people readily understand counterfactuals [2,3] and, importantly, they are implicated in causal understanding [2,14]. Finally, from a legal perspective, [37] have argued that counterfactual explanations are GDPR compliant.

In this section we consider the task of counterfactual generation. We begin by asking what makes a *good* counterfactual – one that is likely to be useful in practice – and we then review recent efforts to generate counterfactuals, paying particular attention to the difference between so-called *"blind" perturbation* approaches [5,26,27,30,37] and more recent *instance-based* approaches [21,26,32]. Because instance-based methods generate counterfactuals using feature values that naturally exist (rather than perturbed values that may not exist naturally), they enjoy certain plausibility benefits; although, state-of-the-art instance-based methods have a number of shortcomings too. We identify and discuss these deficits to motivate the new approach presented in this work.

2.1 What Are Good Counterfactual Explanations?

Intuitively, good counterfactual explanations should be easily understood by users – they should involve fewer, more plausible feature differences – and they should be available for most queries that arise. For example, a counterfactual that says *"if the paper was written more clearly, then the paper would have been accepted"* might be considered better than a more complex one saying *"if the paper was written more clearly, the evaluation more extensive and the review of the literature more comprehensive then the paper would have been accepted"*. There is a general consensus in the XAI literature that good counterfactuals should be:

- *Similar:* maximally similar to the target query, to be understandable to users.
- *Sparse:* differ in as few features as possible from the target, to be easily interpreted.
- *Plausible:* modify features/values that make sense to users (e.g., preferably from known instances).
- *Available:* for a majority of targets, to give a high degree of explanation coverage.

- *Diverse:* use a variety of features to offer counterfactuals that highlight different perspectives, either when multiple alternatives are required, or when it is useful to choose a single explanation from a set of alternatives that involve various feature differences.

The counterfactual literature has many methods that try to meet these properties, but with varying degrees of success.

2.2 Perturbation-Based Approaches

A recent review of the XAI literature has identified >100 distinct methods for computing counterfactuals [20]. Many are designed to meet the various properties of good counterfactuals by perturbing the feature-values of existing instances. For instance, Wachter et al.'s [37] seminal work generates a new counterfactual p', for a target problem p, by perturbing the features of p until a class change occurs, and in a manner that minimises the distance between p and p', $d(p, p')$.

While the approach of [37] can generate a counterfactual p' that is very similar to p, its "blind" perturbation approach can generate counterfactuals that lack sparsity [27] and diversity [30]. It can also generate counterfactuals with (potentially invalid) out-of-distribution feature values; Laugel et al. [26] showed that for some datasets this could occur in 30% of generated instances. Hence, Dandle et al. [5] have proposed modifications to the loss function to minimise the number of different features between p and p' (*diffs(p,p')*). And, Mothila et al. [30] have extended the optimisation function to deal with diversity, so that for a given p, the set of counterfactuals produced minimises the distance and feature differences within the set, while maximising the range of features changed across the set. However, the out-of-distribution problem remains an issue, even for these more advanced perturbation-based solutions.

2.3 Instance-Based Approaches

In response to these out-of-distribution problems, other researchers have argued that counterfactual explanations need to be more grounded in the feature space of the dataset. This has given rise to a family of *instance-guided techniques* that exploit known instances more directly [21,26,32,33]. FACE (Feasible and Actionable Counterfactual Explantions) is one such method that selects candidate counterfactuals that are situated in high-density regions of the dataset, where there is also a feasible path between the query and the generated counterfactual [32]. However, FACE really just approximates to the use of the dataset, as the density analysis merely informs the choice of one generated counterfactual over another.

Keane and Smyth (henceforth, KS20) [21] adopted a more direct instance-guided method, using known, good (native) counterfactuals in the dataset (and their feature values) to generate novel synthetic counterfactuals. KS20 define a *good* counterfactual to be one with ≤ 2 feature differences with respect to a target query, p (based on psychological considerations, see e.g. [11,12]). If a p' exists with

$class(p) \neq class(p')$, and if p and p' differ by no more than 2 features, then p' is a good counterfactual for p. However, often no such p' exists, hence KS20 generates a novel counterfactual by locating a *nearest like neighbour* (NLN) q ($class(p) = class(q)$) such that there exists another instance q' with $class(q) \neq class(q')$, and where q and q' differ by no more than 2 features. The pair $q - q'$ is a *counterfactual-pair* (an *explanation case* in KS20) and we refer to q' as its *counterfactual instance* and to $class(q')$ as its *counterfactual class*. KS20 generates a synthetic counterfactual, p' for p, by using the $q - q'$ pair as a template. The differences between q and q' are used to identify the feature values in p that need to be changed to produce p'; the values of the other (*matching*) features are transferred directly from p to p'. KS20 describe two variations (*direct* and *indirect*) to determine which features values to use in p' for these so-called *difference features*. In the *direct* approach they come from q' itself. In the indirect approach they come from the (like) neighbours of q'.

Thus, even though good counterfactual-pairs are rare in practice, any that do exist can be adapted in different ways, to construct many new good counterfactuals. The approach is not *guaranteed* to produce a valid good counterfactual for p, because the p' may not end up with a (predicted) class that is different from p, but KS20 showed that it regularly generated valid counterfactuals that were very similar to target queries, while remaining sparse (i.e., ≤ 2 feature differences). And because these counterfactuals were always built from existing feature-values they claimed plausibility benefits compared to perturbation methods. As this method works directly from known instances and their feature-values, by design the generated counterfactuals are within distribution (at least with respect to the values of individual features). In tests, KS20 showed that the generated counterfactuals were more similar to target queries than the native counterfactual-pairs in the dataset, thereby further supporting the within-distribution claim. However, KS20's reliance on a single nearest counterfactual-pair as the basis for synthetic counterfactual generation ultimately limits their method's performance in a number of important respects, especially in multi-class settings.

2.4 Instance-Based Shortcomings

Firstly, relying on a single counterfactual-pair means that KS20's generated counterfactuals are, by definition, based on feature values that come from a fixed set of difference features. For a given p, KS20 can only generate one type of counterfactual, because the nearest counterfactual-pair specifies one set of difference features. This limits counterfactual diversity. In a multi-class setting it may be desirable to consider counterfactuals from counterfactual-pairs that are associated with several available counterfactual classes, to generate more diverse counterfactuals, which use a variety of difference features.

If a good counterfactual cannot be generated, directly or indirectly, from the nearest counterfactual-pair, then KS20 fails, thereby limiting the availability of good counterfactuals. This problem may be especially acute in multi-class domains, where it may be feasible to generate good counterfactuals from a variety of different counterfactual classes. However, if only a single counterfactual-pair can be used then all but one of these counterfactual classes will be ignored: in other words KS20 cannot produce a valid counterfactual unless it can be generated from the nearest counterfactual-pair, even though a valid counterfactual may be available by reusing features from a different counterfactual-pair.

Even when KS20 successfully uses a nearest counterfactual-pair $(q - q')$ to construct a good counterfactual, it may not be the best available. It may be possible to generate a counterfactual that is *more* similar to p by starting with a *less* similar counterfactual-pair. In other words, there may exist another counterfactual pair, $q_2 - q_2'$, such that it is possible to generate a good counterfactual from q_2' that is even more similar to p than the one generated from the nearest pair, $q - q'$. Even though this 'better' counterfactual can be generated, it is not available to KS20, because of its reliance of the single, most similar counterfactual-pair.

Similarly, KS20 may suffer from a *plausibility deficit* too. Even if an alternative counterfactual from q_2' offers no similarity advantage, it may be preferable if it is based on a contrasting set of difference features that are more plausible or more "actionable". All good counterfactuals are not creating equally. Some may involve feature differences that are not within the control of the user and don't serve as an actionable explanation. Even if an alternative counterfactual could be produced, from a different counterfactual-pair, using more actionable difference features, KS20 will be blind to it.

In summary then, while KS20 enjoys the plausibility benefits of instance-based approaches, and has been shown to perform well in practice, it's reliance on a single counterfactual-pair can lead to sub-optimal performance in terms of availability, similarity, plausibility, and diversity. This criticism motivates a new approach that is tested here in a systematic set of experiments to parametrically explore its performance, using several key evaluation metrics. As KS20 is currently the state-of-the-art in instance-based counterfactual methods, it is used as the baseline in these tests. The present method simplifies the KS20 algorithm in an elegant way. Stated simply, KS20 proposed a *1NN* approach to counterfactual generation, as a *single* nearest native-counterfactual pair is used as a *template* for the counterfactual. The new method considers an intuitive kNN extension, where $k > 1$ nearest-neighbour counterfactual pairs are reused, each providing a different set of counterfactual candidates (see Algorithm 1) using potentially contrasting difference features. As we shall see, this modification at once unifies the two variations presented in KS20 (direct and indirect) for generating difference-feature values, while at the same time providing a more general-purpose counterfactual generation approach that is well suited to binary *and* multi-class domains.

3 Good Counterfactuals in Multi-class Domains

Most counterfactual methods assume that an underlying decision model (M; e.g. a deep learner) is making predictions to be explained using a generated counterfactual; that is, M is also used to determine predicted classes for the generated counterfactuals. Here, the present method aims to generate *good counterfactuals* ($\leq$2 feature differences) to explain the prediction of a target query, p. Given a set of training cases/instances, I, the approach relies on the reuse of an existing good (native) counterfactual-pair, represented as a so-called *explanation case* (XC) as in KS20. An individual explanation case, xc_d, contains a target query instance, x, and a nearby counterfactual instance x' – that is, x' is a *unlike neighbour* (*UN*) of x', meaning $class(x) \neq class(x')$ – with no more than d feature differences between x and x' as in Eqs. 1–5.

$$UN(x, x') \iff class(x) \neq class(x') \tag{1}$$

$$matches(x, x') = \{f \in x \mid x.f \approx x'.f\} \tag{2}$$

$$diffs(x, x') = \{f \in x \mid x.f \not\approx x'.f\} \tag{3}$$

$$xc_d(x, x') \iff UN(x, x') \wedge |diffs(x, x')| \leq d \tag{4}$$

$$XC_d = \{xc_d(x, x') \; \forall \; x, x' \in I\} \tag{5}$$

Each explanation case, xc_d, is associated with a set of *match* features, whose values are equivalent – within some tolerance – in x and x', and a set of $\leq d$ *difference* features, with differing values. Here we assume $d = 2$ and an xc[1] acts as a template for generating new counterfactuals, by identifying features that *can* be changed (*difference features*) and those that cannot (*match features*).

3.1 Reusing the *kNN* Explanation Cases

To generate a good counterfactual for some target problem/query, p, the method first identifies the $k \geq 1$ nearest xcs with $\leq d$ differences, based on the similarity between p and each $xc.x$; see line 2 and lines 5–8 in Algorithm 1. It then constructs new counterfactuals, *cfs*, from the feature values of p and $xc.x'$ (the good counterfactual for $xc.x$), for each xc; line 3 in Algorithm 1. Importantly, this method is not limited by the specific values of the difference features in $xc.x'$, because it also considers the feature values available from other nearby instances *with the same class* as $xc.x'$ (line 11 in Algorithm 1). Thus, each generated counterfactual, *cf*, is made up of the *match feature* values (ms) from p and the *difference feature* values (ds) from $xc.x'$ *or* its like-neighbours, as shown in lines 15–19 in Algorithm 1.

3.2 Validating Candidate Counterfactuals

Each generated *cf* is associated with a predicted class, $M(cf)$, based on the underlying classification model, M, and this predicted class must be checked to validate the counterfactual. In a multi-class ($n > 2$) setting there are at least two ways to validate a candidate counterfactual. One can look for *any class change*, so *cf* is considered valid if and only if its predicted class ($M(cf)$) *differs* from p's class; this is used by KS20.

[1] For now, we drop the d without loss of generality.

A *stronger* test is to confirm that *cf* has the *same class* as the counterfactual instance used to produce it; i.e. $M(cf) = class(xc.x')$. This is stronger in a multi-class setting, because it accepts only a *single, specific class change*, compared with the $n - 1$ valid classes of the weaker method. The weaker method also feels less appropriate because starting from $class(xc.x')$, but ending with a different class, seems questionable. Thus, the stronger approach (lines 20–21 in Algorithm 1) constrains the *cf* to remain within the vicinity of the original explanation class used to produce it, thereby ensuring greater plausibility.

```
Given  : p, target problem;
         I, training instances;
         d, the number of features differences allowed for a good cf;
         XC_d, explanation cases for d;
         k, number of XCs to be reused;
         M, underlying (classification) model.
Output: cfs, valid, good counterfactuals for p.
1  def gen-kNN-CFs(p, I, d, XC_d, k, M):
2      xcs ← getXCs(p, XC_d, k)
3      cfs ← { genCFs(p, xc, I, M) | xc ∈ xcs }
4      return cfs

5  def getXCs(p, XC, k):
6      XC' ← { xc ∈ XC | class(xc.x) = class(p) }
7      xcs ← sort(XC', key = sim(xc.x, p))
8      return xcs[: k]

9  def genCFs(p, xc, I, d, M):
10     nun ← { xc.x' }
11     nuns ← nun ∪ { i ∈ I | class(i) = class(xc.x') }
12     cfs ← { genCF(p, n, d) | n ∈ nuns }
13     cfs ← { cf | cf ∈ cfs ∧ validateCF(cf, xc, M) }
14     return sort(cfs, key = sim(cf, p))

15 def genCF(p, nun, d):
16     ms ← {f | f ∈ matches(p, nun)}
17     ds ← {f | f ∈ diffs(p, nun)}
18     cf ← ms ∪ ds
19     return cf if (cf ≠ p) ∧ (|ds| ≤ d)

20 def validateCF(cf, xc, M):
21     return M(cf) = class(xc.x')
```

Algorithm 1: Generating multiple, good (for a given d) counterfactuals by reusing the k nearest explanation cases to p.

3.3 Discussion

This new method unifies an important class of instance-based approaches to counterfactual generation. It subsumes and extends KS20 to generate a set of up to $k \times m$ counterfactual candidates for a given p: there are up to m distinct candidates for each of the m unique combinations of difference feature values among the k explanation cases used. The new method also promises better coverage, plausibility and diversity. On *coverage*, generating more counterfactual candidates improves the chances of producing valid counterfactuals and, therefore, should increase the fraction of target problems that can be explained. On *plausibility*, the approach has the potential to generate counterfactuals that are even more similar to the target problem than those associated with a single nearest explanation case. Finally, on *diversity*, since different explanation cases may rely on different combinations of match/difference features, arising from the reuse of different explanation cases, then the resulting counterfactuals should draw from a more diverse set of difference-features.

4 Evaluation

We evaluate the quality of counterfactuals produced by the *knn* approach using 10 common ML datasets, with varying numbers of classes, features, and training instances, in comparison to two (KS20) baselines, using three key evaluation metrics. We generate counterfactuals with, at most, two feature differences ($d = 2$), using KS20's definition of a *good* counterfactual. Some have argued against the strictness of this 2-difference constraint, often pointing to image and time-series data, but, for such data, the count would be based on higher-level latent features (rather than pixels or time-points). Here, for comparison, the experiments also report $d = 3$ results, to accept slightly more complex good counterfactuals.

4.1 Methodology

A form of 10-fold cross-validation is used to evaluate the newly generated counterfactuals, by selecting 10% of the training instances at random to use as target problems. Then, the XC (explanation case) case-base is built from a subset of the XCs that are available from the remaining instances; we use at most 2x as many XCs as there are test instances/target problems. Finally, any remaining instances, which are not part of any selected XCs, are used to train the underlying classifier; in this case we use a gradient boosted classifier [13][2], which was found to be capable of generating sufficiently accurate classification performance across the test datasets, although, in principle, any sufficiently accurate ML model could be used.

We use Algorithm 1, to generate good counterfactuals, by varying k, the number of nearest-neighbour explanation cases, and d, the maximum number of difference features permitted in a good counterfactual. Two variants of the KS20 technique are used as baselines: (i) the *direct 1NN* variant, which generates a counterfactual from a single XC only (a limited, special-case of our kNN

[2] SciKitLearn, with deviance loss, a learning rate of 0.1, and 100 boosting stages.

approach that does not look beyond the counterfactual instance, $xc.x'$, of the nearest explanation case), and (ii) the *indirect* variant (*1NN**) which also considers nearby like-neighbours of $xc.x'$ as a source of extra difference features. This *1NN** variant is actually equivalent to our kNN approach with $k = 1$; note, KS20 found *1NN** to be superior to *1NN*.

Generated counterfactuals are evaluated using 3 different metrics, averaging across the test cases and folds:

- *Test Coverage:* the fraction of test queries/target problems that can be associated with a good counterfactual, to assess explanatory coverage
- *Relative Distance:* the ratio of the distance between the *closest* counterfactual (*cf*) produced and its target problem p, and the distance between the target problem $xc.x$ and the (*original*) counterfactual from the XC used to generate *cf*; thus, a relative distance <1 means the new *cf* is *closer* to p than $xc.x$ was to $xc.x'$. This is our proxy measure for reflecting plausibility[3].
- *Feature Diversity:* the fraction of unique difference features that appear in the counterfactuals produced. Note, *1NN* has the same diversity as *1NN**, since a single XC is reused and thus the same difference features appear.

4.2 Results

Figures 1 and 2 show the results for $1 \leq k \leq 100$ with $d = 2, 3$. Performance per dataset is shown as a separate line graph with statistical significance encoded as follows. If the difference between two *successive* values of k is significant ($p < 0.05$), then the corresponding points are connected by a solid line, otherwise they are connected by a dashed line; for coverage we use a *z-test* and for relative distance and diversity we use a *t-test*. Further, if a marker is filled, it means that the difference between its value and the KS20 baseline is significant ($p < 0.05$). Notice that the x-axis is non-linear, to provide greater detail for $k \leq 10$.

In Fig. 1(a) we see how the ability to produce good counterfactuals increases with k, up to a point, depending on the number of available XCs for each dataset. In all datasets, for $k > 1$, coverage is significantly greater than the baseline, and coverage increases to more than 80% of target problems for a large enough k. On average, the current kNN approach is able to increase coverage by almost a factor of 2, compared to the KS20 *1NN** method, as indicated by the *relative improvement* values for coverage in Fig. 1(d); the approximate values for k shown indicate when this maximum coverage is achieved.

Likewise in Fig. 1(b) we see that these improvements in coverage also offer statistically significant *reductions* (improvements) in relative distance, for increasing k, this time compared with *1NN* because it offers better relative distance values than *1NN** on average. Thus, by considering additional explanation cases, even those that are further away from the target problem, we can generate good

[3] As this is an instance-based technique the out-of-distribution metrics sometimes used in evaluating perturbation-based techniques are not germane.

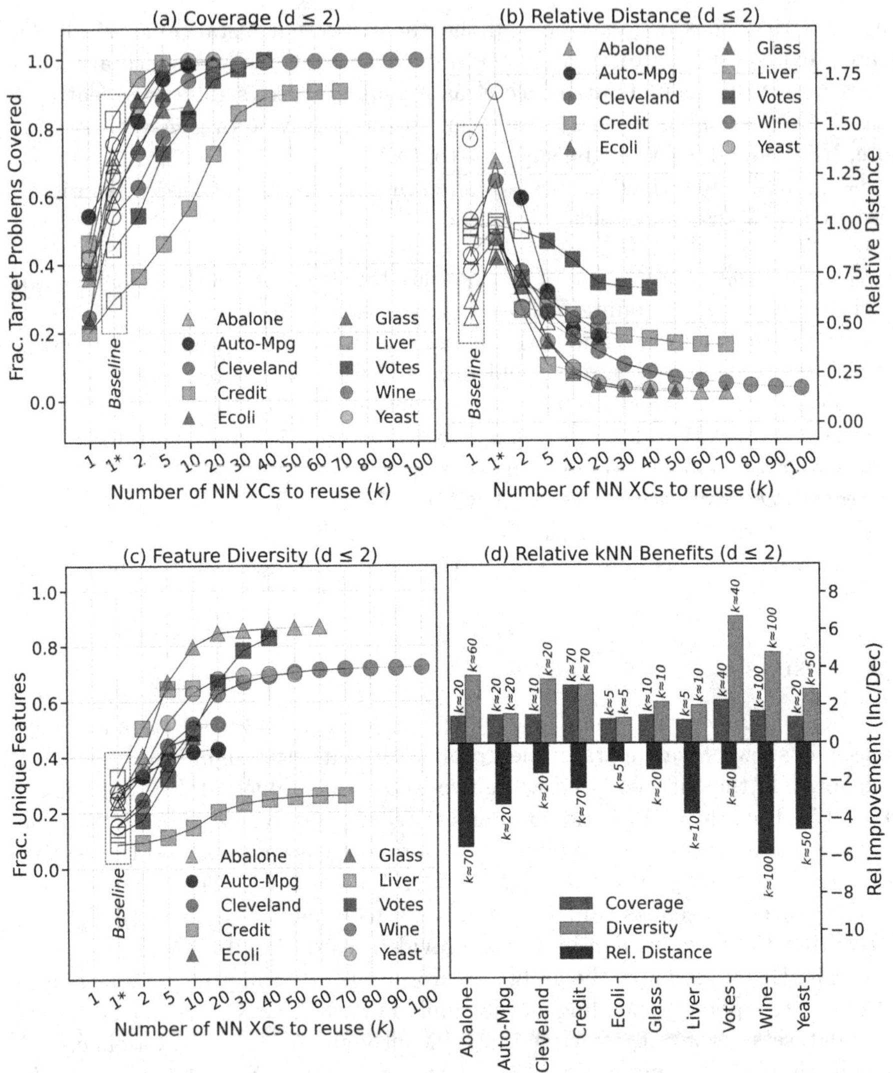

Fig. 1. Counterfactual evaluation results for $d \leq 2$ feature differences: (a) counterfactual coverage, (b) mean relative distance, and (c) counterfactual diversity along with the relative improvements (d) compared to the *1NN/1NN** baseline as appropriate.

counterfactuals that are closer to the target. Incidentally, the increase in relative distance for *1NN**, compared with *1NN*, is due to the significant increase in coverage offered by *1NN**, which means more valid counterfactuals participate in the relative distance calculations. Once again, in Fig. 1(d) we show a relative improvement (decrease) in these distances (compared with *1NN*): on average there is a 3x decrease in relative distance. This is usually achieved for a larger

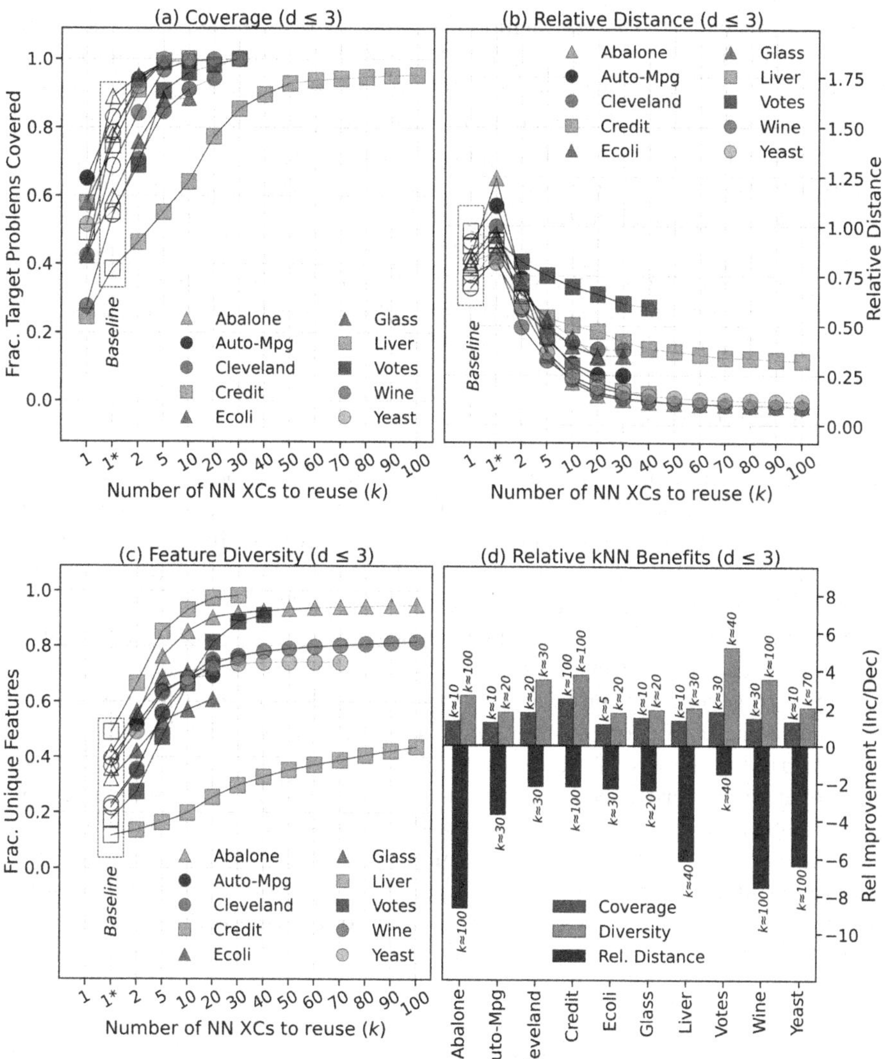

Fig. 2. Counterfactual evaluation results for $d \leq 3$ feature differences: (a) counterfactual coverage, (b) mean relative distance, and (c) counterfactual diversity along with the relative improvements (d) compared to the *1NN/1NN** baseline as appropriate.

value of k than the best coverage, which emphasises the benefits of continuing the search even after an initial good counterfactual has been located.

Finally, the results for feature diversity are shown in Fig. 1(c), once more with significant improvements for increasing values of k, although not every dataset produces counterfactuals with high levels of diversity. For example, in Fig. 1(c) the counterfactuals produced for *Credit* only include up to 25–30% of the available features as difference features. On the other hand, the counterfactuals produced for *Abalone* include over 80% of features as their difference features, while datasets such as *Auto-MPG, Cleveland, and Glass* achieve moderate levels of diversity with 45% to 50% feature participation. Nevertheless, these are considerable improvements (3x on average) compared to the diversity of the baseline (*1NN**) approach, as per Fig. 1(d).

The best value for k varies by dataset, but in practice values of k in the range $10 \leq k \leq 20$ perform well, in terms of coverage, relative distance, and diversity, for all datasets. The $d = 3$ results in Fig. 2, though not discussed in detail, also show similar results and trends, which suggests that the improvements found are not limited to $d = 2$ good counterfactuals; the best results for kNN demonstrate significant improvements over both KS20-baselines.

5 Conclusions

Counterfactuals play an important role in Explainable AI because they can be more causally informative than factual forms of explanation. However, useful native counterfactuals – those similar to a target problem but which differ in only a few (e.g. 1–2) features – can be rare in practice, leading some to propose techniques for generating synthetic counterfactuals [5,30,37]. However, such synthetic counterfactuals often rely on features which may not occur naturally, limiting their explanatory-utility. In response, others have advanced instance-based techniques to generate counterfactuals from naturally occurring feature values. The main contribution of this work is a unifying approach for instance-based counterfactual generation. A second contribution stems from its systematic evaluation of instance-based techniques to demonstrate the optimal parameters for current and previous methods, across a wide range of benchmark datasets.

There are limitations that invite future research. We focused on classification tasks, but the approach should be equally applicable to prediction tasks. The current evaluation focuses on a *like-for-like* comparison with instance-based counterfactual generation methods, but does not include a direct comparison with perturbation-based methods, mostly because the latter cannot guarantee counterfactuals with naturally occurring feature values. Nevertheless, a direct comparison between instance-based and other perturbation-based approaches is warranted and planned. It will also be worthwhile to consider additional metrics to evaluate counterfactuals such as those considered by [4,7].

Though we have provided an offline analysis of counterfactual quality, we have not yet evaluated the counterfactuals produced *in situ*, as part of a real live-user explanation setting. This will also be an important part of future research, as the utility of any counterfactual generation technique will depend critically on the nature of the counterfactuals produced and their informativeness as explanations to "real" end-users. The current tests identify optimal versions of instance-based methods that need to be considered in such future user studies.

Acknowledgements. Supported by Science Foundation Ireland via the Insight SFI Research Centre for Data Analytics (12/RC/2289) and with the Department of Agriculture, Food and Marine via the VistaMilk SFI Research Centre (16/RC/3835).

References

1. Adadi, A., Berrada, M.: Peeking inside the black-box: a survey on explainable artificial intelligence (XAI). IEEE Access **6**, 52138–52160 (2018)
2. Byrne, R.M.: The Rational Imagination: How People Create Alternatives to Reality. MIT Press, Cambridge (2007)
3. Byrne, R.M.: Counterfactuals in Explainable Artificial Intelligence (XAI). In: IJCAI-19, pp. 6276–6282 (2019)
4. Chou, Y.L., Moreira, C., Bruza, P., Ouyang, C., Jorge, J.: Counterfactuals and causability in explainable artificial intelligence: theory, algorithms, and applications. Inf. Fusion **81**, 59–83 (2022)
5. Dandl, S., Molnar, C., Binder, M., Bischl, B.: Multi-objective counterfactual explanations. arXiv preprint arXiv:2004.11165 (2020)
6. Dasarathy, B.V.: Minimal consistent set (MCS) identification for optimal nearest neighbor decision systems design. IEEE Trans. Syst. Man Cybern. **24**(3), 511–517 (1994)
7. Del Ser, J., Barredo-Arrieta, A., Díaz-Rodríguez, N., Herrera, F., Holzinger, A.: Exploring the trade-off between plausibility, change intensity and adversarial power in counterfactual explanations using multi-objective optimization. arXiv preprint arXiv:2205.10232 (2022)
8. Delaney, E., Greene, D., Keane, M.T.: Instance-based counterfactual explanations for time series classification. In: Sánchez-Ruiz, A.A., Floyd, M.W. (eds.) ICCBR 2021. LNCS (LNAI), vol. 12877, pp. 32–47. Springer, Cham (2021). https://doi.org/10.1007/978-3-030-86957-1_3
9. Delaney, E., Greene, D., Keane, M.T.: Uncertainty estimation and out-of-distribution detection for counterfactual explanations. In: ICML21 Workshop on Algorithmic Recourse. arXiv-2107 (2021)
10. Doyle, D., Cunningham, P., Bridge, D., Rahman, Y.: Explanation oriented retrieval. In: Funk, P., González Calero, P.A. (eds.) ECCBR 2004. LNCS (LNAI), vol. 3155, pp. 157–168. Springer, Heidelberg (2004). https://doi.org/10.1007/978-3-540-28631-8_13
11. Förster, M., Hühn, P., Klier, M., Kluge, K.: Capturing users' reality: a novel approach to generate coherent counterfactual explanations. In: Proceedings of the 54th Hawaii International Conference on System Sciences, p. 1274 (2021)
12. Förster, M., Klier, M., Kluge, K., Sigler, I.: Fostering human agency: a process for the design of user-centric XAI systems. In: Proceedings of the International Conference on Information Systems (ICIS) (2020)
13. Friedman, J.H.: Stochastic gradient boosting. Comput. Stat. Data Anal. **38**(4), 367–378 (2002)
14. Gerstenberg, T., Goodman, N.D., Lagnado, D.A., Tenenbaum, J.B.: A counterfactual simulation model of causal judgments for physical events. Psychol. Rev. (2021)
15. Gilpin, L.H., Bau, D., Yuan, B.Z., Bajwa, A., Specter, M., Kagal, L.: Explaining explanations. In: Proceedings of the IEEE 5th International Conference on Data Science and Advanced Analytics, pp. 80–89. IEEE (2018)
16. Goodman, B., Flaxman, S.: European union regulations on algorithmic decision-making and a "right to explanation". AI Mag. **38**(3), 50–57 (2017)
17. Guidotti, R., Monreale, A., Ruggieri, S., Turini, F., Giannotti, F., Pedreschi, D.: A survey of methods for explaining black box models. ACM Comput. Surv. **51**(5), 1–42 (2018)

18. Gunning, D.: Explainable Artificial Intelligence (XAI). DARPA, Web **2**(2) (2017)
19. Karimi, A.H., von Kügelgen, J., Schölkopf, B., Valera, I.: Algorithmic recourse under imperfect causal knowledge. In: NIPS 33 (2020)
20. Keane, M.T., Kenny, E.M., Delaney, E., Smyth, B.: If only we had better counterfactual explanations. In: Proceedings of the 30th International Joint Conference on Artificial Intelligence, IJCAI-21, pp. 4466–4474 (2021). https://doi.org/10.24963/ijcai.2021/609
21. Keane, M.T., Smyth, B.: Good counterfactuals and where to find them: a case-based technique for generating counterfactuals for explainable AI (XAI). In: Watson, I., Weber, R. (eds.) ICCBR 2020. LNCS (LNAI), vol. 12311, pp. 163–178. Springer, Cham (2020). https://doi.org/10.1007/978-3-030-58342-2_11
22. Kenny, E.M., Keane, M.T.: Twin-systems to explain artificial neural networks using case-based reasoning. In: IJCAI-19, pp. 2708–2715 (2019)
23. Kenny, E.M., Keane, M.T.: Explaining deep learning using examples: optimal feature weighting methods for twin systems using post-hoc, explanation-by-example in XAI. Knowl.-Based Syst. **233**, 107530 (2021)
24. Kusner, M.J., Loftus, J.R.: The long road to fairer algorithms. Nature (2020)
25. Larsson, S., Heintz, F.: Transparency in artificial intelligence. Internet Policy Rev. **9**(2) (2020)
26. Laugel, T., Lesot, M.J., Marsala, C., Renard, X., Detyniecki, M.: The dangers of post-hoc interpretability. In: IJCAI-19, pp. 2801–2807. AAAI Press (2019)
27. McGrath, R., et al.: Interpretable credit application predictions with counterfactual explanations. In: NIPS Workshop on Challenges and Opportunities for AI in Financial Services (2018)
28. McKenna, E., Smyth, B.: Competence-guided case-base editing techniques. In: Blanzieri, E., Portinale, L. (eds.) EWCBR 2000. LNCS, vol. 1898, pp. 186–197. Springer, Heidelberg (2000). https://doi.org/10.1007/3-540-44527-7_17
29. Miller, T.: Explanation in artificial intelligence: insights from the social sciences. Artif. Intell. **267**, 1–38 (2019)
30. Mothilal, R.K., Sharma, A., Tan, C.: Explaining machine learning classifiers through diverse counterfactual explanations. In: Proceedings of the Conference on Fairness, Accountability, and Transparency, pp. 607–617 (2020)
31. Muhammad, K.I., Lawlor, A., Smyth, B.: A live-user study of opinionated explanations for recommender systems. In: IUI, pp. 256–260 (2016)
32. Poyiadzi, R., Sokol, K., Santos-Rodriguez, R., De Bie, T., Flach, P.: Face: feasible and actionable counterfactual explanations. In: Proceedings of the AAAI/ACM Conference on AI, Ethics, and Society, pp. 344–350 (2020)
33. Ramon, Y., Martens, D., Provost, F., Evgeniou, T.: A comparison of instance-level counterfactual explanation algorithms for behavioral and textual data: SEDC, LIME-C and SHAP-C. Adv. Data Anal. Classif. **14**(4), 801–819 (2020). https://doi.org/10.1007/s11634-020-00418-3
34. Ribeiro, M.T., Singh, S., Guestrin, C.: Why should i trust you? In: Proceedings of the ACM SIGKDD, pp. 1135–1144 (2016)
35. Russell, C., Kusner, M.J., Loftus, J., Silva, R.: When worlds collide: integrating different counterfactual assumptions in fairness. In: NIPS, pp. 6414–6423 (2017)
36. Verma, S., Dickerson, J., Hines, K.: Counterfactual explanations for machine learning: a review. arXiv:2010.10596 (2020)
37. Wachter, S., Mittelstadt, B., Russell, C.: Counterfactual explanations without opening the black box. Harv. J. Law Tech. **31**, 841 (2017)

How Close Is Too Close? The Role of Feature Attributions in Discovering Counterfactual Explanations

Anjana Wijekoon(✉), Nirmalie Wiratunga, Ikechukwu Nkisi-Orji, Chamath Palihawadana, David Corsar, and Kyle Martin

School of Computing, Robert Gordon University, Aberdeen, Scotland
a.wijekoon1@rgu.ac.uk

Abstract. Counterfactual explanations describe how an outcome can be changed to a more desirable one. In XAI, counterfactuals are "actionable" explanations that help users to understand how model decisions can be changed by adapting features of an input. A case-based approach to counterfactual discovery harnesses Nearest-unlike Neighbours as the basis to identify the minimal adaptations needed for outcome change. This paper presents the DisCERN algorithm which uses the query, its NUN and substitution-based adaptation operations to create a counterfactual explanation case. DisCERN uses Integrated Gradients (IntG) feature attribution as adaptation knowledge to order substitution operations and to bring about the desired outcome with as few changes as possible. We present our novel approach with IntG where the NUN is used as the baseline against which the feature attributions are calculated. DisCERN also uses feature attributions to identify a NUN closer to the query, and thereby minimise the total change needed, but results suggest that the number of feature changes can increase. Overall, DisCERN outperforms other counterfactual algorithms such as DiCE and NICE in generating valid counterfactuals with fewer adaptations.

Keywords: Counterfactual XAI · Feature attribution · Integrated Gradients · Adaptation

1 Introduction

The use of "similar solutions to solve similar problems" naturally promotes an interpretable reasoning strategy [1]. Exemplar or prototype driven Explainable AI (XAI) methods are able to conveniently use the neighbourhood of similar problems to formulate explanations [2]. For instance a Nearest-like Neighbours (NLNs) based explainer extracts factual information to form an explanation from the similarity between the current problem and it's neighbourhood [3].

This research is funded by the iSee project (https://isee4xai.com) which received funding from EPSRC under the grant number EP/V061755/1.

M. T. Keane and N. Wiratunga (Eds.): ICCBR 2022, LNAI 13405, pp. 33–47, 2022.
https://doi.org/10.1007/978-3-031-14923-8_3

Research has shown that similarity metrics guided by feature selection and weighting [4] can significantly improve the relevance and profiling [5] of NLNs.

Whilst a factual explanation responds to "Why" questions, counterfactuals respond to "Why-Not" type queries. Counterfactuals are regarded as more intuitive for people compared to factual explanations because they present alternatives to reality with more desirable outcomes [6]. The prevailing CBR approach to counterfactual discovery harnesses similarities to Nearest-unlike Neighbours (NUN), i.e. similar cases with different class labels (see Fig. 1) [7,8]. A NUN represents potential changes to the current problem, with feature attribution prioritising the changes that, when actioned, can lead to a different outcome [8,9]. Focusing on a small number of key "actionable" features is more desirable from a practical standpoint, and has the benefit of reducing the recipient's cognitive burden for understanding the counterfactual.

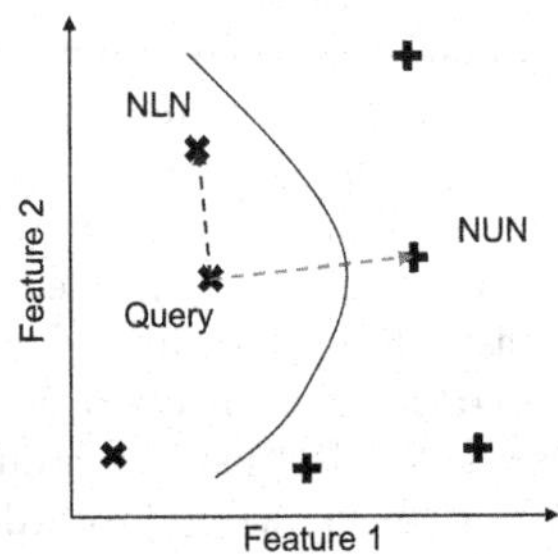

Fig. 1. Nearest-like and nearest-unlike neighbours in 2D space. Explaining the predicted class label of a query based on its similarity to the NLN is a factual explanation, and based on its dissimilarity to the NUN is a counterfactual.

Counterfactual discovery can be viewed as a search in the space of possible feature values guided by feature attribution weights. Here the challenge is to find a counterfactual with minimum feature changes to the query to achieve the needed outcome change. To address this we present DisCERN, a NUN-based counterfactual discovery algorithm that applies substitution-based adaptation operations [10] informed by feature attributions from Integrated Gradients (IntG) [11]. Specifically we seek answers to the following research questions:

- Can the query and NUN case pair form a suitable limit for the integral interval when calculating feature attributions for counterfactual discovery from IntG; and to
- What extent can the approximated integral intervals be used as perturbations to discover counterfactuals closer to the NUN?

The rest of the paper is organised as follows. Section 2 reviews related literature followed by Sect. 3 presenting the DisCERN Algorithm using the IntG feature attribution method for counterfactual discovery. Section 4 presents evaluation methodologies, the datasets and performance metrics with results in Sect. 5. Conclusions and future work appear in Sect. 6.

2 Related Work

Case-based Reasoning (CBR) [7,8] and optimisation techniques [12,13] have been the pillars of discovering counterfactuals. Recent work in CBR has shown how counterfactual case generation can be conveniently supported through the case adaptation stage, where query-retrieval pairs of successful counterfactual explanation experiences are used to create an explanation case-base [7]. Unlike the CBR approach, optimisation techniques like DiCE [12] train a generative model using gradient descent to output multiple diverse counterfactuals. Both approaches uphold two key requirements of good counterfactuals which are: maximising the probability of obtaining the desired label (i.e. different from current label); and minimising the distance (similar to current problem). Additionally the DiCE optimisation also maximises diversity amongst multiple alternative counterfactuals. With the CBR approach additional counterfactuals can be identified by increasing the neighbourhood. In our work presented here, we also adopt a CBR approach to finding counterfactuals, opting for a substitution-based adaptation technique informed by actionable feature recommendations from feature attribution techniques. In doing so, we avoid the need to create similarity-based explanation case-bases, yet maintain the advantage of locality-based explanations which ensure plausible counterfactuals that are often harder to guarantee with optimisation methods.

Feature attribution techniques are used in XAI to convey the extent to which a feature contributes to the predicted class label, with a higher weight indicating higher significance of the feature to the model's decision. Both model-agnostic and model-specific methods are found in literature. Model-agnostic approaches include LIME [14] and SHAP [15]; model-specific approaches often refer to Gradient based techniques, such as DeepLift [16] and Integrated Gradients [11]. Given a query, Integrated Gradients (IntG) are feature attributions calculated as the cumulative change of gradients with respect to interpolated estimates bounded by a baseline and the query. This baseline is formalised as the input where the prediction is neutral. Originally IntG opted to select an all zero input as the baseline for images and text [11], while [17] proposed a mask optimisation approach. Instead in this paper we explore two approaches to selecting the baseline specific to counterfactual discovery based on the uncertainty of the black-box model and the desired outcome change. While the flexibility to use different baselines makes IntG suitable for feature attribution during counterfactual discovery, it limits our approach to explaining only gradient descent optimised models.

3 DisCERN

Consider a neural network classifier F trained to predict the label y for a given input data instance x. The query instance x has m features where the ith feature is denoted by x_i and the label predicted by the classifier for x is $F(x)$. The optimal counterfactual for x is a data instance $\hat{x}$ where $\hat{y}$ is a more desirable label (i.e. $\hat{y} \neq y$) and is closest to x in the feature space. DisCERN's counterfactual discovery for x has the following steps:

1. find the Nearest-unlike Neighbour (NUN), x';
2. compute the feature attribution weight w_i for each x_i of query x, using a feature attribution method Φ. Order the list of features in descending order of their feature attributions, such that the first feature contributes the most to $F(x)$; and
3. iterate over the list of ordered features and at each step, a feature of the query is substituted with the corresponding feature from the NUN, which incrementally forms the adapted query $\hat{x}$. Repeat until $F(\hat{x}) \neq y$, at which point, $\hat{x}$ is selected as the counterfactual for query x.

3.1 Nearest-Unlike Neighbour

DisCERN considers the NUN, x', as the basis for discovering the optimal counterfactual $\hat{x}$ for the query x. Given a query, label pair (x, y) and the training dataset X, a function $\mathcal{N}$ retrieves the query's NUN, (x', y'):

$$\begin{gathered} \mathcal{N} = \underset{(x^i,y^i)\in X}{\arg\min}\ d(x, x^i); y^i \neq y \\ (x', y') \leftarrow \mathcal{N}((x, y), X) \end{gathered} \tag{1}$$

$\mathcal{N}$ calculates the distance $d(.)$ between the query and each candidate (x^i, y^i) in X, and returns the closest (minimum distance) candidate with the desired label, y' (i.e. $y^i \neq y$). Figure 1 illustrates a 2D ($m = 2$) feature space for a binary classed problem. It shows, for a given query, how the NUN (with the desired class label y') appears close to its decision boundary. Although the NUN is a valid counterfactual, there could be an alternative that is closer to the query. Accordingly, DisCERN applies adaptation operations that are bounded by both the query and the NUN to form the counterfactual.

3.2 Feature Ordering by Feature Attribution

Given a query x and its NUN, x', the adaptation step can be as simple as randomly selecting a feature at a time from x' into query $\hat{x}$. Consider the two adaptations presented in Fig. 2. Option 1 (Fig. 2a) needs two substitutions to find its counterfactual; in contrast Option 2 (Fig. 2b) needs just one substitution. This highlights the importance of feature ordering when the query is being iteratively adapted.

Feature attribution techniques identify important features that contributed to a query's class prediction. These attributions can be quantified as weights to enforce an ordering of features. Global feature weighting methods, such as Chi2, and more recent feature attribution explainer methods, such as LIME, SHAP and IntG; are all suitable sources of feature weights. Given feature attributions, w, features are ordered for adaptation in descending order of their feature attributions. The order of the resulting feature indices highlights the features that contribute the most to the current class label. Equation 2 formalises the partial order condition applied to obtain this list of feature indices.

$$x_i \preceq_{\mathcal{R}} x_j \iff \mathcal{R} :: w_i \geq w_j \tag{2}$$

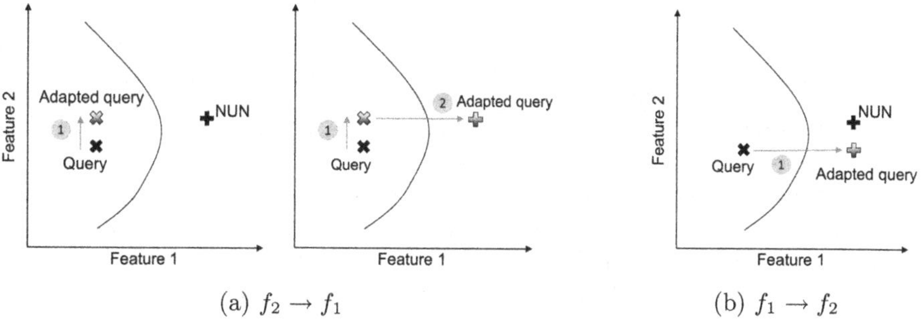

(a) $f_2 \rightarrow f_1$ (b) $f_1 \rightarrow f_2$

Fig. 2. Adaptations based on different feature orderings

3.3 Substitution-Based Adaptation

We illustrate in Fig. 3 the use of feature attributions to adapt query x to its counterfactual $\hat{x}$ following three ordered substitutions. Features of the query are ordered by their attributions where blue and orange colours indicate attributions towards and against the query label. Adaptation involves a series of copy operations from the NUN (from $\mathcal{N}$). Here the adapted query $\hat{x}$ becomes the counterfactual once F($\hat{x}$) outputs the same class as the NUN. In the worst case scenario, the counterfactual is equal to the NUN (i.e. $\hat{x} = x'$) where DisCERN performed m number of substitution operations. In an average case, DisCERN performs only n number of substitution operations where $1 \leq n \leq m$.

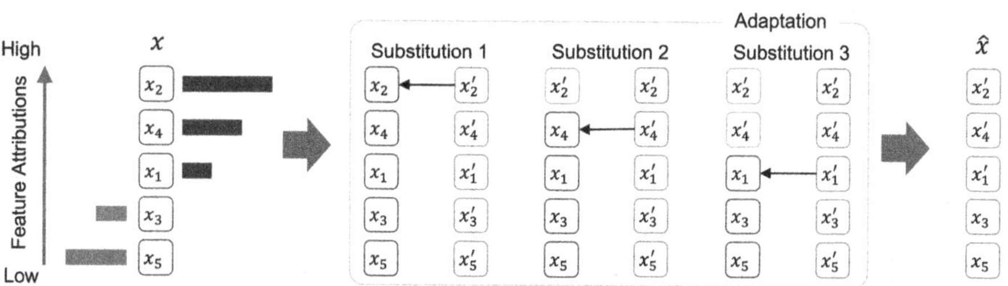

Fig. 3. Substitution-based adaptation operations

3.4 Integrated Gradients for DisCERN

Integrated Gradients (IntG) is a gradient based approach to finding feature attribution weights [11]. An attribution is calculated as the sum of gradients on data points occurring at sufficiently small intervals along the straight-line path from a baseline, x', to the query, x. These intermediate data points are synthetic, perturbed instances between a baseline and the query. With $\mathcal{A}$, number of perturbations, the αth perturbation, x^{α}, can be calculated as in Eq. 3.

$$x^{\alpha} = x' + \frac{\alpha}{\mathcal{A}} \times (x - x') \tag{3}$$

Here α controls the number of integral interval steps the baseline has taken towards the query x. The amount of perturbation is controlled by both the integral step $\frac{\alpha}{\mathcal{A}}$ and the difference between query and baseline. Accordingly a perturbed data instance can be viewed as the baseline taking α number of integral interval steps towards the query x. For symbolic features in tabular data, this requires converting symbolic values into nominal values before applying the integration interval step in Eq. 3. Figure 4 presents an example in the 2D space,

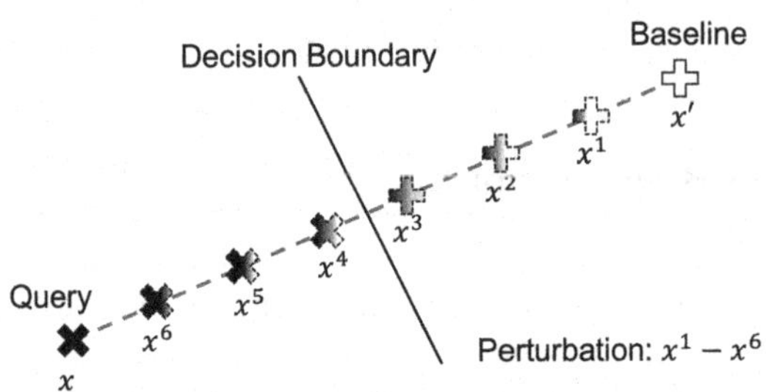

Fig. 4. Perturbation created between the baseline and the query

where six perturbations are created on the straight-line path between a query and a baseline. Given the set of perturbations, an attribution weight w_i for feature x_i, is calculated as in Eq. 4.

$$w_i = (x_i - x_i') \times \sum_{\alpha=1}^{\mathcal{A}} \frac{\partial x^{\alpha}}{\partial x_i} \tag{4}$$

In practice, a large number of perturbations is preferred because the summation of gradients is a discrete approximation of a continuous integration as discussed in [11].

An important decision for IntG feature attribution is the choice of the baseline. Typically an area of uncertainty provides a suitable place to form this baseline. With respect to a neural network classifier a data instance for which the classifier predicts similar probabilities to all class labels at the Softmax activation layer would be an ideal baseline choice. More formally, given the classifier F and a data instance x^i in X, the uncertainty of F in predicting the label of x^i is measured by an entropy $H(x^i|F)$ score. Therefore the chosen baseline, x', is the x^i which maximises entropy from all data instances.

$$x' \leftarrow \underset{x^i \in X}{\arg\max}\ H(x^i|F); x^i \in X \tag{5}$$

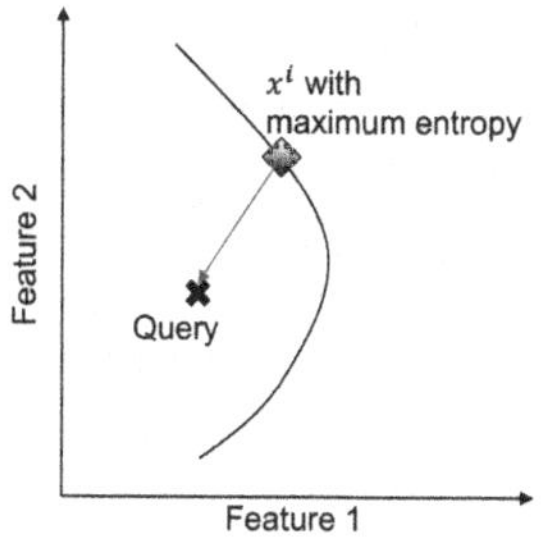

(a) Baseline that maximises entropy for vanilla feature attribution

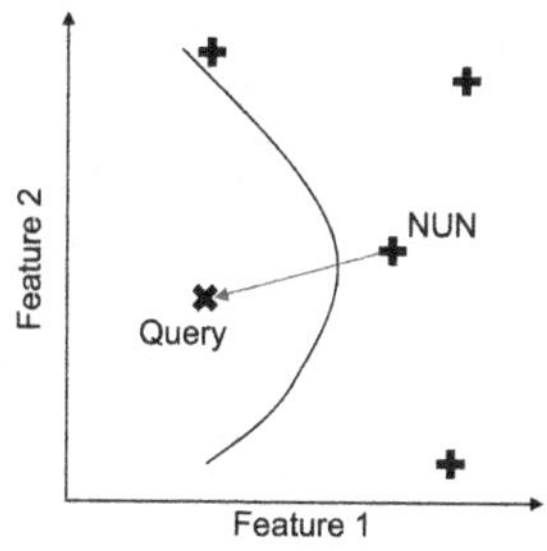

(b) Baseline that minimises distance for guiding counterfactual discovery

Fig. 5. Choice of baselines for IntG

Visually, the selected baseline, x', is either on the decision boundary or very close to it (Fig. 5a). Therefore the resultant feature attributions from a maximal entropy informed baseline, will identify feature values that caused the query to move away from the decision boundary where uncertainty is highest to its current class label.

In DisCERN, we want to choose a baseline for the straight line approximations to better suit our task of counterfactual discovery where feature attributions should highlight actionable features. Additionally this baseline data instance should be closer to the query in the feature space to minimise the changes needed to cross the decision boundary for class change. This is different from having a constant baseline that on average is an uncertain instance to all data points. Instead with DisCERN the baseline should change according to the locality of the query. Therefore the natural baseline choice for DisCERN is to have the NUN as the baseline. More formally, given the NUN function $\mathcal{N}$, and training set X, the baseline x' is retrieved as follows:

$$x' \leftarrow \mathcal{N}((x, y), X) \tag{6}$$

Figure 5b illustrates an example where a NUN is selected as the baseline. Here too the baseline by being close to the query is also in an area of uncertainty. However instead of a globally uncertain area, the NUN ensures that this uncertainty is locally relevant to the query to action the desired class change. Accordingly, the feature attributions can be interpreted as the feature contributions that action the query change from one side of the decision boundary to the other.

3.5 Bringing the NUN Closer

DisCERN's adaptations are bounded by the NUN such that in the worst case scenario, the adaptation-based counterfactual discovery results in the NUN itself (i.e. when all NUN values are copied over to the query). Typically, DisCERN would discover a counterfactual after performing only a subset of the total substitutions suggested by the NUN. This means that an adapted query, with just a small subset of feature value substitutions from the NUN, can be pushed over the boundary to the desired class label. Therefore it is interesting to consider whether an "even closer" NUN can be identified by focusing on just a subset of important features. Here we study two methods to bring the NUN closer to the boundary using: a weighted k-NN retrieval ($\mathcal{N}_w$); and from adapted perturbations ($\mathcal{N}_p$). The NUN found by the former is a true data instance whilst the latter is a perturbed "synthetic" data instance. We will refer to the unweighted k-NN retrieval of the NUN discussed in Sect. 3.1 as $\mathcal{N}$ in order to contrast that with the retrieval methods used by the weighted and perturbed methods aimed at recognising a NUN that is closer to the query.

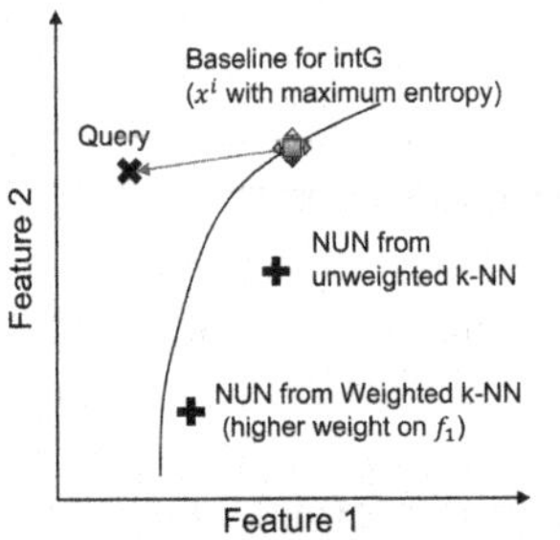

(a) Weighted k-NN retrieval to find NUN

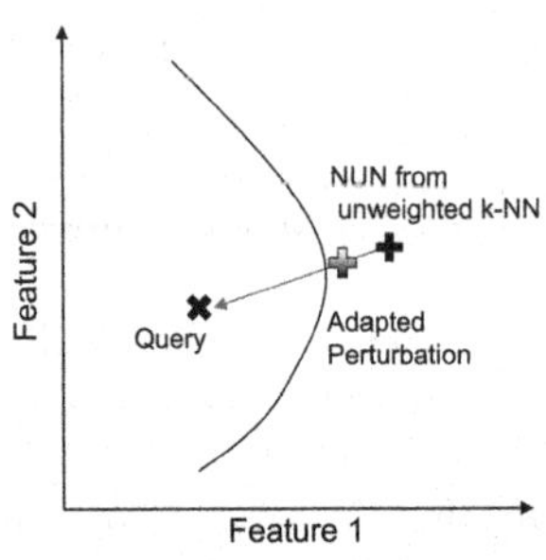

(b) Adapted IntG Perturbation

Fig. 6. Bringing NUN closer

Weighted K-NN Retrieval uses a feature attribution technique to select the subset of features to attend to when calculating distance. It then returns the NUN, x', for query, x, as follows:

$$\begin{aligned} w &= \phi(x, ...) \\ \mathcal{N}_w &= \underset{(x^i, y^i) \in X}{\arg\min}\; d(x, w, x^i); y^i \neq y \\ (x', y') &\leftarrow \mathcal{N}_w((x, y), \phi, X) \end{aligned} \tag{7}$$

Here ϕ returns the feature attributions w by adopting a method such as LIME [14], SHAP [15] or IntG [11]. The ... denotes any other requirements of the ϕ to generate feature attributions (such as method specific hyper-parameters). Note that when ϕ is IntG, a baseline must be specified before feature attribution weights can be computed. This weighted retrieval is illustrated in Fig. 6a for a given query x. The baseline for IntG here is an instance that maximises uncertainty, as measured by entropy in Eq. 5 (vanilla version). In our 2D space the feature attributions for Features 1 and 2 are $w_1 \geq w_2$, as such $\mathcal{N}_w$ will return the new NUN which is closer to the query with respect to f_1.

Adapted Perturbation approach creates a synthetic data instance by creating a perturbed instance between the NUN (retrieved by $\mathcal{N}$) and the query, x, which is closer to the query. This is illustrated in Fig. 6b with an example in 2D space where the "blue" coloured cross shows an ideal synthetic perturbed NUN that is closer to the query compared to the actual NUN. The discovery of this perturbed NUN, x', can be formalised as follows:

$$\alpha^* = \arg\max_{\alpha \in \mathcal{A}} \alpha; F(x^\alpha) \neq y$$
$$\mathcal{N}_p = \begin{cases} x'_i & \text{if } i \text{ is a symbolic feature} \\ x_i^{\alpha*} & \text{otherwise} \end{cases} \tag{8}$$
$$(x', y') \leftarrow \mathcal{N}_p((x, y), \mathcal{N}, X)$$

First, an $\mathcal{A}$ number of perturbations are created using Eq. 3 from the baseline to the query (see Fig. 4). The black box model, F, is used to predict the class for each perturbed data instance in turn. The selected perturbation, α^*, is the closest to the boundary with a prediction matching the desired class. Depending on the feature type (i.e. numeric or symbolic), values from the baseline, x', and $x^{\alpha*}$ are used to form the adapted perturbation. Specifically, symbolic features are substituted from x' and numerical features from the selected perturbation $x^{\alpha*}$. Note that the latter will have interpolated numeric values discovered as part of the perturbations. As a result, $\mathcal{N}_p$ returns a synthetic NUN, which preserves plausibility [6] when used in DisCERN's adaptation operations.

In Fig. 6b the adapted perturbation is on the straight-line path between the NUN from $\mathcal{N}$ and the query. Here both Features 1 and 2 are numeric. However with categorical features, the resulting adapted perturbation may not fall on the straight-line, yet we confirm that $F(x^{\alpha*}) \neq y$ (i.e. ensures a valid NUN from a different class to that of the query).

4 Evaluation

Three questions answered in the evaluations as follows:

- how does IntG compare to other feature attribution methods for counterfactual discovery with DisCERN?;
- how does DisCERN with IntG feature attributions compare against other counterfactual discovery algorithms in literature?; and
- what is the impact of bringing NUN closer in NUN-based counterfactual discovery?

4.1 Datasets

Five public domain datasets were used - Loan and Income datasets are from Kaggle; and Credit, Cancer and ICU datasets are from the UCI Machine Learning Data Repository. Table 2 summarises the properties of each dataset and

Table 1. Dataset details

Datasets	Dataset description	Explanation need	Labels
Loan	Predicts if a loan application is approved or not	What changes to the application will help to get the loan approved?	Q: Rejected CF: Approved
Income	Predicts if a persons income is higher or lower than 50K based on Census data	What changes will help an adult get an income over 50K?	Q: $\leq$50K CF: $\geq$50K
Credit	Predict if a credit card application is successful or not	What changes to the application will help to get a credit card?	Q: Rejected CF: Approved
Cancer	Predict the level of lung cancer risk of a patient based on demographic and triage data	How to reduce lung cancer risk of a patient?	Q: High risk or Medium risk CF: Low risk
ICU	Predict patient outcome in the Intensive Care Unit (ICU) based on demographic and diagnostic data	How to prevent the death of a patient in the ICU?	Q: Deceased CF: Discharged

the explanation needs as questions. Our evaluations consider all features actionable due to the lack of contextual data available. The labels column shows two class labels: the desirable (CF); and less desirable (Q). Typically a counterfactual explanation is needed to explain how a desirable situation could have been achieved when the black box model prediction is the less desired class.

Table 2. Dataset properties

Datasets	Loan	Income	Credit	Cancer	ICU
Features	69	14	14	12	107
Categorical features	8	8	8	11	8
Classes	2	2	2	3	2
Data instances	342865	45222	653	427	6238
Negative test instances	22543	11216	121	109	1003
RF test accuracy (%)	99.51	85.66	77.31	87.94	81.70
NN test accuracy (%)	99.66	85.02	75.00	87.23	73.08

4.2 Experiment Setup

The experimental pipeline to measure performance of a counterfactual discovery method appears in Fig. 7. First the dataset is split as 2/3 train and 1/3 test data. Next, a black-box classifier is trained and used to populate a case-base of labelled train data. In this paper we consider two classifiers: Random Forest

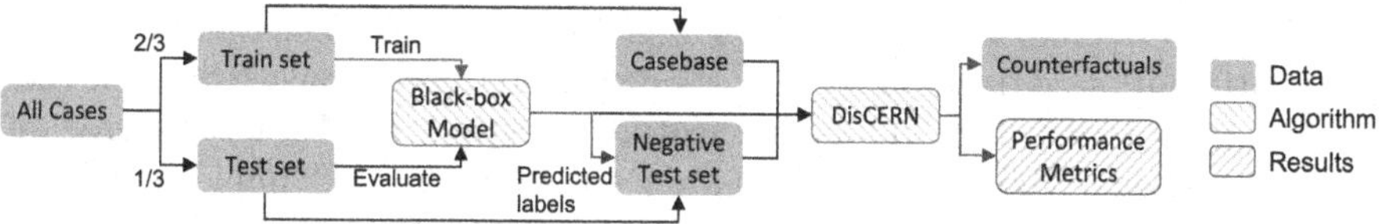

Fig. 7. Experiment setup

and Neural Networks. Test set performance of these 2 classifiers are in Table 2. The test instances classified into the less desirable class are the queries which form the Negative test set (see Table 1 for more details). Finally, the counterfactual discovery algorithm uses the classifier and the populated case-base to find counterfactuals for all query instances in the Negative test set. DisCERN uses Euclidean distance as $d(.)$; and it is available publicly on GitHub[1].

4.3 Performance Measures for Counterfactual Explanations

Validity (V) measures the percentage for which an algorithm is able to find a counterfactual with the desired label [12]. If N is the total number of queries and N_v the number of counterfactuals found, then $V = \frac{N_v}{N} \times 100$.

Sparsity ($\#F$) is the average number of feature differences between a query (x) and its counterfactual ($\hat{x}$) explanation [12]. Here m is the number of features.

$$\#F = \frac{1}{N_v \times m} \sum_{j=1}^{N_v} \sum_{i=1}^{m} 1_{[\hat{x}_i \neq x_i]} \tag{9}$$

Proximity ($\$F$) measures the mean feature-wise distance between a query and its counterfactual explanation [12]. The sum of normalised feature differences are averaged over $\#F$ and the number of counterfactuals (N_v).

$$\$F = \frac{1}{N_v \times \#F} \sum_{j=1}^{N_v} \sum_{i=1}^{m} (|\hat{x}_i - x_i|) \tag{10}$$

Datasets with more categorical features will have higher $\$F$ (difference is always 1), meaning, $\$F$ is not comparable across datasets. Note that higher values of V and smaller values of $\#F$ and $\$F$ are preferred.

5 Results

5.1 A Comparison of Feature Attribution Techniques

Feature attributions determine the order in which values are copied from NUN to query. This adaptation knowledge guides the value substitution operations until

[1] https://github.com/RGU-Computing/DisCERN-XAI.

a valid counterfactual is discovered. In Fig. 8 we compare DisCERN with five feature attribution variants for ordering substitution operations: **Random** (i.e. no adaptation knowledge); $\boldsymbol{\mathcal{X}^2}$ global feature selection; **LIME** local surrogate relevance weights, **SHAP**ely values from the KernelSHAP implementation; and **IntG** with the NUN ($\mathcal{N}$) baseline. Here, DisCERN uses the NUN from unweighted k-NN retrieval (i.e. $\mathcal{N}$) In Fig. 8, 5 marker shapes corresponds to each of the 5 algorithms, and 5 marker colours relate to results corresponding to each dataset. When sparsity and proximity are low the markers appear closer to the origin - this is desirable. Note that for visual clarity the x-axis is in log scale.

IntG achieves the lowest sparsity while random and $\mathcal{X}^2$ techniques achieves lower proximity. IntG's use of the NUN baseline has successfully contributed to reducing sparsity, i.e. IntG's feature attributions had significantly reduced the number of adaptation operations, when compared to using feature attributions from LIME and SHAP. Generally we found that with all datasets, making larger changes to feature values ($F) leads to discovering a counterfactual with fewer feature substitutions (#F). Therefore when we consider the total change (#$F \times$ $$F$), IntG is best on all datasets except on Loan, where $\mathcal{X}^2$ was better. We also see that IntG had higher proximity (0.72 compared to the rest in a range of 0.28–0.39) on the Cancer dataset, but it had significantly lower sparsity (fewer features adapted), with almost half that of the other attribution methods (log scale can mask this difference). This can be a result of IntG selecting categorical features compared to other techniques.

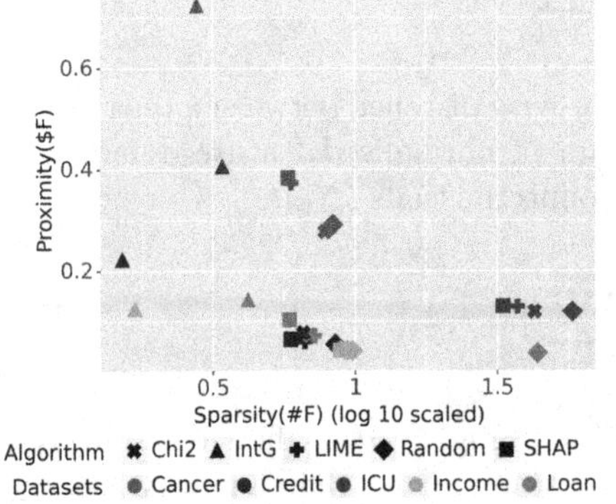

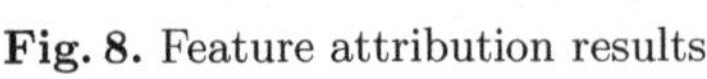

Fig. 8. Feature attribution results

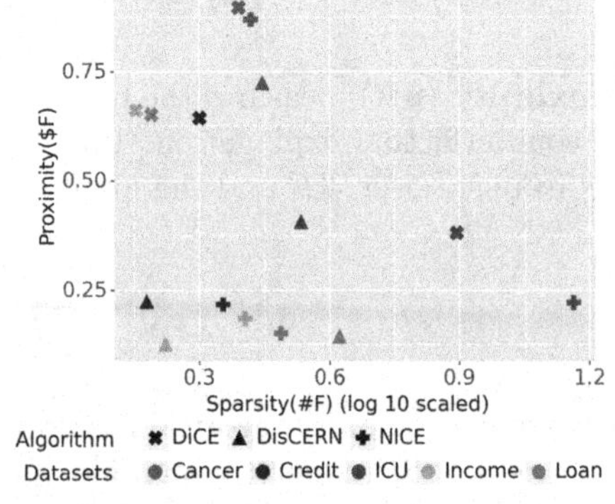

Fig. 9. Counterfactual algorithm results

5.2 A Comparison of Counterfactual Discovery Algorithms

A sparsity and proximity comparison of DisCERN (using $\Phi = IntG$) with popular counterfactual discovery algorithms from literature appear in Fig. 9. DiCE is a generative algorithm that discovers counterfactuals by optimising a randomly initialised input to maximise diversity and minimise sparsity and proximity [12].

Table 3. Validity and total change between counterfactual discovery algorithms

Algorithm	Validity					Total Change				
	Loan	Income	Credit	Cancer	ICU	Loan	Income	Credit	Cancer	ICU
DiCE	99.20	92.55	80.99	**100**	33.80	1.009	0.945	1.286	2.207	2.991
NiCE	97.70	92.50	85.12	82.57	82.35	**0.461**	0.466	0.491	2.278	3.230
DisCERN	**100**	**100**	**100**	**100**	**100**	0.599	**0.209**	**0.338**	**2.014**	**1.387**

NICE is a NUN-based counterfactual discovery algorithm that uses a reward function to minimise sparsity, proximity and to preserve plausibility [8].

Overall minimum proximity is seen with DisCERN (lowest on credit, income and loan). DiCE is better for sparsity (lowest on cancer, income and loan) but at the expense of proximity, which requires larger value adaptations (i.e. higher proximity) of the query applied to a fewer number of features (i.e. lower sparsity). Between NUN-based algorithms NICE and DisCERN, the lower sparsity and proximity achieved with DisCERN makes it a better candidate for counterfactual discovery.

Crucial to counterfactual explainers is the ability to find a valid counterfactual situation (i.e. one with the desired class). Results in Table 3 show that DisCERN dominates in this respect, whereby the NUN guided counterfactual is 100% valid. This is in comparison to DiCE, which uses a generative model given a randomly initialised input and NICE, which like DisCERN, uses a NUN as the basis but uses a reward function to find a counterfactuals. As a result, DiCE and NICE are likely to either fail to generate a counterfactual, or fail to generate a counterfactual that does belong to the desired class (in a multi-class setting). Note that for DiCE and NICE results in Fig. 9, we have reported averaged results using only those queries for which a valid counterfactual was discovered (N_v). We observed a trade-off between sparsity and proximity (in Fig. 9), and accordingly these are combined into total change ($\#F \times \$F$) in Table 3. Here DisCERN is best on all datasets (except Loan where it is marginally worse) as it manages to better balance proximity and sparsity requirements.

5.3 Impact of Bringing NUN Closer

Figure 10 compares DisCERN counterfactual discovery with the weighted ($\mathcal{N}_w$) and non weighted kNN ($\mathcal{N}$) NUN retrieval methods. The additional adapted perturbation ($\mathcal{N}_p$) results is included for IntG feature attribution method. Here in each evaluation DisCERN ensures $\Phi = \phi$. For example, if DisCERN feature ordering (Φ) is using SHAP feature attributions, weighted k-NN retrieval also uses SHAP weights ($\phi = SHAP$) to find the closer NUN. We note that $\mathcal{N}_w$ approach was not evaluated with the Cancer dataset since we were unable to find a valid baseline that maximises entropy in the comparably smaller train set.

Overall $\mathcal{N}_p$ with IntG and $\mathcal{N}_w$ with SHAP and IntG show increased sparsity and decreased proximity compared to $\mathcal{N}$. Lower proximity is a result of bringing the NUN closer with respect to a subset of important features. Here the resulting

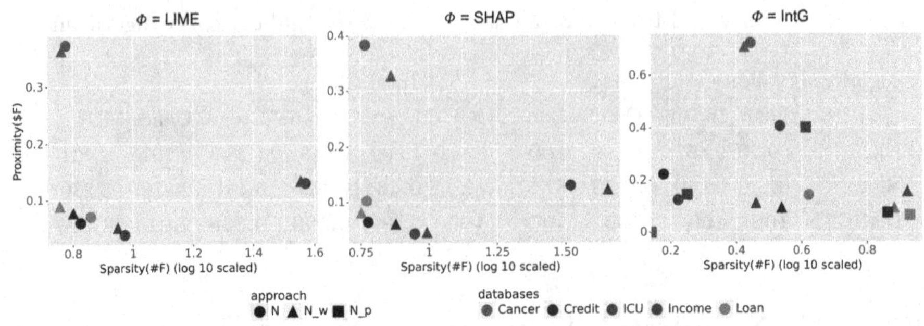

Fig. 10. Results on alternative approaches to form closer NUNs

NUN will have smaller value differences (decreased proximity) with the query. Therefore, initial substitutions will only make smaller actionable changes to the query. These initial features were already part of the subset that influenced the weighted kNN retrieval. As a result, the query will need an increased number of feature changes (increased sparsity). However, empirical evidence remains inconclusive for $\mathcal{N}_w$ with LIME. This might be explained by LIME being a local surrogate attribution method. Accordingly, $\mathcal{N}_w$ with LIME returns a NUN closer to the decision boundary of the local surrogate model, not of the global model. As a result, DisCERN makes larger changes to the query (i.e. increased proximity) in earlier substitutions which decreases the number of feature changes needed (decreased sparsity). In contrast, SHAP or IntG feature attributions seems globally faithful and better aligned to the black box decision boundary. Similarly, adapted perturbation based NUN is also globally faithful which results in increased sparsity and decreased proximity.

6 Conclusions

The XAI DisCERN algorithm discovers counterfactual explanations by applying a set of substitution-based adaptation operations to the NUN. These adaptations help create counterfactual explanations for black box predictions. DisCERN uses feature attribution weights, firstly to guide adaptation choices and, secondly to identify NUNs closer to the decision boundary. Both lead to valid counterfactuals from minimally adapted queries. The use of integrated gradients for feature attribution by limiting the integral approximation to the query and NUN is a unique contribution of this paper. Results suggests that this approach is more effective in guiding counterfactual discovery compared to feature attributions that do not consider both the desired and current prediction boundary locality.

An interesting study of where to position the NUN in support of counterfactual discovery found that it was possible to significantly minimise the total actionable changes required to create the counterfactual explanation, but also increased the number of feature changes needed for the desirable class change. In conclusion, DisCERN discovers effective counterfactuals, and provides the flexibility to select NUN and feature attribution technique based on the AI model and the preference of feature changes in the problem domain. Future work will look to expand DisCERN to generate counterfactual explanations that can also satisfy immutable and constrained feature requirements.

References

1. Li, O., Liu, H., Chen, C., Rudin, C.: Deep learning for case-based reasoning through prototypes: a neural network that explains its predictions. In: 32nd AAAI Conference on Artificial Intelligence, pp. 3530–3537 (2018)
2. Arrieta, A.B., et al.: Explainable artificial intelligence (XAI): concepts, taxonomies, opportunities and challenges toward responsible AI. Inf. Fusion **58**, 82–115 (2020)
3. Kenny, E.M., Keane, M.T.: Twin-systems to explain artificial neural networks using case-based reasoning: comparative tests of feature-weighting methods in ANN-CBR twins for XAI. In: IJCAI-19, pp. 2708–2715, IJCAI (2019)
4. Wettschereck, D., Aha, D.W., Mohri, T.: A review and empirical evaluation of feature weighting methods for a class of lazy learning algorithms. Artif. Intell. Rev. **11**(1), 273–314 (1997)
5. Craw, S., Massie, S., Wiratunga, N.: Informed case base maintenance: a complexity profiling approach. In: AAAI, pp. 1618–1621 (2007)
6. Byrne, R.M.: Counterfactuals in explainable artificial intelligence (XAI): evidence from human reasoning. In: IJCAI, pp. 6276–6282 (2019)
7. Keane, M.T., Smyth, B.: Good counterfactuals and where to find them: a case-based technique for generating counterfactuals for explainable AI (XAI). In: Watson, I., Weber, R. (eds.) ICCBR 2020. LNCS (LNAI), vol. 12311, pp. 163–178. Springer, Cham (2020). https://doi.org/10.1007/978-3-030-58342-2_11
8. Brughmans, D., Martens, D.: Nice: an algorithm for nearest instance counterfactual explanations. arXiv preprint arXiv:2104.07411 (2021)
9. Wiratunga, N., Wijekoon, A., Nkisi-Orji, I., Martin, K., Palihawadana, C., Corsar, D.: Discern: discovering counterfactual explanations using relevance features from neighbourhoods. In: 33rd ICTAI, pp. 1466–1473. IEEE (2021)
10. Craw, S., Wiratunga, N., Rowe, R.C.: Learning adaptation knowledge to improve CBR. Artif. Intell. **170**(16–17), 1175–1192 (2006)
11. Sundararajan, M., Taly, A., Yan, Q.: Axiomatic attribution for deep networks. In: International Conference on Machine Learning, pp. 3319–3328. PMLR (2017)
12. Mothilal, R.K., Sharma, A., Tan, C.: Explaining machine learning classifiers through diverse counterfactual explanations. In: Proceedings of the 2020 Conference on Fairness, Accountability, and Transparency, pp. 607–617 (2020)
13. Karimi, A.-H., Barthe, G., Balle, B., Valera, I.: Model-agnostic counterfactual explanations for consequential decisions. In: International Conference on Artificial Intelligence and Statistics, pp. 895–905. PMLR (2020)
14. Ribeiro, M.T., Singh, S., Guestrin, C.: Why should i trust you? explaining the predictions of any classifier. In: 22nd ACM SIGKDD, pp. 1135–1144 (2016)
15. Lundberg, S.M., Lee, S.-I.: A unified approach to interpreting model predictions. Adv. Neural. Inf. Process. Syst. **30**, 4765–4774 (2017)
16. Li, J., Zhang, C., Zhou, J.T., Fu, H., Xia, S., Hu, Q.: Deep-lift: deep label-specific feature learning for image annotation. IEEE Trans. Cybern. (2021)
17. Qi, Z., Khorram, S., Li, F.: Visualizing deep networks by optimizing with integrated gradients. In: CVPR Workshops, vol. 2 (2019)

Algorithmic Bias and Fairness in Case-Based Reasoning

William Blanzeisky(✉), Barry Smyth, and Pádraig Cunningham

School of Computer Science, University College Dublin, Dublin 4, Ireland
william.blanzeisky@ucdconnect.ie, {barry.smyth,padraig.cunningham}@ucd.ie

Abstract. Algorithmic bias due to underestimation refers to situations where an algorithm under-predicts desirable outcomes for a protected minority. In this paper we show how this can be addressed in a case-based reasoning (CBR) context by a metric learning strategy that explicitly considers bias/fairness. Since one of the advantages CBR has over alternative machine learning approaches is interpretability, it is interesting to see how much this metric learning distorts the case-retrieval process. We find that bias is addressed with a minimum impact on case-based predictions - little more than the predictions that need to be changed are changed. However, the effect on explanation is more significant as the case-retrieval *order* is impacted.

1 Introduction

Transparency and fairness have emerged as areas of concern in AI systems in recent years, changing what it means to evaluate the performance of many AI and machine learning systems in practice. It is no longer sufficient for predictions to be efficient, competent and accurate overall, they much also be fair and transparent in a way that does not inadvertently disadvantage minority groups. Consequently, researchers have been exploring how best to assess and address bias in machine learning systems.

One of the advantages of case-based reasoning (CBR) is that it can deliver transparency through case-based explanation, which has had a lot of attention in CBR research [18,32]. On the other hand, while there has been a lot of machine learning (ML) research on bias and fairness, it has not received a lot of attention in the CBR community. A CBR system will be biased or unfair if it under-predicts the desirable outcome for a protected group, for example loan approvals for women [5,17]. Further detail on different degrees of bias is provided in Sect. 2.

We show that bias can and does arise in the nearest neighbour (NN) retrieval that is central to most CBR systems. We demonstrate how this bias can be removed through a multi-objective metric learning strategy that explicitly considers bias in addition to accuracy, a novel modification of CBR's similarity knowledge container [30]. Since a local change to the similarity knowledge container will impact retrieval, this approach raises the question of whether any distortion in retrieval will lead to a material impact on transparency. For our

M. T. Keane and N. Wiratunga (Eds.): ICCBR 2022, LNAI 13405, pp. 48–62, 2022.
https://doi.org/10.1007/978-3-031-14923-8_4

purposes, transparency equates to explanation. We are particularly concerned with what Keane and Kenny [18] call "*post-hoc* explanation-by-example". In addition to nearest like neighbours, the cases invoked for explanation can be counter-factual cases, near misses, nearest unlike neighbours or even *a fortiori* cases.

In this paper we address two research questions:

1. Can we fix underestimation bias in k-NN and if we can what is the impact on accuracy?
2. How much does fixing underestimation distort the retrieval model?

We find that our method which we call FairRet does fix the prediction bias with minimal impact on predictions – the predictions that need to be changed are changed and little more. However, we find that changing the retrieval metric does alter the nearest neighbour ranking so the cases that have been selected for explanation may change.

The paper proceeds with a review of related work in Sect. 2. Our multi-criteria algorithm for fair metric learning is presented in Sect. 3 and the results are presented in Sect. 4. The paper concludes with some ideas for future work in Sect. 5.

2 Related Research

This research is informed by other work relating to bias in ML, bias in CBR and metric learning. The relevant work in these areas is discussed in the following subsections.

2.1 Bias in ML

As Machine Learning (ML) systems are used to solve problems with high social impacts, in areas such as health care and security [4], there is an increasing need for fairness-aware ML. The demand for discrimination-free ML becomes more apparent as many countries and regions establish regulations to prohibit discrimination. For example, the 1964 US Civil Rights Act (Title VII) prohibits employment discrimination based on race, color, religion, sex, national origin, sexual orientation, and gender identity. An algorithm is deemed discriminatory if it systematically disadvantages people from specific groups instead of relying solely on individual merits [2]. Despite research attention in recent years, the anecdotal evidence of algorithmic bias is still growing [3,15].

ML research on bias can be categorized into *bias discovery* and *bias mitigation* [37]. Most literature on *bias discovery* focuses on quantifying bias and developing a theoretical understanding of the social and legal aspects of ML bias. In contrast, *bias mitigation* focuses on technical approaches to prevent bias. A variety of measures of unfairness have been proposed, with each aiming to measure and emphasize different aspects of fairness [8]. An ML model is generally considered 'fair' if it is not inclined to award desirable outcomes $Y = 1$ (e.g., loan approval/job offers) preferentially to one side of a protected category $S = 0$ (e.g. female/protected group).

Mehrabi *et al.* [26] present a survey of the different types of algorithmic bias that shows that the main source of bias is the training data itself. This may be due to discriminatory practices in the past or shortcomings in the way the data was collected. However, recent work has shown that an ML model can amplify undesirable biases in the training data, even when samples are perfectly representative of the population [7]. So the two primary sources of algorithmic bias are: [5,17]:

- **Negative Legacy**: bias due to the training *data*, either due to poor sampling, incorrect labelling or discriminatory practices in the past.
- **Underestimation**: bias due to the *algorithm*. This happens when the algorithm focuses on strong signals in the data thereby missing more subtle phenomena. Hence, the classifier accentuates bias that might be present in the data and underestimates the infrequent outcome for the minority group.

Disparate Impact (DI_S) is one of the accepted measures of unfairness [14]:

$$\mathrm{DI}_S \leftarrow \frac{P[\hat{Y} = 1|S = 0]}{P[\hat{Y} = 1|S = 1]} < \tau \tag{1}$$

It is the ratio of desirable outcomes $\hat{Y}$ predicted for the protected minority $S = 0$ compared with that for the majority $S = 1$. This measure is independent of what is actually in the training data. When the objective is to quantify bias due to the algorithm, Kamishima *et al.* [17] have proposed the underestimation index (UEI) that considers divergences between actual and predicted distributions for all protected groups S based on the Hellinger distance:

$$\mathrm{UEI} \leftarrow \sqrt{1 - \sum_{y,s \in D} \sqrt{P[\hat{Y} = y, S = s] \times P[Y = y, S = s]}} \tag{2}$$

Here y and s are the possible values of Y and S respectively. $\mathrm{UEI} = 0$ indicates that there is no difference between the probability distribution of the training samples and prediction made by a classifier (no underestimation).

Although this notion is useful when quantifying the extent to which a model's prediction deviates from the training samples, it does not directly tell us how the protected group is doing since it is an aggregate score across all protected attribute S and outcomes Y. An underestimation score (US_S) in line with DI_S (see Eq. 1) that compares predicted and actual outcomes for the protected minority would be [5]:

$$\mathrm{US}_{S=0} \leftarrow \frac{P[\hat{Y} = 1|S = 0]}{P[Y = 1|S = 0]} \tag{3}$$

This is the ratio of desirable outcomes predicted by the classifier for the protected group compared with what is actually present in the data [5]. If $\mathrm{US}_{S=0} < 1$ the classifier is under-predicting desirable outcomes for the minority. It is worth nothing that when $\text{US}_{S=0} = 1$ the classifier may still be biased against the minority group; it is faithful to the data but there may still be a poor DI_S score.

Depending on when the fairness criteria is imposed, there are three categories of strategies to mitigate unfairness [26]:

- *Pre-processing* approaches recognize that data is often the source of the problem. Hence, most methods in this category aim to perform some type of transformation on the dataset to repair the training data prior to feeding it into a ML model.
- *In-processing* approaches focus on mitigating unfairness during the model building process. This can be done by modifying an algorithm's objective function to account for one or more fairness measures.
  one can enforce a fairness measure as a constraint directly into an algorithm optimization function [17,35]. Our multi-objective optimization strategy fits squarely in the in-processing camp.
- *Post-processing* approaches are centered on the fact that the output of an ML model might be biased towards one or more subgroup within the protected attribute. One remediation strategies in this category is threshold adjustment strategy proposed by Corbett-Davies *et al.* [10]

2.2 Bias in CBR

Bias and fairness is not a topic that has received much attention in CBR research. This may be because CBR already scores well in terms of transparency, since it readily supports explanation. In fact the most relevant CBR research on fairness by Dodge *et al.* [11] presents explanation as the solution by proposing that hybrid explanations that have global and case-specific components will support fairness.

In other work [5] we have shown that under-representation of desirable outcomes for the minority class and class imbalance in general in the training data are significant contributors to bias. While the first of these issues has not received much attention in CBR research, the issue of class imbalance has [25] Jalali and Leake [16] show how this class imbalance problem can be addressed by an ensemble strategy with the extra retrieval overhead of the ensemble handled by using locality-preserving hashing for nearest neighbour retrieval. By contrast Lin *et al.* [23] explore the effectiveness of under- and over-sampling the case-base in order to address bias due to class imbalance. They find that, at least for their scenario, undersampling is more effective.

Finally, Ontañón and Plaza [29] have addressed bias in CBR where 'bias' refers to scenarios where the case-base is not a representative sample of the distribution in the real-world. They present a case bartering strategy to redress imbalances and thus remove bias.

2.3 Metric Learning

If a CBR system based on nearest neighbour retrieval is biased then an obvious strategy to address this bias is to adjust the retrieval process. One way to do this would be to induce a new similarity/distance metric that is not biased. A metric is a function that defines a distance between each pair of elements of a set. Formally, it is a mapping $d : X \times X \to \mathbb{R}_{\geq 0}$ over a vector space X that satisfies the properties:

1. $d(x_i, x_j) + d(x_j, x_k) \geq d(x_i, x_k)$ (triangular inequality)
2. $d(x_i, x_j) \geq 0$ (non-negativity)
3. $d(x_i, x_j) = d(x_j, x_i)$ (symmetry)
4. $d(x_i, x_j) = 0 \iff x_i = x_j$ (distinguishability)

$\forall x_i, x_j, x_k \in X$.

A family of metrics over X is defined by computing Euclidean distances after applying a linear transformation $\mathbf{L}$:

$$d_{\mathbf{L}}(x_i, x_j) = \|\mathbf{L}(x_i - x_j)\|_2 \tag{4}$$

Hence, metric learning refers to the field of research concerned with inducing metrics from data [33,34]. The two main strategies are based on:

- **Linear Discriminant Analysis (LDA)** is a linear projection method similar to Principle Component Analysis (PCA). However LDA is *supervised* in the sense that the objective is to discover a linear projection $x \to \mathbf{L}x$ that does a good job of separating the classes. Thus LDA can be used as the basis of a learned metric for k-NN.
- **The Mahalanobis Distance** between two vectors x_i and x_j is defined to be:

$$d_{\mathbf{M}}(x_i, x_j) = \sqrt{(x_i - x_j)^\top \mathbf{S}(x_i - x_j)} \tag{5}$$

  where $\mathbf{S}$ is the covariance matrix of the data. If the data is described by m features then $\mathbf{S}$ is an $m \times m$ matrix. If we replace $\mathbf{S}$ with any Positive Semi-Definite (PSD) matrix $\mathbf{M}$, we have a very general metric that can be learned from the data – this is the Generalized Mahalanobis distance [33]:

$$d_{\mathbf{GM}}(x_i, x_j) = \sqrt{(x_i - x_j)^\top \mathbf{M}(x_i - x_j)} \tag{6}$$

Metric learning has also received some attention in CBR research [13]. For instance Nicolàs Sans *et al.* [28] use a metric learning protocol based on the framework by Xing *et al.* [36] for Melanoma diagnosis. Their objective was to optimise for accuracy as is the objective with metric learning in general. In the next section, we see how metric learning can optimise for accuracy *and* fairness.

3 FairRet: Eliminating Bias with Metric Learning

In this section we present FairRet, a case retrieval process that explicitly considers bias/fairness by using multi-objective metric learning strategy. First we reflect on where this fits in the overall CBR framework.

3.1 Bias and The Similarity Knowledge Container

It is worth noting that this focus on retrieval means that our strategy for dealing with bias is primarily concerned with the similarity knowledge container, one of the four sources of knowledge in a CBR system, according to Richter's *knowledge container model* [30]. Richter's knowledge container model emphasises how case-based reasoning provides for a flexible combination of domain knowledge and data by distributing expertise and knowledge across four distinct knowledge containers: *vocabulary*, *case base*, *similarity*, and *adaptation*. Contemporary CBR research has largely focused on the interplay and interaction between these different knowledge containers in different problem solving settings, as a way to better understand the knowledge trade-offs that exist, and their relative impact, in conventional CBR settings.

Considering bias from the perspective of the similarity knowledge container offers a new perspective on the role of similarity knowledge in CBR. It also leads to the natural question as to whether alternative approaches might exist with respect to other knowledge containers – see [31] for related ideas on case-based explanation – which, for now, we leave as a matter for future consideration.

3.2 A Metric Learning Approach

Given a dataset $\mathcal{D}(X, Y, S)$, where X represents the feature vector, the target label is Y and the protected attribute is S; let $\hat{Y}$ be the prediction output of a model $\mathcal{M}(\theta, X, S)$. The objective in metric learning is to find a linear transformation of the input space $X \rightarrow \mathbf{L}X$ such that nearest neighbours computed from the distances in Eq. 4 share the same class labels. Using the LDA strategy mentioned in Sect. 2.3, this projection matrix $\mathbf{L}$ is typically obtained by solving an optimization problem that maximizes accuracy of the k-NN classifier $Acc(Y, \hat{Y})$.

If the metric learning optimises only for accuracy there is potential for bias. We are particularly concerned with bias where desirable outcomes $Y = 1$ are under-predicted for the protected category $S = 0$. This can happen because reasonable accuracy can be achieved by ignoring errors for under-represented minorities. If we use UEI (see Eq. 2) to quantify underestimation we have a multi-objective optimization problem (MOOP) to find the best solution θ:

$$\theta = arg\max_{\theta} \left(Acc(Y, \hat{Y}), \frac{1}{UEI(Y, \hat{Y}, S)} \right) \tag{7}$$

Unfortunately, this results in a non-convex loss function. Consequently, optimizers that rely on the gradient of the loss function will struggle to converge due to the fact that non-convex functions have potentially many local minima (or maxima) and saddle points. Furthermore, we also have to consider that the two objectives (fairness and accuracy) might be competing so that no improvement on one objective is possible without making things worse in the other. When there is no single solution that dominates in both criteria, the concept of Pareto optimality is used to find a set of non-dominated solutions created by the two competing criteria. Due to this complexity, we propose a multi-objective metric learning strategy using Multi-objective Particle Swarm Optimization (MOPSO) to optimize for accuracy and fairness.

3.3 Multi-objective Particle Swarm Optimization

Particle Swarm Optimization (PSO) [19] has been widely used to solve optimization problems due to its flexibility to be integrated with other optimization techniques (e.g., [27]), its gradient-free mechanism, simplicity of implementation and speed of convergence to reasonably good solutions [24]. These characteristics make PSO particularly suitable for multi-objective optimization.

Similar to PSO, MOPSO starts by randomly generating particles and evaluating their fitness value. For each iteration t, each particle updates its position X_i^t in the search space with a velocity:

$$V_i^{t+1} = wV_i^t + c_1 r_1 (pbest_i^t - X_i^t) + c_2 r_2 (gbest_i^t - X_i^t) \tag{8}$$

where

- w is an inertia constant that determines how much the previous velocity influences the next movement
- c_1 and c_2 control how much own experience and group experience, respectively, influence the movement
- r_1 and r_2 are two randomly generated values sampled from a uniform distribution $\mathcal{U}(0, 1)$
- $pbest_i$ is the best solution particle i has found in iteration t
- $gbest_i$ is the best overall solution found in iteration t

To account for multiple objectives, MOPSO uses the concept of Pareto dominance to determine the flight direction of a particle and a global repository in which every particle deposits its flight experiences after each flight cycle [9]. In each iteration, updates to the repository are made such that newly found non-dominated solutions are added to the repository while dominated solutions are eliminated. The non-dominated solutions explored at each iteration are then organised into hypercubes. Each hypercube is assigned a fitness value that is inversely proportional to the number of non-dominated solutions it contains. A leader will be chosen from this repository, which is later used by other particles to guide their flight. The position of the leader will be used to replace the global best $gbest_i^t$) in Eq. 8. In addition, the repository has limited size and, if it is full, new solutions are inserted based on the retention criterion, that is, giving priority to solutions located in less crowded areas of the objective space. This will result in a more diverse Pareto front (see sample Pareto fronts in Fig. 1).

Our preliminary experiments show that classical MOPSO algorithm suffers from premature-convergence. Intuitively, once the particles move closer to the local optimum, they will lose the ability to search for the global optimum [22]. This phenomenon is in fact a well-known problem of PSO [21]. Most of the

Table 1. Summary details of the four datasets.

Dataset	Samples	Features	% Minority
Synthetic	5,000	3	50%
Exemplar	37,607	18	30%
(reduced) Adult	48,842	7	25%
(reduced) Recidivism	7,214	7	45%

proposed solutions are problem-dependent but are generally based on random-perturbation [38].

Using the idea of random perturbation and the acceptance of inferior solutions to escape local optima from simulated annealing, we modified the classical MOPSO algorithm in [9] by adding random perturbations to the position of the particles whenever the repository is full. Specifically, our modification to the algorithm adds a small Gaussian noise $X \sim \mathcal{N}(0,1)$ to the position of randomly-selected particles located in the most populated areas in the objective space. If an updated solution improves on the original solution, it is accepted as personal best (p_{best} in Eq. 8) with a probability of 1. In contrast, if the updated solution is worse than the original solution, then it may still be accepted with a probability $P_{accept} = 0.5$.

The main parameters of MOPSO are the inertia weight w and learning factors c_1 and c_2. The inertia weight w controls the balance between the exploration and exploitation while the learning factors c_1 and c_2 controls how much each particle personal best and global best influence the next movement. Our preliminary experiments show that the self-adaptive parameters strategy proposed in [1] works well. To ensure reproducibility we have provided access to all of the data and code at the author's Github page[1].

4 Results

We now move on to evaluating our framework on two synthetic and two real-world datasets, which have been extensively studied in fairness research. Specifically, our evaluation considers the synthetic dataset introduced in [14], the medium synthetic exemplar dataset [6], the reduced version of the Adult dataset [20] and the reduced ProPublica Recidivism dataset [12]. The protected attribute that we considered are *Gender*, *Age*, *Sex* and *Caucasian* for the Synthetic, Exemplar, Adult and Recidivism datasets, respectively. Summary statistics for these datasets are provided in Table 1.

To illustrate the effectiveness of the proposed strategy, we compare our framework for fair retrieval (FairRet) with a standard retrieval process (StdRet); in this

[1] https://github.com/williamblanzeisky/Algorithmic-Bias-and-Fairness-in-Case-Based-Reasoning.

study we use the scikit-learn implementation[2] which uses Euclidean distance. For the evaluations that follow the datasets were divided 70:30 for training and testing.

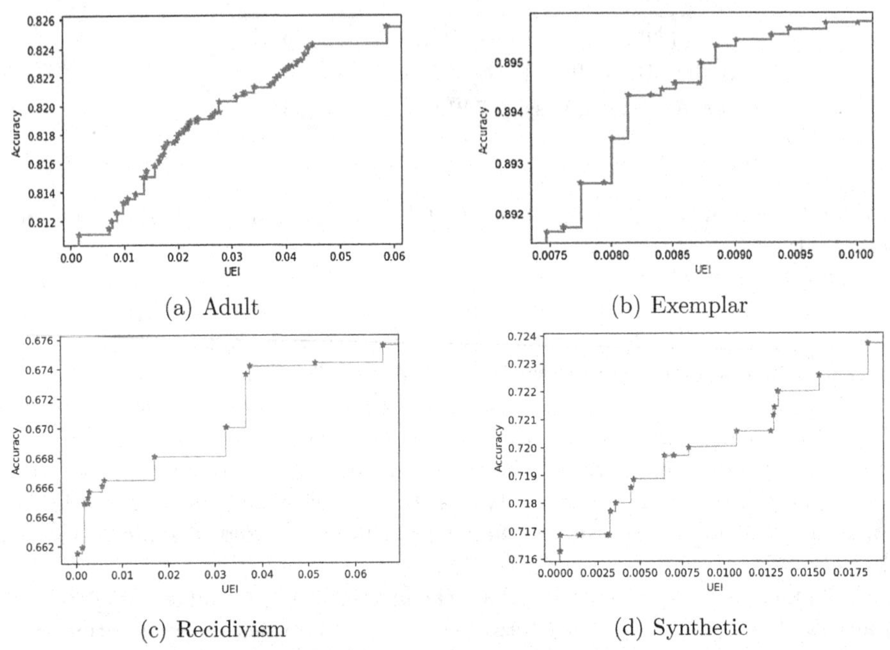

Fig. 1. Pareto fronts obtained with models optimised for both accuracy and UEI using MOPSO on four datasets.

4.1 Dealing with Underestimation Bias

We begin by assessing whether FairRet can effectively deal with underestimation bias and, if so, whether there is any material impact on classification accuracy. Figure 1 shows the Pareto front obtained for the training sets on the four evaluation datasets. Each point in Fig. 1 represents a single classifier with different degrees of underestimation (x-axis) and a corresponding accuracy (y-axis) on the training set. Indeed, the Pareto fronts suggest that these two criteria are in conflict.

Our model selection policy is to select models with lowest UEI on the training data. These are the models on the bottom left of the Pareto front and the performance of these models is then evaluated using the held-back test data. Figure 2 shows how the proposed strategy (FairRet) significantly outperforms standard retrieval (StdRet) on all four datasets, in terms of UEI (the right-hand x-axis), but without a material loss in classification accuracy (left y-axis). Remember, $UEI = 0$ indicates that the distributions for the predictions (in terms of protected features and class labels) match the actual distributions.

[2] https://scikit-learn.org/.

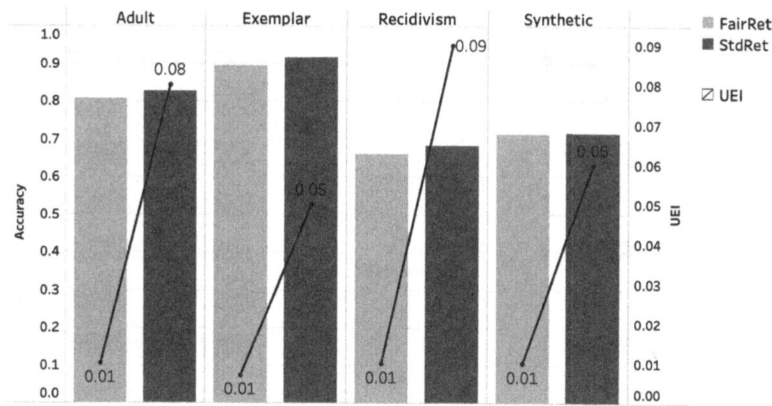

Fig. 2. Accuracy and UEI scores for StdRet and FairRet. It is clear that underestimation is effectively eliminated for all four datasets.

As stated in Sect. 2, the UEI score does not directly tell us how the model is performing on the protected group, because it is a score that is aggregated across all of the protected attributes and outcomes. When the focus is solely on underestimation of desirable outcomes, we evaluate our framework in terms of underestimation score US_S (Eq. 3). Figure 3 shows how FairRet performs on the test data in terms of underestimation for the protected $US_{S=0}$ and unprotected group $US_{S=1}$. For each dataset it shows a pair of bars – the lower bar corresponds to *FairRet* and the upper bar to *StdRet* – for the protected (left) and unprotected (right) groups. FairRet almost completely fixes underestimation bias (by bringing US_S closer to 1). The result for Adult and Recidivism is not perfect, but perhaps it's because the initial $US_{S=0}$ scores (StdRet) are significantly worse than any of the other datasets.

These results show that FairRet can successfully address the underestimation bias in k-NN, and in a manner that does not materially impact classification accuracy.

4.2 Outcome Distortion

One consequence of the FairRet approach to addressing underestimation bias is the potential for distortions in prediction behaviour, because local changes in similarity knowledge can impact the selection and ordering of retrieved cases. Will such retrieval changes distort the classifications that are produced, other than those that need to be fixed to deal with underestimation bias?

For the purpose of illustration, let's focus on the Adult dataset scenario where $Y = 1$ is the award of a loan and $S = 0$ is female. In Fig. 3 on the left we see US is improved from 0.26 to 0.89 by FairRet. Figure 4 shows the minimum number of *outcomes* that need to be flipped to achieve this as the hatched blue bars; in other words, this improvement in US could be achieved by distorting approximately 3,400 outcomes in the case of Adult. But this is just one type of

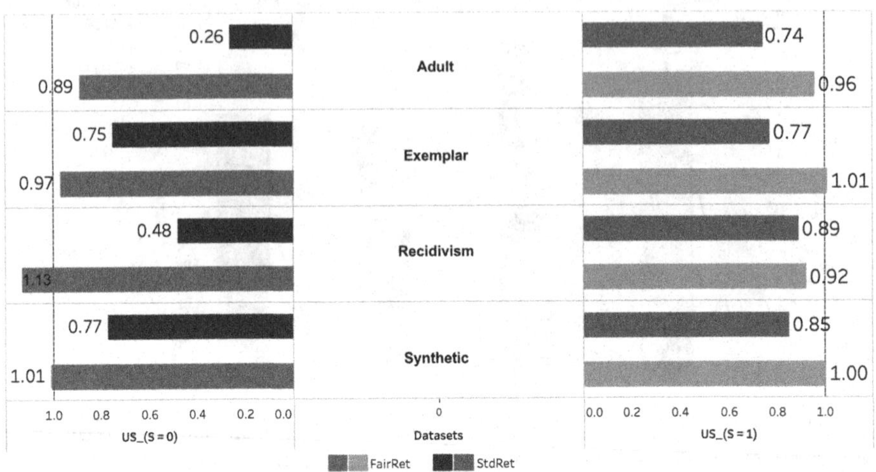

Fig. 3. The Underestimation scores US on test data. $US_{S=0}$ is the protected minority.

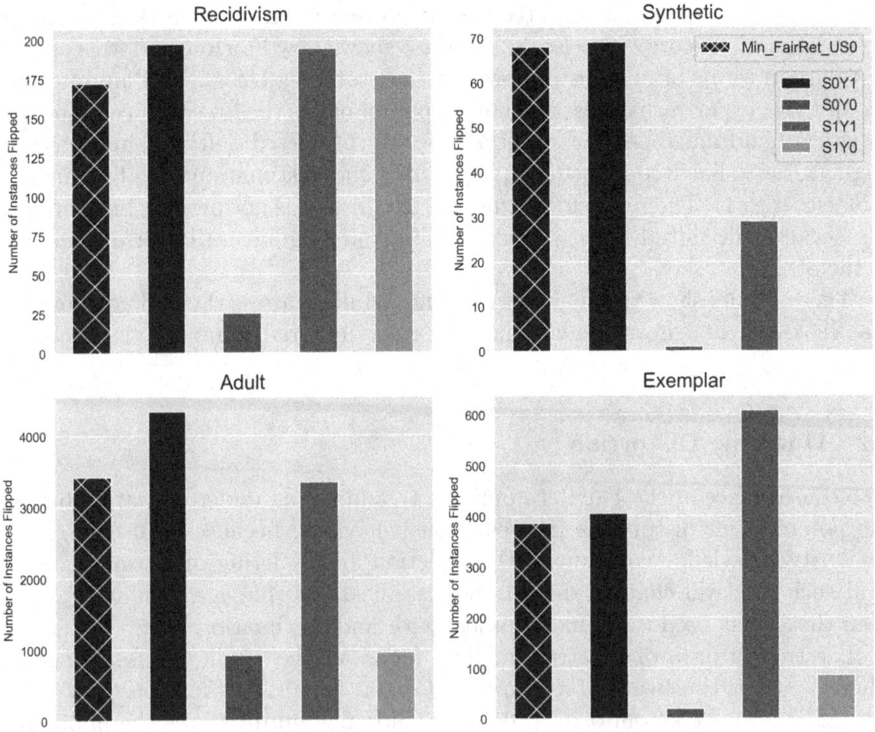

Fig. 4. Count of instances flipped by FairRet compared with StdRet. Hatched bars indicates the minimum required by the improvements shown in Fig. 3.

distortion and for this binary protected feature/binary outcome scenario there are four possible distortions and it is important to understand the extent to which FairRet leads to all possible distortions:

1. S_0Y_1: more females being awarded the loan
2. S_0Y_0: more females not being awarded the loan
3. S_1Y_1: more males being awarded the loan
4. S_1Y_0: more males not being awarded the loan

The four other bars in each of Fig. 4 show the actual counts corresponding to these distortions. The most important bar is the dark blue (second from the left) bar for S_0Y_1 because these show the actual flips that fix the target underestimation $US_{S=0}$ and, as such, they should be as close as possible to the minimum number of flips needed (hatched bar). And, for the most part, they are. Furthermore, ideally the third bar (S_0Y_0 – more females *refused* a loan – should be zero, which is close to being achieved in Recidivism and Adult and very close to being achieved in Synthetic and Exemplar.

What we want for the unprotected group $S = 1$ is more complicated. On the left in Fig. 3 we see there is underestimation to a lesser extent for $S = 1$, so some S_1Y_1 transitions are justified. But as was the case for the protected group ($S = 0$), there should be minimal S_1Y_0 (fifth bars) transitions. We find this to be the case in all datasets except for the Recidivism dataset, where there are similar high numbers of S_1Y_0 and S_1Y_1 flips which is not desirable. Thus, we can say that, even though FairRet introduces some prediction distortion, its impact is limited in all but one of the test datasets.

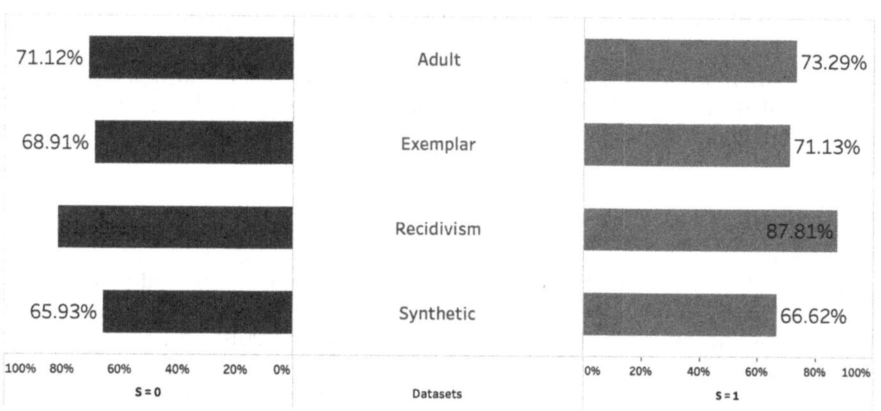

Fig. 5. Overlaps in 1-nearest neighbour retrieval between FairRet and StdRet.

4.3 Retrieval Overlap

Since fixing underestimation necessarily means distorting the retrieval process, it is also important to consider its impact on explanations based on nearest neighbours. Figure 5 illustrates the overlaps between 1-NN retrieved by (FairRet) and

(StdRet) for the protected $S = 0$ and unprotected $S = 1$ group. We see that the impact on the retrieval is more significant compared to overall prediction outcomes. For example, in the case of Adult, the overlap between the cases retrieved by *FairRet* and *StdRet* is just over 71% for the protected and unprotected groups, meaning that just under 30% of the cases retrieved by *FairRet* are not retrieved by *StdRet*. On the one hand, this is not surprising since the changes due to the metric learning process will directly impact case retrieval order, but on the other, it remains an open question as to whether this will matter in practice in terms of case-based explanation.

5 Conclusions

Algorithmic bias due to underestimation refers to situations where an algorithm under-predicts desirable outcomes for a protected minority. In this paper, we focus on mitigating underestimation bias in a case-based reasoning (CBR) context by a metric learning strategy that explicitly considering underestimation as an addition criterion in the ML optimization process. We propose a multi-objective strategy using Multi-objective Particle Swarm Optimization to optimize retrieval on two criteria: (1) maximizing accuracy; (2) ensuring little to no underestimation of desirable outcomes (w.r.t minority group). We demonstrate that our approach can fix underestimation bias as measured by UEI and $\text{US}_{S=0}$, while maintaining classification accuracy, and it does so with minimal retrieval distortion. However, there is likely to be an impact on the retrieval of explanation cases as different cases will be available to explanation. Whether this will matter in practice is an interesting question for future research.

Acknowledgements. This work was funded by Science Foundation Ireland through the SFI Centre for Research Training in Machine Learning (Grant No. 18/CRT/6183) with support from Microsoft Ireland.

References

1. Montalvo, I., Izquierdo, J., Pérez-García, R., Herrera, M.: Improved performance of PSO with self-adaptive parameters for computing the optimal design of water supply systems. Eng. Appl. Artif. Intell. **23**(5), 727–735 (2010). Advances in metaheuristics for hard optimization: new trends and case studies
2. Žliobaitė, I.: Measuring discrimination in algorithmic decision making. Data Min. Knowl. Discov. **31**(4), 1060–1089 (2017). https://doi.org/10.1007/s10618-017-0506-1
3. Bender, E.M., Gebru, T., McMillan-Major, A., Shmitchell, S.: On the dangers of stochastic parrots: can language models be too big? In: Proceedings of the 2021 ACM Conference on Fairness, Accountability, and Transparency, FAccT 2021, pp. 610–623. Association for Computing Machinery, New York (2021)
4. Berk, R., Heidari, H., Jabbari, S., Kearns, M., Roth, A.: Fairness in criminal justice risk assessments: the state of the art. Sociol. Methods Res. **50**(1), 3–44 (2021)

5. Blanzeisky, W., Cunningham, P.: Algorithmic factors influencing bias in machine learning. In: Kamp, M. (ed.) Machine Learning and Principles and Practice of Knowledge Discovery in Databases, pp. 559–574. Springer, Cham (2021). https://doi.org/10.1007/978-3-030-93736-2_41
6. Blanzeisky, W., Cunningham, P., Kennedy, K.: Introducing a family of synthetic datasets for research on bias in machine learning. CoRR abs/2107.08928 (2021)
7. Castelnovo, A., Crupi, R., Greco, G., Regoli, D.: The zoo of fairness metrics in machine learning (2021)
8. Caton, S., Haas, C.: Fairness in machine learning: a survey. arXiv preprint arXiv:2010.04053 (2020)
9. Coello, C., Lechuga, M.: MOPSO: a proposal for multiple objective particle swarm optimization, vol. 2, pp. 1051–1056 (2002)
10. Corbett-Davies, S., Goel, S.: The measure and mismeasure of fairness: a critical review of fair machine learning (2018)
11. Dodge, J., Liao, Q.V., Zhang, Y., Bellamy, R.K., Dugan, C.: Explaining models: an empirical study of how explanations impact fairness judgment. In: Proceedings of the 24th International Conference on Intelligent User Interfaces, pp. 275–285 (2019)
12. Dressel, J., Farid, H.: The accuracy, fairness, and limits of predicting recidivism. Sci. Adv. **4**(1), eaao5580 (2018)
13. Emigh, M.S., Kriminger, E.G., Brockmeier, A.J., Príncipe, J.C., Pardalos, P.M.: Reinforcement learning in video games using nearest neighbor interpolation and metric learning. IEEE Trans. Comput. Intell. AI Games **8**(1), 56–66 (2014)
14. Feldman, M., Friedler, S.A., Moeller, J., Scheidegger, C., Venkatasubramanian, S.: Certifying and removing disparate impact. In: Proceedings of the 21th ACM SIGKDD International Conference on Knowledge Discovery and Data Mining, pp. 259–268 (2015)
15. Holstein, K., Wortman Vaughan, J., Daumé III, H., Dudik, M., Wallach, H.: Improving fairness in machine learning systems: what do industry practitioners need? In: Proceedings of the 2019 CHI Conference on Human Factors in Computing Systems, pp. 1–16 (2019)
16. Jalali, V., Leake, D.: Harnessing hundreds of millions of cases: case-based prediction at industrial scale. In: Cox, M.T., Funk, P., Begum, S. (eds.) ICCBR 2018. LNCS (LNAI), vol. 11156, pp. 153–169. Springer, Cham (2018). https://doi.org/10.1007/978-3-030-01081-2_11
17. Kamishima, T., Akaho, S., Asoh, H., Sakuma, J.: Fairness-aware classifier with prejudice remover regularizer. In: Flach, P.A., De Bie, T., Cristianini, N. (eds.) ECML PKDD 2012. LNCS (LNAI), vol. 7524, pp. 35–50. Springer, Heidelberg (2012). https://doi.org/10.1007/978-3-642-33486-3_3
18. Keane, M.T., Kenny, E.M.: How case-based reasoning explains neural networks: a theoretical analysis of XAI using *Post-Hoc* explanation-by-example from a survey of ANN-CBR twin-systems. In: Bach, K., Marling, C. (eds.) ICCBR 2019. LNCS (LNAI), vol. 11680, pp. 155–171. Springer, Cham (2019). https://doi.org/10.1007/978-3-030-29249-2_11
19. Kennedy, J.: Particle Swarm Optimization. In: Sammut, C., Webb, G.I. (eds.) Encyclopedia of Machine Learning, pp. 760–766. Springer, Boston (2010). https://doi.org/10.1007/978-0-387-30164-8_630
20. Kohavi, R.: Scaling up the accuracy of Naive-Bayes classifiers: a decision-tree hybrid. In: Proceedings of the Second International Conference on Knowledge Discovery and Data Mining, vol. 96, pp. 202–207 (1996)

21. Larsen, R., Jouffroy, J., Lassen, B.: On the premature convergence of particle swarm optimization (2016). https://doi.org/10.1109/ECC.2016.7810572
22. Limlawan, V., Pongchairerks, P.: A PSO with ability to avoid being trapped in a local optimum a PSO with ability to avoid being trapped in a local optimum (2010)
23. Lin, Y.B., Ping, X.O., Ho, T.W., Lai, F.: Processing and analysis of imbalanced liver cancer patient data by case-based reasoning. In: The 7th 2014 Biomedical Engineering International Conference, pp. 1–5. IEEE (2014)
24. Ma, R.J., Yu, N.Y., Hu, J.Y.: Application of particle swarm optimization algorithm in the heating system planning problem. Sci. World J. **2013**, 718345 (2013)
25. Malof, J.M., Mazurowski, M.A., Tourassi, G.D.: The effect of class imbalance on case selection for case-based classifiers: an empirical study in the context of medical decision support. Neural Netw. **25**, 141–145 (2012)
26. Mehrabi, N., Morstatter, F., Saxena, N., Lerman, K., Galstyan, A.: A survey on bias and fairness in machine learning. ACM Comput. Surv. **54**(6), 1–35 (2021). https://doi.org/10.1145/3457607
27. Moslehi, F., Haeri, A., Martínez-Álvarez, F.: A novel hybrid GA-PSO framework for mining quantitative association rules. Soft Comput. **24**, 4645–4666 (2020)
28. Nicolàs Sans, R., Vernet Bellet, D., Golobardes, E., Fornells Herrera, A., de la Torre Frade, F., Puig, S.: Applying distance metric learning in a collaborative melanoma diagnosis system with case-based reasoning. In: Proceedings of the 14th Workshop on Case-based reasoning at the 29th SGAI International Conference on Innovative Techniques and Applications of Artificial Intelligence (2011)
29. Ontañón, S., Plaza, E.: Cooperative case bartering for case-based reasoning agents. In: Escrig, M.T., Toledo, F., Golobardes, E. (eds.) CCIA 2002. LNCS (LNAI), vol. 2504, pp. 294–308. Springer, Heidelberg (2002). https://doi.org/10.1007/3-540-36079-4_26
30. Richter, M.M., Michael, M.: Knowledge containers. In: Readings in Case-Based Reasoning (2003)
31. Roth-Berghofer, T.R.: Explanations and case-based reasoning: foundational issues. In: Funk, P., González Calero, P.A. (eds.) ECCBR 2004. LNCS (LNAI), vol. 3155, pp. 389–403. Springer, Heidelberg (2004). https://doi.org/10.1007/978-3-540-28631-8_29
32. Sørmo, F., Cassens, J., Aamodt, A.: Explanation in case-based reasoning-perspectives and goals. Artif. Intell. Rev. **24**(2), 109–143 (2005)
33. Wang, F., Sun, J.: Survey on distance metric learning and dimensionality reduction in data mining. Data Min. Knowl. Disc. **29**(2), 534–564 (2014). https://doi.org/10.1007/s10618-014-0356-z
34. Weinberger, K.Q., Saul, L.K.: Distance metric learning for large margin nearest neighbor classification. J. Mach. Learn. Res. **10**(2) (2009)
35. Woodworth, B., Gunasekar, S., Ohannessian, M.I., Srebro, N.: Learning non-discriminatory predictors. In: Conference on Learning Theory, pp. 1920–1953. PMLR (2017)
36. Xing, E., Jordan, M., Russell, S.J., Ng, A.: Distance metric learning with application to clustering with side-information. In: Advances in Neural Information Processing Systems 15 (2002)
37. Zliobaite, I.: Fairness-aware machine learning: a perspective. arXiv preprint arXiv:1708.00754 (2017)
38. Ünal, A., Kayakutlu, G.: Multi-objective particle swarm optimization with random immigrants. Complex Intell. Syst. **6**(3), 635–650 (2020). https://doi.org/10.1007/s40747-020-00159-y

"Better" Counterfactuals, Ones People Can Understand: Psychologically-Plausible Case-Based Counterfactuals Using Categorical Features for Explainable AI (XAI)

Greta Warren[1(✉)], Barry Smyth[1,2], and Mark T. Keane[1,2,3]

[1] School of Computer Science, University College Dublin, Dublin, Ireland
greta.warren@ucdconnect.ie, {barry.smyth,mark.keane}@ucd.ie
[2] Insight Centre for Data Analytics, University College Dublin, Dublin, Ireland
[3] VistaMilk SFI Research Centre, University College Dublin, Dublin, Ireland

Abstract. A recent surge of research has focused on counterfactual explanations as a promising solution to the eXplainable AI (XAI) problem. Over 100 counterfactual XAI methods have been proposed, many emphasising the key role of features that are "important" or "causal" or "actionable" in making explanations comprehensible to human users. However, these proposals rest on intuition rather than psychological evidence. Indeed, recent psychological evidence [22] shows that it is abstract feature-types that impact people's understanding of explanations; *categorical features* better support people's learning of an AI model's predictions than *continuous features*. This paper proposes a more psychologically-valid counterfactual method, one extending case-based techniques with additional functionality to transform feature-differences into categorical versions of themselves. This enhanced case-based counterfactual method, still generates good counterfactuals relative to baseline methods on coverage and distances metrics. This is the first counterfactual method specifically designed to meet identified psychological requirements of end-users, rather than merely reflecting the intuitions of algorithm designers.

Keywords: CBR · Explanation · XAI · Counterfactuals · Contrastive

1 Introduction

In recent years, a significant effort has been made to develop methods that can explain to people why/how an automated decision was made by some black-box AI system (see [1–3]). Indeed, given the requirements of GDPR to provide such explanations when automated decisions are made without human intervention, there is an added urgency to solve this eXplainable AI (XAI) problem [3, 4]. Many XAI strategies proposed in recent years have echoed long-standing work in case-based reasoning (CBR) where the provision of explanations for model predictions has always been a motivating concern (see e.g., [5–7]). Hence, case-based explanations proposed over two decades ago have

M. T. Keane and N. Wiratunga (Eds.): ICCBR 2022, LNAI 13405, pp. 63–78, 2022.
https://doi.org/10.1007/978-3-031-14923-8_5

been revisited and extended to be applied to deep learning (see e.g., [8–10]). Similarly, *a-fortori* explanations proposed in CBR [11, 12] have been revived as semi-factuals to explain deep learners [13] and Nearest Unlike Neighbours (NUNs; [11, 14]), have been re-cast as counterfactual explanations realised in 100+ different algorithms in the literature [15]. This last explanation strategy is the focus for the current paper, as it has become one of the most researched post-hoc solutions to the XAI problem.

The classic example of a counterfactual explanation is one for an automated banking application where, on foot of being refused a loan, the customer asks for an explanation and is told "if you asked for a lower loan of $30,000 over a shorter term of two years, you would have been granted the loan". Importantly, the counterfactual tells the end-user about what feature changes will result in a different decision outcome, giving the user some insight into how they might reverse the outcome of an automated decision (so-called *algorithmic recourse* [16]). Counterfactual explanations have attracted a lot of attention in XAI because they appear to be psychologically comprehensible [17], GDPR-compliant [18], and invite a wide variety of computational solutions (see [15, 16]). One family of solutions adopts a case-based approach, where NUNs are used in a variety of different ways to explain some current target (query) case [14, 19–21].

In this paper, we extend the case-based approach of [20] to make it more psychologically-valid by modifying the feature-types its uses in its explanations. The next section places this work in the context of recent relevant research. Recent psychological research shows that, where possible, categorical features should be preferred as the basis for the generated counterfactuals used in explanations [22]. In Sect. 3 we perform a computational study to determine the "natural" occurrence of counterfactuals with categorical feature-differences in several representative datasets; this study shows they are rare and motivates our method that transforms all continuous feature-values into categorical ones (see Sect. 4). Then in Sect. 5, we report a second study to test these feature-transforming methods using an extension of case-based counterfactual generation methods on representative datasets; we assess if there is any decrement in the quality of counterfactuals produced under these transformations. In Sect. 6, we conclude by discussing the implications of these results for counterfactuals in XAI.

2 Background: Computation and Psychology of Counterfactuals

Though it is not always recognised in the AI literature, the computation of counterfactuals has been with us for some time. In earlier guises, it was cast as finding NUNs [23, 24] or inverse classifications [25]. For instance, in a binary classification problem we could have two cases that are very close to one another, but one feature change flips the class of the cases; in the loan domain, a reduction in the value of the *loan-amount* feature, might change the decision from "refuse" to "grant". Depending on the dataset, these two instances could be NUNs, the closest pair of instances in the dataset where specific feature-changes modify the class predicted. Several early papers on NUNs considered their use in the context of explanation for domains using tabular [11, 23] and textual data [14], emphasising the use of instances in the existing dataset.

However, recently, a very different optimisation approach has been proposed that uses similarity constraints to generate synthetic instances that balance similarity to the query against distance to the decision boundary. Wachter et al. [18] propose that counterfactuals can be computed using the loss function, L:

$$L(x, x', y', \lambda) = \lambda(f(x') - y')^2 + d(x, x') \tag{1}$$

$$arg \min_{x'} \max_{\lambda} L(x, x', y', \lambda) \tag{2}$$

where x is the vector for the query case and x' is the counterfactual vector, with y' being the desired (flipped) prediction from f (..) the trained model, where λ acts as the balancing weight. In formula (2), λ balances the closeness of the counterfactual to the query case against making minimal changes to the query case while delivering a prediction change, using the ℓ_1 norm weighted by median absolute deviation. In implementations, this method generates a space of feature perturbations for the original query and then uses gradient descent to settle on a minimally-perturbed (aka the *best*) counterfactual. This method tends to generate low-sparsity counterfactuals, that is, counterfactuals with few feature differences; a property seen as attractive as it allows people to better understand them[1] (e.g., Table 1 shows "good" and "bad" counterfactuals for explaining a blood-alcohol-level prediction based on sparsity). Unfortunately, this original method has been shown to have several limitations. First, it cannot handle categorical features, as it only addresses features with continuous values. Second, it sometimes generates invalid, out-of-distribution data-points and, therefore, invalid explanations in the domain [26]. Many subsequent papers have aimed to rectify these deficits. For example, DiCE [27] handles categorical features using one-hot encoding and adds constraints for diversity, while other models supplement the constraints to be more sensitive to the data [28, 29]. So, there is now a whole family of these optimisation methods that claim to foster better computation of counterfactuals.

One of the persistent themes in this literature has been around the differential importance of features. In the psychological literature on counterfactual thinking, Nobel laureate Daniel Kahneman noted that only some features are "mutable" [30]; some features cannot be changed in creating a counterfactual (e.g., *age* is not a feature that can change to improve one's loan chances). So, counterfactual explanations need to change "plausible" features, namely ones that are "actionable" (i.e., that the user can action; [31–33]), "causally important" (i.e., that play a key role; [34]) or "predictively important" [35, 36]. Overall, this concern with features tries to ensure that these methods produce counterfactual explanations that make sense to people, that people can act on and that increase their understanding of the domain (e.g., how the model makes its decisions). However, there are many issues around the identification and use of the "right" features. Firstly, these featural proposals often end in ad-hoc solutions, such as end-users interacting to mark features as important or to define ranges on feature-values [27]. Secondly, for

[1] Keane and Smyth [19] argued that, for tabular data, counterfactuals should be sparse; no more than 2 feature-differences, to allow people to understand them. Recent user studies show that people prefer counterfactuals with 2–3 feature differences [45].

Table 1. A query case paired with a "Good", "Better" and "Bad" counterfactual from the Blood Alcohol Content (BAC) case-base (the feature-differences shown in bold-italics).

Features	Query case	"Bad" counterfactual	"Good" counterfactual	"Better" counterfactual
Weight	90 kg	90 kg	***100 kg***	90 kg
Duration	1 h	***3 h***	***1.5 h***	1 h
Gender	Female	***Male***	Female	***Male***
Stomach	Empty	***Full***	Empty	***Full***
Units	5	***4***	5	5
BAC level	Over	Under	Under	Under

causal importance, methods assume causal models that are not often or always available. Thirdly, what constitutes the "right" feature seems to be very context-sensitive; for example, if I earn $300k a year, then increasing income by $5k may be actionable, but if I earn $30k a year, earning an additional $5k may be impossible. Perhaps one of the main attractions of case-based approaches is that they exploit implicit dependencies in the data and accordingly, by definition, rely on plausible/mutable/important features and avoid producing out-of-distribution counterfactuals.

Furthermore, as we shall see in the next section, this AI literature on feature importance has overlooked one key aspect of features shown to be psychologically critical. Recent user studies have revealed that abstract feature-types – categorical versus continuous features – are understood very differently by human users [22]. In the next sub-section, we consider related work on the psychology of counterfactuals in XAI and their implications for models of counterfactual generation.

2.1 User Studies of Counterfactual XAI: Mixed Results

Although the AI literature on counterfactual methods has exploded in the last few years, user studies examining how people understand and use counterfactuals have lagged considerably; indeed, the user studies that have been done tend to be too general, report mixed results, or both. Keane et al. [15] report that of 100+ distinct counterfactual methods reported in the XAI literature (of which ~5 are case-based methods) only ~20% report any user tests; even fewer papers test specific aspects of specific techniques (~7%). Many of these studies report quite general findings, showing that counterfactuals broadly improve people's responding in some way [21, 37, 38]. More focused user studies tend to report mixed results on people's performance with counterfactual explanations. Van der Waa et al. [39] tested people's performance with a simulated blood-sugar-prediction app using either contrastive-rule or example-based explanations and found that neither strategy did better than no-explanation controls. Lage et al. [40] found when people were given counterfactual tasks, in which users were asked if a system's recommendation would change given a perturbation of some input feature, they reported greater difficulty; also longer response times and lower accuracy in prediction tasks were recorded. Taken together, these studies present a confusing picture, in which counterfactuals seem to sometimes help and other times hinder. They also suggest a focus on how people really understand the features in counterfactual explanations, to uncover when and how they really work, psychologically.

Though many counterfactual methods have emphasised featural aspects, none of these papers user-test their proposals. To the best of our knowledge only two papers have specifically user-tested feature-types in counterfactual methods [22, 41]. Kirfel and Liefgreen [41] found that people's perceptions of the quality and comprehensibility of explanations was affected by whether they involved actionable and mutable features, as opposed to immutable ones. However, they also pointed out that the actionable/mutaibility distinctions made by AI researchers were not as clear-cut for laypeople. This raises the question about whether there are more fundamental feature-categories that could impact people understanding. Indeed, longstanding evidence from human reasoning suggests that people do not spontaneously change continuous variables (e.g., the speed or timing of vehicles involved in a road accident) when generating counterfactuals [42]. To address this issue, Warren et al. [22] examined the role of abstract feature-types – categorical or continuous – in people's understanding of counterfactual explanations for a black-box model's predictions. They examined the effects of different counterfactual (and causal) explanations on people's understanding of a blood-alcohol-content (BAC) domain. They presented people with a simulated AI model that predicts if someone is over/under the legal alcohol limit for driving, based on five features: weight, duration of drinking, gender, stomach-fullness, and number of units drunk. In the training phase of the experiment, people were presented with query cases with different values for these features and asked to predict the outcome as under/over the BAC limit. After responding, they were shown the model's prediction along with a counterfactual explanation (e.g., see the "good counterfactual" in Table 1). In the training phase, they saw 40 such cases with equally-balanced cases involving counterfactuals for the five features (i.e., 8 cases for each feature). Then, in the testing phase, they received 40 new cases and were asked to predict the outcome while focusing on a specific feature (8 instances per feature), without receiving explanations or feedback, to determine how accurate their predictions were. This experimental paradigm tests a critical aspect of explanation use, namely, if experience with the model's predictions combined with explanations improve people's understanding of the domain, as measured by accuracy in the test phase.

Overall, the results, shown in Fig. 1, show an effect of explanation, where people given counterfactual explanations were more accurate than no-explanation controls. However, the results also showed an independent effect of feature, that also interacted with phase; in the testing phase, accuracy for cases using categorical features improved, whereas those using continuous features did not; note the increase in Fig. 1(B) relative to Fig. 1(A), for *gender* and *stomach-fullness*. Indeed, this feature-type factor accounts for almost all the improvement in accuracy seen between the experiment's training and test phases. These results show that improvements in accuracy were solely due to the presence of categorical features over continuous ones. So, counterfactuals with categorical-differences should be "better" (see Table 1). This finding motivates the current work, to extend counterfactual methods to take feature-type into account.

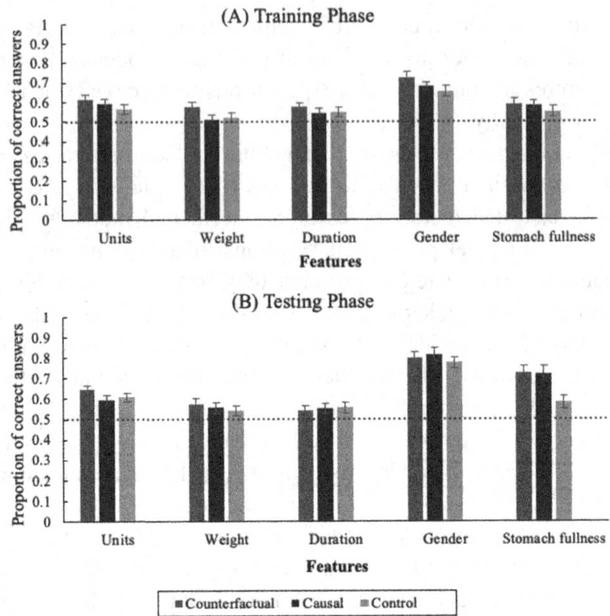

Fig. 1. Mean accuracy for three conditions (counterfactual, causal and control) by each feature in the (A) training and (B) testing phases of Warren et al. [22] (error bars represent standard error of the mean; dashed line represents chance accuracy).

3 Study 1: Plotting Counterfactuals that have Categoricals

Given the importance of categorically-based explanations, in this study we examined a number of UCI datasets [43] – based on (i) prior use in testing counterfactual methods, (ii) their use of categorical features – to determine their potential to yield *native counterfactuals* (i.e., existing pairs of counterfactually-related instances in the dataset that can be used to generate synthetic counterfactuals) that rely on categorical feature-differences (as opposed to continuous ones). Seven datasets were selected: the blood-alcohol-content, contraceptive-choice, cleveland-heart, horse-colic, credit, german credit, and thyroid datasets. Note, datasets containing categorical features may be relatively rare: of the 622 UCI datasets publicly available as of May 2022, 38 (.06%) contain only categorical features, while 55 (.09%), contain mixed features (some of which contain only a single categorical feature, such as the abalone, diabetes datasets). We used the case-based counterfactual method, CB2-CF (see Sect. 4), to compute all pairs of cases either side of a decision boundary (i.e., native counterfactuals) noting the number of feature differences in each, and if they had *at least one* categorical feature. This method uses a *tolerance* to identify feature-differences so small differences [e.g., ±20% of 1 standard deviation (SD)] in continuous features are treated as essentially identical; varying this tolerance ($\leq$1 SD) did not materially change the results.

Table 2. Study 1 results: Frequencies of native categorical counterfactuals (≥1 categorical feature-difference) over 7 datasets, for 1–5 feature-differences, as a % of potential counterfactuals.

Dataset	N cases	N feats	N cat. feat.	1-diff CFs (% tot.)	2-diff CFs (% tot.)	3-diff CFs (% tot.)	4-diff CFs (% tot.)	5-diff CFs (% tot.)
Blood alcohol.	4748	5	2	19 (0.4%)	1302 (27.4%)	4574 (96.3%)	4736 (99.8%)	0 (0%)
Contracept.	1425	9	7	236 (16.6%)	1050 (73.7%)	1345 (94.5%)	1377 (96.7%)	1379 (96.8%)
Cleveland heart	303	13	7	0 (0%)	0 (0%)	0 (0%)	8 (2.65%)	93 (30.8%)
Colic	300	26	19	1 (0.33%)	0 (0%)	0 (0%)	0 (0%)	0 (0%)
Credit	690	15	9	0 (0%)	0 (0%)	0 (0%)	0 (0%)	0 (0%)
German credit	1000	20	13	0 (0%)	0 (0%)	3 (0.3%)	20 (2.0%)	108 (10.8%)
Thyroid	2753	28	22	0 (0%)	0 (0%)	0 (0%)	0 (0%)	69 (2.5%)

3.1 Results and Discussion

Table 2 shows frequencies of native counterfactuals involving at least one categorical feature-difference (and their percentage in the total set of counterfactuals). Note, this is a low bar for categorical counterfactuals, as it admits one with 5 feature-differences where, perhaps, only one of those feature-differences were categorical. Even with this low bar, counterfactuals based on categorical features are rare. For 5 datasets, none of the *good* counterfactuals (i.e., those with 1–3 feature differences) involved categorical features. Of the 2 datasets – blood-alcohol-content and contraceptive – that yield more categorical counterfactuals, there are still very few 1-feature-difference counterfactuals that are categorical (respectively ~0.4% and ~ 16.6%). We found no relationship between the number of categorical features in a dataset and its propensity to generate categorically-based counterfactuals; for instance, the contraceptive dataset has 7/9 categorical features (77%) whereas the thyroid dataset has 22/28 categorical features (78%) but they both show very different results.

Clearly the occurrence of categorical features in counterfactuals must depend on the underlying domain theory, on the presence/absence of dependencies between categorical and continuous variables in the domain. For instance, in the BAC domain *gender* has a big impact on outcomes; females have different metabolic rates to males and this factor impacts other variables in the BAC formula. From these results, it is hard to escape the conclusion that categorically-based, counterfactual explanations do not naturally occur in many datasets. We also note that, unlike those evaluated here, a significant proportion of the datasets widely used in the machine learning literature (e.g., see UCI repository [43]) do not contain any categorical features whatsoever, and hence will not yield native categorical-counterfactuals. So, to present such explanations to end-users, we will need to transform feature-differences involving continuous features into categorical representations of themselves. In the next section, we consider how an existing instance-based counterfactual method can be re-designed to do such transformations in a post-processing step, before an explanation is presented to users.

4 Transforming Case-Based Counterfactuals, Categorically

In AI, NUNs have been considered for some time (see [24] for a review), though the idea of using a NUN as a counterfactual explanation is more recent [11, 21]. However, NUNs on their own are not a general solution to counterfactual explanation; even if available, they may be too distant from the query to provide a good explanation. Hence, most current techniques try to generate synthetic counterfactuals that are close to the query and within-distribution [19, 20, 27]. Case-based counterfactual techniques tend to use NUNs as templates for generating synthetic counterfactuals either by selecting specific features from the NUN in some constrained way [19, 20] or by perturbing the NUN towards the query [14, 36]. In the next subsection, we quickly describe the case-based counterfactual method used in the current experiments, before describing two algorithmic extensions to it, that perform categorical transformations to explanatory cases.

4.1 Case-Based Counterfactual Methods: CB1-CF and CB2-CF

Keane and Smyth [19] proposed a case-based counterfactual method (CB1-CF here) designed to generate plausible and informative counterfactual explanations for any presented query case. Unlike optimisation methods, CB1-CF uses historical counterfactual-pairs in the dataset – so-called *native counterfactuals* – as templates for building new, synthetic counterfactual cases for the query case. As Fig. 2 shows, to explain the outcome of *p*, CB1-CF identifies a nearby pair of cases, *cf(x, x')*, where *x* has the same class as *p* and *x'* is a good counterfactual for *x*; *x* and *x'* differ by a small number of features and these features are adjusted in *p* to obtain a new explanation case, *p'*, that is counterfactually related to *p* (see [19] for details on how these *difference-features* are adjusted). There may be other counterfactual pairs in the case-base, such as *cf(q, q')*, but CB1-CF only uses the closest to build a single explanatory counterfactual.

Recently, Smyth and Keane [20] generalised CB1-CF to go beyond just considering a single, native counterfactual ($k = 1$); this new method (which we refer to as CB2-CF) can arbitrarily vary the number of natives considered (any $k > 1$). The authors show that CB2-CF generates better counterfactual cases (i.e., ones closer to the query) with better coverage (i.e., it can find good counterfactuals for most queries) for $k = 10$–30 in representative datasets. In the current tests, we use a simplified version of CB2-CF to test for the effects of categorical transformations on the generation of explanations[2].

[2] 2 As well as considering multiple natives, CB2-CF also considers nearest-like-neighbours of the native's *x'* (e.g., the three closest, same-class datapoints to *x'*) to expand on the variations of natives considered. This second step in not implemented in our version of CB2-CF.

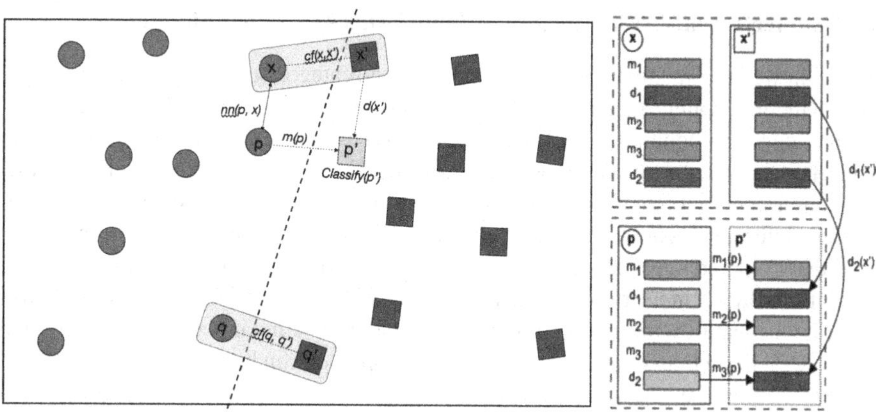

Fig. 2. An illustration of (a) a two-class case-base with 2 native counterfactuals [i.e., *(x, x')* and *(q, q')*], where one *(x, x')* is the nearest-neighbour native to the query, *p*, and *x'* is used to create the explanatory counterfactual case, *p'*; (b) how a synthetic, counterfactual case, *p'*, is generated from the values in the match-features of *p* and the difference-features of *x'*.

Of course, CB2-CF does not consider whether categorical/continuous features are used in the counterfactual. So, in the next section, we extend CB2-CF, using variants that transform feature-difference values to be categorical (see Sect. 5 for tests).

```
CAT-CF^global (q, CB):
cfs, dists ← FindCFs_k(q, CB)
for each cf ∈ cfs:
  for each f_i ∈ DiffFeatures(q, cf):
      cf(f_i) ← BinaryBin(CB, f_i, cf(f_i))
      if cf(f_i) = q(f_i)
         cf ← conflicting
valid_cfs ← remove conflicting CFs
valid_cfs ← Sort(valid_cfs,
      by=['sparsity', 'dist'])
Return valid_cfs
```

```
CAT-CF^Local (q, CB):
cfs, dists ← FindCFs_k(q, CB)
for each cf ∈ cfs:
  for each f_i ∈ DiffFeatures(q, cf):
    if cf(f_i)<q(f_i)
      cf(f_i) ← lower
    else:
      cf(f_i) ← higher
      cf(f_i) ← Direction(q, cf, f_i)
valid_cfs ← Sort(valid_cfs,
      by=[' sparsity', 'direction']
Return valid_cfs
```

Algorithms: Two methods for transforming feature differences in counterfactuals. Notes: *BinaryBin(CB, f, v)* converts a feature value *f(v)* into a binary categorical value *v'* based on the binning of features values for *f* in *CB*. This process can be done once for a given *CB* so that *BinaryBin(CB, f, v)* can be as a simple lookup.

4.2 Counterfactuals with Categorical Transforms #1: Global Binning

Study 1 showed that many datasets produce little or no categorical counterfactuals or only produce them in counterfactuals with poor sparsity (i.e., >2 feature differences). These findings led us to conclude that all continuous-type feature-differences in generated counterfactuals need to be transformed into categorical versions of themselves in the explanation-generation process (as in Table 3). Hence, we propose a post-processor that considers alternative counterfactual explanations for a given query, transforming them into categorical versions and, after some minimal checking, produces the best one as an explanation. Based on the psychological evidence [22], we apply binary transformations to continuous features; though should future work identify similar benefits of categorical features with more than two possible values, our approach can be adapted to reflect this. The first method we considered takes the dataset as is and performs a global binary binning on all the continuously-valued features. For instance, in the dataset the weight feature varies between 40 kg and 191 kg with a median of 94 kg; so, all values greater than the median are labelled as *high-weight* and all those equal-to-or-below the median are labelled as *low-weight* (see Table 3). This binning step is computed at the outset for the dataset. Using the CB2-CF method, for a given query *k* counterfactual-candidates are produced (assume $k = 20$) and the difference-feature-values found in these candidates are all transformed using the binning-labels (obviously categorical-feature-differences are left as is). Note, after the categorical-transformation, some of these candidates will need to be removed because they are *conflicting*; that is, the continuous feature-values in difference-pairs are transformed into the "same" categorical feature (e.g., two weights of 100 kg and 115 kg which were a difference both become labelled as *high-weight*). This means that, after the categorical transformation, the original counterfactual has not been preserved appropriately; therefore, these conflicting candidates are removed. Indeed, as we shall see, this step is probably the main source of performance decrements for this method. See ***Algorithms*** for the steps in this global binning method, called CAT-CBR^{global}. After the conflicting counterfactuals have been removed, it sorts the candidates by sparsity (lowest to highest) and then by distance (i.e., ℓ_2 norm on original untransformed, values of the counterfactual; lowest to highest) choosing the one with the best sparsity and distance score.

4.3 Counterfactuals with Categorical Transforms #2: Local Direction

On the face of it, the CAT-CF^{global} method looks like a plausible solution to the problem of transforming continuous features into categorical ones for psychologically comprehensible counterfactual explanations. However, we have also seen that it can produce conflicts when a continuous feature-difference is not preserved after categorical transformation, which may limit its potential to produce counterfactuals for certain query cases, depending on how a given feature's values are distributed. Hence, we developed and tested a more local method, called CAT-CF^{local}. This method, as its name suggests, works locally within the candidate counterfactual by re-labelling the continuous values in *c(p, p')* as being higher/lower, depending on the direction of difference. For instance, if the *p* query had a value of 110 kg and the candidate *p'* counterfactual instance has a

Table 3. A query case with its paired explanatory case, before and after it is transformed using the Global Categorical (CF-CAT^{global}) and Local Categorical (CF-CAT^{local}) methods.

Features	Query case	Original explanatory counterfactual	Global categorical transformation	Local categorical transformation
Weight	90 kg	***100 kg***	***High***	***Higher***
Duration	1 h	***1.5 h***	***High***	***Higher***
Gender	Female	Female	Female	Female
Stomach	Empty	Empty	Empty	Empty
Units	5	5	5	5
BAC Level	Over	Under	Under	Under

value of 120 kg, then the former would be labelled *lower-weight* and the latter *higher-weight* (and vice versa if the weight values were reversed; see Table 3). This approach avoids the global binning of values (and conflicts that arise) using instead a more relative transformation; it tells the user that one feature was significantly higher/lower than the other and the direction of the difference that produced the counterfactual outcome. Arguably, this method is simpler and easier to compute, though it does give users more relativistic explanations (e.g., people will not know whether *higher* is *high* in some absolute sense, just that the value is high relative to the paired case). The method also prioritises counterfactuals with relative difference-features that are most representative of the set of potential counterfactuals, by assigning each candidate counterfactual a *direction-consistency* score. For example, where there are 20 candidate counterfactuals for a given query case, a certain difference-feature may be relatively *higher* in 15 of these candidates and relatively *lower* in 5. The proportion of candidates with each relative categorical value for that feature is calculated (e.g., .75 for *higher*, .25 for *lower*), and the mean direction-consistency score for each candidate is obtained by averaging this score for all difference-features. The candidates are ordered in terms of (i) sparsity (lowest to highest), and then by (ii) direction (highest to lowest), selecting the one with the best sparsity and direction-consistency score. In the next section, we report our tests of these two methods, implementing variants of the CB2-CF method to test each on those datasets that we saw to be most important in Study 1.

5 Study 2: Evaluating CAT-CF Methods

We evaluated the performance of the two methods described above using seven UCI datasets [43] and in comparison to two baseline techniques (from [20]): (i) CBR$_{\text{Proximity}}$ selects the best candidate counterfactual using the ℓ_2 distance between the query and counterfactual candidate; and (ii) CBR$_{\text{Sparsity \& Proximity}}$ prioritises sparsity between the query and counterfactual case before selecting the most proximal candidate. All methods were evaluated using a k-NN model for varying ks, but here we report the results for $k = 20$, as different values of k yield similar results.

5.1 Method: Data and Procedure

The evaluation datasets vary in the number of features, classes, and overall size (see Table 2), but all contain some categorical features and are used in classification tasks. In order to evaluate the two CAT-CF approaches against baseline CBR methods, we focus on two metrics: (i) *explanation competence* or *coverage*, that is, the proportion of query cases for which at least one counterfactual case can be generated; and (ii) *relative counterfactual distance*, that is, the ratio of distance between a query case and its selected counterfactual case, to the distance between the query case and explanation-case generated for the counterfactual (n.b., ℓ_2 is a standard measure used to evaluate counterfactual methods, with low distance seen as an indicator of better or more plausible explanations). For each dataset we used a tolerance of $\pm 20\%$ 1 SD for a given feature. Ten-fold cross-validation was used in evaluation, randomly selecting 10% of instances as query cases, and the remainder as the basis for the explanation cases. The means for each dataset across all 10 folds are reported here.

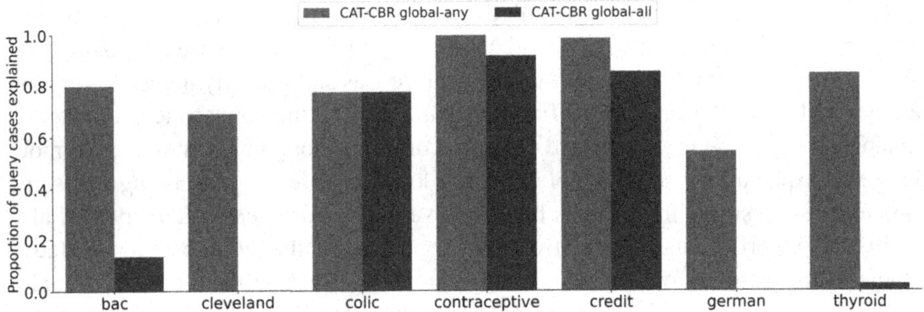

Fig. 3. Study 2 coverage results: The explanatory competence of CAT-CBR$^{\text{global}-\text{any}}$ compared to CAT-CBR$^{\text{global-all}}$, for seven datasets.

To determine the impact of the removal of conflicting-candidates in CAT-CF^{Global}, and its feasibility, we first compared a version of CAT-CF^{Global} that requires *all* feature differences be preserved following the categorical-binning step (CAT-CF$^{\text{Global-all}}$) to one that relaxes this constraint to require that *at least one* feature difference is preserved (CAT-CF$^{\text{Global-any}}$). Figure 3 shows the explanatory competence of these variants, in which CAT-CF$^{\text{Global-all}}$ performs poorly on all datasets relative to the CAT-CF$^{\text{Global-any}}$ ($M_{\text{global-all}} \approx 39\%$; $M_{\text{global-any}} \approx 80\%$; $z = -7.01, p < .001$), failing completely on several. Clearly, the former is too conservative, so we adopt CAT-CF$^{\text{Global-any}}$ in subsequent tests. Though this means the global method will not necessarily transform all continuous feature-differences, a counterfactual explanation with one categorical difference-feature and one continuous difference-feature still holds a distinct psychological advantage over an explanation in which both difference-features are continuous (Fig. 4).

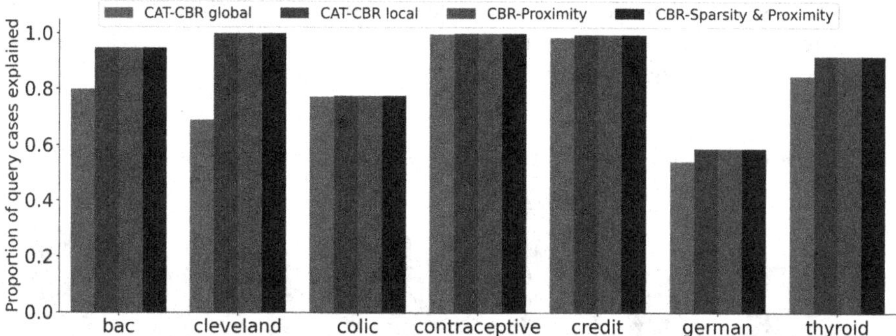

Fig. 4. Study 2 coverage results: The explanatory competence of both categorical methods in comparison to two baseline methods, across 7 datasets.

5.2 Results and Discussion: Counterfactual Distance

Having shown the explanatory competence of the two proposed counterfactual methods, we now move to assessing their explanatory power. *Relative counterfactual distance* (RCF) is used as proxy measure for the quality of generated counterfactuals and is computed by dividing the distance of generated counterfactual pairs, by the baseline distance between native-counterfactuals in the dataset. If RCF is <1, the generated counterfactuals are closer to the query case than the mean baseline distance. RCF for each of the methods and datasets are shown in Fig. 5. Analyses with t-tests showed that both baselines ($RCF_{Proximity} \approx .93$; $RCF_{Sparsity\ \&\ Proximity} \approx .96$) performed better than CAT-CF^{Global} ($RCF_{global} \approx 1.05$), $t(70) = 4.17, p < .001$; $t(70) = 3.33, p < .001$ respectively. There was no significant difference between the mean RCF of the counterfactuals produced by CAT-CF^{Global} and CAT-CF^{Local} ($RCF_{local} \approx .99$), $t(70) = 1.91, p = .058$ (note that this metric only captures the distance between those query-counterfactual pairs that were successfully produced, so the poorer coverage of CAT-CF^{Global} is not accounted for here). CAT-CF^{Local} does not score as well as CBR-Proximity, $t(70) = 2.54, p = .012$, but is not significantly different to CBR-Sparsity & Proximity, $t(70) = 1.65, p = .09$. This suggests that selecting the best counterfactual by prioritising direction-consistency does not sacrifice similarity any more than prioritising sparsity, which is widely accepted to be psychologically important.

Overall, from these results it is clear we can be confident about transforming features into more psychologically-acceptable variants using CAT-CF^{Local}; though, there is a slight hit on the distance measure, this decrement should be compensated for by the improved psychological comprehensibility of the explanations generated using this method. Depending on the task context, as well as the domain-knowledge and the goals of users, their requirements of an explanation are likely to vary [6, 44]. For example, in applications where the user aims to develop a general understanding of how features affect a system's decision (e.g., auditing system fairness), explanations focused on categorical features are likely to be highly effective. They may also be appropriate where there are concerns regarding model extraction or breaches of sensitive personal data, where it may be desirable to avoid explicitly providing raw data points. Even where users require or request more precise information, the categorical explanations proposed here can be easily supplemented with reference to the original data; bearing in mind that developing a basic understanding of the features and how they contribute to a system's decision is clearly a fundamental first step towards actionable recourse.

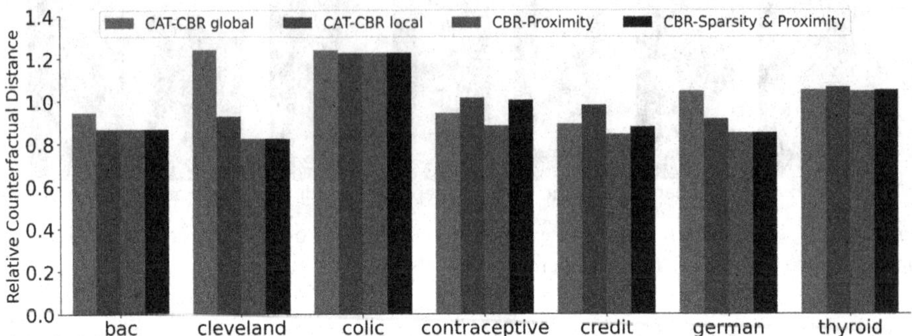

Fig. 5. Study 2 distance results: The counterfactual distance of good counterfactuals produced for 7 datasets, relative to baseline counterfactual distance (between query case and its NUN)

6 Conclusions

In recent years, the XAI literature has been replete with many counterfactual methods that claim to generate plausible explanations based on the "right" features [15] but with little or no psychological evidence to support the claims made. Recent studies have shown that people learn from counterfactuals involving categorical features rather than those using continuous features [22], which motivates the case-based, counterfactual method proposed here; it produces categorical counterfactuals by transforming continuous features into categorical alternatives. We have tested two variants of this transforming approach and found that CAT-CF^{Local}, which performs local transformations, works well on coverage and relative distance measures, compared to standard non-transforming methods. This means we can retain the benefits of current methods but boost them psychologically with categorical transformations of their proposed explanations. The main novelty of this work is that it is the first counterfactual method that has been specifically designed to meet identified psychological requirements of end-users, rather than merely reflecting the intuitions of algorithm designers.

Acknowledgments. This research was supported by (i) the UCD Foundation, (ii) UCD Science Foundation Ireland via the Insight SFI Research Centre for Data Analytics (12/RC/2289) and (iii) the Department of Agriculture, Food and Marine via the VistaMilk SFI Research Centre (16/RC/3835).

References

1. Gunning, D., Aha, D.W.: DARPA's explainable artificial intelligence program. AI Mag. **40**(2), 44–58 (2019)

2. Adadi, A., Berrada, M.: Peeking inside the black-box: a survey on Explainable Artificial Intelligence (XAI). IEEE Access **6**, 52138–52160 (2018)
3. Miller, T.: Explanation in artificial intelligence. Artif. Intell. **267**, 1–38 (2019)
4. Goodman, B., Flaxman, S.: European Union regulations on algorithmic decision-making and a "right to explanation." AI Mag. **38**(3), 50–57 (2017)
5. Leake, D., McSherry, D.: Introduction to the special issue on explanation in case-based reasoning. Artif. Intell. Rev. **24**(2), 103–108 (2005)
6. Sørmo, F., Cassens, J., Aamodt, A.: Explanation in case-based reasoning–perspectives and goals. Artif. Intell. Rev. **24**(2), 109–143 (2005)
7. Schoenborn, J.M., Althoff, K.D.: Recent trends in XAI: In: Case-Based Reasoning for the Explanation of intelligent systems (XCBR) Workshop (2019)
8. Kenny, E.M., Keane, M.T.: Twin-systems to explain neural networks using case-based reasoning. In: IJCAI-19, pp. 326–333 (2019)
9. Keane, M.T., Kenny, E.M.: How case-based reasoning explains neural networks: a theoretical analysis of XAI using post-hoc explanation-by-example from a survey of ANN-CBR twin-systems. In: Bach, K., Marling, C. (eds.) ICCBR 2019. LNCS (LNAI), vol. 11680, pp. 155–171. Springer, Cham (2019). https://doi.org/10.1007/978-3-030-29249-2_11
10. Kenny, E.M., Keane, M.T.: Explaining deep learning using examples: optimal feature weighting methods for twin systems using post-hoc, explanation-by-example in XAI. Knowl.-Based Syst. **233**, 1–14, 107530 (2021)
11. Nugent, C., Cunningham, P.: Gaining insight through case-based explanation. J. Intell. Inf. Syst. **32**(3), 267–295 (2009)
12. Cummins, L., Bridge, D.: KLEOR: a knowledge lite approach to explanation oriented retrieval. Comput. Inform. **25**(2–3), 173–193 (2006)
13. Kenny, E.M., Keane, M.T.: On generating plausible counterfactual and semi-factual explanations for deep learning. In: AAAI-21, pp. 11575–11585 (2021)
14. Martens, D., Provost, F.: Explaining data-driven document classifications. MIS Q. **38**, 73–100 (2014)
15. Keane, M.T., Kenny, E.M., Delaney, E., Smyth, B.: If only we had better counterfactual explanations. In: IJCAI-21, pp. 4466–4474 (2021)
16. Karimi, A.-H., Barthe, G., Schölkopf, B., Valera, I.: A survey of algorithmic recourse. arXiv preprint arXiv:2010.04050 (2020)
17. Byrne, R.M.J.: Counterfactuals in explainable artificial intelligence (XAI): evidence from human reasoning. In: IJCAI-19, pp. 6276–6282 (2019)
18. Wachter, S., Mittelstadt, B., Russell, C.: Counterfactual explanations without opening the black box: automated decisions and the GDPR. Harv. JL Tech. **31**, 841 (2018)
19. Keane, M.T., Smyth, B.: Good counterfactuals and where to find them: a case-based technique for generating counterfactuals for explainable AI (XAI). In: Watson, I., Weber, R. (eds.) ICCBR 2020. LNCS (LNAI), vol. 12311, pp. 163–178. Springer, Cham (2020). https://doi.org/10.1007/978-3-030-58342-2_11
20. Smyth, B., Keane, M.T.: A few good counterfactuals: generating interpretable, plausible and diverse counterfactual explanations. In: ICCBR-22, Springer, Berlin (2022)
21. Wexler, J., Pushkarna, M., Bolukbasi, T., Wattenberg, M., Viégas, F., Wilson, J.: The what-if tool: Interactive probing of machine learning models. IEEE TVCG **26**(1), 56–65 (2019)
22. Warren, G., Keane, M.T., Byrne, R.M.J.: Features of explainability: how users understand counterfactual and causal explanations for categorical and continuous features in XAI. In: IJCAI-22 Workshop on Cognitive Aspects of Knowledge Representation (2022)
23. Nugent, C., Cunningham, P.: A case-based explanation system for black-box systems. Artif. Intell. Rev. **24**(2), 163–178 (2005)
24. Kumar, R.R., Viswanath, P., Bindu, C.S.: Nearest neighbor classifiers: a review. Int. J. Comput. Intell. Res. **13**(2), 303–311 (2017)

25. Aggarwal, C.C., Chen, C., Han, J.: The inverse classification problem. J. Comput. Sci. Technol. **25**(3), 458–468 (2010)
26. Laugel, T., Lesot, M.J., Marsala, C., Renard, X., Detyniecki, M.: The dangers of post-hoc interpretability. In: IJCAI-19, pp. 2801–2807 (2019)
27. Mothilal, R.K., Sharma, A., Tan, C.: Explaining machine learning classifiers through diverse counterfactual explanations. In: FAT*20, pp. 607–617 (2020)
28. Van Looveren, A., Klaise, J.: Interpretable counterfactual explanations guided by prototypes. In: Oliver, N., Pérez-Cruz, F., Kramer, S., Read, J., Lozano, J.A. (eds.) ECML PKDD 2021. LNCS (LNAI), vol. 12976, pp. 650–665. Springer, Cham (2021). https://doi.org/10.1007/978-3-030-86520-7_40
29. Russell, C.: Efficient search for diverse coherent explanations. In: FAT-19, pp. 20–28 (2019)
30. Kahneman, D., Miller, D.T.: Norm theory. Psychol. Rev. **93**(2), 136–153 (1986)
31. Ustun, B., Spangher, A., Liu, Y.: Actionable recourse in linear classification. In: FAT-19, pp. 10–19 (2019)
32. Karimi, A.H., Barthe, G., Balle, B., Valera, I.: Model-agnostic counterfactual explanations for consequential decisions. In: AISTATS-20, Palermo, Italy, vol. 108. PMLR (2020)
33. Wiratunga, N., Wijekoon, A., Nkisi-Orji, I., Martin, K., Palihawadana, C., Corsar, D.: Actionable feature discovery in counterfactuals using feature relevance explainers. In: CEUR Workshop Proceedings (2021)
34. Karimi, A.H., von Kügelgen, J., Schölkopf, B., Valera, I.: Algorithmic recourse under imperfect causal knowledge. In: NeurIPS-20, 33 (2020)
35. Ramon, Y., Martens, D., Provost, F., Evgeniou, T.: A comparison of instance-level counterfactual explanation algorithms for behavioral and textual data: SEDC, LIME-C and SHAP-C. Adv. Data Anal. Classif. **14**(4), 801–819 (2020). https://doi.org/10.1007/s11634-020-00418-3
36. Delaney, E., Greene, D., Keane, M.T.: Instance-based counterfactual explanations for time series classification. In: Sánchez-Ruiz, A.A., Floyd, M.W. (eds.) ICCBR 2021. LNCS (LNAI), vol. 12877, pp. 32–47. Springer, Cham (2021). https://doi.org/10.1007/978-3-030-86957-1_3
37. Dodge, J., Liao, Q.V., Zhang, Y., Bellamy, R.K., Dugan, C.: Explaining models: an empirical study of how explanations impact fairness judgment. In: IUI-19, pp. 275–285 (2019)
38. Lucic, A., Haned, H., de Rijke, M.: Contrastive local explanations for retail forecasting. In: FAT*20, pp. 90–98 (2020)
39. Van der Waa, J., Nieuwburg, E., Cremers, A., Neerincx, M.: Evaluating XAI: a comparison of rule-based and example-based explanations. Artif. Intell. **291** (2021)
40. Lage, I., et al.: Human evaluation of models built for interpretability. In: HCOMP-19, pp. 59–67 (2019)
41. Kirfel, L., Liefgreen, A.: What if (and how...)? Actionability shapes people's perceptions of counterfactual explanations in automated decision-making. In: ICML-21 Workshop on Algorithmic Recourse (2021)
42. Kahneman, D., Tversky, A.: The simulation heuristic. In: Kahneman, D., Slovic, P., Tversky, A. (eds.), Judgment Under Uncertainty: Heuristics and Biases, pp. 201–208. CUP (1982)
43. Dua, D., Graff, C.: UCI Machine Learning Repository. University of California, School of Information and Computer Science, Irvine, CA (2019). http://archive.ics.uci.edu/ml
44. Keil, F.C.: Explanation and understanding. Ann. Rev. Psychol. **57**, 227–254 (2006)
45. Förster, M., Klier, M., Kluge, K., Sigler, I.: Evaluating explainable artificial intelligence: what users really appreciate. In ECIS-2020 (2020)

Representation and Similarity

Extracting Case Indices from Convolutional Neural Networks: A Comparative Study

David Leake, Zachary Wilkerson(✉), and David Crandall

Luddy School of Informatics, Computing, and Engineering, Indiana University, Bloomington, IN 47408, USA
{leake,zachwilk,djcran}@indiana.edu

Abstract. Machine learning for extracting case features can provide great benefit over feature engineering for retrieval in poorly understood or hard to characterize domains. The effectiveness of machine learning with deep neural networks has prompted much interest in neural network approaches to feature learning in case-based reasoning, with several works showing the value of feature extraction from input data using convolutional neural networks. Those approaches are based on plausible assumptions about where in the networks to extract features for maximal usefulness. This paper presents an empirical evaluation of those underlying assumptions. We compare three extraction approaches, for an image classification task: the most common feature extraction method, extracting after the convolution layer; a recently proposed alternative, extracting after the densely-connected layers; and a new approach, extracting after the densely-connected layers using multiple networks. Our results show that the latter two approaches substantially increase case retrieval accuracy in example-sparse domains, to which case-based reasoning systems are commonly applied.

Keywords: Case-based reasoning · Deep learning · Feature learning · Hybrid systems · Indexing · Integrated systems · Retrieval

1 Introduction

Effective case-based reasoning (CBR) requires high-quality retrieval. Retrieval quality in turn generally depends on case indexing, using atomic features and possibly more complex indexing structures to characterize cases. Indexing knowledge may be acquired manually through knowledge acquisition and engineering (e.g., [7,16,20]). The manual acquisition process can provide high quality indices, but it can be expensive and is not always feasible. For example, even domain experts may not be capable of providing comprehensive feature vocabularies for poorly-understood domains or for tasks such as image recognition.

Given the effectiveness of deep learning (DL) at extracting features from data, it is natural to consider how automated indexing based on DL might supplement

M. T. Keane and N. Wiratunga (Eds.): ICCBR 2022, LNAI 13405, pp. 81–95, 2022.
https://doi.org/10.1007/978-3-031-14923-8_6

or replace human feature engineering. In CBR research, substantial attention has been focused on using convolutional neural networks (CNNs) to extract feature information from multi-dimensional raw input data. For example, CNNs have been used for extracting features from images for classifying examples with novel classes [23,24], and from outputs of three-dimensional movement sensors for human activity recognition in digital health technologies [19]. As exemplified in research by Turner et al. [23,24] and Sani et al. [19], values from feature vectors created by passing the raw input data through convolution and pooling layers early on in the network can be extracted before those vectors are further processed by densely-connected classification layers; these values become the feature set for similarity metrics in the CBR component of the hybrid system.

Ideally, the convolution and pooling steps in a CNN capture the most salient input features and structures (e.g., for image data, features such as shapes, edges, etc.). The outputs from these steps traditionally are conceptualized as the atomic features of the input. This contrasts with the outputs of the densely-connected hidden layers, which "mix and match" these features to facilitate classification. As convolution and pooling steps theoretically highlight atomic features of an input image, especially in the context of the rest of the network, it is appealing to map their features into similarity features for CBR, which has led to the use of this mapping for feature extraction.

However, it is possible that mappings at other, less-explored locations in the CNN might produce more useful features for similarity assessment in CBR. For example, the fact that features are combined in the densely-connected layers and that the final classification depends on the outputs of such combinations suggests that useful features might be extracted from the densely-connected layers in a CNN. This was proposed by Kenny and Keane [13] in the context of extracting and modifying features to generate counterfactual explanations. We hypothesize that feature extraction from the densely-connected layers will improve feature quality for the goal of increasing accuracy of case-based image classification.

This paper compares three methods that extract information in different ways from a single testbed network architecture. The extraction methods include (1) a traditional technique that extracts output values from after the convolution and pooling layers as features [19,23,24], (2) a previously proposed but less deeply-explored method that extracts the result of processing by the densely-connected layers—the inputs to the output layer of the CNN—as features [13], and (3) a novel approach that extracts as features the inputs to the output layer of n binary CNN classifiers (as opposed to one n-class classifier). Results show that extracting from before the output layer and from multiple binary classifiers can produce features that enable superior case-based classification accuracy, with especially notable performance improvements for lower-dimensional feature spaces and more class-dense scenarios.

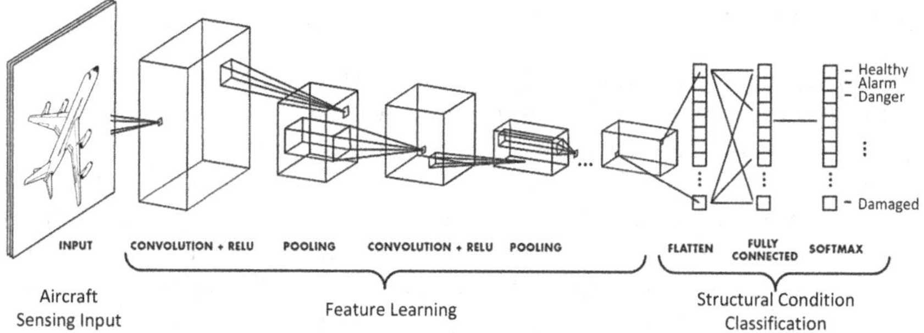

Fig. 1. Procedural diagram for a CNN in an aircraft sensor domain. Figure by Iuliana Tabian, Hailing Fu, and Zahra Sharif Khodaei is licensed under CC BY 4.0 [22].

2 Potential Feature Extraction Points in CNNs

CNNs refine the information from raw input data into a classification prediction through multiple layers. At the highest level of abstraction, a CNN may be divided into two sections. The feature extraction section consists of a series of layers designed to process the multi-dimensional raw data into a set of features passed to the classification section, which is a multilayer perceptron network (Fig. 1).

The feature extraction section typically consists of convolution and pooling layers that iteratively transform values from multi-dimensional input data. Each convolution layer consists of several different filters that are applied iteratively across the input to produce feature map output values. For each unit (e.g., pixel) in the input P indexed by (i, j), and for a filter F of size $(2k+1) \times (2l+1)$ (generally $k = l$), the output O is calculated by:

$$O_{ij} = \sum_{m=-k}^{k} \sum_{n=-l}^{l} F_{mn} * P_{(i-m)(j-n)} \tag{1}$$

Thus, the output of each convolution layer is a set of modified feature maps, one for each filter in the layer. In pooling steps, the resolution of each feature map generated by the preceding convolution layer is reduced by replacing each unit in a non-overlapping $r \times s$ region (again, usually $r = s$) by the value of a representative unit from the region. For the post-convolution method described below, features are extracted following the last pooling layer.

The resulting feature maps from all convolution and pooling layers in the feature extraction section are then flattened into a one-dimensional feature vector and passed as inputs into the classification section. The features are passed through multiple fully-connected dense layers until the final outputs are used as inputs to the output layer. The same final outputs are extracted as features for the post-dense and multi-net methods described below.

3 Related Work

Case retrieval quality is critically dependent on the quality of the indices used [7,14,16,17,20]. Feature vocabularies form the foundation of case indices and are commonly generated through knowledge engineering processes, reflecting comprehensive domain analysis [7,16,20]. However, manually generating the right set of features can be costly. In addition, the resulting feature set may be incomplete or unreliable when domain knowledge is imperfect. Symbolic learning methods have long been applied to refining feature selection and weighting (e.g., [1,3–5,8]), and recent work has begun to explore extraction of features and feature weights from deep neural networks. For example, Grace et al. [9] use a DL system in a recipe design domain to identify ingredient associations from the case base, and the DL system uses this information to retrieve example cases that address competing creativity and plausibility criteria. Shin et al. [21] apply an artificial neural network architecture to learn feature weightings for a CBR-based data mining task. Turner et al. [23,24] leverage CNN-generated features in a CBR classifier that classifies images for which the CNN has low confidence, defining an implicit class of images that may fall outside of known classes. Their method extracts features from different network architectures analogously to our post-convolution method, illustrating how various CNN models may be leveraged to generate CBR feature information. Sani et al. [19] apply CNNs to process multi-dimensional data from tri-axis sensors that measure human movement. Features extracted from after the convolution and pooling layers in their model are then used to classify the type and intensity of the activity using CBR retrieval.

Feature extraction from networks has also been pursued in the context of explainable AI. Kenny and Keane propose the use of CBR "twin systems", which explain network outputs by presenting cases retrieved using information extracted from the networks [12]. They also study the use of extracted feature information to generate counterfactual cases, with a method that extracts features from the output of the densely-connected layers of a CNN [13], a concept that we explore in this paper for extracting features for classification. Graziani et al. [10] use regression analyses to select entries from a field of potential concepts to identify those that a given neural network system is most likely to be learning; to achieve this mapping, the regression algorithm draws from feature data extracted from multiple regions in the network architecture.

One of the motivations for our work is the integration of knowledge-engineered and network-generated features. Weber et al. [25] leverage additional knowledge-engineered features to augment network-based explanation selection, and Barnett et al. [2] integrate interpretable, CBR-derived principles directly into a CNN image classifier. Specifically, in Barnett et al.'s work, network information is funneled toward sub-sections of the network architecture represented by prototype images in a way reminiscent of CBR retrieval. Wilkerson, Leake and Crandall [26] explore feature and weight learning using a CNN system to extract information from images to augment knowledge-engineered features. That work focuses on how learned features and knowledge-engineered features can be used in concert for greater retrieval quality and echoes the feature extraction design

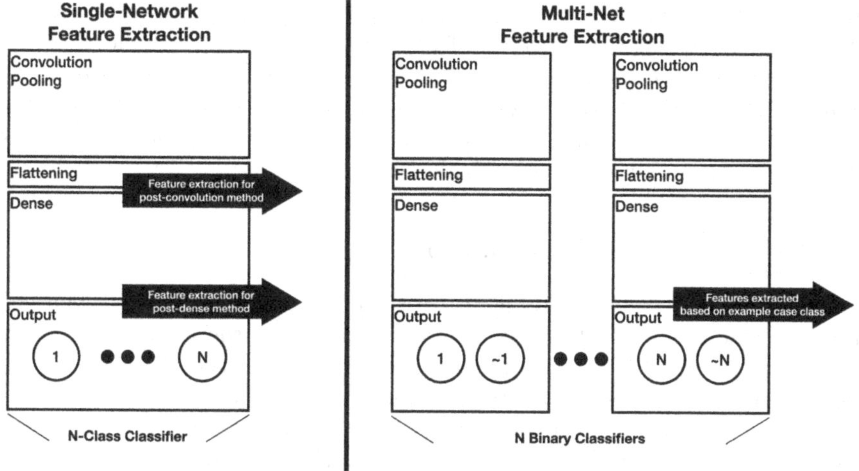

Fig. 2. Feature extraction locations for post-convolution, post-dense (both left), and multi-net (right) feature extraction methods.

of Kenny and Keane [13]. This paper solely explores feature extraction from networks.

4 Three Structure-Based Feature Extraction Methods

This paper examines three approaches for extracting CBR features/indices from a CNN architecture: one well-studied prior method [19,23,24], one method that has been explored for explanation [13] but, to our knowledge, not for classification, and a new approach proposed in this paper:

1. **Post-convolution:** Extracting feature values from between the feature extraction and classification sections in the CNN architecture
2. **Post-dense:** Extracting feature values from the outputs of the densely-connected hidden layers in the CNN's classification section
3. **Multi-net:** Expanding the single CNN architecture into multiple binary CNNs for each prediction class, and extracting features as in the post-dense approach

Figure 2 illustrates the architectures and extraction locations for each of these approaches.

4.1 Post-convolution Feature Extraction

As described in Sect. 2, iterations of convolution and pooling steps ideally remove noise and highlight atomic features from raw input data before passing the resulting output to the classification section. Therefore, if we assume that these output values represent the atomic features of the original data (e.g., as in [19,23,24]), features extracted from between the feature extraction and classification sections (i.e., features in the flattened feature vector passed into the dense layers) are appropriate features to provide to the CBR retrieval process. The retrieval process can then use the values of those features as inputs to, for example, the distance calculation for k-nearest neighbors.

4.2 Post-dense Feature Extraction

The post-dense method extracts as features the outputs from the last densely-connected hidden layer in the classification section (i.e., the inputs to the output layer in the CNN). This design is inspired by the observation that if the feature extraction section generates atomic features from raw data, then the classification section aggregates/combines those features into richer structures more directly relevant to the classification task. From the perspective of index extraction, those structures might correspond to richer indices with more useful information. This method has not received as much attention as the post-convolution method in DL-CBR hybrid research, but some previous works have begun to explore this approach (e.g.,. [13,26]).

4.3 Multi-net Feature Extraction

During retrieval, feature applicability for classification can depend on the class to which a query case is being compared. For example, features corresponding to airplanes in an image are much more useful when classifying an airport than a library. Traditionally, the issue of relative feature importance is addressed through feature weighting, but sensitizing the feature space itself may be similarly effective. Consequently, feature extraction that enables generating local features, rather than requiring that the same features be used across the entire space, might be more useful for case indexing.

To generate local features, we propose a novel feature extraction approach, multi-net feature extraction. Rather than training a single n-class CNN classifier and extracting features, multi-net feature extraction is based on training n binary CNN classifiers that each distinguish between examples of a unique class and all examples that are not in that class. Multi-net extraction creates a unique feature generation approach for each class, and it uses different feature values based on the class of the candidate case to which the query case is compared (i.e., calculating similarity as if the query and candidate are both members of the same class). This potentially provides a benefit analagous to local similarity measures (e.g., [18]), but rather than resulting in locally adjusted feature weights, it results in an adjusted feature vocabulary. This increases flexibility by enabling richer or different representations when needed. A tradeoff of this method is increased processing cost: the training time for multi-net is increased by roughly a factor of n relative to a standard CNN architecture.

5 Evaluation

Our evaluation compares the quality of features extracted by the methods described previously, based on classification accuracy using the extracted features.

5.1 Hypotheses

Our evaluation tests the following hypotheses:

1. **Post-convolution feature extraction will lead to the weakest accuracy.** As discussed, the post-convolution method can be seen as extracting a set of initial atomic features, rather than the more refined/complex features generated by extracting from later in the network.
2. **Post-dense feature extraction will result in higher accuracy than post-convolution methods.** As discussed, the features from post-dense extraction can be seen as representing a richer range of factors.
3. **Multi-net feature extraction will yield the highest retrieval accuracy.** As discussed, the quality of the multi-net features can benefit both from the richer features of the post-dense method and from the flexibility of using different feature sets for different classes.

5.2 Test Domain and Test Set Selection

The approaches are evaluated on the Places data set for image recognition, which has been used as a standard for competition for DL-based image recognition algorithms [27]. This data set consists of images representing various common locations (e.g., alley, library, airport, etc.).

To test the approaches across problems with different numbers of classes, we generate three distinct subsets of the raw data set, respectively containing image examples from ten, twenty-five, or fifty classes. Classes for each subset are selected randomly, and for each experiment, these class subsets are frozen for consistency between iterations. In each experimental iteration, training images are selected randomly from the classes represented in the subset to create the training set. To build the training sets, an equal number N of images is chosen from each class represented in the set. Two groups of experiments are conducted. The first group keeps constant the number of examples per class regardless of the number of classes (resulting in the system having more total examples when there are more classes). The second keeps the total number of examples constant by decreasing the number of examples per class as the number of classes is increased.

For each group, three values of N are considered—10, 20, and 50. In the first group, $N = 10$ and all experiments use the same number of images per class, regardless of the number of classes. In the second group, the value of N depends on the number of classes; in the fifty-class experiment, $N = 10$, for twenty-five, $N = 20$, and for ten, $N = 50$, so that 500 training images are used for each experiment. Because CBR systems are often used in example-sparse scenarios, training set sizes are purposefully kept small in our experiments.

5.3 Testbed System

As this work only pertains to retrieval, the testbed case-based classifier has no adaptation component. The classifier performs retrieval using 1-NN and a Euclidean distance metric to determine case similarity. For these experiments, all features are weighted equally, but future work could assess the effect of feature weighting or extraction of both features and weights from CNN systems.

The CNN used to test each of the three approaches has the same structure. It derives closely from the AlexNet architecture [15] but deviates from AlexNet in excluding the bias term for output layer neurons. The rationale for this change is that the bias term influences the other input values during training but is not extracted along with other features. Consequently, a bias term could affect feature values in the CNN but remain unaccounted for when those features are transferred to the CBR system, reducing the ability of the extracted features to truly reflect the CNN's behavior.

During experimentation involving post-convolution feature extraction, the number of filters in the last convolution layer is modified to vary the number of features extracted for the CBR system; for the other two approaches, the number of neurons in the dense layers is similarly modified for the same purpose.

The activation function for all dense layers is RELU, and, as our previous work using post-dense extraction showed that training for fifty epochs produced the best results [26], we continue that training structure for this work. Each experiment iteration (i.e., training, feature extraction, and CBR-based retrieval testing) is repeated thirty times, recording mean and standard deviation values. For some multi-net tests involving the largest numbers of features, the tests terminated prematurely due to memory constraints, resulting in only twenty or twenty-five iterations overall. However, any impact would be felt only at the rightmost data point in the graph, and the results remain consistent with observed trends.

5.4 Accuracy Testing and Informal Upper Bound

In the evaluation, accuracy values are calculated by leave-one-out testing performed on the training set. These values show the relative performance of the three feature extraction methods. The figures with accuracy results also show the performance of our CNN architecture, trained on the training set—as done to generate the features extracted for the CBR system—and also tested on the *training set*. These results give an informal indication of an upper bound performance—the best performance that could result from the features available to the CBR system, were they applied in a neural network architecture to the data from which they were generated. This can be taken to roughly reflect the predictive power of the feature set under ideal conditions.

Results for the CNN upper bound should not be taken as suggesting that CNNs necessarily outperform CBR in this task, for two reasons. First, the CNN was trained on all examples, including each query being processed; in contrast, the CBR systems process each query with its corresponding case omitted from the case base. Second, the strongest CBR performance would require tuning similarity weighting, which is not done in our experiments.

6 Results and Discussion

6.1 Comparative Performance

Figures 3 and 4 show training accuracy versus number of features for different numbers of classes, comparing the three methods and the CNN classifier. In general, the post-dense approach significantly outperforms the post-convolution extraction method, and in many instances, the multi-net method outperforms both the post-dense and post-convolution methods, especially for smaller numbers of features. There are only a few instances in which the post-convolution method rivals either novel method, and only for limited numbers of features. The overall pattern supports the three hypotheses and suggests that the novel approaches improve feature quality. The results also illustrate several tradeoffs:

When the Total Number of Examples Varies, There Is a Tradeoff Between More Classes Increasing the Number of Training Examples and Increasing the Degrees of Freedom: Especially in the trends for post-dense extraction, the maximum accuracy values are highest in the 25-class case when holding the number of training examples per class constant. This illustrates a tradeoff between the number of classes and the number of examples per class. Specifically, a larger number of classes affords a greater number of training examples overall but creates more degrees of freedom in the classification problem itself. The opposite is true when the number of classes is reduced. Thus, we see a local maximum in the 25-class data for the post-dense results, as it represents a "happy medium" between these two factors. This is further supported by results when the number of training examples is held constant (Fig. 4). In this instance, accuracy curves for each approach essentially parallel one another across the different numbers of classes, with overall decreases in accuracy with a higher number of classes easily attributable to fewer training examples per class.

Fewer Features Can Harm CNN convergence, while many features can lead to a "curse of dimensionality": For each method (except the CNN classifier), accuracy broadly decreases as the number of features increases. Also evident in the post-dense method's accuracy curves, an even more pronounced decrease in accuracy occurs for small numbers of features (we hypothesize that a similar trend exists for the multi-net method for smaller numbers of features than we show here). We believe that the first phenomenon is a consequence of the "curse of dimensionality", with individual features having increasingly small influence on distances between examples in feature-dense spaces. Note that we do not see this in the CNN classifier, as CNNs tend to be robust to (and often more performant with) large numbers of features. Relative to the second phenomenon, if a neural network has access to too few parameters during training,

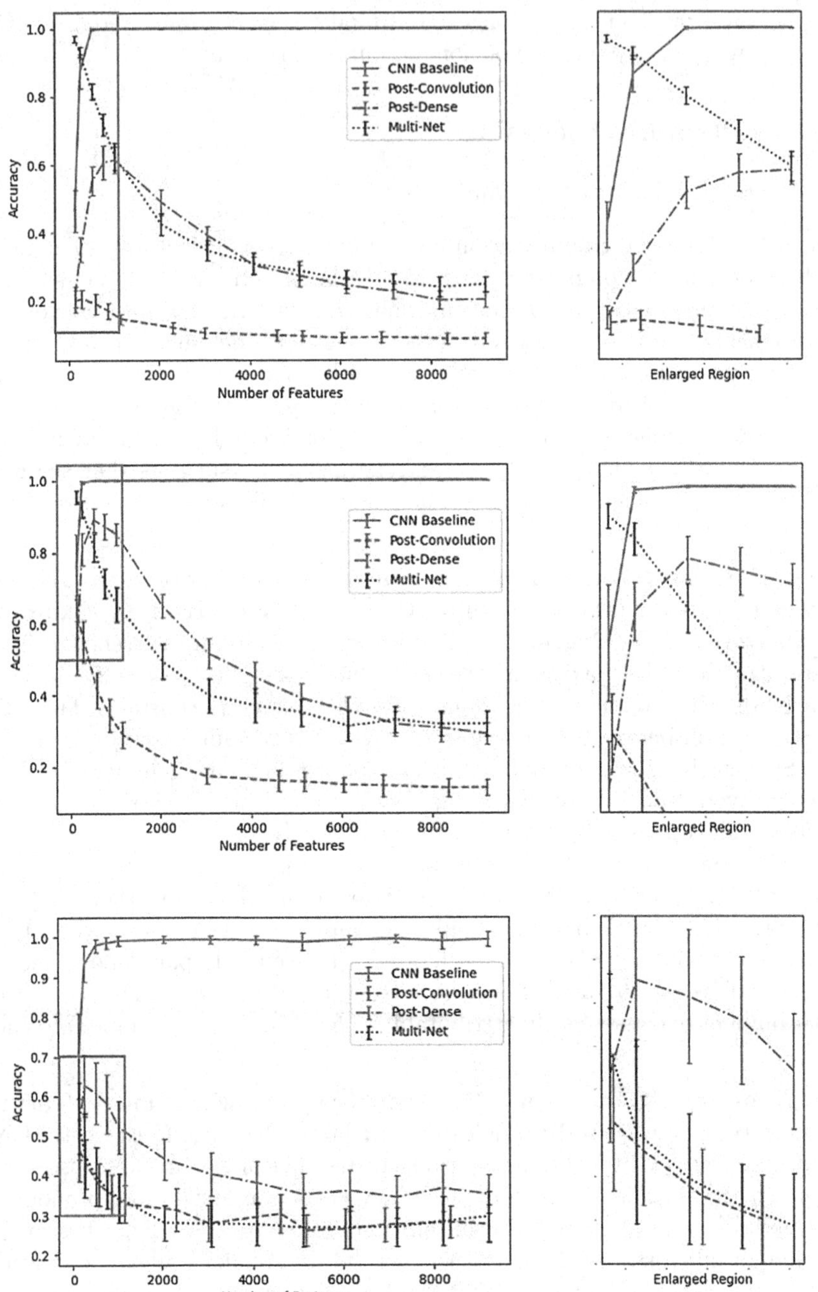

Fig. 3. Accuracy versus number of features for the 50-class case (top), 25-class case (middle) and 10-class case (bottom), using ten training examples per class. Error bars represent one standard deviation. Boxed regions at left on each graph are shown enlarged at right.

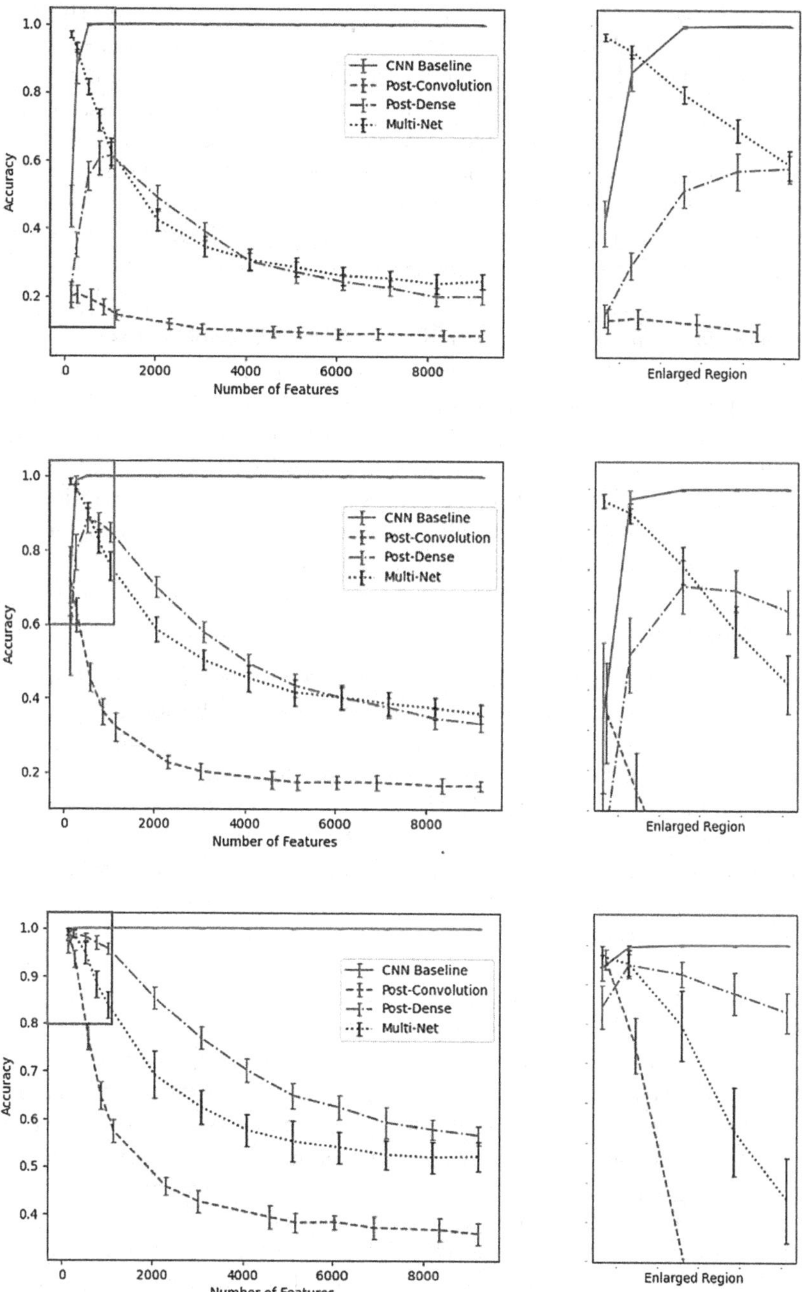

Fig. 4. Accuracy versus number of features for the 50-class case (top), 25-class case (middle) and 10-class case (bottom), using 500 training examples for each. Error bars represent one standard deviation. Boxed regions at left on each graph are shown enlarged at right.

it may not converge on a representative feature set. Thus, we hypothesize the existence of a tradeoff for the number of features in the CBR system—with too few features, retrieval performance suffers because there are not enough features for the network to converge while training, and with too many features, the distance calculations are in so many dimensions that the individual features are ineffective. Furthermore, the "happy medium" for this tradeoff should also be dependent on the number of classes (i.e., more features are required to distinguish between a larger number of classes); this assertion is supported by the data (e.g., the location of the maxima for the post-dense method).

Multi-net Has an Accuracy-Training Time Tradeoff Instead of an Accuracy-Explainability Tradeoff: The end-to-end CNN classifier, expected to be an upper bound, outperforms all methods almost all of the time in each experiment. However, surprisingly, the multi-net approach outperforms the CNN for small numbers of features. In this way, multi-net performance contrasts with the traditional conceptualization of the accuracy-explainability tradeoff [11]: compared to the CNN it trades off increased training time against accuracy, while (through the use of CBR) retaining explainability.

6.2 Discussion

A primary observation from the experiments is the superior performance of the multi-net approach. Case-based classification using the local features generated by the multi-net approach frequently outperforms the other case-based approaches, and it outperforms the CNN classifier for small numbers of features. This is reasonable because fewer degrees of freedom in doing binary rather than multiclass classification would suggest that fewer features are required to discriminate between the classes. Instead of trading off accuracy and explainability, as in other models that use extracted features for CBR, for small numbers of features multi-net trades off accuracy and training efficiency.

In addition, we hypothesize that the local feature extraction of the multi-net approach is critical to its performance. Specifically, the multi-net feature extraction model, which selects a set of features based on the class of a candidate case, can be seen as predicating features on the CBR component of the model, as a form of the traditional CBR situation assessment process, which elaborates and rerepresents features of an input query to be commensurate with the feature vocabulary of the case base. Here, instead of asking the feature extraction model "what features are present in the query?" it asks multi-net "what features related to class x are present in the query?"

It is natural to ask whether a process similar to the multi-net process could be achieved in an end-to-end CNN approach. It would be possible to use a collection of CNN binary classifiers and select the one that predicts that the query is in its class. However, in practice, multiple models may answer in the affirmative, requiring some tiebreaker (e.g., a softmax), raising the question of whether the result would be significantly different from a multiclass CNN. More research is needed to quantify the exact factors that enable multi-net's strong performance.

7 Ramifications for Interpretability

Hybrid systems as explored in this work sit at the intersection between DL and CBR systems. The nearest-neighbor retrieval and classification process presented here is interpretable in being able to present cases to explain decisions, a capability missing from DL systems alone. However, using learned features for similarity assessment makes such systems less interpretable than a CBR system applying knowledge-engineered features exclusively, for which case similarity—the reason the case was selected—could be more readily explained. However, in domains where a human user can holistically ascribe similarities between a query case and the retrieved case, this "middle ground" between DL and knowledge-engineered CBR may provide sufficient interpretability, and there is evidence for the value of case presentation alone as an explanation mechanism [6].

Furthermore, these approaches (especially multi-net) may be applicable in domains for which classification accuracy is more important than explainability, and for which minimal training data exists. However, further research is needed into the accuracy-interpretability tradeoff when using network-learned features, as well as into the potential use of methods such as counterfactual/semi-factual explanation generation [13] to generate additional cases to holistically illuminate the boundaries for cases considered similar, even if it is not possible to point to variations of user-understandable features.

8 Conclusions and Future Work

Feature extraction from neural networks can facilitate the application of case-based reasoning to hard to characterize domains, where knowledge-engineered feature information may be difficult and/or expensive to produce. Prior work in feature extraction has focused primarily on extracting features immediately after the convolution and pooling layers, based on the intuition that such layers will be best suited to feature extraction because they provide atomic descriptions of domain features. This paper challenges that assumption, proposing feature extraction after the dense layers. It presents a new multi-net approach for this extraction, and, to our knowledge, presents the first comparative evaluation to assess the performance of alternative extraction locations. The results highlight the strength of post-dense feature extraction in example-sparse domains, where CBR systems are often the method of choice; furthermore, they support that multi-net can provide even stronger performance in lower-dimensional spaces.

In future research, we expect to investigate the use of multi-net feature extraction with different CNN architectures. In addition, building on our prior work on combining network-learned and expert-provided features [26], we plan to test its effects on hybrid retrieval using both extracted features and knowledge-engineered features. We also intend to consider more example-dense training scenarios and larger datasets, as well as exploring how similarity weights might be extracted along with features from network architectures to further improve performance.

Acknowledgments. This work was funded by the US Department of Defense (Contract W52P1J2093009), and by the Department of the Navy, Office of Naval Research (Award N00014-19-1-2655). We thank the Indiana University Deep CBR group, especially Vibhas Vats and Lawrence Gates, for valuable discussions of this work.

References

1. Barletta, R., Mark, W.: Explanation-based indexing of cases. In: Kolodner, J. (ed.) Proceedings of a Workshop on Case-Based Reasoning, pp. 50–60. DARPA, Morgan Kaufmann, Palo Alto (1988)
2. Barnett, A.J., et al.: Interpretable mammographic image classification using case-based reasoning and deep learning. In: IJCAI Workshops 2021 (2021)
3. Bhatta, S., Goel, A.: Model-based learning of structural indices to design cases. In: Proceedings of the IJCAI-93 Workshop on Reuse of Design, pp. A1–A13. IJCAI, Chambery, France (1993)
4. Bonzano, A., Cunningham, P., Smyth, B.: Using introspective learning to improve retrieval in CBR: a case study in air traffic control. In: Leake, D.B., Plaza, E. (eds.) ICCBR 1997. LNCS, vol. 1266, pp. 291–302. Springer, Heidelberg (1997). https://doi.org/10.1007/3-540-63233-6_500
5. Cox, M., Ram, A.: Introspective multistrategy learning: on the construction of learning strategies. Artif. Intell. **112**(1–2), 1–55 (1999)
6. Cunningham, P., Doyle, D., Loughrey, J.: An evaluation of the usefulness of case-based explanation. In: Ashley, K.D., Bridge, D.G. (eds.) ICCBR 2003. LNCS (LNAI), vol. 2689, pp. 122–130. Springer, Heidelberg (2003). https://doi.org/10.1007/3-540-45006-8_12
7. Domeshek, E.: Indexing stories as social advice. In: Proceedings of the Ninth National Conference on Artificial Intelligence, pp. 16–21. AAAI Press, Menlo Park, CA (1991)
8. Fox, S., Leake, D.: Introspective reasoning for index refinement in case-based reasoning. J. Exp. Theor. Artif. Intell. **13**(1), 63–88 (2001)
9. Grace, K., Maher, M.L., Wilson, D.C., Najjar, N.A.: Combining CBR and deep learning to generate surprising recipe designs. In: Goel, A., Díaz-Agudo, M.B., Roth-Berghofer, T. (eds.) ICCBR 2016. LNCS (LNAI), vol. 9969, pp. 154–169. Springer, Cham (2016). https://doi.org/10.1007/978-3-319-47096-2_11
10. Graziani, M., Andrearczyk, V., Marchand-Maillet, S., Müller, H.: Concept attribution: explaining CNN decisions to physicians. Comput. Biol. Med. **123**, 103865 (2020)
11. Gunning, D., Aha, D.W.: DARPA's explainable artificial intelligence (XAI) program. AI Mag. **40**(2), 44–58 (2019)
12. Kenny, E.M., Keane, M.T.: Twin-systems to explain artificial neural networks using case-based reasoning: comparative tests of feature-weighting methods in ANN-CBR twins for XAI. In: Proceedings of the Twenty-Eighth International Joint Conference on Artificial Intelligence (2019)
13. Kenny, E.M., Keane, M.T.: On generating plausible counterfactual and semi-factual explanations for deep learning. In: Proceedings of the Thirty-Fifth AAAI Conference on Artificial Intelligence (AAAI-21), pp. 11575–11585. AAAI (2021)
14. Richter, M.M., Weber, R.O.: Relations and comparisons with other techniques. In: Case-Based Reasoning, pp. 523–538. Springer, Heidelberg (2013). https://doi.org/10.1007/978-3-642-40167-1_23

15. Krizhevsky, A., Sutskever, I., Hinton, G.E.: Imagenet classification with deep convolutional neural networks. In: Proceedings of the 25th International Conference on Neural Information Processing Systems, vol. 1, pp. 1097–1105 (2012)
16. Leake, D.: An indexing vocabulary for case-based explanation. In: Proceedings of the Ninth National Conference on Artificial Intelligence, pp. 10–15. AAAI Press, Menlo Park, CA (1991)
17. de Mántaras, L.R., et al.: Retrieval reuse revision and retention in CBR. Knowl. Eng. Rev. **20**(3), 215–240 (2005)
18. Ricci, F., Avesani, P.: Learning a local similarity metric for case-based reasoning. In: Veloso, M., Aamodt, A. (eds.) ICCBR 1995. LNCS, vol. 1010, pp. 301–312. Springer, Heidelberg (1995). https://doi.org/10.1007/3-540-60598-3_27
19. Sani, S., Wiratunga, N., Massie, S.: Learning deep features for kNN-based human activity recognition. In: Proceedings of ICCBR 2017 Workshops (CAW, CBRDL, PO-CBR), Doctoral Consortium, and Competitions co-located with the 25th International Conference on Case-Based Reasoning (ICCBR 2017), Trondheim, Norway, June 26–28, 2017. CEUR Workshop Proceedings, vol. 2028, pp. 95–103. CEUR-WS.org (2017)
20. Schank, R., et al.: Towards a general content theory of indices. In: Proceedings of the 1990 AAAI Spring Symposium on Case-Based Reasoning. AAAI Press, Menlo Park, CA (1990)
21. Shin, C., Yun, U.T., Kim, H.K., Park, S.: A hybrid approach of neural network and memory-based learning to data mining. IEEE Trans. Neural Netw. Learn. Syst. **11**(3), 637–646 (2000)
22. Tabian, I., Fu, H., Khodaei, Z.S.: A convolutional neural network for impact detection and characterization of complex composite structures. Sensors **19**(22), 4933 (2019)
23. Turner, J.T., Floyd, M.W., Gupta, K.M., Aha, D.W.: Novel object discovery using case-based reasoning and convolutional neural networks. In: Cox, M.T., Funk, P., Begum, S. (eds.) ICCBR 2018. LNCS (LNAI), vol. 11156, pp. 399–414. Springer, Cham (2018). https://doi.org/10.1007/978-3-030-01081-2_27
24. Turner, J.T., Floyd, M.W., Gupta, K., Oates, T.: NOD-CC: a hybrid CBR-CNN architecture for novel object discovery. In: Bach, K., Marling, C. (eds.) ICCBR 2019. LNCS (LNAI), vol. 11680, pp. 373–387. Springer, Cham (2019). https://doi.org/10.1007/978-3-030-29249-2_25
25. Weber, R.O., Shrestha, M., Johs, A.J.: Knowledge-based XAI through CBR: there is more to explanations than models can tell. In: ICCBR Workshops 2021, pp. 75–86 (2021)
26. Wilkersoon, Z., Leake, D., Crandall, D.: On combining knowledge-engineered and network-extracted features for retrieval. In: Case-Based Reasoning Research and Development, ICCBR 2021, pp. 248–262 (2021)
27. Zhou, B., Lapedriza, A., Xiao, J., Torralba, A., Oliva, A.: Learning deep features for scene recognition using places database. Adv. Neural Inf. Process. Syst. **27** (NIPS) (2014)

Exploring the Effect of Recipe Representation on Critique-Based Conversational Recommendation

Fakhri Abbas(✉), Nadia Najjar, and David Wilson

University of North Carolina at Charlotte, Charlotte, NC 28223, USA
{fabbas1,nanajjar,davils}@uncc.edu

Abstract. Diet diversification can facilitate both positive health outcomes and greater enjoyment in food consumption. Case-based recommendation can play an important role to promote a more diverse diet by connecting users with more diverse options in meal planning. Our research investigates conversational CBR approaches to support greater diversity in recommendations for recipes and meal planning. This paper presents and evaluates a critique based conversational recommender approach to support diet diversification. The approach incorporates both (1) dynamic generation of diversity driven critique for conversational interaction, and (2) identification of key recipe features in contexts that promote greater diversity of results through dynamic critique. Our approach is evaluated using an initial offline simulation study, followed by a full online user study. Results show that meal diversity outcomes for users can be increased using dynamic critique, and that recipe representation plays an important role in the diversity of recommended recipes and has a direct impact on user choices and outcomes.

Keywords: Diversity · Recipe recommendation · Critique-based · Case-based reasoning

1 Introduction

Diet diversification has been linked to positive health outcomes such as reducing incidence of cancer or mortality [10]. However, due to a range of physiological, psychological, social and environmental factors, changing food-related behaviour such as adopting a diverse diet is a challenging task [6]. Hence, facilitating individual access to and exploration of diverse food choices is a step toward diet diversification. To help address this, our research investigates CBR recommender support for diversity during recipe exploration. Incorporating diversity in recipe recommenders provides a number of advantages. Diversity enables the user to explore alternative options that could be healthier and increase dietary diversity [10]. It also increases user awareness and knowledge of existing recipes by providing more recipes that could be explored from different cultures, cuisines, or communities [13]. But these advantages come with the challenge of balancing accuracy and diversity. The recommended diverse recipes must also meet user

M. T. Keane and N. Wiratunga (Eds.): ICCBR 2022, LNAI 13405, pp. 96–110, 2022.
https://doi.org/10.1007/978-3-031-14923-8_7

requirements. In particular, finding the balance between diversity and accuracy is an open research challenge [13].

In previous work, we developed a CBR approach that enabled users compile diverse meal plans through the use of dynamic critique [1–3]. The research reported in this paper builds upon our previous work in critique generation, and expands upon it in two primary ways. First, we propose and evaluate a new model for critique generation to promote diversity. Second, we present an investigation of the impacts of different recipe case representations for critique generation and effectiveness. Our investigation addresses the following research questions (RQ) and hypotheses (H):

RQ 1: How does the proposed critique-based CBR approach impact the diversity of recommendations?

- **H 1.1** Critique-based recommendation results in recommending more diverse recipes compared to a non critique-based recommender.
- **H 1.2** Critique-based recommendation achieves higher diversity scores in fewer iterations compared to a non critique-based recommender.

RQ 2: In critique-based conversational recommendation, how does the underlying representation of recipe cases impact diversity in terms of user outcomes?

- **H 2.1** In diversity-focused critique, different recipe representations result in differences in the diversity of meal plans created by users.
- **H 2.2** In diversity-focused critique, recipe representations lead users to choose different types of critique features.
- **H 2.3** In diversity-focused critique, meal plan diversity is realized based on different features that are related to certain demographic characteristics.
- **H 2.4** In diversity-focused critique, recipe representation affects user perceptions of diversity.

The remainder of this paper is organized as follows. Section 2 presents an overview of related work. Section 3 presents our proposed approach for diversity-focused conversational recommendation. Section 4 presents our simulation study to address RQ 1, and the full user study evaluation to address RQ2. The paper concludes in Sect. 5 with discussion and future directions.

2 Background

This paper brings together three lines of related research: diversity in recommender systems, critiquing in conversational recommender systems, and the domain of recipe recommendation.

2.1 Diversity in Recommender Systems

The concept of diversity in recommender systems has been linked to the concept of similarity [25]. Smyth and McClave suggested measuring the diversity of recommended cases as the average pairwise distance [25]. Using pairwise distances between cases to measure diversity has been widely adopted with variations in the distance metric (e.g., cosine metric, Jaccard similarity, etc.) [11,19,27,29]. These differences in distance metrics depend on case representation. For example, when cases are represented by their content, the distance has been measured using the complement of Jaccard similarity [27], the complement of cosine similarity [11], or taxonomy-based metrics [29]. When cases are represented by rating, hamming distance [19], the complement of Pearson correlation [27], or the complement cosine similarity have been adopted as a distance measure. Our proposed approach adopts the average pairwise distance as a diversity measure.

2.2 Critique-Based Conversational Recommender Systems

Recommender systems are most often considered as a type of one shot interaction, in which the system recommends a set of items and the user navigates through that set to find an item of interest. Conversational CBR [4] and more generally conversational recommender systems (CRSs) take a different approach, providing a richer user interaction through iterative feedback and refinement of results. During successive iterations the system can elicit and refine the user's preference and context. This in turn has a positive impact on enabling users to better understand the search space, and reduce the effect of the cold start problem [18,29]. For example, McGinty and Smyth [22] incorporated diversity in CRS while balancing the tradeoff between diversity and relevance. In each cycle of that approach the user selects a critique which is the basis for the next conversational step. The search is widened if the same critique is applied to the same case, and narrowed if a different critique is used on a different case. In [20], McCarthy et al. addressed diversity in critiquing, but the focus was on creating diversity in critiques rather than diversity in conversational outcomes.

Smyth and McGinty [26] compared different types of CRS. In particular, one promising approach employed a critiquing form of feedback. In critiquing feedback, the user provides a directional preference over a feature of the recommendation [9,21]. For example, in a recipe recommender a user may ask for recipes with less meat and more protein. CRS in turn will adopt and recommend more vegetarian recipes with high protein. Here, meat and protein are the relevant recipe features, and less and more are the direction preferences. The feature(s) along with the direction(s) together comprise the critique.

Critiquing can be static or dynamic. Static critique is an approach in which there is a pre-designed set of potential critiques, which are fixed within the user interaction session. In contrast, the dynamic critique approach generates a unique set of potential critiques for each recommended item individually, based on a specified metric. An example dynamic critique approach was proposed by McCarthy et al. [21], in which the system combines features depending on the available items in the search space. Here, we investigate a novel dynamic critiquing approach to support diet diversification, which expands upon our initial work in case-based recommendation [1].

2.3 Diversity in Recipe Recommenders

Incorporating diversity into food recommender systems is a natural extension of Health-Aware recommenders. The importance of diversity in recipe recommendation has several advantages such as: providing meals with varied sources of nutrition for a balanced meal diet [12], increasing user awareness of existing recipes, and covering a wide variety of options that could reduce the cold start problem [5]. A number of studies have considered recommender support for making healthier meal choices. For example, Grace et al. [15] proposed a system (Q-Chef) that encourages dietary diversity by generating and recommending recipes based on models of surprise and novelty of the ingredients that appear in recipes. While Q-Chef focused on identifying new recipes that are surprising to the user and could result in diversifying their diet, the set of recommended recipes itself is not necessarily diverse. Similarly, Musto et al. [23] introduced a natural language justification approach to support food recommendation with the goal to promote healthy choices. This approach focused on transparent recommendation and not on diversity outcomes as such. Elsweiler et al. [12] acknowledged the importance of diversity in meal plans as a way to provide healthy alternatives. They proposed a meal planner algorithm to recommend recipes, but acknowledged that diversity was not specifically engineered into the recommendations.

3 DiversityBite Framework: Recommend, Review, Revise

This research expands upon our *DiversityBite* CBR framework [1]. DiversityBite involves a three-stage *recommend-review-revise* cycle for CRS, as shown in Fig. 1. The *recommend stage*, consists of two main steps: recommending candidate cases and dynamically generating potential user critiques for each case. In the *review stage*, the user reviews the cases and can select a critique for one of them as the basis for a new set of recommended cases (or select a recipe as an outcome). Finally, in the *revise stage*, the selected critique serves as a constraint that is applied for the next recommend stage.

In practice, the cycle begins with a zooming phase [7] based on initial user context. The user context consists of both hard constraints (e.g., vegetarian) to filter out irrelevant recipes, and soft constraints (e.g., meal course) that provide relative weighting as part of retrieving baseline cases. The baseline recommendation step consists of applying a straightforward similarity metric to find recipes matching the user context. Potential critiques are then dynamically generated for each of the initial recommendations.

The dynamic critique generation step is the key part of the conversational process, and is the focus of our investigation. To support diversity in outcomes, a potential critique (e.g., more spicy) is presented as an option for the user only if it also promotes diversity in candidate recommendations. The critique is essentially "like this, but more diverse" across different recipe dimensions. Selecting diversity-positive critiques is accomplished by identifying a diversity goal—a representative subset of recipes that serves as a footprint for the space of

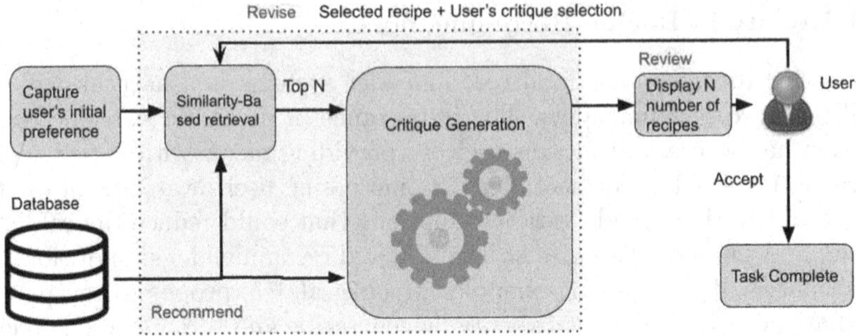

Fig. 1. Illustration of recommend-review-revise cycle found in DiversityBite along with the main components. The framework starts with user initial preference and ends with user acceptance. The shaded area represents retrieval and critique generation cycle.

available recipes. The baseline in [1] employed a stochastic process for generating the diversity goal, which we refer to as *Diversity Goal Footprint* (DGF).

3.1 Adaptive Diversity Goal Approach

In this research, we are proposing a new model for generating diversity goals, which we refer to as the *Adaptive Diversity Goal* (ADG) approach. Critique generation starts by identifying a diverse set of recipes within the domain of recipes that matches the user's initial preference. This set represents a diversity goal, and it provides a basis for selecting critique features to move the recommendation toward a more diverse set of recipes. More specifically, the diversity goal is a set of recipes that serves as a reference point to select a critique and identify a direction (more/less) across the critique dimensions. The next step is to extract features related to critique from the diversity goal set, such as the average protein content in the set of recipes. The process then compares extracted diversity goal features with features found in a candidate recommended recipe. The comparison provides insight on which features should be forwarded as *critique features*, which, if selected, will increase diversity by moving the recommendation toward the diversity goal. The process concludes by identifying text for each critique feature along with the direction.

The proposed ADG approach establishes a diversity goal as a maximally diverse set of recipes from available recipes by applying a shortest path algorithm. This is a separate, contextually-dependent analysis in relation to each Top-N recipe case being suggested to the user. This addresses two limitations in the previous DGF approach. First, it considers the diversity analysis as an optimization problem that tries to find the optimal diverse set by utilizing a shortest path algorithm. Second, for each recommended recipe a new diversity goal is calculated. This process better aligns generated critique features to the proposed recipe cases.

Figure 2 shows a comparison between our previous DGF approach and the ADG approach proposed here. Figure 2 (left), compares between the new pro-

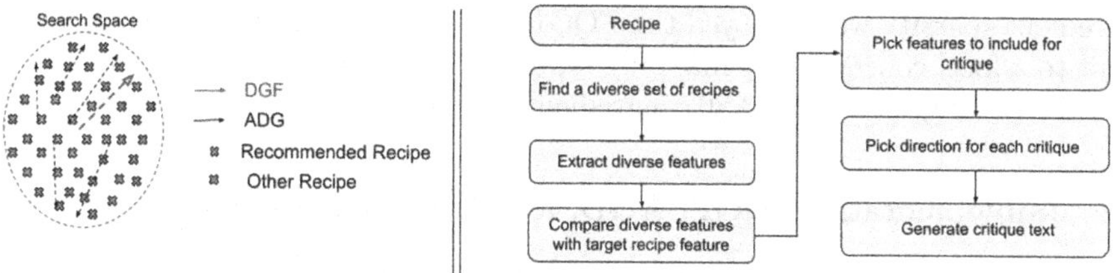

Fig. 2. A comparison between DGF vs. ADG (left). The general steps to generate critique proposed in [1] (right)

posed approach—Adaptive Diversity Goal (ADG) and the approach presented in [1]—Diversity Goal Footprint (DGF). It shows that each recipe will have a different diversity goal and this goal is guaranteed to be a maximally diverse set of recipes. Figure 2 (right) shows the common steps in generating critique proposed in this work. Section 4 will discuss the implementation details of ADG along with the algorithms used.

4 Evaluation

To evaluate our research questions, we conducted two primary evaluations. The first is an offline evaluation, a simulation study focused on addressing RQ 1. The second is an online evaluation, a full user study focused on addressing RQ 2. In the online evaluation, all user actions are logged for further analysis and exploration. This section first describes the case base used for experimentation. Next, it presents the implementation details for DGF, AGD, and diversity scoring, followed by the results of both the simulation study and the user study.

4.1 Case Base

Our experiments employ a recipe case library based on a dataset with strong potential for meal diversity—it contains a wide variety in terms of both recipes and cuisines. Sajadmanesh et al. [24] prepared a dataset with 120K recipes crawled from yummly.com, a personalized recipe recommender platform. The dataset consists of recipes from 204 countries. Each recipe has an average review rating, ingredients, preparation time, course type, nutritional values, and flavor features. The raw data contains 11,113 ingredients. The course type feature has values related to the recipe type such as afternoon tea, bread, breakfast, etc. The nutritional value features are: saturated fat, trans fat, fat, carbohydrate, sugar, calories, fiber, cholesterol, sodium, and protein of a recipe per serving. Recipes are characterized by six flavor features on a scale from 0 to 1: saltiness, sourness, sweetness, bitterness, spiciness, and savoriness. Preparatory analysis did not reveal substantive inconsistencies or errors in the feature data, so all features were included in the case base for evaluation. In addition, to reduce overall ingredient sparsity we employed the FOODON [16] ontology to map each ingredient to a food concept. The mapping reduced the number of unique ingredients from 11,113 ingredients to 3,807 ingredients in case features.

4.2 Implementation: DGF, AGD, and Diversity Scoring

This section discusses comparative implementation detail for DGF and ADG in the evaluation studies. To create the diversity goal set using DGF [1], **L** number of recipes were randomly selected from the search space and a diversity score would be calculated for that set. This process is repeated **R** number of times. The list with the highest diversity score is then selected to represent the actual diversity goal. This approach follows Vargas et al. [28], who noted that maximum diversity can be approximated through random selection.

In ADG, the diversity goal is created using a greedy re-ranking algorithm, which employs Dijkstra's shortest path analysis [8] to select the next recipe to be added to the list **S**. In particular, given a current recipe **r** then the next recipe **n** should be the farthest (most dissimilar) recipe from **r** within the search space. To help address nearest-neighbor search efficiency, a K-D tree algorithm [14] was employed to calculate the distances between recipes. In the ADG approach, each recipe in the recommended Top-N recipes serves as the start node of the shortest path algorithm to estimate the diversity goal.

The diversity score is calculated using the average pairwise distances between recipes following Smyth and McClave [25], as shown in Eq. 1.

$$Diversity(R) = \frac{\sum\limits_{i \epsilon R} \sum\limits_{j \epsilon R/\{i\}} dist(i,j)}{|R|(|R|-1)} \tag{1}$$

where R, represents the recipe cases in the list.

4.3 Simulation Study: Incorporating Diversity in Critique

To address our first research question, a simulation study for critique generation was conducted. The purpose of the simulation study is (1) to understand the diversity scores of the recommended recipes over the course of the users' interactions, and (2) the feasibility of the proposed algorithm by examining the change of diversity scores over the number of iterations. The following sections describe the experimental setup and evaluation results.

Experiment Setup. To evaluate the critique approach, three variations of DiversityBite were implemented, one without critique and two with critique. The first variation without critique (DiversityBite-) simulates a similarity-based recipe recommender. The second (with critique) variation implements the DGF (DiversityBite+DGF) approach, while the third (with critique) variation implements the ADG (DiversityBite+ADG) approach. In all variations the same DiversityBite *recommend-review-revise* cycle was employed; the only difference is the variation in critique. The first iteration in the recommendation starts recommending the closest N recipes to the centroid of the user search space, where the centroid represents the average score for the ingredients vector. For each iteration, given a selected recipe from the previous iteration the algorithm selects the closest N recipes to the selected recipe. The closest N recipes were determined using the cosine similarity metric, where each recipe case is represented by a vector of 3,807 ingredients. After the selection of a recipe and a critique, the algorithm recommends the N closest recipe cases to the selected recipe with the critique applied.

The simulation consisted of building 100 user profiles. Each profile is evaluated by simulating 50 iterations of using DiversityBite-, DiversityBite+DGF, and DiversityBite+ADG. Since the yummly.com data does not provide user interaction with recipes, user profiles were created by randomly selecting a region. Then, a subset of recipes with an average rating of 4 or more (on a 1–5 scale) were randomly selected to build the user profile. The search space for each user is the rest of recipes found in the region but not in the user profile. To simulate user selection of recipes at each iteration, the closest recipe to the user profile centroid was chosen using cosine similarity. In the critique approach, a random critique was chosen from the critique list of the selected recipes.

For the implementation of the three variations the following settings were used: $\mathbf{N} = 10$, $\mathbf{L} = 100$. The total number of critique features is 16 (6 flavour + 10 nutrition). To ensure the reproducibility of the results, the user's unique identifier was used as the random seed in the cases where randomness was used. Recipe cases were represented as a vector of ingredients with binary values where 1 means the ingredient is present in the recipe. Cosine similarity was used for recommendation while diversity calculation employed euclidean distance.

Analysis and Results. Results for RQ 1 addressed both diversity improvement (H 1.1) and number of iterations (H 1.2).

H1.1 - Diversity Improvement Analysis. The diversity score for the recommended set of recipes was measured at each iteration using the diversity Eq. 1. The left side of Fig. 3 shows the diversity score of the first 15 iterations for the same user in DiversityBite-, DiversityBite+DGF, and DiversityBite+ADG. In all iterations (except one) the diversity scores from DiversityBite+ADG were higher than the diversity score for DiversityBite- and DiversityBite+DGF. Lower scores are sometimes due to the simulator selecting a critique with a lower diversity score at one iteration compared to the rest. However, the overall score for other iterations show that DiversityBite+ADG is consistently higher. Figure 3 shows a comparison of diversity scores between the three recommender variations. The right side of Fig. 3 shows the overall distribution for each variation. To address the first hypothesis (H1.1), a one-way repeated measure ANOVA test shows there is a significant difference between the diversity scores in the recommended recipe for each iteration ($F(2,98) = 4.17$, $p < 0.05$). Tukey's post hoc test shows that diversity in DiversityBite+DGF ($M = 2.27$, $SD = 0.37$), and DiversityBite+ADG ($M = 2.28$, $SD = 0.37$) is significantly higher than the diversity

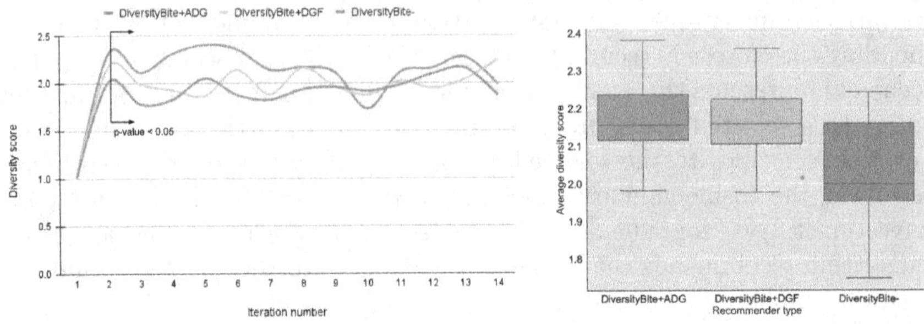

Fig. 3. Comparison between DiversityBite-, DiversityBite+DGF, and DiversityBite+ADG diversity scores

scores in DiversityBite- (M = 2.08, SD = 0.39). This analysis indicates that using critique has the potential to enable recommendation of more diverse recipes. While in simulation we did not find a statistically significant difference between DiversityBite+DGF, and DiversityBite+ADG, results indicate that both diversity critique methods can be used to increase diversity compared to the baseline DiversityBite-.

H 1.2 - Diversity Improvement and Number of Iterations. To address the second hypothesis H1.2, we investigated the relation between the number of iterations and the diversity scores. Our analysis shows that from the second iteration there is a statistically significant difference ($p < 0.05$)) between the critique-based recommenders (DiversityBite+DGF, DiversityBite+ADG) and the non-critique recommender (DiversityBite-), as shown in Fig. 3. The results at each iteration support H1.2, with higher diversity in the critique-based approach. This indicates that the critique-based approach can be applied in real scenarios even with comparatively few critique interactions.

4.4 User Study: Comparing Different Recipe Representations

To address the second research question, a full version of DiversityBite was developed and deployed to conduct a user study, in which users were asked to prepare a weekly meal plan by interacting with the system to explore recipes.

Experiment Setup. A web-based recommender application of DiversityBite was developed for users to interact with. Figure 4 shows a screenshot of the web application used in the study. The user study analyzed performance of the approach and compared the impact of different types of underlying recipe representation for dynamic critique. For this study, the Adaptive Diversity Goal approach was employed. Approach parameters were set for Top-N recommendation **N** = 10 (# recommended recipe cases), and ADG **S** = 10 (cardinality for diversity goal set). The parameters were selected based on pilot testing to ensure reasonable computation time during user interaction with the website.

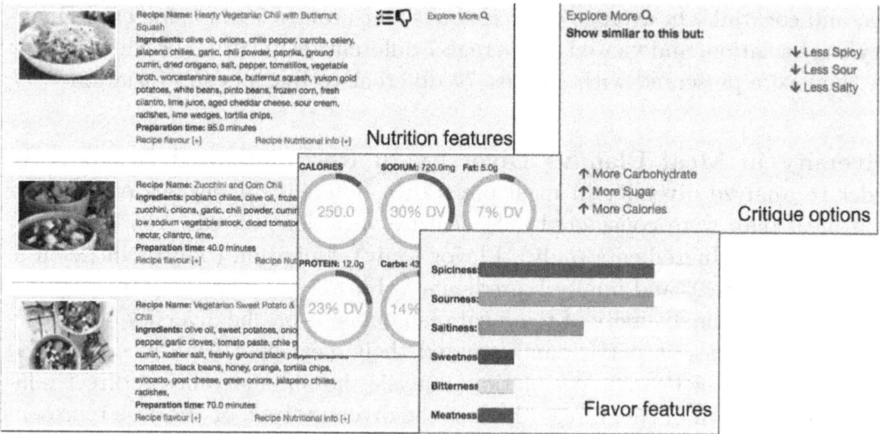

Fig. 4. A screenshot shows the interface of the web application. Participants can see details about the recipe including ingredients, flavor, and nutritional info. The explore more link displays the critique features the user can select to load more recipes.

Four variations of DiversityBite were implemented with four different representations: ingredient (*Ingr-DiversityBite*), flavor (*F-DiversityBite*), nutrition (*N-DiversityBite*), and flavor & nutrition (*FN-DiversityBite*) features. The baseline was taken as *Ingr-DiversityBite*, since it has been used in the simulation study while the other three variations are the treatment. In all variations, the user explores more recipes by using critique. Flavor and nutritional features were used as a critique for each variation regardless of the representation.

Participants. One-hundred participants were recruited from students, staff and faculty at a U.S. public university. Total time spent by each participant was on average 30 min. Participants included 67 females and 33 males, with the majority of participants in the age range of 18 to 24 years old. The majority of participants had at least a bachelor's degree. All participants reported using online resources to look for new recipes or to refresh their memory regarding a recipe they know. Additionally, all participants indicated that they frequently look for new recipes. Participants reported the most frequently used online resources as: Google search, YouTube videos, and social networks. The main criteria reported as considerations in seeking recipes were: recipe ingredients, preparation time, and balanced dish. This suggests that participants had a good exposure to online resources when looking for recipes. Among the chosen cuisines, Italian, American, Mexican, and Indian were the most frequently chosen cuisines, while the least chosen cuisines were Ethiopian, Swedish, and Ukrainian. This would seem to align with the demographic distribution of the area participants were recruited from (a U.S. urban public university). Since the task was to develop a weekly meal plan, the most frequently chosen meal courses were: main dish, Lunch, and Breakfast/Brunch, while the least frequently chosen ones are beverages such as tea, and cocktail. On average participants spent around 5 min using each DiversityBite variation, and viewed on average 7 different recipe lists in each variation; so, they were presented with at least 70 different recipes in each variation.

Diversity in Meal Plan vs Diversity in Recommended Recipes. In order to analyze diversity in meal plans, five different dimensions of diversity in a meal plan were considered. The feature variations on case representation considered are: Ingredients (only), Flavor (only), Nutrition (only), Nutrition & Flavor (combined), and finally Ingredients & Flavor & Nutrition (combined).

Intuitively, the diversity of the meal plan depends on the diversity of the recommended recipes as participants created their meal plan from recommended recipes. Results of Pearson correlation analysis showed a significant direct relation between both of them, regardless of the diversity type or the case representation type. In terms of meal plan diversity, participants were able to create a more diverse meal plan in each variation. Table 1 summarizes the average diversity meal plan for each variation along with diversity definition. The Table shows the results in groups depending on the diversity definition, rows with the highest diversity scores highlighted. For example, using ingredient representation for recipes *Ingr-DiversityBite* participants created meal plans with highest diversity in ingredients. Similarly, participants created meal plan with high diversity in nutrition using *Ingr-DiversityBite* variation. The table also shows that, using *N-DiversityBite* variation participants created diverse meal plan in terms of flavor, and in the case of all features combined. Finally, using *F-DiversityBite* the meal plan created were diverse in terms of both nutrition and flavor.

Results show that different representation choices yield differences in meal plan diversity. For the Diversity-Ingr variation, a one-way repeated measure ANOVA test shows a significant difference between the diversity scores in the meal plan for each variation ($F(3,297) = 6.82$, $p < 0.05$). Tukey's post hoc test shows that diversity score in *Ingr-DiversityBite*, is significantly higher than the diversity scores in *F-DiversityBite.* For Diversity-N, a one-way repeated measure ANOVA test shows a significant difference between the diversity scores in the meal plan for each variation ($F(3,297) = 3.62$, $p < 0.05$). Tukey's post hoc test shows that diversity score in *Ingr-DiversityBite*, is significantly higher than the diversity scores in *F-DiversityBite.* For Diversity-NF, a one-way repeated measure ANOVA test shows a significant difference between the diversity scores in the meal plan for each variation ($F(3,297) = 4.36$, $p < 0.05$). Tukey's post hoc test shows that diversity score in *F-DiversityBite*, is significantly higher than the diversity scores in *FN-DiversityBite.* Finally, for all features combined, a one-way repeated measure ANOVA test shows there's a significant difference between the diversity scores in the meal plan for each variation ($F(3,297) = 5.64$, $p < 0.05$). Tukey's post hoc test shows that diversity score in *N-DiversityBite*, is significantly higher than the diversity scores in *Ingr-DiversityBite.* Despite the similarity and the high correlation between flavor, nutrition, and ingredient, overall results show that diversity in meal plan differ depending on the representation which supports hypothesis H2.1.

Table 1. Average meal plan diversity for each variation along with the definition of diversity

Diversity Type	Variation	Average Diversity	Diversity Type	Variation	Average Diversity
Ingredients	*Ingr-DiversityBite*	0.0951	Nutrition	*Ingr-DiversityBite*	0.3942
Ingredients	*F-DiversityBite*	0.0819	Nutrition	*F-DiversityBite*	0.3817
Ingredients	*N-DiversityBite*	0.0915	Nutrition	*N-DiversityBite*	0.3917
Ingredients	*FN-DiversityBite*	0.0930	Nutrition	*FN-DiversityBite*	0.3872
Flavor	*Ingr-DiversityBite*	0.3937	Nutrition+Flavor	*Ingr-DiversityBite*	0.3759
Flavor	*F-DiversityBite*	0.3955	Nutrition+Flavor	*F-DiversityBite*	0.3795
Flavor	*N-DiversityBite*	0.3957	Nutrition+Flavor	*N-DiversityBite*	0.3724
Flavor	*FN-DiversityBite*	0.3944	Nutrition+Flavor	*FN-DiversityBite*	0.3666
All features	*Ingr-DiversityBite*	0.1248	All features	*F-DiversityBite*	0.1344
All features	*N-DiversityBite*	0.1348	All features	*FN-DiversityBite*	0.1341

User Behaviour in Critique Selection. To address hypothesis H2.2, we studied participants' behavior in the selection of different types of critique. Critiques can be viewed as two main types: Nutrition and Flavor. Nutrition critiques include: Protein, Calories, Carbohydrate, Sugar, Fiber, and Fat. Flavor critiques include: Bitter, Sour, Salty, Meaty, Spicy, and Sweet. Figure 5, shows that participants preferred to explore using flavor critique over nutrition critique in all variations except in flavor representation (*F-DiversityBite*). This suggests that *F-DiversityBite* was able to provide participants recipes with flavors that matched their preferences, and therefore participants chose nutrition critique to explore more. Result differences were statistically significant ($p < 0.05$) across all variations, with the exception of the flavor variation. These results support hypothesis H2.2 in which representation types can lead users to prefer one type of critique over the other. The *F-DiversityBite* variation recommended recipes that matched participants' flavor interest but not nutrition. Therefore, participants chose to explore recipes using the nutrition critique feature. These results are also corroborated through participant responses in the reflection survey. The survey asked "What influenced your main decision when you explored more recipes?" and participants chose flavor as the main reason that influenced their decision to explore.

Demographic Differences in Diversity and Critique Selection. To address hypothesis H2.3, participant data was grouped and analyzed based on demographic categories collected in the survey. We asked participants for their age, gender, and education level. The results show no differences between the different groups in terms of their age and education when it comes to critique selection. However, the analysis showed differences among participants when grouped based on gender. In terms of meal plan diversity, male partici-

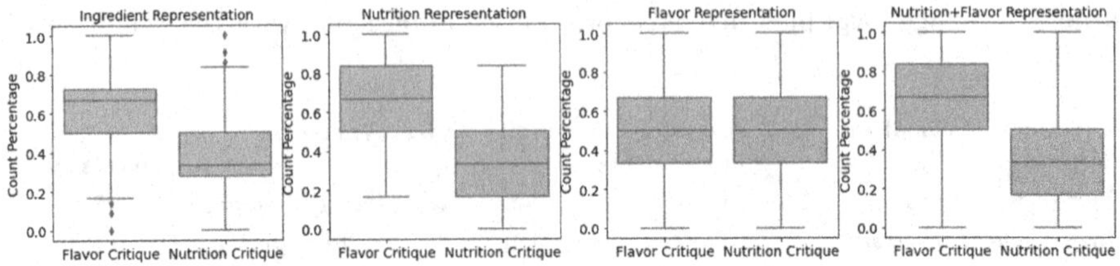

Fig. 5. A comparison between participants selection on flavor and nutrition critique on different variations

pants created more diverse meal plans using the nutrition representation, while female participants created more diverse meal plans using the flavor representation. One-way ANOVA with repeated measures shows a statistical significant in flavor and nutrition diversity scores (NF-Diversity) in meal plans for females ($F(3,198) = 6.25$, $p < 0.05$). Tukey's post hoc test shows that diversity scores for the *F-DiversityBite* variation are significantly higher than the diversity scores in *FN-DiversityBite*. For males, a one-way ANOVA with repeated measures shows a statistically significant difference in nutrition diversity scores (N-Diversity) in meal plans ($F(3,96) = 3.70$, $p < 0.05$). Tukey's post hoc test shows that diversity scores for *N-DiversityBite* variation are significantly higher in terms of diversity scores than *F-DiversityBite*. This suggests that male participants were more interested in diversifying the meal plan in terms of nutrition, while female participants were interested in diversifying meal plan in terms of flavor. To further explore this observation, critique selections for males and females were analyzed. The analysis shows that females chose to explore more recipes using flavor critiques compared to nutrition critiques. On the other hand, male participants used flavor and nutrition critiques across two representations equally. This finding supports hypothesis H2.3 in which demographic differences show different behavior in terms of meal plan diversity and critique behavior selection.

User Perceptions. To capture participant perceptions of diversity, participants were asked questions that address the variety of the recommended recipes and the created meal plan. According to [17], there are two types of diversity *categorical diversity* and *item-to-item diversity*. In the recipe domain, categorical diversity refers to diversity in terms of cuisine while item-to-item diversity refers to differences between the recipes such as ingredient, nutrition, and flavor. In the three questions, the term variety and different were used instead of diversity to avoid priming users specifically about diversity. Q1 ("I have seen recipes of different variety"), and Q2 ("I was able to create a meal plan from different variety of recipes") address categorical diversity. Q3 ("Recipes in my meal plan were similar to each other") addresses item-to-item diversity. The average rating for the questions Q1, Q2, and Q3 were 3.1, 3.2, and 3.7, respectively. In all variations none of the questions showed statistically significant differences, which aligns with previous findings [17]. Therefore, even though introducing diversity in recommendations while exploring shows a positive influence on diversity outcomes, it may not make a noticeable difference to participants' perceptions.

5 Conclusion

This paper presented a new approach and evaluation for generating dynamic critique to increase diversity in conversational case-based meal selection. Results of our initial simulation study confirmed that diversity can be increased using the proposed critique generation technique. Results of our user study showed that recipe representation has an effect on the diversity of a meal plan created by participants. In addition, different recipe case representations can lead users to select different types of critique. These two findings were also extended to show behaviours between different demographic groups. While this provides positive support for user outcomes, interestingly user perception of diversity was not significantly different between different recipe representations.

References

1. Abbas, F., Najjar, N., Wilson, D.: The bites eclectic: critique-based conversational recommendation for diversity-focused meal planning. In: Sánchez-Ruiz, A.A., Floyd, M.W. (eds.) ICCBR 2021. LNCS (LNAI), vol. 12877, pp. 1–16. Springer, Cham (2021). https://doi.org/10.1007/978-3-030-86957-1_1
2. Abbas, F., Najjar, N., Wilson, D.: Increasing diversity through dynamic critique in conversational recipe recommendations. In: Proceedings of the 13th International Workshop on Multimedia for Cooking and Eating Activities (2021)
3. Abbas, F.G., Najjar, N., Wilson, D.: Critique generation to increase diversity in conversational recipe recommender system. In: The International FLAIRS Conference Proceedings (2021)
4. Aha, D.W., McSherry, D., Yang, Q.: Advances in conversational case-based reasoning. Knowl. Eng. Rev. **20**(3), 247–254 (2005)
5. Anderson, C.: A survey of food recommenders. arXiv preprint arXiv:1809.02862
6. Braude, H.D.: Intuition in Medicine: A Philosophical Defense of Clinical Reasoning. University of Chicago Press (2012)
7. Burke, R.D., et al.: Knowledge-based navigation of complex information spaces. In: Proceedings of the National Conference on Artificial Intelligence (1996)
8. Chen, J.C.: Dijkstra's shortest path algorithm. J. Formalized Math. **15**, 237–247 (2003)
9. Chen, L., Pu, P.: Critiquing-based recommenders: survey and emerging trends. User Model. User-Adap. Interact. **22**, 125–150 (2012)
10. Drescher, L.S., et al.: A new index to measure healthy food diversity better reflects a healthy diet than traditional measures. J. Nutr. **137**, 647–651 (2007)
11. Ekstrand, M.D., et al.: User perception of differences in recommender algorithms. In: Proceedings of the 8th ACM Conference on Recommender Systems (2014)
12. Elsweiler, D., et al.: Bringing the "healthy" into food recommenders. In: DMRS (2015)
13. Freyne, J., Berkovsky, S.: Intelligent food planning: personalized recipe recommendation. In: Proceedings of the 15th International Conference on Intelligent User Interfaces (2010)

14. Goldberger, J., et al.: Neighbourhood components analysis. In: Advances in Neural Information Processing Systems (2004)
15. Grace, K., Maher, M.L., Wilson, D., Najjar, N.: Personalised specific curiosity for computational design systems. In: Gero, J.S. (ed.) Design Computing and Cognition '16, pp. 593–610. Springer, Cham (2017). https://doi.org/10.1007/978-3-319-44989-0_32
16. Griffiths, E.J., et al.: FoodON: a global farm-to-fork food ontology. In: ICBO/BioCreative (2016)
17. Hu, R., Pu, P.: Helping users perceive recommendation diversity. In: DiveRS@ RecSys (2011)
18. Jannach, D., Manzoor, A., Cai, W., Chen, L.: A survey on conversational recommender systems. arXiv preprint arXiv:2004.00646 (2020)
19. Kelly, J.P., Bridge, D.: Enhancing the diversity of conversational collaborative recommendations: a comparison. Artif. Intell. Rev. **25**, 79–95 (2006)
20. McCarthy, K., Reilly, J., Smyth, B., Mcginty, L.: Generating diverse compound critiques. Artif. Intell. Rev. **24**, 339–357 (2005)
21. McCarthy, K., et al.: An analysis of critique diversity in case-based recommendation. In: FLAIRS Conference (2005)
22. McGinty, L., Smyth, B.: On the role of diversity in conversational recommender systems. In: Ashley, K.D., Bridge, D.G. (eds.) ICCBR 2003. LNCS (LNAI), vol. 2689, pp. 276–290. Springer, Heidelberg (2003). https://doi.org/10.1007/3-540-45006-8_23
23. Musto, C., et al.: Exploring the effects of natural language justifications in food recommender systems. In: Proceedings of the 29th ACM Conference on User Modeling, Adaptation and Personalization (2021)
24. Sajadmanesh, S., et al.: Kissing cuisines: exploring worldwide culinary habits on the web. In: Proceedings of the 26th International Conference on WWW Companion (2017)
25. Smyth, B., McClave, P.: Similarity vs. diversity. In: Aha, D.W., Watson, I. (eds.) ICCBR 2001. LNCS (LNAI), vol. 2080, pp. 347–361. Springer, Heidelberg (2001). https://doi.org/10.1007/3-540-44593-5_25
26. Smyth, B., McGinty, L.: An analysis of feedback strategies in conversational recommenders. In: The Fourteenth Irish Artificial Intelligence and Cognitive Science Conference (AICS 2003) (2003)
27. Vargas, S., Castells, P.: Rank and relevance in novelty and diversity metrics for recommender systems. In: Proceedings of the 5th ACM Conference on Recommender Systems (2011)
28. Vargas, S., et al.: Coverage, redundancy and size-awareness in genre diversity for recommender systems. In: Proceedings of the 8th ACM Conference on Recommender Systems (2014)
29. Ziegler, C.N., et al.: Improving recommendation lists through topic diversification. In: Proceedings of the 14th International Conference on World Wide Web (2005)

Explaining CBR Systems Through Retrieval and Similarity Measure Visualizations: A Case Study

Paola Marín-Veites(✉) and Kerstin Bach(✉)

Department of Computer Science, Norwegian University of Science and Technology (NTNU), Trondheim, Norway
{paola.m.veites,kerstin.bach}@ntnu.no

Abstract. Explainability in AI is becoming increasingly important as we delegate more safety-critical tasks to intelligent decision support systems. Case-Based Reasoning (CBR) systems are one way to build such systems. Understanding how results are created by a CBR system has become an important task in their development process. In this work, we present how visualizations can help developers and domain experts to evaluate the CBR systems behavior and provide insights to further develop CBR systems in their application scenarios. This paper presents an overview of SupportPrim, a CBR system for the management of musculoskeletal pain complaints, and presents methods that explain its retrieval and similarity measures through visualizations that help to evaluate the system's performance. In the case study, we conduct experiments within the SupportPrim CBR system using differently weighted global similarity measures to compare their effect on the retrieval. This work shows that providing suitable explanations for the CBR system's stakeholders increases the likelihood of its adoption, and visualizations allow the creation of different explanations for the different users throughout the development phase, thus allowing for better modeling and usage of the system.

Keywords: Explainable AI · XCBR · Similarity modeling · Retrieval · Visualization

1 Introduction

Case-Based Reasoning (CBR) is an artificial intelligence method that provides a solution based on past experiences. In CBR, a case is defined as a problem description with its solution. A CBR system finds a solution by matching the new problem description (the query) to all or some of the existing cases in the case base. For searching a solution, similarity measures are used to compare problem descriptions. Once one or more solutions are found, they can be adapted or directly provided to the users. Successful cases are learned by the CBR system

M. T. Keane and N. Wiratunga (Eds.): ICCBR 2022, LNAI 13405, pp. 111–124, 2022.
https://doi.org/10.1007/978-3-031-14923-8_8

to increase its competence [1]. In this process the definition of the similarity measure is central as it determines which cases are returned.

Defining similarity measures and assessing them are key elements in CBR systems development. However, a CBR system usually involves users outside the technical domain that have little to no knowledge about how a CBR system is built. Stakeholders in a CBR application might understand the core concepts of CBR, but not how it works on their data. The gaps between the known methodology and how it is used in an application in their own domain can become blurry. If transparency is achieved, stakeholders and researchers would fully understand how their CBR system is operating and be able to tackle its shortcomings. This task should not only be the developer's responsibility. In many cases when creating the initial CBR system, we do not have a gold standard to compare the system against, but still need to show that the system is performing well. Visual tools can help to explore whether the retrieval differentiates well between the cases.

CBR systems are developed to serve a certain purpose, once the CBR system has been deployed, we would like to know how the CBR systems evolves over time. This includes possible updates on the similarity measures. To address this topic, we will use a CBR application example and present visualizations to create explanations on its behavior, so stakeholders understand how their data is being used within the system. For our application example, we modeled our CBR system using the local and global similarity principle.

Our overall aim is to improve the analytical tools of CBR systems and make its contents transparent to the stakeholders during the software development process. Our visualization approach can be applied to CBR systems where a concept, similarity measures, a set of attributes and a query case exist. The challenges we are addressing in this paper are as follow: (1) we visualize how the similarity of attributes contribute to an overall similarity score. (2) We present a visual explanation of the similarity scores for the query cases by comparing the global and local similarity measures of the attributes.

This paper is structured as follows: in Sect. 2 we discuss relevant work. Section 3 describes our application domain in more detail, in Sect. 4 we explain our approach and data processing, in Sect. 5 we test and evaluate it, in Sect. 6 we discuss the results and finally, our conclusions and future work are presented in Sect. 7.

2 Related Work

Explanations generated from CBR systems are important so the end users are encouraged to use and adopt them. As Kenny et al. mention [9], adoption barriers can be addressed by the explanation capabilities designed to improve adoption, such as adequate predictions and providing "personalised explanation-by-example". They identify three main challenges that systems have. The first one is accuracy, the second is their interpretability for the users and the third is that they function as a good decision support system regarding its context of application. On their work, Bach et al. [4] focus on methods to explain the similarity-based retrieval reasoning process, using visualizations that allow for a better understanding of the system, thus enabling explanations. Sørmo et al. [18] also discuss the transparency of the reasoning process and making the usage of the result understandable for the end user. They present a framework based on important explanation goals so that the context of the application aligns with it. Cunningham et al. [5] outline their experiment setting on a case-based explanation system where the decision process and patterns were transparent. In their work, subjects score the explanations. The case-based explanation system showed to perform better than having no explanation and better than rule-based systems. They concluded that the explanation potential of CBR "could have significant impact" [5]. Hoffman et al. [7] present another example on how explaining the retrieval process used in Process-Oriented Case-Based Reasoning—using graphs and workflows—helps to pinpoint how different approaches used in CBR perform. They also mention the potential for optimizing these approaches. Lamy et al. [10] propose a CBR user interface where they provide visual explanations. The interface provides both qualitative and quantitative visualizations of the similarity scores between the query case and the respective retrieval results. This approach explains why these cases were similar through visualizations that allow for easier visual reasoning. When tested with medical experts they found out that these visualizations made the shared patient characteristics easier to understand.

For the modeling and development of a CBR system, the open source case-based reasoning tool myCBR offers various explanation capabilities, as described by Roth-Berghofer et al. [16]. It is a prototyping tool with a similarity-based retrieval engine. Combining the existing tools of the software with our approach of visual explanations helps in answering questions that might arise for myCBR from the users involved in the development, such as the quality of retrieval outcome and the system's modeling behavior. Visualizations allow to understand the system configuration as a whole, not just for the knowledge engineer. As Roth-Berghofer et al. also point out, explanations for developer engineers and explanations for the knowledge experts are different: the former is more interested in modeling errors while the latter in understanding the system's concepts and behavior. Moreover, CBR itself has also been used as a tool to recommend explanations, for example for image classifiers [15] or to explain and assess the confidence of black-box methods [6,14].

3 SupportPrim CBR System

The CBR system used as a case study in this paper has been developed as part of the SupportPrim project, a collaborative research between the Department of Public Health and Nursing (ISM) and the Department of Computer Science (IDI) at the Norwegian University of Science and Technology (NTNU). The system's goal is to improve management of musculoskeletal pain disorders (MSD) in primary care and provide decision support for clinical practice. In particular, we focus on creating a dashboard for clinicians that provides an overview of the patients current situation based on previously answered questionnaires and an assessment by the clinician[1].

The SupportPrim project is a spin-off of a previous project called FysioPrim. As mentioned by Jaiswal et al. [8], the knowledge experts involved "extracted non-specific MSD patients". The dataset is a collection of features that describe the problem for which the patient seeks consultation, such as, classification of pain areas, questionnaire responses to assess followup information and treatment, if there is a perceived improvement in the patients quality of life and functionality during treatment, as well as the patients demographics and physiological factors to mention a few.

In a second step, we use CBR to find the most similar, successful treatment plans and combine them with best practices to create an individual treatment plan. The dashboard facilitates co-decision making between clinician and patient as they are able to review the data and treatment plan together. In Fig. 1 we show how data is collected from patients and used to create datasets for our CBR systems. Questionnaires are sent out to patients before their first visit to collect baseline data. The baseline questionnaire is comprehensive and contains the items listed in Table 1 plus additional ones which are not included in the similarity matching. After 2, 4 and 8 weeks a short questionnaire including from three and up to seven questions is sent. Those questionnaires are repetitions of baseline questions and help obtaining a trajectory during treatment. After three months a larger follow-up questionnaire is deployed[2].

When developing the CBR system for finding most similar patients at each time point, we worked with domain experts to determine relevant attributes. Meisingset et al. [13] proposed classifying MSD patients according to phenotypes, making subgroups where treatment is adapted to the similar characteristics and prognostic factors. Attributes defining phenotypes are also relevant to find similar patient cases and we therefore used them in the case representation.

3.1 Data

For the creation of the datasets and modeling in myCBR we extracted the data collected in the SupportPrim Randomized Controlled Trial (RCT). As shown in Fig. 1 we have six datasets used to build the CBR systems: one for each time point and the demographics that can be added to extend the case representation. The datasets contains the 571 patients assessed in the different time points mentioned above. For the experiment setting, we only considered the intervention group (50% of the patients) and among those, all that have completed all stages of the intervention. Patients with missing data at each stage were dropped, which results in different case base sizes for each time point.

[1] For more information about the dashboard and the project, please see https://www.ntnu.no/supportprim.

[2] The full Randomized Controlled Trial (RCT) registration can be found at https://www.isrctn.com/ISRCTN17927832.

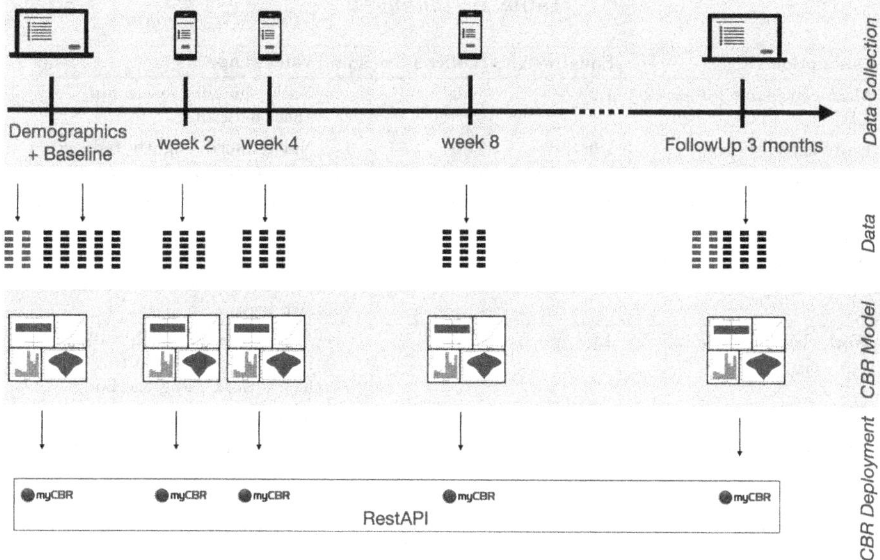

Fig. 1. Data collection and CBR system development

Table 1 contains all attributes included in the case representations. The table includes the description of the attribute, the weight distribution (i.e. its importance) used in each global similarity and their value ranges. The attributes have their origin in questionnaires used to assess patient reported outcome measures. Together with domain experts we selected relevant questionnaires for the SupportPrim study and defined relevant attributes for comparing similar patients.

Table 1. The case representation of a patient. This is a subset of the patient case dataset used in the similarity measure.

Description	Equal weights	Different weights	Value range
Case ID	0.0	0.0	0–100000
Patient ID	0.0	0.0	1–∞
Age	1.0	1.0	0–150
Gender	1.0	1.0	Female, male
BMI	1.0	1.0	0.00–100.1
Smoking	1.0	1.0	No, yes
Education	1.0	2.0	Primary school, high school, up to 4 years higher education, more than 4 years higher education, other

(continued)

Table 1. (*continued*)

Description	Equal weights	Different weights	Value range
Main complaint for seeking GP	1.0	4.0	Neck, shoulder, back, hip, knee, multisite
Daily activity level	1.0	2.0	Not reduced, slightly reduced, quite reduced, very reduced
Activity and function	1.0	1.0	0–10
Walk aid	1.0	4.0	No, yes
Work situation	1.0	1.0	Working or other, disability pension or work assessment, sick leave
Work characteristic	1.0	2.0	Mostly seated, much walking, much walking and lifting, heavy work using the body
Work ability	1.0	4.0	0–10
Comorbidity count	1.0	1.0	0 comorbidity, 1 comorbidity, 2 to 3 comorbidities, 4 or more comorbidities
EQ5D - Mobility	1.0	1.0	No problem, slight problem, moderate problem, severe problem, unable
EQ5D - Self-care	1.0	1.0	No problem, slight problem, moderate problem, severe problem, unable
EQ5D - Anxiety	1.0	2.0	Not, slightly, moderately, severely, extremely
15D - Sleep	1.0	4.0	Sleep normally, slight problem, moderate problems, great problems
15D - Vitality	1.0	1.0	Healthy and energetic, slightly weary, moderately weary, very weary, extremely weary
Örebro-1: Pain Duration	1.0	4.0	Less than 1 month (1–3), 1 to 3 months (4–6), 3 to 6 months (7–9), 6 to 12 months (10), more than 12 months
Örebro-Q2: Pain	1.0	1.0	0–10
Örebro-2: Pain last week	1.0	1.0	0–10
Örebro-7: Long-lasting ailments	1.0	4.0	0–10
Örebro-10: Stop activity	1.0	1.0	0–10
Number of pain sites	1.0	2.0	0–10
Temporary pain	1.0	1.0	No, yes
Mental distress	1.0	8.0	1.0–4.0
Keele STarT MSK	1.0	4.0	Low, medium, high
MSK-HQ-7: Social activities and hobbies	1.0	1.0	Not at all, slightly, moderately, severely, extremely
MSK-HQ-15: Physical activity level	1.0	2.0	None, 1 day, 2 days, 3 days, 4 days, 5 days, 6 days, 7 days
Pain self-efficacy Q1	1.0	1.0	0–6
Pain self-efficacy Q2	1.0	1.0	0–6

(*continued*)

Table 1. (*continued*)

Description	Equal weights	Different weights	Value range
Pain self-efficacy and fear avoidance score	1.0	2.0	0–12
Fear avoidance	1.0	1.0	0–10
Global Perceive Effect	1.0	1.0	Very much improved, much improved, minimally improved, no change, minimally worse, much worse, very much worse

3.2 Case Representation and Similarity Modeling

For the modeling of the attributes, we used the data from the 571 patients included in the RCT to ensure the broad value ranges are considered. The CBR systems contains 35 attributes considered as the most relevant by the domain experts involved in SupportPrim and were assessed through different time points in the RCT. Each time point reflect the overall evolution assessment of the patients and contains different number of attributes. The datasets contain symbolic, integer and float attribute types.

The local similarity measures are modeled by plotting each of the chosen attributes' Empirical Cumulative Distribution Function (ECDF). The ECDF allows to assess several characteristics of our dataset, such as the value range and distribution of the data. As mentioned by Scheidegger et al. domain models can be based on ECDF to simulate both behavior and data, because it gives a good reproduction of the observed measurements[17]. By using the ECDF plot we can model the local similarity measures using the data distributions from the underlying datasets.

Figure 2 shows the similarity modeling for the attribute *work_ability_1* (left) and its corresponding ECDF plot (right). To align the value distribution and the similarity modeling in the value range of $[0, 1]$ where 1 is most similar, we inverted the ECDF plot. We took the proportion values in the y-axis and assumed that the distribution growth is proportional to the similarity distance. Considering the x-axis being the range values for the attribute and the y-axis being the ECDF, for example $x = 4$ and its corresponding $y = 0.3$ in the ECDF graph to the right, in the similarity measure we then model $x = 4$ as $1 - 0.3$ and thus, ending up with a similarity of 0.7 as illustrated in the graph to the left. This approach to the similarity measure modeling can be used since no more data will be further collected.

3.3 Case Base and Similarity Population

Six datasets were created for their respective case bases and concepts, each one corresponding to each time point assessment of the patient evolution. We only included the intervention group (about half of the 571 included patients) and created the following case bases: demographics (269 cases), baseline (269 cases),

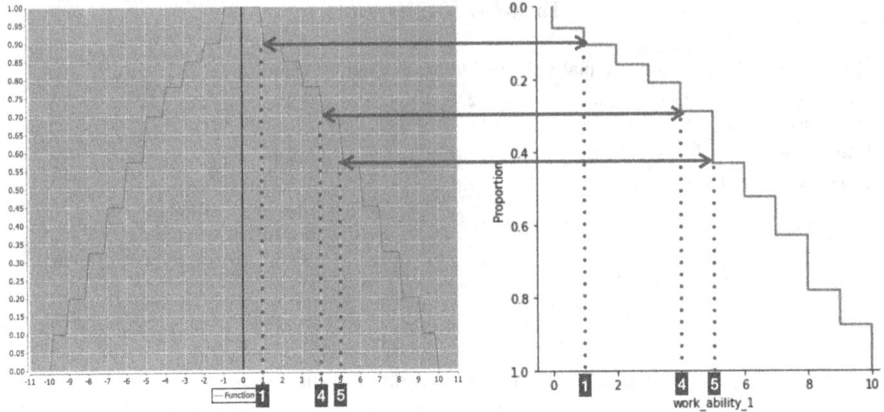

Fig. 2. Modeling of an attribute using the ECDF in the myCBR workbench

week2 (22 cases), week4 (22 cases), week8 (22 cases), and follow-up 3 months (63 cases: see Fig. 3 for the data collection timeline).

The similarity measures were modeled in the myCBR workbench, a Java-based development framework [2,19]. It is designed to expose modeling functionality, creating concepts and similarity functions that run through an HTTP REST API and can be used with all programming languages that support Rest API and parsing JSON objects, as described by Bach et al. [3]. Local similarity measures were created for each attribute and two global similarity functions were created for each time point, one with different weights and the other equally weighted for comparison purposes. Python and Jupyter Notebook were used for the analysis and visualizations of the data facilitating the similarity modeling.

4 Explanatory Case Base Visualizations

Once the CBR agents are deployed, we can investigate the content of the case bases and how the most similar patients are retrieved. In this section we present visualizations of the CBR system that can explain a domain expert how the system is working and thereby build trust in the application. While CBR is considered to be an explainable artificial intelligence methodology [11,12], the assessment of similarity often lacks transparency. In this work, we aim to make the modeled similarity more explicit for stakeholders that are involved in the development of the CBR system. The following visualizations are not intended for end users, but for domain experts to verify that the implemented system works as intended. To create the visualizations we use the SupportPrim CBR systems including the data for the patients that have completed all stages of the intervention. This allows to compare different patient trajectories.

4.1 Accessing the CBR System's Model

For the visualizations, we created functions in Python that retrieve the data from the myCBR REST API[3]. The API provides access to all knowledge containers. To compare similarity functions, we used the following parameters for each time point: concept (case representation), the case base, the similarity function, a query case and k for the number of cases to retrieve in the results. We created functions to compare two instances taking into account the local similarity, the global similarity and the weights of the attributes.

4.2 Visualization of Retrievals

The retrieved results shown to the end user, e.g. the clinician and/or patient, focus on presenting cases with solutions. However, our focus is more on how the retrieval results operate on entire case bases. Figure 3 shows the retrieval results for the SupportPrim CBR systems for all five time points. For each visualization we run a leave-one-out cross-validation using the respective case base and show the average similarity score for each ranking. Each plot contains the top 5 rank of most similar cases to the query case. The first bar to the left, $rank_0$, is the query case similarity compared to itself (to serve as a visual aid for comparison), while the following bars indicate the average similarity of the top 5 most similar cases. These five bars also show the similarity range. Such charts help to visualize how the variation of similarity can influence the results as they show the robustness of the ranking for a specific case base.

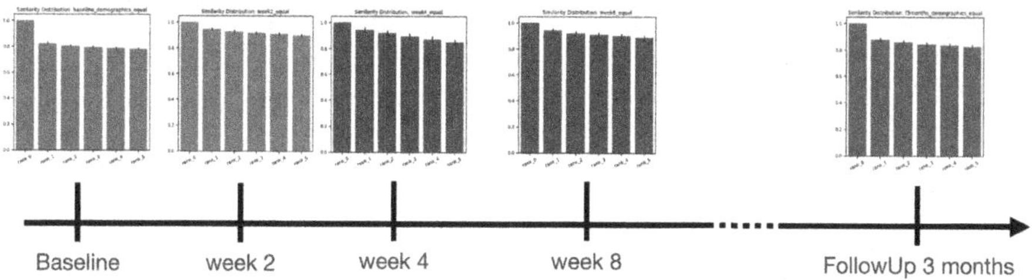

Fig. 3. Similarity score ranges for the top five cases at each time stamp

The purpose of the Fig. 3 is to show the distribution of the results per time point, providing an overview of how the system performs at each time point of the intervention. If the comparison of the mean similarity scores would be equal, we could conclude that the similarity functions are not properly representing the data distribution and the CBR system cannot differentiate relevant from irrelevant cases. In Fig. 3 we can also see the effect of different case representations to the similarity measure. The *Baseline* and *FollowUp 3 months* case representations are much larger than the weekly questionnaire case information.

[3] https://github.com/ntnu-ai-lab/mycbr-sample-python.

4.3 Visualization of the Similarity Scores for Individual Case Comparisons

The next step after comparing the retrieval results, is to provide a visualization for understanding the detailed similarity score of a query/case pair when using the system. Figure 4 presents a set of five case comparisons. Each comparison has three charts comparing the global similarity, the local similarity scores, and the weighted score respectively. The y-axis indicates a set of attributes, selected regarding their weights—shown in the x-axis according to Table 1—from highest (8) to lowest (1). The charts show the comparison of the five most similar cases to the query case.

The visualization shows how the weighted attributes affect the global similarity and allows to assess its influence in the overall similarity score per attribute. As mentioned by Bach et al. [4], visual explanations can offer a better understanding of the system in the development phase. With this visual aid, CBR developers can pinpoint if a set of attributes heavily weighted are overpowering other attributes' contributions.

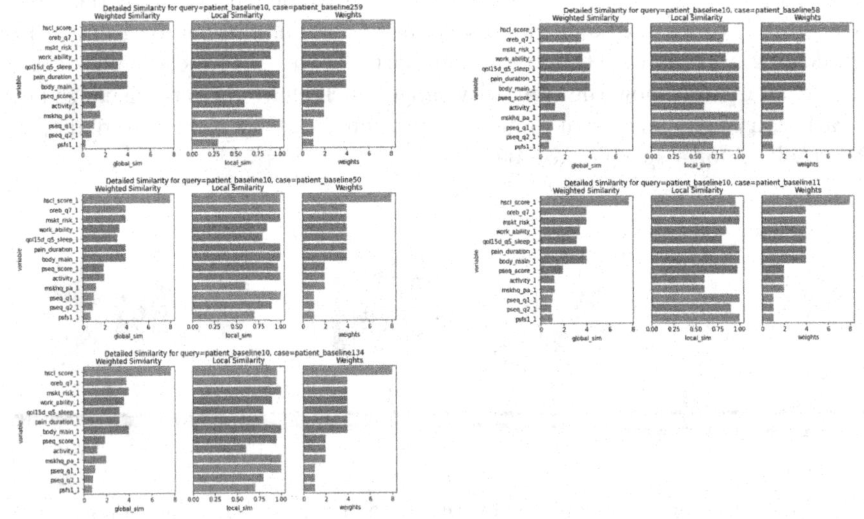

Fig. 4. Visual explanations of case comparisons. Left: rank 1 to 3; Right: rank 4 and 5

5 Experiments

In this section we will describe the experiments we conducted on the Support-Prim CBR system. When developing the local similarity measures we used the same methodology and data foundation for all time points. After discussing with our domain experts, we concluded that the assessment of patients phenotypes—as described in [13]—is a good way to compare how the CBR system performs. A phenotype describes a homogeneous patient group and we assume that they also receive similar treatment recommendations. Moreover the five phenotypes are ordered with phenotype 1 being a low risk group and phenotype 5 a high risk group. In the experiments we focus on the two largest case representation as they include all relevant attributes to compute the phenotypes, i.e. baseline and baseline plus demographics, both with $n = 269$. We conducted the experiments with both the same local similarity measures, but differently weighted global similarity measures for each case base, resulting in four different outcomes. Our case base includes five different phenotypes and the phenotypes are ordered so that neighboring phenotypes are more similar. For example, phenotypes 1 and 2 are more similar than phenotypes 1 and 3. Figure 5 illustrates the phenotype distribution in the case base. At least 27 cases exist for each phenotype, with phenotype 5 being the smallest. Phenotype 2 is the largest with 85 cases. For the SupportPrim application, the phenotype is only assessed at baseline and hence we only conducted experiments on that CBR system.

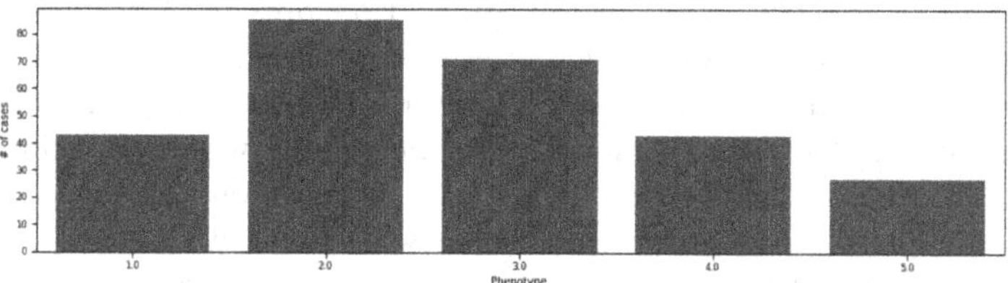

Fig. 5. Phenotype distribution in the case base

For each of the n most similar cases we calculated the difference $DiffRank_i$ between the query case's phenotype and the case's phenotype value. As seen from Fig. 5, we have five phenotypes so the maximum $DiffRank_i$ is 4. For each case base cb we calculated the mean phenotype error as follows:

$$MeanPhenotypeError(cb) = \frac{\sum_{i=1}^{n} DiffRank_i}{n} \quad (1)$$

The *MeanPhenotypeError* of both settings (equal and different weights) were identical and are shown in Table 2. The baseline column shows the mean phenotype error as calculated with Eq. 1. Additionally to the mean we also included the standard deviation.

The results show that using the best matching case provides on average the best results. However, the larger standard deviation indicates that there is quite some variation between the phenotypes. The variation, however, is at most of one phenotype.

Table 2. Results of the experiments using the baseline CBR system showing the error and standard deviation of the top n cases compared to their respective phenotypes.

	Baseline	Baseline + Demographics
Top 1 Error	0.565 (±0.738)	0.625 (±0.751)
Top 2 Error	0.651 (±0.591)	0.677 (±0.61)
Top 3 Error	0.685 (±0.543)	0.669 (±0.54)
Top 5 Error	0.714 (±0.451)	0.714 (±0.51)

6 Discussion

For the SupportPrim CBR system, we used the visualizations presented above to assess how each attribute is contributing to the overall score and to the similarity ranking among the cases. The visual aid helped in understanding the system's performance and corroborate that the modeling of the attributes was adequate, since the matching cases are very similar to the query case. The retrieval visualizations per time point allowed to assess our case bases differentiation distributions, through the bar plots. In the application presented, we see that the cases' similarity scores are well differentiated and the global similarity scores' comparison charts further help assess how the different weighted global similarity is influencing the results compared to the equally weighted similarity per time point. Since the phenotypes differed by at most one, there is room for improvement. Furthermore, our evaluation results showed that the weights of the attributes in global similarity measures are not a factor in our CBR system, as the equally weighted global similarity and the different weighted global similarity had the same mean phenotype error. Visualization charts can be a tool that if paired with other analysis, e.g. correlations, can help to further explain a CBR system's behavior. Having these pointers allows to discuss the results with domain experts and if necessary make the appropriate modifications.

7 Conclusion

From the application presented on this paper, the insights provided by the visualizations help in explaining the overall CBR system's behavior and performance. In the development phase, having such understanding is key for modeling and assessing the similarity measures to achieve the desired CBR system goal. Visualizations allow to create explanations for different users through the development phase. The charts presented are not only information for development but also for providing explanations to knowledge experts. A visual layout of how experts' data is used within the system can be valuable in further developing and/or updating similarity measures in CBR. Future work we would like to explore is creating visualizations on attributes' correlations within a CBR system. Although we presented how different weights of global similarity measures influenced the overall similarity score, if we visualize how the attributes are correlated with each other we can further pinpoint how each attribute, specially highly weighted ones, influences the global similarity score, and assess if a CBR system is double matching on the same feature. Moreover, creating a tool for exploring the CBR system for domain experts and developers is another way forward.

References

1. Aamodt, A., Plaza, E.: Case-based reasoning: foundational issues, methodological variations, and system approaches. Artif. Intell. Commun. **7**(1), 39–59 (1994)
2. Bach, K., Althoff, K.-D.: Developing case-based reasoning applications using myCBR 3. In: Agudo, B.D., Watson, I. (eds.) ICCBR 2012. LNCS (LNAI), vol. 7466, pp. 17–31. Springer, Heidelberg (2012). https://doi.org/10.1007/978-3-642-32986-9_4
3. Bach, K., Mathisen, B.M., Jaiswal, A.: Demonstrating the myCBR rest API. In: Workshops Proceedings for the Twenty-Seventh International Conference on Case-Based Reasoning, vol. 2567. CEUR-WS (2016)
4. Bach, K., Mork, P.J.: On the explanation of similarity for developing and deploying CBR systems. In: The Thirty-Third International Flairs Conference (2020)
5. Cunningham, P., Doyle, D., Loughrey, J.: An evaluation of the usefulness of case-based explanation. In: Ashley, K.D., Bridge, D.G. (eds.) ICCBR 2003. LNCS (LNAI), vol. 2689, pp. 122–130. Springer, Heidelberg (2003). https://doi.org/10.1007/3-540-45006-8_12
6. Gates, L., Kisby, C., Leake, D.: CBR confidence as a basis for confidence in black box systems. In: Bach, K., Marling, C. (eds.) ICCBR 2019. LNCS (LNAI), vol. 11680, pp. 95–109. Springer, Cham (2019). https://doi.org/10.1007/978-3-030-29249-2_7
7. Hoffmann, M., Malburg, L., Klein, P., Bergmann, R.: Using Siamese graph neural networks for similarity-based retrieval in process-oriented case-based reasoning. In: Watson, I., Weber, R. (eds.) ICCBR 2020. LNCS (LNAI), vol. 12311, pp. 229–244. Springer, Cham (2020). https://doi.org/10.1007/978-3-030-58342-2_15
8. Jaiswal, A., Bach, K., Meisingset, I., Vasseljen, O.: Case representation and similarity modeling for non-specific musculoskeletal disorders-a case-based reasoning approach. In: The Thirty-Second International Flairs Conference (2019)
9. Kenny, E.M., et al.: Predicting grass growth for sustainable dairy farming: a CBR system using Bayesian case-exclusion and *post-hoc*, personalized explanation-by-example (XAI). In: Bach, K., Marling, C. (eds.) ICCBR 2019. LNCS (LNAI), vol. 11680, pp. 172–187. Springer, Cham (2019). https://doi.org/10.1007/978-3-030-29249-2_12
10. Lamy, J.B., Sekar, B., Guezennec, G., Bouaud, J., Séroussi, B.: Explainable artificial intelligence for breast cancer: a visual case-based reasoning approach. Artif. Intell. Med. **94**, 42–53 (2019)
11. Leake, D., Mcsherry, D.: Introduction to the special issue on explanation in case-based reasoning. Artif. Intell. Rev. **24**, 103–108 (2005)
12. Leake, D.B.: CBR in context: the present and future. In: Case-Based Reasoning: Experiences, Lessons and Future Directions, pp. 3–30. MIT Press (1996)
13. Meisingset, I., et al.: Novel approach towards musculoskeletal phenotypes. Eur. J. Pain **24**(5), 921–932 (2020)

14. Nugent, C., Cunningham, P.: A case-based explanation system for black-box systems. Artif. Intell. Rev. **24**, 163–178 (2005)
15. Recio-García, J.A., Parejas-Llanovarced, H., Orozco-del-Castillo, M.G., Brito-Borges, E.E.: A case-based approach for the selection of explanation algorithms in image classification. In: Sánchez-Ruiz, A.A., Floyd, M.W. (eds.) ICCBR 2021. LNCS (LNAI), vol. 12877, pp. 186–200. Springer, Cham (2021). https://doi.org/10.1007/978-3-030-86957-1_13
16. Roth-Berghofer, T.R., Bahls, D.: Explanation capabilities of the open source case-based reasoning tool myCBR. In: Proceedings of the Thirteenth UK Workshop on Case-Based Reasoning UKCBR, pp. 23–34 (2008)
17. Scheidegger, M., Baumgartner, F., Braun, T.: Simulating large-scale networks with analytical models. Int. J. Simul. Syst. Sci. Technol. Special Issue on: Advances in Analytical and Stochastic Modelling (2005)
18. Sørmo, F., Cassens, J., Aamodt, A.: Explanation in case-based reasoning-perspectives and goals. Artif. Intell. Rev. **24**(2), 109–143 (2005)
19. Stahl, A., Roth-Berghofer, T.R.: Rapid prototyping of CBR applications with the open source tool myCBR. In: Althoff, K.-D., Bergmann, R., Minor, M., Hanft, A. (eds.) ECCBR 2008. LNCS (LNAI), vol. 5239, pp. 615–629. Springer, Heidelberg (2008). https://doi.org/10.1007/978-3-540-85502-6_42

Adapting Semantic Similarity Methods for Case-Based Reasoning in the Cloud

Ikechukwu Nkisi-Orji(✉), Chamath Palihawadana, Nirmalie Wiratunga, David Corsar, and Anjana Wijekoon

School of Computing, Robert Gordon University, Aberdeen, UK
{i.nkisi-orji,c.palihawadana,n.wiratunga,d.corsar1,a.wijekoon1}@rgu.ac.uk

Abstract. CLOOD is a cloud-based CBR framework based on a microservices architecture which facilitates the design and deployment of case-based reasoning applications of various sizes. This paper presents advances to the similarity module of CLOOD through the inclusion of enhanced similarity metrics such as word embedding and ontology-based similarity measures. Being cloud-based, costs can significantly increase if the use of resources such as storage and data transfer are not optimised. Accordingly, we discuss and compare alternative design decisions and provide justification for each chosen approach for CLOOD.

Keywords: CBR architectures and frameworks · Cloud microservices · Semantic similarity · Ontologies

1 Introduction

Modern computing has evolved rapidly with the adoption of cloud computing across sectors such as healthcare, finance and travel. As organisations transition to the latest technology stacks and update the underpinning infrastructure, keeping existing development tools and frameworks up to date can pose significant challenges. Case-based reasoning (CBR) is an example of one such application area where once popular frameworks have become unusable with new, state-of-the-art technologies. Recently CLOOD [13] was introduced with the aim of addressing this challenge by adopting a cloud-first approach based on a microservices oriented architecture.

CLOOD has demonstrated more robust performance and scalability than other CBR systems like jCOLIBRI [4] and has been successfully integrated into industry projects, enabling the application of aspects of the CBR cycle in large scale systems. The practical demands of applying CBR in real-world applications often leads to the requirement to extend the built-in local similarity functions. One such

This research is funded by the iSee project (https://isee4xai.com) which received funding from EPSRC under the grant number EP/V061755/1. iSee is part of the CHIST-ERA pathfinder programme for European coordinated research on future and emerging information and communication technologies.

M. T. Keane and N. Wiratunga (Eds.): ICCBR 2022, LNAI 13405, pp. 125–139, 2022.
https://doi.org/10.1007/978-3-031-14923-8_9

project is *iSee*[1] which aims to enhance the explainability of machine learning models. *iSee* is developing a CBR system that uses the experiences of multiple users who have received explanations for the outputs of machine learning models, as the basis for new explanation strategies (combinations of explainability techniques), generated using CBR methods. The new strategy can then be executed to provide new users with explanations for model output(s). The *iSee* project is developing iSeeOnto[2] to describe AI Models, explanations, explainability techniques, explanation strategies, and user experiences. We argue that the similarity and adaptation containers of the *iSee* CBR system would benefit from using advanced semantic similarity methods, such as ontology-based and vector-based approaches to improve the quality of the generated explanation strategies.

CLOOD models its casebase using an open-source search engine (OpenSearch[3]) which leverages the efficient Lucene index for case retrieval. While the similarity module of OpenSearch (and similar search engines) supports several similarity metrics such as exact and fuzzy matching techniques out-of-the-box, it lacks several similarity metrics that are useful for case-based reasoning applications such as *iSee*. Extending the similarity module to include new metrics requires the use of custom similarity scripts that accomplish the retrieval needs within the microservices architecture and without a significant overhead in resource use.

A key challenge when extending the capabilities of a framework like CLOOD is to retain the core design principles: cloud-first, microservices-oriented, and serverless (on-demand workloads) application model. Furthermore, a framework will be sustainable and adopted by the community only if it maintains the operational overheads (e.g. compute time and resource cost) as new features are added. In this work, both of these challenges are addressed while enhancing the functionality of the CLOOD CBR framework with support for semantic similarity metrics for local similarity which includes:

- similarity table, word embedding based similarity, and ontology-based similarity measures,
- architectural considerations to retain the microservices nature of the platform,
- minimising the retrieval overhead due to the introduction of the semantic similarity measures,
- reviewing the potential impact of extending CLOOD as a platform for rapid integration of CBR.

The remainder of this paper is structured as follows; in Sect. 2 we discuss the related work in semantic relatedness measures, ontologies in CBR and CLOOD; Sect. 3 presents the introduced semantic similarity metrics; Sect. 4 discusses the integration of the metrics into the existing microservices architecture of CLOOD; Sect. 5 experimentally evaluates the impact of adopting alternative approach on the most resource-intensive metrics; Sect. 6 concludes the paper with a review of contributions and outlines future directions of CLOOD.

[1] https://isee4xai.com/.
[2] https://github.com/isee4xai/iSeeOnto.
[3] https://opensearch.org/.

2 Related Work

2.1 Clood CBR

Introduced in [13], CLOOD is the first cloud-based generic CBR framework developed for scalability using a microservices-oriented design. Prior to CLOOD, CBR frameworks were based on monolithic architectures which was restrictive for applications that require high scalability. CLOOD opened up a new avenue in the CBR landscape by enabling CBR applications to reach higher levels of scale. An empirical study showed that CLOOD can scale extensively without compromising performance (e.g. retrieval from a casebase of half a million cases was over 3,700 times faster than jCOLIBRI). Further, limited integration support (e.g. APIs) in the previous CBR frameworks has been an obstacle for adopting CBR for some real-world applications. The extensible and open source nature of CLOOD has facilitated its improvement and enhancement over time. Implementation using the microservices paradigm makes CLOOD more sustainable considering the rapid adoption of cloud computing and serverless computing, particularly in enterprise settings [19]. A complete CLOOD based implementation consists of the following:

- **Casebase** contains the cases of a CBR application and is implemented using a full-text search engine (e.g. Elasticsearch, OpenSearch).
- **CBR Functions** consists of the CBR cycle operations (retrieve, reuse, revise, retain), which were implemented using Serverless functions.
- **Similarity Functions** provides the mechanism to match and rank cases during case retrieval. The microservices based architecture in CLOOD is advantageous for extending similarity functions.
- **External Access** consists of a set of HTTP API endpoints that trigger the CBR functions. This external interface is implemented using cloud-native microservices that is available on most cloud service providers (e.g. AWS API gateway, Google API Gateway).
- **Data sources** are the persistence tools where applications store their data (e.g. MySQL, MongoDB) and these data sources can be synchronised with the Casebase through the external access APIs.
- **Client applications** are front facing components of any system such as the CLOOD dashboard. Client applications on any platform can use the external APIs to achieve CBR integration.

2.2 Ontologies in CBR

Ontologies have long been used in various aspects of CBR such as the vocabulary for describing cases [1,12,16], case structure and indexing [14], semantic knowledge for similarity measurements [1,6,12,14,16], and domain knowledge for case adaptation [16]. Our focus is the use of ontologies to determine the semantic similarity during case retrieval. Ontology-based semantic similarity approaches consider factors such as the taxonomic relations between concepts and the degree of shared properties. The ontology-based similarity approaches differ according to the type of information used to determine similarity (or relatedness) with path based, information content (IC) based and feature based as the main categories of alternative approaches [9]. Path based approaches rely on relative distances between the concepts of an ontology to determine similarity [15,21]. The first path based methods solely relied on the shortest distance between concepts. Subsequent methods added extensions such as the use of most specific common subsumer (MSCS) information and depth scaling. MSCS is the most distant node from the root that subsumes the concepts of a comparison. Typically, concepts become increasingly specific as an ontology is traversed from the root to leaf nodes. Depth-scaling approaches consider concepts in close proximity to be more closely related when they are nearer the leaf nodes than when they are nearer the root. IC approaches integrate a measure of information content in their similarity models [10,17]. Some IC approaches rely on the occurrence information of concepts in an external corpus to determine their information content and this introduces the challenge of correctly annotating the corpus. Feature based approaches determine similarity by comparing the features of concepts [18]. Similarity is determined by offsetting the degree of common features by the distinct features. The symmetric property is one of the differentiating features of different algorithms for ontology-based similarity. With the symmetric property, the similarity between concepts remains the same irrespective of the direction of comparison (i.e. $sim(x, y) = sim(y, x)$). Ontology-based similarity or relatedness measures correlate positively with human judgements to a good extent [7].

2.3 Retrieval with Word Embedding

A word embedding is a distributed representation for text that allows words with similar meanings to have similar embeddings. Most of the recent word embedding methods use neural networks to generate embedding vectors (dense vector of real numbers) that encode the context-induced meaning of words [11]. Context is determined by a corpus from which the word embedding is generated. Similarity is computed by comparing the vector representation of terms with the expectation that words with similar meanings will have similar embeddings. There are different types of learning techniques for creating word embedding models (e.g. Word2Vec, GloVe, BERT) [8] and several pre-trained models are available for reused. The embedding vectors can be used to determine local similarity measures during case retrieval as discussed in [2].

The use of vector-based similarity is not limited to textual CBR as it can apply to other media (e.g. image and audio). Also, there are ontology-based similarity approaches that use word embedding techniques to embed knowledge graphs into a dense vector space [9].

2.4 Serverless Function Benefits and Limitations

Serverless concepts provide many benefits such as the ability to scale systems according to workloads, flexibility of development, isolation of services, minimum maintenance overheads and major cost reductions. However, there are a few drawbacks which can pose implementation challenges such as provider-defined limits on compute resources (e.g. execution timeout in AWS Lambda, a widely used Function-as-a-Service) [20,22]. Serverless functions are used to compute fine-grained tasks which require very little computation unlike a large monolith application. Based on the study in [5], scalability is the main goal when using the microservices architecture while performance and response time are the chief optimisation concerns.

Clood depends on serverless functions for similarity calculations and other CBR functions, which only require small amounts of computation resources. Also, the casebase is not loaded into memory in Clood for scalability and performance reasons. However, operations such as pre-loading a large database from a CSV file, generating vector representations of strings, or computing similarity between nodes of a logically complex ontology will require additional computational resources, which can increase costs and affect the overall system performance. In this work we explore these limitations and propose options to overcome the challenges of using rich knowledge sources (word embedding and ontology) for similarity measures in Clood without imposing a significant negative impact on scalability, performance and response time.

3 Semantic Similarity Metrics in a Microservices Architecture

Several design challenges have to be overcome in order to implement enhanced similarity measures in the microservices architecture which Clood uses. In this section we present how the current limitations of cloud-based microservice architectures can be overcome to enable the inclusion of semantically rich knowledge resources for similarly measures. Specifically, we consider similarity metrics using similarity tables, word embeddings and ontologies. By leveraging the indexing capabilities of a NoSQL database equipped with a search engine, the current and future similarity methods can be incorporated into Clood without sacrificing overall CBR performance.

3.1 Clood Similarity Functions Overview

Table 1 is an overview of the local similarity metric functions that are available on Clood. This paper focuses on the similarity metrics in bold font face. The similarity metrics that are not marked as "Core" are implemented as separate microservices that are used by the base retrieval system through API calls during case retrieval. The decision to implement these metrics as separate services due to their resource needs is one of the measures used to ensure efficiency in performance.

Table 1. CLOOD's Local Similarity Metrics - the enhanced metrics presented in this paper are highlighted in bold text.

Data type	Similarity metric	Description	Core
All	Equal	Similarity based on exact match (used as a filter)	✓
String	EqualIgnoreCase	Case-insensitive string matching	✓
	BM25	TF-IDF-like similarity based on Okapi BM25 ranking function	✓
	Semantic USE	**Similarity measure based on word embedding vector representations**	–
Numeric	Interval	Similarity between numbers in an interval	✓
	INRECA	Similarities using INRECA More is Better and Less is Better algorithms	✓
	McSherry	Similarities using McSherry More is Better and Less is Better algorithms	✓
	Nearest number	Similarity between numbers using a linear decay function	✓
Categorical	EnumDistance	Similarity of values based on relative positions in an enumeration	✓
	Table	**User-defined similarity between entries of a finite set of domain values**	✓
Date	Nearest date	Similarity between dates using a decay function	✓
Location	Nearest location	Similarity based on separation distance of geo-coordinates using a decay function	✓
Ontology	**Path-based**	**Similarity using Wu & Palmer path-based algorithm**	–
	Feature-based	**Similarity using Sanchez et al. feature-based algorithm**	–

3.2 Similarity Table

A similarity table is a cartesian square of similarity measures of a finite set domain values/entities that specifies how any pair of values are related. A similarity table can capture the knowledge of a domain expert by recording their assessment of the similarity of entity pairs. Practical considerations mean this approach is best suited when the number of values is low. The complexity for specifying the similarity knowledge for the similarity table is $O(n^2)$ which can make managing the table to become tedious and time-consuming for domain experts as the number of possible values n, increases. The number of new similarity measures to be specified increases by $2n+1$ whenever n increases by 1 for asymmetric similarity. When relying on domain experts to explicitly create similarity tables is unfeasible, word embeddings and ontology-based similarity measures can be used to reduce the burden of acquiring the semantic similarity knowledge for case retrieval.

Since user-defined similarity tables are not expected to grow too large, each similarity table is persisted as part of the similarity knowledge for case retrieval. The similarity table forms a lookup table for the local similarity measures between query and case values at retrieval time.

3.3 Word Embedding Based Similarity

A word embedding based similarity method can be added to the CBR system as a loosely-coupled service. Persisting the word embedding model, generating embedding vectors for terms and comparing the vector representations are the main resource considerations for using a similarity measure based on Word Embedding. By using a separate service, we ensure that the word embedding component is easier to manage and able to scale up or down according to the model's requirements without affecting the other components. Also, adding the component as a separate service offers the flexibility to exclude it from an instantiation of the CBR framework when it is not needed leading to further reduction in resource use and lower-cost application when deployed on cloud infrastructure.

The processes that run on serverless functions are expected to be ephemeral and free up resources as the execution of functions end. When using word embedding model, most of the time is spent to load up the model and reloading the model each time we want to compute similarity measures can cause significant delays. In order to minimise delays during case retrieval, we generate any required vector representations when cases are being added during the pre-cycle stage or during a retain operation. The resulting dense vector representations are persisted as part of the retrieval knowledge in the casebase. While pre-computing vector representations slightly increases the time it takes to add cases to the casebase, it significantly reduces the time it takes to retrieve cases. At retrieval time, we only determine the vector representations of the applicable query values and compute word embedding based local similarity measures by taking the cosine similarity between the query vectors and the pre-loaded vector representations of cases.

3.4 Ontology-Based Similarity Measure

An ontology-based similarity method can be integrated into the microservices architecture as a separate service that is accessed by the base system through API calls. Similar to the word embedding similarity component, this separation increases flexibility and allows the service is manage its resource needs independent of the base system. Accordingly, there were two main challenges to overcome when implementing ontology-based similarity: how to maintain the ontology-based similarity independent in a scalable manner; and how computationally intensive operations like large tree traversal can be implemented using cloud functions.

On the first challenge, a key decision was made to change the system architecture to support computing similarity measures outside the base retrieval system. Prior to this challenge, all the similarity function scripts were maintained inside the core retrieval functions, but for enhanced similarity methods like ontology-based similarity, support for the use of local similarity measures that are returned through API responses was needed. This requirement is because there was no practical way of directly apply ontology-based similarity computation to case retrieval without having to load the cases into memory and this will have significant negative impact on the system's scalability. Instead, the ontology-based similarity component computes and returns all the similarity measures that are relevant for a query as a similarity table that is looked up for local similarity measures at retrieval time.

Given an ontology, θ with concepts $c_i, \ldots, c_n$, the similarity table for all the possible similarity measures of the n concepts require n^2 comparisons. However, when the query concept $c_q \in \theta$ is known, we only need a row of the similarity table that compares c_q with the other concepts of θ for case retrieval (i.e. n comparisons). This ability to use a subset of the similarity measures during each retrieval instance reduces the amount of data that is transmitted from the ontology-based similarity service to the base CBR system. In addition to reducing computation cost, using a row of the similarity table for each retrieval instance reduces the data transfer between the ontology-based similarity service and the base retrieval system.

In considering the computational cost that is associated with using ontology-based similarity methods and knowing that we only need a subset of ontology concept comparisons when retrieving for a query, we considered three options:

1. **Pre-loaded**: Pre-load determines all the similarity measures that can be determined by the ontology and persists the measures in a searchable index (flattened). We expect this method to have a high computation cost for large ontologies. The pre-loading of similarity measures takes place only once after the ontology added. Also, any updates to the ontology will require a complete refresh of the index to determine new similarity measures.
2. **Cached**: Similarity knowledge for retrieving for any newly seen concept (i.e. similarity between query concept and all the concepts of the ontology) is computed and cached in a searchable index. Whenever a request is made with a query concept, new ontology-based similarity measures are computed only if it is not stored previously in the index. Otherwise, it performs a simple lookup of previously cached similarity measures. Any updates to the ontology may require clearing the cached similarity measures.
3. **Non-Cached**: This approach will not persist any similarity measures so that similarity computation occurs on each request. This method will not use up storage space for an index.

An enhancement that can improve efficiency and reduce retrieval times is the ability to limit similarity computations to a sub-graph of the ontology. For example, a travel ontology can specify entities for both accommodation and activity amongst others. If we are only interested in the activity entities for case description, the ability to limit similarity computations to the activity sub-graph of the ontology can result in significant savings with respect to computation resources and retrieval times.

Note that the ontology-based similarity measure discussed here is applicable when the case attribute values map to classes (or concepts) instead of instances of classes. However, the ontology-based similarity component can be extended to support the computation of similarity measures for instances of classes.

4 Implementation of Semantic Similarity Measures on Clood Framework

This section discusses how the semantic similarity measures are implemented in CLOOD taking the design consideration in Sect. 3 into account. Figure 1 presents the CLOOD system architecture with its microservices. Updated components of the diagram are numbered as from 1–3. Component (1) represents the proposed isolation of enhanced similarity functions, this component represents all the extended functions as microservices. Components (2) and (3) represents the proposed Ontology-based similarity measure (Sect. 3.4) and Word Embedding similarity measure (Sect. 3.3) respectively. The discussion in this section includes how the similarity measures are used through the CLOOD dashboard. As indicated in Fig. 1, the user interfaces can be implemented differently with API access to the CLOOD functions. Description of the API end-points are available on the CLOOD repository[4].

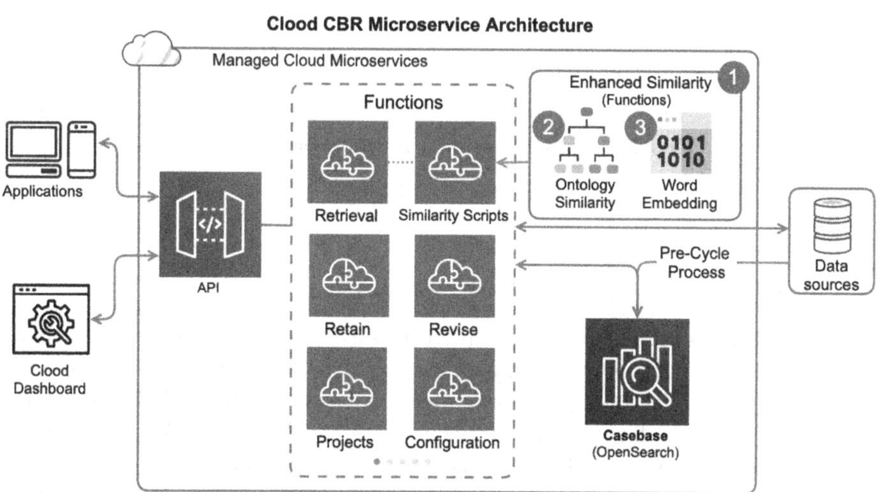

Fig. 1. Updated CLOOD CBR Architecture diagram

Building a similarity table on CLOOD is facilitated by an interactive user interface that enables a user to enumerate the possible values that attributes

[4] https://github.com/RGU-Computing/clood.

and the pairwise similarity measures of values as shown in Fig. 2. The configuration interface to create a similarity table is only available for attributes with table similarity metric type. There is the option to make the similarity table symmetric or asymmetric. The user is required to provide only half of the similarity measures when using the symmetric option. The similarity table is persisted as a parameter of the case definition/configuration for lookup during case retrieval. The case definition is where the similarity type, reuse strategy and feature importance/weight of each case attribute is held for computing and aggregating local similarity measures, and for composing a recommended solution.

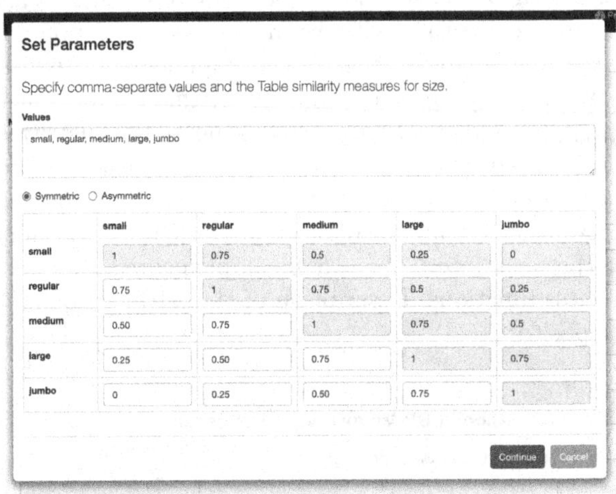

Fig. 2. Specifying a similarity table on CLOOD.

4.1 Word Embedding Similarity on Clood

We implemented semantic similarity on CLOOD using a pretrained Universal Sentence Encoders (USE) for word embedding[5]. USE is a general-purpose context-aware encoding model for word representations based on the transformer architecture [3]. Additional word embedding models can be included and the USE model can be replaced by a different type of word embedding model. The vector representations are stored as dense vector types in the casebase and the built-in functionality of OpenSearch is used to determine the cosine similarity between vector representations for local similarity measures during case retrieval.

Although similarity is based on vector representations when using word embedding, presenting the dense vectors of real numbers to users will not be very useful. Accordingly, appropriate conversions are made in the layer between

[5] https://npmjs.com/package/@tensorflow-models/universal-sentence-encoder.

the user interface and the casebase. In order to support this conversion, the values of attributes with word embedding vector based similarity are persisted as object (non-primitive) data type in the casebase consisting of both the human-readable attribute values and their corresponding vector representations. The user only sees the human-readable values while the retrieval function uses the vector representations to match and rank cases in the casebase. As a result, no modifications were made to the user interfaces to support the use of word embedding based similarity measures. The user only has to indicate that an attribute will use a word embedding similarity metric function during the attribute configuration for a casebase.

4.2 Ontology-Based Similarity on Clood

We implemented the service for ontology-based semantic similarity measures on CLOOD with the options for Pre-loaded, Cached and Non-Cached methods as discussed in Sect. 3.4. If the user specifies that an attribute will use an ontology-based similarity approach for local similarity, a configuration option to specify the ontology detail becomes available on the user interface. The configuration interface allows the user to specify the URI locations of the ontology files, each file's format and an optional name for the ontology source. The support for including multiple sources/files is useful for instances where an ontology is stored in multiple files of overlapping concepts (e.g. the modular structure of iSeeOnto). There is option to specify a root concept which is useful when the intention is to use a sub-graph of the ontology for computing similarity measures. When a root is not specified, it is inferred as the uppermost reachable node from the concepts of the ontology. Also, there is option to specify a relation type for determining taxonomic structure if it is different from "rdfs:subClassOf" relation.

We demonstrated support for ontology-based semantic similarity measures by integrating path-based and feature-based similarity measures on CLOOD. Path-based approach uses Wu and Palmer algorithm [21] as shown in Eq. 1

$$sim(c_i, c_j)_{wup} = \frac{2 * depth(mscs(c_i, c_j))}{depth(c_i) + depth(c_j)} \tag{1}$$

where $mscs(c_i, c_j)$ is the most specific common subsumer of concepts c_i and c_j. The depth of concept c_i (i.e. $depth(c_i)$) is the number of edges between c_i and the root node.

Feature-based approach is based on Sanchez et al. normalised dissimilarity [18] as shown in Eq. 2

$$sim(c_i, c_j)_{san} = 1 - \log_2(1 + \frac{|\phi(c_i) \setminus |\phi(c_j)| + |\phi(c_j) \setminus |\phi(c_i)|}{|\phi(c_i) \setminus |\phi(c_j)| + |\phi(c_j) \setminus |\phi(c_i)| + |\phi(c_i) \cap |\phi(c_j)|}) \tag{2}$$

where $\phi(c)$ is the taxonomic ancestors of concept c.

5 Evaluation of Resource Impact

In considering the semantic similarity measures we have discussed, design decision based difference in performance is expected to be most noticeable for ontology-based similarity measures. Accordingly, we compare the three implementation options (i.e. pre-loaded, cached or non-cached) to highlight their strengths and weaknesses.

5.1 Experiment Setup

We use the Pizza Price Prediction dataset[6] that describes pizza using attributes for company, price, topping, size, etc. for the case description. We use the pizza ontology[7] for the ontology-based similarity of different types of pizza toppings during case retrieval. First, we anchor the dataset attribute's pizza topping values to the concepts of the pizza ontology. To achieve this, we used an edit distance similarity measure (based on Levenshtein) to map pizza toppings of the dataset to the most suitable concepts of the pizza ontology. The topping attribute was set up to CLOOD's path-based similarity to determine local similarity measures during retrieval. Then, we randomly selected 500 toppings with replacement from the pizza ontology to compose queries for case retrieval. Random selection with replacement ensures that queries can repeat multiple times which is expected in real-life applications. Several toppings repeat multiple times in the query selection because the ontology specifies 48 unique pizza toppings. Figure 4 shows the proportion of the query values that are unique as the query selection increases. At 500 query selection, all the pizza toppings had been seen more once as indicated by the line that shows the proportion of unique queries go to 0.

5.2 Result and Discussion

We performed case retrieval and noted the retrieval times as the number of queries increase as shown in Fig. 3. Retrieval times were measured at different intervals and the average time for 5 runs of each set of queries was reported.

In Pre-loaded, most of the time is spent to pre-compute all the pairwise similarity measures between the ontology concepts. In the experiment, we also compared using the entire ontology graph (i.e. Pre-loaded (All Nodes)) with the option that pre-loads only a sub-hierarchy of the ontology (i.e. Pre-loaded (Sub-hierarchy)). For the sub-hierarchy, we used a portion of the ontology for pizza toppings only by specifying the most general concept of pizza topping as the root for similarity measures. Specifying the root restricted computations to a smaller relevant portion of the ontology which reduced the total retrieval times. Given that there are 48 pizza toppings in the ontology, the pairwise similarity computation determines 2,304 (48×48) similarity measures when using the sub-hierarchy option. The entire ontology describes 99 concepts (classes) with a

[6] https://www.kaggle.com/datasets/knightbearr/pizza-price-prediction.

[7] https://protege.stanford.edu/ontologies/pizza/pizza.owl.

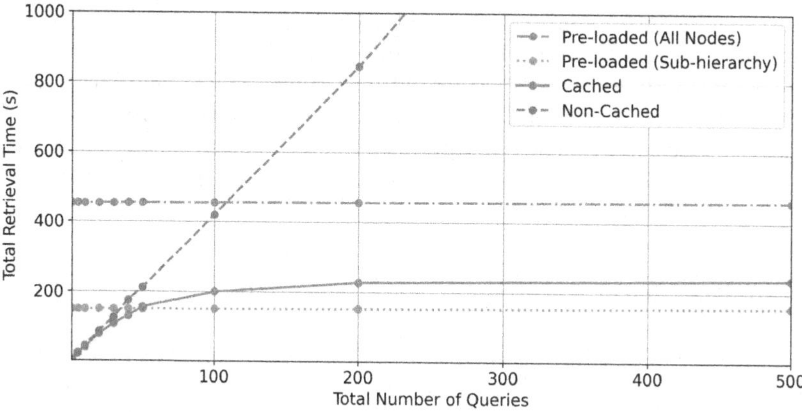

Fig. 3. Times for case retrieval for different methods of implementing ontology-based similarity.

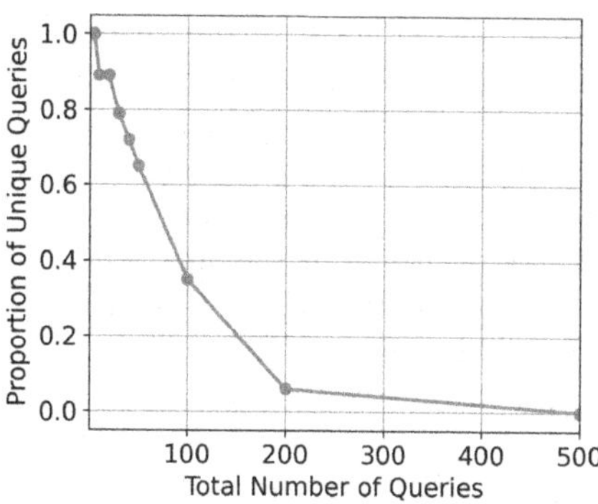

Fig. 4. Proportion of unique queries with total number of queries

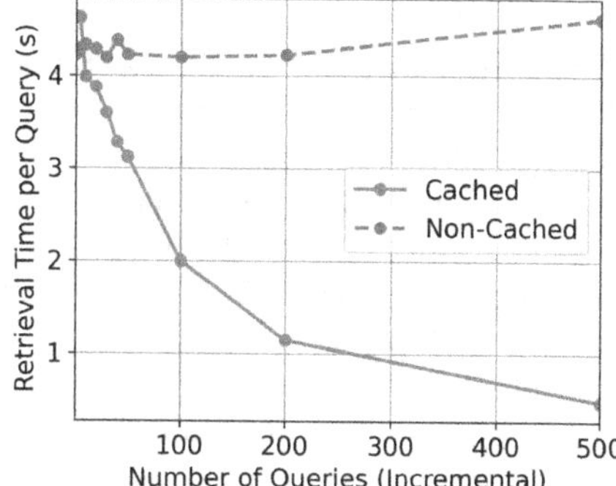

Fig. 5. Comparison between Cache and Non-Cache methods

possible 9,801 pairwise similarity measures most of which are outside the pizza topping sub-domain. We added the pre-loading time to the retrieval time of the first query. The time spent in executing additional queries mostly consists of the lookup time from the index of similarity measures. In the Cached option, the total retrieval time is initially similar to Non-Cache. However, it becomes almost horizontal as queries begin to recur. At some point, all the concepts become available in the cache so that it becomes a lookup of similarity values like the pre-loaded option. The Non-Cached option neither pre-computes similarity measures nor maintains an index of seen comparisons. Unsurprisingly, the total retrieval time increases linearly as the number of queries increases. Figure 5 shows how the average time of retrieval for each query reduces over time providing additional insight into the advantage of caching over non-caching. The average time per query remains consistently high for Non-Cached. In contrast, the average time per query significantly reduces over time for Cached. By the 100th query, Cache was already more than 2 times better than Non-Cached.

Similarity results were obtained for ontology feature-based similarity. In general, Pre-loaded option is useful if most of the ontology nodes are being used in the casebase. Cached is an efficient approach if queries often repeat and for large scale ontologies where only a few nodes are used. Non-Cached can be useful for smaller rapidly changing ontologies.

6 Conclusion

In this paper, we discussed how architectural challenges influenced decisions on how to include semantic similarity measures for case retrieval in a microservices architecture. We showed how the similarity measures can be implemented on the CLOOD framework and presented an experimental evaluation to demonstrate the impact of different options for using ontology-based semantic similarity measures.

Future work will provide support for additional methods of computing the ontology-based similarity measures including approaches for embedding knowledge graphs. As a supplement to the open-sourced and extensible CLOOD framework, the team is currently building the first CBR-as-a-Service platform. CLOOD API will be a software-as-a-service offering where organisations, developers and researchers can harness the power CBR and CLOOD within few minutes. The key reason for this direction is due to the time consumed for setting up CBR frameworks for each project/product. This can be solved by using a CBR-as-a-Service platform where the entire CBR system is itself a single microservice. Infrastructure, security, maintenance and bug-fixes can be centrally handled reducing any overhead for organisations to adapt and integrate CBR into their applications. This will be a solution for small-medium scale businesses with limited expertise on CBR and cloud to setup the systems. With an interactive and simple dashboard the entire CBR cycle can be ready and exposed as API endpoints in very few steps. You can submit your interest in this platform at https://cloodcbr.com.

References

1. Amailef, K., Lu, J.: Ontology-supported case-based reasoning approach for intelligent m-government emergency response services. Decis. Support Syst. **55**(1), 79–97 (2013)
2. Amin, K., Lancaster, G., Kapetanakis, S., Althoff, K.-D., Dengel, A., Petridis, M.: Advanced similarity measures using word embeddings and siamese networks in CBR. In: Bi, Y., Bhatia, R., Kapoor, S. (eds.) IntelliSys 2019. AISC, vol. 1038, pp. 449–462. Springer, Cham (2020). https://doi.org/10.1007/978-3-030-29513-4_32
3. Cer, D., et al.: Universal sentence encoder. arXiv preprint arXiv:1803.11175 (2018)
4. Díaz-Agudo, B., González-Calero, P.A., Recio-García, J.A., Sánchez-Ruiz-Granados, A.A.: Building CBR systems with jcolibri. Sci. Comput. Program. **69**(1–3), 68–75 (2007)

5. Ghofrani, J., Lübke, D.: Challenges of microservices architecture: a survey on the state of the practice. ZEUS **2018**, 1–8 (2018)
6. González-Calero, P.A., Díaz-Agudo, B., Gómez-Albarrán, M., et al.: Applying DLS for retrieval in case-based reasoning. In: Proceedings of the 1999 Description Logics Workshop (Dl 1999). Linkopings universitet. Citeseer (1999)
7. Hliaoutakis, A., Varelas, G., Voutsakis, E., Petrakis, E.G., Milios, E.: Information retrieval by semantic similarity. Int. J. Semant. Web Inf. Syst. (IJSWIS) **2**(3), 55–73 (2006)
8. Khattak, F.K., Jeblee, S., Pou-Prom, C., Abdalla, M., Meaney, C., Rudzicz, F.: A survey of word embeddings for clinical text. J. Biomed. Inform. **100**, 100057 (2019)
9. Lastra-Díaz, J.J., Goikoetxea, J., Taieb, M.A.H., García-Serrano, A., Aouicha, M.B., Agirre, E.: A reproducible survey on word embeddings and ontology-based methods for word similarity: linear combinations outperform the state of the art. Eng. Appl. Artif. Intell. **85**, 645–665 (2019)
10. Lin, D., et al.: An information-theoretic definition of similarity. In: ICML, vol. 98, pp. 296–304 (1998)
11. Mikolov, T., Sutskever, I., Chen, K., Corrado, G.S., Dean, J.: Distributed representations of words and phrases and their compositionality. In: Advances in Neural Information Processing Systems 26 (2013)
12. Montero-Jiménez, J.J., Vingerhoeds, R., Grabot, B.: Enhancing predictive maintenance architecture process by using ontology-enabled case-based reasoning. In: 2021 IEEE International Symposium on Systems Engineering (ISSE), pp. 1–8. IEEE (2021)
13. Nkisi-Orji, I., Wiratunga, N., Palihawadana, C., Recio-García, J.A., Corsar, D.: Clood CBR: towards microservices oriented case-based reasoning. In: Watson, I., Weber, R. (eds.) ICCBR 2020. LNCS (LNAI), vol. 12311, pp. 129–143. Springer, Cham (2020). https://doi.org/10.1007/978-3-030-58342-2_9
14. Qin, Y., et al.: Towards an ontology-supported case-based reasoning approach for computer-aided tolerance specification. Knowl.-Based Syst. **141**, 129–147 (2018)
15. Rada, R., Mili, H., Bicknell, E., Blettner, M.: Development and application of a metric on semantic nets. IEEE Trans. Syst. Man Cybern. **19**(1), 17–30 (1989)
16. Recio-Garía, J.A., Díaz-Agudo, B.: Ontology based CBR with jCOLIBRI. In: Ellis, R., Allen, T., Tuson, A. (eds.) SGAI 2006, pp. 149–162. Springer, London (2006). https://doi.org/10.1007/978-1-84628-666-7_12
17. Resnik, P.: Using information content to evaluate semantic similarity in a taxonomy. arXiv preprint cmp-lg/9511007 (1995)
18. Sánchez, D., Batet, M., Isern, D., Valls, A.: Ontology-based semantic similarity: a new feature-based approach. Expert Syst. Appl. **39**(9), 7718–7728 (2012)
19. Schleier-Smith, J., et al.: What serverless computing is and should become: the next phase of cloud computing. Commun. ACM **64**(5), 76–84 (2021)
20. Taibi, D., El Ioini, N., Pahl, C., Niederkofler, J.R.S.: Patterns for serverless functions (function-as-a-service): a multivocal literature review (2020)
21. Wu, Z., Palmer, M.: Verb semantics and lexical selection. arXiv preprint cmp-lg/9406033 (1994)
22. Xie, R., Tang, Q., Qiao, S., Zhu, H., Yu, F.R., Huang, T.: When serverless computing meets edge computing: architecture, challenges, and open issues. IEEE Wirel. Commun. **28**(5), 126–133 (2021)

Adaptation and Analogical Reasoning

Case Adaptation with Neural Networks: Capabilities and Limitations

Xiaomeng Ye(✉), David Leake, and David Crandall

Luddy School of Informatics, Computing, and Engineering, Indiana University, Bloomington, IN 47408, USA
{xiaye,leake,djcran}@indiana.edu

Abstract. Neural network architectures for case adaptation in case-based reasoning (CBR) have received considerable attention. However, architectural gaps and general questions remain. First, existing architectures focus on adaptation of numeric attributes alone. Second, some proposed neural network adaptation architectures operate directly on pairs of cases, so could be performing direct prediction instead of adaptation. Third, it is unclear how the effectiveness of CBR systems with neural network components compares to that of networks alone. This paper addresses these questions. It extends a neural network-based case difference heuristic (NN-CDH) approach to handle both numeric and nominal attributes, in an architecture that applies to both regression and classification domains. The network predicts solution difference based on problem difference, ensuring that it learns adaptations. The paper presents experiments for both classification and regression tasks that compare performance of a neural network to a baseline CBR system and CBR variants with different retrieval schemes and adaptation schemes, on both real data and controlled artificial data sets. In these tests, CBR with the extended NN-CDH generally performs comparably to the baseline neural network, and NN-CDH consistently improves the results from naive retrieval but may worsen the results of network-based retrieval.

Keywords: Case adaptation · Case difference heuristic · Hybrid systems · Neural network-based adaptation · Nominal differences

1 Introduction

Neural network architectures for case adaptation have been the subject of considerable study within the case-based reasoning community. However, gaps remain both in architectural capabilities and in fundamental questions of system behavior. First, existing architectures focus on adaptation of numeric attributes; adapting nominal attributes is an open challenge, made harder because of the lack of standard methods for expressing such adaptations in network architectures. Second, some proposed neural network adaptation architectures take as input a query and retrieved case and generate a solution, which raises a question about

M. T. Keane and N. Wiratunga (Eds.): ICCBR 2022, LNAI 13405, pp. 143–158, 2022.
https://doi.org/10.1007/978-3-031-14923-8_10

whether they truly learn adaptation—in principle, they could learn to ignore the prior case and simply generate a solution from scratch. Third, the performance benefit of using CBR systems with neural network components over other models is unclear. This paper presents research on these questions.

This paper introduces a method for neural network adaptation of nominal attributes based on expressing the difference between two one-hot encoded nominal values as a vector, and extends the NN-CDH adaptation approach [12] to predict a solution difference given a problem difference, where the differences can involve nominal attributes. In contrast to the previous version of NN-CDH for classification, this guarantees learning adaptation knowledge. Extensive experiments on standard regression and classification data sets, and on artificial data sets, compare the extended NN-CDH with other models. Some trends of results paralleled those obtained in previous tests [12,20], providing additional support for those trends as general characteristics of neural network adaptation.

The experimental results suggest that NN-CDH is most useful when (1) retrieval is relatively good, in the sense of providing a starting point harmonized to learned adaptation knowledge (cf. [9,18]) and (2) queries are relatively novel, so adaptation is needed, and yet not too novel, which could require adaptation capabilities beyond the learned adaptation knowledge.

The results illustrate three lessons. First, good case retrieval alone may surpass other ML methods such as neural networks. Second, learned adaptation may actually worsen the retrieval result if the two processes are not harmonized. This point is beyond the scope of this paper but examined in our previous work [11]. Third, directly integrating neural networks into a CBR system may lead to results comparable to the counterpart neural network, but is not a "magic bullet" for superior performance. Even with comparable performance, CBR offers benefits such as interpretability. However, the results suggest that to reliably surpass statistical AI methods, symbolic knowledge will be necessary.

2 Background

Neural Network Adaptation Learning by the Case Difference Heuristic: CBR researchers have explored many machine learning techniques for acquiring case adaptation knowledge. Because of the difficulty of codifying adaptation knowledge, especially in poorly understood domains, there has been particular interest in data-driven methods [2–4,13,17]. Hanney and Keane's case difference heuristic (CDH) approach [5] is a method for learning adaptation knowledge from the case base, by comparing pairs of cases and attributing their solution difference to their problem difference. Originally, the CDH approach was applied to learning adaptation rules, but other variants have been explored, including network-based approaches. Liao, Liu, and Chao [13] train a neural network on case pairs to predict solution difference based on problem difference. Leake, Ye, and Crandall [12] take a similar approach but train the neural network with adaptation context in addition to problem/solution differences. They call this method the neural network-based case difference heuristic (NN-CDH) approach.

Case Adaptation Involving Nominal Attributes: The work mentioned in Sect. 2 all focuses on case adaptation for regression tasks, based on numeric attributes. As noted by Craw et al. [3], adaptation involving nominal attributes is difficult compared to numerical attributes because there is no natural calculation for symbolic similarity (for retrieval) or dissimilarity (for adaptation). Some previous works have studied non-neural methods for learning case adaptation involving nominal attributes. For example, Jarmulak, Craw and Rowe [8] present a case-based method that learns adaptation cases for both numeric and nominal features. Jalali, Leake, and Forouzandehmehr [6] combine a statistical method with an ensemble approach. Craw et al. [3] propose two methods to adapt nominal attributes: first, a coarse-grained method indicating whether a nominal attribute should remain the same or change, and second, a multi-class adaptation which proposes the target solution directly.

Initial Version of NN-CDH for Classification: The initial version of NN-CDH for classification followed the second route proposed by Craw et al. [3]; Ye et al. [20] modify NN-CDH into an approach called C-NN-CDH which predicts a target solution (class label) based on a source case and a target problem. It was tested in comparison to other classification algorithms including SVMs and neural networks. Those experiments supported that C-NN-CDH can achieve state-of-art case adaptation and classification results.

However, C-NN-CDH operates differently from other CDH methods (including NN-CDH) that work directly with problem/solution differences. C-NN-CDH takes a source case and a target problem as inputs. It is not guaranteed to make use of the source case to truly perform adaptation; in principle it could learn to find a target solution based on the target problem only. In response, this paper proposes a single adaptation model that learns from differences of nominal features/labels and therefore guarantees the learning of adaptation knowledge.

NN-CDH can handle nominal feature differences but not nominal label differences. To address this, we use the following encoding scheme. If a nominal feature is one-hot encoded into a vector of numbers (with a single "1" and multiple "0"s), it can be treated as multiple numerical features and processed by the neural network. Two such vectors can be subtracted from one another to form a nominal difference, which can be then passed to the input layer of NN-CDH. However, NN-CDH's last layer uses a single neuron with the linear activation function to predict a numerical output. This numerical output is the solution difference in a regression task. This output neuron cannot represent a nominal difference in the solution.

Both the studies on NN-CDH and C-NN-CDH methods (we will refer to both as NN-CDHs for short) compared CBR systems using NN-CDHs with their counterparts, neural network systems that predict target solution directly from target problem [12,20]. Ye et al. [20] show that NN-CDH performs comparably to the counterpart neural network system on certain data sets. Leake, Ye and Crandall [12] hypothesize that NN-CDHs can outperform end-to-end network methods, for example, when the query is novel in a high dimensional space.

However more evidence is needed to assess this hypothesis. This paper reports experiments to elucidate NN-CDH behavior.

Siamese Networks for Similarity Assessment: Siamese networks [1] are a neural network architecture that can predict the distance between two input samples. A siamese network is composite of two identical feature extraction networks and a subtraction layer. Given two input vectors (in our context, two feature vectors, one describing a query and the other the problem addressed by a prior case), the feature extraction networks extract their features and the subtraction layer compares their features and outputs a value indicating the distance (often using a sigmoid function) between the two cases. Siamese networks have been used as the similarity measure in case retrieval [14,15], with good performance. This study refers to a KNN retrieval process that uses a siamese network as similarity measure as *SN retrieval*.

The Relationship Between Retrieval and Adaptation: Smyth and Keane observed that for efficient adaptation, CBR retrieval and adaptation knowledge must be tightly connected [18], and Leake, Kinley and Wilson [9] illustrated the efficiency benefit of coordinating similarity and adaptation learning. Leake and Ye [11] showed that even when strong network models are trained for both retrieval and adaptation, adapted solutions might be less accurate than the retrieved solution if the retrieval and adaptation knowledge are not coordinated—*i.e.*, if the retrieved cases are close to the real solution by the similarity metric but not easily adaptable, or if the adaptation model is not trained to adapt such retrieval results. The experiments in this study tested a CBR system adapting results from either 1-NN retrieval or SN retrieval. The experiments further support that when both the retrieval model and the adaptation model are well trained individually but not in harmony with each other, adaptation may worsen the result of retrieval.

3 NN-CDH for both Classification and Regression

The research reported in this paper extends NN-CDH to perform adaptation for both regression and classification task domains. If the domain is regression, the model works identically to the original NN-CDH [12]. The following first explains the case adaptation process applicable to both classification and regression domains, then introduces a network method for handling nominal difference, and last discusses the neural network structure of NN-CDH and how it works with both numerical and nominal differences.

3.1 General Model of Case Adaptation

Given a query describing a target problem, the standard CBR adaptation process first retrieves a case whose problem is similar to the query. The system calculates the difference between the retrieved problem and the query problem, and modifies the solution of the retrieved case based on the problem difference. NN-CDH augments the difference information by using the retrieved problem as context for the adaptation. It uses both that context and the problem difference to predict a solution difference.

If the system task is a regression task, NN-CDH calculates the difference of two values over a numerical attribute by subtracting the two values. However, in classification tasks, each case contains a solution description that is a nominal label (Multi-class labeling is not within the scope of this study). The neural network of NN-CDH needs to handle outputs of differences of nominal attributes.

3.2 1-Hot/1-Cold Nominal Difference

NN-CDH handles nominal differences as follows. Given a nominal-valued attribute n that can take any of a set d different possible values for that attribute, one-hot encoding converts n into a group of d binary bits $\{n_1, n_2, ...n_d\}$, where n_i is '1' and all others bits are '0's. Given two nominal values $n = \{n_1, n_2, ...n_d\}$ and $m = \{m_1, m_2, ...m_d\}$ of the same attribute, their 1-hot/1-cold nominal difference (or "nominal difference" for short) is defined as

$$n - m = \{n_1 - m_1, n_2 - m_2, ...n_d - m_d\} \tag{1}$$

Given two cases in a classification task, their problem difference is calculated as a vector of individual feature differences concatenated, which may or may not involve nominal differences; Their solution difference is the nominal difference of their class labels. If the two cases are of the same class, then the solution difference is all '0's, indicating no difference between their solutions; Otherwise, the solution difference contains exactly one '1' and one '-1' (hence the name "1-hot/1-cold"), indicating changing from one class into another. Nominal differences are vectors that can be either input or output of NN-CDH, allowing NN-CDH to learn the projection from problem difference to solution difference in a classification task.

As a side benefit, the problem difference may contain both nominal and numerical differences, allowing interaction between the two categories of feature differences. This benefit is similar to that of a classification neural network which learns one-hot encoded nominal values and numerical values together.

3.3 Neural Network Structure of NN-CDH

Given a neural network structure for a given domain and task, the network structure of the NN-CDH for it is similar. The main difference is in its first and last layers. The first layer needs to have more neurons to accommodate both adaptation context and problem difference. The last layer needs to express predicted solution difference. The last layer is a dense layer using the *tanh* activation function, as opposed to the linear activation function in the original NN-CDH.

For regression, the last layer is a single neuron, producing a solution difference between -1 and 1 to increase or decrease a retrieved solution. For classification,

Algorithm 1. Pseudocode for the Training and Usage of NN-CDH

```
procedure Training(cases)
    pairs ← assembled pairs of cases
    NN-CDH ← new neural network
    CDH_data ← {}
    for each source and target in pairs do
        CDH_data.append(
        [prob(source),prob(source) − prob(target):sol(source) − sol(target)])
    NN-CDH.fit(CDH_data)
    return NN-CDH
procedure Adapt(query,retrieval)
    retrieved ← retrieval(CB, query)
    sol_diff ← NN-CDH.predict(prob(retrieved), prob(retrieved) − prob(query))
    if Task is regression then
        r ← sol(retrieved) − sol_diff
    else if Task is classification then
        r_vector ← sol(retrieved) − sol_diff  #element-wise subtraction
        r ← argmax(r_vector)
    return r
```

the last layer is a dense layer with d neurons, where d is the dimension of a one-hot encoding of the classification label. Each neuron can have a value between -1 (indicating "change to this class") and 1 (indicating "change from this class").

3.4 Training and Adaptation Procedure

The training and adaptation procedures follow the original NN-CDH, but with some modification. They are illustrated in Algorithm 1.

During training, pairs of training cases are assembled as training data for NN-CDH. For each pair, their problem difference and solution difference are calculated. One problem description of the two cases is used as the adaptation context. The problem difference and the adaptation context are concatenated to form the input of the NN-CDH and the solution difference is the expected output of the NN-CDH. Last, the NN-CDH is trained using backpropagation and the mean squared error as the loss function.

During adaptation, the NN-CDH predicts a solution difference based on a problem difference and an adaptation context. Depending on the task domain, the retrieved solution is modified according to the solution difference in one of two ways. If it is a regression task, the retrieved solution subtracting the predicted solution difference forms the final solution (as in the original NN-CDH). If it is a classification task, the retrieved solution is a one-hot encoding of the class of the retrieved case. The retrieved solution subtracts the predicted solution difference element by element. The maximum bit of the resulting vector is used to determine the final solution (Ties are broken arbitrarily).

4 Evaluation

Our evaluation addresses two questions: Does NN-CDH consistently improve the result of retrieval, and how does a CBR system using NN-CDH perform when compared to a neural network of equivalent computational power?

4.1 Systems Being Compared

This study tests six different methods and compares their performance in terms of prediction accuracy. They are: 1) a baseline neural network, 2) k-nearest neighbor (k-NN), 3) a CBR system whose retrieval is either 1-NN retrieval or SN retrieval and whose adaptation is either a rule-based CDH or an NN-CDH. The rule-based CDH is a baseline adaptation method (referred as NN_A in the work of Craw et al. [3]) where the case pairs are stored in an adaptation case base. The rule-based CDH uses a non-optimised 1-NN retrieval to select the case pairs based on the adaptation context and problem difference and applies the solution difference as the adaptation. Because there are two variations of retrieval and two of adaptation, four variations of CBR systems are tested. The six different methods are referred as "all models" in the following text.

The neural networks may have more or fewer layers and neurons per layer to accommodate the varying complexity of different data sets. In our implementation, the neural networks have 2–4 hidden layers, each of which has 8–128 neurons. For every task domain, the baseline neural network is almost identical to the NN-CDH and they share the same number of layers, neurons and activation functions, except for the first layer because NN-CDH takes in adaptation context and problem difference. This is to ensure fair comparison of the two models because they share similar complexity. The structure of the NN-CDH is as discussed in Sect. 3.3. The last layer of the baseline neural network uses a sigmoid activation function for regression or softmax activation function for classification. The baseline neural network model is trained with the loss function of mean squared error in regression or with the loss function of categorical cross entropy for classification. Such designs of neural networks for regression and classification are widely used.

Both k-NN and 1-NN are default implementations from the scikit-learn package [16]. They use Euclidean distance over problem feature values to calculate distance between cases. All cases are weighted equally. Our k-NN used k = 3. When the CBR system uses a siamese network over the Euclidean distance for similarity measure, a separate siamese network is trained to predict the similarity of two given cases.

The siamese network for case retrieval measures the similarity between two cases. The feature extraction network is composite of three dense layers (of dimension 32, 32 and 16) with dropout layers (dropout rate = 0.1) in between. For harder problems, the number of neurons in each layer is multiplied by 4.

The two features extracted from two cases are then passed to the subtraction layer which outputs the element-wise feature distance. Last, this is passed into a final dense layer to output a single similarity score. The final layer uses the

ReLU activation function for regression or the sigmoid activation function for classification. The siamese network is trained with the mean average error loss for regression or the contrastive loss for classification.

4.2 Assembling Case Pairs for Training

While the baseline neural network and the k-NN are trained from cases directly, both the siamese network and the NN-CDH need case pairs for training. Using all possible pairs may be infeasible, as a case base of n cases would have n^2 pairs. Multiple strategies exist for selective case pair assembly [7]. In all experiments of this study, we use n neighboring pairs (each case is paired with its nearest neighbor) and $10n$ random pairs (each case is randomly paired with another case). From these pairs, 90% are used for training and the rest for validation. We observed that this design choice can heavily influence the models, for example, a model may not accommodate two highly different input cases if the model is not trained with enough random pairs. However, this design choice is not the focus of this study.

To train the siamese network, we assemble pairs of cases' problem descriptions as input and determine their distance as the expected output of the siamese network. For regression, the distance is the absolute value of the distance between the two cases' solutions. For classification, the distance is 0 if the two solutions are the same and 1 otherwise. To train the NN-CDH, we use problem differences and solution differences of the case pairs.

4.3 Data Sets

This experiments test on five standard regression data sets (Airfoil, Car, Student Performance, Yacht, Energy Efficiency) and five classification data sets (Credit, Balance, Car, Yeast, Seeds), as well as on artificial data described in Sect. 4.4. As preprocessing, all numeric attributes are scaled to the range of [0,1] and all nominal attributes are one-hot encoded. This way the expected output values match the output range of the NN-CDH. Each data set is tested with 10-fold cross validation, and on three different settings:

- The normal setting: The standard setting where 90% of the cases are used as the training set (out of which 90% of the cases are used for training and the rest for validation) and 10% as the test set. The case pairs are assembled from the training set. The models are first trained and then tested on the whole test set.
- The novel setting (X): Similar to the normal setting with the difference that: For every test case, we remove its top $R\%$ neighbors (based on Euclidean distance on their *problem* descriptions) in the train set to form a trimmed train set. All models are trained on the *trimmed train set* and then tested on *that single test case*. This follows the design of a previous novel setting experiment [12].

– The novel setting (Y): Similar to the novel setting (X), we still remove top $R\%$ neighbors of a test case but the Euclidean distance is based on the solution description rather than the problem description. All models are trained on the trimmed train set and then tested on that single test case. This is a modification of another previous novel setting experiment [21].

The novel setting (X) simulates when the models are not trained with cases whose problem descriptions are similar to the query problem. The novel setting (Y) simulates when the models are not trained with cases sharing similar solutions as the query solution. The novel setting (Y) is arguably harder than the novel setting (X) because a CBR system in the later setting may still retrieve a case with good enough solution. The results for 1-NN retrieval under the novel setting (Y) are not reported because the trend is already clear in the novel setting (X). Moreover, the novel setting (Y) does not apply to classification data sets because two cases can be very different but still share the same class label. Removing cases based on class label does not necessarily make the query novel.

The data sets and various settings have been used in previous studies [12, 20, 21]. This study tests both classification and regression using the same models. We chose $R\%$ as 40%. For the normal setting of simpler data sets, experimental results are averaged over one ten-fold cross validation run. However, the novel settings have very high computational costs. Even one run on the whole test set is extremely expensive, because each test case requires a re-training of all the models. We resort to randomly choosing only 50 cases from a test set for testing.

In the novel settings, the performance of any model on test cases can vary tremendously as the novelty and difficulty of the test cases vary. Consequently almost all the differences in novel settings are not statistically significant.

Experimental Results on Real Data Sets. We observed the error rate of models on regression in Table 1 (lower is better) and accuracy of models on classification in Table 2 (higher is better). It is important to note that in novel settings the variance is very high (not shown in the tables) and performance differences of the models are not statistically significant. However, the general trend still reveals some interesting comparisons between the models:

1. SN retrieval is almost always better than 1-NN retrieval.
2. The relation between retrieval methods and NN-CDH is complicated:
   (a) NN-CDH consistently improves the result of 1-NN retrieval in regression, but less so in classification. We believe this is largely because (1) it is easier to retrieve a case with the same label in classification than to retrieve a case with the exact same solution in regression, and (2) nominal attributes hide subtle differences between cases (ex. a major problem difference may lead to no class change or a minor problem difference may lead to a class change) and therefore case pairs are harder for NN-CDH to learn.
   (b) NN-CDH often fails to improve the result of SN retrieval. When the retrieval process is very good but not in synchronization with the adaptation, in this case NN-CDH, the adaptation model does not necessarily improve the retrieval result. See discussion in Sect. 2.

Table 1. Error rates of models on regression data sets

	Setting	Retrieval	Neural Network	k-NN	Retrieval	Rule CDH	NN-CDH
Airfoil	Normal	1-NN	7.42%	6.87%	6.94%	5.80%	5.71%
	Normal	Siamese	7.60%	6.97%	6.49%	17.06%	8.82%
	Novel(X)	1-NN	9.34%	16.88%	17.99%	23.85%	12.02%
	Novel(X)	Siamese	9.51%	16.20%	8.45%	18.16%	13.84%
	Novel(Y)	Siamese	8.90%	16.49%	17.18%	22.29%	13.44%
Car	Normal	1-NN	1.52%	1.95%	1.63%	1.81%	1.38%
	Normal	Siamese	1.47%	1.92%	2.19%	6.89%	1.72%
	Novel(X)	1-NN	5.00%	7.42%	8.48%	8.87%	4.31%
	Novel(X)	Siamese	5.41%	7.36%	2.76%	8.45%	3.61%
	Novel(Y)	Siamese	5.06%	7.05%	6.20%	9.32%	4.77%
Student Performance	Normal	1-NN	21.61%	25.47%	31.59%	31.03%	29.63%
	Normal	Siamese	21.38%	25.64%	26.39%	31.66%	30.62%
	Novel(X)	1-NN	16.42%	18.73%	23.30%	27.00%	24.33%
	Novel(X)	Siamese	16.32%	19.30%	21.00%	21.90%	25.82%
	Novel(Y)	Siamese	23.73%	26.17%	32.00%	28.70%	33.38%
Yacht	Normal	1-NN	7.53%	13.77%	11.48%	6.85%	8.05%
	Normal	Siamese	5.94%	13.87%	2.18%	17.11%	7.71%
	Novel(X)	1-NN	10.50%	13.15%	16.72%	26.96%	10.50%
	Novel(X)	Siamese	10.14%	12.96%	3.52%	24.25%	6.43%
	Novel(Y)	Siamese	15.64%	19.56%	13.68%	19.77%	23.22%
Energy Efficiency	Normal	1-NN	7.36%	7.53%	14.62%	15.06%	13.04%
	Normal	Siamese	7.20%	7.55%	2.17%	12.51%	4.89%
	Novel(X)	1-NN	17.96%	23.46%	25.83%	22.29%	14.88%
	Novel(X)	Siamese	17.82%	23.44%	16.40%	22.41%	13.20%
	Novel(Y)	Siamese	17.07%	24.19%	23.72%	20.74%	12.95%

3. Neural network, SN retrieval and NN-CDH all may achieve best performance in various settings of different data sets. It is unclear which model will be most suitable in a given situation but some general trends are observed:
   (a) Under normal settings, the neural network is often best performing. Under novel settings, performance of all models degrades.
   (b) Under the novel setting (X), 1-NN is much worse than in the normal setting, but siamese retrieval performs relatively well and is often best.
   (c) Under the novel setting (Y), the siamese retrieval also suffers. We observe that NN-CDH may improve (but sometimes worsen) the retrieval results.
   (d) The neural network and the NN-CDH have comparable performance. This is because the two models share the same structure and computational power, although trained with different data for different purposes. Often NN-CDH is slightly worse. This may be because NN-CDH is working on the retrieval result. If the retrieval result is bad or if the retrieval and the adaptation are not in synchronization, it is harder to adapt.
   (e) As the neural network and the NN-CDH are similar in terms of problem solving power, if the neural network is underperforming (for example, if it performs worse than the retrieval method), then NN-CDH is likely underperforming as well and likely to worsen the retrieval result.

Table 2. Accuracy rates of models on classification data sets

	Setting	Retrieval	Neural Network	k-NN	Retrieval	Rule CDH	NN-CDH
Credit	Normal	1-NN	86.06%	85.34%	85.34%	80.37%	81.10%
	Normal	Siamese	85.91%	85.06%	80.78%	75.73%	76.34%
	Novel(X)	1-NN	77.80%	58.60%	58.60%	58.80%	70.20%
	Novel(X)	Siamese	68.00%	48.00%	70.00%	52.00%	76.00%
Balance	Normal	1-NN	97.21%	79.00%	79.00%	72.21%	97.15%
	Normal	Siamese	97.12%	79.44%	98.40%	73.66%	97.28%
	Novel(X)	1-NN	84.00%	46.00%	46.00%	56.00%	70.00%
	Novel(X)	Siamese	88.00%	46.00%	90.00%	42.00%	70.00%
Car	Normal	1-NN	99.87%	86.36%	86.36%	79.21%	99.27%
	Normal	Siamese	99.71%	84.84%	97.63%	71.12%	97.05%
	Novel(X)	1-NN	82.00%	52.00%	52.00%	52.00%	84.00%
	Novel(X)	Siamese	78.00%	60.00%	82.00%	64.00%	62.00%
Yeast	Normal	1-NN	58.83%	54.65%	54.65%	50.68%	52.90%
	Normal	Siamese	58.84%	54.42%	48.18%	45.19%	49.03%
	Novel(X)	1-NN	42.00%	40.00%	40.00%	38.00%	34.00%
	Novel(X)	Siamese	40.00%	26.00%	26.00%	26.00%	30.00%
Seeds	Normal	1-NN	93.71%	92.67%	92.67%	89.33%	94.29%
	Normal	Siamese	94.76%	93.33%	94.29%	90.48%	95.71%
	Novel(X)	1-NN	46.00%	26.00%	28.00%	28.00%	48.00%
	Novel(X)	Siamese	42.00%	14.00%	44.00%	32.00%	40.00%

4.4 Artificial Data Sets

Considering the nature of different models, we hypothesize that the locality of the task domain (whether local regions follow a specific pattern that is sufficiently different from the global landscape) is one factor causing disparity between the performances of models. Obviously, there are many other factors of a data set that might influence a model's performance, for example, the sparsity of feature values, the dimension, and the time-spatial relationship between features.

To further study the trends and find scenarios where one model may outperform the others, we created a way to generate artificial data sets with variable locality. The artificial cases take the form of

$$\{x_1, x_2, ...x_k : y\}, 0 \leq x_i \leq 1$$

where $\{x_1, x_2, ...x_k\}$ is a problem description with k features and y is the solution. k weights $\{w_1, w_2, ...w_k\}$ and k biases $\{b_1, b_2, ...b_k\}$ are randomly sampled from 0 to 1, each corresponding to one feature. For each case, x_i are randomly sampled from 0 to 1 and y is determined by two steps: 1) Find the first integer i such that $x_1 \leq i/k$; 2) Calculate the value of y as $y = w_i * x_i + b_i$.

This data set can be converted to include nominal features and even nominal solutions. For example, the first feature x_1 can be converted to an nominal feature of k possible values. If converted this way, the data set shows a perfect example where the nominal and numerical features are independent and yet interact, as the first feature (nominal) determines which numerical feature to use in calculating the solution.

Table 3. Error rates (and standard deviation) of Models on the Artificial Regression Data Sets. CBR uses 1-NN retrieval and adaptation is based on the retrieval result.

	Setting	Neural Network	k-NN	1-NN Retrieval	Rule CDH	NN-CDH
3 features	normal	17.47%(5.37)	9.677%(1.55)	9.818%(2.81)	12.31%(2.42)	9.906%(3.35)
remove on X	novel 0.1	17.23%(16.4)	14.86%(15.3)	18.57%(19.6)	24.90%(27.3)	9.148%(12.0)
	novel 0.2	19.90%(15.8)	19.09%(19.9)	23.94%(21.4)	27.62%(25.1)	11.41%(13.3)
	novel 0.3	22.42%(16.0)	21.00%(17.5)	24.40%(22.3)	30.25%(26.3)	15.41%(15.7)
5 features	normal	12.41%(1.66)	16.87%(2.13)	20.68%(1.98)	25.92%(2.12)	11.82%(2.82)
remove on X	novel 0.1	11.39%(9.71)	17.76%(14.7)	19.28%(22.6)	26.61%(23.4)	9.961%(9.01)
	novel 0.2	12.68%(11.6)	22.81%(15.7)	24.98%(23.7)	31.35%(23.9)	12.61%(11.8)
	novel 0.3	13.08%(11.9)	21.13%(18.7)	24.36%(22.4)	35.70%(27.8)	12.89%(11.7)
7 features	normal	24.42%(2.69)	25.70%(1.87)	32.08%(2.09)	39.37%(3.18)	25.49%(2.58)
remove on X	novel 0.1	20.02%(13.6)	25.53%(15.8)	34.56%(22.7)	37.55%(29.3)	23.15%(14.5)
	novel 0.2	21.38%(12.2)	25.70%(19.1)	33.92%(23.3)	40.67%(26.6)	23.84%(20.0)
	novel 0.3	22.98%(12.2)	28.35%(16.1)	31.02%(20.7)	36.22%(22.6)	21.82%(15.4)
3 features	normal	17.47%(5.37)	9.677%(1.55)	9.818%(2.81)	12.31%(2.42)	9.906%(3.35)
remove on Y	novel 0.1	15.59%(17.6)	13.77%(19.8)	15.27%(22.6)	14.24%(23.7)	10.63%(17.3)
	novel 0.2	20.65%(18.0)	17.97%(22.5)	21.64%(23.8)	21.19%(25.4)	16.74%(21.8)
	novel 0.3	22.33%(19.2)	24.68%(21.8)	26.23%(23.2)	25.05%(24.9)	19.62%(22.0)
5 features	normal	12.41%(1.66)	16.87%(2.13)	20.68%(1.98)	25.92%(2.12)	11.82%(2.82)
remove on Y	novel 0.1	12.11%(12.3)	16.81%(14.9)	18.15%(19.6)	21.64%(23.1)	11.83%(11.8)
	novel 0.2	18.73%(17.3)	24.74%(18.0)	28.06%(21.5)	26.95%(20.2)	20.88%(18.5)
	novel 0.3	23.25%(20.7)	31.04%(19.4)	33.68%(19.6)	34.40%(19.2)	21.99%(19.2)
7 features	normal	24.42%(2.69)	25.70%(1.87)	32.08%(2.09)	39.37%(3.18)	25.49%(2.58)
remove on Y	novel 0.1	29.76%(14.4)	29.85%(19.4)	33.85%(22.2)	37.84%(21.4)	31.37%(20.5)
	novel 0.2	32.92%(17.9)	35.60%(19.3)	38.07%(20.4)	38.89%(22.9)	39.12%(20.7)
	novel 0.3	35.73%(15.9)	39.03%(17.8)	40.11%(18.6)	41.49%(21.0)	39.42%(19.8)

On a high level, the first feature x_1 is globally used while the other features are only locally used depending on the value of x_1. Therefore this data set demonstrates a good example of task domains involving both global and local landscapes. By tuning the number of features k, we can modify the locality of the data set. When $k = 1$, the data set follows a single global rule; When k is large, the data set follows many local rules.

We generate data sets of 1000 cases respectively using $k = 3$, 5, and 7. For each data set, we test it with all models and three settings: normal, novel (X), and novel (Y). For each novel setting, we also vary $R\%$ to be 10%, 20%, and 30% in order to render gradual influences of the novel settings. To ensure fair comparison between models, we use the same seed to generate random cases for each choice of k and to select test queries.

Experimental Results on Artificial Data Sets. We observed the performance of models in Table 3 where the CBR system uses 1-NN retrieval and in Table 4 where the CBR system uses SN retrieval. We recorded both the error rate and standard deviation of each model. Each model is tested with 50 samples under each novel setting. The standard deviation of all models is very high in

Table 4. Error rates (and standard deviation) of Models on the Artificial Regression Data Sets. CBR uses SN retrieval and adaptation is based on the retrieval result.

	Setting	Neural Network	k-NN	SN Retrieval	Rule CDH	NN-CDH
3 features	normal	16.93%(4.94)	9.677%(1.55)	4.338%(1.09)	15.28%(4.23)	9.087%(3.05)
remove on X	novel 0.1	16.83%(16.5)	14.86%(15.3)	8.870%(15.4)	21.35%(29.8)	8.562%(10.9)
	novel 0.2	17.36%(14.3)	19.09%(19.9)	11.36%(15.8)	32.46%(27.5)	13.35%(12.3)
	novel 0.3	22.95%(14.9)	21.00%(17.5)	16.28%(18.0)	36.49%(25.8)	19.17%(18.0)
5 features	normal	13.01%(2.44)	16.87%(2.13)	7.322%(1.72)	25.59%(2.94)	12.51%(2.68)
remove on X	novel 0.1	11.03%(10.6)	17.76%(14.7)	6.017%(10.1)	28.25%(22.7)	9.115%(8.58)
	novel 0.2	11.38%(11.3)	22.81%(15.7)	6.954%(9.07)	25.10%(21.2)	12.42%(10.4)
	novel 0.3	12.72%(10.9)	21.13%(18.7)	9.769%(13.1)	22.93%(21.4)	12.48%(11.0)
7 features	normal	21.16%(2.38)	25.70%(1.87)	17.92%(4.98)	36.13%(3.47)	23.44%(2.90)
remove on X	novel 0.1	21.60%(13.3)	25.53%(15.8)	19.76%(19.8)	32.57%(25.6)	24.73%(19.0)
	novel 0.2	22.37%(13.0)	25.70%(19.1)	22.13%(20.3)	40.46%(33.8)	25.75%(17.9)
	novel 0.3	25.39%(10.8)	28.35%(16.1)	23.00%(20.6)	38.59%(27.1)	27.47%(18.3)
3 features	normal	16.93%(4.94)	9.677%(1.55)	4.338%(1.09)	15.28%(4.23)	9.087%(3.05)
remove on Y	novel 0.1	15.02%(18.3)	13.77%(19.8)	10.46%(13.9)	13.31%(16.6)	9.129%(11.6)
	novel 0.2	22.83%(19.4)	17.97%(22.5)	18.77%(21.5)	25.64%(24.3)	16.33%(24.6)
	novel 0.3	21.29%(20.2)	24.68%(21.8)	22.06%(18.3)	28.12%(25.8)	21.04%(23.8)
5 features	normal	13.01%(2.44)	16.87%(2.13)	7.322%(1.72)	25.59%(2.94)	12.51%(2.68)
remove on Y	novel 0.1	10.88%(10.4)	16.81%(14.9)	6.869%(8.68)	21.01%(20.2)	9.752%(9.32)
	novel 0.2	19.78%(17.1)	24.74%(18.0)	17.66%(19.0)	33.89%(26.6)	20.01%(16.9)
	novel 0.3	22.53%(20.2)	31.04%(19.4)	23.35%(20.4)	34.45%(24.1)	24.40%(22.3)
7 features	normal	21.16%(2.38)	25.70%(1.87)	17.92%(4.98)	36.13%(3.47)	23.44%(2.90)
remove on Y	novel 0.1	29.28%(15.8)	29.85%(19.4)	27.28%(22.3)	35.69%(22.4)	33.14%(21.8)
	novel 0.2	34.26%(17.3)	35.60%(19.3)	36.82%(21.0)	46.45%(27.8)	40.74%(22.9)
	novel 0.3	36.16%(15.5)	39.03%(17.8)	40.23%(20.4)	41.37%(22.8)	41.06%(20.7)

novel settings. This renders the comparisons in novel setting statistically insignificant, but we still believe the average error rates provide interesting data.

Many of the observations mesh with those in Sect. 4.3. We also observed additional phenomena in the experiments with the artificial data sets:

1. To our surprise, the baseline network performs relatively well (and sometimes best) in data sets with high locality. This contradicts our hypothesis.
2. Rule-based CDH always downgrades the retrieval result. Rule-based CDH finds the best case pairs to apply using the naive 1-NN, which works poorly in this special domain where only two features matter.
3. All models perform better in low-dimension data sets than high-dimension ones. 1-NN performs well in low-dimension spaces. The NN-CDH further improves the result of 1-NN retrieval, and often achieves the best performance. However, as the dimensionality increases, only two features are relevant and 1-NN retrieves worse results, making adaptation harder for NN-CDH. We observe when $k = 7$, the neural network outperforms 1-NN retrieval and NN-CDH consistently. This trend is not as obvious for SN retrieval.

4. SN retrieval can consistently outperform other models, except under novel settings (Y). Under a novel setting (Y), even the best possible neighbor's solution will be different from the target solution, as all cases with close solutions are removed. In such situations, we see the neural network and NN-CDH can outperform SN retrieval.
5. The artificial data set can be perfectly solved if a symbolic system somehow learns the rule to 1) find the first integer i such that $x_1 \leq i/k$; and 2) calculate the value of y as $y = w_i * x_i + b_i$. However, none of the systems tested achieve similar proficiency.

5 Conclusion

This paper proposed a way to handle nominal differences in network-based adaptation and extended NN-CDH to case adaptation for both classification and regression domains. Experiments with both real and artificial data sets align with results from previous studies of NN-CDH. In general, NN-CDH achieves comparable performance to its counterpart, the traditional neural network. Moreover, SN retrieval may outperform both the neural network and NN-CDH, and NN-CDH can worsen the result from SN retrieval. This illustrates the need to harmonize retrieval and adaptation methods [11].

In extensive experimental results, integrating neural network methods into CBR did not give CBR power beyond the neural network, even on data designed to test a hypothesized advantage for CBR. There are more sample pairs to train NN-CDH than samples to train a baseline neural network, which might provide an advantage [19] but we do not observe that here. On the other hand, CBR generally achieves performance comparable to the network, making it a competitive option, especially in tasks for which the intrinsic interpretability of CBR would make it preferable to a network approach.

The artificial data set, which can be perfectly solved using simple rules, illustrates a situation in which neither the neural network or knowledge-light CBR learns the underlying abstraction well. Symbolic CBR provides the opportunity to integrate knowledge and task-optimized representations. We envision that a balanced blend of domain knowledge, brought to bear by symbolic AI methods, with network-learned methods, has the potential to achieve a performance edge. We consider the study of such integration to be a key step in advancing the performance of case adaptation [10].

Acknowledgments. This work was funded by the Department of the Navy, Office of Naval Research (Award N00014-19-1-2655). We thank the members of the Indiana University Deep CBR group for valuable discussions.

References

1. Bromley, J., Guyon, I., LeCun, Y., Säckinger, E., Shah, R.: Signature verification using a "siamese" time delay neural network. In: Proceedings of the 6th International Conference on Neural Information Processing Systems, NIPS 1993, pp. 737–744. Morgan Kaufmann, San Francisco (1993)

2. Corchado, J., Lees, B.: Adaptation of cases for case based forecasting with neural network support. In: Pal, S.K., Dillon, T.S., Yeung, D.S. (eds.) Soft Computing in Case Based Reasoning, pp. 293–319. Springer, Berlin (2001). https://doi.org/10.1007/978-1-4471-0687-6_13
3. Craw, S., Wiratunga, N., Rowe, R.: Learning adaptation knowledge to improve case-based reasoning. Artif. Intell. **170**, 1175–1192 (2006)
4. Zhang, F., Ha, M., Wang, X., Li, X.: Case adaptation using estimators of neural network. In: Proceedings of 2004 International Conference on Machine Learning and Cybernetics (IEEE Cat. No. 04EX826), vol. 4, pp. 2162–2166 (2004)
5. Hanney, K., Keane, M.T.: Learning adaptation rules from a case-base. In: Smith, I., Faltings, B. (eds.) EWCBR 1996. LNCS, vol. 1168, pp. 179–192. Springer, Heidelberg (1996). https://doi.org/10.1007/BFb0020610
6. Jalali, V., Leake, D., Forouzandehmehr, N.: Learning and applying case adaptation rules for classification: an ensemble approach. In: Proceedings of the Twenty-Sixth International Joint Conference on Artificial Intelligence, IJCAI 2017, pp. 4874–4878 (2017)
7. Jalali, V., Leake, D.: Extending case adaptation with automatically-generated ensembles of adaptation rules. In: Delany, S.J., Ontañón, S. (eds.) ICCBR 2013. LNCS (LNAI), vol. 7969, pp. 188–202. Springer, Heidelberg (2013). https://doi.org/10.1007/978-3-642-39056-2_14
8. Jarmulak, J., Craw, S., Rowe, R.: Using case-base data to learn adaptation knowledge for design. In: Proceedings of the 17th International Joint Conference on Artificial Intelligence - Volume 2, IJCAI 2001, pp. 1011–1016. Morgan Kaufmann, San Francisco (2001)
9. Leake, D., Kinley, A., Wilson, D.: Learning to integrate multiple knowledge sources for case-based reasoning. In: Proceedings of the Fourteenth International Joint Conference on Artificial Intelligence, pp. 246–251. Morgan Kaufmann (1997)
10. Leake, D., Crandall, D.: On bringing case-based reasoning methodology to deep learning. In: Watson, I., Weber, R. (eds.) ICCBR 2020. LNCS (LNAI), vol. 12311, pp. 343–348. Springer, Cham (2020). https://doi.org/10.1007/978-3-030-58342-2_22
11. Leake, D., Ye, X.: Harmonizing case retrieval and adaptation with alternating optimization. In: Sánchez-Ruiz, A.A., Floyd, M.W. (eds.) ICCBR 2021. LNCS (LNAI), vol. 12877, pp. 125–139. Springer, Cham (2021). https://doi.org/10.1007/978-3-030-86957-1_9
12. Leake, D., Ye, X., Crandall, D.: Supporting case-based reasoning with neural networks: an illustration for case adaptation. In: Proceedings of AAAI Spring Symposium AAAI-MAKE 2021: Combining Machine Learning and Knowledge Engineering (2021). https://www.aaai-make.info/program
13. Liao, C., Liu, A., Chao, Y.: A machine learning approach to case adaptation. In: 2018 IEEE First International Conference on Artificial Intelligence and Knowledge Engineering (AIKE), pp. 106–109 (2018)
14. Martin, K., Wiratunga, N., Sani, S., Massie, S., Clos, J.: A convolutional siamese network for developing similarity knowledge in the SelfBACK dataset. In: Proceedings of the ICCBR 2017 Workshops, Doctoral Consortium, and Competitions, pp. 85–94. CEUR Workshop Proceedings (2017). http://hdl.handle.net/10059/2490
15. Mathisen, B.M., Aamodt, A., Bach, K., Langseth, H.: Learning similarity measures from data. Prog. Artif. Intell. **9**, 129–143 (2019). https://doi.org/10.1007/s13748-019-00201-2
16. Pedregosa, F., et al.: Scikit-learn: machine learning in python. J. Mach. Learn. Res. **12**, 2825–2830 (2011)

17. Policastro, C.A., Carvalho, A.C., Delbem, A.C.: Automatic knowledge learning and case adaptation with a hybrid committee approach. J. Appl. Log. **4**(1), 26–38 (2006)
18. Smyth, B., Keane, M.: Adaptation-guided retrieval: questioning the similarity assumption in reasoning. Artif. Intell. **102**(2), 249–293 (1998)
19. Ye, X., Leake, D., Huibregtse, W., Dalkilic, M.: Applying class-to-class siamese networks to explain classifications with supportive and contrastive cases. In: Watson, I., Weber, R. (eds.) ICCBR 2020. LNCS (LNAI), vol. 12311, pp. 245–260. Springer, Cham (2020). https://doi.org/10.1007/978-3-030-58342-2_16
20. Ye, X., Leake, D., Jalali, V., Crandall, D.J.: Learning adaptations for case-based classification: a neural network approach. In: Sánchez-Ruiz, A.A., Floyd, M.W. (eds.) ICCBR 2021. LNCS (LNAI), vol. 12877, pp. 279–293. Springer, Cham (2021). https://doi.org/10.1007/978-3-030-86957-1_19
21. Ye, X., Zhao, Z., Leake, D., Wang, X., Crandall, D.J.: Applying the case difference heuristic to learn adaptations from deep network features. CoRR abs/2107.07095 (2021). https://arxiv.org/abs/2107.07095

A Deep Learning Approach to Solving Morphological Analogies

Esteban Marquer[1](✉), Safa Alsaidi[1], Amandine Decker[1], Pierre-Alexandre Murena[2], and Miguel Couceiro[1]

[1] Université de Lorraine, CNRS, LORIA, 54000 Nancy, France
{esteban.marquer,miguel.couceiro}@loria.fr
[2] HIIT, Aalto University, Helsinki, Finland
pierre-alexandre.murena@aalto.fi

Abstract. Analogical proportions are statements of the form "A is to B as C is to D". They support analogical inference and provide a logical framework to address learning, transfer, and explainability concerns. This logical framework finds useful applications in AI and natural language processing (NLP). In this paper, we address the problem of solving morphological analogies using a retrieval approach named ANNr. Our deep learning framework encodes structural properties of analogical proportions and relies on a specifically designed embedding model capturing morphological characteristics of words. We demonstrate that ANNr outperforms the state of the art on 11 languages. We analyze ANNr results for Navajo and Georgian, languages on which the model performs worst and best, to explore potential correlations between the mistakes of ANNr and linguistic properties.

Keywords: Analogy solving · Neural networks · Retrieval · Morphological word embeddings

1 Introduction

An analogy, or analogical proportion, is a relation between four elements A, B, C, and D meaning "A is to B as C is to D", often written as $A : B :: C : D$. For example, *cat* : *kitten* :: *dog* : *puppy* and *cat* : *cats* :: *dog* : *dogs* are two analogies between words. Notice that the transformation between *cat* and *kitten* is a semantic one (*kitten* is a young *cat*) while the one between *cat* and *cats* is morphological (*cats* is the plural of *cat*, obtained with the suffix "*-s*"). We call the first example a *semantic analogy* and the second a *morphological analogy*. It can be argued that morphological analogies are covered by semantic analogies, but morphological analogies can be manipulated even without knowledge

This research was partially supported by TAILOR, a project funded by EU Horizon 2020 research and innovation program under GA No 952215, and the Inria Project Lab "Hybrid Approaches for Interpretable AI" (HyAIAI).

M. T. Keane and N. Wiratunga (Eds.): ICCBR 2022, LNAI 13405, pp. 159–174, 2022.
https://doi.org/10.1007/978-3-031-14923-8_11

about the semantics of a word. For example, *cat* : *cats* :: *Balrog* : *Balrogs* is understandable even without knowing what a *Balrog* is.

There are two main tasks associated with analogical proportions. One is *analogy detection* that refers to task of deciding whether a quadruple A, B, C, D forms a valid analogy $A : B :: C : D$. The other is *analogy solving* that refers to the task of finding possible values x for which $A : B :: C : x$ constitutes a valid analogy. Expressions $A : B :: C : x$ for an indeterminate x are referred to as *analogical equations*. We further detail the two tasks and related approaches to tackle them in Sect. 2.

Analogy solving can be seen as a form of case-based reasoning (CBR) [18]. Indeed, in CBR the goal is to find a solution s_t to a problem p_t using a set of problems P, a set of solutions S, and cases $(p, s) \in P \times S$ associating a problem p with one of its solutions s. The first step, called *retrieval*[1], is to select k cases in the case base according to some criteria related to p_t. The k retrieved cases are then used to propose a target solution s_t, this is the *adaptation* step. When $k = 1$, we can formulate the adaptation step as solving the analogical equation $p_1 : s_1 :: p_t : x$, with s_t one of the equation's solution. There are other ways to relate analogies and CBR, albeit less related to this paper. For example, if $k = 3$ one can look at cases where $p_1 : p_2 :: p_3 : p_t$ is valid and $s_1 : s_2 :: s_3 : x$ is solvable in S [18]. Like above, s_t would be solution to the equation.

As mentioned in the first paragraph, analogies can subsume relations of different nature (semantic or morphological in the example, but one could build syntactic analogies on sentences or geometric analogies on numbers or images). In this article, we focus on solving morphological analogies. While recent approaches to tackle this problem using symbolic methods achieve state of the art performance on analogy solving [9,12,23], they are inherently restricted to a subset of morphology as they are not able to account for "irregular" cases like *cat* : *cats* :: *child* : *children*. We use deep learning to learn morphological features of words to address this issue. Following a similar idea, Lim *et al.* [19] proposed a deep learning model to tackle semantic analogies on words, based on the analogical framework of Miclet *et al.* [21] and Prade and Richard [24]. Unlike previous works in deep learning, the architecture integrates the characteristics of analogies by design and relies heavily on pretrained GloVe embeddings to compute word representations. We argue that their approach, which already deals with analogies on words, can be applied to morphological analogies. As mentioned in our previous work [1], although the embedding model used by Lim *et al.* is well suited for semantic analogies, it results in lower performance on the morphological counterpart. In our previous work [1] we addressed morphological analogy detection by proposing an embedding model targeting word morphology, and we extend those results for analogy solving in the present work.

To summarize, the main contributions of this paper are the following: (*i*) we demonstrate the importance of well suited embedding space for analogy manipulation, and provide empirical evidence that analogy detection is helpful in obtain-

[1] Except in this paragraph, we use *retrieval* in the general meaning and not the one of CBR in this article.

ing a well suited embedding model for analogy solving, and (*ii*) we propose a deep learning framework that outperforms state of the art approaches to solve analogies that capture morphological features.

In the remainder of this paper we first introduce the problem of morphological analogies with a brief state of the art in Sect. 2. We describe the three components of our retrieval approach (ANNc, ANNr and the morphological embedding model) in Sect. 3, and detail our experiments in Sect. 4. First, we describe the dataset used in Sect. 4.1, then compare performance with different training procedures and against baselines in Subsects. 4.2 to 4.4. Finally, in Subsect. 4.5, we explore mistakes made by ANNr on Navajo and Georgian to get insight on the behavior and flaws of our approach. As per tradition, we conclude our paper and offer perspectives on some key aspects in Sect. 5.

2 The Problem of Morphological Analogy

An *analogical proportion* is a 4-ary relation denoted by $A : B :: C : D$ and interpreted as "A is to B as C is to D". In this paper, we focus on morphological analogies, *i.e.*, analogies on words A, B, C, and D that capture morphological transformations of words (*e.g.*, conjugation or declension).

Analogical Proportions. The importance of analogy in morphology has been long known [26], and it has been mathematically formalized following the early works of Lepage [14,16]. These works paved the way towards the current view of *analogical proportions* [21,24] as a 4-ary relation that verifies the following postulates for all A, B, C, and D: reflexivity ($A : B :: A : B$), symmetry ($A : B :: C : D \rightarrow C : D :: A : B$), and central permutation ($A : B :: C : D \rightarrow A : C :: B : D$). It is not difficult to verify that other equivalent forms can be derived using symmetry and central permutation: $D : B :: C : A$, $C : A :: D : B$, $B : A :: D : C$, $D : C :: B : A$ and $B : D :: A : C$. The two main trends in the research on analogies, namely *analogy detection* and *analogy solving*, are described below.

Analogy Detection. The analogy detection task corresponds to classifying quadruples $\langle A, B, C, D\rangle$ into valid or invalid analogies. In particular, in the context of semantic analogies, Bayoudh *et al.* [3] proposed to use Kolmogorov complexity as a distance measure between words in order to define a conceptually significant analogical proportion and to classify quadruples as valid or invalid analogies. A data-driven alternative was implemented by Lim *et al.* [19], by learning the classifier directly as a neural network. In particular, analogy detection has been used in the context of analogical grids [9], *i.e.*, matrices of transformations of various words, similar to paradigm tables in linguistics [8].

Analogy Solving. The analogy solving task corresponds to inferring the fourth term that makes an analogy valid. This task is by far the most investigated in the analogy literature and several methodologies have been proposed to solve it.

The approaches in the next paragraph *generate* the fourth element to solve the analogy, but it is also possible to leverage a list of candidates and *retrieve* the most fitting fourth term to solve the analogy. Many approaches in embedding spaces, including ours, use the latter method as generation from an embedding space can be challenging. In our case the candidates are the set of all the words in the dataset, called the *vocabulary*.

In the context of solving morphological analogies, the main trend follows the seminal work of Lepage and Ando [16] by exploiting the aforementioned postulates of analogical proportions. For instance, Lepage [15] uses these postulates to address multiple characteristics of words, such as their length, the occurrence of letters and of patterns. Following the results of Yvon [29] about closed form solutions, the *Alea* algorithm [12] proposes a Monte-Carlo estimation of the solutions of an analogical equation by sampling among multiple sub-transformations. Recently, a more empirical approach was proposed by Murena *et al.* [23], which does not rely on the axioms of analogical proportions. Their method consists in finding the simplest among all possible transformations from A to B which could also apply to C, using the Kolmogorov complexity of the transformations. We provide more details on the latter two approaches in Subsect. 4.3.

Analogy in Embedding Spaces. A particular and noteworthy form of analogical proportions in vector spaces is the *parallelogram rule* that states that four vectors e_A, e_B, e_C, and e_D are in analogical proportion if $e_D - e_C = e_B - e_A$. This relation has been used since the first works on analogy [25], and it is a key element in the methodology employed by the recent neural-based approaches [6, 22]. In this setting, the parallelogram rule is applied in some learned embedding space, with e_A, e_B, e_C, and e_D being the embeddings of four elements A, B, C, and D. We detail two of the most used methods for solving analogies in embedding spaces, namely 3CosAdd [22] and 3CosMul [17], in Subsect. 4.3. These two approaches implicitly generate a solution e_x and retrieve the closest candidate from the vocabulary. However, Chen *et al.* [4] argue that the latter two methods significantly differ from human performance. Nonetheless, frameworks based on analogy datasets like those mentioned in [19] appear to bridge this gap in performance. Similarly to the method of Lim *et al.* [19], ours learns a model for both the analogy detection and solving tasks in morphology. This approach models analogy as described by the analogy data, unlike 3CosAdd and 3CosMul that rely on fixed formulas and on the expected properties of the embedding space.

3 Proposed Approach

In this section we present the approach we use, illustrated in Fig. 1. There are 3 components in our framework, and they are described in Subsect. 3.1: a classification model (ANNc) and a retrieval model (ANNr), both taking as input embeddings computed by a morphological embedding model. We then detail our training and evaluation procedures in Subsect. 3.2. Additional information about the parameters of our model are given in Subsect. 4.2.

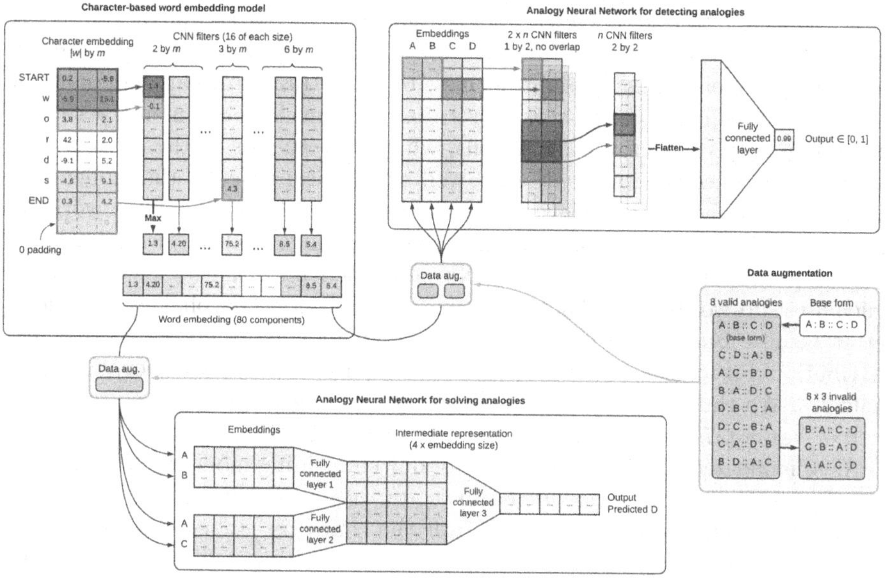

Fig. 1. Morphological embedding model, data augmentation, analogy classification (ANNc) and analogy retrieval (ANNr) models.

3.1 Classification, Retrieval and Embedding Models

The models described in this subsection follow the structure of the ones proposed in [1,19] and are schematized in Fig. 1.

Classification. The neural network classifier follows the idea that an analogy $A : B :: C : D$ is valid if A and B differ in the same way as C and D. We call this model *Analogy Neural Network for classification* (ANNc). Technical details on this model can be found in our previous works [1,2].

Retrieval. An approach to solving $A : B :: C : \mathbf{x}$ is to find how e_B differs from e_A and to generate an $e_{\mathbf{x}}$ that differs from e_C in the same way. Central permutation (see Sect. 2) allows us to apply the same operations on $A : C :: B : \mathbf{x}$, to obtain $e_{\mathbf{x}}$ from e_B using the difference between e_A and e_C.

Following this intuition, the model applies two separate fully connected layers with ReLU activation to determine the relation between e_A and e_B on the one side (*fully connected layer 1* in Fig. 1) and the one between e_A and e_C on the other side (*fully connected layer 2*). Those layers also encode the necessary information from e_B and e_C, respectively, while taking e_A into account. Finally, *fully connected layer 3* (with no activation function) generates $e_{\mathbf{x}}$ the embedding of the predicted $\mathbf{x}$ from all the extracted information. We refer to this model as the *Analogy Neural Network for retrieval* (ANNr).

Embedding Model. Most deep learning methodologies rely on real-valued vector representations of the data called *embeddings*. For many applications, there are embedding models available and that have been pretrained on large amounts of data, as it saves users the cost of fully training them. It is commonly accepted that the quality of such representations, which corresponds to the amount and nature of the encoded information as well as the properties of the embedding space, is a key factor to achieve higher performance. In our previous work [1] and early experiments with pretrained word embeddings models (*fasttext*, GloVe, Bert Multilingual and *word2vec*) ANNc performed poorly. Note that *fasttext*, which uses sub-words instead of words and is thus closer to morphology, produced better results. Such general-purpose embedding models, oriented towards the distributional semantics of words, seem ill-suited to manipulate morphological analogies. We thus proposed in [1] a word embedding model inspired from the work of Vania [27], that is more suited to morphological tasks.

As schematized in Fig. 1, the inputs of our embedding model are the characters of a word, which are embedded into vectors of size m using a learned embedding matrix. Multiple CNN filters go over the character embeddings, spanning over the full embeddings of 2 to 6 characters, and resulting in filter sizes between 2 by m and 6 by m. For each filter, the model computes the maximum output to serve as a component of the word embedding. This last operation keeps only salient patterns detected by each of the filters, and forces each CNN filter to specialize in identifying a specific pattern of characters. As we use character embeddings to encode character features, the model can capture patterns such as "-ing" but also "vowel-vowel-consonant". This flexibility is useful to deal with phenomena like *euphony* which is, in very simple terms, a change of sound to make a word easier to pronounce (*e.g.*, *far* becomes *further* when adding the suffix *-ther*). These character patterns correspond to *morphemes*, which are the minimal units of morphology. For further details see [1].

3.2 Training and Evaluation

Data Augmentation. The postulates of analogical proportions described in Sect. 2 enable the generation multiple analogies from each quadruple in our analogy dataset. We refer to this process as data augmentation. It extends the amount of data available, but also makes the models learn how to fit the formal postulates of analogy.

Given a valid analogy $A : B :: C : D$, we generate 7 more valid analogies, namely, $A : C :: B : D$, $D : B :: C : A$, $C : A :: D : B$, $C : D :: A : B$, $B : A :: D : C$, $D : C :: B : A$, $B : D :: A : C$. In practice, data augmentation is applied after the embedding model as shown in Fig. 1. Further details on the training of the classifier can be found in [1].

Training Criterion. As in previous works [1,2,19], we use the Binary Cross-Entropy (BCE) loss to train the classification model. For the retrieval model (to solve analogies), we experiment with multiple training objectives designed to avoid a collapse of the embedding space when training the embedding model[2].

Our first loss is based on the *Cosine Embedding Loss* (CEL):

$$\mathrm{CEL}(e_D, \widehat{e_D}, y) = \begin{cases} 1 - \cos(e_D, \widehat{e_D}), & \text{if } y = 1 \\ \max(0, \cos(e_D, \widehat{e_D})), & \text{if } y = -1 \end{cases} \tag{1}$$

where e_D is the embedding of D and $\widehat{e_D}$ a prediction for e_D. Here, $y = 1$ if e_D and $\widehat{e_D}$ are to be close, and $y = -1$ otherwise. Given an analogy $A : B :: C : D$, we encourage $\widehat{e_D}$ to be close to the actual e_D and far from e_A, e_B, and e_C the embeddings of A, B, and C by using the sum:

$$\begin{aligned} \mathcal{L}_{\mathrm{CEL}} = &\ \mathrm{CEL}(e_A, \widehat{e_D}, -1) + \mathrm{CEL}(e_B, \widehat{e_D}, -1) \\ &+ \mathrm{CEL}(e_C, \widehat{e_D}, -1) + \mathrm{CEL}(e_D, \widehat{e_D}, 1) \end{aligned} \tag{2}$$

We follow a similar intuition for two losses based on the L^2 distance or *Mean Squared Error* (MSE):

$$MSE(e_D, \widehat{e_D}) = \frac{1}{n} \sum_{i \in [1,n]} (e_{D,i} - \widehat{e_{D,i}})^2 \tag{3}$$

where $e_{D,i}$ is the i-th component of e_D and n is the number of dimensions of the embeddings. We encourage $\widehat{e_D}$ to be close to the actual e_D and far from other embeddings by normalizing $\mathrm{MSE}(e_D, \widehat{e_D})$ based on distances between other embeddings. Normalizing using the full distribution of distances between embeddings would be very accurate, but computing embeddings of the full vocabulary for each training step would be computationally heavy.

Instead, we experiment with two smaller-scale normalization. A first option is to normalize with regards to the possible pairs of elements in the quadruple:

$$\mathcal{L}_{\text{norm. other}} = \frac{1 + 6 \times MSE(e_D, \widehat{e_D})}{1 + \sum_{a,b \in \{(A,B),(A,C),(A,D),(B,C),(B,D),(C,D)\}} MSE(e_a, e_b)} \tag{4}$$

A second option is to normalize with regards to some random embedding e_z:

$$\mathcal{L}_{\text{norm. random}} = \frac{1 + MSE(e_D, \widehat{e_D})}{1 + MSE(e_z, \widehat{e_D})} \tag{5}$$

As the model is trained with batches of randomly selected samples, we associate each prediction with an unrelated embedding e_z by permuting e_D along the batch dimension.

Finally, we consider the sum of all the above loss terms, in order to determine whether their combination overcomes the limitations of each:

$$\mathcal{L}_{\text{all}} = \mathcal{L}_{\mathrm{CEL}} + \mathcal{L}_{\text{norm. other}} + \mathcal{L}_{\text{norm. random}} \tag{6}$$

[2] An example of embedding space collapse: moving all the embeddings in a smaller area of the embedding space by multiplying them by 10^5 minimizes $\mathrm{MSE}(e_D, \widehat{e_D})$ but does not improve retrieval performance, as the relative distance between embeddings does not change.

Inference and Evaluation. The output of ANNr is a real-valued vector in the embedding space, but not necessarily the exact embedding of a word. As the model is not equipped with a decoder for the embedding space, we do not have direct access to the word corresponding to a generated embedding. Instead, we use cosine distance[3] to retrieve the closest embeddings among the embeddings of the whole vocabulary as the model prediction. To evaluate the performance we use top-k retrieval accuracy.

4 Experiments

In this section, we describe some of our experiments on the retrieval model. The code can be found on GitHub[4]. In Sect. 4.1, we briefly describe the dataset used and explain our choice of training procedure in Subsect. 4.2. The performance of our model is compared with state of the art baselines in Subsect. 4.3, and we explore how far the model prediction is from the expected output in Subsect. 4.4. Model mistakes on Navajo and Georgian are studied in Subsect. 4.5. Our experiments are implemented in PyTorch and PyTorch Lightning, and were carried out using computational clusters equipped with GPUs from the Grid'5000 testbed (*grele* and *grue* clusters, see https://www.grid5000.fr).

4.1 Data

For our experiments, we used the analogies from 11 languages available in the Siganalogies dataset [20]: Spanish, German, Finnish, Russian, Turkish, Georgian, Navajo, Arabic (Romanized), Hungarian, and Maltese extracted from Sigmorphon2016 [5], and Japanese from the Japanese Bigger Analogy Test Set [10]. It is noteworthy that we use the data of the original Sigmorphon2016 dataset, which produces a different set of analogies than the one used by [9,23]. In particular, Siganalogies contains analogies that are hard to solve for a non-data-driven approach (*e.g.*, "be : was :: go : went").

For training and evaluation we use the original split of the Sigmorphon2016 [5] dataset, from which we extract the analogies independently. For the Japanese Bigger Analogy Test Set [10] however, no such split is available and so we split[5] the extracted analogies into 70% for the training, 5% for the development, and 25% for the test set. To maintain reasonable training and evaluation times, we used up to 50000 analogies of each set, randomly selected when loading the data.

---

[3] We experimented with both Euclidean and cosine distance, the former giving slightly better results in most cases, even though the difference is not significant.

[4] https://github.com/EMarquer/nn-morpho-analogy-iccbr.

[5] The samples were randomly selected using a fixed random seed.

Table 1. Top-1 accuracy (*i.e.*, precision, in %) of ANNr when training for 50 epochs with the embedding from ANNc and from scratch. We report mean ± std. over 10 random seeds. Boldface results are the best for each language.

	$\mathcal{L}_{\text{CEL}}$	$\mathcal{L}_{\text{norm. other}}$	$\mathcal{L}_{\text{norm. random}}$	$\mathcal{L}_{\text{all}}$
Arabic (from scratch)	8.53 ± 0.89	16.01 ± 4.20	27.90 ± 4.66	16.45 ± 4.35
Arabic (transfer)	6.86 ± 1.08	68.84 ± 5.54	**73.08 ± 4.19**	68.59 ± 3.17
Finnish (from scratch)	21.31 ± 2.31	64.14 ± 7.07	47.25 ± 9.82	57.35 ± 5.46
Finnish (transfer)	6.23 ± 1.27	87.37 ± 2.11	**90.15 ± 1.42**	89.90 ± 1.61
Georgian (from scratch)	34.14 ± 3.44	76.33 ± 7.92	68.56 ± 9.85	77.66 ± 5.42
Georgian (transfer)	16.82 ± 3.33	95.64 ± 1.12	**97.12 ± 0.26**	95.09 ± 0.65
German (from scratch)	29.31 ± 3.42	64.05 ± 11.12	51.95 ± 11.21	54.91 ± 8.81
German (transfer)	14.17 ± 2.02	90.66 ± 0.66	91.47 ± 0.55	**91.52 ± 0.62**
Hungarian (from scratch)	24.35 ± 1.64	50.11 ± 4.72	41.25 ± 9.39	55.54 ± 4.46
Hungarian (transfer)	11.61 ± 1.93	**89.85 ± 1.52**	89.42 ± 1.43	88.79 ± 1.78
Japanese (from scratch)	23.33 ± 2.71	9.76 ± 2.52	34.00 ± 8.54	11.46 ± 3.54
Japanese (transfer)	26.89 ± 1.66	83.10 ± 0.92	**86.12 ± 0.76**	74.14 ± 1.09
Maltese (from scratch)	5.70 ± 0.88	48.21 ± 9.24	72.74 ± 3.52	51.82 ± 10.22
Maltese (transfer)	5.63 ± 0.84	95.94 ± 0.73	**97.16 ± 0.30**	91.69 ± 1.55
Navajo (from scratch)	6.81 ± 0.69	19.36 ± 3.07	23.66 ± 2.99	24.69 ± 2.49
Navajo (transfer)	6.34 ± 0.64	**53.73 ± 1.58**	52.22 ± 1.18	52.45 ± 1.97
Russian (from scratch)	12.21 ± 1.72	38.46 ± 4.77	36.80 ± 3.84	41.04 ± 4.00
Russian (transfer)	4.47 ± 0.68	74.08 ± 1.24	71.66 ± 0.76	**76.12 ± 1.11**
Spanish (from scratch)	26.76 ± 1.70	84.26 ± 2.93	78.31 ± 5.91	81.76 ± 4.19
Spanish (transfer)	20.67 ± 4.32	91.03 ± 1.63	**92.63 ± 1.25**	91.12 ± 1.65
Turkish (from scratch)	13.30 ± 1.07	31.71 ± 4.40	42.82 ± 5.49	39.16 ± 6.82
Turkish (transfer)	7.41 ± 1.63	86.17 ± 1.66	88.36 ± 1.17	**88.45 ± 1.12**

4.2 Refining the Training Procedure

We experiment with the four losses mentioned in Subsect. 3.2. We also consider two training procedures: we transfer the embedding model learned in the ANNc task, and we compare the results with training the embedding model from scratch with ANNr to confirm the benefits of transferring. When transferring, we obtained the best results by first freezing[6] the embedding model and training until ANNr converges[7], then unfreezing the embedding model and resuming training. We limited the total training time to 50 epochs for ANNr, and 20 for ANNc. For Japanese which has less than 50,000 training analogies (18,487), we limit ANNr training to 150 epochs. In average, half of the training epochs are needed to converge with the embedding frozen, but this varies between runs and

[6] By freezing we mean that the parameters of the model are not updated.

[7] By convergence we mean that there is no improvement in the development set loss.

ranges between 11 and 42 epochs out of 50 (18 and 68 for Japanese). Comparative results are reported in Table 1.

We use a character embedding size (m in Fig. 1) of 64 and 16×5 filters spanning over 2 to 6 input characters, resulting in embeddings of 80 dimensions. We use 128 filters for ANNc (n in Fig. 1). We use Adam [11] with the recommended learning rate of 10^{-3}. For retrieval, we use a learning rate of 10^{-5} for the embedding model which produced better results experimentally in both transfer and non-transfer settings.

Transferring Embeddings from ANNc Significantly Improves ANNr Performance. A first conclusion from the results in Table 1 is that reusing the embedding model from ANNc significantly improves the final performance, in addition to reducing the convergence time, which is expected when performing transfer learning between closely related tasks. When training the embedding from scratch, we observe low performance as shown in Table 1. Removing the limit on the total training time does not significantly improve those results. This indicates that ANNr is not suited to learning the embedding model and requires a pretrained embedding. ANNc seems suitable for this task.

Normalized MSE Performs better than Cosine Embedding Loss. A second effect we observe in Table 1 is that even though we use cosine similarity to retrieve the solution, $\mathcal{L}_{\text{CEL}}$ is by far the worst performing criterion. In most cases when performing transfer, using $\mathcal{L}_{\text{norm. random}}$ performs better than or comparably to $\mathcal{L}_{\text{norm. other}}$ and $\mathcal{L}_{\text{all}}$. $\mathcal{L}_{\text{all}}$ only performs better than the other criteria on Russian. Based on these observations, we only report the results for $\mathcal{L}_{\text{norm. random}}$ afterwards, but results with $\mathcal{L}_{\text{norm. other}}$ and $\mathcal{L}_{\text{all}}$ follow similar trends.

4.3 Performance Comparison with State of the Art Methods

We use two state of the art methods mentioned in Sect. 2 as baselines: the models of [12] and [23], that we respectively refer to as *Alea* and *Kolmo*. We also report the performance of standard arithmetic methods for analogies in embedding spaces, namely, 3CosAdd [22] and 3CosMul [17] described below.

Alea [12]. The *Alea* algorithm implements a Monte-Carlo estimation of the solutions of an analogy, by sampling among multiple sub-transformations. Those sub-transformations are obtained by considering the words as bags of characters and generating permutations of characters that are present in B but not in A on one side, and characters of C on the other. Intuitively, if we consider $bag(A)$ the bag of characters in A, *Alea* considers $bag(D) = (bag(B) - bag(A)) + bag(C)$ and thus D is a permutation of the characters of $bag(D)$. For each quadruple $A : B :: C : D$, we generate $\rho = 100$ potential solutions for $A : B :: C : \mathbf{x}$ and select the most frequent one.

Kolmo [23]. The generation model proposed by Murena *et al.* considers some transformation f such that $B = f(A)$ and $f(C)$ is computable. The simplest transformation f is usually the one human use to solve analogies [23], and is

Table 2. Top-1 accuracy (in %) of ANNr using $\mathcal{L}_{\text{norm. random}}$ against the baselines. We report mean ± std. over 10 random seeds for our models, and when relevant the timeout rate for the baselines.

		Arithmetic on ANNc emb.		Symbolic baselines		Timeout (%)	
	ANNr	3CosAdd [22]	3CosMul [17]	Alea [12]	Kolmo [23]	Alea	Kolmo
Arabic	**73.08** ± 4.19	66.11 ± 3.09	55.78 ± 2.97	26.43	29.03	–	0.039
Finnish	**90.15** ± 1.42	87.10 ± 2.61	82.76 ± 3.38	23.76	22.65	0.040	3.802
Georgian	**97.12** ± 0.26	95.51 ± 0.73	91.36 ± 2.38	85.19	80.15	–	0.026
German	**91.47** ± 0.55	82.24 ± 4.35	79.17 ± 5.31	84.19	55.05	0.023	1.998
Hungarian	**89.42** ± 1.43	85.60 ± 2.77	74.92 ± 5.69	35.49	31.68	0.002	0.102
Japanese	**86.12** ± 0.76	73.29 ± 4.36	65.02 ± 5.34	4.03	14.35	–	–
Maltese	**97.16** ± 0.30	95.60 ± 2.22	78.37 ± 1.45	73.47	68.48	–	0.330
Navajo	**52.22** ± 1.18	45.20 ± 3.05	43.71 ± 2.54	15.82	17.82	–	0.018
Russian	**71.66** ± 0.76	58.52 ± 2.65	58.49 ± 2.81	41.59	33.52	–	0.334
Spanish	**92.63** ± 1.25	91.07 ± 1.85	85.86 ± 4.18	82.54	73.89	–	0.188
Turkish	**88.36** ± 1.17	78.62 ± 2.24	57.37 ± 3.04	41.88	39.33	0.028	0.496

found by minimizing the Kolmogorov complexity of f. This complexity is estimated by first expressing f using a language of operations (insertion, deletion, *etc.*), and computing the length of the resulting program. Unlike *Alea*, *Kolmo* is able to handle mechanisms like reduplication (repeating part of a word).

Arithmetic on Embeddings. 3CosAdd [22] and 3CosMul [17] are standard methods to retrieve the fourth element of an analogy within an embedding space, and are still used even if their limitations are known. In Table 2, we report results of 3CosAdd and 3CosMul applied on the embeddings trained with ANNc to measure the improvement brought by ANNr. 3CosAdd (7) can be seen as the parallelogram rule ($D = B - A + C$) with a cosine similarity to recover the closest existing solution. As 3CosMul (8) is harder to describe intuitively, we refer the reader to [17] for a detailed description. To avoid a 0 denominator, a ε (small) is added in (8).

$$\text{3CosAdd} = \underset{e_D}{\text{argmax}}\, cos(e_D, e_B - e_A + e_C) \tag{7}$$

$$\text{3CosMul} = \underset{e_D}{\text{argmax}}\, \frac{cos(e_D, e_B) cos(e_D, e_C)}{cos(e_D, e_A) + \varepsilon} \tag{8}$$

Timeout on Alea *and* Kolmo. On a small portion of the dataset, *Alea* and *Kolmo* can take a significantly longer time to compute the results (more than 10 s against usually less than a second). For practical purposes, we interrupt the resolutions that take longer than 10 s and consider that the baseline failed to solve the analogy. Details of the portion of such cases on the test data are reported in Table 2, and it can be seen that this technical shortcut does not have a major impact on the measured baseline performance.

Table 3. Top-k accuracy (in %) of ANNr using $\mathcal{L}_{\text{norm. random}}$ for $k \in \{1, 3, 5, 10\}$. We report mean ± std. over 10 random seeds.

	Top-1	Top-3	Top-5	Top-10
Arabic	73.08 ± 4.19	89.05 ± 2.43	92.68 ± 1.74	95.69 ± 1.04
Finnish	90.15 ± 1.42	96.73 ± 0.87	97.57 ± 0.63	98.28 ± 0.40
Georgian	97.12 ± 0.26	98.86 ± 0.16	99.25 ± 0.16	99.58 ± 0.10
German	91.47 ± 0.55	96.99 ± 0.41	97.84 ± 0.39	98.50 ± 0.31
Hungarian	89.42 ± 1.43	97.48 ± 0.73	98.57 ± 0.54	99.15 ± 0.34
Japanese	86.12 ± 0.76	98.48 ± 0.19	99.70 ± 0.15	99.88 ± 0.09
Maltese	97.16 ± 0.30	99.50 ± 0.11	99.75 ± 0.08	99.89 ± 0.04
Navajo	52.22 ± 1.18	77.67 ± 1.13	85.89 ± 0.90	92.87 ± 0.80
Russian	71.66 ± 0.76	95.18 ± 0.54	97.24 ± 0.44	98.18 ± 0.29
Spanish	92.63 ± 1.25	97.54 ± 0.43	98.19 ± 0.32	98.65 ± 0.26
Turkish	88.36 ± 1.17	97.88 ± 0.55	98.79 ± 0.40	99.29 ± 0.25

Performance Against the Baseline. As can be seen in Table 2, ANNr significantly outperforms the symbolic baselines (all Student t-test p-values under 0.001 except for German, with $p < 0.19$), with the added benefit of a shorter and bounded computation time. We observe the opposite as what is presented in [17], as 3CosAdd significantly outperforms 3CosMul (all t-test p-values under 0.005 except for Russian, with $p > 0.8$). This could be due to having an embedding model trained with a focus on analogies, but no further experiments were performed to confirm this assumption. ANNr significantly outperforms 3CosAdd in all cases (t-test p-value all under 0.001 except for Maltese, with $p < 0.04$), with larger differences in Japanese and Russian (+13%), followed by Turkish (+10%), German (+9%), Navajo and Arabic (+7%). The largest increase with regards to symbolic baselines can be observed on Japanese. Symbolic methods based on characters are expected to have trouble handling complex modification of the characters themselves, while methods using character embeddings have more leeway. All approaches perform poorly on Navajo which is a language with complex verb morphology [7] (further details in Subsect. 4.5).

4.4 Distance of the Expected Result

While for some languages (mainly Navajo but also Russian and Arabic) ANNr struggles to reach a high overall accuracy, further analysis of the results indicates that the expected solution can be found in the close vicinity of the prediction. Notably, some analogical equations can have multiple viable solutions (*e.g.*, *sing* : *sing* :: *am* : $\mathbf{x}$ for which *am* and *are* are viable). For such cases, finding a particular solution as the top candidate is less likely as other viable solutions could be preferred, which can explain part of the increase of performance.

Indeed, as can be seen in Table 3, looking at the top 3 solutions increases the accuracy of the Navajo models from 52% to 78% in average, from 73% to 89% for Arabic and from 72% to 95% for Russian. Increasing the margin to the top 10 brings the accuracy of all models to at least 98%, except for Arabic and Navajo which are at 95% and 92% respectively. Compared to the size of the vocabulary of each language, a margin of 3 or even 10 is very small, yet enough to find the correct solution in most cases.

4.5 Case Analysis: Navajo and Georgian

To get further insight on the behavior of the model, we perform a more detailed analysis of where the model makes mistakes for Navajo and Georgian, the languages on which ANNr performs worst and best respectively. To be able to analyze more in-depth, we consider only one of the 10 models trained in the transfer setting with $\mathcal{L}_{\text{norm. random}}$.

Overall, there is no significant predominance of a particular permutation nor of a particular postulate (symmetry, central permutation, nor any usual combination of both) in the mistakes on either Navajo or Georgian. Additionally, less than 0.3% of mistakes on Navajo involve expected cases of reflexivity (*i.e.*, forms like $A : B :: A : B$ or $A : A :: B : B$), and no such case was observed for Georgian, indicating that reflexivity is well handled by ANNr.

Violations of Stronger Versions of Reflexivity. We notice that 47.49% of all mistakes in Georgian are cases where either: (*i*) $A = B$ but $C \neq D$ and the model predicts $\widehat{D} = C$ or, similarly, by central permutation (41.06% of all mistakes), or (*ii*) $A \neq B$ but $C = D$ and the model predicts $\widehat{D} \neq C$, or $A \neq C$ but $B = D$ and the model predicts $\widehat{D} \neq B$ (6.42% of all mistakes). For example for (*i*), კოხტა : კოხტა :: გონიერი : **x** expects გონიერმა but გონიერი is predicted. In English, a similar situation would be *sing* : *sing* :: *am* : **x**, in which expecting **x** = *are* is counter-intuitive if the underlying transformation from A to B ("pos=V, per=1, num=SG" to "pos=V, per=1, num=PL") is not provided. It is interesting to note that the model makes more mistakes when presented with an apparent instance of identity (*sing* : *sing* :: *am* : **x**) than when the expected answer is the same as one of the elements (*am* : *are* :: *sing* : **x**). This corresponds to the behavior of humans, who would prefer a simpler relation (identity is simpler that any morphological transformation) while being able to transfer from a complex case to a simpler one. This matches the data augmentation process for ANNc, $A : A :: B : C$ is invalid while $A : B :: C : C$ is not generated.

The permutations described in (*i*) above correspond to violations of stronger versions of reflexivity, introduced in [14]: strong inner reflexivity ($A : A :: B : \mathbf{x} \rightarrow \mathbf{x} = B$) and strong reflexivity ($A : B :: A : \mathbf{x} \rightarrow \mathbf{x} = B$). ANNr appears to implicitly learn the above properties. However, we can see in Table 3 that the expected answer is usually very close to the predicted $e_{\mathbf{x}}$, including cases when it violates strong inner reflexivity and strong reflexivity.

Complex Morphology of Navajo Verbs. Verbs correspond to 73.79% of all mistakes in Navajo (75.35% if we exclude cases described in the previous paragraph). Navajo is originally an oral language of the Native-American languages, and according to Eddington and Lachler [7] "Verb stem inflectional patterns in Navajo are arguably one of the most intractable problems in modern Athabaskan linguist studies". They also refer to a work by Leer [13] which states that this complexity can be attributed to "analogical innovation, which is thus quite difficult to analyze synchronically". This could explain why symbolic baselines have a low performance on Navajo even if ANNr reaches above 92% of accuracy using the 10 most likely solutions.

The remaining mistakes in Navajo are composed of 21.11% of nouns in the first or second person of singular, both mixing prefixing and alternation but including variations which are hard to predict from the A, B, and C alone (*e.g.*, ajá́ád: shijá́ád:: atsoo': sitsoo' ach'íí': nich'íí':: sáanii: nizáanii).

5 Conclusion and Perspectives

In conclusion, we propose ANNr and a fitting training procedure for morphological analogies. Our approach outperforms state of the art symbolic baselines as well as more traditional methods on embedding spaces. We demonstrate the added value of ANNr compared to 3CosAdd and 3CosMul and provide in-depth analysis of results for two languages, displaying interesting properties of our framework on morphology. We provide *ad hoc* explanations of the behaviour of ANNr using mistakes made by the model, and explain why some unexpected predictions made by the model could be desirable, like the fact that our model prevents violations of strong reflexivity and strong inner reflexivity.

We think that the ANNc/ANNr framework can generalize to analogies on a wide range of data types and applications. In that direction, our work defines a more general framework for analogy solving by proposing a generic pipeline: we propose to pretrain an embedding model using ANNc and use it as a basis for ANNr. This makes training analogy solving from analogical data possible even without standard pretrained embedding models like GloVe as long as analogical data is available. Our framework could be expanded by using ANNc to check ANNr predictions. Our preliminary experiments confirm that mistakes can be detected that way. In practice, this could also determine viable solutions among the retrieval results, in cases where more than one solution is possible (*e.g.*, *sing* : *sing* :: *am* : $\mathbf{x}$ for which *am* and *are* are viable solutions).

A key challenge in the future will be unsupervised analogy discovery, which would complement our framework and allow analogy solving without the need of manually labeled data. Another useful extension is complementing ANNr with a model to generate solutions from predicted embeddings as was done in [28], as it would enable analogical innovation and bridge the gap with symbolic approaches.

References

1. Alsaidi, S., Decker, A., Lay, P., Marquer, E., Murena, P.A., Couceiro, M.: A neural approach for detecting morphological analogies. In: IEEE 8th DSAA, pp. 1–10 (2021)
2. Alsaidi, S., Decker, A., Lay, P., Marquer, E., Murena, P.A., Couceiro, M.: On the transferability of neural models of morphological analogies. In: AIMLAI, ECML PKDD, vol. 1524, pp. 76–89 (2021). https://doi.org/10.1007/978-3-030-93736-2_7
3. Bayoudh, M., Prade, H., Richard, G.: Evaluation of analogical proportions through kolmogorov complexity. Knowl.-Based Syst. **29**, 20–30 (2012)
4. Chen, D., Peterson, J.C., Griffiths, T.: Evaluating vector-space models of analogy. In: 39th CogSci, pp. 1746–1751. Cognitive Science Society (2017)
5. Cotterell, R., Kirov, C., Sylak-Glassman, J., Yarowsky, D., Eisner, J., Hulden, M.: The sigmorphon 2016 shared task-morphological reinflection. In: SIGMORPHON 2016. ACL (2016)
6. Drozd, A., Gladkova, A., Matsuoka, S.: Word embeddings, analogies, and machine learning: Beyond king - man + woman = queen. In: 26th COLING, pp. 3519–3530 (2016)
7. Eddington, D., Lachler, J.: A computational analysis of navajo verb stems, pp. 143–161. CSLI Publications (2010)
8. Fam, R., Lepage, Y.: Morphological predictability of unseen words using computational analogy. In: 24th ICCBR Workshops, pp. 51–60 (2016)
9. Fam, R., Lepage, Y.: Tools for the production of analogical grids and a resource of n-gram analogical grids in 11 languages. In: 11th LREC, pp. 1060–1066. ELRA (2018)
10. Karpinska, M., Li, B., Rogers, A., Drozd, A.: Subcharacter information in japanese embeddings: when is it worth it? In: Workshop on the Relevance of Linguistic Structure in Neural Architectures for NLP, pp. 28–37. ACL (2018)
11. Kingma, D.P., Ba, J.: Adam: a method for stochastic optimization. In: 3rd ICLR (2015)
12. Langlais, P., Yvon, F., Zweigenbaum, P.: Improvements in analogical learning: application to translating multi-terms of the medical domain. In: 12th EACL, pp. 487–495. ACL (2009)
13. Leer, J.: Proto-athabaskan verb stem variation. Part One: Phonology. Fairbanks: Alaska Native Language Center (1979)
14. Lepage, Y.: De l'analogie rendant compte de la commutation en linguistique. Université Joseph-Fourier - Grenoble I, Habilitation à diriger des recherches (2003)
15. Lepage, Y.: Character-position arithmetic for analogy questions between word forms. In: 25th ICCBR (Workshops), vol. 2028, pp. 23–32 (2017)
16. Lepage, Y., Ando, S.: Saussurian analogy: a theoretical account and its application. In: 16th COLING (1996)
17. Levy, O., Goldberg, Y.: Dependency-based word embeddings. In: 52nd ACL (Volume 2: Short Papers), pp. 302–308. ACL (2014)
18. Lieber, J., Nauer, E., Prade, H.: When revision-based case adaptation meets analogical extrapolation. In: Sánchez-Ruiz, A.A., Floyd, M.W. (eds.) ICCBR 2021. LNCS (LNAI), vol. 12877, pp. 156–170. Springer, Cham (2021). https://doi.org/10.1007/978-3-030-86957-1_11
19. Lim, S., Prade, H., Richard, G.: Solving word analogies: a machine learning perspective. In: Kern-Isberner, G., Ognjanović, Z. (eds.) ECSQARU 2019. LNCS (LNAI), vol. 11726, pp. 238–250. Springer, Cham (2019). https://doi.org/10.1007/978-3-030-29765-7_20

20. Marquer, E., Couceiro, M., Alsaidi, S., Decker, A.: Siganalogies - morphological analogies from Sigmorphon 2016 and 2019 (2022)
21. Miclet, L., Bayoudh, S., Delhay, A.: Analogical dissimilarity: definition, algorithms and two experiments in machine learning. J. Artif. Intell. Res. **32**, 793–824 (2008)
22. Mikolov, T., Chen, K., Corrado, G., Dean, J.: Efficient estimation of word representations in vector space. In: 1st ICLR, Workshop Track (2013)
23. Murena, P.A., Al-Ghossein, M., Dessalles, J.L., Cornuéjols, A.: Solving analogies on words based on minimal complexity transformation. In: 29th IJCAI, pp. 1848–1854 (2020)
24. Prade, H., Richard, G.: A short introduction to computational trends in analogical reasoning. In: Prade, H., Richard, G. (eds.) Computational Approaches to Analogical Reasoning: Current Trends. SCI, vol. 548, pp. 1–22. Springer, Heidelberg (2014). https://doi.org/10.1007/978-3-642-54516-0_1
25. Rumelhart, D.E., Abrahamson, A.A.: A model for analogical reasoning. Cogn. Psychol. **5**(1), 1–18 (1973)
26. de Saussure, F.: Cours de linguistique générale. Payot (1916)
27. Vania, C.: On understanding character-level models for representing morphology. Ph.D. thesis, University of Edinburgh (2020)
28. Wang, L., Lepage, Y.: Vector-to-sequence models for sentence analogies. In: ICACSIS, pp. 441–446 (2020)
29. Yvon, F.: Finite-state transducers solving analogies on words. Rapport GET/ENST<CI (2003)

Theoretical and Experimental Study of a Complexity Measure for Analogical Transfer

Fadi Badra[1(✉)], Marie-Jeanne Lesot[2(✉)], Aman Barakat[2], and Christophe Marsala[2]

[1] Université Sorbonne Paris Nord, LIMICS, Sorbonne Université, INSERM, Bobigny, France
badra@univ-paris13.fr

[2] Sorbonne Université, CNRS, LIP6, Paris, France
{marie-jeanne.lesot,aman.barakat,christophe.marsala}@lip6.fr

Abstract. Analogical transfer addresses classification and regression tasks, performing a plausible inference according to which similar instances are likely to be associated with similar labels. This paper proposes a detailed study of the ordinal implementation of this principle by the so-called CoAT algorithm, that is based on a data set complexity measure quantifying the number of inversions observed when ranking the data according to their instance or label similarities. At a theoretical level, it establishes an upper bound of the complexity measure, providing a reference value to which the observed one can be compared. At an algorithmic level, it proposes an optimization that allows decreasing the computational complexity by one order of magnitude. At an experimental level, it studies the correlation of the complexity measure with the accuracy of the conducted label inference, as well as with the classification task difficulty, as captured by the class overlapping degree.

Keywords: Computational analogy · Analogical transfer · Similarity-induced ranking · Data set complexity

1 Introduction

Analogical reasoning [7] has been recognized by psychologists to be at the core of human thoughts [6]; computational analogy proposes, among others, to transpose its principles to artificial intelligence and machine learning models [3,15]. In particular, computational analogical transfer addresses prediction tasks, such as classification and regression, and implements a special type of plausible inference according to which similar instances are likely to be associated with similar labels. Since the pioneering logical formulation of analogical transfer [4], many formulations of this principle have been proposed: a first type of approach consists in looking for local alignment of the instance and the labels similarities [2,8,13,14]. A second one expresses the similarity principle as a negative constraint that excludes labels that are not similar enough to the ones of the

M. T. Keane and N. Wiratunga (Eds.): ICCBR 2022, LNAI 13405, pp. 175–189, 2022.
https://doi.org/10.1007/978-3-031-14923-8_12

similar instances [10]. A third approach, related to the second one, consists in measuring the extent to which a potential label is supported as compared to the other available data [5,9]. Other works study how to take into account domain knowledge in the inference [11,12].

This paper focuses on another approach, implemented in the Complexity-based Analogical Transfer algorithm CoAT [1], presented in more details in Sect. 2. CoAT relies on an ordinal formalization of the above mentioned principle according to which the ranking induced by the similarity measure applied to the data instances should be identical to the ranking induced by the similarity measure applied to their associated labels. As a consequence, the predicted label must be such that it does not entail ranking inversions. More precisely, the CoAT algorithm relies on the definition of a complexity measure that counts the number of so-called inversions, i.e. case triples violating the ordering requirement.

This paper proposes an extended study of the CoAT method, from three complementary points of view, namely theoretically, computationally and experimentally: it first establishes an upper bound of the complexity measure, providing a reference value to assess the relevance of the analogical assumption for the considered data set and similarity measures. It then addresses algorithmic concerns about the CoAT method and shows that it can be optimized to reduce its computational complexity to a tractable value. Finally, it presents an experimental study of the complexity measure, in particular regarding its correlation with the accuracy of the conducted label inference, its correlation with the prediction task difficulty for classification tasks (measured as the class overlap). Experimental results about its computational cost are also presented.

The paper is structured as follows: Sect. 2 recalls the principle of the CoAT algorithm, Sect. 3 presents the established upper bound on the complexity measure, successively for regression and classification tasks. Section 4 discusses the algorithmic optimization that allows reducing the computational cost of the CoAT approach for inference. Section 5 describes the conducted experimental study. Finally, Sect. 6 concludes the paper.

2 Reminder on Complexity-Based Analogy

This section recaps the principles of the Complexity-based Analogical Transfer algorithm CoAT [1] studied in this paper. After introducing the notations used throughout the paper, it recalls the definition of the complexity measure on which CoAT relies and then describes the inference algorithm itself.

2.1 Notations

Throughout the paper, D denotes a case base containing n instances, or *cases*, c_i, $i = 1..n$, defined as ordered pairs (s_i, r_i): s_i denotes the *situation*, i.e. a feature-based description of the considered instance, or problem, and r_i its associated label, or *outcome* or solution, either a numerical value, in the case of regression tasks, or a categorical value, in the case of classification tasks. Throughout the paper, the situation and outcome that constitute a case are identified by their identical index.

In addition, σ_S denotes a similarity measure applied to the situations, for instance derived from the Euclidean distance in case all features are numerical. σ_R denotes a similarity measure applied to the outcomes. Formally, a similarity measure applied to elements from a domain $\mathcal{X}$ is defined as a function $\sigma : \mathcal{X} \times \mathcal{X} \to \mathbb{R}^+$ that satisfies a reflexivity constraint: there exists a value $M \in \mathbb{R}^+$ such that $\forall (x, y) \in \mathcal{X}$, $\sigma(x, y) \leq \sigma(x, x) = M$ and $\sigma(x, x) = \sigma(y, y)$, i.e. the similarity of any object to itself is maximal. In addition, a similarity measure is most of the time supposed to be symmetrical.

2.2 Ordinal Analogical Principle: Complexity Definition

As mentioned in the introduction, the `CoAT` algorithm [1] relies on an ordinal understanding of the basic analogical principle, according to which similar instances are to be associated with similar labels: the complexity measure at the core of the algorithm quantifies the extent to which the ordering induced by the situation similarity measure σ_S is similar to the ordering induced by the outcome similarity measure σ_R.

More formally, the following qualitative continuity constraint is tested on each triple of cases (c_0, c, c'), with $c_0 = (s_0, r_0)$, $c = (s, r)$, and $c' = (s', r')$:

$$\text{if } \sigma_S(s_0, s) \geq \sigma_S(s_0, s'), \text{ then } \sigma_R(r_0, r) \geq \sigma_R(r_0, r')$$

This constraint expresses that each time a situation s_0 is more similar to a situation s than to a situation s', this order is preserved on their associated outcomes. Any violation of the constraint is called an inversion of similarity, defined as a Boolean value:

$$inv(c_0, c, c') = (\sigma_S(s_0, s) \geq \sigma_S(s_0, s')) \wedge (\sigma_R(r_0, r) < \sigma_R(r_0, r'))$$

It leads to the following definition of *inversion set* for a given case c with respect to a case base D and two similarity measures σ_S and σ_R (omitted in the notation to ease it) using the same function name, with a different arity:

$$inv(c) = \{(c_i, c_j) \in D \times D \mid inv(c, c_i, c_j) \text{ holds } \} \quad (1)$$

Finally, the complexity measure for a case base D and two similarity measures σ_S and σ_R counts the number of such inversions observed in the case base:

$$\Gamma(D, \sigma_S, \sigma_R) = \sum_{c \in D} |inv(c)| \quad (2)$$

2.3 Ordinal Analogical Inference Algorithm

The complexity measure Γ defined in Eq. (2) can then be used either to select appropriate similarity measures, as the ordered pair (σ_S, σ_R) among a list of

Algorithm 1. Complexity-based Analogical Transfer CoAT [1]

```
inputs: s (new situation), D (case base), R (set of candidate outcomes), σ_S, σ_R
(situation and outcome similarity measures)
output: predicted outcome r_s for the new situation s
minΓ = Γ(D ∪ {(s, r_0)}, σ_S, σ_R) for a specific arbitrary r_0 ∈ R
for r ∈ R do
   D' = D ∪ {(s, r)}
   Γ' = computeGamma(D', σ_S, σ_R)      using Alg. 2
   if Γ' < minΓ then
      minΓ = Γ'
      r_s = r
   end if
end for
return r_s
```

Algorithm 2. Complexity computation : computeGamma [1]

```
inputs: D (case base), σ_S, σ_R (situation and outcome similarity measures)
output: value of Γ(D, σ_S, σ_R)
Γ = 0
for c_0 ∈ D do
   for c ∈ D do
      for c' ∈ D do
         if inv(c_0, c, c') then
            Γ = Γ + 1
         end if
      end for
   end for
end for
return Γ
```

candidates that minimizes Γ, or to perform inference for a new situation [1]. In the latter case, for a new situation s, the transfer inference consists in predicting the outcome r_s that minimizes Γ applied to the considered data set enriched with the additional case (s, r_s):

$$r_s = \arg\min_{r \in R} \Gamma(D \cup \{(s, r)\}, \sigma_S, \sigma_R)$$

where R denotes a set of candidate outcomes. R is e.g. defined as the set of possible classes in case of classification tasks or as an interval of possible numerical values for regression tasks.

The CoAT inference algorithm [1] reproduced in Algorithm 1 then consists in testing all possible values r for the outcome and outputting the one that leads to the minimal complexity when the considered data set is completed with the candidate case (s, r).

3 Theoretical Property of the Complexity Measure: Upper Bound

This section proposes a theoretical study of the complexity measure introduced in [1] and recalled in the previous section, establishing the value of its upper bound for a given case base and given similarity measures. Such a bound provides a reference value that defines a quality scale for the observed complexity value. Indeed, the CoAT algorithm relies on comparisons of candidate complexity values and selects the smallest one. The same principle is applied when the complexity measure is used to select appropriate similarity measures, as the ones that minimize Γ. However, such comparative approaches do not give indication about the quality of these selections, i.e. whether these best choices are actually relevant ones. Establishing a complexity upper bound provides a reference value, corresponding to the worst case, to define a quality scale.

This section establishes the values of this bound, first in the general case, then focusing on the case of binary classification. Indeed, for the latter, a tighter bound can be provided: the worst case established in general appears to be too pessimistic in the case of binary classification.

3.1 General Case

The following theorem states the value of the complexity upper bound and shows it can be considered as tight, stating the case in which the bound can be attained.

Theorem 1. *For a case base D and two similarity measures σ_S and σ_R, the maximum value that the complexity $\Gamma(D, \sigma_S, \sigma_R)$ can take is $\Gamma_{max} = \frac{n^2(n-1)}{2}$ where $n = |D|$.*

There exists a pair (σ_S, σ_R) such that this bound can be attained if all outcome values observed in D are distinct.

To demonstrate this theorem, we first show that this value is an upper bound, and exhibit the configuration in which it can be attained.

Value of the Upper Bound. Establishing the value of the upper bound relies on the observation that, for any case c, among the two ordered pairs (c_i, c_j) and (c_j, c_i), at most one belongs to the set of inversions $inv(c)$. Indeed, assuming without loss of generality that $(c_i, c_j) \in inv(c)$, then by definition $\sigma_S(s, s_i) \geq \sigma_S(s, s_j)$ and $\sigma_R(r, r_i) < \sigma_R(r, r_j)$. Having $(c_j, c_i) \in inv(c)$ would require that $\sigma_R(r, r_j) < \sigma_R(r, r_i)$, which contradicts this hypothesis.

In addition, $c_i \neq c_j$ since an equality would lead to $\sigma_R(r, r_i) = \sigma_R(r, r_j)$, which is not compatible with the inversion definition

As a consequence, the cardinality of $inv(c)$ is bounded by the number of combinations of 2 elements of the case base that are distinct, i.e. $n(n-1)/2$. Summing over the n possible values for c leads to the expected inequality $\Gamma \leq n^2(n-1)/2$.

Tightness of the Upper Bound. The bound can be shown to be tight by exhibiting similarity measures σ_S and σ_R for which it is attained: in the case where all outcome values observed in D are distinct, which can for instance occur in the case of regression tasks, consider

- $\sigma_S(s_i, s_j) = 1$ for all pairs of situations s_i and s_j
- $\sigma_R(r_i, r_j) = e^{-f(i,j)}$ where f is a pairing function, i.e., is such that the values it assigns for the pairs (i, j) are all distinct. An example of such function is the Cantor pairing function $f(i, j) = \frac{1}{2}(i + j)(i + j + 1) + j$.

Then for any pair of distinct cases (c_i, c_j), the fact that all values assigned by σ_R are distinct entails that exactly one of the two possible ordered pairs belongs to $inv(c)$ for any c, the one with the minimal index $min(i, j)$. Indeed, considering without loss of generality that $i < j$, then it holds that $\sigma_S(s, s_i) = \sigma_S(s, s_j) = 1$ and $\sigma_R(r, r_i) < \sigma_R(r, r_j)$ due to the above definitions of σ_S and σ_R. The total number of inversions for a given c thus equals $\frac{n(n-1)}{2}$ and the upper bound is attained.

It can be observed that this bound remains a pessimistic one, insofar as these similarity measures are of course not relevant ones (indeed, considering all situations are fully similar does not constitute a relevant choice). However, it allows to set a scale and a reference value to compare the complexity values of relevant similarity measures.

3.2 Binary Classification Case

In the case of binary classification, by definition, the outcomes r can only take two values. The bound established in Theorem 1 can thus not be attained (except in the extreme case where D contains 2 instances, one of each class), and is not tight enough. This section establishes a tighter bound:

Theorem 2. *For a case base D in which all outcomes values observed in D can only take two distinct values, for two similarity measures σ_S and σ_R, the maximum value that the complexity $\Gamma(D, \sigma_S, \sigma_R)$ can take is $\Gamma_{cls} = \frac{n^3}{4}$, where $n = |D|$.*

There exists a pair (σ_S, σ_R) such that this bound can be attained if the two classes have the same number of elements.

Value of the Upper Bound. Let n_0 and n_1 denote the number of cases in the case base associated with each of the two outcomes respectively.

For any triple (c, c_i, c_j), the inequality $\sigma_R(r, r_i) < \sigma_R(r, r_j)$ can hold only if $r \neq r_i$ and $r = r_j$ because of the reflexivity property of a similarity measure, as recalled in Sect. 2.1. As a consequence, the maximal number of such triples is $n_0 n_1$, which in turn is bounded by $\frac{n^2}{2}$. Indeed, $n_0 n_1 = n_0(n - n_0)$ which is a quadratic function of n_0 whose maximum is reached for $n_0 = \frac{n}{2}$ and equals $\frac{n^2}{4}$.

Summing over all n situations c leads to the expected result.

Tightness of the Upper Bound. In the case where σ_S is the same as in the previous section, i.e. $\sigma_S(s,s') = 1$ for all pairs of situations and where $\sigma_R(r,r') = 1$ if $r = r'$ and 0 otherwise, the bound is attained if the two classes have the same number of elements, $n_0 = n_1 = \frac{n}{2}$.

Indeed, for a given case c, an inversion is observed for any ordered pair (c_i, c_j) where c_j has the same class as c and c_i the opposite class: $\sigma_S(c,c_i) = \sigma_S(c,c_j) = 1$ and $\sigma_R(r,r_i) = 0 < \sigma_S(r,r_j) = 1$. There are $n_0 n_1 = \frac{n^2}{4}$ such triples for a given c and thus $\frac{n^3}{4}$ inversions altogether.

Note that the order of magnitude of this bound is the same as the one in the general case, cubic in the number of cases, but it is halved (also note they are equal in the extreme case where $n = 2$). As previously, it is a pessimistic bound as it relies on non-relevant similarity measures.

4 Algorithmic Optimisation

This section studies the CoAT algorithm from an algorithmic point of view and shows that its computational complexity can be decreased drastically. It first presents the justification, and then describes the proposed optimized version of the CoAT algorithm.

4.1 Principle

The computational complexity of the CoAT algorithm, as recalled from [1] in Algorithm 1, is high, as it computes the complexity measure of the candidate modified data set D' for each candidate outcome value: the complexity is $O(n^3 \times |R|)$, i.e. not tractable for real data sets. Indeed, computing the complexity of a data set is a cubic function of its number of cases as it considers all triples (see the triple loop in Algorithm 2).

However, one can decrease the complexity by one order of magnitude when observing that actually not all triples are needed to identify the optimal r value minimizing $\Gamma(D', \sigma_S, \sigma_R)$: indeed all triples that do not involve the new situation are not needed, as they are common to all candidate modified data sets D'. Formally,

$$\begin{aligned}
\Gamma(D \cup \{(s,r)\}, \sigma_S, \sigma_R) &= \sum_{i=1}^{n} |inv(c_i)| + |inv((s,r))| \\
&= \Gamma(D, \sigma_S, \sigma_R) + \\
&\quad \sum_{i=1}^{n} |\{c_j \in D | \sigma_S(s_i, s) \geq \sigma_S(s_i, s_j) \wedge \sigma_R(s_i, r) < \sigma_R(s_i, r_j)\}| \\
&\quad + |inv((s,r))|
\end{aligned}$$

As the term $\Gamma(D, \sigma_S, \sigma_R)$ does not depend on the candidate outcome r, its computation is not needed: denoting

$$\Delta\Gamma(s, r, D, \sigma_S, \sigma_R) = \Gamma(D \cup \{(s,r)\}, \sigma_S, \sigma_R) - \Gamma(D, \sigma_S, \sigma_R)$$

Algorithm 3. Optimized variant of the `CoAT` algorithm

inputs: s (new situation), D (case base), R (set of candidate outcomes), σ_S, σ_R (situation and outcome similarity measures)
output: predicted outcome r_s for the new situation s
$min\Delta\Gamma = n^2(n-1)/2$ with $n = |D|$
for $r \in R$ **do**
  $\Delta\Gamma' = \text{computeDeltaGamma}(D, s, r, \sigma_S, \sigma_R)$ using Alg. 4
  if $\Delta\Gamma' < min\Delta\Gamma$ **then**
    $min\Delta\Gamma = \Delta\Gamma'$
    $r_s = r$
  end if
end for
return r_s

it holds that

$$\arg\min_{r\in R} \Gamma(D \cup \{(s,r)\}, \sigma_S, \sigma_R) = \arg\min_{r\in R} \Delta\Gamma(s, r, D, \sigma_S, \sigma_R)$$

Now the computation of $\Delta\Gamma(s, r, D, \sigma_S, \sigma_R)$ is quadratic in the number of cases contained in the considered case base D, as both its terms are. Indeed, the first term of the sum defining $\Delta\Gamma(s, r, D, \sigma_S, \sigma_R)$ is a sum over all n cases contained in D, which altogether has a quadratic complexity in n. The second term needs to go through all pairs of cases in D to compute $|inv((s,r))|$, which also has a quadratic complexity.

4.2 Proposed Optimized Algorithm

Algorithm 3 shows how the principle discussed in the previous subsection can be implemented. First the minimal value of the candidate $min\Delta\Gamma$ can be initialized to the upper bound established in Sect. 3. The algorithm then goes through all possible candidate outcome values $r \in R$, but each value is used to compute $\Delta\Gamma$ instead of Γ.

This computation is performed in Algorithm 4, which relies on a double loop, where the computation of Γ performed in Algorithm 2 relies on a triple loop. Indeed, it only considers the triples that contain the considered candidate case $c_0 = (s, r)$, testing all three possibilities, depending on whether c_0 is in first, second or third position in the triple.

This procedure can be further optimized if the best observed value for $min\Delta\Gamma$ is given as additional argument to the function computeDeltaGamma described in Algorithm 4. Indeed, it is then possible to take advantage of an early discard principle, i.e. to exit the double loop on c and c' as soon as the current $\Delta\Gamma$ value becomes greater than the already observed best value stored in this additional parameter $min\Delta\Gamma$. This principle can be especially useful when `CoAT` is applied to regression tasks, i.e. when the number of candidate outcome values is high.

A further direction for computational optimization, left for future works, is to define a relevant order, possibly based on a heuristic criterion, for testing the

Algorithm 4. Complexity increase computation : computeDeltaGamma

```
inputs: D (case base), s additional situation, r associated candidate outcome, σ_S, σ_R
(situation and outcome similarity measures)
output: value of ΔΓ(s, r, σ_S, σ_R) with respect to D
c_0 = (s, r)
ΔΓ = 0
for c ∈ D do
  for c' ∈ D do
    if inv(c_0, c, c') then
      ΔΓ = ΔΓ + 1
    end if
    if inv(c, c_0, c') then
      ΔΓ = ΔΓ + 1
    end if
    if inv(c, c', c_0) then
      ΔΓ = ΔΓ + 1
    end if
  end for
end for
return ΔΓ
```

candidate outcome values: if the optimal one is tested first, all other candidates can be discarded early without fully computing their associated $\Delta\Gamma$ values.

5 Experimental Study

The experimental study of the `CoAT` algorithm and its optimization described in this section rely on their Python implementation available on github[1].

The experimental study consists in three parts: the first one, described in Sect. 5.1, illustrates the decrease of computational complexity offered by the algorithmic optimization proposed in Sect. 4; the second one (Sect. 5.2) shows there is a correlation between the data set complexity and the accuracy of the inferred label; the third one shows there is a correlation between the data set complexity and the classification task difficulty, as captured by the class overlapping degrees (Sect. 5.3).

5.1 Computational Cost

This section describes the experimental study of the computational cost of the `CoAT` algorithm and its optimization proposed in Sect. 4. Note that the latter is correct in the sense that its output is always identical to that of `CoAT`.

[1] https://github.com/fadibadra/coat_iccbr.

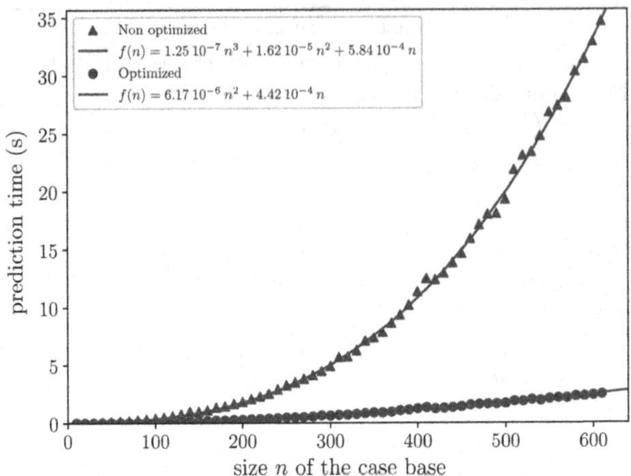

Fig. 1. CoAT prediction time for its non-optimized and optimized versions, according to the size of the case base. (Color figure online)

Experimental Protocol. The experiment is conducted on case bases of increasing sizes obtained as random subsamples of the UCI Balance Scale dataset[2] that defines a 3-class classification task. For each case base, the prediction time of both the non-optimized and the optimized versions of the CoAT algorithm is measured on 10 test instances. The similarity measure σ_S is defined as a decreasing function of the Euclidean distance, and the similarity measure σ_R is the class membership similarity: for two classes r_i and r_j, $\sigma_R(r_i, r_j) = 1$ if $r_i = r_j$, and 0 otherwise.

Results. Figure 1 shows the average prediction time of the CoAT algorithm as a function of the size of the case base: the red triangles correspond to the non-optimized version of CoAT, the blue dots to the optimized version. The latter clearly show the decrease in the computational time.

A polynomial regression shows that the computing time of non-optimized version of CoAT on a case base of size n can be approximated by the function $f(n) = 1.25\,10^{-7}\,n^3 + 1.62\,10^{-5}\,n^2 + 5.84\,10^{-4}\,n$ (red line on the figure), with a root mean square error of 0.3; the computing time of optimized version of CoAT can be approximated by the function $f(n) = 6.17\,10^{-6}\,n^2 + 4.42\,10^{-4}\,n$ (blue line on the figure), with a root mean square error of 0.04. . These results are consistent with the theoretical analysis of their respective computational costs (see Sect. 4).

5.2 Correlation Between Case Base Complexity and Performance

This experiment shows that there is a correlation between the value of the complexity measure and the performance of the CoAT prediction algorithm.

[2] https://archive.ics.uci.edu/ml/datasets/balance+scale.

Experimental Protocol. The experiment is conducted on 200 instances extracted from the Balance Scale data set. As the instances of these data sets are described only by d numeric features, each situation can be represented by a vector of $\mathbb{R}^d$. Let $\mathbf{x}, \mathbf{y} \in \mathbb{R}^d$ be two such vectors. The performance of the `CoAT` algorithm is measured for each dataset by generating 100 different classification tasks $\{(D, \sigma_i, \sigma_R)\}_{1 \leq i \leq 100}$, each of which is obtained by keeping D and σ_R fixed, and choosing for σ_S a decreasing function of a randomly weighted Euclidean distance. More precisely, a set of random linear maps $\{L_i : \mathbb{R}^d \longrightarrow \mathbb{R}^d\}_{1 \leq i \leq 100}$ are generated, and for each map L_i, σ_i is defined as a decreasing function of the Euclidean distance computed in the L_i's embedding space:

$$\sigma_i(\mathbf{x}, \mathbf{y}) = e^{-d_i(\mathbf{x}, \mathbf{y})} \text{ with } d_i(\mathbf{x}, \mathbf{y}) = \|L_i\mathbf{x} - L_i\mathbf{y}\|_2 = \sqrt{(\mathbf{x} - \mathbf{y})^T L_i^T L_i(\mathbf{x} - \mathbf{y})}$$

The performance is also measured on the task (D, σ_E, σ_R), in which $\sigma_E(\mathbf{x}, \mathbf{y}) = e^{-\|\mathbf{x}-\mathbf{y}\|_2}$ is a decreasing function of the Euclidean distance, which amounts to taking as linear map the identity matrix. The similarity measure σ_R is the class membership similarity. For each task, the performance is measured by the prediction accuracy, with 10-fold cross validation.

Results. Figure 2 shows for each classification task the average accuracy and standard deviation of the `CoAT` algorithm according to the dataset complexity. The blue points correspond to the randomly generated σ_i similarity measures. The red point gives the results for the σ_E similarity measure based on the standard Euclidean distance. The green line shows the result of a linear regression on the data. The Pearson's coefficient is -0.97. On these datasets, the results clearly show a correlation between the dataset complexity and the performance

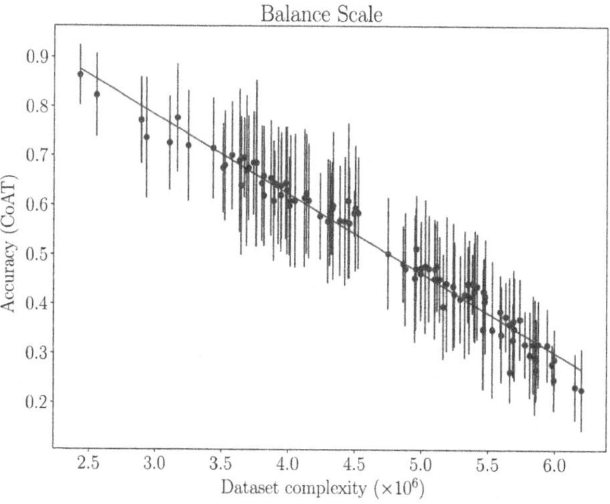

Fig. 2. Relation between `CoAT` performance (accuracy) and dataset complexity on the Balance Scale data set.

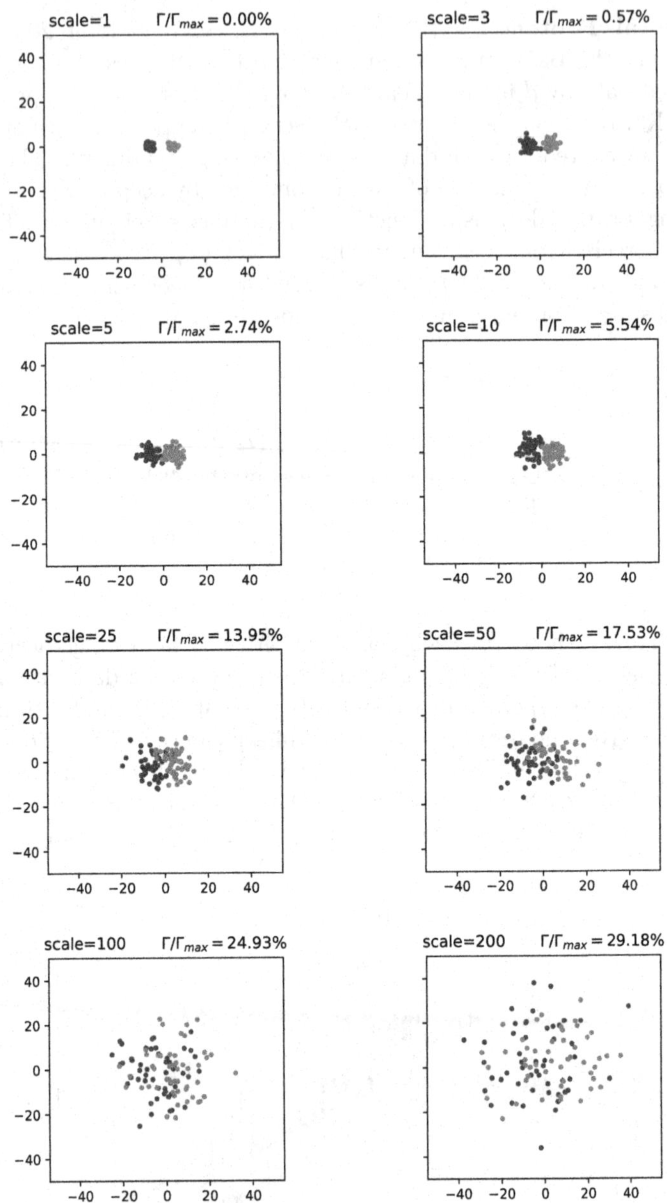

Fig. 3. Data distribution and ratio Γ/Γ_{max} for different synthetic data sets.

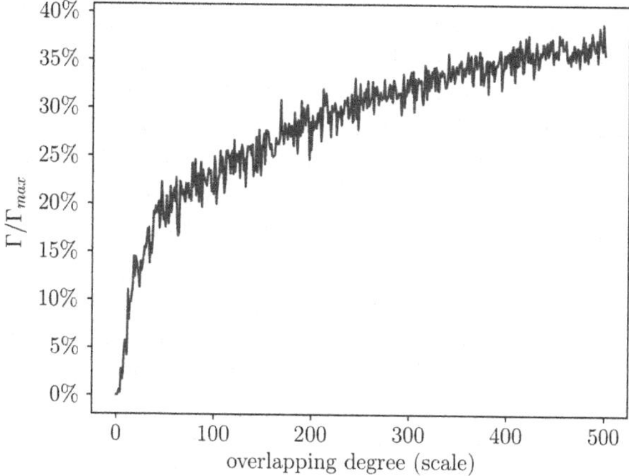

Fig. 4. Relation between data set complexity and classification task difficulty.

of the CoAT algorithm. The dataset complexity values range between 6.10% and 15.58% of the upper bound $\Gamma_{max} = 3,980,000$. The complexity upper bound thus provides a reference value, that can be used to define a quality scale for the similarity measure σ_S.

5.3 Correlation Between Complexity and Task Difficulty

This experiment shows the correlation between the data set complexity and the classification task difficulty, as captured by the class overlapping degree.

Experimental Protocol. The experiment is conducted on a set of $2D$ synthetic data sets, whose instances are equally split into two classes (blue and orange). A set of classification tasks $\{(D_i, \sigma_S, \sigma_R)\}_{1 \leq i \leq 500}$ is generated, in which both the size $|D_i| = 100$ of the case bases and the two similarity measures σ_S and σ_R are fixed, but the overlapping degree of the two classes vary. Random samples are drawn for each class from a multivariate normal distribution centered on the point $(-10, 0)$ for the blue class and $(10, 0)$ for the orange class, and the covariance matrix of each normal distribution for the data set D_i is the identity matrix multiplied by the scale factor `scale` $= i$. This parameter thus controls the overlapping degree of the two classes The similarity measure σ_S is a decreasing function of the Euclidean distance, and the similarity measure σ_R is the class membership similarity. The data set complexity $\Gamma(D_i, \sigma_S, \sigma_R)$ is computed for each classification task $(D_i, \sigma_S, \sigma_R)$.

Results. Figure 3 shows the data distribution and ratios $\Gamma(D_i, \sigma_S, \sigma_R)/\Gamma_{max}$ obtained for different data sets D_i. When the value of the `scale` parameter is very small, the two classes are well separated, but as its value increases, the two classes start to overlap. When the two classes are well separated, no instance is more similar to an instance of a different class than it is to an instance of the same class, hence, $\Gamma = 0$. When the instances of the two classes get closer to each other, or overlap, some class similarities happen to be lower than some intra-class similarities, leading to a non-zero data set complexity Γ. Note however that the data set complexity Γ does not exactly measure the overlapping degree of the two classes, since it can be non-zero when the two class are close to one another, but non overlapping.

As shown on Fig. 4, the more the two classes overlap, the higher the data set complexity. The ratio $\Gamma(D_i, \sigma_S, \sigma_R)/\Gamma_{max}$ thus provides a scale on which to estimate the difficulty of the task, as captured by the overlapping degree `scale` of the two classes on the data set D_i. This experiments also illustrates that Γ_{max} is not a tight bound: even for highly overlapping classes, the complexity value is still lower that 40% of Γ_{max}.

6 Conclusion and Future Works

This paper proposes an extended study of the `CoAT` algorithm that provides an ordinal implementation of the analogical transfer principle for classification and regression tasks. From a theoretical point of view, the paper establishes an upper bound of the complexity measure `CoAT` relies on. From an algorithmic point of view, an efficient optimization of the `CoAT` algorithm is proposed, that allows decreasing its computational cost by one order of magnitude: the optimized variant has a quadratic complexity, equivalent to that of any relational learning method. This property is illustrated experimentally. The paper also provides an experimental characterization of the complexity measure, regarding its relation to the inference performance and to the inference difficulty. When D and σ_R are fixed, the complexity measure is an intrinsic indicator of the quality of the similarity measure σ_S. When σ_S and σ_R are fixed, the complexity measure is an indicator of the inference difficulty, as captured by D's class overlapping degree.

The results obtained in this study provide additional arguments regarding the relevance of the ordinal approach to analogical transfer and motivations for further developing this principle of plausible inference. Future directions of research in particular include working on tighter bounds of the complexity measure, e.g. focusing on more realistic (and thus less pessimistic) similarity measures and on the case of non binary classification. From an algorithmic point of view, future works will aim at proposing methods, possibly heuristics, to optimize the order in which the candidate outcomes are tested: as mentioned earlier, if the optimal value is considered first, other candidates can be discarded early, further decreasing the computational cost.

References

1. Badra, F.: A dataset complexity measure for analogical transfer. In: IJCAI International Joint Conference on Artificial Intelligence, pp. 1601–1607 (2020)

2. Badra, F., Sedki, K., Ugon, A.: On the role of similarity in analogical transfer. In: Cox, M.T., Funk, P., Begum, S. (eds.) ICCBR 2018. LNCS (LNAI), vol. 11156, pp. 499–514. Springer, Cham (2018). https://doi.org/10.1007/978-3-030-01081-2_33
3. Helman, D.H. (ed.): Analogical Reasoning: Perspectives of Artificial Intelligence, Cognitive Science, and Philosophy. Springer, Dordrecht (2010). https://doi.org/10.1007/978-94-015-7811-0
4. Davies, T.R., Russell, S.J.: A logical approach to reasoning by analogy. In: IJCAI International Joint Conference on Artificial Intelligence (1987)
5. Dubois, D., Hüllermeier, E., Prade, H.: Flexible control of case-based prediction in the framework of possibility theory. In: Blanzieri, E., Portinale, L. (eds.) EWCBR 2000. LNCS, vol. 1898, pp. 61–73. Springer, Heidelberg (2000). https://doi.org/10.1007/3-540-44527-7_7
6. Hofstadter, D.R., Sander, E.: Surfaces and Essences: Analogy as the Fuel and Fire of Thinking. Basic Books, New York (2013)
7. Holyoak, K.J., Thagard, P.: The analogical mind. Am. Psychol. **52**(1), 35–44 (1997)
8. Hug, N., Prade, H., Richard, G., Serrurier, M.: Analogical classifiers: a theoretical perspective. In: 22nd European Conference on Artificial Intelligence – ECAI, vol. 285, pp. 689–697 (2016)
9. Hüllermeier, E.: Possibilistic instance-based learning. Artif. Intell. **148**(1–2), 335–383 (2003)
10. Hüllermeier, E.: Credible case-based inference using similarity profiles. IEEE Trans. Knowl. Data Eng. **19**(6), 847–858 (2007)
11. Lieber, J.: Application of the revision theory to adaptation in case-based reasoning: the conservative adaptation. In: Weber, R.O., Richter, M.M. (eds.) ICCBR 2007. LNCS (LNAI), vol. 4626, pp. 239–253. Springer, Heidelberg (2007). https://doi.org/10.1007/978-3-540-74141-1_17
12. Lieber, J., Nauer, E., Prade, H.: When revision-based case adaptation meets analogical extrapolation. In: Sánchez-Ruiz, A.A., Floyd, M.W. (eds.) ICCBR 2021. LNCS (LNAI), vol. 12877, pp. 156–170. Springer, Cham (2021). https://doi.org/10.1007/978-3-030-86957-1_11
13. Miclet, L., Bayoudh, S., Delhay, A.: Analogical dissimilarity: definition, algorithms and two experiments in machine learning. J. Artif. Intell. Res. **32**, 793–824 (2008)
14. Ontañón, S., Plaza, E.: On knowledge transfer in case-based inference. In: Agudo, B.D., Watson, I. (eds.) ICCBR 2012. LNCS (LNAI), vol. 7466, pp. 312–326. Springer, Heidelberg (2012). https://doi.org/10.1007/978-3-642-32986-9_24
15. Prade, H.: Reasoning with data - a new challenge for AI? In: Schockaert, S., Senellart, P. (eds.) SUM 2016. LNCS (LNAI), vol. 9858, pp. 274–288. Springer, Cham (2016). https://doi.org/10.1007/978-3-319-45856-4_19

Graphs and Optimisation

Case-Based Learning and Reasoning Using Layered Boundary Multigraphs

Thomas Gabel(✉) and Fabian Sommer

Faculty of Computer Science and Engineering, Frankfurt University of Applied Sciences, Frankfurt am Main, 60318 Frankfurt, Germany
{tgabel,fabian.sommer}@fb2.fra-uas.de

Abstract. Instance-based and case-based learning algorithms learn by remembering instances. When scaling such approaches to datasets of sizes that are typically faced in today's data-rich and data-driven decade, basic approaches to case retrieval and case learning quickly come to their limits. In this paper, we introduce a novel scalable algorithm for both, the retrieval and the retain phase of the CBR cycle. Our approach builds an efficient graph-based data structure when learning new cases which it exploits in a stochastic any-time manner during retrieval. We investigate its characteristics both, theoretically and empirically using established benchmark datasets as well as a specific larger-scale dataset.

1 Introduction

Retrieval in Case-Based Reasoning (CBR) takes time. For some applications, specifically data intensive ones, retrieval times can quickly become the system's bottleneck. Since this has been known for decades, a lot of research effort has been put into the development of CBR approaches to increase retrieval efficiency while retaining its efficacy. Those approaches tackle the problem in different ways, including but not limited to (a) reducing the number of cases stored in the case base, (b) using hierarchical, filtering, or multistep retrieval methods to reduce the number of query-case comparisons, (c) constructing and utilizing index structures to guide the search for similar cases, (d) improving case representation and developing tailored methods for efficient similarity assessments, or (e) using anytime algorithms whose retrieval efficacy grows with available computation time.

The core contribution of the paper at hand is a novel retrieve and retain procedure that combats the aforementioned challenges using a combination of the strategies (a), (c), and (e) listed above. According to [17], indexing cases is one of the most challenging tasks in CBR. To this end, we aim at building up a *graph-based* index structure that enhances the similarity-driven search for nearest neighbors (c), while also reducing the number of cases stored overall (a). Additionally, we design the method to be an anytime approach (e) which means that the retrieval process can be stopped at any time and that the quality of the results obtained is likely to be better if more time has been allocated to the retrieval process.

M. T. Keane and N. Wiratunga (Eds.): ICCBR 2022, LNAI 13405, pp. 193–208, 2022.
https://doi.org/10.1007/978-3-031-14923-8_13

At the heart of our contribution is the construction of an index structure that we call a *boundary graph* or, respectively, a *labeled boundary multigraph* extension of it. We build up the graph structure from case data, i.e. its topology is not fixed a priori. It is worth noting that the construction process can be applied in an online setting, i.e. no batch access to the full dataset is needed and, hence, the graph index structure can be extended as more and more cases come in. Both, the buildup as well as the employment of that graph-based index structure are inherently stochastic – a fact that we found to substantially improve the robustness of the approach as well as to reduce its dependency on other factors like the order of case presentation during learning.

We start this paper with a brief literature review on related work. Section 3 introduces boundary graphs and labeled boundary multigraphs and presents corresponding retain and retrieve procedures for constructing such graph structures as well as for utilizing them during the actual retrieval. We have tested our algorithms on a variety of classical benchmark datasets as well as on a large scale dataset from the application field of robotic soccer simulation (RSS). In Sect. 4, we present the corresponding empirical results as well as further analyzes of our algorithms' properties and their scaling behavior.

2 Background and Related Work

Since retrieval takes such a prominent position in CBR, the optimization of its efficacy and efficiency has attracted a lot of research in the past. Providing a comprehensive overview on these issues is beyond the scope of this paper, which is why we only point to work that is strongly related ours.

Case Base Maintenance (CBM [13]) aims to control the number of cases in the case base while guaranteeing a high competence of the system. Following the initial proposal of the nearest neighbor rule [6], several authors have proposed ideas to reduce the set of stored cases [12]. Among those, the family of *Instance-Based Learning* algorithms (IBL [1]) is a classic whose IB2 variant centered around the idea of adding a new case only, if its problem part would not be solved by the so far existing case base. This simple but powerful idea is also fundamentally embedded into the core of the algorithms we are proposing in this paper. Other CBM algorithms take the opposite approach and iteratively decide which cases to delete from a case base [21] which comes at the cost of requiring batch access to the case data. Another technique to limit the case base size utilizes the notion of coverage and reachability of cases [18] which henceforth was exploited by the incremental COV-FP [19] algorithm.

Index Structures for Efficient Retrieval are supposed to guide the search for similar cases. Thus, before the actual retrieval utilizing an index structure can take place that structure must be generated. Tree-based structures have frequently been employed to speed up the access to large datasets (e.g. geometric near-neighbor access trees [5] or nearest vector trees [14]). Tree-based algorithms that do also feature online insertion capabilities include cover trees [4], boundary trees [16] (see below), or kd-trees [20] where the latter have the additional advantage of not requiring full similarity calculations at tree nodes. Many more complex retrieval methods and belonging index structures do exist, including, for example, case retrieval nets [15] or retrieval using Bayesian networks [7].

Boundary Trees [16] are a powerful tree-based index structure for similarity-based search. They consist of nodes representing training cases connected by edges such that any pair of parent and child node belongs to different classes[1]. This fact is eponymous as with each edge traversal a decision boundary is crossed.

Given a boundary tree $\mathcal{T}$ and a new query q, the tree is traversed from its root by calculating the similarity between q and all children of the current node, moving to that child which has the highest similarity to q. Boundary trees use a hyper parameter $k \in [1, \infty]$ that determines the maximal number of children any node is permitted to have. The retrieval is finished, if a leaf node has been reached or if the current (inner) node v has less than k children and the similarity between q and v is larger than the similarity between q and all children of v. This way, a "locally closest" case c^* to the query is found, meaning that neither the parent(s) of c^* nor the children of c^* are more similar.

The tree creation procedure for boundary trees is inspired by the classical IB2 algorithm [1] (see above). The next training case c_i is used as query using the so far existing boundary tree $\mathcal{T}_{i-1}$. If the result of the tree-based retrieval returns a case c^* whose solution does not match the solution of c_i, then c_i is added as a new child node of c^*. In [16], Mathy et al. propose to extend the described approach to an ensemble of boundary trees, a so-called boundary forest (BF). They train an ensemble of (in that paper, usually, ten or 50) boundary trees on shuffled versions of the training data and employ different voting mechanisms using the retrieval results of the boundary trees. The Boundary Graph approach we are presenting in the next section takes some inspiration from boundary trees which is why we also use it as a reference method in our empirical evaluations.

3 Boundary Graphs and Labeled Boundary Multigraphs

We propose a case-based technique that covers both, a method to decide which cases to store in the case base and which not as well as algorithms to build up and employ an index structure that facilitates an efficient retrieval. In what follows, we assume an attribute value-based case representation over a problem space $\mathcal{P}$ and a solution space $\mathcal{S}$ where each case $c = (p, s)$ consists of a problem part $p \in \mathcal{P}$ and a solution part $s \in \mathcal{S}$ which we can both access using the dot operator (i.e. $c.p$ or $c.s$). As usual, similarity between cases is measured using a problem similarity measure $sim_p : \mathcal{P} \times \mathcal{P} \to [0, 1]$, while the similarity between cases' solutions can be assessed using a solution similarity measure $sim_s : \mathcal{S} \times \mathcal{S} \to [0, 1]$. Note that we do not impose any further requirements on $sim_{s/p}$ throughout the rest of the paper, except that, for ease of presentation, we assume it to be symmetric.

[1] While the definition given here focuses on classification tasks, a straightforward generalization to other tasks like regression or mere retrieval can easily be made.

3.1 Boundary Graphs

We now introduce the concept of boundary graphs which we will later extend to so-called labeled boundary multigraphs. These graph structures, plus techniques to create and utilize them, represent the backbone of our entire approach.

3.1.1 Notation

For a given case base CB, a *Boundary Graph (BG)* $\mathcal{B} = (V, E)$ is an undirected graph without loops with a set of nodes $V \subseteq CB$ and a set of edges

$$E \subseteq \{(c_i, c_j) | c_i, c_j \in V \text{ and } i \neq j\}, \tag{1}$$

where, by construction, each edge from E connects only cases with differing solutions. This means, for each $(c_i, c_j) \in E$ it holds

$$sim_s(c_i.s, c_j.s) < 1 - \varepsilon \tag{2}$$

where $\varepsilon \in [0, 1]$ is a threshold that defines when two solutions are considered to be different. The definition given so far and the relations in Formula 1 and 2 are not finalized, since Eq. 1 gives just a subset specification. We concretize this specification in the next paragraphs, emphasizing that the graphs we are creating will be a sparse representation of the data and contain a tiny fraction of the edges that would be allowed to be in E according to Eqs. 1 and 2.

3.1.2 Retrieval and Reuse

Given a query $q \in \mathcal{P}$ and a boundary graph $\mathcal{B} = (V, E)$, the retrieve algorithm moves *repeatedly* through the graph structure, calculating the similarity between q and the current node $c \in V$ as well as between q and the neighbors of c, i.e. for all $v \in V$ for which an edge $(c, v) \in E$ exists. It successively "moves" onwards to the node with the highest similarity to q until some maximum $c^\star$ has been reached, which means that $sim_p(q, c^\star) \geq sim_p(q, c) \forall (c^\star, c) \in E$.

Importantly, this procedure is repeated for r times, where the starting node is selected randomly from V each time. Hence, r determines the number of random retrieval starting points from which the similarity-guided search is initiated. Consequently, as retrieval result a vector $\mathcal{N}_q^r = (n_1, \ldots, n_r)$ of r estimated nearest neighbors is obtained.

The delineated retrieve step (function BG_Retrieve in Algorithm 1) is embedded into the superjacent function BG_Predict for boundary graph-based prediction which performs both, the retrieve and revise step of the classic CBR cycle. The mentioned vector of r nearest neighbor estimates are combined to form an overall prediction $\mathcal{R}(q)$ using some amalgamation function $\mathcal{A}$, such that

$$\mathcal{R}(q) = \mathcal{A}(\mathcal{N}_q^r) = \mathcal{A}((n_1, \ldots, n_r)). \tag{3}$$

For classification we can use a simple majority vote

$$\mathcal{A}((n_1, \ldots, n_r)) \in \arg\max_{l \in \mathcal{S}} |\{n_j | n_j.s = l, j = 1, \ldots, r\}| \tag{4}$$

BG_PREDICT(q, $\mathcal{B}$, r)
Input: query $q \in \mathcal{P}$,
boundary graph $\mathcal{B} = (V, E)$,
number r of random retrieval restarts,
amalgamation function $\mathcal{A}$
Output: BG-based prediction $\mathcal{R}(q)$
// retrieve step
$\mathcal{N}_q^r \leftarrow$ BG_RETRIEVE$(q, \mathcal{B}, r)$
// reuse step (cf. Eq. 4-6)
$\mathcal{R}(q) \leftarrow \mathcal{A}(\mathcal{N}_q^r)$
return $\mathcal{R}(q)$

BG_RETRIEVE(q, $\mathcal{B}$, r)
Input: query $q \in \mathcal{P}$,
boundary graph $\mathcal{B} = (V, E)$ with $V \neq \emptyset$,
number r of random retrieval restarts
Output: r-dimensional vector $\mathcal{N}_q^r$ of potential nearest neighbors
$\mathcal{N}_q^r \leftarrow r$-dimensional vector
for $i = 1$ **to** r **do**
$c^\star \leftarrow$ random node from V
$stop \leftarrow false$
while $stop = false$ **do**
$c \leftarrow \arg\max_{v \in V \text{ s.t. } (c^\star, v) \in E} sim_p(q, v)$
if $sim_p(q, c) > sim_p(q, c^\star)$
then $c^\star \leftarrow c$
else $stop \leftarrow true$
$\mathcal{N}_q^r[i] \leftarrow c^\star$
return $\mathcal{N}_q^r$

Algorithm 1: Boundary Graph-Based Prediction and Retrieval

or a similarity-weighted voting scheme, like

$$\mathcal{A}((n_1, \ldots, n_r)) \in \arg\max_{l \in \mathcal{S}} \sum_{j=1}^{r} \begin{cases} sim_p(q, n_j) & \text{if } n_j.s = l \\ 0 & \text{else} \end{cases}. \tag{5}$$

In a similar manner, for regression tasks the estimated value becomes

$$\mathcal{A}((n_1, \ldots, n_r)) = \frac{\sum_{j=1}^{r} sim_p(q, n_j) \cdot n_j.s}{\sum_{j=1}^{r} sim_p(q, n_j)}. \tag{6}$$

A pseudo-code summary of the entire case-based retrieval and revise approach utilizing a boundary graph as index structure is given in Algorithm 1.

3.1.3 Graph Construction

We assume that the cases c_1 to c_n from the case base CB are presented to the boundary graph construction algorithm successively. Given a single training case c_i, the algorithm first queries the boundary graph $\mathcal{B}_{i-1} = (V_{i-1}, E_{i-1})$ which has been trained for the preceding $i-1$ cases, yielding a vector $\mathcal{N}_{c_i}^r = (n_1, \ldots, n_r)$ of r possible nearest neighbors. The algorithm then iterates over these n_j ($j = 1, \ldots, r$) and, if $sim_s(c_i.s, n_j.s) < 1 - \varepsilon$ (i.e. n_j does "not solve" c_i, which for classification tasks boils down to $c_i.s \neq n_j.s$), then c_i is added as a new node to V_{i-1} and a (bidirectional) edge (c_i, n_j) is added to E_{i-1}. The resulting, extended boundary graph is denoted as $\mathcal{B}_i$. To sum up, training cases are added as nodes to the graph (including connecting edge), if the algorithm stochastically discovers a random retrieval starting point for which the currently existing boundary graph's prediction would be wrong and where, hence, a correction is needed.

Again, pseudo-code for constructively building up a boundary graph for a sequence of training cases is provided in Algorithm 2, denoted as BG_CONSTRUCT. Note that the algorithm can be easily deployed in an online setting where new cases arrive during runtime by simply calling the BG_RETAIN function.

The left part of Fig. 1 is meant as an attempt to visualize an exemplary boundary graph for a synthetic two-dimensional, linearly separable two-class problem. Using 80 randomly created training cases, the BG_CONSTRUCT algorithm created a boundary graph of 19 nodes and 40 edges. Using 20 independently sampled test cases, the resulting graph-based classifier yields an average classification error of 9.42% for 1000 random repetitions of the experiment.

BG_CONSTRUCT(CB, r)
Input: case base
$CB = \{c_1, \dots, c_n\}$,
number r of random
retrieval restarts
Output: boundary tree $\mathcal{B}$
$\mathcal{B} \leftarrow (\emptyset, \emptyset)$
// loop over all cases
for $i = 1$ **to** n **do**
  $\mathcal{B} \leftarrow$ BG_RETAIN$(\mathcal{B}, c_i, r)$
return $\mathcal{B}$

BG_RETAIN($\mathcal{B}$, c, r)
Input: single (new) case c,
boundary graph $\mathcal{B} = (V, E)$,
number r of random retrieval restarts
Requires (global variables):
amalgamation function $\mathcal{A}$,
solution discrimination threshold ε
Output: (possibly extended) boundary graph $\mathcal{B}$
if $V = \emptyset$ **then** $V \leftarrow V \cup c$
else
  $\mathcal{N}_c^r \leftarrow$ BG_RETRIEVE$(c, \mathcal{B}, r)$
  for $i = 1$ **to** r **do**
    $\sigma \leftarrow sim_s(c.s, \mathcal{N}_c^r[i].s)$
    if $\sigma < 1 - \varepsilon$ **then**
      $V \leftarrow V \cup c$, $E \leftarrow E \cup (c, \mathcal{N}_c^r[i])$
(**return** (V, E)):

Algorithm 2: Construction of and Retain Procedure for Boundary Graphs

3.2 Labeled Boundary Multigraphs

We observed that increasing the value of the parameter r for the number of random retrieval restart improves the prediction accuracy and the stability of predictions. However, just like IB2 (cf. Sect. 2), the presented approach suffers from a dependency of the resulting boundary graph on the order in which the cases are presented to the retain procedure. The boundary forest algorithm (cf. Sect. 2) mitigates this dependency by forming an ensemble of (tree-based) classifiers. This is a straightforward idea whose impact we will also analyze for the IB2 algorithm below. At this point, however, we take inspiration from these ideas to extend our boundary graph algorithm such that it becomes more robust with respect to the order of the training data, while the computational overhead is acceptable and a single holistic retrieval index structure is retained.

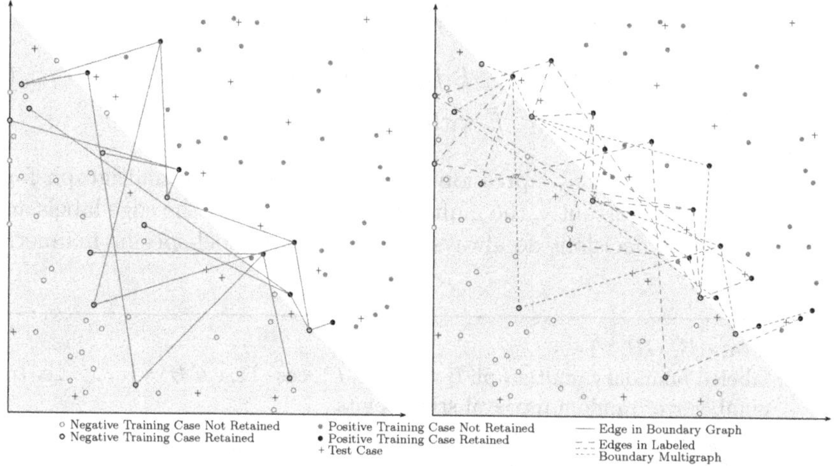

Fig. 1. Left: Visualization of an Examplary Boundary Graph: From the 80 training cases, 19 are included in the graph's set of vertices (11 from the negative class, 8 from the positive one), when trained using $r = 9$. Among that set of nodes, there are 88 possible edges that would cross the decision boundary. Out of those, 40 are included in the graph's set of edges. Right: Examplary Labeled Boundary Multigraph trained on the same data set for $\lambda = 3$ different labels and, accordingly, using $r_t := \frac{r}{\lambda} = \frac{9}{3} = 3$. In total, 27 nodes are included in the multigraph's set of vertices which are interconnected using 71 edges (32/8/31 for the three labels).

The core idea is to use uniquely identifiable labeled edges in the graph structure. This means we allow for multiple edges between vertices (which turns the graph into a multigraph), but make them distinguishable by attaching a label out of a set of λ labels to each edge. This promotes a more efficient dispersion of the retrieval knowledge across the graph structure. Then, instead of performing r random retrieval restarts (as we did before), the algorithm now (on average) performs $r_t := r/\lambda$ such random retrieval restarts per edge label. In so doing, the total amount of inner-graph retrieval computations stays roughly the same.

In the following, we first introduce the necessary notation, then present the retain part and, afterwards, conclude with the retrieve/revise procedures.

3.2.1 Notation

We define a *Labeled Boundary Multigraph (LBM)* $\tilde{\mathcal{B}} = (\tilde{V}, \tilde{E}, \tilde{L})$ to be a labeled undirected multigraph [2] with $\tilde{V}$ a set of vertices, $\tilde{E}$ a multiset of bidirectional edges, and $\tilde{L} : \tilde{E} \rightarrow \mathcal{L}$ a labeling function mapping to each edge a label out of a finite set of λ unique labels $\mathcal{L} = (l_1, \ldots, l_\lambda)$. We use the notation $\tilde{\mathcal{B}}|_l$ to indicate the submultigraph of $\tilde{\mathcal{B}} = (\tilde{V}, \tilde{E}, \tilde{L})$ for some specific edge label l. Note that, due to the restriction to edge label l, $\tilde{\mathcal{B}}|_l$ represents a boundary graph, no longer a labeled boundary multigraph. Formally,

$$\tilde{\mathcal{B}}|_l = (V_l, E_l) \text{ where } E_l = \{e \in \tilde{E} | \tilde{L}(e) = l\} \text{ and} \\ V_l = \{v \in \tilde{V} | \exists (x,y) \in \tilde{E} \text{ with } \tilde{L}((x,y)) = l \text{ and } x = v \text{ or } y = v\} \tag{7}$$

Figure 1 (right) conveys an impression of a labeled boundary multigraph for a toy domain. Most importantly, the multigraph is factored by the edge labels and, retrieval and retain decisions do always take place in a label-specific manner.

LBM_RETAIN($\tilde{\mathcal{B}}$, CB, r)
Input: labeled boundary multigraph $\tilde{\mathcal{B}} = (\tilde{V}, \tilde{E}, \tilde{L})$, case base $CB = \{c_1, \dots, c_n\}$, number r of random retrieval start points
Output: (possibly extended) labeled boundary multigraph $\tilde{\mathcal{B}}$
1: **repeat** λ times // $\lambda = |\mathcal{L}|$
2: $CB \leftarrow$ shuffle cases in CB
3: **for** $i = 1$ **to** n **do**
4: $l \leftarrow$ random edge label from $\mathcal{L} = \{1, \dots, \lambda\}$
5: $(V_l, E_l) \leftarrow \tilde{\mathcal{B}}|_l$ // *induced subgraph for label l, cf. Equation 7*
6: $(V_l', E_l') \leftarrow$ BG_RETAIN$((V_l, E_l), c_i, \frac{r}{\lambda})$
7: **forall** $e \in \tilde{E} \cup E_l'$ **do if** $e \in E_l'$ **then** $\tilde{L}'(e) = l$ **else** $\tilde{L}'(e) = \tilde{L}(e)$
8: $\tilde{\mathcal{B}} \leftarrow (\tilde{V} \cup V_l', \tilde{E} \cup E_l', \tilde{L}')$
9: **return** $\tilde{\mathcal{B}}$

Algorithm 3: Construction of Labeled Boundary Multigraphs

3.2.2 Multigraph Construction

The LBM_RETAIN algorithm, provided in Algorithm 3, takes as input the number r of random retrieval restarts, a set of cases $CB = \{c_1, \dots, c_n\}$ as well as a (possibly empty) labeled boundary multigraph $\tilde{\mathcal{B}}$ which it extends and returns. It thus works for both scenarios, either being given a set of training cases and starting out with an empty graph or in an online setting where a non-empty labeled multigraph is extended for a single or a few further training case(s).

When considering the next training case c_i, the algorithm first selects a random edge label l. If the algorithm later finds that this case should be added to the graph, then it will be connected to other nodes by edges that are labeled with l. Accordingly, line 5 determines the induced boundary subgraph for label l (cf. Eq. 7), consisting of edges with label l exclusively and of vertices that are adjacent to those edges. For this subgraph $\tilde{\mathcal{B}}|_l = (V_l, E_l)$ the BG_RETAIN algorithm is invoked, handing over the current case c_i plus the number of random retrieval restarts to be made during that retain step. Note that the latter number is reduced by a factor of λ (i.e. $\frac{r}{\lambda}$ is handed over in line 6) which is balancing the fact that the loop over all training cases $(c_1, \dots, c_n)$ is repeated for as many times as we do have labels (i.e. for λ times, repeat loop from lines 1 to 8). The result of the BG_RETAIN call on the subgraph is finally incorporated into the labeled boundary multigraph $\tilde{\mathcal{B}}$ (lines 7 and 8) before the algorithm continues with the next iteration. Note that each case is handled for λ times (each time using a randomly selected label) and might, thus, be connected with other nodes by a number of possibly differently labeled edges. Moreover, the contents of CB is shuffled at the beginning of each of the λ outer loop repetitions in order to mitigate against the dependency on the presentation order of the instances.

3.2.3 Multigraph Retrieval

Retrieval in an LBM $\tilde{\mathcal{B}}$ traverses the graph structure – searching greedily for more similar cases to the query q, jumping to neighboring vertices, if their similarity to q is higher than the similarity q and the current vertex – for a total of r times, starting at a random node v each time. Moreover, each of these traversals sticks to using edges with a specific label l exclusively. So, the r repetitions are equally distributed among the subsets of $\tilde{E}$ that contain edges with label l only. We point to the fact that lines 5 to 9 in the LBM_RETRIEVE procedure (Alg. 4) could be rewritten using a call to BG_RETRIEVE on $\tilde{\mathcal{B}}|_l$ with $\frac{r}{\lambda}$ random retrieval restarts, but that we decided for the more lengthy write-up for better comprehension.

As a result, an r-dimensional vector of estimated nearest neighbors is formed which, finally, can be utilized by some prediction function to form an overall estimate (reuse step) using some amalgamation function. To this end, we may alter the function BG_PREDICT (Algorithm 1) to LBM_PREDICT with the only difference that it calls LBM_RETRIEVE instead of BG_RETRIEVE in line 2.

As mentioned, the right part of Fig. 1 shows an exemplary labeled boundary multigraph (for $\lambda = 3$ labels) for the same toy problem as in Sect. 3.1.3. The increase in number of vertices and edges stored brings (while staying computationally at nearly the same level) a reduction of the classification error by almost 17% compared to the basic boundary graph approach: Using 20 independently sampled test cases, the resulting boundary graph-based classifier yields an average classification error of 7.87% (for 1000 random repetitions of the test).

LBM_RETRIEVE(q, $\tilde{\mathcal{B}}$, r)
Input: query $q \in \mathcal{P}$, LBM $\tilde{\mathcal{B}} = (\tilde{V}, \tilde{E}, \tilde{L})$, number r of random retrieval restarts
Output: r-dimensional vector $\mathcal{N}_q^r$ of potential nearest neighbors
1: $\mathcal{N}_r^q \leftarrow r$-dimensional vector
2: **for** $l = 1$ **to** λ **do**
3: $(V_l, E_l) \leftarrow \tilde{\mathcal{B}}|_l$
4: **for** $i = 1$ **to** $\frac{r}{\lambda}$ **do**
5: $v \leftarrow$ random node from V_l, $stop \leftarrow false$, $c^* \leftarrow v$
6: **while** $stop = false$ **do**
7: $c^* \leftarrow \arg\max_{(v,c) \in E_l} sim_p(q, c)$
8: **if** $sim_p(q, c^*) > sim_p(q, v)$ **then** $v \leftarrow c^*$ **else** $stop \leftarrow true$
9: $\mathcal{N}_r^q[(l-1)r/\lambda + i] \leftarrow v$
10: **return** $\mathcal{N}_q^r$

Algorithm 4: Labeled Boundary Multigraph Retrieval

3.3 Discussion

For both algorithms described, the boundary graph as well as the labeled multi-graph extension, we find empirically that the retrieval time using such a graph as index structure scales either as a power law βn^α in the amount of training cases n with a power value $\alpha < 1$ or logarithmically For the most comprehensive data set we analyzed we found the complexity to be in $O(\log n)$. Accordingly, training time scales as $n^{1+\alpha}$ or $n \log n$, respectively, because each retain step essentially includes a retrieve step, rendering the complexity of training to be a loop of n repetitions wrapped around the retrieval procedure.

The boundary graph approach has the favorable characteristic to be an *any-time retrieval algorithm*. By handling the parameter r of random retrieval starting points within the graph different during training (r_t) and the application (r_a) of the learned graph, i.e. separating $r_t := \frac{r}{\lambda}$ from r_a, one can gain a significant performance boost by letting $r_a > r_t$, given that a sufficient amount of time is available for the system to respond to a query. This is a desirable property in real-time and online application settings since the accuracy of the retrieval grows with r_a as we will show in the next section.

4 Empirical Evaluation

Our experimental investigations were driven by two questions: What final performance can be achieved using labeled boundary multigraphs as index structure in case-based retrieval? And at what costs can these results be obtained? We are going to address these questions in the next subsections.

4.1 Experimental Set-Up

Our experiments focus on classification problems. Hence, no specific value for ε must be set as two cases' solutions are considered different, if their class labels do not match. We selected a variety of established classification benchmark datasets from the UCI Machine Learning Repository [8] with varying amounts of case data, classes, and numbers and types of features. Additionally, we used a larger (500 k instances) nine-dimensional dataset from the field of robotic soccer simulation where the goal is to predict the type of an opponent agent's next action (e.g. kick or dash or turn, cf. [9]) In all our experiments we employ a knowledge-poor default similarity measure according to the local-global principle [3] with uniform attribute weights, identity similarity matrices for discrete features and linear difference-based similarity functions for numeric ones. We are fully aware that the classification accuracy might be improved significantly, when applying knowledge-intensive, domain-specific similarity measures or even learned ones [10]. For each domain, we split the available case data into two randomly created disjoint sets, using the first (80%) one for construction the graph-based index structure and the second (20%) for applying (testing) it. To account for the stochastic nature of our proposed algorithms, all experiments were repeated 100 times, forming average values of performance indicators.

4.2 Classical Benchmark Data Sets

In this series of experiments, we compared our proposed methods (BG and LBM) to several other retrieval mechanisms. As a baseline, we employed the k-nearest neighbor classifier with $k = 1$, yielding a classification error μ of 26.07% averaged over the 24 datasets[2] (cf. Table 1). Searching for the best value of k for that set of domains in a brute force manner, we found that $k^* = 13$ yields best results ($\mu = 21.07\%$). We proceeded in the same way for the boundary tree/forest approach (cf. Sect. 2). Using forests of 10 and 50 trees (as the authors in [16] propose), a classification error of 23.32 and 21.32%, respectively, is obtained, while the best one found (brute force search) is 20.83% for a forest of 325 trees.

With respect to storage requirements it is worth noting that the only algorithm that yields a substantial case base compactification γ (last line in Table 1) is the classical IB2 algorithm which retains 34.6% of the given case data on average. To this end, we also tested a straightforward extension of IB2, called $IB2_e$, which runs IB2 on e shuffled versions of the training data, forms an ensemble of e compactified case bases and classifies cases by applying a majority vote as in Eq. 4. As expected, increasing e clearly impairs the achieved level of case base compactification (γ is now determined on the basis of the union of the e IB2 instances' case bases), trading this off for lower classification errors with the lowest one found (again, in a brute force manner) for $e^* = 94$.

Using a single boundary graph as index structure (columns BG_r), that was trained using $r = 10$ and 50 random retrieval restarts (these numbers have been chosen in accordance to the boundary forests), approximately 25% of the training cases need not to be stored. However, with an average classification error of 24.10 and 23.52%, respectively, the approach does not surpass the boundary forests.

Next, we investigated the labeled boundary multigraph approach where, for reasons of comparison to the previous algorithms, we set $r = 50$. We first report the setting where these 50 random retrieval restarts are distributed over $\lambda = 7$ labels during training *and* application, i.e. $r_t = r_a = \frac{r}{\lambda} = \frac{50}{7} \approx 7$. Apparently, μ drops to 21.08%, outperforming all other approaches considered so far. On the supposition that during the application of the system was more time or computational power available, one might consider increasing r_a beyond r_t. The impact of that computational extra effort can be read from the neighboring table column where μ is reported to drop to 20.49%. We emphasize that this is a unique characteristic of the BG/LBM approach, i.e. a feature that the other algorithm do not possess, and that further increasing r_a would reduce the error even more. This particular effect of varying computational budgets during retrieval in the application phase of the system is more thoroughly analyzed in Fig. 2.

The third and second from last columns indicate that doubling the number of labels while retaining the overall effort at the same level (i.e. $\lambda = 13$ and $r_t = 4$ with $\lambda r_t = 13 \cdot 4 \approx 7 \cdot 7$) improves the average performance of the

[2] A-Balance, B-BanknoteAuth, C-Cancer, D-Car, E-Contraceptive, F-Ecoli, G-Flare, H-Glass, I-Haberman, J-Hayes, K-Heart, L-Iris, M-MammogrMass, N-Monks, O-Pima, P-QualBankruptcy, Q-TeachAssistEval, R-TicTacToe, S-Transfusion, T-UserKnowledge, U-VertebralCol, V-Wholesale, W-Wine, X-Yeast.

Table 1. For all considered retrieval approaches and for each of the considered domains the classification error in percent (averaged over 100 experiment repetitions) is provided, plus an average μ over all domains. Additionally, in the last line the average case base compactification γ is reported. For each domain, the two top-performing algorithms are highlighted. The first column contains domain identifiers (see footnote for plain text names).

Dom.	k-NN		BF_t			$IB2_e$			BG_r		$LBM^{\lambda=7}_{r_t,r_a}$		$LBM^{\lambda=13}_{r_t,r_a}$		LBM $\lambda^*=37$
	k=1	k^*=13	t=10	t=50	t^*=325	e=1	e=13	e^*=94	r=10	r=50	r_t=7 r_a=7	r_t=7 r_a=50	r_t=4 r_a=4	r_t=4 r_a=50	r_t=6 r_a=50
A	35.47	17.12	26.11	20.47	19.13	48.59	47.05	45.75	24.43	25.18	19.54	17.24	18.39	**14.85**	**15.69**
B	0.16	0.30	0.12	0.12	0.15	0.57	0.15	0.17	0.20	0.14	0.12	**0.10**	0.11	**0.09**	0.12
C	31.48	**24.84**	29.76	27.94	26.91	32.85	29.64	28.91	30.16	31.58	27.02	26.58	25.62	**25.27**	25.29
D	22.78	9.18	10.06	**5.21**	**3.93**	22.94	15.14	14.57	12.84	5.76	8.61	6.51	11.99	9.13	6.59
E	56.34	52.00	54.87	53.06	52.67	57.18	54.69	53.90	54.57	54.81	52.43	51.24	51.84	**50.24**	**51.11**
F	20.08	16.12	20.31	19.98	19.98	28.07	23.74	23.13	20.84	21.99	16.16	16.03	15.57	**15.37**	**15.24**
G	28.86	17.52	21.51	21.37	21.21	40.65	36.60	33.82	18.36	21.16	17.25	17.17	16.99	**16.85**	**17.12**
H	28.66	33.52	27.60	27.06	**26.54**	32.61	29.62	29.41	31.07	30.02	28.19	27.98	27.90	27.10	**26.40**
I	35.34	**26.20**	35.77	35.29	35.17	40.00	37.63	38.12	35.56	36.66	33.93	34.00	**32.66**	32.79	33.39
J	33.15	43.28	27.58	**25.10**	**24.28**	32.21	29.78	29.29	32.50	31.00	33.50	34.54	34.19	35.35	35.19
K	21.27	**16.89**	23.41	20.61	20.02	28.81	24.71	23.77	23.87	24.72	19.22	18.76	18.39	18.39	**18.31**
L	5.93	**4.88**	6.43	5.72	5.79	8.75	6.70	6.46	8.13	8.87	5.93	5.90	**5.63**	**5.63**	5.70
M	26.93	20.10	23.93	22.35	21.82	32.57	28.61	27.42	22.77	23.64	20.22	**19.29**	20.61	19.49	**19.14**
N	27.37	6.11	3.97	**0.03**	**0.00**	26.57	15.74	13.03	9.49	1.03	2.64	0.47	5.56	1.06	0.22
O	30.46	26.58	31.24	28.97	28.14	36.16	35.02	34.00	30.68	32.47	27.40	27.10	26.49	**25.87**	**26.38**
P	0.20	0.40	0.60	0.67	0.63	1.88	0.42	0.28	0.52	0.20	0.26	**0.18**	0.24	0.20	**0.10**
Q	**38.42**	52.88	40.43	40.44	40.47	42.59	39.00	**38.45**	42.83	40.43	42.30	41.50	42.80	42.43	39.87
R	18.88	2.33	7.63	**1.82**	**1.07**	18.70	15.77	16.02	12.19	2.46	7.08	4.92	10.61	9.42	4.61
S	31.24	**22.30**	29.28	29.14	29.03	36.38	33.56	33.51	27.83	30.98	24.70	24.46	23.46	**23.41**	24.08
T	19.95	18.14	16.08	13.62	13.48	25.78	18.75	18.24	18.61	17.33	12.92	12.37	12.29	**11.61**	**11.51**
U	24.58	**21.26**	25.26	23.28	22.53	29.75	26.07	25.59	25.32	26.19	22.94	22.95	22.32	**21.74**	22.37
V	46.65	**29.24**	45.40	43.04	42.91	51.65	49.65	49.19	43.86	46.31	38.00	37.47	34.70	**34.56**	35.75
W	3.99	2.72	2.66	2.02	**1.60**	7.52	2.69	2.41	4.03	3.51	2.17	2.14	2.20	**1.77**	1.86
X	47.57	**41.85**	47.51	44.43	43.92	53.80	51.52	51.60	47.77	47.98	43.38	42.93	42.62	**41.86**	42.17
μ	26.49	21.07	23.23	21.32	20.89	30.69	27.18	26.54	24.10	23.52	21.08	20.49	20.97	**20.19**	**19.93**
γ	100.0	100.0	79.5	92.3	96.4	**34.6**	79.3	93.2	**72.4**	74.9	92.4	92.4	94.8	94.8	96.4

obtained index structure even further. For completeness, we also included the best possible LBM (using a set of $\lambda = 37$ edge labels, $r_t = 6$ random retrieval restarts during training and $r_a = 50$ during application) that we found by brute force search (therefore, again marked with a star) whose average classification error is 19.93%.

4.3 Scaling Analysis

When introducing novel algorithms, their space and time requirements are of high interest. In our case, space complexity boils down to the number of cases retained which can be equated with the number of nodes in a BG/LBM. Storing edges represents a negligible overhead as we realize this by storing pointers to the original case data. We measure the algorithms' time complexity in terms of

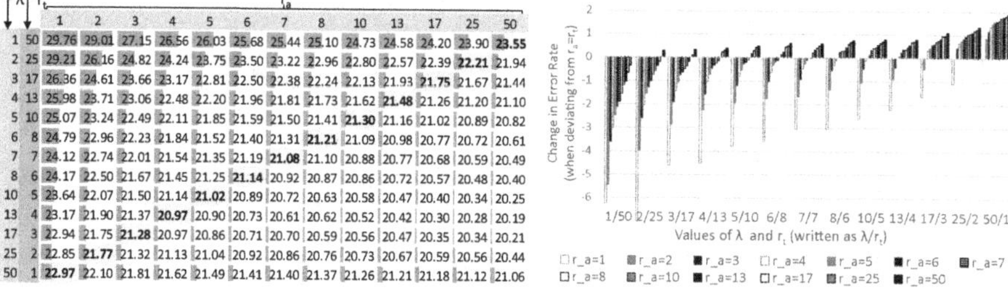

λ	r_t	r_a = 1	2	3	4	5	6	7	8	10	13	17	25	50
1	50	29.76	29.01	27.15	26.56	26.03	25.68	25.44	25.10	24.73	24.58	24.20	23.90	**23.55**
2	25	29.21	26.16	24.82	24.24	23.75	23.50	23.22	22.96	22.80	22.57	22.39	**22.21**	21.94
3	17	26.36	24.61	23.66	23.17	22.81	22.50	22.38	22.24	22.13	21.93	**21.75**	21.67	21.44
4	13	25.98	23.71	23.06	22.48	22.20	21.96	21.81	21.73	21.62	**21.48**	21.26	21.20	21.10
5	10	25.07	23.24	22.49	22.11	21.85	21.59	21.50	21.41	**21.30**	21.16	21.02	20.89	20.82
6	8	24.79	22.96	22.23	21.84	21.52	21.40	21.31	**21.21**	21.09	20.98	20.77	20.72	20.61
7	7	24.12	22.74	22.01	21.54	21.35	21.19	**21.08**	21.10	20.88	20.77	20.68	20.59	20.49
8	6	24.17	22.50	21.67	21.45	21.25	**21.14**	20.92	20.87	20.86	20.72	20.57	20.48	20.40
10	5	23.64	22.07	21.50	21.14	**21.02**	20.89	20.72	20.63	20.58	20.47	20.40	20.34	20.25
13	4	23.17	21.90	21.37	**20.97**	20.90	20.73	20.61	20.62	20.52	20.42	20.30	20.28	20.19
17	3	22.94	21.75	**21.28**	20.97	20.86	20.71	20.70	20.59	20.56	20.47	20.35	20.34	20.21
25	2	22.85	**21.77**	21.32	21.13	21.04	20.92	20.86	20.76	20.73	20.67	20.59	20.56	20.44
50	1	**22.97**	22.10	21.81	21.62	21.49	21.41	21.40	21.37	21.26	21.21	21.18	21.12	21.06

Fig. 2. Comparison of LBMs with Equal Computational Construction Effort: The product of λ and r_t is always (nearly) the same, i.e. $r = \lambda r_t \approx 50$. The left matrix shows classification errors averaged over all 24 UCI domains, subject to differing values of r_a (columns). While the diagonal is highlighted as a default setting with $r_t = r_a$, the diagram on the right visualizes the gains/losses in accuracy that are obtained when deviating from the default and varying the values of r_a between 1 to 50, subject to the different combinations of λ and r_t (all with $\lambda r_t \approx 50$).

similarity calculations as a function of the number of training cases n, as this is the computational bottleneck for case-based retrieval algorithms.

Part a) in Fig. 3 visualizes the average number of required similarity calculations for a test query for the 24 UCI domains we selected (trained/tested for $\lambda = 1$ and $r_t = r_a = 15$). The best power law fit of the data is nearly identical to the best logarithmic fit (in terms of the coefficient of determination R^2) leaving us somewhat undecided whether the computational effort scales with $O(n^{\frac{3}{5}})$ or logarithmically, especially since there is a lot of variation included due to the varying characteristics of the different domains.

By contrast, part b) visualizes the scaling behavior of the boundary graph approach ($\lambda = 1$, $r_t = r_a = 50$) for the mentioned robotic soccer simulation domain. Here, the number of required similarity calculations per test query seems to scale clearly logarithmically in the number of the training cases (i.e. $O(\log n)$ and $O(n \log n)$ for the overall training process).

The behavior plotted in part b) of Fig. 3 can be fully appreciated only, when relating this to the achieved case base compactification γ which can be read from part c). Apparently, the number of cases stored grows linearly with n (note the log scale abscissa) at a level of $\gamma \approx 0.6$, such that, e.g., for a training set of $n = 51200$ cases on average only 4548 similarity calculations (4.9% of n) must be performed. For $n = 409600$ cases, we observe 251 k stored cases ($\gamma = 61\%$) and 7278 required similarity calculations (1.8%) for a single test query on average. This is in strong contrast to the other algorithms where many more similarity calculations are required during retrieval. Essentially, this is achieved by the fact that the number of edges per vertex grows logarithmically with n (see dashed line in the plot of part c) in Fig. 3).

Finally, part d) highlights the relation between the training set size and the final performance of the constructed graph-based index structure in the robotic soccer domain. While it is to be expected that the classification error on the test

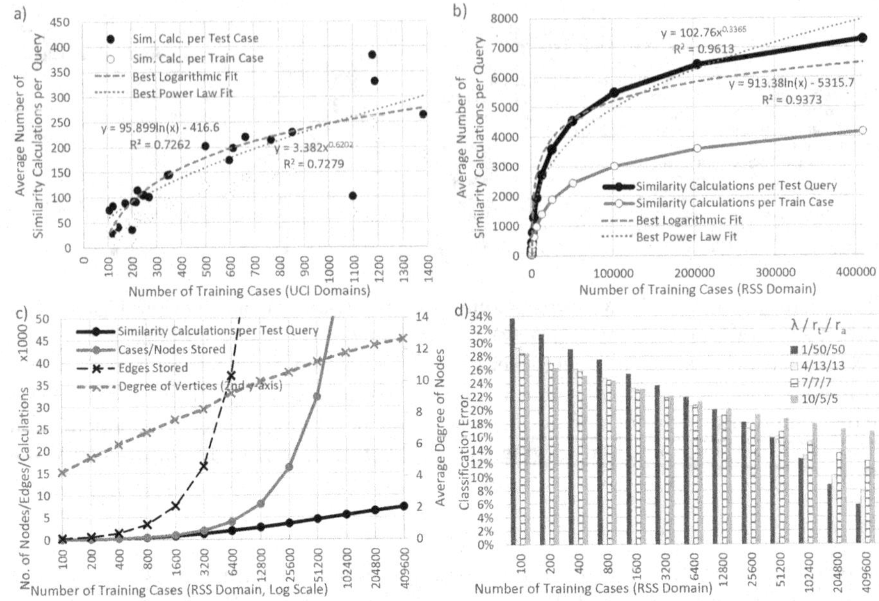

Fig. 3. Scaling Behavior of BGs/LBM: See the text for details.

set decreases with the number of training cases, it is interesting to observe that for smaller training sets a distribution among a larger number λ of label layers is less beneficial. This fact is revealed for $n \geq 100\,\text{k}$ where the simpler structured boundary graph (i.e. with $\lambda = 1$) supersedes other variations and finally achieves an excellent low classification error of less than 6%.

It is worth noting that, under these settings ($n = 409.6\,\text{k}$, $\lambda = 1$, $r_t = r_a = 50$), a case-based classification can be made within 18.6 ms of time on a single core of a contemporary 3 GHz CPU which adheres to the real-time constraints imposed by the soccer simulation environment where an agent must execute each action within 100 ms. With the already discussed additional opportunity to increase/decrease r_a online depending on necessary other computations done by the agent during decision-making, we obtain a reliable and performant module for case-based opponent modeling. Further analyses for that domain and of our algorithms' scaling properties can be found in a separate paper [11].

5 Conclusion

Retrieval efficiency in Case-Based Reasoning remains an important topic even after decades of research. In this paper, we have introduced the concept of boundary graphs which we suggest to use as an efficient index structure during case-based retrieval. The core idea of these graph structures as well as of their labeled multigraph extensions that we develop on top of them is that their edges do always connect cases with differing solutions. We have proposed appropriate retrieve and retain algorithms and evaluated them using a selection of benchmark classification problems as well as a robotic soccer dataset. While our methods are presented in a way that makes them applicable to various problem types, our empirical evaluations focused on classification tasks, leaving the analysis of other problem types (like regression etc.) for future work.

References

1. Aha, D., Kibler, D., Albert, M.: Instance-based learning algorithms. Mach. Learn. **6**, 37–66 (1991). https://doi.org/10.1007/BF00153759
2. Balakrishnan, V.: Theory and Problems of Graph Theory. McGraw, USA (1997)
3. Bergmann, R., Richter, M., Schmitt, S., Stahl, A., Vollrath, I.: Utility-oriented matching: a new research direction for case-based reasoning. In: Proceedings of the 9th German Workshop on Case-Based Reasoning (GWCBR) (2001)
4. Beygelzimer, A., Kakade, S., Langford, J.: Cover tree for nearest neighbor. In: Proceedings of the Twenty-Third International Conference on Machine Learning (ICML), pp. 97–104. ACM Press, Pittsburgh, USA (2006)
5. Brin, S.: Near neighbors search in large metric spaces. In: Proceedings of the Twenty-First International Conference on Very Large Data Bases (VLDB), pp. 574–584. Morgan Kaufmann, Zurich, Switzerland (1995)
6. Cover, T., Hart, P.: Nearest neighbor pattern classification. IEEE Trans. Inf. Theory **13**, 21–27 (1967)
7. Djebbar, A., Merouani, H.: Optimising retrieval phase in CBR through pearl and JLO algorithms. J. Adv. Intell. Paradigms **5**(3), 161–181 (2013)
8. Dua, D., Graff, C.: UCI repository (2017). http://archive.ics.uci.edu/ml
9. Gabel, T., Godehardt, E.: I know what you're doing: a case study on case-based opponent modeling and low-level action prediction. In: Workshop on Case-Based Agents at ICCBR (CBA 2015), pp. 13–22. Frankfurt, Germany (2015)
10. Gabel, T., Godehardt, E.: Top-down induction of similarity measures using similarity clouds. In: Hüllermeier, E., Minor, M. (eds.) ICCBR 2015. LNCS (LNAI), vol. 9343, pp. 149–164. Springer, Cham (2015). https://doi.org/10.1007/978-3-319-24586-7_11
11. Gabel, T., Sommer, F.: Instance-based opponent action prediction in soccer simulation using boundary graphs. In: Paetzel, M., Lau, N., Wanichanon, T., Eguchi, A. (eds.) RoboCup 2022: Robot Soccer World Cup XXVI. Springer, Bangkok (2022)
12. Gates, G.: The reduced nearest neighbor rule. IEEE Trans. Inf. Theory **18**(3), 431–433 (1972)
13. Leake, D.B., Wilson, D.C.: Categorizing case-base maintenance: dimensions and directions. In: Smyth, B., Cunningham, P. (eds.) EWCBR 1998. LNCS, vol. 1488, pp. 196–207. Springer, Heidelberg (1998). https://doi.org/10.1007/BFb0056333
14. Lejsek, H., Jonsson, B., Amsaleg, L.: NV-tree: nearest neighbors in the billion scale. In: Proceedings of the First ACM International Conference on Multimedia Retrieval (ICMR), pp. 57–64. ACM Press, Trento, Italy (2011)
15. Lenz, M.: Case retrieval nets as a model for building flexible information systems. Ph.D. thesis, Humboldt University of Berlin, Germany (1999)
16. Mathy, C., Derbinsky, N., Bento, J., Rosenthal, J., Yedidia, J.: The boundary forest algorithm for online supervised and unsupervised learning. In: Proceedings of the 29th AAAI Conference on AI, pp. 2864–2870. AAAI Press, Austin, USA (2015)

17. Richter, M.M., Weber, R.O.: Case-Based Reasoning. Springer, Heidelberg (2013). https://doi.org/10.1007/978-3-642-40167-1
18. Smyth, B., McKenna, E.: Building compact competent case-bases. In: Althoff, K.-D., Bergmann, R., Branting, L.K. (eds.) ICCBR 1999. LNCS, vol. 1650, pp. 329–342. Springer, Heidelberg (1999). https://doi.org/10.1007/3-540-48508-2_24
19. Smyth, B., McKenna, E.: Competence guided incremental footprint-based retrieval. Knowl.-Based Syst. **14**(3–4), 155–161 (2001)
20. Wess, S., Althoff, K.-D., Derwand, G.: Using k-d trees to improve the retrieval step in case-based reasoning. In: Wess, S., Althoff, K.-D., Richter, M.M. (eds.) EWCBR 1993. LNCS, vol. 837, pp. 167–181. Springer, Heidelberg (1994). https://doi.org/10.1007/3-540-58330-0_85
21. Wilson, D., Martinez, T.: Reduction techniques for instance-based learning algorithms. Mach. Learn. **38**(3), 257–286 (2000). https://doi.org/10.1023/A:1007626913721

Particle Swarm Optimization in Small Case Bases for Software Effort Estimation

Katharina Landeis[1,2], Gerhard Pews[1], and Mirjam Minor[2(✉)]

[1] Capgemini, Cologne, Germany
[2] Department of Business Informatics, Goethe University Frankfurt, Frankfurt, Germany
minor@cs.uni-frankfurt.de

Abstract. To facilitate research in the field of user story effort estimation (USEE), this work analyzes the applicability of case-based reasoning to effort estimation of user stories. The analysis uses real-world user stories of a software development project of the Capgemini Group. The focus of the analysis is the development of an effort estimation tool that could generate accurate effort estimates serving the purposes of project planning and control. In addition to a classical structural CBR approach, the paper applies the weights optimization method Particle Swarm Optimization to small case bases. The highly accurate effort estimates resulting from a couple of experiments on real data show that estimation by analogy presents with the aid of an automated environment an eminently practical technique. As a consequence, this approach impacts estimation accuracy and thus success of industrial software development projects.

Keywords: CBR applications · Software engineering · Few data · Particle swarm optimization

1 Introduction

Software effort estimation (SEE) is the process of approximating the amount of effort needed to complete project activities [24]. In agile software development, a project comprises several iterations, each of which delivers a set of requirements known as user stories [1]. The success or failure of an agile software project depends on accuracy in estimating the effort of user stories [16]. Underestimates bear the risk that projects reveal to exceed the budget. When efforts are overestimated, the company might mistakenly reject potentially profitable user stories or even projects.

Numerous studies on effort estimation of user stories have been published in the recent past [1,6,12,16,25]. They report on many different estimation techniques of expert-based or data-driven kind. The data-driven approaches have in common that they require a large amount of data. Malgonde and Chari's work [12] with around 500 stories are among those with smaller data sets. In practice, however, many repositories with user stories are distinctly sparser for

M. T. Keane and N. Wiratunga (Eds.): ICCBR 2022, LNAI 13405, pp. 209–223, 2022.
https://doi.org/10.1007/978-3-031-14923-8_14

privacy or further business concerns. Our research is investigating how accurate estimations can be derived from small repositories of user stories. We have developed a Case-based Reasoning (CBR) approach for estimating user stories' effort that uses particle swarm optimization. It turned out during our experiments with four small case-bases (below 60 cases each) that CBR outperforms the estimation accuracy of expert judgements achieved with the Planning Poker technique.

The remainder of the paper is organized as follows. Related work is discussed in Sect. 2. The application scenario is introduced in further detail in Sect. 3. The CBR approach is presented in Sect. 4. Next, Sect. 5 reports on the experiments with real-world data from a software project of the Capgemini Group. Finally, a conclusion is drawn in Sect. 6.

2 Related Work

SEE by analogy has already a long tradition in CBR [7,8,15,20,27,28]. These approaches have in common that a software project is represented as a case and is characterized by a set of features that are regarded as effort drivers, such as the programming languages or complexity of the project. In contrast to our approach those publications focus on entire software projects. Today, agile software development is of increasing importance. This means that the requirements whose effort can be estimated are described in the form of user stories. Those smaller, less complex units have to our knowledge not yet been considered in case-based research on SEE.

Recently, the optimization of CBR approaches in SEE has attracted considerable research attention as approaches like particle swarm optimization (PSO) and genetic algorithm (GA) have been used to optimize weights, parameters, and select features [7,8,27,28]. These research results have shown that CBR method with optimized weights derived by PSO or GA can improve estimation results. Furthermore, there exist results verifying that PSO is able to outperform GA in searching the optimized weight of CBR [14]. Again, there do not exist weights optimization approaches in the context of user story effort estimation (USEE). As the PSO method is known to outperformed GA [14], this method is chosen to identify optimal weights for effort drivers in our CBR approach.

Additionally, related approaches for optimization have gained attention in CBR research [9,22,26]. The work of Jarmulak et al. [9] optimizes the case-base index and the feature weights for similarity measure simultaneously for the application area of tablet formulation. Stahl and Gabel [22] implement a novel approach for optimizing the similarity assessment in CBR. Their work employs evolutionary algorithms for optimizing similarity measures by means of relative case utility feedback. The work of Wiratunga et al. [26] introduces learning-to-learn personalised models from few data. It applies a personalized meta-learning approach to self-management cases for patients of back-pain. These approaches provide alternative solutions to PSO in the context of CBR approaches, the latter with few available data. They have not yet been considered in our work but might inspire future work on alternative or hybrid approaches for USEE.

3 Software Effort Estimation of User Stories

SEE is an active research field since the 1970s. This dynamic field of SEE has undergone several changes in the last four decades, whereas one significant development emerged in the course of the agile movement.

The shift from traditional to agile methodologies used in the development process changed the perspective on estimation and planning in the last twenty years. In agile development settings, the project is characterized by incremental development in small iterations implying that estimations should be done progressively. Whereas in each iteration a number of user stories is implemented. Thus, the estimation in agile projects especially focuses on estimating user stories rather than whole projects [4].

A user story is a common way for agile teams to express user requirements [4] and describes functionality that will be valuable to either a user or purchaser of a software [5]. Figure 1 shows an exemplary story of this project.

Due to the importance of reliable effort estimates for effective software project management, the field of SEE was investigated actively in the last four decades, leading to the evolvement of various estimation models and techniques [23]. Nevertheless nowadays, it is common practice to apply expert-based estimation techniques to a great extent and the application of effort estimation techniques other than expert judgement is still immature [25].

Expert-based approaches require a subjective assessment of experts [17]. For this approach, different methods exist that guide the consultation process of experts. Expert-based estimation with a structured group-consensus approach is represented by the principles of Wideband Delphi [24]. A widely practiced expert-based technique in agile software development is Planning Poker (PP) which principles are in fact derived from the group-consensus methods of Wideband Delphi [24].

This gamified estimation method involves discussion among the team members [3,16]. For each user requirement, all team members make their estimate by choosing a single card from their own deck of cards. Each card from the deck shows one number which represents the estimated effort typically measured in days or story points. Story points are a relative unit of measure. All cards, this means all estimates, are revealed concurrently. If any discrepancy occurs, then discussion among team members takes place to find consensus. Finally, the agreed estimation is set down as finalized and the next user requirement is taken into consideration.

PP does not require any historical data and is applicable in any phase of software development. Typically, estimation based on group discussion contributes to a better understanding of software development problems or the identification of weaknesses in software requirements. Moreover, human experts can handle differences between past project experiences and new techniques, architectures or unique project characteristics. Besides its strengths, this group estimation method involves multiple experts with advanced expertise in the developed software which makes the estimation relatively expensive. This approach does not provide a reusable estimation model as the estimation procedure must be

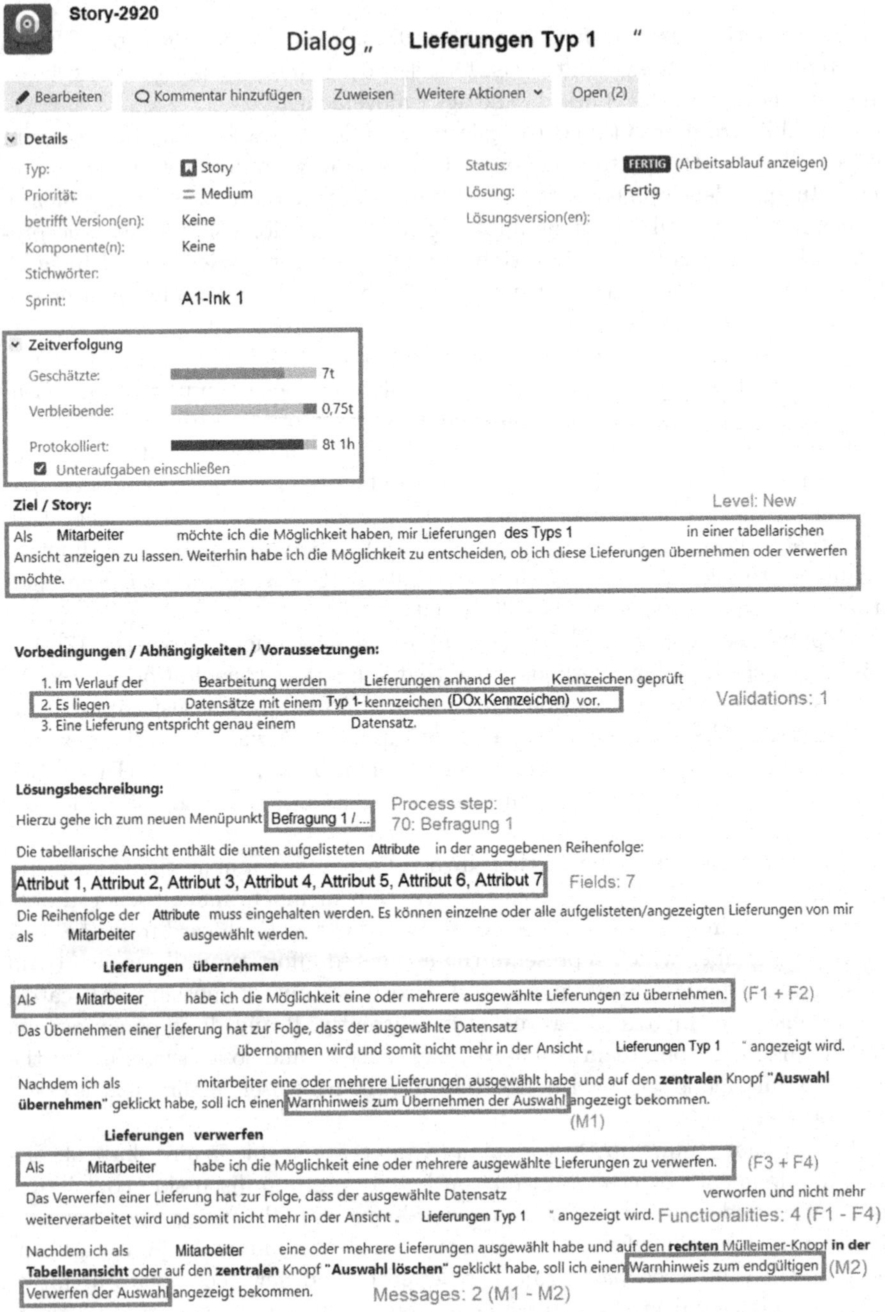

Story-2920

Dialog „ **Lieferungen Typ 1** "

Bearbeiten | Kommentar hinzufügen | Zuweisen | Weitere Aktionen | Open (2)

Details

Typ:	Story	Status:	FERTIG (Arbeitsablauf anzeigen)
Priorität:	Medium	Lösung:	Fertig
betrifft Version(en):	Keine	Lösungsversion(en):	
Komponente(n):	Keine		
Stichwörter:			
Sprint:	A1-Ink 1		

Zeitverfolgung

Geschätzte:	7t
Verbleibende:	0,75t
Protokolliert:	8t 1h

Unteraufgaben einschließen

Ziel / Story: Level: New

Als Mitarbeiter möchte ich die Möglichkeit haben, mir Lieferungen des Typs 1 in einer tabellarischen Ansicht anzeigen zu lassen. Weiterhin habe ich die Möglichkeit zu entscheiden, ob ich diese Lieferungen übernehmen oder verwerfen möchte.

Vorbedingungen / Abhängigkeiten / Voraussetzungen:

1. Im Verlauf der Bearbeitung werden Lieferungen anhand der Kennzeichen geprüft
2. Es liegen Datensätze mit einem Typ 1- kennzeichen (DOx.Kennzeichen) vor. Validations: 1
3. Eine Lieferung entspricht genau einem Datensatz.

Lösungsbeschreibung:

Hierzu gehe ich zum neuen Menüpunkt Befragung 1 / ... Process step: 70: Befragung 1

Die tabellarische Ansicht enthält die unten aufgelisteten Attribute in der angegebenen Reihenfolge:

Attribut 1, Attribut 2, Attribut 3, Attribut 4, Attribut 5, Attribut 6, Attribut 7 Fields: 7

Die Reihenfolge der Attribute muss eingehalten werden. Es können einzelne oder alle aufgelisteten/angezeigten Lieferungen von mir als Mitarbeiter ausgewählt werden.

Lieferungen übernehmen

Als Mitarbeiter habe ich die Möglichkeit eine oder mehrere ausgewählte Lieferungen zu übernehmen. (F1 + F2)

Das Übernehmen einer Lieferung hat zur Folge, dass der ausgewählte Datensatz übernommen wird und somit nicht mehr in der Ansicht „ Lieferungen Typ 1 " angezeigt wird.

Nachdem ich als mitarbeiter eine oder mehrere Lieferungen ausgewählt habe und auf den **zentralen** Knopf **"Auswahl übernehmen"** geklickt habe, soll ich einen Warnhinweis zum Übernehmen der Auswahl angezeigt bekommen. (M1)

Lieferungen verwerfen

Als Mitarbeiter habe ich die Möglichkeit eine oder mehrere ausgewählte Lieferungen zu verwerfen. (F3 + F4)

Das Verwerfen einer Lieferung hat zur Folge, dass der ausgewählte Datensatz verworfen und nicht mehr weiterverarbeitet wird und somit nicht mehr in der Ansicht „ Lieferungen Typ 1 " angezeigt wird. Functionalities: 4 (F1 - F4)

Nachdem ich als Mitarbeiter eine oder mehrere Lieferungen ausgewählt habe und auf den **rechten** Mülleimer-Knopf **in der Tabellenansicht** oder auf den **zentralen** Knopf **"Auswahl löschen"** geklickt habe, soll ich einen Warnhinweis zum endgültigen (M2) Verwerfen der Auswahl angezeigt bekommen. Messages: 2 (M1 - M2)

Fig. 1. Exemplary user story

repeated each time estimates are needed. Additionally, expert estimates can not provide objective and quantitative analysis of project effort dependencies and can be biased by numerous factors like individual expertise or preferences [24].

4 CBR Approach

The key to successful estimation is to identify relevant effort drivers [24]. In terms of CBR, this is achieved by defining suitable case representations for the description of user stories first. Next, the similarity functions are specified. An adaptation rule is described to derive estimation values from multiple cases. In addition to the classical CBR approach, the weights of the similarity functions are optimized in order to balance the impact of the relevant effort drivers on the system's estimation. The specific contribution of our optimization approach is that it works successfully for very small case-bases.

4.1 Case Representation

Interviews with experts revealed that effort drivers in agile software development are dependent on the project context. It is difficult to define uniform effort drivers for all user stories. Hence, the user stories have been grouped into different case-bases depending on their main purpose. For instance, stories that primarily have an effect on the user interface can be classified as stories of the category 'UI'. The UI stories can be further distinguished according to sub-categories such as 'Dialog' or 'View'. For each sub-category, an own case-base is specified. The cases record those feature-value pairs that are the most relevant effort drivers for the purpose of the case-base, i.e. the case representation implements a structural CBR approach [18]. The solution part of the cases comprises a numerical value expressing the actual effort recorded post mortem.

4.2 Similarity

The similarity functions follow the local-global principle [18]. The similarity sim for a problem q and a case $c = (p, l)$ from the case-base is calculated as follows:

$$sim(q, p) = \Phi(sim_{A_1}(q_1, p_1), \ldots, sim_{A_n}(q_n, p_n))$$

where $\Phi : \mathbb{R}^n \mapsto \mathbb{R}$ denotes an amalgamation function and $sim_{A_i} : T_i \times T_i \mapsto \mathbb{R}$ a local similarity function for the i-th feature (with range T_i) of the case representation. We have chosen to use the most prevalent amalgamation function namely the linear sum $\Phi(s_1, \ldots s_n) = \sum_{i=1\ldots n} \omega_i \cdot s_i$ where ω_i is the weight of the i-th feature.

4.3 Adaptation

The effort estimate for the new user story that is described in the query case is based on the best matching cases identified in the retrieval step. We have chosen a multiple case adaptation approach which generates the effort estimate using the weighted mean of the actual effort values of the k most similar source cases:

$$\text{PredictedEffort} = \sum_{i=1}^{k} \frac{sim(q, p_i)}{\sum_{i=1}^{k} sim(q, p_i)} \cdot \text{ActualEffort}_i$$

This adaptation rule calculates the weight factor on the basis of the similarity measure between the user story q to be estimated and the historical user story p_i. The weight factors are only used for normalization purposes. Moreover, as this adaptation rule is based on multiple cases, for instance $k = 3$, it allows to cope with varying development productivities among software engineers which arise from different levels of experience.

4.4 Weight Optimization with PSO

As defined in Sect. 4.2 the global similarity function is deduced from local similarity functions of each feature where the weights determine the feature's influence on global similarity. It is eminent to identify the best weights in the term of improved estimation accuracy. The optimization problem of discovering appropriate weights for the features can be solved by the Particle Swarm Optimization (PSO) method [10].

PSO simulates the behaviour of fishes and birds in swarms. The position of a particle represents a potential solution of the optimization problem. The goal is that a particle meets an optimal point in the solution space. Please note, that the solution space of the optimization problem differs from the solution space of the case-base since it addresses optimal weights for the similarity function. In PSO, a population of particles representing different solution proposals is created and updated iteratively. In any iteration, the fitness of each particle is calculated by putting its information into a designated objective function. In response to the fitness value and in accordance with the movement of the other particles, each particle is updated by adjusting its position in the solution space.

In an n-dimensional problem space, the position of the j-th particle at the iteration t is described by an n-dimensional particle vector $X_j^t = (x_{j1}^t, x_{j2}^t, ..., x_{jn}^t)$. The particle's velocity is as well defined as an n-dimensional vector $V_j^t = (v_{j1}^t, v_{j2}^t, ..., v_{jn}^t)$. The position of a particle is updated using the velocity vector in accordance with Wu et al. [28]:

$$X_j^{t+1} = X_j^t + V_j^{t+1}.$$

The velocity vector is adjusted (like in [28]) by considering its previous best position p_j according to the objective function, its current position, its current velocity and the previous global best position g of all particles:

$$V_j^{t+1} = i_t \cdot V_j^t + c_1 r_1 \cdot (p_j - X_j^t) + c_2 r_2 \cdot (g - X_j^t)$$

where i_t is a time-varying inertia weight (decreasing from iteration to iteration in order to slow down the impact of the former velocity, cmp. [28]), c_1, c_2 are positive constants and r_1, r_2 random numbers between 0 and 1.

After the particle population is initialized randomly, the fitness value of each particle is calculated. Then these values are compared with the fitness values of the best positions resulting in the updates of the individual best positions and the global best position. At least, the adjusted velocities and particles' positions lead to a new particle population.

In the context of USEE, the objective is to derive weights that generate highly accurate estimates. Therefore, one needs to decide on an accuracy metric on which the optimization problem is based. As the mean magnitude of relative error (MMRE) between estimated and actual efforts is the most frequently used accuracy metric, this metric is chosen to serve as the objective function.

It is defined by the magnitude of relative error (MRE) for a case

$$\text{MRE} = \frac{|ActualEffort - PredictedEffort|}{ActualEffort},$$

averaging the MRE values for a case-base with N cases:

$$\text{MMRE} = \frac{1}{N} \sum_{i=1}^{N} MRE_i.$$

Thus, the objective is to minimize the mean prediction error of all user stories whose effort values are aimed to be estimated.

The PSO method is applied separately to each case-base. A population with the same swarmsize of particles is generated for every case-base by randomly selecting initial weights. Each particle represents a potential similarity function. More precisely, a particle is a vector of weights to aggregate the values of the (given) local similarity functions where ω_i is the weight of the i-th feature, or in other words, the weight of the i-th local similarity measure. The ω_i's are chosen within lower and upper bounds pre-defined for each feature of the particular case representation.

The defined objective function shows that there is data required that serves as case-base and data that represents the new user stories whose effort values are aimed to be predicted accurately. Consequently, the fitness of the local similarity function (a particle) is determined by applying it to a case-base and measuring the accuracy of the predicted estimation values. Dividing the data set into these two containers could lead to the problem of over-fitting. This means that a CBR cycle initialized on weights derived in this way would provide a perfect accuracy score but would fail to predict anything useful on yet-unseen data.

The problem of over-fitting is encountered through a 3-fold cross-validation. Therefore, the whole data set is divided into a training set (80%) and a test set (20%). The test set contains user stories that the model has never seen before and is used for the final evaluation of the CBR approach. The training set is used for the search of optimized weights with the aid of PSO. This data set is split up into 3 folds. Hence, the optimal weights are derived 3 times, every time two folds are used as case-base and one fold is utilized for accuracy evaluation purposes. Even though it is common practice in cross-validation to choose the parameters of the iteration with the lowest error rate, this principle is not applicable in the context of small case bases. Since each fold contains only a very small number of cases the error values can explode due to outliers. Thus, the optimal weight vectors of all iterations are utilized by calculating their median value.

5 Experiments

The experiments have been guided by two hypotheses:

H1 The PSO optimization improves the results of the case-based estimation approach.
H2 The case-based estimation approach with PSO outperforms human experts who use Planning Poker as an estimation technique.

The experimental environment has been created in myCBR [2]. Two experimental setups have been defined and conducted on the same experimental data that is described in the following. Experiment 1 addresses hypothesis H1 as described in Sect. 5.2. Experiment 2 focuses on hypothesis H2 (see Sect. 5.3). The results of both experiments are discussed in Sect. 5.4.

5.1 Experimental Data

The experimental data comprises 127 user stories from a currently running software development project of the Capgemini Group. The project whose user stories formed the data basis of the analysis has involved around 100 employees, consisting of project manager, software developers, business analysts and software testers. The project has been executed in the context of agile software development. Concretely, the software has been developed using Scrum, a process framework managing product development in an iterative, incremental procedure [19]. Consequently, the software was planned, estimated and delivered incrementally in small iterations, whereas in each iteration a certain number of user stories was realized.

The evaluated period of 17 months offered a total of 298 user stories that were realized in 11 increments. A major problem that SEE research community encounters is the heterogeneity of data. Many studies emphasize the demand for more homogeneous datasets to achieve higher accuracy levels [13,20,21]. The fact that all stories belong to the same project and at least show a similar context, complies the requirement of homogeneity. To strengthen this requirement, a subset of 127 stories that primarily have an effect on the user interface were selected as experimental data. This data set was divided into four self-contained case-bases whose technical implementations differed from each other. The topics and size of the four experimental case-bases are depicted in Table 1. Each case-base shows effort values of similar range (cmp. Table 5).

Table 1. Distribution of user stories across the category *UI*.

Dialog	Filtering	Report	View	$\sum$
32	18	59	18	127

'Dialog' user stories implement or extend any user interface which gives the user the possibility for data entry, for record selection and deletion with the aid of check-boxes, for triggering data processing through clicking on buttons and so forth. 'Filtering' user stories implement or extend user interfaces which consist of filters. An example case describes the requirement that the filter attributes for postal addresses should include an additional attribute for name affixes. 'Report' user stories only display data and inform the user on the current status of specified variables. 'View' user stories have the central purpose to display data and are characterized by limited user interactions. To be more precise, the allowed interactions are restricted to the actions belonging to the project's standard structure of interfaces. For instance, they do permit the user to remove or select columns and navigate forth and back. Stories involving more complex user interactions are put into category 'Dialog'.

The four case-bases contain slightly different feature sets (cmp. the second column of Table 4). Table 2 exemplarily depicts the feature set of one of the case bases.

Table 2. Feature set of the *Dialog* cases.

Feature	Domain
Level	New/Extension
Process step	20/25/27/30/35/40/50/60/70/80/90
Fields	0–30
Buttons	0–5
Messages	0–8
Validations	0–8
Functionalities	0–5
Complexity	Low/Medium/High

'Level' states whether a story specifies a new user interface which meets the properties of the user story or extends an existing one. 'Process step' references the identification number of the process step in the business process model that underlies the software and describes the software's functionality at a high-level, business-oriented perspective. Stories that fulfill requirements of advanced process steps tend to require more development effort than those of earlier steps. The domain of the feature is restricted to those identification numbers that occur within the software project's business process. 'Fields' captures the number of fields needed to be implemented. 'Buttons' accounts for the number of buttons specified in the story. 'Messages' describes the number of messages needed to be implemented. 'Validations' comprise various checks for the compliance of inserted values by the user on the permitted range of values as well as checks for data records that are allowed to be displayed on the user interface. 'Functionalities' captures the number of functionalities specified in the story. This involves all actions that can manipulate data and are triggered by the user through clicking on buttons. 'Complexity' describes the story's complexity. The assignment of complexity to a user story is either more or less subjective but factors like the difficulty of functionalities, the complexity of SQL-scripts or html-files are the most relevant indicators.

Obviously, categorical local similarity functions are specified for 'Level', 'Process step' and 'Complexity'. MyCBR's 'polynomial' similarity function is used for 'Fields', 'Buttons' and 'Messages'. 'Validations' and 'Functionalities' are compared by another of MyCBR's standard similarity functions called 'smooth-step-at' [2]. The adaptation rule considers the three best matching cases, i.e. we have specified $k = 3$.

5.2 Experiment 1

Experiment 1 investigates the impact of the optimization and aims to quantify the improvement in terms of accuracy. As already introduced in Sect 4.4 the experimental data set is split up into a training set and a test set. Each test set of the four experimental case-bases is partitioned into three folds of the same size. Consequently, the optimal weights are derived three times, whereas in each iteration two folds act as case-base and one fold is used for accuracy evaluation.

The lower and upper bounds for the feature weights are specified depending on the subjective assessment of the relevance of the effort drivers. Figure 2 shows the bounds used for 'Dialog'.

```
lb = [3.0, 3.0, 3.0, 3.0, 1.0, 1.0, 4.0, 4.0]
ub = [6.0, 6.0, 6.0, 6.0, 3.0, 3.0, 6.0, 6.0]
```

Fig. 2. Exemplary definition of lower and upper bound.

The experiment is conducted with the *pyswarm* package an optimization package for python that implements PSO [11]. The number of particles in the swarm (*swarmsize*), the particle velocity scaling factor (*omega*), the scaling factor to search away from the particle's best known position (*phip*) and the scaling factor to search away from the swarm's best known position (*phig*) are assigned to their default values [11]. The minimum stepsize of swarm's best position before the search terminates (*minstep*) is set to 1e-8 and the minimum change of swarm's best objective value before the search terminates (*minfunc*) is set to 1e-15. The maximum number of iterations for the swarm to search (*maxiter*) has the value of 200. An exemplary optimizer for the first iteration, in which the on MMRE based objective function is named *error_global_S1*, is illustrated in Fig. 3.

```
pso(error_global_S1, lb, ub, ieqcons=[], f_ieqcons=None, args=(), kwargs={},
    swarmsize=100, omega=0.5, phip=0.5, phig=0.5, maxiter=200, minstep=1e-8,
    minfunc=1e-15, debug=False)
```

Fig. 3. Exemplary call of the PSO optimizer.

Table 3. Improvement in accuracy through weights optimization

Dialog	Filtering	Report	View
+ 9.20%	+ 1.17%	+ 3.29%	+ 2.35%

Table 4. Results of weights optimization.

Case base	Feature	Optimized weights			
		Per iteration			Median
		Fold1	Fold2	Fold3	
Dialog	Level	3.00	3.00	3.00	3.00
	Process step	3.00	3.82	3.00	3.00
	Fields	5.51	5.22	5.31	5.31
	Buttons	6.00	3.00	6.00	6.00
	Messages	3.00	1.00	1.00	1.00
	Validations	3.00	3.00	1.00	3.00
	Functionalities	4.00	6.00	5.26	5.26
	Complexity	5.98	4.00	5.26	5.26
Filtering	Level	1.00	1.00	1.00	1.00
	Process step	3.00	1.00	1.00	1.00
	Filters	4.00	4.00	6.00	4.00
	Additional columns	3.00	3.00	1.00	3.00
	Dialogs	3.00	1.00	1.00	1.00
	Filterconcept	2.00	2.00	1.25	2.00
	Concept maturity	3.00	3.00	1.00	3.00
Report	Level	6.00	6.00	2.55	6.00
	Reportconcept	5.15	6.00	5.38	5.38
	Type	1.35	1.94	2.71	1.94
	Contentfields	4.82	6.00	3.75	4.82
	Export option	1.00	1.00	1.65	1.00
	Export file	3.00	3.39	3.64	3.39
	Export execution	3.00	3.00	3.00	3.00
	Entities	1.79	3.00	2.13	2.13
View	Level	1.23	1.00	1.00	1.00
	Process step	3.00	1.67	1.00	1.67
	Columns/Fields	3.00	3.00	6.00	3.00
	Buttons	3.00	3.00	3.00	3.00
	Entities	6.00	6.00	3.00	6.00
	Filteroption	1.80	2.60	1.93	1.93

The resulting, optimized weights are depicted in Table 4. The evaluation of the CBR model on the test set led to a moderate improvement of accuracy compared to the original weights as shown in Table 3.

5.3 Experiment 2

Experiment 2 addresses the evaluation of the optimized CBR model in comparison to the estimation values obtained from human experts.

Table 5 shows the results for the test sets. All effort values are shown in hours. The MRE values for the test cases are fully listed. The accumulated values for all cases (for PP even including the three training folds) are provided in the boxes below the rows with the particular test cases. In addition to MMRE, the values of two further accuracy metrics are depicted. $MdMRE$ denotes the median of the MRE's which is less sensitive to outliers than the mean MRE. $PRED(x)$ measures the accuracy by the percentage of predictions that fall within x percent of the actual value [20]. In other words, the $PRED(x)$ is the percentage of MRE which is less than or equal to value x for all stories. It is common practice to use $x = 25$ as performance indicator [6]. The CBR method outperforms the experts for all four sample case-bases with respect to the MMRE. The MdMRE and $PRED(25)$ for the 'Report' case-base achieved a slightly better accumulated value with the PP method compared to the CBR method while for the other three case-bases CBR performed better.

5.4 Discussion of Results

Both hypotheses are confirmed by the experiments. Experiment 1 succeeded well in avoiding over-fitting since the accuracy of the estimation values for the user stories is improved by the optimization (cmp. Table 3). While the amount of improvement in a single digit range might seem marginal at a first glance the impact on software projects is significant at a closer look. In terms of staff-hours as well as in terms of reputation losses the economic consequences of such an improvement are high.

The results of experiment 2 show that the CBR approach clearly outperforms the PP approach. In addition to the direct benefits from improving the accuracy of the estimation values, the support and validation of PP sessions by an automated estimation approach could provide further advantages for the software projects.

Table 5. Results from Experiment 2.

Story-No.	Actual effort	PP Predicted effort	PP MRE	PP PRED(25)	CBR Predicted effort	CBR MRE	CBR PRED(25)
Dialog:							
7040	12	12	0.00	1	11.86	0.01	1
4769	22	16	0.27	0	17.25	0.22	1
7870	25	40	0.60	0	26.56	0.06	1
7572	36	36	0.00	1	32.39	0.10	1
3232	47	67	0.43	0	48.38	0.03	1
2570	72	100	0.39	0	79.14	0.10	1
Accumulated:		MMRE = 0.25 MdMRE = 0.15 PRED(25) = 0.56			MMRE = 0.09 MdMRE = 0.08 PRED(25) = 1.00		
Filtering:							
7880	32	24	0.25	0	33.13	0.04	1
3233	48	48	0.00	1	48.79	0.02	1
4759	62	56	0.10	1	56.67	0.09	1
3241	76	58	0.24	1	65.66	0.14	1
Accumulated:		MMRE = 0.17 MdMRE = 0.10 PRED(25) = 0.72			MMRE = 0.07 MdMRE = 0.06 PRED(25) = 1.00		
Report:							
2740	42	40	0.05	1	41.97	0.00	1
5498	51	52	0.02	1	58.69	0.15	1
5444	64	64	0.00	1	78.66	0.23	1
5455	68	68	0.00	1	95.28	0.40	0
5471	77	77	0.00	1	71.31	0.07	1
5463	84	68	0.19	1	92.29	0.10	1
5466	92	96	0.04	1	94.87	0.03	1
8716	92	92	0.00	1	51.34	0.44	0
8827	98	106	0.08	1	96.57	0.01	1
8171	106	106	0.00	1	96.76	0.09	1
8597	120	120	0.00	1	115.17	0.04	1
8104	144	144	0.00	1	93.89	0.35	0
Accumulated:		MMRE = 0.20 MdMRE = 0.05 PRED(25) = 0.80			MMRE = 0.16 MdMRE = 0.09 PRED(25) = 0.75		
View:							
8449	27	24	0.11	1	28.05	0.04	1
4777	40	40	0.00	1	40.54	0.01	1
3036	50	32	0.36	0	43.16	0.14	1
8469	84	100	0.19	1	78.91	0.06	1
Accumulated:		MMRE = 0.16 MdMRE = 0.16 PRED(25) = 0.67			MMRE = 0.06 MdMRE = 0.05 PRED(25) = 1.00		

6 Conclusion

The aim of the paper was to analyze the applicability of a case-based reasoning estimation technique on effort estimation of user stories and to provide an automated effort estimation tool which could offer reliable support for project planning. On the basis of real-world data, the applicability was approved. The distribution of the user stories from a large software project into multiple small case-bases and the PSO based weights optimization of the local similarity measures was very successful. We think it might play a role that the user stories in the case-bases are homogeneous due to this separation. Moreover, the documentation of the stories is of an outstanding quality. Further, it seems that it is an advantage that the adaptation rule is considered by the objective function during optimization with PSO. In our future work, we are planning to conduct research to investigate this assumption. Concluding, the results show that CBR in combination with an automated environment reveals to be a suitable estimation technique for user story software estimation that can offer a reliable estimation support.

References

1. Alsaadi, B., Saeedi, K.: Data-driven effort estimation techniques of agile user stories: a systematic literature review. Artif. Intell. Rev. 1–32 (2022). https://doi.org/10.1007/s10462-021-10132-x
2. Althoff, K., Roth-Berghofer, T., Bach, K., Sauer, C.: myCBR (2015). http://www.mycbr-project.org/. Accessed 06 May 2022
3. Bilgaiyan, S., Sagnika, S., Mishra, S., Das, M.: A systematic review on software cost estimation in agile software development. J. Eng. Sci. Technol. Rev. (JESTR) **10**(4), 51–64 (2017)
4. Choetkiertikul, M., Dam, H., Trany, T., Phamy, T., Ghose, A., Menzies, T.: A deep learning model for estimating story points. IEEE Trans. Softw. Eng. **45**(7), 637–656 (2016)
5. Cohn, M.: User Stories Applied - For Agile Software Development. Addison-Wesley (2004). iSBN: 978-0-321-20568-1
6. Fernández-Diego, M., Méndez, E.R., González-Ladrón-De-Guevara, F., Abrahão, S., Insfran, E.: An update on effort estimation in agile software development: a systematic literature review. IEEE Access **8**, 166768–166800 (2020)
7. Huang, S.J., Chiu, N.H.: Optimization of analogy weights by genetic algorithm for software effort estimation. Inf. Softw. Technol. **48**, 1034–1045 (2006)
8. Huang, S.J., Chiu, N.H., Chen, L.W.: Integration of the grey relational analysis with genetic algorithm for software effort estimation. Eur. J. Oper. Res. **188**, 898–909 (2008)
9. Jarmulak, J., Craw, S., Rowe, R.: Genetic algorithms to optimise CBR retrieval. In: Blanzieri, E., Portinale, L. (eds.) EWCBR 2000. LNCS, vol. 1898, pp. 136–147. Springer, Heidelberg (2000). https://doi.org/10.1007/3-540-44527-7_13
10. Kennedy, J., Eberhart, R.: Particle swarm optimization. In: Proceedings of ICNN 1995-International Conference on Neural Networks, vol. 4, pp. 1942–1948. IEEE (1995)

11. Lee, A.: Pyswarm documentation (2014). https://pythonhosted.org/pyswarm/, Accessed 06 May 2022
12. Malgonde, O., Chari, K.: An ensemble-based model for predicting agile software development effort. Empirical Softw. Eng. **24**(2), 1017–1055 (2018). https://doi.org/10.1007/s10664-018-9647-0
13. Marco, R., Suryana, N., Ahmad, S.: A systematic literature review on methods for software effort estimation. J. Theor. Appl. Inf. Technol. **97**(2), 434–464 (2019)
14. Medeiros, J.A.C.C., Schirru, R.: Identification of nuclear power plant transients using the particle swarm optimization algorithm. Ann. Nucl. Energy **35**, 576–582 (2008)
15. Mukhopadhyay, T., Vicinanza, S., Prietula, M.: Examining the feasibility of a case-based reasoning model for software effort estimation. MIS Quart. **16**, 155–171 (1992)
16. Munialo, S.W., Muketha, G.M.: A review of agile software effort estimation methods. Int. J. Comput. Appl. Technol. Res. **5**(9), 612–618 (2016)
17. Nerkar, L.R., Yawalkar, P.M.: Software cost estimation using algorithmic model and non-algorithmic model a review. IJCA Proc. Innovations Trends Comput. Commun. Eng. ITCCE **2**, 4–7 (2014). publisher: Foundation of Computer Science (FCS)
18. Richter, M.M., Weber, R.O.: Case-Based Reasoning. Springer, Heidelberg (2013). https://doi.org/10.1007/978-3-642-40167-1
19. Schwaber, K.: Agile Project Management with Scrum. Microsoft Press (2004). iSBN: 978-0-735-61993-7
20. Shepperd, M., Schofield, C.: Estimating software project effort using analogies. IEEE Trans. Softw. Eng. **23**(12), 736–743 (1997)
21. Shepperd, M., Schofield, C., Kitchenham, B.: Effort estimation using analogy. In: Proceedings 18th International Conference Software Engineering, pp. 170–178. IEEE CS Press (1996)
22. Stahl, A., Gabel, T.: Optimizing similarity assessment in case-based reasoning. In: Proceedings of the National Conference on Artificial Intelligence, vol. 21(2), p. 1667. Menlo Park, CA; Cambridge, MA; London; AAAI Press; MIT Press; 1999 (2006)
23. Suri, P., Ranjan, P.: Comparative analysis of software effort estimation techniques. Int. J. Comput. Appl. (IJCA) **48**(21), 12–19 (2012)
24. Trendowicz, A., Jeffery, R.: Software Project Effort Estimation. Springer, Cham (2014). https://doi.org/10.1007/978-3-319-03629-8
25. Usman, M., Mendes, E., Weidt, F., Britto, R.: Effort estimation in agile software development: a systematic literature review. In: Proceedings of the 10th international conference on predictive models in software engineering, pp. 82–91 (2014)
26. Wiratunga, N., Wijekoon, A., Cooper, K.: Learning to compare with few data for personalised human activity recognition. In: Watson, I., Weber, R. (eds.) ICCBR 2020. LNCS (LNAI), vol. 12311, pp. 3–14. Springer, Cham (2020). https://doi.org/10.1007/978-3-030-58342-2_1
27. Wu, D., Li, J., Bao, C.: Case-based reasoning with optimized weight derived by particle swarm optimization for software effort estimation. Soft. Comput. **22**(16), 5299–5310 (2017). https://doi.org/10.1007/s00500-017-2985-9
28. Wu, D., Li, J., Liang, Y.: Linear combination of multiple case-based reasoning with optimized weight for software effort estimation. J. Supercomput. **64**(3), 898–918 (2013). https://doi.org/10.1007/s11227-010-0525-9

MicroCBR: Case-Based Reasoning on Spatio-temporal Fault Knowledge Graph for Microservices Troubleshooting

Fengrui Liu[1,2], Yang Wang[1,2], Zhenyu Li[1,2], Rui Ren[1,2], Hongtao Guan[1,2], Xian Yu[3,4], Xiaofan Chen[4], and Gaogang Xie[2,5](✉)

[1] Institute of Computing Technology, Chinese Academy of Sciences, Beijing, China
{liufengrui18z,wangyang2013,zyli,renrui2019,guanhongtao}@ict.ac.cn

[2] University of Chinese Academy of Sciences, Beijing, China
xie@cnic.cn

[3] Shenzhen Institutes of Advanced Technology, CAS, Shenzhen, China
yuxian@sangfor.com.cn

[4] Sangfor Technologies Inc., Shenzhen, China
chenxiaofan@sangfor.com.cn

[5] Computer Network Information Center, Chinese Academy of Sciences, Beijing, China

Abstract. With the growing market of cloud-native applications, microservices architectures are widely used for rapid and automated deployments, scaling, and management. However, behind the prosperity of microservices, diagnosing faults in numerous services has brought great complexities to operators. To tackle this, we present a microservices troubleshooting framework called MicroCBR, which makes use of history faults from a knowledge base to construct spatio-temporal knowledge graph offline, and then troubleshoot online through case-based reasoning. Compared to existing frameworks, MicroCBR (1) takes advantage of heterogeneous data to fingerprint the faults, (2) carefully extracts a spatio-temporal knowledge graph with only one sample for each fault, (3) can handle novel faults through hierarchical reasoning, and incrementally update it to the fault knowledge base thanks to case-based reasoning paradigm. Our framework is explainable to operators, they can easily locate the root causes and refer to historical solutions. We also conduct three different microservices architectures with fault experiments on Grid'5000 testbed, the results show that MicroCBR achieves 91% top-1 accuracy, and outperforms three state-of-the-art methods. We report success stories in a real cloud platform and the code is open-sourced.

Keywords: CBR · Knowledge graph · Microservices · Troubleshooting

1 Introduction

Cloud-native applications enable loosely coupled systems that are resilient, manageable, and observable. This technology embraces microservices, a popular architectural style for constructing modern applications in dynamic environments such

M. T. Keane and N. Wiratunga (Eds.): ICCBR 2022, LNAI 13405, pp. 224–239, 2022.
https://doi.org/10.1007/978-3-031-14923-8_15

as public, private, and hybrid clouds. The philosophy behind microservices is decoupling the resources from applications, where each unit has a single task and responsibility. Microservices architectures become increasingly complex with the growth of user demands, causing that fault diagnosis across numerous services exhaust the operators. Thus, an effective and automated troubleshooting method is required to offload the labor and reduce the mean time to repair (MTTR) of microservices.

We share several observations from a real cloud platform to clarify the challenges of microservices troubleshooting. First, the available data for fault diagnosis can be very different due to deployment, security, and performance requirements. Therefore, the methods [1,2] of using only homologous data are easy to fail when the required data is missing. Second, faults are rare, which brings huge obstacles for training-based methods [3,4], While these history faults are well maintained in a knowledge base, we should consider how to learn from them with only one sample for each fault. Third, we point out that the spatial topology of instances and the temporal order of anomalies can also effectively diagnose different faults. Further, in practical applications, the troubleshooting framework needs to be incrementally updated to accommodate novel fault cases. In addition, an explainable troubleshooting process and recommendation solutions for the emerging fault are important to operators.

To tackle the aforementioned challenges, we propose **MicroCBR**, a **c**ase-**b**ased **r**easoning (CBR) driven troubleshooting framework for **micro**services. In particular, MicroCBR constructs a fault spatio-temporal knowledge graph using heterogeneous data, which is embedded with temporal anomaly events sequences and spatial instances topologies. Explainable case-based reasoning is performed on the knowledge graph to diagnose emerging faults, followed by recommended solutions. The salient contributions of our work are summarized as follows:

- We fully take advantage of heterogeneous data, i.e. metrics, logs, traces, and commands. Comprehensive data entries can greatly enrich the fault fingerprints, thus expanding the scope of applicable targets and improving the troubleshooting accuracy.
- With retaining the physical and logical topologies of microservices instances, we innovatively embed anomaly events sequences into the fault knowledge graph. The analysis of spatial topology make diagnosing target instance without historical data possible, and temporal anomaly events sequences improve the troubleshooting accuracy with limited data.
- Our framework is not confined to retrieving the most similar historical case to an emerging fault, it can further assign a novel fault to a fault type by hierarchical reasoning. With CBR paradigm, we revise and retain the novel fault in the knowledge base to achieve incremental updates.
- We report experiments that compare to three state-of-the-art (SOTA) methods on Grid'5000 testbed. The results demonstrate that MicroCBR outperforms SOTA methods with 91% top-1 accuracy. Success stories from a real private cloud platform prove that our framework can troubleshoot the faults effectively and offload the labor of operators. The code[1] is also available.

[1] MicroCBR repository: https://github.com/Fengrui-Liu/MicroCBR.

2 Related Work

In this section, we study the strengths and weaknesses of existing methods that aim for microservices troubleshooting from three perspectives, i.e. data entries, graph-based analysis, and reasoning methods.

Data Entries. The most common work focus on homologous data and diagnosis faults by mining anomalies. [5,6] start from the logs. They collect anomaly scores from different log detectors and identify root causes using correlation analysis. Another great deal of efforts have been devoted to metrics analysis. [2,7] perform anomaly detection on structured time-series metrics, and further determine the faults according to the monitored targets. In addition, [1,8] turn their attention to the traces, they model the service invocations and assume that instances with abnormal latency are more likely to be root causes. However, these methods are limited to a narrow perspective with only using homologous data, and fail when required data is missing or faults affect multiple kinds of data. Recently, some work [9–11] take into account the combination of metrics and logs, showing the advantages of using heterogeneous data in industrial settings. We argue that they still have deficiencies in data entries, especially for the post-hoc commands anomalies.

Graph-Based Analysis. Graph is a popular and effective representation of entities and their relationships, researchers propose various views of graph construction to assist microservices troubleshooting. Causeinfer [12] regards physics instances as target entities while network connections as relationships, and [8,10] track invocations among different traces as a service call graph. [11,13] try to deduce event causality and build a graph to describe event relationships, with an underlying assumption that the order of anomalies can infer specific faults. Although different graph-based methods have strengths in modeling microservices, they still separate physics entities, services logic, and anomaly events sequences, which limits them to a single granularity. In our framework design, multi-level abstractions and a fusion of spatio-temporal heterogeneous data are used to construct the fault knowledge graph.

Reasoning. In recent years, the most popular faults diagnosis methods are those driven by machine learning. [4] takes advantage of variational autoencoder to detect anomalies and Seer [3] locates root causes using counterfactuals. Netrca [14] adopts an ensemble model to improve troubleshooting generalization. Most of these supervised methods suffer from labeling overhead in the training phase. They also have limited discussion on incremental model updates and the reusability when novel faults occur. In addition, unsupervised methods [1,9,13] utilize probabilistic graphical models, such as Bayesian networks. Nevertheless, from practical experience, the prior probability of a fault is hard to collect due to the bug fixes and the growth of maintenance experience. Based on this observation, probabilistic graphical models must be used with care. Case-based reasoning is different from the above. It follows a 4R paradigm which contains *Retrieve*, *Reuse*,*Revise* and *Retain*. In [15,16], authors introduce how CBR can be used for troubleshooting, and iSQUAD [17] integrates CBR to provide explanation for reasoning results.

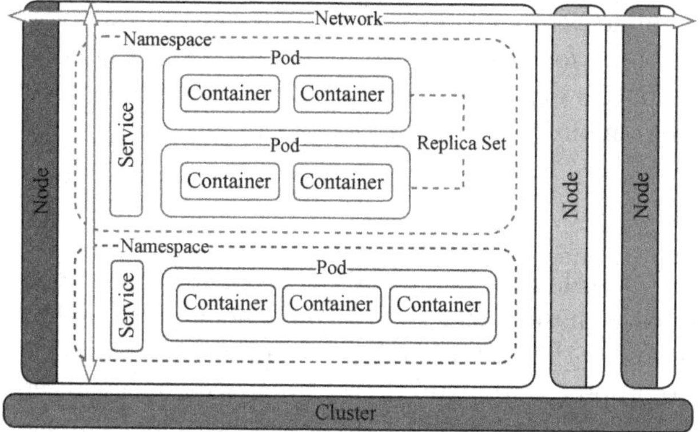

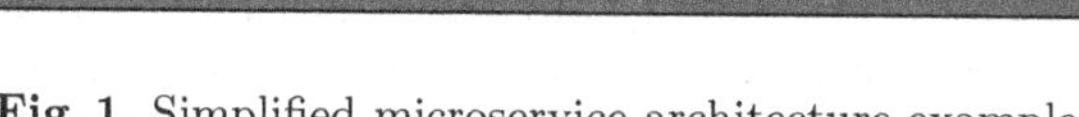

Fig. 1. Simplified microservice architecture example.

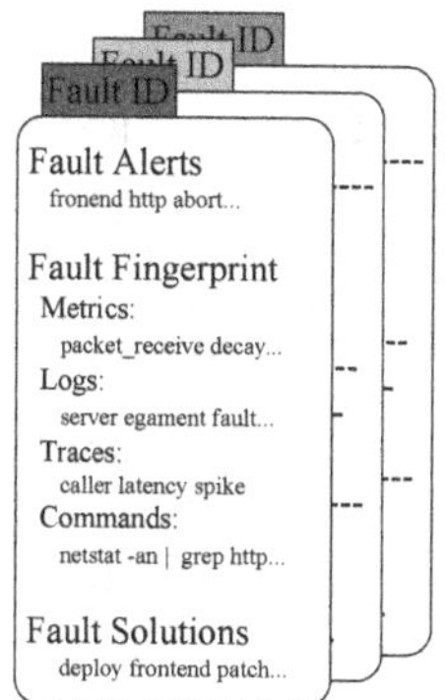

Fig. 2. Fault knowledge base.

3 Background and Motivation

This section first introduces the background of microservices troubleshooting with clarifying basic concepts. After that, we detail our motivation.

3.1 Background with Basic Concepts

Take Fig. 1 as a simplified example, we introduce the objects of microservices troubleshooting. The workloads run in **containers** at the lowest level. They are bundled together as **pods** which is the smallest deployable unit to create, schedule and manage. A **namespace** is a virtual cluster, it provides a mechanism for isolating groups of resources within a single **node**. In microservice deployment, the **replica set** is a common controller, which plays a central role in automatically orchestrating workloads. Since pods are constantly being created and destroyed, **services** provide a level of abstraction and act as an endpoint for the pods. Due to the scalability of microservices, a configuration management database (CMDB) is often used to manage their physical and logical topologies.

The **knowledge base** is a collection of all fault cases through long-term microservices maintenances. For each fault, it contains the fault alerts, a fault fingerprint, and the corresponding solutions, as shown in Fig. 2. Note that the **fault fingerprint** records all anomalies that are related to the fault. It is drawn from four types of heterogeneous data, i.e. metrics, logs, traces, and commands. **Metrics** are numeric representations of data over intervals of time. They are widely used in performance monitoring. **Logs** are timestamped records of discrete events. They tend to give more in-depth information than metrics, e.g., predefined events or program exceptions. **Traces** add critical visibility into the health of microservices end-to-end, which are introduced by caller and callee pairs. **Commands** are post-hoc supplements to the above data sources, which show great strength when required data is missing, e.g. security or performance limitations. While existing troubleshooting frameworks [1,2,5–8] turn a blind eye to commands. Note that the above four heterogeneous data sources are summarized from practical troubleshooting experiences. However, each fault fingerprint only includes the available and anomaly items, not necessarily for all.

3.2 Motivation

Microservices troubleshooting, also known as fault diagnosis, is aiming to diagnose inevitable faults from both physical and logical components. The highest priority of operators is to stabilize the system and avoid faults escalation. The motivation of this paper is to propose a troubleshooting framework for microservices, which can offload the labor by automated faults identification, minimize the losses by reducing MTTR, as well as bridge the gap between prior works and following practical constraints.

In practice, faults may recur because containers that have bugs can be deployed multiple times to different services, or because complicated scenario restrictions always lead to unexpected misconfigurations. If operators can quickly determine whether the emerging fault is similar to a previously-seen case, those known solutions may be reused to quickly fix the emerging fault. With this, several interesting observations guide us to design the troubleshooting framework.

First, we learn that the required data for diagnosing various faults can be very different [9–11]. In particular, we note that commands are widely used in practice, they should be adopted together with metrics, logs and traces to enrich the fault fingerprints. Second, the same fault data are always too scarce to train a supervised model [3,14] in reality. In our practical experiences, if an emerging fault can be solved by referring to the historical solutions, operators would hardly enrich it anymore. Supervised methods suffer from handling novel faults, and fail on incremental updates. Besides, the prior probability of each fault is difficult to determine after the bugs are fixed or the maintenance experiences growth. Thus, probabilistic graphical models [1,9,13], like the Bayesian network, should be used with care. Next, we focus on how to draw the fault fingerprints as accurately as possible in limited data. The effective answer is endowing spatio-temporal characteristics to the fingerprints.

Thanks to the above valuable practical observations, we are expected to design a microservices troubleshooting framework that can take advantage of heterogeneous data, and learn from one sample of each fault. In addition, it should be able to provide recommended solutions and handle novel faults. To tackle these challenges, we propose MicroCBR which uses case-based reasoning on spatio-temporal fault knowledge graph for microservices troubleshooting, and the details are described in the next section.

4 Troubleshooting Framework

In this section, we firstly introduce the overview workflow of our troubleshooting framework, followed by detailed descriptions of its main components.

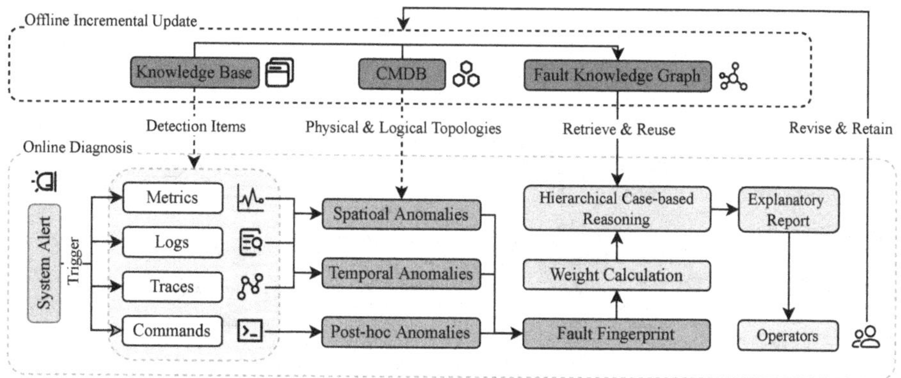

Fig. 3. Overview workflow of proposed MicroCBR troubleshooting framework.

4.1 Framework Overview

As Fig. 3 shows, our framework combines offline update with online diagnosis through case-based reasoning. For the offline part, we leverage the CMDB of target system to construct a graph that contains its physical and logical topologies. Then we embed the existing knowledge base into the graph, and enrich it into a spatio-temporal fault knowledge graph. An online troubleshooting workflow is usually triggered by a system alert. The universal set of fault fingerprints from existing knowledge base points out the objects to be detected. After various detecting methods applying on metrics, logs, traces and commands, we select those anomalies to depict a fingerprint of emerging fault. In order to distinguish the importance of different anomalies, we assign weights scores to them. After performing hierarchical case-based reasoning on constructed fault knowledge graph to realize the retrieve and reuse of existing fault cases, we provide a explanatory report with fault fingerprint and recommended solutions. The operators can revise the fault details and retain a novel fault in the knowledge base for incremental updates. Next we elaborate on each technology of the framework.

4.2 Spatio-Temporal Fault Knowledge Graph

In our framework, the fault knowledge graph is the cornerstone of fault diagnosis. The backbone of the knowledge graph is constructed from the CMDB of a target system. Its entities include logical nodes, namespaces, services topologies, and physical clusters. The spatial topologies of these entities are represented by links that indicate their affiliations, and the links of different services represent their call relation. On this foundation, we append the fingerprints from the knowledge base to the graph. For each fingerprint, its upstream is the anomaly entity, and its downstream is the corresponding fault. We further illustrate the power of temporal event sequences and spatial topologies for troubleshooting by giving a fault case respectively in Fig. 4. Note that these two analytical perspectives are not independent, and should be combined in some fault cases.

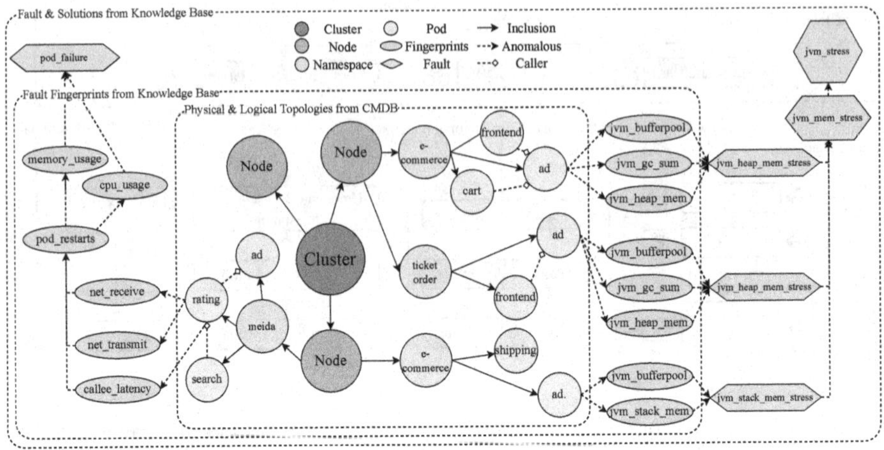

Fig. 4. A subgraph of spatio-temporal fault knowledge graph. The left pod failure fault fingerprint has temporal event sequences, while the right JVM memory stress fault shows us the spatial topologies and hierarchical reasoning for troubleshooting.

Temporal. A key insight of the fingerprints is that some anomaly events occur orderly. Having the same composition, anomaly events with different orders may point to different faults. The *rating pod* in Fig. 4 shows us a remarkable event sequence of its *pod failure*. At first, both the *net_receive* and *net_transmit* metrics have unexpected declines, accompanied by a significant increase in its *callee_latency*. However, this symptom is too common in various faults to diagnose correctly. What inspires us is that there are a series of follow-ups. Its *pod_restart* counter is incremented by one, followed by continuous increases in *memory_usage* and *cpu_usage*. These sequential events point out that the daemon is trying to restart the *rating pod*, and diagnose it as a *pod_failure* fault. The key challenge of embedding event sequences into the knowledge graph is mining their temporal order. For a fault fingerprint, supposing each anomaly a_i and its beginning time t_i is presented by a tuple (t_i, a_i). We ascending sort the anomalies according to their beginning time t_i. After that, an unsupervised DBSCAN [18] algorithm is performed on their time dimension for clustering, as $C_1, C_2, ..., C_m$ = DBSCAN$([t_1, t_2, ..., t_i], n, \epsilon)$, with two important empirical parameters minimum points ($n = 1$) and neighborhood radius ($\epsilon = 15$s) in our settings. The positions m of clusters C_m on the time dimension are used as temporal order of a_i. Anomaly events in the same cluster share the same temporal order, as the *memory_usage* and *cpu_usage* in the above pod failure example.

Spatial. We turn to how spatial topology helps us with fault diagnosis when lacks historical data. A useful observation is that the entities with similar spatial topology can be used as references for anomaly detection. Due to the Java-based *advertising* services being widely deployed in different namespaces, we study its Java virtual machine (JVM) stress faults in Fig. 4. Owing to resources limitations, the pod under *ticket-order* namespace has a JVM stress fault during the startup phase, it is impossible to detect anomalies on related time series metrics without historical data. Similar *advertising* pods that work well in other namespaces can serve as normal references. It turns out that the target pod has a higher ratio of bufferpool, memory, and garbage collection usage than those normals. To determine those references, for a target instance i, we retrieve its one-hop neighbors n and form a subgraph $subg(i)$. Thanks to CMDB provides us the physical and logical topologies of microservices, we search the whole topology graph for reference instances r, *s.t.* $sim(subg(i), subg(r)) > \theta$, empirically findings that $sim(\cdot)$ can be calculated by Jaccard distance and $\theta = 0.7$.

Hierarchical. In some certain circumstances, like a novel fault that has never been seen before occurring in the target system, we are unable to retrieve a sufficiently similar case from the existing fault knowledge graph to reuse its solutions. Thus, we introduce a hierarchical abstraction of all known faults. Take the JVM stress fault in Figure 4 as an example. At the finest granularity, the knowledge base has only collected heap and stack memory stress faults. Once there occurs another kind of memory stress fault, metaspace overflow, similarity-based retrieving (introduced in Sect. 4.3) fails to assign it to any known faults with a predefined threshold. An ideal way is to classify this novel fault to a higher level, such as a JVM memory stress or a JVM stress fault. Although this is a coarse-grained diagnosis, it can also effectively reduce the scope of troubleshooting. After revising the fault fingerprint and solutions by operators, the novel fault is added to the knowledge base and finishes the incremental updates to the fault knowledge graph.

4.3 Fingerprinting the Fault

When an alarm triggers the troubleshooting workflow as Fig. 3 shows, the first step is to detect anomalies for the target system. All the items to be detected are from the fingerprints of the existing knowledge base. Here we list a series of anomaly detection methods that are used in practice. For metrics data, we detect their anomalies in a time series manner [19,20]. Log anomalies [21,22] can be reported from their template sequences and specific events. As for traces, according to [1,8], their anomalies are reflected in call latency. Thus we select their one-hop caller and callee latency to monitor. The commands are post-hoc detections for faults, they should be sent to different targets and collect returns to automate the troubleshooting workflow. Predefined rules are the best practice for commands owing to security and customization requirements.

The above methods usually represent the state of detected items in a binary way, a.k.a normal and anomaly. We introduce an algorithm to evaluate the weights of anomalies in a fault fingerprint. Suppose a knowledge base that contains k known fault fingerprints F. For each fingerprint F, it contains a collection of anomalous items f. The first consideration is frequency. It reflects the belief that the lower the frequency, the more important the word is, as

$$W_{freq}(f) = \frac{\sum_i^k \mathbb{1}_{[f \in i]}}{k} \tag{1}$$

Another factor to consider is the relatedness of anomalous items, which reflects in their degrees. The more numbers of different terms that co-occur with the candidate detection item, the more meaningless the item is likely to be. The length of co-occur list of f is $C_l(f) = \sum_i^k \sum_j^i \mathbb{1}_{[j,f\in i]}$, and the length of co-occur set of f is $C_s(f) = \sum_i^k \sum_j^i \mathbb{1}_{\{j,f\in i\}}$ which only counts the unique detection items. We define the relatedness weight of f as

$$W_{rel}(f) = 1 + \frac{C_s(f)}{C_l(f)} + \frac{C_s(f)}{max(W_{freq}(\cdot))} \tag{2}$$

We heuristically combine the two important factors into a single measure as

$$W(f) = \frac{W_{rel}(f)}{\frac{W_{freq}(f)}{W_{rel}(f)} + C_l(f)} \tag{3}$$

The motivation of this equation is to assign high weights to anomalous items that appear infrequently as long as the item is relevant. Those anomalies with high weights have great contributions to fault discrimination.

4.4 Case-Based Reasoning

After fingerprinting the emerging fault, we show how to use the paradigm of case-based reasoning to complete once fault diagnosis.

Retrieve. The key idea of this step is to select the most similar known fault F from the knowledge base to the emerging fault F'. As we have discussed the temporal characteristic of fault fingerprints in Sect. 4.2, it can be solved by converting to a weighted longest common subsequence (WLCS) problem [23]. The similarity can be defined in a weighted bitwise way:

$$Sim(F', F) = \frac{\sum_f^{F'} W(f)\mathbb{1}_{[f\in F\cap WLCS(F,F')]}}{max(\sum_f^{F'} W(f)\mathbb{1}_{[f\in F']}, \sum_f^{F} W(f)\mathbb{1}_{[f\in F]})} \tag{4}$$

Reuse. For each fault F in the knowledge base, we can get its similarity score to emerging fault F'. The solutions of a fault F that has the highest similarity score can be used as references for troubleshooting. Furthermore, to ensure the recall rate for similar faults, a common practice is to sort their scores in descending and select top-k for recommendations. At the same time, we should avoid recommending too many options under the consideration of labor cost. Thus, we argue the power of top-2 in experiments.

Revise & Retain. The weighted detection items, similar faults, and recommended solutions together form the explanatory report. The good benefits are that the operators can understand the root causes of an emerging fault. Some anomalies that hardly distinguish various faults can be eliminated from the fingerprint by operators. After that, the revised fault fingerprint is retained within the knowledge base.

5 Evaluation

This section presents the detailed results of extensive experiments to evaluate our troubleshooting framework by answering the following questions:

Q1. What is the accuracy of MicroCBR compared to SOTA baselines?
Q2. How much accuracy is affected by each component of the framework?
Q3. How MicroCBR is affected by the data scale?
Q4. Does it offload the labor in practical applications?

5.1 Evaluation Setup

We configure a testbed in Grid'5000 [24] and deploy three open-source microservices architectures to evaluate our framework. Besides, three selected SOTA methods for comparison are introduced in this section.

Testbed & Microservices. We prepare 3 private nodes in the Nancy site of Grid'5000, with 16GB RAM and 4 cores Xeon E5-2650 CPU for each node. Online-Boutique[2](OB), Sock-Shop[3](SS), and Train-Ticket[4](TT) are deployed respectively, which have different microservice architectures. Each service of them is deployed with multiple instances. We continuously run a workload generator to simulate the real-world user access behaviors.

Fault injection & Data collection. To explore the faults of different microservices architectures, we select 31 faults at both pods and containers from Chaos-Mesh[5]. Besides, 10 misconfiguration faults have been prepared manually. These faults can be categorized in a high hierarchy with 6 types, including network faults, stress scenarios, etc. For different faults, we carefully analyze their anomalies and collect them to form a knowledge base. Then, we successfully inject them into different instances and finish 3572 experiments. For each injection, we collect the anomalies from metrics, logs, traces, and commands within 10 min.

Baselines. We select three SOTA methods, Bayesian-based CloudRCA [9], case-based CloodCBR [15] and graph-based GraphRCA [10] for comparison. To make these methods suitable for our experimental settings, we assume that CloudRCA treats all faults with the same prior probability, CloodCBR adopts equal matching as the similarity calculation strategy, and GraphRCA needs no additional assumptions. Another thing to note is that all of them ignore the traces and commands, and we comply with their original frameworks.

5.2 Q1. Comparative Experiments

For the four troubleshooting methods applied on different microservices, we use *top-k* (A@k), specially A@1 and A@3, to evaluate their accuracy. It refers to the probability that the groundtruth fault is included in the *top-k* results.

[2] Online-Boutique: https://github.com/GoogleCloudPlatform/microservices-demo.
[3] Sock-Shop: https://github.com/microservices-demo/microservices-demo.
[4] Train-Ticket: https://github.com/FudanSELab/train-ticket.
[5] Chaos-Mesh: https://chaos-mesh.org/.

Table 1. Overall accuracy comparison of microservices troubleshooting.

Fault type	Fault (#)	Micro-services	Instance (#)	MicroCBR		CloodCBR		CloudRCA		GraphRCA	
				A@1	A@3	A@1	A@3	A@1	A@3	A@1	A@3
Net	17	OB	187	***.91***	**1.0**	.47	.59	.72	.82	.81	**1.0**
		SS	238	***.94***	**1.0**	.39	.54	.61	.78	.80	**1.0**
		TT	1139	***.92***	**1.0**	.49	.61	.70	.81	.79	**1.0**
Pod	3	OB	33	***1.0***	**1.0**	.84	.84	.82	.82	.91	.97
		SS	42	***1.0***	**1.0**	.88	.88	.83	.83	.88	.93
		TT	201	***1.0***	**1.0**	.81	.81	.88	.88	.81	.93
Stress	2	OB	22	.95	**1.0**	***1.0***	**1.0**	.95	**1.0**	.73	.95
		SS	28	***.96***	**1.0**	.89	**1.0**	.89	**1.0**	.57	.93
		TT	134	***.97***	**1.0**	.90	**1.0**	.94	**1.0**	.66	.96
JVM	4	OB	4	***1.0***	**1.0**	.91	**1.0**	.84	**1.0**	.67	**1.0**
		SS	16	***.93***	**1.0**	.69	**1.0**	.57	**1.0**	.74	.98
		TT	148	***.94***	**1.0**	.78	**1.0**	.80	**1.0**	.64	.94
I/O	5	OB	55	***.96***	**1.0**	.62	.75	.87	**1.0**	.84	**1.0**
		SS	70	***.98***	**1.0**	.66	.84	.84	**1.0**	.87	**1.0**
		TT	335	***.90***	**1.0**	.70	.80	.87	**1.0**	.83	**1.0**
Config	10	OB	110	***.84***	**1.0**	.00	.00	.00	.00	.00	.00
		SS	140	***.81***	**1.0**	.00	.00	.00	.00	.00	.00
		TT	670	***.82***	**1.0**	.00	.00	.00	.00	.00	.00
All (of 3572 instances)				***.91***	**1.0**	.45	.54	.57	.66	.59	.74
Improvement of our method				(ours)		102%	85%	60%	51%	54%	35%
Var. across 3 microservices				***1.3e−4***	**0.0**	7.6e−4	4.7e−5	1.1e−3	4.9e−6	3.2e−4	8.8e−5

Table 1 details the experiment results. The A@1 of our method outperforms the compared SOTA methods by 54% to 102%, and A@3 prove that our method can always provide the correct answer within three options. Furthermore, the pod faults catch our attention, which contain plenty of temporal anomaly events collected by the knowledge base. The design of our method that can handle temporal characteristics ensures our accuracy advantages. Besides, those configuration faults heavily depend on the post-hoc commands. Compared to SOTA methods that leak commands information, our method benefits from adequate heterogeneous data and achieves higher accuracy. We also study the accuracy variance of these methods across different microservices, while our method has the lowest variance. This indicates that MicroCBR is more robust than others and can be used widely on various microservices.

Next, with other SOTA methods ignoring the fault type analysis, we report A@1 of MicroCBR hierarchical reasoning in Table 2 on its own. Different from the first experiment, we study the fault type accuracy of novel faults that have never been seen before. By analyzing the results, we find out that although novel faults are not included in the knowledge base, whether their fingerprints are similar to known faults matters. For the novel stress and JVM faults, parts of their fingerprints overlap with known same type faults, resulting in high accuracy. In

Table 2. A@1 of MicroCBR hierarchical reasoning for novel faults.

	Net	Pod	Stress	JVM	I/O	Config	All (of 6 types)
OB	0.81	0.76	0.95	0.93	0.83	0.79	0.82
SS	0.83	0.74	0.93	0.95	0.76	0.72	0.80
TT	0.85	0.75	0.97	0.93	0.80	0.78	0.84
All (of 3 systems)	0.96	0.75	1.00	0.94	0.80	0.77	0.83

a comprehensive view across 3 microservices with 6 fault types, the hierarchical reasoning of MicroCBR can diagnose the fault type with 83% accuracy.

5.3 Q2. Ablation Experiment

For ablation experiments, we first study the A@1 with different ablation rates and further talk about the effect of spatio-temporal knowledge graph on troubleshooting accuracy.

Anomaly detectors play the entry role of MicroCBR, by drawing the fingerprints of emerging faults. However, due to various limitations, such as parameter selections or data bias, they fail to give a perfect fingerprint. We study their impact by customizing the ablation rates of fingerprints, e.g. 0.2 ablation rate means that only 80% of the complete fingerprint can be collected. One additional setting is that the size of each fault fingerprint is no less than one. Figure 5 reports the A@1 of MicroCBR with different ablation rates. With the increase of ablation rate, the accuracy of stress and JVM faults decrease significantly. While the pod faults benefit from temporal anomaly events orders, our framework is still able to locate root causes correctly. Besides, limited to the size of fingerprints, those configuration faults that have small fingerprints change slightly on their A@1. However, it is particularly noteworthy that the accuracy of I/O faults increases when the ablation rate changes from 0.2 to 0.4. This is because this change affects fingerprint importance weight, as expressed in Eq. 3. This experiment illustrates that the anomaly detectors do affect the accuracy of

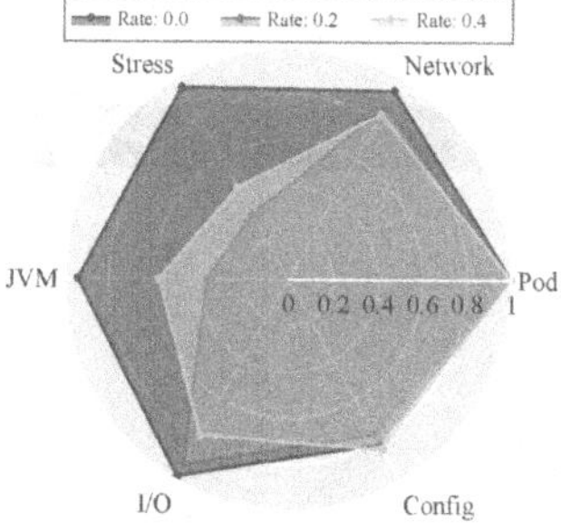

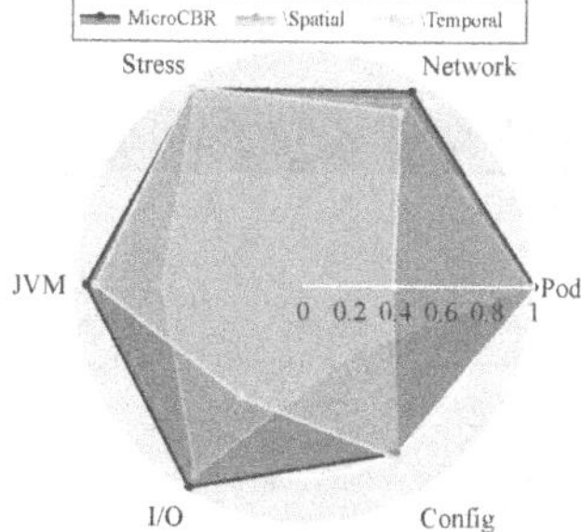

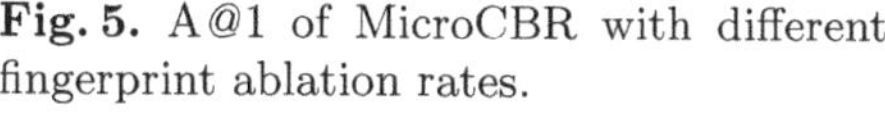

Fig. 5. A@1 of MicroCBR with different fingerprint ablation rates.

Fig. 6. A@1 of MicroCBR with spatial and temporal ablations.

MicroCBR. This conclusion guides us to select anomaly detectors with care in practical applications, ensuring high-quality fault fingerprints.

Next is the ablation study on spatio-temporal knowledge graph. We separately eliminate the spatial and temporal characteristics from our framework, represented by \ Spatial and \ Temporal. Figure 6 shows that these two characteristics in varying degrees impact A@1. The JVM and configuration faults need to compare similar instances to detect anomalies, while pod and I/O faults contain anomaly events sequences. The results show that the design of spatio-temporal knowledge graph improves the troubleshooting accuracy of MicroCBR.

5.4 Q3. Efficiency Experiments

Retain new cases of CBR make the incremental update possible, accompanied by the accumulation of knowledge base. To ensure the long-term usability of our method, we study how the scale of knowledge base and the size of fault fingerprints affect the troubleshooting efficiency.

Fingerprinting the emerging fault is the first step after a system alert. In our framework, it requires interaction with the microservice systems, which includes requesting data from databases and executing commands post-hoc. From Fig. 7 we can see that the troubleshooting mean time of MicroCBR far outstrips others because collecting commands results takes plenty of time. Fortunately, the

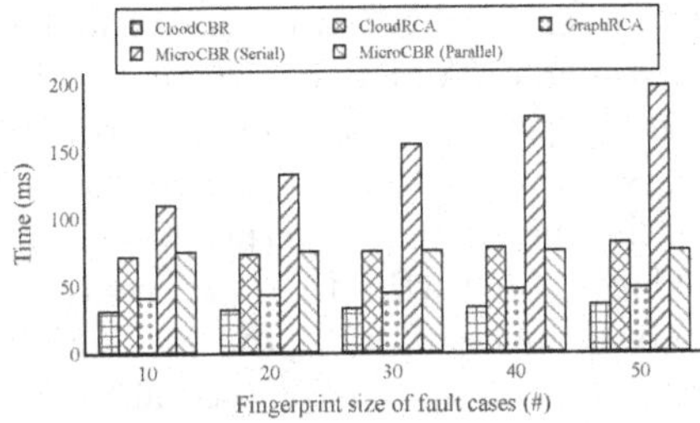

Fig. 7. Troubleshooting mean time with different fingerprint sizes (knowledge base size = 3000).

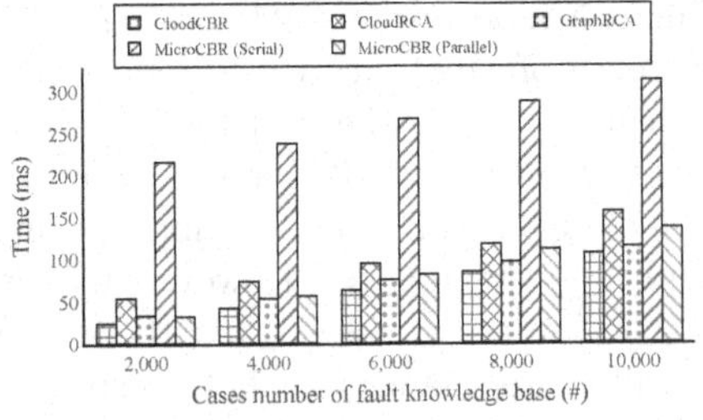

Fig. 8. Troubleshooting mean time with different knowledge base sizes (fingerprint size = 30).

CBR troubleshooting management system

Faults Management Graph View Report Authentication

Search...

ID	Abstract	Instance	Metrics	Logs	Traces	CMDs	Tags	Solutions
10001	network loss	pod/frontend:v2.3.0	M.1, M.2, M.3, M.6	L.2, L.3	callee	C.3	net	correct connection port
10002	network delay	cluster/node2	M.1, M.2, M.4, M.5	L.1, L.3	callee	C.1, C.2	net	upgrade to 100Mbps full duplex
10003	dns error	pod/mailsvc:v2.1.0	M.7, M.8	L.5, L.6	caller	C.4	dns, net	correct proxy configuration
10004	pod cpu stress	pod/cartsvc:v2.1.0	M.9, M.10, M.11, M.12	L.2, L.3	caller, callee	C.5	cpu	resource cpu request and limit
10005	pod failure	pod/cartsvc:v2.1.0	M.10, M.11, M.13, M.14	L.6, L.7, L.8		C.6	failure	wait until probe success

« 1 2 3 4 5 »

Fig. 9. Prototype of MicroCBR management system.

overhead of time can be optimized through parallelism. Figure 8 shows us the troubleshooting mean time with different knowledge base sizes. The mean troubleshooting time of our MicroCBR and other compared methods are increase linearly with the knowledge base accumulation, which is consistent with the theoretical analysis from Eq. 4. In particular, linear time complexity also ensures the usability of our algorithm in practical scenarios. Although the cost of our framework in time comparison is not the best, we argue that its performance of once troubleshooting at a second level is still acceptable.

5.5 Q4. Case Studies and Learned Lessons

Our framework has been widely tested in a real private cloud platform, which has more than 100,000 users from the field of education, health care and finance. During the long-term maintenance of this platform, we collect 710 known faults as a knowledge base. To evaluate the usability of our method in practical applications, we apply MicroCBR on this platform. Figure 9 shows a prototype that provides an easy access for operators to use MicroCBR. We collect the user experience feedback and select two typical cases for study.

The first case is a misconfiguration fault. We successfully detect a disk mount error after once container upgrade. It is noteworthy that most of the metrics fail to be sampled during the upgrade, thus anomaly detection cannot be performed from the time dimension when a new pod start. Thanks to our framework having designed a strategy of referencing similar instances, it finds out a misconfiguration by comparing pods that have not been upgraded. The whole diagnosis is completed in 60 s, which shortens the time by 90% compared with experiential 10-minutes manual troubleshooting. This case shows the power of our framework in reducing MTTR and improving the quality of service.

Another case is related to the mining virus. The system monitors that the CPU utilization of a *cnrig* process on a cluster is as high as 3181% and continues to be abnormal. Since no mining-related cases have been included in the knowledge base before. MicroCBR reports it as a stress fault at a high level. Operators revise this report by adding more mining virus names and traffic features of mining pools, with adding it to the knowledge base. We successfully detect another mining virus called *syst3md* after one week. This case proves the ability of our framework to deal with novel faults.

An important lesson learned from real deployment is that anomalies with high weighted scores always indicate root causes. Meanwhile, these anomalies provide sufficient discrimination for fault fingerprints, which is the basis for similarity-based retrieval.

6 Conclusion

This paper presents our framework named MicroCBR for microservices troubleshooting. Heterogeneous data from metrics, logs, traces, and commands are integrated into a spatio-temporal fault knowledge graph. Hierarchical case-based reasoning is performed to recommend historical similar cases and solutions to operators. The extensive experiments show that MicroCBR outperforms the SOTA methods on troubleshooting accuracy. We also share case studies and learned lessons from our deployment in a real private cloud.

Acknowledgement. This work was supported in part by Austrian-Chinese Cooperative RTD Projects: 171111KYSB20200001, and the National Natural Science Foundation of China No. U20A20180 and No. 61802366.

References

1. Liu, P., Xu, H., Ouyang, Q., et al.: Unsupervised detection of microservice trace anomalies through service-level deep Bayesian networks. In: 2020 IEEE 31st International Symposium on Software Reliability Engineering, pp. 48–58. IEEE (2020)
2. Xu, H., Chen, W., Zhao, N., et al.: Unsupervised anomaly detection via variational auto-encoder for seasonal KPIs in web applications. In: Proceedings of the 2018 World Wide Web Conference, pp. 187–196 (2018)
3. Gan, Y., Zhang, Y., Hu, K., et al.: Seer: leveraging big data to navigate the complexity of performance debugging in cloud microservices. In: Proceedings of the Twenty-Fourth International Conference on Architectural Support for Programming Languages and Operating Systems, pp. 19–33 (2019)
4. Wu, L., Bogatinovski, J., Nedelkoski, S., Tordsson, J., Kao, O.: Performance diagnosis in cloud microservices using deep learning. In: Hacid, H., et al. (eds.) ICSOC 2020. LNCS, vol. 12632, pp. 85–96. Springer, Cham (2021). https://doi.org/10.1007/978-3-030-76352-7_13
5. Zhao, N., Wang, H., Li, Z., et al.: An empirical investigation of practical log anomaly detection for online service systems. In: Proceedings of the 29th ACM Joint Meeting on European Software Engineering Conference and Symposium on the Foundations of Software Engineering, pp. 1404–1415 (2021)
6. Zhou, P., Wang, Y., Li, Z., et al.: Logchain: cloud workflow reconstruction & troubleshooting with unstructured logs. Comput. Netw. **175**, 107279 (2020)
7. Luo, C., Lou, J.-G., Lin, Q., et al.: Correlating events with time series for incident diagnosis. In: Proceedings of the 20th ACM SIGKDD International Conference on Knowledge Discovery and Data Mining, pp. 1583–1592 (2014)
8. Li, Z., Chen, J., Jiao, R., et al.: Practical root cause localization for microservice systems via trace analysis. In: 2021 IEEE/ACM 29th International Symposium on Quality of Service, pp. 1–10. IEEE (2021)
9. Zhang, Y., Guan, Z., Qian, H., et al.: CloudRCA: a root cause analysis framework for cloud computing platforms. In: Proceedings of the 30th ACM International Conference on Information & Knowledge Management, pp. 4373–4382 (2021)
10. Brandón, Á., Solé, M., Huélamo, A., et al.: Graph-based root cause analysis for service-oriented and microservice architectures. J. Syst. Softw. **159**, 110432 (2020)
11. Wang, H., Wu, Z., Jiang, H., et al.: Groot: an event-graph-based approach for root cause analysis in industrial settings. In: 2021 36th IEEE/ACM International Conference on Automated Software Engineering, pp. 419–429. IEEE (2021)
12. Chen, P., Qi, Y., Zheng, P., Hou, D.: CauseInfer: automatic and distributed performance diagnosis with hierarchical causality graph in large distributed systems. In: IEEE INFOCOM Conference on Computer Communications. IEEE (2014)

13. Qiu, J., Du, Q., Yin, K., et al.: A causality mining and knowledge graph based method of root cause diagnosis for performance anomaly in cloud applications. Appl. Sci. **10**(6), 2166 (2020)
14. Zhang, C., Zhou, Z., Zhang, Y., et al.: Netrca: an effective network fault cause localization algorithm. arXiv preprint arXiv:2202.11269 (2022)
15. Nkisi-Orji, I., Wiratunga, N., Palihawadana, C., Recio-García, J.A., Corsar, D.: CLOOD CBR: towards microservices oriented case-based reasoning. In: Watson, I., Weber, R. (eds.) ICCBR 2020. LNCS (LNAI), vol. 12311, pp. 129–143. Springer, Cham (2020). https://doi.org/10.1007/978-3-030-58342-2_9
16. Bennacer, L., Amirat, Y., Chibani, A., et al.: Self-diagnosis technique for virtual private networks combining Bayesian networks and case-based reasoning. IEEE Trans. Autom. Sci. Eng. **12**(1), 354–366 (2014)
17. Ma, M., Yin, Z., Zhang, S., et al.: Diagnosing root causes of intermittent slow queries in cloud databases. Proc. VLDB Endow. **13**(8), 1176–1189 (2020)
18. Ester, M., Kriegel, H.-P., Sander, J., et al.: A density-based algorithm for discovering clusters in large spatial databases with noise. In: KDD, vol. 96, pp. 226–231 (1996)
19. Ren, H., Xu, B., Wang, Y., et al.: Time-series anomaly detection service at Microsoft. In: Proceedings of the 25th ACM SIGKDD International Conference on Knowledge Discovery & Data Mining, pp. 3009–3017 (2019)
20. Blázquez-García, A., Conde, A., Mori, U., Lozano, J.A.: A review on outlier/anomaly detection in time series data. ACM Comput. Surv. **54**, 1–33 (2021)
21. Du, M., Li, F., Zheng, G., Srikumar, V.: DeepLog: anomaly detection and diagnosis from system logs through deep learning. In: Proceedings of the 2017 ACM SIGSAC Conference on Computer and Communications Security (2017)
22. He, S., Zhu, J., He, P., Lyu, M.R.: Experience report: system log analysis for anomaly detection. In: 2016 IEEE 27th International Symposium on Software Reliability Engineering, pp. 207–218. IEEE (2016)
23. Amir, A., Gotthilf, Z., Shalom, B.R.: Weighted LCS. J. Discret. Algorithms **8**(3), 273–281 (2010)
24. Balouek, D., et al.: Adding virtualization capabilities to the grid'5000 testbed. In: Ivanov, I.I., van Sinderen, M., Leymann, F., Shan, T. (eds.) CLOSER 2012. CCIS, vol. 367, pp. 3–20. Springer, Cham (2013). https://doi.org/10.1007/978-3-319-04519-1_1

GPU-Based Graph Matching for Accelerating Similarity Assessment in Process-Oriented Case-Based Reasoning

Maximilian Hoffmann[1,2](✉), Lukas Malburg[1,2], Nico Bach[1], and Ralph Bergmann[1,2]

[1] Artificial Intelligence and Intelligent Information Systems, University of Trier, 54296 Trier, Germany
{hoffmannm,malburgl,s4nibach,bergmann}@uni-trier.de
[2] German Research Center for Artificial Intelligence (DFKI), Branch University of Trier, Behringstraße 21, 54296 Trier, Germany
{maximilian.hoffmann,lukas.malburg,ralph.bergmann}@dfki.de
http://www.wi2.uni-trier.de

Abstract. In *Process-Oriented Case-Based Reasoning (POCBR)*, determining the similarity between cases represented as semantic graphs often requires some kind of inexact graph matching, which generally is an NP-hard problem. Heuristic search algorithms such as A* search have been successfully applied for this task, but the computational performance is still a limiting factor for large case bases. As related work shows a great potential for accelerating A* search by using GPUs, we propose a novel approach called *AMonG* for efficiently computing graph similarities with an A* graph matching process involving GPU computing. The three-phased matching process distributes the search process over multiple search instances running in parallel on the GPU. We develop and examine different strategies within these phases that allow to customize the matching process adjusted to the problem situation to be solved. The experimental evaluation compares the proposed GPU-based approach with a pure CPU-based one. The results clearly demonstrate that the GPU-based approach significantly outperforms the CPU-based approach in a retrieval scenario, leading to an average speedup factor of 16.

Keywords: GPU graph matching · A* search · Similarity-based retrieval · Semantic workflow graphs · Process-Oriented Case-Based Reasoning

1 Introduction

During the past 15 years, the application of workflows, initially proposed to automate business processes, has significantly expanded to new areas such as scientific workflows [31], medical guideline support [22], cooking recipes [25], robotic process automation [1], or IoT environments [4] such as manufacturing [13,24,28,29]. Workflow management, which involves creating, adapting,

M. T. Keane and N. Wiratunga (Eds.): ICCBR 2022, LNAI 13405, pp. 240–255, 2022.
https://doi.org/10.1007/978-3-031-14923-8_16

optimizing, executing, and monitoring them, is getting increasingly challenging in these areas and provides ample opportunities for Artificial Intelligence (AI) support. During the past decade, *Case-Based Reasoning (CBR)* [2,27] demonstrated various benefits in the workflow domain, which led to the subfield of *Process-Oriented Case-Based Reasoning (POCBR)* [5] addressing the integration of process-oriented information systems with CBR. Among other things, POCBR enables the experience-based creation of workflows by reusing successful workflows from the past, stored as cases in a case base. Respective research conducted so far addresses the similarity-based retrieval of reusable workflows as well as their adaptation towards new problems [7]. In both CBR-phases, the similarity assessment between a query and case from the case base is an essential operation, applied frequently during the problem-solving process. The fact that in POCBR query and case are workflows typically represented as semantically annotated graphs, turns the similarity assessment problem into a graph similarity problem based on some domain-specific model of similarity. For addressing this problem, graph matching [10,26] approaches have demonstrated significant benefits, as in addition to the similarity value also a related (best) mapping between query and case graph is computed, which is quite useful, e.g., during adaptation [7]. The involved search process required to compute the mapping can be implemented with A* search [5] but as the problem is inherently NP-hard [11,26] large graphs can still lead to unacceptable computation times for practical applications. Particularly for case retrieval, in which a query has to be compared with each case in the case base, several POCBR approaches have been proposed to either speed up the computation of a single similarity assessment [30,33] or to speed up the overall retrieval using MAC/FAC approaches [14,19] based on faster but approximative similarity measures for preselection [8,18,20]. However, up to now, only moderate speed improvements could be demonstrated.

To address this problem, this paper explores the opportunity to achieve larger performance benefits based on a highly parallelized A*-based graph matching approach for execution on *Graphic Processing Units (GPUs)*, which is inspired by impressive performance improvements obtained for A* search for path-finding [9,35] based on GPUs. Therefore, we describe and analyze a novel approach called AMonG (A*-Based Graph Matching on GPUs) and thereby contribute to other recent endeavors to exploit GPU computing for CBR [3,23]. The following section presents foundations on the used semantic graph representation and similarity assessment via A* graph matching. Next, we describe the AMonG approach in detail, before Sect. 4 demonstrates an experimental evaluation comparing AMonG with the currently based CPU-based approach. Finally, Sect. 5 concludes with a summary of the results and a discussion of future work.

2 Foundations and Related Work

Our approach addresses similarity assessment between pairs of semantic workflow graphs via A*-based graph matching. Although the method is generic regarding the semantic graph representation, we use NEST graphs [5] for the presentation and evaluation. In the following, the NEST graph representation (see Sect. 2.1) as well as the similarity assessment between NEST graphs using A* search (see Sect. 2.2) is introduced. Additionally, we present related work that covers accelerating the similarity assessment between semantic graphs and generic A* search approaches on GPUs (see Sect. 2.3).

2.1 Semantic Workflow Graph Representation

In our approach, we use semantically annotated graphs named *NEST* graphs introduced by Bergmann and Gil [5] to represent workflows. A *NEST* graph consists of four elements: *N*odes, *E*dges, *S*emantic descriptions, and *T*ypes. Figure 1 illustrates a fragment of a cooking recipe. Task nodes represent cooking steps (e. g., `cut`) and data nodes specify the corresponding ingredients that are processed or produced during the execution of the cooking step (e. g., `tomato`). In addition, workflow nodes are used to represent general information about the cooking recipe, e. g., calories or the needed preparation time. Each task and data node is connected with their corresponding workflow node by a part-of edge. Control-flow edges define the execution order in a workflow and data-flow edges indicate that a task consumes or produces this data node. For example, the task `dice` processes `cucumber` in one piece and produces it again, but as diced cucumber. Semantic descriptions can be used to attach specific information to nodes and edges. They are based on a semantic metadata language (e. g., an ontology) that expresses domain-independent and domain-dependent knowledge. In the *NEST* graph illustrated in Fig. 1, semantic descriptions are used to express properties of the data nodes or tasks (e. g., the duration or auxiliaries of a cooking step).

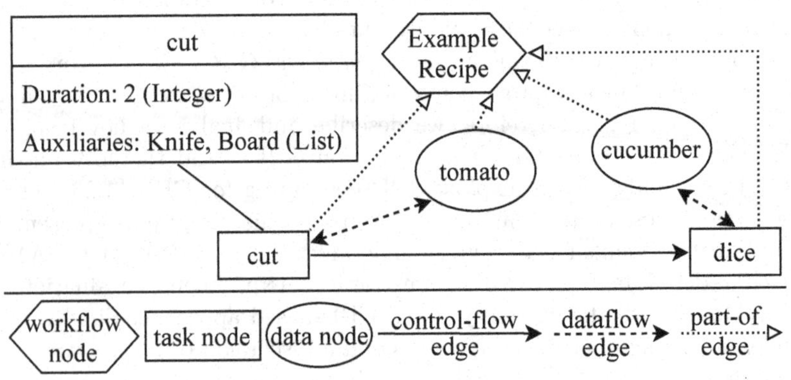

Fig. 1. A cooking recipe represented as a semantic workflow graph.

2.2 State-Space Search by Using A*

By using the presented semantic graph format, it is possible to perform a graph matching between a *query graph* and a *case graph* to get the similarity value. We determine this similarity value with the approach proposed by Bergmann and Gil [5] that aggregates local similarities of mapped nodes and edges to a global similarity value according to the well-known local-global principle by Richter [27]. The local similarities are computed with a model that defines similarities based on the semantic descriptions of nodes and edges. The graph matching process is restricted w. r. t. *type equality*, which means that only nodes and edges of the same type (see Sect. 2.1) can be mapped to each other. Edge mappings are further restricted such that two edges can only be mapped to each other if the nodes linked by the edge are already mapped. However, several valid mappings are possible for two graphs and an algorithm has to be used for finding the best overall injective partial mapping M that maximizes the global similarity $sim(QW, CW)$ between query workflow QW and case workflow CW:

$$sim(QW, CW) = max\,\{sim_M(QW, CW) \mid \text{mapping } M\}$$

The algorithm that is used for this purpose is the A* search algorithm (originally proposed by Hart et al. [15]) that provides a complete and in particular optimal search. The way that A* is used in a graph matching environment is very similar to the original scenario of path search: The search goal is to find a mapping (solution) that maximizes the similarity between two semantic graphs. Starting with a set of unmapped nodes and edges of both graphs, the partial solutions are iteratively build up by adding possible legal mappings. This is done until all nodes and edges of the query graph are mapped. The process is guided by the following equation that evaluates a mapping solution: $f(M) = g(M) + h(M)$. The estimation of the similarity $f(M)$ of a mapping M is given by the sum of the approved similarities of already mapped nodes and edges $g(M)$ and the estimation of the similarities of all unmapped nodes and edges computed by an admissible heuristic $h(M)$. Thereby, $g(M)$ represents the aggregated similarities of the nodes and edges that are already mapped. The function $h(M)$ is a heuristic estimation of the maximum similarity that can be achieved by mapping the currently not mapped nodes and edges. This means, that $f(M) = g(M)$ after the mapping process is finished and $f(M) = h(M)$ before the mapping process is started. Figure 2 depicts two possible mappings ($M1$ and $M2$) between the nodes of the query graph to the nodes of the case graph with their similarities. Please consider that, for simplicity reasons, only the node mappings are illustrated. In addition, it is important to note that the similarity between two graphs is usually not symmetric: Thus, it makes a difference whether the nodes and edges of the query graph are mapped to the case graph or the node and edges of the case graph are mapped to the query graph. The illustrated graph is a typical example for a query that is mostly only a partial graph that is a subgraph of the case workflow graph. We take a closer look at the data node `cheddar` from the query graph and its two possible mappings $M1$ and $M2$: The data node `cheddar` can due to the necessary *type equality* only be mapped to the other data nodes,

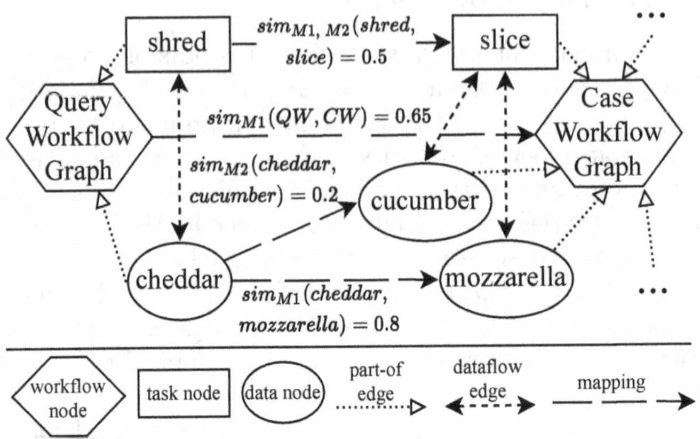

Fig. 2. Exemplary mappings and similarity calculations between two semantic workflow graphs

i. e., `mozzarella` or `cucumber` in the case graph. If the data node `cheddar` is mapped to the data node `mozzarella` a similarity value of 0.8 can be reached. Whereas, a mapping from `cheddar` to `cucumber` results also in a legal mapping but with a lower similarity of 0.2. Thus, the first mapping increases the overall similarity ($sim_{M1} = 0.65$) between the two graphs more than the other mapping ($sim_{M2} = 0.35$).

2.3 Related Work

In this section, we present related work for our proposed approach. Thereby, we distinguish between: 1) related work from POCBR for accelerating case retrieval and similarity assessment by using deep learning or other techniques and 2) related work that uses GPU capabilities in CBR or for performing a state-space search with A*.

To accelerate the similarity assessment between two workflow graphs, several approaches have been proposed, mostly as a similarity measure to be used in the MAC-phase of a MAC/FAC retrieval approach [14]: Bergmann and Stromer [8] present an approach that uses a manually-modeled feature-vector representation of semantic graphs. By using this simplified representation, it is possible to efficiently determine an approximate similarity between two graphs. However, the manual modeling and knowledge acquisition effort for generating appropriate features is high. Klein et al. [20] and Hoffmann et al. [18] try to reduce the manual effort by using neural networks for similarity assessment that can automatically learn feature vectors for graphs. These approaches have good quality and performance characteristics. However, they are also only an approximation of the mapping-based similarity, thus using them for case retrieval may lead to retrieval errors. They also require an offline training phase with high computational cost. In contrast to these approaches, Zeyen and Bergmann [33] present an enhanced version of the A* graph matching process introduced by Bergmann and Gil [5] to improve the search performance while still computing the exact similarity. The improvements consist of four aspects: 1) an improved initialization of the solutions also w. r. t. *type equality*, 2) a *case-oriented mapping* to swap the mapping direction if the case workflow has fewer nodes than the query workflow, 3) a *more-informed heuristic* to reduce the degree of overestimation and to make the h-values more precise, and 4) a *revised selection function* that decides when to map which nodes and edges during the process. However, even with these improvements of the matching process, it tends to be not possible to find optimal solutions in reasonable time for larger graphs.

A possible solution to this problem is GPU computing. To the best of our knowledge, CBR research dealing with GPU-based case retrieval is only rarely investigated [3,23]. The motivation for this work are our previous findings [23] where GPU computing is used for case retrieval of feature-vector cases and achieves a speedup of 37 when compared to CPU-based retrieval. Agorgianitis et al. [3] also work with graph similarities in conjunction with GPU computation but they do not cover semantic annotations as part of the graph similarity computation and they do not use the approach in a retrieval context. Other related work performs a state-space search using A* on the GPU. Bleiweiss [9] presents an approach for accelerating the navigation planning and pathfinding in games. This work focuses on finding the shortest path of several agents, achieving a speedup of up to 24 times. Caggianese and Erra [12] propose a similar A* variant for multi-agent parallel pathfinding in a single graph. Individual threads represent different agents and search different paths in a shared graph by using a hierarchical graph abstraction. Zhou and Zeng [35] propose an A* algorithm that is able to run on a GPU in a massively-parallel fashion, reporting a speedup of up to 45 times. They explore the possibility of not only extracting a single state from the priority queue in each iteration, but rather extracting and processing multiple of the best states at once. All presented approaches are similar to our approach but they are not used for similarity assessment via graph matching. In addition, the gained speedups also promise a great potential for our use case.

3 AMonG: A*-Based Graph Matching on Graphic Processing Units

This section introduces our approach AMonG (A*-Based Graph Matching on GPUs) for performing an A*-based graph matching between semantic workflow graphs by exploiting the highly-parallel computing architecture of GPUs[1]. Our approach integrates the key concepts and the heuristic of the CPU-based A* similarity search presented by Zeyen and Bergmann [33] into a modified version of the GPU-based A* search by Zhou and Zeng [35] where we reuse the structure of parallel search instances (see Sect. 2.3). We first introduce an overview of the

[1] Nico Bach formally described the approach in his bachelor thesis "Using Graphic Processing Units for A*-Based Similarity Assessment in POCBR" submitted 2021 at Trier University.

approach with all associated components (see Sect. 3.1). Since the most important component of this architecture is the parallel graph matching algorithm, we describe its design in detail afterwards (see Sect. 3.2).

3.1 Overview and Components

The graph matching algorithm computes the maximum similarity for a *query graph* and a *case graph*. Both graphs are semantic NEST graphs, as introduced in Sect. 2.1. Due to the fact that NEST graphs have several types of nodes and edges, some mappings during the A* search are not legal, e. g., the mapping of a task node from the query graph to a data node in the case graph. For this reason, we compute all legal mappings between the individual nodes and edges of both graphs and their similarities (also called isolated mappings resp. *isolated similarities*) on the CPU and transfer them to the GPU. This way, the GPU-computation focuses on the pure graph matching process and not on the computation of similarities between nodes and edges. In addition, this also reduces the amount of data stored on the GPU since the semantic information of nodes and edges remain in the CPU memory. In order to parallelize the matching process, we introduce n separate *search instances* that operate individually and in parallel for certain tasks (similar to [35]). Each of these instances operates on its own *priority queue* that stores *state descriptions* containing partially matched solutions. The search instances can be considered as separate A* search runs that run in parallel as often as possible but share their search progress in form of expanded states occasionally. The parameter n has a high influence on the parallelism potential of the matching procedure. A higher value of n corresponds to a higher degree of parallelism and possibly increased performance but comes with the risk of generating more overhead, e. g., for communication and exchange of solutions between the individual priority queues of the instances. The partially matched solution represented by a state description is denoted as s and composed of a set of already *applied mappings* $A(s)$, i. e., all pairs of nodes and edges that are already mapped between query and case graph [5], and a set of *possible mappings* $P(s)$. $P(s)$ is computed by deleting all mappings from the isolated similarities in which a node or an edge is already mapped in $A(s)$ such that it cannot be mapped anymore. Prior to the iterative graph matching procedure, we initialize the priority queues by putting an empty solution, i. e., $A(s_i)$ is empty and $P(s_i)$ is equal to the isolated similarities, into one of the priority queues and leave all other priority queues empty. This is motivated by the findings of related work [35] to prevent the need for computationally-intensive deduplication. By starting with a single solution and deterministically adding new node or edge mappings, it is not possible to generate the same solution twice by different search instances.

3.2 Parallel Graph Matching

The matching procedure is depicted in Fig. 3. The process consists of three distinct phases that are executed iteratively for all search instances. These components are explained in more detail in the following.

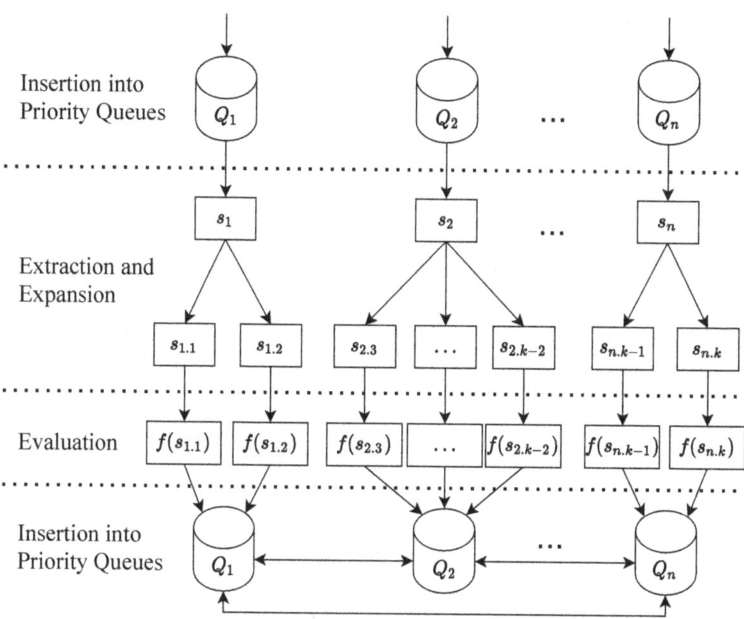

Fig. 3. Execution phases of the GPU-based graph matching algorithm (Based on: [35])

The initial phase in the procedure consists of an *extraction* of the best partial solution s_i by each search instance from its priority queue. The priority queues evaluate and return the best solutions according to their f-value, which is composed of the g-value and the h-value. Please note that although the extracted solutions are all optimal within the scope of the search instances, they are not guaranteed to be optimal in the global scope of all search instances. This might lead to non-optimal solutions being expanded, which can increase matching time. This also motivates a careful parameterization of the approach, in particular with the value of n. Each extracted solution s_i with $i \in [1, n]$ is *expanded* by selecting the next node or edge to match in the query graph. The selected node or edge is then mapped to all legal nodes or edges of the case graph by using $P(s_i)$ that provides information which nodes and edges can be legally mapped according to their types (*type equality*). This leads to k new solutions, denoted as $s_{i.j}$ with $j \in [1, k]$. Each $s_{i.j}$ is stored in a list specific to its search instance.

In the *evaluation* phase, the function f of all previously expanded solutions is computed. Updating the f-value means updating the g- and h-values and is done with $A(s_{i.j})$ and $P(s_{i.j})$. The g-value can be computed by summing-up the similarities of all applied mappings $A(s_{i.j})$. The h-value is denoted as the estimated maximum similarity of all possible remaining mappings $P(s_{i.j})$. However, $P(s_{i.j})$ has to be updated after the expansion by removing mappings with already mapped nodes and edges before computing the correct value of h. In order to parallelize the computation of the h-value, we propose three different strategies: The first naive strategy (Eval_1) only semi-parallelizes the phase by letting each search instance compute the h-value and the updated set of $P(s_{i.j})$ for its expanded mappings in *sequence*. This strategy is semi-parallel as it parallelizes across the search instances but the evaluation of each mapping is computed in serial within each instance. The second strategy (Eval_2) aims at an improved load distribution by collecting the expanded mappings from all search instances and then invoking individual computations of h-value and $P(s_{i.j})$ for each expanded mapping $s_{i.j}$ in *parallel*. The third strategy (Eval_3) follows Eval_2 but additionally splits up the computation of the h-value and the update of $P(s_{i.j})$ into separate parallel subphases by evaluating each node and edge separately. The last two strategies aim at reducing the computations into small, parallelizable parts (*divide and conquer*) in order to improve load distribution. All strategies contribute to the trade-off between parallelism and communication overhead generated by the parallel execution.

In the *insertion* phase, the previously evaluated mappings are inserted into the priority queues of the individual search instances. The evaluated mappings should be distributed between the search instances in order to also distribute the workload for subsequent iterations of the search. An even distribution of partially matched solutions is crucial for the performance of this algorithm and has to be well coordinated. Although there are typically more insertions than extractions [9], priority queues might become empty or are not able to hold more solutions if the distribution is not well coordinated. We propose two different insertion strategies: The first strategy (Ins_1) distributes the expanded mappings of one search instance into the priority queue of only one randomly chosen search instance. Thus, only fixed pairs of search instances share data with each other for one iteration. Consequently, less synchronization is needed but the solutions are not evenly distributed to all other search instances. In contrast, the second strategy (Ins_2) distributes the expanded mappings of a single search instance evenly to the priority queues of *all other* instances. This achieves the maximum degree of distribution and aims to keep the similarities of the solutions in the priority queues uniformly distributed. However, accessing the priority queues of all instances simultaneously, requires a nearly-equal runtime of the instances in the previous expansion phase to avoid waiting for some instances. The insertion phase also has the purpose of checking the termination criteria of the algorithm. It terminates if one of the solutions from all priority queues is fully matched, i. e., all nodes and edges of the query graph are part of a mapping, and this solution also features the maximum similarity value among all solutions, i. e., it satisfies the goal function.

4 Experimental Evaluation

In the experimental evaluation, we compare our AMonG approach with the CPU-based graph matching method [33] in the context of similarity-based retrieval. Our central claim states that using GPUs for similarity assessment via graph matching increases the performance compared to the CPU-based approach (see Sect. 2.3). We investigate the following hypotheses in our experiment:

H1 Distributing all expanded mappings of one search instance into the priority queues of *all other* instances (Ins_2) leads to a lower runtime in comparison to limiting the distribution by only inserting the mappings into the priority queue of another *random* instance (Ins_1).

H2 Evaluating the expanded mappings in parallel and parallelizing the computation of the h-value and the update of the possible mappings in strategy Eval_3 increases the speedup compared to the other *evaluation* strategies Eval_1 and Eval_2.

In Hypothesis H1, we validate the proposed *insertion* strategies in our experiments. The hypothesis is derived from the assumption that the wider distribution by sharing the expanded mappings with all other priority queues (Ins_2) leads to overall lower runtimes compared to less parallelization by inserting the expanded mappings only to *random* instances in strategy Ins_1. Similar to this, we assume in Hypothesis H2 that the selected strategy in the *evaluation* phase should parallelize the workload as much as possible. For this reason, we assume that Eval_3 increases the speedup compared to the other strategies. Thus, we expect that the experiments benefit more from an increased parallelization than the associated communication and synchronization overhead harms performance. In the following, we first describe our experimental setup (see Sect. 4.1) and subsequently the results of our experiments in Sect. 4.2 w. r. t. the hypotheses. Finally, a discussion and further considerations are presented in Sect. 4.3.

4.1 Experimental Setup

For our experiments, we implemented the previously presented approach in the open-source POCBR framework ProCAKE[2] [6], which is suitable for representing semantic graphs and enabling A*-based graph matching between them (see [33]). We use the bindings of JCUDA [32] for GPU-acceleration, since ProCAKE is implemented in Java. The case base for the experiments is an exemplary case base available in ProCAKE, containing 40 manually-modeled cooking recipes represented as NEST graphs [6]. These recipes are similar to the recipe that is illustrated in Fig. 1. To highlight the mapping complexity of this scenario,

[2] http://procake.uni-trier.de.

Table 1. Graph size and mapping complexity of the case base

	Graph Nodes	Graph Edges	Graph Node Mappings	Graph Edge Mappings
min	9	21	70	$9.8 \cdot 10^4$
avg	21.15	55.63	$2 \cdot 10^8$	$1 \cdot 10^{28}$
max	38	110	$7 \cdot 10^{28}$	$1.2 \cdot 10^{31}$

we present important properties of the case base in Table 1. The numbers show the enormous search space of the mapping problem. The evaluation is restricted to similarity assessments between graphs from this case base that do not reach the memory limitations of the system (GPU and CPU memory). As already described in Sect. 2.2, query graphs are typically partial graphs with fewer nodes and edges than the case graphs. For this reason, we also restrict the experiments to similarities where this condition holds. The final number of evaluated similarity assessments is 704 where all other assessments either reach the memory limitations or do not meet the criteria of a query smaller than the case. Our central evaluation metric is the *speedup* in computation time that can be achieved by applying AMonG in addition to the CPU-based similarity assessment. AMonG is introduced such that it always computes the similarity in parallel to the pure CPU-based A* computation and considers the one that first finishes the computation (the slower computation can be stopped and discarded). Thus, the speedup is defined by the full computation time on the CPU divided by the minimum of the time of AMonG and the full computation time on the CPU. All experiments are repeated five times and averaged afterwards. The computation results of AMonG are verified by comparing them with the results of the CPU-based A* computation. The experiments are conducted on a computer running Windows 10 64-bit with an Intel i7 6700 CPU and 48 GB RAM. For the GPU, an NVIDIA GeForce GTX 1080 with compute capability 6.1 and 8 GB graphics RAM is used. In preliminary experiments, we determined that a number of $n = 2048$ priority queues is sufficient for our experiments.

4.2 Experimental Results

In this section, we present and discuss the results of our experiments. With Hypothesis H1, we want to examine which *insertion* strategy is best suited. Figure 4 depicts the runtime of all examined similarity computations on the GPU for both insertion strategies in relation to the number of expanded mappings. Both strategies are comparable w. r. t. their runtime for relatively small numbers of expansions. However, as the required number of expansions to find a solution increases, Ins_2 provides a better runtime overall. Further, we investigate the total number of expanded mappings for both strategies: Ins_1 expands fewer mappings than Ins_2. This could be attributed to having more idle priority queues in the beginning of the search, as mappings are not spread out efficiently over the

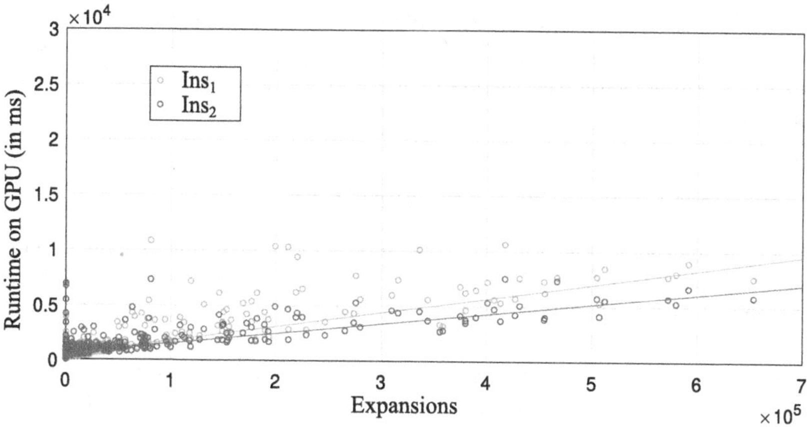

Fig. 4. Experimental results of different insertion strategies

priority queues, leading to fewer expansions in early phases. Due to the better distribution of the workload in early iterations, Ins_2, by contrast, expands more mappings on average than Ins_1. For our experiments, we confirm Hypothesis H1 as the runtime difference of Ins_2 becomes larger as expansions grow and the runtime is overall lower than that of Ins_1.

To check Hypothesis H2, we run the experiments by using the best *insertion* strategy from the first experiment Ins_2 with all three proposed *evaluation* strategies (Eval_1, Eval_2, and Eval_3). We measure the *average speedup* that is calculated with the speedups of all 704 similarity assessments. Additionally, the *average retrieval speedup* is given based on the mean of the conducted retrievals where the case base is queried with every graph. These values can be interpreted as the expected speedup for a single similarity assessment of a query-case pair and a typical retrieval, respectively. The results in Fig. 5 show that the strategy

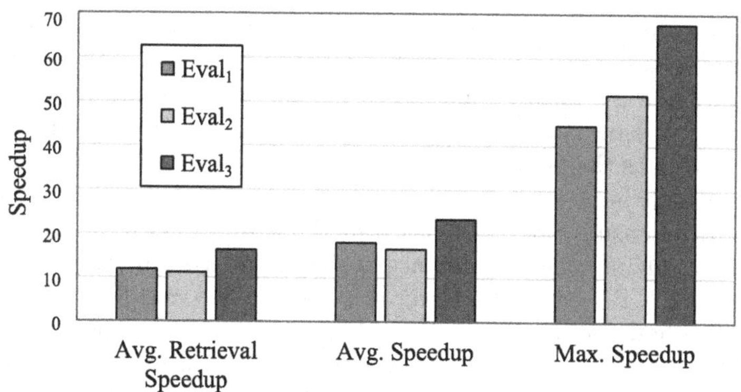

Fig. 5. Experimental results of different evaluation strategies

Eval_3 achieves the highest values overall, with an average retrieval speedup of 16.29 and an average speedup of 23.33. This strategy also achieves a maximum speedup of a single similarity assessment of 67.72. For this reason, we clearly accept Hypothesis H2.

4.3 Discussion and Further Considerations

In our experimental evaluation, we have shown the performance gains that are possible by using the GPU for A* search and we support our central claim with the hypotheses. However, of the 704 similarity computations 379 were not accelerated using AMonG. Nevertheless, the similarity assessment on the GPU is faster in a typical retrieval scenario (see *retrieval speedup*), as 178 calculations can be performed with a speedup greater than 1 and less than 10, and 147 calculations can even be executed with a speedup greater than 10. Our approach thereby benefits from being used for larger problem spaces, where it clearly outperforms the CPU-based method. In our experiments, we determine that a similarity assessment, in which more than 2500 expansions on the CPU are needed, should be performed on the GPU. The required expansions on the CPU vary between 29 and 1,765,595 with an average of 44920.

5 Conclusion and Future Work

We presented the AMonG approach to accelerate A*-based similarity assessment between semantic graphs by using GPUs in POCBR. AMonG exploits the architecture of GPUs to evaluate multiple mappings in parallel during the search process. To factor in the trade-off between parallelism and synchronization overhead, we also discuss several strategies that contribute to either of these two aspects, making the approach customizable w. r. t. multiple scenarios. The evaluation investigates the potential of the proposed approach in speeding up similarity assessment between semantic workflow graphs. It demonstrates that our GPU-based approach significantly outperforms the CPU-based approach, leading to speedup factors of up to 67. GPU retrieval acceleration is novel to POCBR and is only little investigated in CBR (e. g., [3,23]. The approach can serve as the basis for future applications dealing with a wide variety of CBR tasks. It can be especially useful in scenarios that deal with many similarity assessments such as the learning process of adaptation knowledge [7]. Further, it enables to process large case bases in complex domains that could be inefficient or even infeasible using only CPU-based methods (e. g., [33]).

To further enhance the performance of the overall system, we propose to use GPU-based and CPU-based matching in parallel. This could be achieved with a suitable method for distributing graph pairs to both components a-priori, e. g., by using a heuristic or a learning approach. It can lead to both approaches fully utilizing their potential. This can also be important in the context of a dependency-guided retrieval [21], where the search space can be particularly large due to consideration of dependencies between cases during the retrieval phase. Furthermore, we aim to provide more flexibility with the algorithm's hyperparameters to better fit the computation for different domains of semantic graphs. This also emphasizes an automated method for hyperparameter optimization [16]. To validate the findings from this paper, future work should also cover more extensive evaluations with further POCBR domains (e. g., scientific workflows [34] or cyber-physical manufacturing workflows [24,29]). In addition, the usage of the approach in combination with other techniques for accelerating similarity-based retrieval (e. g., [17,18,20,23]) promises further benefits.

Acknowledgments. This work is funded by the Federal Ministry for Economic Affairs and Climate Action under grant No. 22973 SPELL.

References

1. Van der Aalst, W.M.P., Bichler, M., Heinzl, A.: Robotic process automation. BISE **60**(4), 269–272 (2018). https://doi.org/10.1007/s12599-018-0542-4
2. Aamodt, A., Plaza, E.: Case-based reasoning: foundational issues, methodological variations, and system approaches. AI Commun. **7**(1), 39–59 (1994)
3. Agorgianitis, I., et al.: Business process workflow monitoring using distributed CBR with GPU computing. In: 30th FLAIRS, pp. 495–498. AAAI Press (2017)
4. Janiesch, C., et al.: The Internet of Things meets business process management: a manifesto. IEEE Syst. Man Cybern. Mag. **6**(4), 34–44 (2020)
5. Bergmann, R., Gil, Y.: Similarity assessment and efficient retrieval of semantic workflows. Inf. Syst. **40**, 115–127 (2014)
6. Bergmann, R., Grumbach, L., Malburg, L., Zeyen, C.: ProCAKE: a process-oriented case-based reasoning framework. In: ICCBR Workshops, vol. 2567, pp. 156–161. CEUR-WS.org (2019)
7. Bergmann, R., Müller, G.: Similarity-based retrieval and automatic adaptation of semantic workflows. In: Nalepa, G.J., Baumeister, J. (eds.) Synergies Between Knowledge Engineering and Software Engineering. AISC, vol. 626, pp. 31–54. Springer, Cham (2018). https://doi.org/10.1007/978-3-319-64161-4_2
8. Bergmann, R., Stromer, A.: MAC/FAC retrieval of semantic workflows. In: 26th FLAIRS. AAAI Press (2013)
9. Bleiweiss, A.: GPU accelerated pathfinding. In: Proceedings of the 23th EUROGRAPHICS/ACM SIGGRAPH, pp. 65–74. Eurographics Association (2008)
10. Bunke, H.: Recent developments in graph matching. In: Proceedings of the 15th ICPR, pp. 117–124 (2000)
11. Bunke, H., Messmer, B.T.: Similarity measures for structured representations. In: Wess, S., Althoff, K.-D., Richter, M.M. (eds.) EWCBR 1993. LNCS, vol. 837, pp. 106–118. Springer, Heidelberg (1994). https://doi.org/10.1007/3-540-58330-0_80
12. Caggianese, G., Erra, U.: Parallel hierarchical A* for multi agent-based simulation on the GPU. In: Mey, D., et al. (eds.) Euro-Par 2013. LNCS, vol. 8374, pp. 513–522. Springer, Heidelberg (2014). https://doi.org/10.1007/978-3-642-54420-0_50
13. Erasmus, J., Vanderfeesten, I., Traganos, K., Grefen, P.W.P.J.: Using business process models for the specification of manufacturing operations. Comput. Ind. **123** (2020)
14. Forbus, K.D., Gentner, D., Law, K.: MAC/FAC: a model of similarity-based retrieval. Cogn. Sci. **19**(2), 141–205 (1995)

15. Hart, P.E., Nilsson, N.J., Raphael, B.: A formal basis for the heuristic determination of minimum cost paths. IEEE Trans. Syst. Sci. Cybern. **4**(2), 100–107 (1968)
16. Hoffmann, M., Bergmann, R.: Improving automated hyperparameter optimization with case-based reasoning. In: Keane, M., Wiratunga, N. (eds.) ICCBR 2022. LNAI, vol. 13405, pp. 143–158. Springer, Cham (2022)
17. Hoffmann, M., Bergmann, R.: Using graph embedding techniques in process-oriented case-based reasoning. Algorithms **15**(2), 27 (2022)
18. Hoffmann, M., Malburg, L., Klein, P., Bergmann, R.: Using Siamese graph neural networks for similarity-based retrieval in process-oriented case-based reasoning. In: Watson, I., Weber, R. (eds.) ICCBR 2020. LNCS (LNAI), vol. 12311, pp. 229–244. Springer, Cham (2020). https://doi.org/10.1007/978-3-030-58342-2_15
19. Kendall-Morwick, J., Leake, D.: A study of two-phase retrieval for process-oriented case-based reasoning. In: Montani, S., Jain, L. (eds.) Successful Case-based Reasoning Applications, vol. 494, pp. 7–27. Springer, Heidelberg (2014). https://doi.org/10.1007/978-3-642-38736-4_2
20. Klein, P., Malburg, L., Bergmann, R.: Learning workflow embeddings to improve the performance of similarity-based retrieval for process-oriented case-based reasoning. In: Bach, K., Marling, C. (eds.) ICCBR 2019. LNCS (LNAI), vol. 11680, pp. 188–203. Springer, Cham (2019). https://doi.org/10.1007/978-3-030-29249-2_13
21. Kumar, R., Schultheis, A., Malburg, L., Hoffmann, M., Bergmann, R.: Considering inter-case dependencies during similarity-based retrieval in process-oriented case-based reasoning. In: 35th FLAIRS. FloridaOJ (2022)
22. Lyng, K.M., Hildebrandt, T., Mukkamala, R.R.: From paper based clinical practice guidelines to declarative workflow management. In: Ardagna, D., Mecella, M., Yang, J. (eds.) BPM 2008. LNBIP, vol. 17, pp. 336–347. Springer, Heidelberg (2009). https://doi.org/10.1007/978-3-642-00328-8_34
23. Malburg, L., Hoffmann, M., Trumm, S., Bergmann, R.: Improving similarity-based retrieval efficiency by using graphic processing units in case-based reasoning. In: 34th FLAIRS. FloridaOJ (2021)
24. Malburg, L., Seiger, R., Bergmann, R., Weber, B.: Using physical factory simulation models for business process management research. In: Del Río Ortega, A., Leopold, H., Santoro, F.M. (eds.) BPM 2020. LNBIP, vol. 397, pp. 95–107. Springer, Cham (2020). https://doi.org/10.1007/978-3-030-66498-5_8
25. Minor, M., Bergmann, R., Görg, S., Walter, K.: Adaptation of cooking instructions following the workflow paradigm. In: Proceedings of the ICCBR Workshops, pp. 199–208 (2010)
26. Ontañón, S.: An overview of distance and similarity functions for structured data. Artif. Intell. Rev. **53**(7), 5309–5351 (2020). https://doi.org/10.1007/s10462-020-09821-w
27. Richter, M.M., Weber, R.O.: Case-Based Reasoning. Springer, Heidelberg (2013). https://doi.org/10.1007/978-3-642-40167-1
28. Rinderle-Ma, S., Mangler, J.: Process automation and process mining in manufacturing. In: Polyvyanyy, A., Wynn, M.T., Van Looy, A., Reichert, M. (eds.) BPM 2021. LNCS, vol. 12875, pp. 3–14. Springer, Cham (2021). https://doi.org/10.1007/978-3-030-85469-0_1
29. Seiger, R., Malburg, L., Weber, B., Bergmann, R.: Integrating process management and event processing in smart factories: a systems architecture and use cases. J. Manuf. Syst. **63**, 575–592 (2022)
30. Serina, I.: Kernel functions for case-based planning. Artif. Intell. **174**(16–17), 1369–1406 (2010)

31. Taylor, I.J., Deelman, E., Gannon, D.B., Shields, M.S. (eds.): Workflows for e-Science, Scientific Workflows for Grids. Springer, London (2007). https://doi.org/10.1007/978-1-84628-757-2
32. Yan, Y., Grossman, M., Sarkar, V.: JCUDA: a programmer-friendly interface for accelerating java programs with CUDA. In: Sips, H., Epema, D., Lin, H.-X. (eds.) Euro-Par 2009. LNCS, vol. 5704, pp. 887–899. Springer, Heidelberg (2009). https://doi.org/10.1007/978-3-642-03869-3_82
33. Zeyen, C., Bergmann, R.: A*-based similarity assessment of semantic graphs. In: Watson, I., Weber, R. (eds.) ICCBR 2020. LNCS (LNAI), vol. 12311, pp. 17–32. Springer, Cham (2020). https://doi.org/10.1007/978-3-030-58342-2_2
34. Zeyen, C., Malburg, L., Bergmann, R.: Adaptation of scientific workflows by means of process-oriented case-based reasoning. In: Bach, K., Marling, C. (eds.) ICCBR 2019. LNCS (LNAI), vol. 11680, pp. 388–403. Springer, Cham (2019). https://doi.org/10.1007/978-3-030-29249-2_26
35. Zhou, Y., Zeng, J.: Massively parallel A* search on a GPU. In: Proceedings of the 29th AAAI, pp. 1248–1255. AAAI Press (2015)

Never Judge a Case by Its (Unreliable) Neighbors: Estimating Case Reliability for CBR

Adwait P. Parsodkar[1(✉)], Deepak P.[1,2], and Sutanu Chakraborti[1]

[1] Indian Institute of Technology, Madras, Chennai 600036, TN, India
{cs20d404,sutanuc}@cse.iitm.ac.in

[2] Queen's University Belfast, Belfast, UK
deepaksp@acm.org

Abstract. It is known, in the Case-based Reasoning community, that the effectiveness of a Case-Based Reasoner is heavily dictated by the quality of cases in its Case Base, and therefore the presence of poor quality cases can adversely influence its predictions. While it is common practice for a domain expert to periodically check the cases in the case base of a reasoner, it often becomes a time-intensive exercise in practice. Existing literature provides potential measures of reliability of cases in the case base, however, they fail to provide robust estimates of the reliability of a case when its neighborhood comprises of mixed quality cases. In this work, we propose *RelCBR* which builds upon a *circular* definition of case reliability - *a case is reliable if it is well-aligned with its reliable neighbors.* This formulation allows us to arrive at more robust estimates of reliability and results in streamlining the case base maintenance process by drawing the attention of the expert to cases that are more likely of being incorrect. In addition, these reliability values can also be used to discount the contribution of unreliable cases in the reasoning process that would consequently boost the performance of the reasoner.

Keywords: Case-Based Reasoning · Case Base Maintenance · Case Reliability

1 Introduction

The effectiveness of a Case-based Reasoner (CBR system) is heavily determined by the quality of the cases within its case base. Case bases within practical CBR systems are often constructed through drawing upon plurality of expertise sources, such as multiple human case authors, multiple authoritative information sources (e.g., books), or by collating multiple smaller case bases [12]. The plurality of sources makes heterogeneity an inevitable character of large case bases. While heterogeneity could exist in case structures, topical focus, and others, our focus is on the heterogeneity in the quality of cases within a case base. It may be observed that not all human experts necessarily provide highly reliable information at all times, case sources could vary in subjectivity and thus reliability,

M. T. Keane and N. Wiratunga (Eds.): ICCBR 2022, LNAI 13405, pp. 256–270, 2022.
https://doi.org/10.1007/978-3-031-14923-8_17

and cases could come from smaller case bases that have been curated for quality to differing standards. As a case in point, [6] posits that the provenance of cases be remembered to enhance robust CBR operation. The impracticality of manual quality curation of individual cases within large case bases has prompted much research into automated and semi-automated solutions for the task of case-base maintenance [15].

A simple and effective pathway for quantifying the goodness of cases has been provided by the body of work on *case base alignment* [13]. These quantify the extent to which the assumption that *similar problems have similar solutions* hold within the local neighborhood of a case. This is operationalized by considering the relationship between the local similarity structure in the problem space and their dispersion within the solution space. The dependence of alignment on the local neighborhood of a case is intuitively appealing since the eventual goal of a case-based reasoner is to use cases in a neighborhood of a problem case towards arriving at a solution. We observe that the construction of case base alignment measures makes it eminently capable of distinguishing between localized spaces that comprise good quality cases, and those that comprise poor quality cases. However, they are less robust in localized spaces that contain a mix of good and poor quality cases as will see.

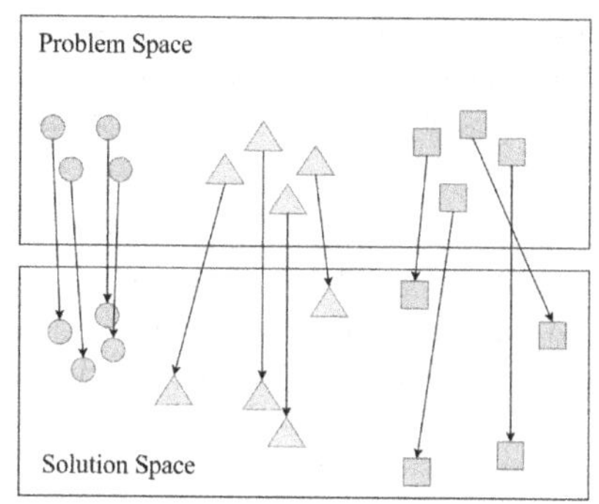

Fig. 1. Alignment and case quality

Towards illustrating this important shortcoming using a simplistic and stylized example, consider three localized clusters of cases in Fig. 1, represented using their problem-solution spaces, and the application of case alignment measures over them. The cluster comprising of circular cases is visibly well-aligned, and cases within them would be accorded high alignment scores. Analogously, the cluster of square cases exhibits poor alignment, and case alignment measures would rightly assign them poor scores. The middle cluster poses a challenge for alignment measures since they contain two cases that are well-aligned and two cases that exhibit poor alignment. The simple aggregation within alignment measures would yield a medium alignment score for all cases within the middle cluster. In other words, the case alignment mechanism formulation is incapable of identifying the sub-cluster of well-aligned cases within the cluster. Further, cases in a cluster composed of well-aligned poor quality cases that digress from the global trend might still be inaptly asserted high reliability scores by such alignment measures.

In this paper, we consider this incongruence between case alignment metrics and intuitive goodness of cases within mixed quality neighborhoods, and develop an alternative and robust formulation that is capable of doing more robust quantifications of case goodness. We draw inspiration from the usage of circular definitions of object quality - which could be stated as *'an object is good if it is related to other good objects'* - as used within varied contexts such as web-page scoring (e.g., HITS [4], PageRank [11]) and information aggregation (e.g., truth discovery [8]) towards developing our formulation. While extant contexts of circularity usage are directed towards collections of singular data objects, we extend it for usage within the significantly different context of case bases that comprise case objects with a dichotomous problem-solution structure. We develop a computational formulation based on the aforementioned notion and an optimization method towards addressing it, in order to arrive at quantifications of case goodness that we term as *case reliability.* Our contributions are as follows:

- We propose robust case quality estimation as a novel challenge within the ambit of case base maintenance.
- We develop a case reliability estimation method, *RelCBR*, powered by a novel formulation founded upon a circular definition of case quality.
- Our extensive empirical evaluation over synthetic and real-world datasets establishes the effectiveness of the proposed method.

We now describe the organization of this work. In Sect. 2, we present the problem statement followed by a brief overview of Truth Discovery and some potential measures of case reliability from existing CBR literature in Sect. 3. In Sect. 4, we define a constrained optimization problem solution of which is expected to provide more robust estimates of reliability. Section 5 illustrates the effectiveness of the proposed method followed by discussions in Sect. 6.

2 Problem Statement

Consider a case base $\mathcal{C} = \{\ldots, c = (p_c, v_c), \ldots\}$ where each case c is represented as a problem-solution pair and the value in the solution is represented by v_c. Our task is to quantify the *reliability* of each case in $\mathcal{C}$ as a vector r such that $r_c \in [0,1]$ indicates the reliability of case c. A higher value of r_c indicates that the case c is more reliable, where reliability is defined using a circular notion. The circular definition of reliability may be outlined as: *'a case is reliable if it can be solved by its reliable problem-space neighbors'*. Using vocabulary from case base alignment literature, we may paraphrase this definition as: *'a case is reliable if it is well-aligned with its reliable neighbors'*. We summarize the notations used in this paper in Table 1.

3 Background

We now provide an overview of the background literature to our work. As alluded to earlier, circular definitions - such as our reliability definition - have been used in contexts as varied information aggregation and web page quality estimation. We first discuss *truth discovery* within information aggregation as an illustrative example of the usage of circular definitions. Next, we discuss case base maintenance literature, especially those closest to ours in terms of quantifying the goodness of cases such as case alignment.

Table 1. Notations and their meanings

Notation	Meaning
$\mathcal{C}$	The Case Base
c	A case in $\mathcal{C}$
p_c	The problem part of the case $c \in \mathcal{C}$
v_c	The value in the solution part of the case $c \in \mathcal{C}$
r_c	The reliability of case $c \in \mathcal{C}$
$\mathcal{N}_c^P$	The nearest problem-space neighbors of $c \in \mathcal{C}$
s_{xy}^P	Similarity between the problem parts of two cases $x, y \in \mathcal{C}$

3.1 Truth Discovery

Truth Discovery [8] deals with the task of identifying trustworthy answers for a *question* when there are multiple *sources* (e.g., experts) of information that provide potentially conflicting *answers*. While choosing the majority answer might work well in many scenarios, it is not necessarily a foolproof solution. For example, the majority answer for *'capital of Canada?'* might turn out to be *Toronto*, and a knowledgeable expert who provides the correct answer, *Ottawa*, might find herself in the minority. Truth Discovery improves upon majority voting in such information aggregation settings through replacing simple aggregation by an reliability driven aggregation. Here, reliability is defined using a circular form, viz., *the extent to which the source agrees with reliable sources in providing answers to various questions.* As evident from this construction, such estimation of reliability requires a corpus of questions, with sources providing answers to each (or most) questions. It is also worth noting that this formulation of reliability estimation in truth discovery does not require supervision, in that it does not assume access to the gold-standard answers to the questions. Once reliability scores are estimated, the answer to a given question may be estimated using a reliability-weighted aggregation of answers from across sources (as opposed to simple uniform-weighted aggregation). Existing truth discovery methods solve the reliability estimation problem using approaches that involve optimizing a cost function [7] and modeling the problem as a Probabilistic Graphical Model (PGM) [18], among others. There have also been recent semi-supervised extensions to the truth discovery framework [16,17].

3.2 Case Base Maintenance

Traditionally, a case is added to the case base when an expert ensures that the case is correct and adds value to the CBR system. However, in real-world systems, expert supervision is not necessarily available due to which potentially incorrect cases can be added to the case base. In addition, over time, the reasoner gains more knowledge in the form of cases but some cases tend to become out-of-date or inconsistent with the other cases in the case base. This demands correction or removal of cases to ensure that CBR decisions are always informed by good quality cases.

Case Cohesion: A simple and intuitive measure, called *case cohesion* [5], scores each case c using the Jaccard similarity between the set of problem-space and solution-space neighbors.

$$caseCohesion(c) = \frac{|\mathcal{N}_c^P \cap \mathcal{N}_c^S|}{|\mathcal{N}_c^P \cup \mathcal{N}_c^S|} \tag{1}$$

where $\mathcal{N}_c^S$ ($\mathcal{N}_c^P$) denote the cases within the solution-space (problem-space) neighbors of c. Cases whose neighborhoods on the problem side and solution side are highly overlapping are thus assigned a higher score. This may be seen as an early attempt at quantifying the extent to which a case's neighborhood agrees with the CBR assumption that *similar problems have similar solutions.*

Case Alignment: A major limitation of case cohesion is that all neighborhood cases of a case c, the almost identical neighbor and a moderately similar neighbor, all contribute equally to case cohesion score for c. The case alignment notion by Massie et al. [9] refines this notion to weigh the neighborhood cases proportional to similarity to c, resulting in a form as follows:

$$alignMassie(c) = \frac{\sum_{c' \in \mathcal{N}_c^P} s_{cc'}^P \times s_{cc'}^S}{\sum_{c' \in \mathcal{N}_c^P} s_{cc'}^P} \tag{2}$$

where s_{xy}^S (s_{xy}^P) denote solution-space (problem-space) similarity between $x, y \in \mathcal{C}$. While this and other notions of case alignment ([3], for instance), as noted in Sect. 1 and Fig. 1, do well in quality-homogeneous neighborhoods, they tend to become inaccurate indicators of quality in neighborhoods that comprise cases from across a broader quality spectrum.

Other Case Scoring Measures: There have been other work on case base maintenance that consider discriminating cases based on other criteria, which are somewhat tangential to our work. We provide a brief overview here. [1] considers trade-offs between generalizability and usability of cases in determining cases to discard/retain. [14] tries to arrive at a condensed set of cases from the case base, called the footprint set, that has (roughly) the same problem solving ability as the entire case base. They, however, restrict their focus on situations that involve adaptation of the solution of a single case to the problem. [10] improves upon the prior work by allowing compositional adaptation, and preserves a case if the case is advantageous to solve problems and ensuring overall case base competence.

4 RelCBR: Our Approach

Given that our approach, *RelCBR*, is founded upon the circular definition of reliability, we take this opportunity to restate the definition: *a case is reliable if it can be solved by its reliable problem-space neighbors.* Since our intent is to solve cases using reliable problem-space neighbors, we will use case solution estimation as a starting point to outline our approach.

4.1 Towards an Optimization Objective for Reliability Estimation

Consider a case base scenario where the solution part of cases are numeric. This would correspond to answering questions such as *distance between A and B?*. Given a good estimation of reliabilities as a reliability vector, r, the solution part of a case c may be estimated by using its problem-space neighbors as follows:

$$v_c^e = \frac{\sum_{c' \in \mathcal{N}_c^P} r_{c'} \times s_{cc'}^P \times v_{c'}}{\sum_{c' \in \mathcal{N}_c^P} r_{c'} \times s_{cc'}^P} \tag{3}$$

In other words, the estimated solution for c, denoted v_c^e, is computed as the weighted sum of solutions of its problem-space neighbors, each neighbor weighted by the product of *their reliability* (i.e., $r_{c'}$) and *their similarity to c* ($s_{cc'}^P$).

This easily extends to case base scenarios where the solution part is categorical. Analogous to the numeric case, we use a reliability weighted averaging; however, this yields a probability distribution over the space of categorical solution values, unlike a single value for the numeric case. The categorical value associated with the highest probability is then chosen as v_c^e:

$$p(v_c^e = i) = \frac{\sum_{c' \in \mathcal{N}_c^P} r_{c'} \times s_{cc'}^P \times \mathbb{I}(v_{c'}, i)}{\sum_{c' \in \mathcal{N}_c^P} r_{c'} \times s_{cc'}^P} \tag{4}$$

$$v_c^e = \arg\max_{i \in V} \; p(v_c^e = i) \tag{5}$$

where V is the space of all solution values across cases in $\mathcal{N}_c^P$, and $\mathbb{I}(x, y)$ returns 1 when x and y are identical, 0 otherwise. Despite the slightly different construction, observe that $p(v_c^e = i)$ simply denotes the probability mass associated with i among the neighbors of c under weighted solution aggregation, using the same product weighting formulation as earlier.

A scheme for solution estimation for a case using its neighbors and their reliability estimates is only as good as the accuracy with which it estimates solutions. Given that some cases in a case base may be inherently unreliable (i.e., of low quality), we would like to ensure that our solution estimation scheme works well for estimating the solutions for reliable cases (recall our definition of reliability). Towards this, we outline a reliability weighted accuracy measure:

$$L(\mathcal{C}, r) = \sum_{c \in \mathcal{C}} r_c \times (v_c - v_c^e)^2 \tag{6}$$

$L(\mathcal{C}, r)$ denotes the reliability weighted squared errors of deviation between the actual solution of c (i.e., v_c) and the reliability-oriented estimate (i.e., v_c^e). This, as probably already evident by the notation, serves as a loss function that is sought to be optimized to arrive at good reliability estimates. The corresponding loss function for the categorical case is defined as the squared euclidean distance between the probability vector from the solution estimation scheme, and the one-hot vector determined by the actual solution:

$$L(\mathcal{C}, r) = \sum_{c \in \mathcal{C}} r_c \times \sum_{i \in V} \left(h_c(i) - p(v_c^e = i)\right)^2 \tag{7}$$

where $h_c(i)$ is the one-hot vector defined as:

$$h_c(i) = \begin{cases} 1 & \text{if } i = v_c \\ 0 & \text{otherwise} \end{cases}$$

These can be extended to other case bases involving non-numeric and non-categorical solutions. However, as a first step towards reliability estimation for CBR, we restrict the scope of this paper to numeric and categorical scenarios.

We note here that the estimated solution v_c^e (or the probability distribution $p(v_c^e = i)$) does not depend on v_c or r_c. The loss function is dependent on the disparity between the estimates and the actual solution, weighted by reliabilities. This makes the operation of the circularity evident, and may be interpreted as a leave-one-out strategy for defining the loss function.

4.2 RelCBR Optimization

Having arrived at the numeric and categorical scenario versions of the loss function $L(\mathcal{C}, r)$, the best reliability vector is one that leads to the smallest value of $L(\mathcal{C}, r)$. Due to the construction of $L(\mathcal{C}, r)$ as a reliability weighted sum of case-specific losses, it can be trivially optimized by setting all reliabilities to 0. Towards preventing this meaningless solution, we impose two constraints:

$$\forall\, c \in \mathcal{C},\ r_c \in [0, 1] \tag{8}$$

$$\left(\sum_{c \in \mathcal{C}} r_c\right) \geq a \tag{9}$$

In other words, we restrict each case's reliability to be within $[0, 1]$ and additionally enforce that the case reliabilities across the case base add up to at least a, which is set up as a positive-valued numeric hyperparameter.

This leads to a constrained optimization setting, where the optimization procedure searches for estimates of the r vector, subject to the constraints. We use projected gradient descent as the optimization algorithm where, within each iteration, there are two steps:

- the parameters are updated by moving opposite to the direction of the gradient (as in gradient descent), and
- reliability values are projected to a feasible set of values, denoted by Δ, that agree to the constraints.

Each iteration may be expressed concisely using an update expression as follows:

$$r^{t+1} = \pi_{\Delta}\left(r^t - \alpha_t \times \nabla_r \widehat{L(\mathcal{C}, r)}\ |_{r=r^t}\right) \tag{10}$$

where α_t is the learning rate, $\nabla_x f(x)$ denotes the gradient of $f(x)$ w.r.to x, $\hat{u}$ indicates a unit vector along the direction of the vector u, and $\pi_\Delta(.)$ is the projection operation. We describe the gradient and projection operations below.

Gradients: For the numeric setting, the gradient of the loss function with respect to the reliability r_c can be shown to be:

$$\frac{\partial L(\mathcal{C}, r)}{\partial r_c} = (v_c - v_c^e)^2 - 2 \sum_{c' : c \in \mathcal{N}_{c'}^P} \frac{r_{c'} \; s_{cc'}^P}{\sum_{c'' \in \mathcal{N}_{c'}^P} r_{c''} \; s_{c'c''}^P} (v_{c'} - v_{c'}^e)(v_c - v_{c'}^e) \quad (11)$$

We omit the steps for arriving at the expression above since it entails from the loss function. Analogously, the gradient for the categorical setting is:

$$\frac{\partial L(\mathcal{C}, r)}{\partial r_c} = \sum_{i \in V} p(v_c^e = i)^2 + 1 - 2 \times p(v_c^e = v_c) +$$
$$2 \sum_{c' | c \in \mathcal{N}_{c'}^P} \frac{r_{c'} \; s_{cc'}^P}{\sum_{c'' \in \mathcal{N}_{c'}^P} r_{c''} \; s_{c'c''}^P} \left(p(v_{c'}^e = v_c) + p(v_{c'}^e = v_{c'}) - \sum_{i \in V} p(v_{c'}^e = i)^2 - \mathbb{I}(v_c, v_{c'}) \right) \quad (12)$$

Despite these complex expressions, these gradient formulations lend to efficient computational implementations, as may be visible on closer inspection.

Projection: We now describe the projection operation $\pi_\Delta(u)$ (Ref: Eq. 10). $\pi_\Delta(u)$ is the projection of u with respect to a predefined distance function $d(\cdot, \cdot)$ onto the feasible set (i.e., set of values respecting the extant constraints) Δ, and is defined by,

$$\pi_\Delta(u) = \arg\min_{x \in \Delta} d(u, x) \quad (13)$$

In our case, revised estimates of the vector r need to be projected to the feasible set. Observe that the feasible set for r corresponds to a portion of the unit-side hypercube since the elements of the reliability vector are within $[0, 1]$ (Ref: Eq. 8). The second constraint, that in Eq. 9, discards a pyramidal portion from the hypercube where the apex of the pyramid is the origin, and its base is a simplex of side a (equivalently, a surface whose vertices are vectors of length a along all the axes). The projection could be described as three disjoint cases:

1. *r lies in the feasible region*: In this case, nothing needs to be done, and the projection operation just copies the vector from input to the output.
2. *r faces the simplex*: If $r^\top \mathbf{1} < a$ and $r^\top \preceq a\mathbf{1}$, then the closest surface on the portion of hyper-cube from r is the simplex. r is projected on the simplex by first plugging all the negative elements of r to 0, and then scaling the entries proportionally in order to ensure that they sum to a.
3. If the vector does not satisfy the above two conditions, then the surface closest to r is one of the vertices/edges/faces of the hyper-cube. Projection onto a face can be obtained using the following formulation.

$$\pi_\Delta(r)_c = \begin{cases} 0 & \text{if } r_c \leq 0 \\ r_c & \text{if } 0 \leq r_c \leq 1 \\ 1 & \text{if } r_c \geq 1 \end{cases}$$

4.3 RelCBR: Overall Approach

The overall pseudocode for *RelCBR* is outlined in the pseudocodes below, which correspond to numeric and categorical settings. The case base, a termination threshold ϵ, the hyperparameter a and the nearest neighbors of each case (as entailed from the similarity function) are inputs to the algorithm. The time-step t is set to 1 and two consecutive reliability vectors r^0 and r^1 (r^k denotes r at time-step k) are initialized as shown, with initial reliability values set to 0.5 for all the cases. The reliability vector is iteratively updated until the maximum element in the absolute difference vector of two consecutive reliability vectors (r^t and r^{t-1}) is no more than ϵ. Each iteration comprises two steps, one corresponding to the movement according to the gradient, followed by a projection operation (and a trivial step of time-step increment). The pseudocode references the equations which have been introduced earlier.

Algorithm 1. RelCBR when solutions are numerical in nature

```
Require: C, ϵ > 0, a > 0, {N_c^P}_{c∈C}
  r^0 ← 0   ∈ R^{|C|}
  r^1 ← 1/2 ∈ R^{|C|}
  t ← 1
  while max(| r^t − r^{t−1} |) > ϵ do
     v_c^e ← Eq. (3)
     ∇_r L(C, r) |_{r=r^t} ← Eq. (11)
     r^{t+1} ← Eq. (10)
     t ← t + 1
  end while
  return r^t
```

Algorithm 2. RelCBR when solutions are categorical in nature

```
Require: C, ϵ > 0, a > 0, {N_c^P}_{c∈C}
  r^0 ← 0   ∈ R^{|C|}
  r^1 ← 1/2 ∈ R^{|C|}
  t ← 1
  while max(| r^t − r^{t−1} |) > ϵ do
     p(v_c^e = i) ← Eq. (4)  ∀i
     ∇_r L(C, r) |_{r=r^t} ← Eq. (12)
     r^{t+1} ← Eq. (10)
     t ← t + 1
  end while
  return r^t
```

4.4 Discussion: RelCBR and Truth Discovery

Despite taking inspiration from circular definitions as used in truth discovery, RelCBR is quite different. We now discuss the relationship. In the *RelCBR* approach, every case is proposed a solution based on the solutions of its problem-side neighbors. Therefore, each case acts as a *problem*, and all the cases that contribute to the solution of at least one case serve as *sources* of information. This is significantly different from a traditional truth discovery setting wherein the set of questions does not overlap with the set of sources. Further, the proposed solution for a question case $c \in \mathcal{C}$ involves $\{s^P_{cc'}\}_{c' \in \mathcal{N}^P_c}$, that indicates the relevance of the neighboring case c' to c. Such a notion of relevance of a source with a problem is not considered in truth discovery. Finally, truth discovery techniques operate predominantly in situations where the questions are not labelled with a solution. This is starkly different from our setting that involves a potentially incorrect solution paired with every case.

5 Experimentation

In this section, we empirically verify the effectiveness of *RelCBR* over our baselines (Ref: Sect. 3.2), *caseCohesion* and *alignMassie.*

We first note that assessment of case reliability is particularly difficult since it is typically hard to source datasets where cases are explicitly labeled as either reliable or not. In fact, to our best knowledge, there is no public dataset in the CBR domain where cases are labeled for reliability by experts. Thus, we first provide a quantitative analysis on two synthetic datasets (one each for regression and classification) where we have access to the corrected case base for the purpose of evaluation. Second, we consider multiple real-world datasets (assumed to be fairly reliable), and randomly add noise to reduce the reliability of specific cases. This is followed by evaluating whether the contribution of such poor quality cases affects the overall performance of prediction.

For the purpose of experimentation, we need a pre-specific similarity function. Towards this, we consider the attribute level similarity between two attribute values as 1 - the normalized absolute distance between the two values (normalized with the maximum attribute level absolute difference in the case base). Unless otherwise specified, we use the number of neighbors and local attribute weights from the set

$$\{(k, \frac{w}{||w||_1}) \mid k \in \{1, 2, \ldots, 10\} \ , \ w_i \in \{0, 1, 2, \ldots, 10\} \ \forall \ i \ , \ ||w||_1 \neq 0\}$$

that leads to the best performing CBR reasoner in the leave-one-out style evaluation.

5.1 Synthetic Dataset for Numeric Solution Scenario

We construct a synthetic dataset in the housing domain where each house is represented by two features - the rating of the locality (*loc*), and the area of the house (*area*). The solution corresponding to each case contains the cost of the house. The synthetic dataset containing poor quality cases is summarized in Table 2 with the highlighted entries being truly unreliable. The poor quality of highlighted values is apparent when contrasted against neighboring house prices. For the purpose of evaluation, we use the corrected version of the dataset which is given in Table 3.

For estimation of the reliability vector using *RelCBR*, we use $\epsilon = 1 \times 10^{-4}$, $\alpha_t = 1 \times 10^{-3} \ \forall \ t$, and $a = 10$. Reliability vectors are also obtained using the *caseCohesion* and *alignMassie* scores for each case. The three reliability vectors are then used to propose solution (using Eq. 3) corresponding to every query

Table 2. The housing dataset

loc \ area	1200	1400	1600	1800	2000	2200	2400	2600
1	40	50	60	70	80	90	100	110
2	80	90	100	110	120	130	140	150
3	120	130	200	150	160	170	180	190
4	160	170	180	190	200	210	220	230
5	200	210	220	230	240	250	260	270
6	240	250	260	390	280	410	300	310
7	280	290	300	310	320	330	340	350
8	320	330	340	350	360	370	380	390

Table 3. Corrected housing dataset

loc \ area	1200	1400	1600	1800	2000	2200	2400	2600
1	40	50	60	70	80	90	100	110
2	80	90	100	110	120	130	140	150
3	120	130	140	150	160	170	180	190
4	160	170	180	190	200	210	220	230
5	200	210	220	230	240	250	260	270
6	240	250	260	270	280	290	300	310
7	280	290	300	310	320	330	340	350
8	320	330	340	350	360	370	380	390

case in a leave-one-out setup. The Mean of Squared Error (MSE) values over all the cases with respect to the corrected dataset are listed in Table 4. The values clearly indicate the effectiveness of *RelCBR* over other models. It was also found that the reduced error of RelCBR was statistically significant against all competitors at $p < 0.05$. In addition, Fig. 2 illustrates the values of reliability assigned to the corresponding cases in the case base by the various techniques in the form of a heatmap; a darker shade in a cell indicates that the corresponding case is unreliable. RelCBR is able to distinguish the poor quality cases from the others very sharply, indicating its effectiveness.

Table 4. Error with respect to the corrected dataset

Model	MSE
CBR	225.71
CBR with caseCohesion	245.78
CBR with alignMassie	196.07
RelCBR	67.32

5.2 Synthetic Dataset for Categorical Solution Scenarios

Table 5 and 6 show the synthetic categorical solution dataset in presence and absence of poor quality cases. Like before, the cases that are highlighted are unreliable. The leave-one-out error in prediction (using Eq. 5) based on the different reliability vectors (as obtained using *caseCohesion*, *alignMassie* and *RelCBR*) are summarized in Table 7. The reliability scores assigned to cases in the Case Base are also illustrated in Fig. 3. While all techniques perform poorly in the diagonal area where the crisp decision change does not augur well with similarity based decision making ethos in CBR, RelCBR is able to demarcate the noisy cases from the others much better.

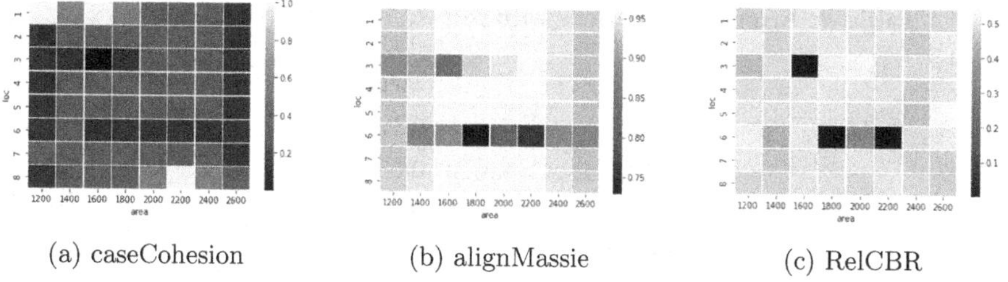

(a) caseCohesion (b) alignMassie (c) RelCBR

Fig. 2. Case reliability estimates as given by the three different models for the synthetic regression dataset.

Table 5. The categorical dataset

f_2 \ f_1	1	2	3	4	5	6	7	8	9	10	11
1	0	0	0	0	0	0	0	0	0	0	1
2	0	0	0	0	0	0	0	0	0	1	1
3	0	0	**1**	**1**	**1**	0	0	0	1	1	1
4	0	0	0	**1**	0	0	0	1	1	1	1
5	0	0	0	0	0	0	1	1	1	1	1
6	0	0	0	0	0	1	1	1	1	1	1
7	0	0	0	0	1	1	1	1	1	1	1
8	0	0	0	1	1	1	**0**	1	1	1	1
9	0	0	1	1	1	**0**	**0**	**0**	1	1	1
10	0	1	1	1	1	1	1	1	1	1	1
11	1	1	1	1	1	1	1	1	1	1	1

Table 6. Corrected categorical dataset

f_2 \ f_1	1	2	3	4	5	6	7	8	9	10	11
1	0	0	0	0	0	0	0	0	0	0	1
2	0	0	0	0	0	0	0	0	0	1	1
3	0	0	**0**	**0**	**0**	0	0	0	1	1	1
4	0	0	0	**0**	0	0	0	1	1	1	1
5	0	0	0	0	0	0	1	1	1	1	1
6	0	0	0	0	0	1	1	1	1	1	1
7	0	0	0	0	1	1	1	1	1	1	1
8	0	0	0	1	1	1	**1**	1	1	1	1
9	0	0	1	1	1	**1**	**1**	**1**	1	1	1
10	0	1	1	1	1	1	1	1	1	1	1
11	1	1	1	1	1	1	1	1	1	1	1

5.3 Real-World Dataset for Numerical Solution Scenarios

For demonstrating the robustness of *RelCBR* in real-world settings with unreliable cases, we use the Boston Housing Dataset that contains 506 cases, where the reasoner is required to predict the price of a house given its 13 numerical attributes. The attribute-level similarity are combined by taking a convex combination of local similarities where the relative weights of $\{INDUS, DIS\}$, $\{RM, PTRATIO, LSTAT\}$ and the remainder feature set is considered to be in the ratio $3:2:1$ [2]. In our experiments, the termination condition in *RelCBR* is set using $\epsilon = 1 \times 10^{-3}$. We use $\alpha_t = 1/(t+1)$ and $a = 10$ and consider the 3 nearest neighboring cases to address the query.

We randomly select 20 cases from the Case Base, and add to their solutions a Gaussian noise with 0 mean and varying standard deviation. The MSE values over all the cases with respect to the unaltered case base are obtained based on the predictions made by the three methods as earlier. This process is repeated 100 times, and the mean of MSE values is computed and presented in Fig. 4. The effectiveness of *RelCBR* over other methods is clearly evident and is found to give a statistically significant improvement over others at $p < 0.01$.

Table 7. Error in estimations with respect to the corrected dataset

Model	Mean error
CBR	0.124
CBR with caseCohesion	0.083
CBR with alignMassie	0.091
RelCBR	0.049

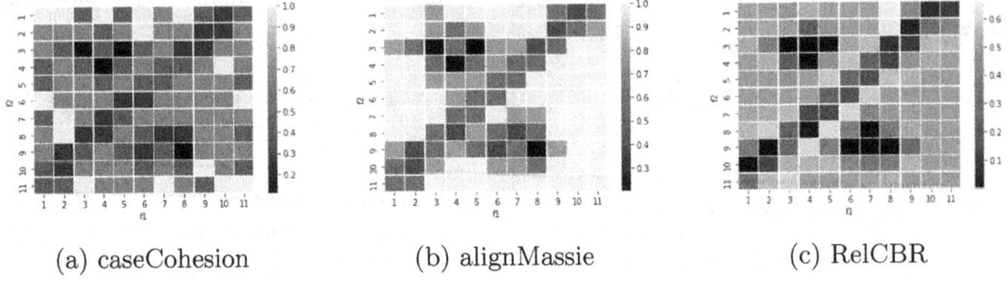

(a) caseCohesion (b) alignMassie (c) RelCBR

Fig. 3. Case reliability estimates as given by the three different models for the synthetic classification dataset.

5.4 Real-World Dataset for Categorical Solution Scenarios

The Iris dataset is a widely used classification dataset that contains the classes to which flowers belongs given their 4 attributes. The values of ϵ and α_t for *RelCBR* are unaltered from those used in Sect. 5.3. In order to construct an Iris dataset with unreliable cases, we randomly sample 20 cases from the case base and alter their classes to an incorrect class randomly. This is followed up by computing the fraction of mispredictions by the three methods in a leave-one-out style evaluation, as earlier. This process is repeated 100 times, and the error in prediction are averaged and reported in Table 8. The prediction error using *RelCBR* is found to be significantly lower than that of other methods at $p < 0.01$.

Table 8. Average fraction of misprediction over 100 noise added Iris datasets.

Model	Mean error
CBR	0.0451
CBR with caseCohesion	0.0344
CBR with alignMassie	0.0390
RelCBR	0.0297

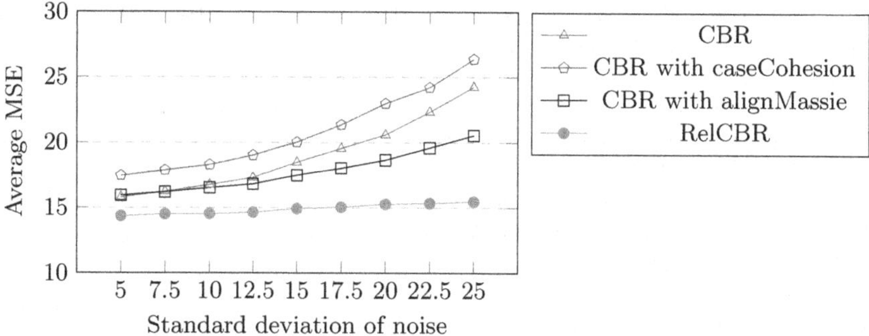

Fig. 4. Variation of average MSE over 100 noise added Boston Housing datasets with the standard deviation of the zero mean Gaussian noise.

6 Discussion

Empirical results presented in Sect. 5 illustrate the effectiveness of *RelCBR* in identifying unreliable cases in the case base. Notice that while *caseCohesion* and *alignMassie* fail to identify a reliable case ($loc = 6, area = 2000$) within an unreliable neighborhood in the situation sketched out in Sect. 5.1 due to its disagreement with the neighborhood, *RelCBR* proves to be much more effective in arriving at its true reliability estimate by discounting the contribution of its unreliable neighbors. Similarly, in Sect. 5.2, two unreliable cases (($f_1 = 4, f_2 = 3$) and ($f_1 = 7, f_2 = 9$)) embedded with a poor quality neighbors are claimed reliable by *caseCohesion* and *alignMassie* by virtue of their agreement to their respective unreliable neighborhood. *RelCBR* with compositional adaptation, in contrast, provides more robust estimates of the reliability of these cases by largely disregarding the contribution of their unreliable neighbors.

We would finally like to draw attention to the fact that these reliability scores can be used to guide the Case Base Maintenance process, in that the expert is first exposed to cases that are reckoned unreliable, thereby allowing the expert to avoid a one-by-one inspection over the entire case base.

7 Conclusion

In this work, empirical evidences were provided to illustrate the necessity and effectiveness of defining the reliability of cases in a circular fashion. The results suggest that *RelCBR* is better at both identification of unreliable cases, and providing more robust predictions for cases in comparison to *caseCohesion* and *alignMassie*. This allows *RelCBR* to act as a potentially effective assistance system in the Case Base Maintenance process.

References

1. Deepak, P., Chakraborti, S., Khemani, D.: More or better: on trade-offs in compacting textual problem solution repositories. In: CIKM, pp. 2321–2324 (2011)

2. Ganesan, D., Chakraborti, S.: An empirical study of knowledge tradeoffs in case-based reasoning. In: IJCAI, pp. 1817–1823 (2018)
3. Ganesan, D., Chakraborti, S.: A reachability-based complexity measure for case-based reasoners. In: The Thirty-Second International Flairs Conference (2019)
4. Kleinberg, J.M.: Authoritative sources in a hyperlinked environment. J. ACM (JACM) **46**(5), 604–632 (1999)
5. Lamontagne, L.: Textual CBR authoring using case cohesion. In: Proceedings of 3rd Textual Case-Based Reasoning Workshop at the 8th European Conference on CBR, pp. 33–43 (2006)
6. Leake, D., Whitehead, M.: Case provenance: the value of remembering case sources. In: Weber, R.O., Richter, M.M. (eds.) ICCBR 2007. LNCS (LNAI), vol. 4626, pp. 194–208. Springer, Heidelberg (2007). https://doi.org/10.1007/978-3-540-74141-1_14
7. Li, Q., Li, Y., Gao, J., Zhao, B., Fan, W., Han, J.: Resolving conflicts in heterogeneous data by truth discovery and source reliability estimation. In: Proceedings of the 2014 ACM SIGMOD International Conference on Management of Data, pp. 1187–1198 (2014)
8. Li, Y., et al.: A survey on truth discovery. ACM SIGKDD Explor. Newsl. **17**(2), 1–16 (2016)
9. Massie, S., Wiratunga, N., Craw, S., Donati, A., Vicari, E.: From anomaly reports to cases. In: Weber, R.O., Richter, M.M. (eds.) ICCBR 2007. LNCS (LNAI), vol. 4626, pp. 359–373. Springer, Heidelberg (2007). https://doi.org/10.1007/978-3-540-74141-1_25
10. Mathew, D., Chakraborti, S.: Competence guided model for casebase maintenance. In: IJCAI, pp. 4904–4908 (2017)
11. Page, L., Brin, S., Motwani, R., Winograd, T.: The pagerank citation ranking: bringing order to the web. Technical report, Stanford InfoLab (1999)
12. Racine, K., Yang, Q.: Maintaining unstructured case bases. In: Leake, D.B., Plaza, E. (eds.) ICCBR 1997. LNCS, vol. 1266, pp. 553–564. Springer, Heidelberg (1997). https://doi.org/10.1007/3-540-63233-6_524
13. Raghunandan, M.A., Wiratunga, N., Chakraborti, S., Massie, S., Khemani, D.: Evaluation measures for TCBR systems. In: Althoff, K.-D., Bergmann, R., Minor, M., Hanft, A. (eds.) ECCBR 2008. LNCS (LNAI), vol. 5239, pp. 444–458. Springer, Heidelberg (2008). https://doi.org/10.1007/978-3-540-85502-6_30
14. Smyt, B., McKenna, E.: Footprint-based retrieval. In: Althoff, K.-D., Bergmann, R., Branting, L.K. (eds.) ICCBR 1999. LNCS, vol. 1650, pp. 343–357. Springer, Heidelberg (1999). https://doi.org/10.1007/3-540-48508-2_25
15. Smyth, B.: Case-base maintenance. In: Pasqual del Pobil, A., Mira, J., Ali, M. (eds.) IEA/AIE 1998. LNCS, vol. 1416, pp. 507–516. Springer, Heidelberg (1998). https://doi.org/10.1007/3-540-64574-8_436
16. Yang, Y., Bai, Q., Liu, Q.: On the discovery of continuous truth: a semi-supervised approach with partial ground truths. In: Hacid, H., Cellary, W., Wang, H., Paik, H.-Y., Zhou, R. (eds.) WISE 2018. LNCS, vol. 11233, pp. 424–438. Springer, Cham (2018). https://doi.org/10.1007/978-3-030-02922-7_29
17. Yin, X., Tan, W.: Semi-supervised truth discovery. In: Proceedings of the 20th International Conference on World Wide Web, pp. 217–226 (2011)
18. Zhao, B., Rubinstein, B.I., Gemmell, J., Han, J.: A Bayesian approach to discovering truth from conflicting sources for data integration. arXiv preprint arXiv:1203.0058 (2012)

CBR and Neural Networks

Improving Automated Hyperparameter Optimization with Case-Based Reasoning

Maximilian Hoffmann[1,2(✉)] and Ralph Bergmann[1,2]

[1] Artificial Intelligence and Intelligent Information Systems, University of Trier, 54296 Trier, Germany
{hoffmannm,bergmann}@uni-trier.de

[2] German Research Center for Artificial Intelligence (DFKI), Branch University of Trier, Behringstraße 21, 54296 Trier, Germany
{maximilian.hoffmann,ralph.bergmann}@dfki.de
http://www.wi2.uni-trier.de

Abstract. The hyperparameter configuration of machine learning models has a great influence on their performance. These hyperparameters are often set either manually w. r. t. to the experience of an expert or by an *Automated Hyperparameter Optimization (HPO)* method. However, integrating experience knowledge into HPO methods is challenging. Therefore, we propose the approach HypOCBR (**Hyp**erparameter **O**ptimization with **C**ase-**B**ased **R**easoning) that uses *Case-Based Reasoning (CBR)* to improve the optimization of hyperparameters. HypOCBR is used as an addition to HPO methods and builds up a case base of sampled hyperparameter vectors with their loss values. The case base is then used to retrieve hyperparameter vectors given a query vector and to make decisions whether to proceed trialing with this query or abort and sample another vector. The experimental evaluation investigates the suitability of HypOCBR for two deep learning setups of varying complexity. It shows its potential to improve the optimization results, especially in complex scenarios with limited optimization time.

Keywords: Case-based reasoning · Automated hyperparameter optimization · Machine learning · Deep learning

1 Introduction

In recent years, machine learning and especially *Deep Learning (DL)* models have been used as a method of choice for solving various tasks, e. g., in decision support systems [18] and in helpdesk scenarios [2]. An important part of these models are the *hyperparameters* that are used to configure the model architecture or the learning process such as the number of layers or the learning rate. Hyperparameters are numerous in modern DL setups and there is an ongoing trend towards even more complex models, making it increasingly difficult to find suitable configurations for the large number of hyperparameters. Despite the existence of *Automated Hyperparameter Optimization (HPO)* methods [7,9,16],

M. T. Keane and N. Wiratunga (Eds.): ICCBR 2022, LNAI 13405, pp. 273–288, 2022.
https://doi.org/10.1007/978-3-031-14923-8_18

it is still common practice to tune these hyperparameters manually based on user experience. This task is, on the one hand, challenging since it requires in-depth knowledge of the underlying task and DL setup to set hyperparameter values appropriately. On the other hand, it is time-consuming as the process involves manually triggered iterations of selecting a hyperparameter configuration, training the parameterized model, and validating its performance. Whereas the latter aspect can be automated even by the simplest HPO methods, expert knowledge of the DL setup to be tuned can be hardly considered in current HPO methods (e. g., [8,12,15]). For instance, there might be knowledge in the form of a statement such as this: *The second convolutional layer has a great influence on the overall results.* To use this knowledge in current HPO approaches, it would be necessary to transform it into meta-parameters of the HPO method, such as the number of sampled hyperparameter vectors. However, this transformation is not trivial and requires in-depth knowledge of the HPO method, which the neural network modeler might be lacking.

To address these shortcomings, we propose an approach called HypOCBR (**Hyp**erparameter **O**ptimization with **C**ase-**B**ased **R**easoning) for combining HPO methods with a *Case-Based Reasoning (CBR)* [1] system that allows an explicit integration of expert knowledge into optimization procedures. The main assumption is that similar hyperparameter vectors lead to similar optimization results. Based on this assumption and modeled domain and similarity knowledge that expresses an expert's experience knowledge, HypOCBR uses a CBR system to filter sampled hyperparameter vectors from an HPO method and make decisions to proceed training with them or abort them. The proposed approach is designed to be used as an extension of existing HPO methods without required modifications to their core functionality. The remainder of the paper is structured as follows: Sect. 2 describes the fundamentals of HPO, including the hyperparameters of an example DL model and random search as a popular HPO method. Additionally, this section discusses related work about HPO in CBR research. Section 3 describes our approach by introducing the proposed system architecture and the used retrieval and decision-making process. The presented approach is evaluated in Sect. 4 where optimization procedures with and without CBR methods are compared on two DL setups of varying complexity. Finally, Sect. 5 concludes the paper and examines future research directions.

2 Automated Hyperparameter Optimization of Deep Learning Models

Our approach aims at optimizing *Deep Learning (DL)* models with the help of *Case-Based Reasoning (CBR)* methods that are built on top of existing *Automated Hyperparameter Optimization (HPO)* methods. In this section, we introduce the formal concepts and terminology of HPO (see Sect. 2.1). Additionally, different types of hyperparameters (see Sect. 2.2) are examined and random search, a popular HPO method (see Sect. 2.3), is presented. We further discuss related work in Sect. 2.4.

2.1 Formal Definition

Hyperparameter optimization involves two basic components in its simplest form, i. e., a training setup of a DL model including its hyperparameters and training data, and a search procedure for selecting a hyperparameter vector from the hyperparameter search space. Our introduction and notation of these components follows Feurer and Hutter [9]: A DL model $\mathcal{A}$ is parameterized by a set of hyperparameters N, where each hyperparameter $n \in N$ is defined by its domain Λ_n. The overall hyperparameter search space is given by $\Lambda = \Lambda_1 \times \Lambda_2 \times \Lambda_n$. We denote $\lambda \in \Lambda$ as a hyperparameter vector that represents a distinct sample from the hyperparameter search space. Instantiating the model $\mathcal{A}$ with this sample is denoted as $\mathcal{A}_\lambda$. The optimization procedure is defined as follows:

$$\lambda^* = \operatorname*{argmin}_{\lambda \in \Lambda} \mathcal{L}(\mathcal{A}_\lambda, \mathcal{D}) \tag{1}$$

Thereby, the optimal hyperparameter vector $\lambda^* \in \Lambda$ is determined by selecting a hyperparameter vector $\lambda \in \Lambda$ that minimizes the loss function $\mathcal{L}(\mathcal{A}_\lambda, \mathcal{D})$. The loss value is the result of training $\mathcal{A}_\lambda$ and validating its performance on the dataset $\mathcal{D}$. Therefore, $\mathcal{D}$ is usually split up into a training dataset for training $\mathcal{A}_\lambda$ and a validation dataset for computing the loss value. We refer to the training, validation, and loss computation with a single hyperparameter vector by the term *trial*. Please note that instead of loss values, which are always minimized, also other metrics, e. g., classification accuracy, can be used for optimization according to Eq. 1. The only necessary change is to compute argmax(·) instead of argmin(·) in some cases. When referring to loss values in this paper, we mean both types, i. e., metrics to minimize and to maximize.

2.2 Hyperparameter Search Spaces

The computational effort of an optimization as shown in Eq. 1 is mainly determined by the number of possible hyperparameter vectors $|\Lambda|$ and the time needed to perform trials with the parameterized models. But, even if the training time is small and it is a simple DL setup, Λ can become very large and the whole optimization process very slow. Consider the following example[1]: A DL setup for image classification is made up of two consecutive layers of convolution followed by pooling. The convoluted images are then flattened, i. e., reshaped to a one-dimensional vector, and fed into several fully-connected layers. The final output is a vector of ten elements that represents the probabilities for the individual classes of a classification task. The model is trained by processing batches of images and applying stochastic gradient descent according to the computed loss. A possible hyperparameter search space for this example setup is illustrated in Fig. 1. The hyperparameters are structured hierarchically, with model and training hyperparameters forming the main groups. Each hyperparameter

[1] The example is derived from an introduction on convolutional neural networks, accessible at https://www.tensorflow.org/tutorials/images/cnn.

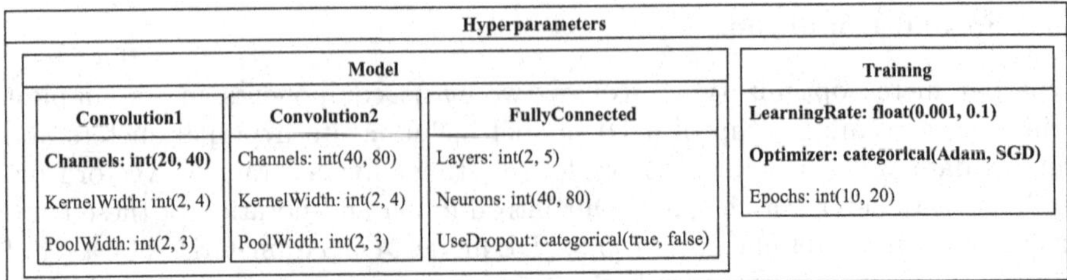

Fig. 1. Example hyperparameter search space

belongs to a certain type of search space (Λ_n) and is constrained to certain values. For instance, the number of channels in the first convolution is an integer value between 20 and 40 and the learning rate is a float value between 0.001 and 0.1. These types of search spaces influence the number of possible values of each hyperparameter. For instance, categorical and integer hyperparameters such as the optimizer or the number of channels represent a definitive set of possible values. Continuous search space types such as the learning rate, in turn, have an infinite number of theoretically possible values, assuming an infinitely small step size. This makes it infeasible to trial with every possible hyperparameter vector to compute argmin$(\cdot)$ and to find λ^* [6].

2.3 Random Search

Therefore, most search algorithms only examine a small subset of Λ that does not guarantee finding the optimal hyperparameter vector [9]. Random search (see Alg. 1 and cf. [6] for more information) is a simple example of these algorithms. The algorithm is an approximation of the function argmin$(\cdot)$ from Eq. 1 and works in the following way: Random hyperparameter vectors λ are selected from Λ by the function selectFrom$(\cdot)$ and trialed. If the loss of the selected sample is smaller than the loss of the current best hyperparameter vector λ^+, λ will be assigned to λ^+. This loop repeats until the search is finished (function isOptimized$(\cdot, \cdot)$) and the best selected sample λ^+ is returned. The used termination criterion is dependent on the underlying scenario and can be, for instance, the maximum search

Algorithm 1. Random Search

$\lambda \leftarrow$ selectFrom(Λ)
$\lambda^+ \leftarrow \lambda$
while not isOptimized$(\lambda^+, \mathcal{L})$ **do**
    $\lambda \leftarrow$ selectFrom(Λ)
    if $\mathcal{L}(\mathcal{A}_\lambda, \mathcal{D}) < \mathcal{L}(\mathcal{A}^+_\lambda, \mathcal{D})$ **then**
        $\lambda^+ \leftarrow \lambda$
    end if
end while
return λ^+

time, the maximum number of selected samples, or a threshold of the loss value. If random search has an unlimited budget, it will converge towards λ^+ being equal to the optimal hyperparameter vector λ^*.

2.4 Related Work

We discuss related work that covers popular HPO methods and CBR approaches in the field of HPO. Literature from the former category is discussed in detail in several survey publications (e. g., [9,16,26]), which is why we only want to highlight two popular example approaches: Multi-fidelity optimization aims at approximating the actual loss value of a setup by conducting low-fidelity and high-fidelity optimizations with a specific budget allocation, e. g., a maximum number of training iterations. Hyperband [15] uses an iterative process where the budget for each trial is determined based on the results of this run in the last iteration. Well-performing runs are allocated more resources and poorly-performing runs are terminated, until only the best-performing optimization is left. Model-based black box optimization methods aim to improve on other methods, e. g., Hyperband, that usually sample random hyperparameter vectors. Instead, promising hyperparameter vectors are chosen based on a surrogate model that is built during the optimization to copy the hyperparameter distribution of the black box method to optimize, e. g., a DL model. Bayesian optimization [24] methods use a surrogate model that is based on probabilistic methods, e. g., Gaussian processes. Our approach is compatible with both categories of HPO methods and, additionally, provides the opportunity of expert knowledge integration into the optimization process. Expert knowledge is directly integrated as CBR domain and similarity knowledge instead of being indirectly modeled in existing HPO methods.

The joint applications of CBR and HPO methods in literature are mostly concerned with hyperparameter tuning of CBR algorithms, e. g., feature weighting [25]. The opposite relation of CBR used for HPO is, to the best of our knowledge, not commonly discussed. We highlight some selected approaches: Pavón et al. [20] use CBR to enable automatic selection of Bayesian model configurations for individual problem instances. Their application builds up a case base of configurations, which is used to find the best-matching configuration for an upcoming problem instance. This idea is further pursued by Yeguas et al. [27] and applied to the task of tuning parameters of evolutionary optimization algorithms. Auslander et al. [3] explore a case-based approach of setting parameter values in the scenario of multi-agent planning. They retrieve parameter settings from a case base to parameterize upcoming planning problems. Molina et al. [19] use a set of past decision tree executions to predict suitable parameters for the application of the decision tree on new datasets. The parameter settings are retrieved based on the characteristics of the datasets. In contrast to the approach in this paper, most of the presented approaches can be classified as AutoML methods [13] that are used as a replacement for hyperparameter optimization. These methods automatically select a model configuration according to the training data or the learning task instead of tuning parameters from scratch. Our approach is novel in the sense that it aims to integrate CBR within the optimization procedure to make expert knowledge about the hyperparameter search space available and guide the optimization by eliminating unpromising hyperparameter vectors.

3 Automated Hyperparameter Optimization with Case-Based Reasoning

This section introduces our approach HypOCBR (**Hyp**erparameter **O**ptimization with **C**ase-**B**ased **R**easoning) that aims at improving *Automated Hyperparameter Optimization (HPO)* of *Deep Learning (DL)* hyperparameters with *Case-Based Reasoning (CBR)* methods. Our goal is to accelerate the optimization process by utilizing HypOCBR as a filter for the hyperparameter vectors that classifies whether a vector should be considered for trialing or not. Thereby, the strategy is to disregard hyperparameter vectors in situations where they are highly similar to known low-performing examples that are collected in a case base throughout the optimization procedure. Figure 2 shows an architectural overview of the three

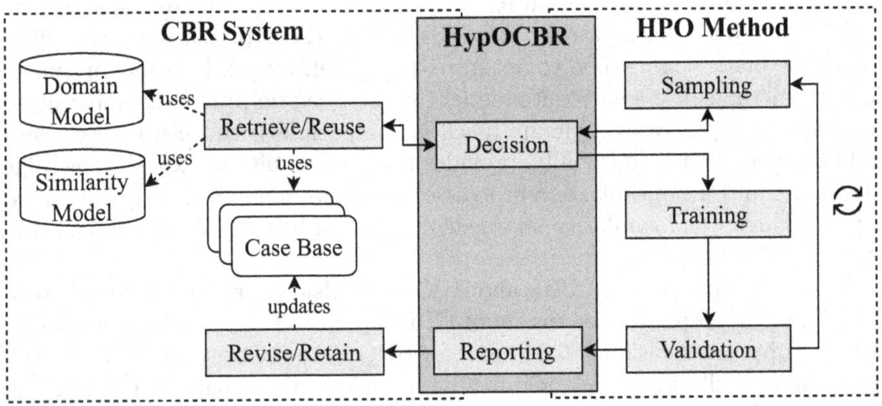

Fig. 2. Architecture of the CBR system, the HPO method, and HypOCBR

involved components, i. e., the CBR system, the HPO method, and HypOCBR. The HPO method carries out the optimization procedure by sampling hyperparameter vectors from the search space, performing training, and validating the model's performance (see Sect. 2.3). The architecture, in this regard, allows using arbitrary HPO methods, since their functionality does not have to be fitted to HypOCBR. The CBR system supports the optimization procedure by maintaining a case base with completed trials of hyperparameter vectors and their corresponding loss values as well as domain and similarity models to include domain expert knowledge. HypOCBR connects the CBR system and the HPO method by making use of a lightweight implementation of the 4R cycle [1]: After a new hyperparameter vector is sampled during the optimization, HypOCBR makes a decision to proceed with this vector or abort it early and sample another vector. Each sampled vector serves as a query to the CBR system based on which the case base is searched for similar hyperparameter vectors and their corresponding loss values, i. e., retrieving trials. HypOCBR then reuses the most similar trials and makes the decision based on their loss values. Please note that the retrieved hyperparameters are not adapted but their loss values are used to assess the potential of the queried hyperparameter vector. Each optimization gradually builds up a case base to use by starting with an empty case base and retaining each completed trial therein. Thereby, we do not consider an explicit revision of cases in the approach but rather store all reported validation results from the HPO component. Please note that this can lead to large case bases in long optimization runs, such that methods for speeding up retrieval (e. g., [17]) or decreasing the size of the case base (e. g., [22]) can be necessary but are not further discussed in this work. In the following, we will examine how a retrieval in the CBR system is performed by inspecting the case representation as well as the similarity definitions (see Sect. 3.1). The retrieval is part of the decision-making process of HypOCBR that is explained in Sect. 3.2.

3.1 Experience-Based Retrieval: Case Representation and Similarity Definition

The case representation models trials as pairs of their hyperparameter vector and the respective loss value. The case base, in this regard, stores information on the quality of hyperparameter vectors that were sampled during the optimization. The hyperparameter vectors are represented as object-oriented cases, as shown by the example in Fig. 1. The domain model describing these vectors is one point to integrate expert knowledge. The concrete form is highly dependent on the structure of the modeled hyperparameter vectors. For instance, simple knowledge about the data types, value ranges, and expected distributions of individual hyperparameters (see Sect. 2.2) can build the baseline. It can be extended by knowledge about the structure of individual hyperparameters (e. g., taxonomies of optimizer types) or the constraints among hyperparameters (e. g., the width of the kernel has to be less than the image width and height). Even more complex knowledge such as ontologies can be used to model the cases. The loss value that is also part of each case, usually is a single numeric value, e. g., accuracy, but can also be represented as a more complex object, e. g., a list of accuracy values from each epoch of training.

During retrieval, similarities are computed between the hyperparameter vectors of the cases and the hyperparameter vector that is given as the query by HypOCBR. We do not specify the similarity measures to use, but rather allow them to be customized regarding the use case and the available expert knowledge. Thereby a global object-oriented similarity between two hyperparameter vectors is usually put together from multiple local similarities between the individual hyperparameters, e. g., numeric measures for integer and float search spaces, binary measures for boolean search spaces, and tables or taxonomies for categorical values (cf. [4, pp. 93f.] for more information). This enables a precise customization of the global pairwise similarity based on the expert's experience:

For instance, the weights of all hyperparameters from the training category (see Fig. 1) can be increased to focus more on this part of the hyperparameter vectors for similarity assessment.

3.2 Making a Decision for New Trials

The decision task of HypOCBR applies an algorithm to make a decision between *proceeding* with a sampled hyperparameter vector or *aborting* the trial. The used approach is conceptualized in Alg. 2 and can be parameterized according to the well-known principles of *exploration* and *exploitation* (see, for instance, Leake and Schack [14] for more information). This means that it can be configured towards favoring hyperparameter vectors that are different from all previously encountered vectors (exploration) or similar to known good hyperparameter vectors (exploitation). The meta-parameters to influence the behavior of the algorithm are given in Table 1.

The algorithm's first step is to check if the case base has reached a certain size (lines 1 – 3) which is given as the meta-parameter θ_1. This check is necessary as a case base is built up throughout the optimization to improve the quality of upcoming decisions. The case base, however, suffers from the cold start problem [23] which can cause undesired behavior in CBR systems with little or no data at the launch of the application (e. g., [21]). If the case base has reached the desired size, it can be used for retrieving r (line 4) with the query λ_q, the case base CB, and the similarity measure for case pairs sim. The retrieval incorporates the meta-parameter θ_4 that defines the number of nearest neighbors to retrieve.

Algorithm 2. Decision-Making for New Trials

Input: case base CB, similarity function $\text{sim}(\cdot,\cdot)$, query λ_q
Output: PROCEED or ABORT
Meta-Parameters: θ_1, θ_2, θ_3, θ_4

1: **if** $|\,\text{CB}\,| < \theta_1$ **then**
2:     **return** PROCEED ▷ Minimum size of case base not reached
3: **end if**
4: $r \leftarrow \text{retrieve}(\text{CB}, \text{sim}, \lambda_q, \theta_4)$
5: $s \leftarrow \text{aggregateSimilarities}(r)$
6: **if** $s \geq \theta_2$ **then**
7:     $l \leftarrow \text{aggregateLosses}(r)$
8:     $p \leftarrow \text{percentile}(l, \text{CB}, \theta_3)$
9:     **if** $p = \textit{true}$ **then**
10:         **return** PROCEED ▷ Exploitation
11:     **else**
12:         **return** ABORT ▷ Similar to underperforming cases
13:     **end if**
14: **else**
15:     **return** PROCEED ▷ Exploration
16: **end if**

Larger values of θ_4 help to prevent overfitting and make the retrieved cases more robust to outliers. These cases are then used to compute an aggregate similarity value s that measures how similar λ_q is to the retrieved cases from the case base r (line 5). The aggregated similarity is computed to ensure that the retrieved cases are sufficiently similar to make a decision. The retrieval is also the main part of the algorithm where expert knowledge is used. It determines the computed similarities, which direct the algorithm to the hyperparameter vectors and their loss values that, in turn, best match the queried vector. As the retrieved cases are the basis of the decision, the knowledge directly influences the measured potential of the query vector. If s does not exceed θ_2 (line 6) then the exploration strategy is followed and `PROCEED` is returned (see line 15). Otherwise, the retrieved cases are further inspected in lines 7 – 13. The loss values of the retrieved cases are aggregated to l (line 7) to get an average loss of the cases that are similar to the query. Given l, the case base CB, and the meta-parameter θ_3 as parameters, the function percentile$(\cdot,\cdot,\cdot)$ in line 8 returns a boolean value that expresses if the average loss value l is in the percentile range given by θ_3. For instance, setting θ_3 to a value of 55 expresses that p is true if l is among the best 45 % of the loss values in the case base. This gives a hint towards the potential quality of λ_q which is based on the average quality of cases similar to λ_q (retrieved cases r) w. r. t. to all cases in the case base CB. Eventually, `PROCEED` is returned if p is true (exploitation strategy; line 9) and `ABORT` is returned if p is false. The algorithm only aborts in one particular scenario, which highlights the main goal of the filter process, i. e., to abort trials if they are expected to lead to bad results.

Table 1. Meta-parameters of HypOCBR

Meta-Parameter	**Description**	**Constraints**
θ_1	Minimum number of cases in the case base to avoid cold start	$\theta_1 > 0$
θ_2	Minimum similarity threshold of aggregated retrieved cases	$\theta_2 \in [0, 1]$
θ_3	Minimum percentile of aggregated metric of retrieved cases	$\theta_3 \in [0, 100]$
θ_4	Number of cases to retrieve	$\theta_4 <= \theta_1$

Furthermore, the meta-parameters (see Table 1) provide a straightforward way of configuring the behavior of the algorithm w. r. t. certain goals. For instance, it can be configured towards exploration by increasing θ_2 which requires a higher similarity of retrieved cases. A parameterization towards an `ABORT` decision is also possible by decreasing θ_2 and increasing θ_3. Additionally, pretests of an implementation of Alg. 2 with standard similarity measures of the process-oriented CBR framework ProCAKE [5] have shown that the performance is adequate, enabling working with case bases containing hundreds or thousands of trials within a few milliseconds.

4 Experimental Evaluation

The experimental evaluation compares the results and procedure of hyperparameter optimization with and without the usage of the proposed *Case-based Reasoning (CBR)* component HypOCBR. To include optimization tasks with different levels of complexity, we evaluate a rather simple baseline setup of an image classification task and a much more complex similarity learning task based on *Graph Neural Networks (GNNs)*. The goal is to analyze the influence of HypOCBR on the number of sampled hyperparameter vectors and the loss values of the trialed cases. The following hypotheses are examined:

H1 The computation overhead introduced by HypOCBR is negligible.
H2 The usage of HypOCBR in an optimization procedure leads to better results compared to an identical optimization without it.
H3 The benefit of integrating HypOCBR in an optimization procedure increases with the complexity, i. e., longer running trials with less overall optimization budget, of the setup to optimize.

Hypothesis H1 addresses the computation overhead introduced by the CBR system, which is expected to not influence the completed number of trials compared to HPO without HypOCBR. Hypothesis H2 examines the potential of the presented approach to conduct better trials w. r. t. their loss values. Hypothesis H3 aims at investigating the influence of the setup complexity on the benefit of HypOCBR.

4.1 Experimental Setup

The experiments feature two *Deep Learning (DL)* setups. The baseline setup (S-I) is a convolutional neural network classifying CIFAR10 images (derived from the example in Sect. 2.2). The model is fully trained for ten epochs within one optimization run with the goal of maximizing the percentage of correctly classified images (*accuracy*). The hyperparameter vectors of the model contain 11 parameters with only integer search spaces. The number of possible hyperparameter combinations, i. e., the number of unique hyperparameter vectors, is approx. $3 \cdot 10^7$. Additionally, we also want to look at a more complex problem by incorporating a second setup (S-II) that uses GNNs. S-II is based on our previous work on using graph embeddings for similarity learning [10,11]. Due to the required time for a full training run being approx. 12 – 18 h, the iterations in each epoch are limited and the model is only trained for ten epochs in trials. Each hyperparameter vector contains 26 hyperparameters, i. e., 18 integer hyperparameters, five float hyperparameters, and 3 categorical hyperparameters. This results in a total number of approx. $2 \cdot 10^{37}$ possible hyperparameter vectors. The target metric is the *Mean Absolute Error (MAE)* between the predicted similarities and the label similarities that should be minimized (see more details in [10,11]). Both setups are validated on a part of the dataset that is disjoint from the data that is used for training. We use simple domain models for both setups that include the data types and value ranges of all hyperparameters as well as an object-oriented structure of the vectors. The similarity model is also simple with linear numeric measures for integers and floats and binary measures for categorical hyperparameters. The similarity between two hyperparameter vectors is computed by a weight-adjusted average of the object-oriented structure of the hyperparameters.

The HPO method used in the experiments is random search (see Sect. 2.3) as it is a baseline method that is often used and performs reasonably well among other state-of-the-art optimization methods [9]. This way, we can focus on the effects of HypOCBR without the need for factoring in differently parameterized HPO methods which might be required, e. g., if using Bayesian methods. Each optimization procedure is conducted twice, with the only difference being that HypOCBR is just used in one procedure. All other factors are kept identical, which includes the dataset, the training procedure, and the HPO procedure. Randomized parts, e. g., the initial model weights and biases or the sampled hyperparameter vectors, are made deterministic by using random seed values. This means that it is possible to perform an optimization run with the same results if the same random seed is used. The used meta-parameters of HypOCBR are set according to results of pretests. For S - I, that is $\theta_1 = 20$, $\theta_2 = 0.81$, $\theta_3 = 50$, $\theta_4 = 15$ and for S - II that is $\theta_1 = 15$, $\theta_2 = 0.7$, $\theta_3 = 45$, $\theta_4 = 10$.

The termination criterion for each optimization with and without HypOCBR is the maximum elapsed time. A value of one hour is set for all optimizations of S - I and four hours for all optimizations of S - II. These values reflect the different complexities of both setups, where training and validation takes longer for S - II. After the optimization process is terminated, the trained and validated hyperparameter vectors are analyzed. We assume a scenario where an expert reviews the best hyperparameter vectors to make the final decision. Therefore, the validation results, i. e., the accuracy or MAE, of all trials and the ten best trials are compared among optimization procedures with and without HypOCBR. The implementation is realized as an extension of the open-source process-oriented CBR framework ProCAKE[2] [5]. All experiments are conducted on a computer with an Intel Xeon Gold 6138 CPU and an NVIDIA Tesla V100 SXM2, running Ubuntu 18.04 LTS.

4.2 Experimental Results

The results of the conducted experiments are depicted in Table 2 for S - I and in Table 3 for S - II. The information in both tables is structured analogously: The lines show ten optimization procedures, once conducted with and without HypOCBR under the same circumstances, i. e., with the same random seed. We give information on the number of trials that were evaluated (two leftmost columns), which is further split up into the trials with a *proceed* and an *abort* decision for the optimizations with HypOCBR. The loss values of the individual optimizations are percentage differences between optimizations with and without

[2] http://procake.uni-trier.de.

Table 2. Evaluation results for S - I

Trials		Loss (All)			Loss (Top)	
#	# (Proceed, Abort)	Best	Mean	Median	Mean	Median
161	620 (155, 465)	0.00%	0.50%	1.10%	0.70%	0.81%
152	609 (149, 460)	-0.44%	1.85%	1.60%	0.87%	0.99%
141	646 (143, 503)	0.00%	1.64%	1.50%	0.49%	0.66%
149	728 (141, 587)	1.37%	1.18%	1.29%	0.74%	0.55%
153	640 (149, 491)	2.33%	1.02%	0.72%	0.76%	0.57%
158	613 (158, 455)	-0.10%	0.90%	0.49%	0.29%	0.37%
161	456 (157, 299)	0.00%	1.49%	1.10%	1.00%	1.17%
164	413 (160, 253)	-0.43%	2.00%	1.94%	0.30%	0.41%
163	863 (159, 704)	-0.34%	1.96%	2.21%	0.52%	0.69%
159	690 (158, 532)	0.77%	1.13%	0.71%	0.37%	0.43%

HypOCBR. A negative value corresponds to a negative impact of HypOCBR and vice versa. The table shows best, mean, and median values aggregated from all trials (left) and the ten best trials (right) of the individual optimizations. All presented differences are statistically significant ($p < 0.01$).

The results for S - I (see Table 2) show that the HypOCBR approach aborts many trials and only proceeds with a small share. The number of trials that are not aborted is in a similar range as the number of trials when HypOCBR is not used. However, the optimizations that use HypOCBR are capable of pre-filtering a larger number of trials (increase between 251 % and 529 %) which provides a better coverage of the search space. The aggregated accuracies (higher values are better) show better results of the mean and median values for HypOCBR on average, while the approach without found a better vector in four optimizations. All in all, the differences between both variants are small, ranging from 0.29 %

Table 3. Evaluation results for S - II

Trials		Loss (All)			Loss (Top)	
#	# (Proceed, Abort)	Best	Mean	Median	Mean	Median
105	685 (110, 575)	-0.19%	17.15%	16.21%	22.95%	22.00%
108	923 (103, 820)	2.97%	16.17%	34.29%	17.13%	27.17%
113	671 (111, 560)	0.38%	16.97%	17.47%	14.13%	11.70%
113	865 (103, 762)	0.00%	16.52%	12.31%	20.13%	17.71%
107	155 (116, 39)	0.00%	7.01%	21.39%	18.11%	19.73%
112	169 (118, 51)	2.75%	4.33%	21.23%	8.62%	14.06%
115	750 (112, 638)	22.60%	16.07%	14.66%	26.00%	49.14%
113	876 (105, 771)	0.00%	11.80%	9.76%	14.57%	4.52%
114	716 (114, 602)	-0.03%	15.58%	19.27%	-0.70%	3.48%
113	171 (110, 61)	0.00%	6.53%	22.57%	0.07%	0.00%

to 2 % for the mean and median accuracies and from -0.44 % to 2.33 % for the best accuracy.

The results for S - II (see Table 3) show that the number of proceeded trials for optimizations with HypOCBR is approximately equal to the number of trials for optimizations without HypOCBR while pre-selecting numerous trials (increase from 144 % to 854 %). The aggregated MAE values (lower values are better) generally show improvements when using HypOCBR: The best MAE values show decreases between -0.19 % and 22.6 %. The mean and median MAE values mostly show large decreases of up to 49.14 %.

4.3 Discussion

The overall results of the optimization procedures that use HypOCBR are promising. Regarding Hypothesis H1, HypOCBR optimizations manage to train and validate approx. The same number of trials as the corresponding optimizations without HypOCBR. The small deviations of the results follow no trend and are most likely caused by computational variations of the underlying hardware. Thus, the introduced performance overhead is negligible and H1 is accepted. When analyzing the MAE and accuracy values, HypOCBR improves the optimization results in most cases with a few exceptions that stem largely from the best trials. The overall small improvements for S - I might be due to the full training run that is conducted during trialing. Thereby, the optimizer has the complete dataset to train the model and, thus, might be able to find suitable model weights even for inferior hyperparameters. The results for S - II show much clearer improvements than for S - I. With median MAEs being decreased by up to 49 %, HypOCBR significantly improves the optimization procedures. This especially reveals potential in scenarios with a limited time budget for optimization where only a small amount of trials is possible, e. g., in prototyping. There, the CBR component allows sampling more hyperparameter vectors that can be assessed for trialing. Although some of these trials might be misclassified by HypOCBR, it still improves the overall results of the optimization. The consistently improved mean and median results of all trials also hints at a success of eliminating bad trials. Therefore, we conclude that Hypothesis H2 is only partly accepted, since the integration of HypOCBR does not improve the optimization results in every case. The results are consistent with Hypothesis H3 due to the noticeably improved optimization for the more complex setup S - II compared to S - I. However, additional tests are needed to solidify the results.

5 Conclusion and Future Work

This paper introduced our approach called HypOCBR for enabling the use of *Case-Based Reasoning (CBR)* to improve *Automated Hyperparameter Optimization (HPO)*. HypOCBR acts as a filter for sampled hyperparameter vectors, deciding whether a vector should be considered for training and validation or not. The decision is based on a case base of hyperparameter vectors that were already trained and validated during optimization and on expert-modeled domain and similarity knowledge. These components are utilized in the following decision-making process: retrieve similar hyperparameter vectors given a query vector, aggregate their loss values, compare the aggregated loss value to the distribution of loss values, proceed training and validation with the query if it is similar to well-performing hyperparameter vectors. When evaluated for two *Deep Learning (DL)* setups of varying complexity, optimization procedures with HypOCBR show great potential: Due to the filtering function, more hyperparameter vectors can be analyzed, which leads to better optimization results for both setups.

A focus of future research should be on further optimizing, extending, and evaluating the approach. For instance, the approach might benefit from self-learning capabilities for the decision-making process that enable automatic tuning of the meta-parameters during optimization and easier application of the approach to new data. Further, the role of the case base can be extended to reuse existing case bases during startup and export the case base after the optimization procedure. It could also be beneficial to investigate more advanced methods for the reuse and revise phases of the described lightweight CBR cycle, which might, for instance, include methods for case adaptation or managing the growth of the case base (e. g., [22]). Additionally, HypOCBR could be evaluated on a larger scale by covering other HPO methods (e. g., [8,15]), other DL setups (see [10,11] for more examples), and the influence of differently modeled domain and similarity knowledge.

References

1. Aamodt, A., Plaza, E.: Case-based reasoning: Foundational issues, methodological variations, and system approaches. AI Commun. **7**(1), 39–59 (1994)
2. Amin, K., Lancaster, G., Kapetanakis, S., Althoff, K.-D., Dengel, A., Petridis, M.: Advanced similarity measures using word embeddings and siamese networks in CBR. In: Bi, Y., Bhatia, R., Kapoor, S. (eds.) IntelliSys 2019. AISC, vol. 1038, pp. 449–462. Springer, Cham (2020). https://doi.org/10.1007/978-3-030-29513-4_32
3. Auslander, B., Apker, T., Aha, D.W.: Case-based parameter selection for plans: coordinating autonomous vehicle teams. In: Lamontagne, L., Plaza, E. (eds.) ICCBR 2014. LNCS (LNAI), vol. 8765, pp. 32–47. Springer, Cham (2014). https://doi.org/10.1007/978-3-319-11209-1_4
4. Bergmann, R.: Experience Management: Foundations, Development Methodology, and Internet-Based Applications. LNCS, vol. 2432. Springer, Heidelberg (2002)
5. Bergmann, R., Grumbach, L., Malburg, L., Zeyen, C.: ProCAKE: a Process-oriented case-based reasoning framework. In: Workshop Proceedings of ICCBR, vol. 2567, pp. 156–161. CEUR-WS.org (2019)
6. Bergstra, J., Bengio, Y.: Random search for hyper-parameter optimization. J. Mach. Learn. Res. **13**(2), 281–305 (2012)
7. Claesen, M., de Moor, B.: Hyperparameter search in machine learning. CoRR abs/1502.02127 (2015)
8. Falkner, S., Klein, A., Hutter, F.: Bohb: robust and efficient hyperparameter optimization at scale. In: ICML, pp. 1437–1446 (2018)

9. Feurer, M., Hutter, F.: Hyperparameter optimization. In: Hutter, F., Kotthoff, L., Vanschoren, J. (eds.) Automated Machine Learning. TSSCML, pp. 3–33. Springer, Cham (2019). https://doi.org/10.1007/978-3-030-05318-5_1
10. Hoffmann, M., Bergmann, R.: Using graph embedding techniques in process-oriented case-based reasoning. Algorithms **15**(2), 27 (2022)
11. Hoffmann, M., Malburg, L., Klein, P., Bergmann, R.: Using siamese graph neural networks for similarity-based retrieval in process-oriented case-based reasoning. In: Watson, I., Weber, R. (eds.) ICCBR 2020. LNCS (LNAI), vol. 12311, pp. 229–244. Springer, Cham (2020). https://doi.org/10.1007/978-3-030-58342-2_15
12. Kennedy, J., Eberhart, R.: Particle swarm optimization. In: Proceedings of International Conference on Neural Networks (ICNN'95), Perth, WA, Australia, 27 November - 1 December, 1995, pp. 1942–1948. IEEE (1995)
13. Leake, D., Crandall, D.: On bringing case-based reasoning methodology to deep learning. In: Watson, I., Weber, R. (eds.) ICCBR 2020. LNCS (LNAI), vol. 12311, pp. 343–348. Springer, Cham (2020). https://doi.org/10.1007/978-3-030-58342-2_22
14. Leake, D., Schack, B.: Exploration vs. exploitation in case-base maintenance: leveraging competence-based deletion with ghost cases. In: Cox, M.T., Funk, P., Begum, S. (eds.) ICCBR 2018. LNCS (LNAI), vol. 11156, pp. 202–218. Springer, Cham (2018). https://doi.org/10.1007/978-3-030-01081-2_14
15. Li, L., Jamieson, K., DeSalvo, G., Rostamizadeh, A., Talwalkar, A.: Hyperband: a novel bandit-based approach to hyperparameter optimization. J. Mach. Learn. Res. **18**(1), 6765–6816 (2018)
16. Luo, G.: A review of automatic selection methods for machine learning algorithms and hyper-parameter values. Netw. Model. Anal. Health Inform. Bioinf. **5**(1), 1–16 (2016). https://doi.org/10.1007/s13721-016-0125-6
17. Malburg, L., Hoffmann, M., Trumm, S., Bergmann, R.: Improving similarity-based retrieval efficiency by using graphic processing units in case-based reasoning. In: Proceedings of the 34th FLAIRS Conference FloridaOJ (2021)
18. Mathisen, B.M., Bach, K., Aamodt, A.: Using extended siamese networks to provide decision support in aquaculture operations. Appl. Intell. **51**(11), 8107–8118 (2021). https://doi.org/10.1007/s10489-021-02251-3
19. Molina, M.M., Luna, J.M., Romero, C., Ventura, S.: Meta-learning approach for automatic parameter tuning: a case study with educational datasets. In: Proceedings of the 5th International Conference on Educational Data Mining, pp. 180–183. Chania, Greece (2012)
20. Pavón, R., Díaz, F., Laza, R., Luzón, V.: Automatic parameter tuning with. a bayesian case-based reasoning system a case of study. Expert Syst. Appl. **36**(2), 3407–3420 (2009)
21. Quijano-Sánchez, L., Bridge, D., Díaz-Agudo, B., Recio-García, J.A.: A case-based solution to the cold-start problem in group recommenders. In: Agudo, B.D., Watson, I. (eds.) ICCBR 2012. LNCS (LNAI), vol. 7466, pp. 342–356. Springer, Heidelberg (2012). https://doi.org/10.1007/978-3-642-32986-9_26
22. Roth-Berghofer, T.R.: Knowledge Maintenance of Case-Based Reasoning Systems: The SIAM Methodology, Dissertationen zur künstlichen Intelligenz. Akad. Verl.-Ges. Aka, Berlin (2003)
23. Schafer, J.B., Frankowski, D., Herlocker, J., Sen, S.: Collaborative filtering recommender systems. In: Brusilovsky, P., Kobsa, A., Nejdl, W. (eds.) The Adaptive Web. LNCS, vol. 4321, pp. 291–324. Springer, Heidelberg (2007). https://doi.org/10.1007/978-3-540-72079-9_9

24. Snoek, J., Larochelle, H., Adams, R.P.: Practical bayesian optimization of machine learning algorithms. In: Advances in Neural Information Processing Systems, vol. 25. Curran Associates, Inc. (2012)
25. Wettschereck, D., Aha, D.W.: Weighting features. In: Veloso, M., Aamodt, A. (eds.) ICCBR 1995. LNCS, vol. 1010, pp. 347–358. Springer, Heidelberg (1995). https://doi.org/10.1007/3-540-60598-3_31
26. Yang, L., Shami, A.: On hyperparameter optimization of machine learning algorithms: theory and practice. Neurocomputing **415**, 295–316 (2020)
27. Yeguas, E., Luzón, M.V., Pavón, R., Laza, R., Arroyo, G., Díaz, F.: Automatic parameter tuning for evolutionary algorithms using a bayesian case-based reasoning system. Appl. Soft Comput. **18**, 185–195 (2014)

A Factorial Study of Neural Network Learning from Differences for Regression

Mathieu d'Aquin[(✉)], Emmanuel Nauer, and Jean Lieber

LORIA, Université de Lorraine, CNRS, INRIA, Vandœuvre-lés-Nancy, France
{mathieu.daquin,emmanuel.nauer,jean.lieber}@loria.fr

Abstract. For regression tasks, using neural networks in a supervised way typically requires to repeatedly (over several iterations called epochs) present a set of items described by a number of features and the expected value to the network, so that it can learn to predict those values from those features. Inspired by case-based reasoning, several previous studies have made the hypothesis that there could be some advantages in training such neural networks on differences between sets of features, to predict differences between values. To test such a hypothesis, we applied a systematic factorial study on seven datasets and variants of datasets. The goal is to understand the impact on the performance of a neural network trained on differences, as compared to one trained in the usual way, of parameters such as the size of the training set, the number of epochs of training or the number of similar cases retrieved. We find that learning from differences achieves similar or better results than the ones of a neural network trained in the usual way. Our most significant finding however is that, in all cases, difference-based networks start obtaining good results from a low number of epochs, compared to the one required by a neural network trained in the usual manner. In other words, they achieve similar results while requiring less training.

Keywords: Case-based reasoning · Neural network · Case difference heuristic · Learning from differences · Factorial study

1 Introduction

As described in more details in the related work section of this paper (Sect. 2), the idea of learning from differences in regression is not new. Inspired by case-based reasoning (CBR), and viewed for example in [4] as a way to acquire adaptation knowledge, the idea is to estimate an unknown value (the solution) associated to a target set of features (the problem) by predicting its difference with the value associated with a known, similar source case from the training set (the case base). From a machine learning point of view, this corresponds to training a model (here we focus on neural network models) with differences of features, to predict differences in target values.

As an example, based on a real dataset used in the experiments later in this paper, while a neural network trained in the usual way would try to predict the

M. T. Keane and N. Wiratunga (Eds.): ICCBR 2022, LNAI 13405, pp. 289–303, 2022.
https://doi.org/10.1007/978-3-031-14923-8_19

sale price of a used car directly based on information such as its age, mileage, or engine size, the approach of learning from differences consists in building a similar neural network, but that is able to predict the differences in prices between similar cars, given the differences in their age, mileage or engine size. Such a network can therefore be used in a process based on the CBR methodology, predicting the price difference between the car under consideration and a similar car retrieved from the case base/training set.

While doing so does not formally increase the amount of information provided to the neural network for learning, it can be expected to have a number of advantages. At a meta-level, the results might be more interpretable, since the prediction of the price of a used car, in our example, might be easier to explain in reference to a similar car for which the price is known. What we consider here however is of a different nature: We want to test the hypothesis that CBR-inspired learning from differences might have advantages with respect to the training performance of neural network models, and under what circumstances (size of the data, training time, number of similar cases used) those advantages might materialise.

To achieve this, we set up a factorial study on seven datasets and variants of datasets. By factorial study we mean that we systematically train and measure the performance of neural networks in the usual way (using the original features of the data) and using case differences, while varying a number of factors: number of epochs, size of the testing and training sets, etc. This allows us to check in which way those factors influence the performance of the networks trained in those two ways. The contributions of this paper therefore include:

- A publicly available python library facilitating the process of training neural networks (and possibly other machine learning models) from case differences under various parameters,
- a large set of performance results (also publicly available) from the thousands of models trained under different sets of parameters,
- the main findings that a key effect of learning from differences requires significantly less epochs (from half to two orders of magnitude less) to reach the same/similar performance results as a neural network trained in the usual way, and
- a report on which parameter values in the configuration of the training and prediction processes achieve the best performance on the selected seven datasets and variants.

We start by describing related works on learning from differences in the next section. We then describe the process we applied and the parameters that have been used as varying factors in our factorial study in Sect. 3. We also describe the methodology for the factorial study in Sect. 4 and the results of applying this methodology in Sect. 5. Finally, we conclude on the main findings of this study in Sect. 6.

2 Related Work

Many works have addressed the use of neural network in a CBR process, especially for acquiring adaptation knowledge. These works are based on the exploitation of the case base, following the idea that adaptation knowledge can be acquired from differences between pairs of cases using the case difference heuristic (CDH) [2]. The CDH has been applied first outside of the context of neural networks to produce adaptation rules with various approaches [2,3,6].

More recently, neural networks have been used with CDH to learn the differences between solutions from the differences between problems [4,5,8]. In these works, particular points have been studied. [5], which is a preliminary work, shows the feasibility of using a neural network to correct the solution of the most similar retrieved case. The impact of the size of the training set is also studied, showing, unsurprisingly, that using more cases (80% of the case base) works better than using less cases (20%).

[4] compares 5 systems: nearest neighbour (1-NN) retrieval with copy adaptation, average of the solutions of a 3-NN process (i.e. k Nearest Neighbours, kNN, with $k = 3$), a classical neural network which takes problem features as input to predict the solution, a CBR system inspired from [1] using adaptation rules generated with CDH in addition to the problem features as context to adapt the most similar case, a CBR system which adapts the most similar case using a neural network which has learned how to adapt with CDH (i.e. from differences). This study concludes that the last system outperforms the two first ones (without adaptation) and outperforms the system which adapts by rules, being only outperformed by the neural network which solves the regression problem directly. This is the closest work to our own, since it provides some elements of comparison between neural networks learning from differences (last system), and learning in the usual way (third system). However, this study addresses a very particular issue: solving *novel* problems, by removing a certain number of cases that are the most similar to the target problem (sometimes up to a third of the case base), and does not therefore report on factors such as the ones studied in the present paper.

To the best of our knowledge, no work has really examined in details the impact of parameters usually involved in CBR experiments (case base size for training, number of cases retrieved for prediction, etc.) in the framework of using neural network with CDH for case adaptation. Additionally, as the neural network is central to the process, some parameters of its learning process (e.g. number of epochs) could also play an important role and deserve to be considered.

3 Learning from Differences for Regression

We consider here a dataset as a set D of pairs (X_i, y_i) where X_i is a vector of n numerical values corresponding to the features of a given example in the dataset, and y_i is a value corresponding to the result we expect to be able to predict.

In the example of the cars, a given set of features X_i includes for example the brand, model[1], engine size and mileage, and the corresponding value y_i is the price at which that car was sold.

Considering this, the typical process to train and validate a neural network is the following:

1. Split the dataset D into two subsets $D^{train} = \{(X_i^{train}, y_i^{train})\}_i$ and $D^{test} = \{(X_j^{test}, y_j^{test})\}_j$ through random sampling.
2. Fit the neural network to D^{train} over a number of iterations *epochs*.
3. Use the trained neural network to predict the value corresponding to each X_j^{test}; the predicted value is denoted by y_j^{pred}.
4. Compare y_j^{pred} to y_j^{test} to assess the accuracy of the predictions (in our experiments, we use the R^2 measure).

We do not detail those steps since they are relatively standard and are implemented using commonly used libraries (in our experiments, keras[2] and scikitlearn[3]).

Learning from differences includes similar steps, with additional elements to prepossess the data in order to transform it into sets of case differences, and to compute predictions of actual values from predicted case differences. In more details, the process involves the following:

1. Split the dataset D into two subsets $D^{train} = \{(X_i^{train}, y_i^{train})\}_i$ and $D^{test} = \{(X_j^{test}, y_j^{test})\}_j$ through random sampling.
2. For each case $C_i = (X_i^{train}, y_i^{train}) \in D^{train}$, retrieve *ntr* similar cases from D^{train} (the similarity being only computed over the set of problem features) and compute their difference with C_i to create ΔD^{train}: for $C_j = (X_j^{train}, y_j^{train})$ one of the *ntr* similar cases to C_i, add to ΔD^{train} the case difference $(X_i^{train} - X_j^{train}, y_i^{train} - y_j^{train})$.
3. Fit the neural network to ΔD^{train} over a number of iterations *epochs*.
4. For each X_j^{test}, retrieve *nte* similar cases $(X_i^{train}, y_i^{train}) \in D^{train}$, and compute the differences $\Delta X_{ij}^{test} = X_j^{test} - X_i^{train}$. Let $\Delta X_j^{test} = \{\Delta X_{ij}^{test}\}_i$ be the set of these differences.
5. Use the trained neural network to predict the differences in values corresponding to each of the difference feature sets $\Delta X_{ij}^{test} \in \Delta X_j^{test}$, calling the result ΔX_{ij}^{pred}. Compute y_j^{pred} as the average over i of $y_i^{train} + \Delta X_{ij}^{pred}$, with y_i^{train} being the value from the original training set associated with the corresponding similar case to X_i^{test}.
6. Compare y_j^{pred} to y_j^{test} to assess the accuracy of the predictions.

Several of those steps (splitting of the dataset, training, prediction) can be implemented in the same way as for the previous process. To facilitate the implementation of steps 2, 4 and 5, we created a python library called *deltaML*[4].

[1] those features being one-hot encoded.
[2] https://github.com/keras-team/keras.
[3] https://github.com/scikit-learn/scikit-learn.
[4] https://github.com/mdaquin/deltaML.

This library uses the *NearestNeighbour* function from the *scikitlearn* library as a reliable implementation for steps 2 and 4. It is worth mentioning that this process aligns with the one of CBR in the sense that Step 4 corresponds to the retrieval step of CBR, and Step 5 to the adaptation step.

Our experiments correspond to varying a number of factors, as parameters, in both those processes to see how the training performance of the resulting networks is affected. In all experiments, we use the same topology (same number of hidden layers and same number of neurons in each hidden layer) for the neural network whether it is trained in the usual way (Process 1) or from differences (Process 2). The two parameters shared between the two processes are the size of the training/test sets in percentage of the overall dataset (*test_size*) and the number of epochs used for training (*epochs*).

In addition, for the difference-based process, two additional parameters are included: The number of similar cases used during training (*ntr* in Step 2), and the number of similar cases used in prediction (*nte* in Step 4).

Finally, a variant (originally described in [4]) of the difference-based process is also tested in which, in addition to the differences between feature sets, the original feature sets of the considered case are also included as context. In other words, in Step 2, the created entry in ΔD^{train} corresponds to $((X_i^{train}, X_i^{train} - X_j^{train}), y_i^{train} - y_j^{train})$ and a similar change is made in Step 4 to include the *context* of the difference (i.e. the original set of features).

4 Factorial Study Methodology

The proposed factorial study consists, for each given dataset, in training and testing a neural network with a range of values for each of the parameters/factors described above. To do so, a preliminary phase was carried out where for each of the datasets, we first experimentally identify a network structure (reused for all tests on that dataset) and a set of parameters that obtained good results on a network trained in the usual way. In other words, through trial and error in the application of Process 1 of Sect. 3, we first identify the kind of neural network to use (number of layers, size of layers, etc.) so to achieve good results when training in the usual way. Once those base parameters are established, we iteratively vary the values of the considered parameters, training and/or testing a neural network model at each iteration.

We apply this factorial analysis on three different processes to compare their performance under different conditions:

Base: In this version, we train a neural network in the usual way, using the first process described in the previous section.

Differences: In this version, we train a neural network to predict differences in values from differences in features, using the second process described in the previous section.

Differences+context: In this version, we train a neural network to predict differences in values from differences in features and the features of the original case, using the variant of the second process used above, as described at the end of the previous section.

All the code and configurations to reproduce those tests and the results obtained are available in the repository hosting the *deltaML* library. In the following, we described the datasets used in the experiments, and the range of values used for each parameter and dataset.

4.1 Datasets

Below is a short description of each dataset used in our experiments, including their variants. All those datasets come from shared public libraries, and have been used as downloaded from the links provided. For all datasets, categorical values were one-hot-encoded and the dataset was standardized. Unless explicitly stated, no other modification was made. For each dataset, we also specify the structure of the neural network used in all experiments of that dataset and its variants. For all neural networks, we only used the *ReLu* activation function, and the *mean squared error* as the loss function.

Used Cars: This dataset[5] contains information about used cars (model, year, fuel type, transmission type, fuel consumption, mileage, tax band) and the price at which they were sold. The goal is to be able to predict the sale price of a car given those features. The neural network model used for this dataset is a sequential, feedfoward network including two hidden layers of sizes 50 and 30 respectively. We tested two variants of this dataset, one for cars of the brand Toyota and one for cars of the brand Vauxhall, since those gave significantly different results.

Airfoil: This dataset[6] provides information about the parameters of tests in wind tunnels of airfoil blade sections (frequency, angle of attack, chord length, free-stream velocity, suction side displacement thickness) and the noise emitted (scaled sound pressure level) as a result. The goal is to predict the level of noise from those characteristics. The neural network used for this dataset is a sequential, feedfoward network including two hidden layers of sizes 20 and 10 respectively.

Students: This dataset[7] provides information about students in a school in Portugal (demographics, family situation, transport, etc.) and the results of their tests (intermediary and final) in Math and Portuguese. The goal is to predict the results of students at the final tests based on the other characteristics. The neural network used for this dataset is a sequential, feedfoward network including two hidden layers both of size 10. We consider the prediction of final test results in Math and in Portuguese as two separate variants of this dataset.

[5] https://www.kaggle.com/code/najibmozahem/used-cars-neural-network/data.

[6] https://www.kaggle.com/datasets/fedesoriano/airfoil-selfnoise-dataset.

[7] https://www.kaggle.com/datasets/impapan/student-performance-data-set.

Flights: This dataset[8] provides information obtained at a given date (11th February 2022) about flights (date and time, duration, origin and destination, airline, number of stops) and the price of a single ticket at that date. The goal is to predict the price of the ticket based on the other characteristics. The neural network used for this dataset is a sequential, feedfoward network including two hidden layers of sizes 50 and 10 respectively. Two variants of this dataset are included: one with the price of tickets in economy class, and one with the price of tickets in business class. To keep the training time reasonable, we reduced the dataset, for both variants, to a randomly selected subset of 15,000 flights (from 206,774 flights in economy and 93,487 flights in business).

4.2 Factors and Parameters

As mentioned above, the objective of this study is to compare the performance of the neural networks trained in the usual way and from differences under varying conditions, and to see how those factors impact on the performance of those networks. Those factors are represented by the following parameters:

test_size: The test size corresponds to the relative amount of data from the original dataset D which is kept for testing, as opposed to training. In other words, higher values for the test size imply smaller amounts of data used in training. It is expected that performance should therefore decrease as *test_size* increases. This parameter is used for both networks trained in the usual way and from differences (with and without context).

epochs: The number of epochs corresponds to the number of times the training process will iterate over the training set to fit the network. The need for a high number of epochs, when neural networks are trained in the usual way, highly depends on the task, the structure of the network and the dataset. We therefore fixed the range of values to be tested based on the best results obtained through trial and error (as described at the beginning of Sect. 4). This parameter is used for both networks trained in the usual way and from differences (with and without context).

ntr: The number of similar cases used in training corresponds to the number of retrieved nearest neighbours used during the training phase for each case included in the training set (see Step 2, Sect. 3). It is worth mentioning that *ntr* can be seen as a multiplier for the size of the training set: for each case in the original set, *ntr* case differences will be included in the difference-based training set. This parameter is only used for networks trained from differences (with and without context).

nte: The number of similar cases used in testing corresponds to the number of retrieved nearest neighbours used for prediction (see Step 4, Sect. 3). For each of them, the difference in values will be predicted and an average difference calculated over the *nte* retrieved cases. This average difference is then used to compute the final prediction. This parameter is only used for networks trained from differences (with and without context).

[8] https://www.kaggle.com/datasets/shubhambathwal/flight-price-prediction.

Table 1 summarises the range of values used for each of the parameters above when testing using each of the datasets described before. For a given dataset, we used the same ranges of parameter values for all three kinds of trained networks (see Sect. 4) so to be able to compare their performance under the same conditions. We also used the same ranges of parameter values for any variant of a given dataset.

Table 1. Ranges of values for each parameter/factor and each dataset in the format (min, max, increment).

	test_size	epochs	ntr	nte
Used cars	(0.05, 0.95, 0.05)	(1, 20, 1)	(1, 5, 1)	(1, 5, 1)
Airfoil	(0.05, 0.95, 0.05)	(2, 402, 10)	(1, 5, 1)	(1, 10, 1)
Students	(0.05, 0.95, 0.05)	(1, 121, 5)	(1, 5, 1)	(1, 10, 1)
Flights	(0.05, 0.95, 0.05)	(1, 51, 5)	(1, 5, 1)	(1, 10, 1)

5 Results

In the following, we summarise the results obtained based on the factors considered in our experiments. In all cases, we use the R^2 score to measure the performance of each of the trained neural networks (Steps 4 and 6 respectively in the two processes described in Sect. 3). The summary of the results is that the same networks trained from differences on the same datasets are in some circumstances able to outperform the ones trained in the usual way, but the best achievable performance are generally not significantly different. What is different however is that the networks trained from differences appear to require less training than the ones trained in the usual way: They reached close to their best results from significantly less epochs of training. We also show that the numbers of similar cases used during training and prediction affect the results, but that different datasets appear to have different requirements with respect to those numbers. Finally, we show that adding the context (the features of the source item) in addition to the differences in training and prediction does not always have a significant effect on performance, but does in a positive way in some cases.

5.1 Performance in Relation to Test Size

Figure 1 shows an example of the evolution of the performance (according to the R^2 score) of the neural networks trained in the three different ways according to the size of the test set (i.e. the portion of the dataset that is reserved for testing, as opposed to training) for the economy variant of the Flights dataset.

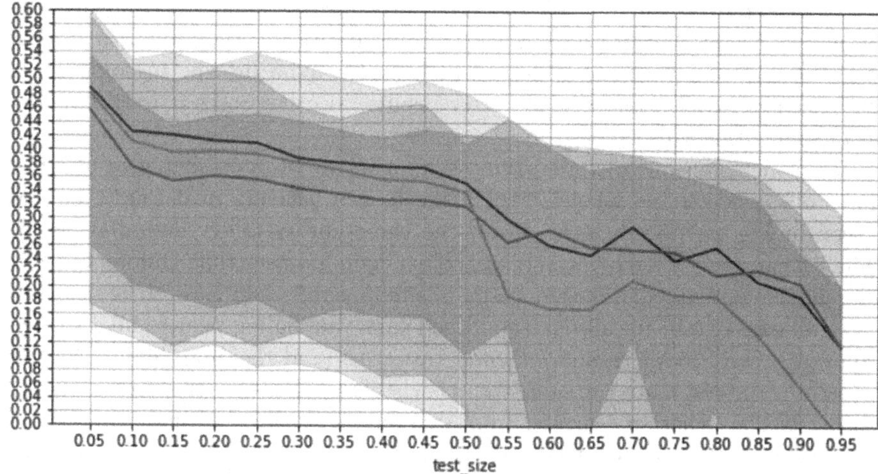

Fig. 1. Evolution of performance (R^2 score) depending on size of the test set for the Flight/economy dataset. Blue represents Base, red represents Differences and yellow represents Differences+context. For each, the average R^2 score across all other parameters than *test_size* is represented by the line, and the minimum and maximum are represented by the borders of the area around it. (Color figure online)

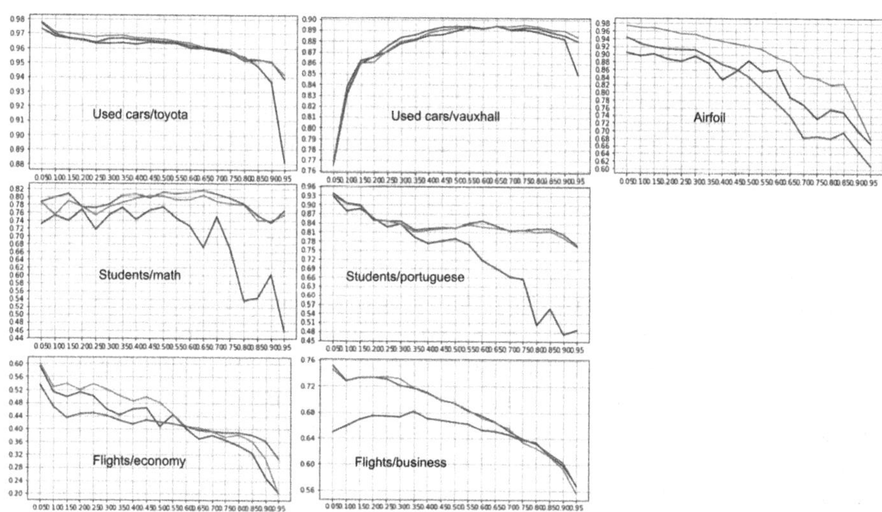

Fig. 2. Best performance obtained by Base (blue), Differences (red) and Differences+context (yellow) by test size. (Color figure online)

As can be expected, there is for the three versions a general trend downwards (the network is less accurate with less training data) and they follow a similar shape. Other than that, no general conclusion can be drawn: In some cases Difference+context seems to give better results, in other cases it is Differences and in some others it is Base.

This conclusion on a single example appears to be representative of what can be observed on the whole set of datasets and variants of datasets, as can be seen in Fig. 2. Indeed, in all cases, the three curves follow a similar trend. While we can see for both variants of the Students dataset that Differences and Differences+context both obtain better results overall than Base, it is not true to a significant extent for all datasets. Used cars/vauxhall appear to be a special case overall, with lower results for lower test sizes (and therefore higher sizes of the training dataset), but the same trend is visible for the three training methods. In other words, whether learning from differences, with or without context, is more adapted to situations where lower amounts of data are available appears to depend on the dataset and task under consideration.

5.2 Performance in Relation to the Number of Epochs

Figure 3 shows the example of the toyota variant of the Used Cars dataset for the evolution of the neural networks performance based on the number of epochs, i.e. the number of times the training process iterates over the dataset. As can be expected, Base, the neural network trained in the usual way, sees its performance increase with the number of epochs. It starts to plateau around 11 epochs and generally reaches its best performance at close to 20 epochs. Also, it can be noticed that at lower numbers of epochs, the performance of Base is more affected by other parameters (namely, the test size) than it is at higher ones (higher spread between minimum and maximum results).

What is however more surprising in this figure is that the trend for both networks trained from differences is significantly different. In both cases, high values of the R^2 score are achieved as early as Epoch 1, and they remain high. We can also notice, in this case, that the impact of other parameters ($test\_size$, ntr, nte) is relatively low both in high and low numbers of epochs.

As can be seen in Fig. 4, the same conclusion can be drawn for all the datasets and variants of datasets. In every case, while Base might require anything between 20 and 400 epochs to reach its peak performance, Differences and Differences+context achieve their best results, or close to their best results, from a comparatively low numbers of epochs. This is the most surprising result of this study, as it is hard to explain why, in such a systematic way, the training requirements of a network trained from differences are so significantly lower than for the same network trained in the usual way. We could imagine that this is due to the larger amounts of information used to train the network, since if ntr is greater than 1, several case differences are created for every case in the original dataset. However, as can be seen in Fig. 3 looking at the range of results for

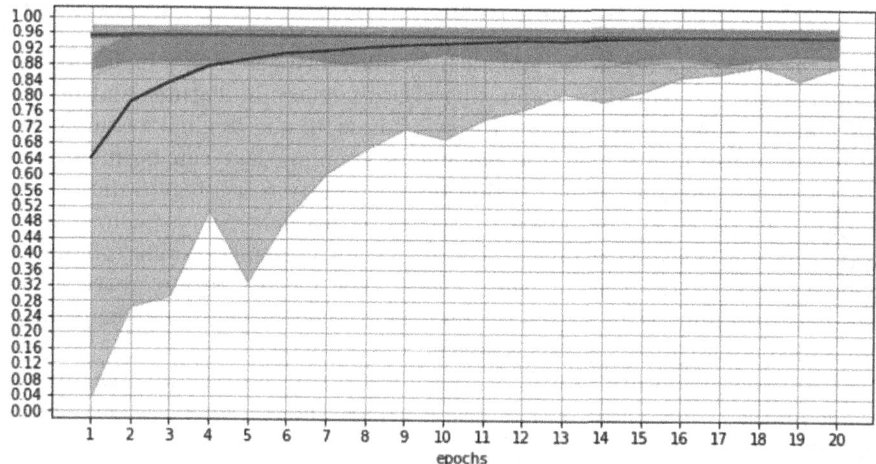

Fig. 3. Evolution of performance (R^2 score) depending on the number of epochs for the Used cars/toyota dataset. Legend is as per Fig. 1.

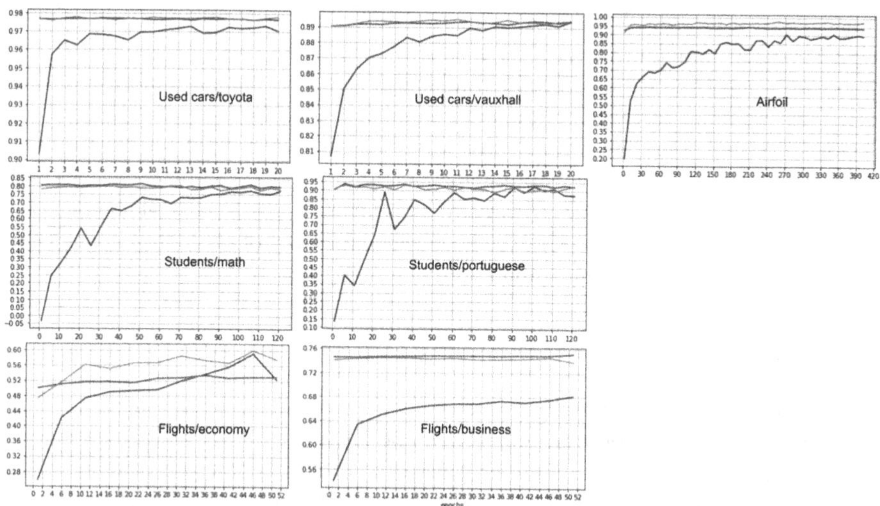

Fig. 4. Best performance obtained by Base (blue), Differences (red) and Differences+context (yellow) by number of epochs. (Color figure online)

Differences and Differences+context, the stability of the results with respect to the number of epochs remains even in the worst case. A closer inspection of the results would indeed reveal that even if ntr is 1, the observed phenomena is still visible.

5.3 Performance in Relation to the Number of Similar Cases Used

One of the advantages that the approach by difference has is that multiple case differences can be created by computing the differences in features and results with multiple similar data entries for every item in the original training set. This, in practice, means that the amount of training data can be multiplied without adding any new data. In addition, the ability to aggregate the results from multiple retrieved cases given a target set of features can also help smooth out possible outliers and irregularities in the results at prediction time, obtaining better accuracy. To test this, we varied the number of cases used to create differences in the training set (*ntr*) and the number of items retrieved and aggregated during prediction (*nte*) to see their effect on performance.

Table 2 shows which values of *ntr* and of *nte* obtained the best results on average and as a maximum over all the other parameters for both Differences and Differences+context. As can be seen, there does not seem to be a clear trend in those data. While in some cases, very small numbers of similar cases are required in training and prediction, in others, the best values were obtained with the highest number within the ranges tested. There appears to be a slight trend indicating that Differences+context sometimes require a lower number of similar cases, especially in training, but this difference does not seem significant enough to draw conclusions.

In summary, the best number of similar cases to use, both in training and in prediction, appears to be dependent on the dataset under consideration. Since the role of using those multiple cases can be seen as enabling a greater use of the information about the input space available and as helping smooth out outliers, we can expect those variations to be related to the density of the original dataset, i.e. how many cases tend to share the same area of that data space that are relevant to be used in the same context for prediction.

5.4 Peak Performance

To get an overview of the main results of the presented factorial study, we look at the minimal requirements in number of epochs, number of similar cases used during training and number of similar cases used during prediction to reach peak performance for each of Base, Differences, and Differences+context. We look at those results for test sizes of 20% and 80% of the original dataset (consistently with [5], corresponding to training sets of 80% and 20% of the original dataset respectively). We consider peak performance to have been reached when the R^2 score obtained is within 0.2% of the maximum, to account for the non-significant variations that naturally appear in those scores. The result of this analysis is presented in Table 3.

The first result from this table is that, as noticeable in the previous figures, at least one of the methods using differences often slightly outperforms the base method where the neural network is trained in the usual way. In the few cases

Table 2. Number of cases used to create the difference-based training set (ntr) and number of cases retrieved/aggregated for prediction (nte) obtaining the best results on average and in the best case.

	Differences				Differences+context			
	ntr		nte		ntr		nte	
	Mean	Best	Mean	Best	Mean	Best	Mean	Best
Used Cars/toyota	4	5	5	4	3	3	5	4
Used Cars/vauxhall	5	5	5	5	2	3	5	5
Airfoil	5	5	2	2	5	2	2	2
Students/maths	4	3	9	10	4	1	10	10
Students/portuguese	5	5	9	10	5	1	8	9
Flight/economy	5	5	8	6	3	5	10	6
Flight/business	5	5	4	2	4	2	5	2

where it does not, the R^2 scores actually obtained are very close to the best results obtained with Base.

What can be noticed as well is that adding the context (the features of the source item used to construct differences) to the input variables does not always lead to greater performances. However, if lower, the results of Differences+context are close to the ones of Differences, while if higher, they can be significantly higher (e.g. for Airfoil with both 20% and 80% test sizes). In other words, including the context seems a valid option since it does not generally lead to drastically lower results, while potentially bringing significant improvements.

As already mentioned in the previous section, it is difficult to find a pattern of interest in the number of similar cases used in training and prediction to achieve the best results in Differences and Differences+context. This is true also when comparing the results between the two difference-based methods: sometimes Differences+context requires slightly more similar cases, and sometimes slightly less, but the numbers are always relatively similar.

Finally, the most striking result is, as already discussed in Sect. 5.2, that in most cases, the methods learning from differences require significantly less training than the Base method. Indeed, the number of epochs required to achieve a score close to the best result is in most cases less than half of the one required by Base. Here too, it is difficult to find a pattern in comparing the required number of epochs between the two difference-based methods: Differences+context sometimes require less, and sometimes more. It is worth reminding the reader in addition that, according to Figs. 3 and 4, it is not only the case that learning from differences achieves its best results earlier (in number of epochs), but also that those results are more stable: While a slight decrease in number of epochs with Base might result in a significant drop in performance, the R^2 score tends to stay within a short range of the best result even when drastically reducing the amount of training carried out.

Table 3. Overview of parameters reaching within 0.2% of the best results for Base, Differences and Differences+context with sizes of test sets of 20% and 80% (i.e. sizes of training sets of 80% and 20% respectively). *ep.* corresponds to the number of epochs.

	Base		Differences				Diff+context			
	R^2	*ep.*	R^2	*ep.*	*ntr*	*nte*	R^2	*ep.*	*ntr*	*nte*
20% test size										
Cars/toyota	96.5%	10	96.6%	1	3	5	**96.8%**	6	5	5
Cars/vauxhall	**86.6%**	17	**86.6%**	16	3	5	86.1%	3	1	5
Airfoil	88.8%	392	91.4%	152	2	2	**96.2%**	232	5	10
Students/math	76.7%	96	77.3%	6	5	9	**77.4%**	66	1	10
Students/port	**85.7%**	116	85.2%	21	4	9	84.9%	21	3	10
Flights/economy	51.3%	51	44.6%	46	5	9	**52.0%**	46	5	9
Flights/business	67.5%	46	**73.4%**	11	5	3	73.3%	6	5	3
80% test size										
Cars/toyota	**95.4%**	19	95.1%	1	4	5	95.3%	4	4	5
Cars/vauxhall	88.9%	20	89.2%	7	5	5	**89.4%**	4	4	5
Airfoil	75.5%	262	68.0%	232	5	10	**82.1%**	382	5	10
Students/math	53.5%	66	**78.2%**	16	5	9	78.0%	41	3	9
Students/port	50.3%	111	**82.3%**	46	5	8	81.2%	76	3	8
Flights/economy	34.7%	51	**38.8%**	21	5	9	38.2%	11	5	10
Flights/business	**63.4%**	46	63.2%	31	5	6	62.5%	6	5	10

6 Conclusion

In this paper, we presented a factorial study comparing the influence of the size of the training set, the number of epochs of training and the number of similar cases used on the performance of neural networks trained in three different ways for regression tasks: The usual way (Base), where values are predicted from the raw input data, from differences (Differences), where differences in values are predicted from differences of pairs of input vectors, and from differences with their context (Differences+context), where differences in values are predicted from differences of pairs of input vectors and the raw feature data.

The main findings from this study are that, from all the seven datasets and variants of datasets tested: 1- the performance of the difference-based methods tend to be comparable, and often slightly higher than the performance of the Base method; 2- there seem to be an advantage in adding the context (in the form of the original set of features) to case differences as it achieves either very similar or better results (as already discussed in [4]); 3- Both methods based on learning from differences in most cases required significantly less epochs of training to reach their peak performance, and arrive within a short range of that best result in just a few epochs. This last point is significant since it implies that those difference-based methods can achieve performances at least as good as the Base method, while being trained for less time. This, however, has to be considered carefully since the retrieval of similar cases and the inclusion of multiple case differences in both training and prediction also comes with a time overhead. It would therefore be interesting to study in more details the time implications of those aspects and to test more efficient implementations of similarity based retrieval than the one used in the *deltaML* library developed for this study.

In addition, the present study has a number of limitations and would therefore benefit from being further expanded. First, we only considered regression tasks. Since it is not guarantied that the results found here would generalise to neural networks trained for classification tasks (as in [7]), a similar study on such networks would be beneficial. Also, while the datasets selected are varied in size, dimensionality, topics and the results obtained, the neural networks used on them remain similar. In addition to including classification tasks, the inclusion of datasets and tasks requiring different types of networks and a broader range of network size/depth would help confirm the results obtained. Finally, not all of the factors influencing the performance of a neural network have been considered here. In particular, we deliberately did not vary the structure of the network in terms of number of layers, neurons per layers, activation functions and loss function. It could be possible, however, that a different structure be more suitable for learning from differences than for learning in the usual way, leading to possibly even better results.

References

1. Craw, S., Wiratunga, N., Rowe, R.C.: Learning adaptation knowledge to improve case-based reasoning. Artif. Intell. **170**(16–17), 1175–1192 (2006)
2. Hanney, K., Keane, M.T.: Learning adaptation rules from a case-base. In: Smith, I., Faltings, B. (eds.) EWCBR 1996. LNCS, vol. 1168, pp. 179–192. Springer, Heidelberg (1996). https://doi.org/10.1007/BFb0020610
3. Jalali, V., Leake, D., Forouzandehmehr, N.: Learning and applying case adaptation rules for classification: an ensemble approach. In: Proceedings of the Twenty-Sixth International Joint Conference on Artificial Intelligence, pp. 4874–4878. IJCAI-17 (2017)
4. Leake, D., Ye, X., Crandall, D.J.: Supporting case-based reasoning with neural networks: an illustration for case adaptation. In: AAAI Spring Symposium: Combining Machine Learning with Knowledge Engineering, Vol. 2 (2021)
5. Liao, C.K., A. Liu, Y.C.: A machine learning approach to case adaptation. In Springer, ed.: IEEE First International Conference on Artificial Intelligence and Knowledge Engineering (AIKE), pp. 106–109 (2018)
6. Lieber, J., Nauer, E.: Adaptation knowledge discovery using positive and negative cases. In: Sánchez-Ruiz, A.A., Floyd, M.W. (eds.) ICCBR 2021. LNCS (LNAI), vol. 12877, pp. 140–155. Springer, Cham (2021). https://doi.org/10.1007/978-3-030-86957-1_10
7. Ye, X., Leake, D., Jalali, V., Crandall, D.J.: Learning adaptations for case-based classification: a neural network approach. In: Sánchez-Ruiz, A.A., Floyd, M.W. (eds.) ICCBR 2021. LNCS (LNAI), vol. 12877, pp. 279–293. Springer, Cham (2021). https://doi.org/10.1007/978-3-030-86957-1_19
8. Ye, X., Zhao, Z., Leake, D., Wang, X., Crandall, D.: Applying the case difference heuristic to learn adaptations from deep network features. In: IJCAI 2021 workshop on Deep Learning, Case-Based Reasoning, and AutoML: Present and Future Synergies, arXiv (2021)

Case-Based Inverse Reinforcement Learning Using Temporal Coherence

Jonas Nüßlein(✉), Steffen Illium, Robert Müller, Thomas Gabor, and Claudia Linnhoff-Popien

Institute of Computer Science, LMU Munich, Munich, Germany
{jonas.nuesslein,steffen.illium,robert.mueller,thomas.gabor, linnhoff}@ifi.lmu.de

Abstract. Providing expert trajectories in the context of Imitation Learning is often expensive and time-consuming. The goal must therefore be to create algorithms which require as little expert data as possible. In this paper we present an algorithm that imitates the higher-level strategy of the expert rather than just imitating the expert on action level, which we hypothesize requires less expert data and makes training more stable. As a prior, we assume that the higher-level strategy is to reach an unknown target state area, which we hypothesize is a valid prior for many domains in Reinforcement Learning. The target state area is unknown, but since the expert has demonstrated how to reach it, the agent tries to reach states similar to the expert. Building on the idea of Temporal Coherence, our algorithm trains a neural network to predict whether two states are similar, in the sense that they may occur close in time. During inference, the agent compares its current state with expert states from a Case Base for similarity. The results show that our approach can still learn a near-optimal policy in settings with very little expert data, where algorithms that try to imitate the expert at the action level can no longer do so.

Keywords: Case-based reasoning · Inverse reinforcement learning · Incomplete trajectories · Learning from observations · Temporal coherence

1 Introduction

In Reinforcement Learning (RL), the goal of the agent, given a Markov Decision Process, is to maximize the expected cumulative reward. The higher the expected reward, the better the agent's policy. In Imitation Learning, on the other hand, the agent does not have access to a reward signal from the environment. Instead, it either has access to an expert who can be asked online for the best action for a given state or a set of trajectories generated by the expert is available. Imitation Learning has been proven to be particularly successful in domains where the demonstration by an expert is easier than the construction of a suitable reward function [AD21]. There are two main approaches to Imitation Learning:

M. T. Keane and N. Wiratunga (Eds.): ICCBR 2022, LNAI 13405, pp. 304–317, 2022.
https://doi.org/10.1007/978-3-031-14923-8_20

Behavioral Cloning (BC) [Pom91] and Inverse Reinforcement Learning (IRL) [FLL17, AD21, AN04]. In BC, the agent learns via supervised learning to produce the same actions that the expert would have produced. The advantage of this approach is that no further rollouts in the environment are necessary. However, the approach suffers greatly from compounding error, i.e., the slow drift of states visited by the expert [RGB11]. In the second approach, IRL, a reward function is learned under which the expert is uniquely optimal. Then, a policy can be learned using classical Reinforcement Learning and this reconstructed reward function. However, the drawback of this approach is that it usually requires a lot of rollouts in the environment, as it often includes RL as a subroutine.

GAIL [HE16] is another approach to Imitation Learning. It builds on the ideas of Generative Adversarial Networks. In this approach, a policy and a discriminator are learned. The goal of the discriminator is to be able to distinguish state-action pairs of the expert from state-action pairs of the agent, while the goal of the policy is to fool the discriminator. GAIL requires expert actions, but there is an extension, named GAIfO, which does not [TWS18]. While GAIL discriminates between state-action pairs produced by the agent or the expert respectively, GAIfO does so with state transitions. In this paper we consider, as GAIfO does, the setting where no expert actions are available to the agent. This setting is also called Learning from Observation (LfO) or Imitation from Observation (IfO) [YMH+19, TWS18].

Providing expert trajectories is often very expensive and time-consuming, especially if the expert is a human. The goal must therefore be to create algorithms which require as little expert data as possible.

The aim of this paper is to present an algorithm that imitates the higher-level strategy of the expert rather then just imitating the expert on action level.

Our motivation for this is that we hypothesize that it takes less expert data to learn the higher-level strategy than to imitate the expert on action level. We also hypothesize that it makes the training more stable, with less "forgetting" of what has already been learned. As a prior for the higher-level strategy, we assume that the higher-level strategy is to reach an unknown target state area, which we hypothesize is a valid prior for many domains in Reinforcement Learning.

We present an algorithm that learns these higher-level strategies from expert trajectories. To prove that the algorithm does not imitate the expert on action level, we consider a special setting of Imitation Learning, which is characterized by incomplete expert trajectories. Here, the agent does not see every state of the expert trajectory, but, for example, only every fifth. Thus, it cannot imitate the expert on action level.

The idea behind machine learning is to derive general rules from a large amount of data, which can then be applied to new, unknown scenarios. This induction-based learning principle differs from Case-Based problem solving. In Case-Based Reasoning, a set of problems solved in the past is stored in a database. If a new, unknown problem is to be solved, the problem most similar to the current situation is retrieved from the database and used to solve the current problem. Applications of Case-Based Reasoning range from explaining neural network outputs [LLCR18, KK19] over financial risk detection [LPS21] to medical diagnosis [CB16]. In our algorithm we build on ideas from Case-Based Reasoning as well as on the idea of Temporal Coherence.

Temporal Coherence [GBT+15, MCW09, ZNY11] originates from Video Representation Learning, where the idea is that two images, which occur shortly after each other in a video, are very likely to show the same object or objects. The two images should therefore have a similar representation. On the other hand, distant images should have different representations. The combination of this convergence and divergence, also called contrastive learning, can be used as a self-supervised training signal to learn semantically meaningful representations [KHW+21].

Our contribution in this paper is twofold. First, we propose the setting with incomplete expert trajectories without expert actions as a way to prove that the agent really learns the expert's strategy and does not imitate the expert on action level. The prior we are using for the higher-level strategy is to reach an unknown target state area. Second, we present an algorithm that can learn such higher-level strategies and we test it on four typical domains of RL. The results show that our approach can still learn a near-optimal policy in settings with very little expert data, where IRL algorithms that try to imitate the expert at the action level can no longer do so.

2 Background

In this section we want to provide a brief introduction to Markov Decision Processes (MDP) [ADBB17]. A MDP is a tuple (S, A, T, R, γ). S is a set of states, combined with a distribution of starting states $p(s_0)$. A is a set of actions the agent can perform. T is the transition function of the environment which computes the next state s_{t+1} given a state s_t at time t and an action a_t: $T(s_{t+1}|s_t, a_t)$. The property of T that the computation of s_{t+1} depends only on the last state s_t and not on $s_{\tau<t}$ is also called the Markov property, hence the name Markov Decision Process. $r_t = R(s_t, a_t, s_{t+1})$ is a reward function and $\gamma \in [0;1]$ is a discount factor. If $\gamma < 1$, immediate rewards are preferred compared to later rewards. An agent acts in a MDP using its policy π. The policy is a function which outputs an action a given a state s: $\pi(s) = a$. MDPs are often episodic, which means that the agent acts for T steps, after which the environment is reset to a starting state. The goal of the agent in a MDP is to maximize the expected return by finding the policy

$$\pi^* = \underset{\pi}{\text{argmax}}\ E[R|\pi] \tag{1}$$

where the return R is calculated via:

$$R = \sum_{t=0}^{T-1} \gamma^t r_{t+1} \tag{2}$$

3 Related Work

Combination of Case-Based Reasoning (CBR) and Reinforcement Learning (RL): In [BRLdM09] the authors use Case-Based Reasoning (CBR) in the setting of Heuristic Accelerated Reinforcement Learning, where a heuristic function assists in action selection to accelerate exploration in the state-action space. In [ALUHMA08], Case-Based Reasoning is used to efficiently switch between previously stored policies learned with classical RL. A similar approach is taken by [WW14]. Most Imitation Learning algorithms try to imitate the expert skill step-by-step. In [LHYL19], a hierarchical algorithm is presented where this goal is mitigated. Instead, a policy is learned that reaches sub-goals, which in turn are sampled by a meta-policy from the expert demonstrations.

Temporal Coherence in Reinforcement Learning: Some papers have already investigated the use of Temporal Coherence in the context of Reinforcement Learning. For example, in [FDH+19] it was proposed to learn an embedding for the inputs of the Markov Decision Process, such that the euclidean distance in the embedding space is proportional to the number of actions the current agent needs to get from one state to the other. The byproduct of this is a policy that can theoretically reach any previously seen state on demand. A similar idea is followed in the context of goal-conditioned RL: In [LSSL21] a proximity function $f(s, g)$ is learned that outputs a scalar proportional to the distance of the state s to the goal g. The distance then serves as a dense reward signal for a classical RL agent. This is especially beneficial when the environment's reward function is sparse.

In [SLC+18], a special setting is considered where multiple observations are available simultaneously, showing the same state from different perspectives. An embedding is then learned so that contemporaneous observations have the same embedding and temporally distant observations have different embeddings. Thus, a perspective-invariant representation is learned, which contains semantic information. That paper also considers the case where only one perspective is available. In this case, the embeddings of two nearby inputs should be as similar as possible and temporally distant inputs should be as dissimilar as possible. We build on this idea of Temporal Coherence, although we do not learn an embedding. [DTLS18] extends the idea of [SLC+18] to input sequences to contrast movements.

In [SRM+18], the concept of Reachability Networks is already introduced, i.e., a network that classifies whether two states can occur in short succession in a trajectory. This network is then used as a curiosity signal to guide exploration in sparse reward domains. We build on this concept, but use it differently. While in [SRM+18] the agent searches for dissimilar states, the goal of the agent in our approach is to reach similar states (compared to expert states).

Curriculum via Expert Demonstrations: As we will see in the next section, the reconstructed reward function in our approach can be interpreted as an implicit curriculum. A related approach, which creates an explicit curriculum using expert demonstrations, is [DHW21]. In that paper the expert trajectory is divided into several sections and state resetting to expert states is used to increase the difficulty of reaching the goal state. The sector from which expert states are sampled for resetting is gradually pushed away from the goal as the curriculum progresses. A similar approach is [HAE+20], which again uses resetting to starting states of varying difficulty.

Unsupervised Perceptual Rewards for Imitation Learning: the closest work to ours is [SXL16]. In that paper the authors examine how to use pre-trained vision models to reconstruct a reward function from few human video demonstrations. They do so by first splitting the human demo videos into segments, then selecting features of a pre-trained model which best discriminate between the segments and then using a reward function, which is based on these selected features, to learn a policy via standard RL algorithms. The biggest difference to our algorithm is that [SXL16] reconstructs the reward function entirely before training in the RL domain. In contrast, we learn the reward function and the policy at the same time.

4 Case-Based Inverse Reinforcement Learning (CB-IRL)

In this work, we consider a special setting of Imitation Learning that is characterized by two main features. First, there are no expert actions available to the agent and, second, the expert trajectories are incomplete, i.e., from the original sequence of MDP states of the expert $[s_0, s_1, s_2, ..., s_T]$, the agent only sees, for example, every fifth state: $[s_0, s_5, s_{10}, ...]$. This makes it impossible for the agent to imitate the expert at the action level. Given such a setting, we now propose the algorithm Case-Based Inverse Reinforcement Learning (CB-IRL). The architecture of CB-IRL consists of the Case Base (C) and two neural networks, the Equality Net (E) and the Policy (π), see Fig. 1. C is filled with the expert trajectories.

The basic idea is that the agent should not act in every step exactly as the expert would do, but instead imitate the higher-level strategy of the expert. We chose the task of reaching a target state area as the prior for the higher-level strategy. For example, for the OpenAI domain 'MountainCar' the target state area are the states where the car is on top of the mountain. For the Atari game 'Pong' the target state area would be the states where the agent has 21 points. The agent does not know the target state area, but since the expert has demonstrated how to reach the target state area, CB-IRL trains the agent to reach similar states as the expert.

Two states are "similar" in the context of Reinforcement Learning if it takes only few steps (actions) to get from one state to the other. Other approaches [FDH+19, SLC+18, DTLS18] try to learn a state-embedding such that the euclidean distance of the representations is proportional to the number of steps needed to get from one state to the other. We take a different approach and instead train a neural network that accepts two states s_1 and s_2 as input and outputs a scalar $E(s_1, s_2) = d$; $E : S \times S \to [0; 1]$ to classify whether s_2 can be reached within *windowFrame* steps from s_1. Thus, this is a classification and not a regression. We believe a classification is easier and more stable to learn compared to a regression, since it suffers less from the "moving target" problem. For example if we would predict the number of steps which are required to go from one state to the other, the target of this supervised learning tasks is heavily based on the current performance of the agent. In contrast, for near/far classification, it does not matter if the states are, for example, 30 or 40 steps apart if *windowFrame* = 10. In both cases the state pair gets the target 0 for supervised learning, since it shall be classified as dissimilar.

Algorithm 1: CB-IRL

```
Data: Case-Base C (containing expert trajectories)
Result: Policy π, Equality Net E
while training do
    s ← sample start state
    r_pre ← Reward(s)
    trajectory ← [s]
    while episode is not finished do
        a ← π(s)
        s' ← execute a
        trajectory.append(s')
        r_post ← Reward(s')
        r ← r_post − α * r_pre
        use (s, a, r, s') for training π
        s ← s'
        r_pre ← r_post
    end
    append trajectory to the Replay Buffer of E
    train E using the Replay Buffer, C and the hyperparameters windowFrame
      and ν
end

Function Reward(s):
    mostSimilar = μ
    similarity = τ
    foreach trajectory ∈ C do
        foreach o_e^(i) ∈ trajectory do
            if E(s, o_e^(i)) > similarity then
                mostSimilar = i
                similarity = E(s, o_e^(i))
            end
        end
    end
    return mostSimilar
```

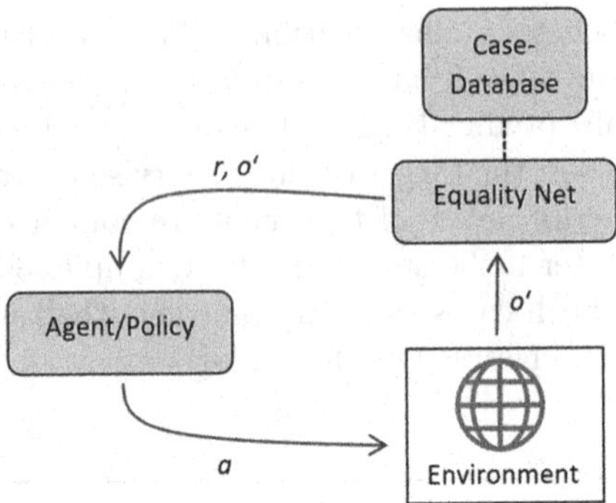

Fig. 1. This figure shows the usual cycle of Reinforcement Learning, with a small adjustment. The Equality Net (E) is interposed between the environment and the agent. The agent performs an action a, which is executed in the environment. E receives the next observation o' from the environment, then calculates the reward r using the case database and forwards both to the agent.

A second advantage of Reachability Networks in contrast to embeddings is that they are suitable for asymmetric state-action spaces. For example, it may be easy to reach s_2 from s_1, but difficult or impossible to reach s_1 from s_2.

The policy π is learned via Inverse Reinforcement Learning using the case database C and the Equality Net E. If the agent is in state o, it executes the action $a = \pi(o)$ with its current policy π and receives the next observation o' from the environment. Using E, all expert observations $o_e^{(i)}$ from C are now checked to see if they are similar to o', where the similarity must be above a threshold τ. If there is a similar expert state $o_e^{(j)}$ (if more than one, choose the most similar), the reward is given by the position number j. Thus, the further back the similar expert state is in the expert trajectory, the higher the reward the agent receives. If there is no similar expert state, the agent receives a penalty μ (a negative reward). Figure 2 shows the idea schematically. The complete algorithm is summarized in Algorithm 1.

The algorithm contains several hyperparameters, whose task and influence we discuss in the following: $\tau \in [0; 1]$ is the threshold that determines the minimum similarity of an expert state $o_e^{(i)}$ to the current state o of the agent, so that the agent receives a positive reward. If no expert state has a similarity higher than τ, the agent receives a penalty (a negative reward μ). The hyperparameter $\alpha \in [0; 1]$ controls whether the actual reward for the agent is always the reward difference ($\alpha = 1$) or whether the agent always receives the full reward ($\alpha = 0$). For $\alpha = 0$, the agent tends to achieve large rewards as quickly as possible, but maybe not reliably, whereas for $\alpha = 1$, the agent tries to achieve a large reward as reliably as possible by the end of the episode.

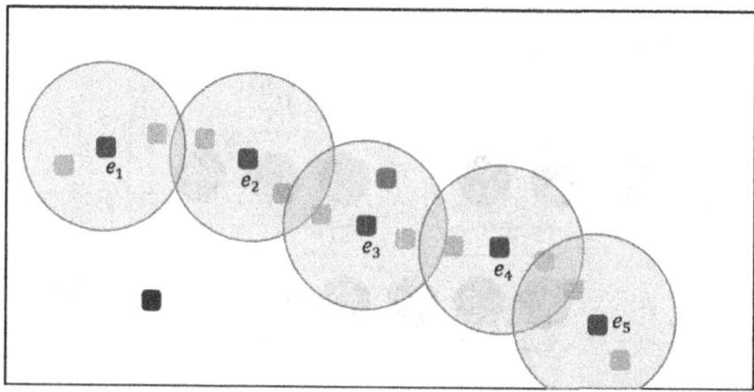

Fig. 2. This figure shows schematically how the algorithm works. Assume the rectangle is a two-dimensional state space. The light and dark gray boxes represent the trajectory of expert states but only the dark states are visible to the agent. Using its own rollouts the agent now learns the Equality Net, which classifies whether two states can occur close to each other in a trajectory. The outputs of the Equality Net for the expert states are represented in the image by the circles around them. During inference, the agent checks whether the current state is similar to an expert state or not. For example, if the agent is in the yellow state, it is similar to expert state e_3 and therefore receives reward 3. If the agent is in the blue state, it is not similar to any expert state and receives a negative reward μ. (Color figure online)

The hyperparameters *windowFrame* and ν are used to train E. They model on the one hand the threshold which indicates whether two states are considered similar or dissimilar and on the other hand the number of explicit divergence between states of the agent and states of the expert.

Training of the Equality Net: The task of the Equality Net E is to classify whether two inputs can occur in short succession in a trajectory and are thus "similar". To train E, we use the Replay Buffer that contains the trajectories sampled by the agent. E is trained using supervised learning. The training set consists of similar and dissimilar state pairs. For the similar state pairs, two states are selected from the same trajectory of the Replay Buffer which are no further apart than *windowFrame* steps. For the dissimilar state pairs, two states are sampled from two different trajectories. For the similar state pairs, the network E is trained to output the value 1, for dissimilar state pairs it is trained to output 0. The structure of E is graphically visualized in Fig. 3.

In addition, training can also be performed in an analogous manner on the expert trajectories. The hyperparameter ν models the number of explicit divergence between agent and expert state. That is, there are ν state pairs where one state is sampled from the Replay Buffer and the other state is sampled from C. The target for these state pairs during supervised learning is 0, since they shall be classified as dissimilar.

The output of the Equality Net can be understood as a (lossy) binary distance measure. The distance measure is binary because it only distinguishes between similar (1) and dissimilar (0).

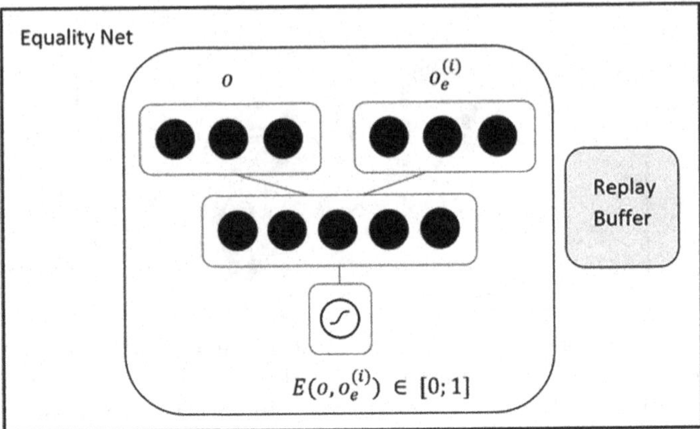

Fig. 3. The Equality Net E accepts as input two states and classifies whether they are similar in the sense that they can appear close to each other in a trajectory. During inference, E receives as input the current state o of the agent and compares it to all expert states $o_e^{(i)}$. E is trained using supervised learning on the trajectories produced by the agent, which are stored in the Replay Buffer.

5 Experiments

We tested our algorithm in four OpenAI Gym domains [BCP+16]: Acrobot, Mountain Car, Lunar Lander, and Half Cheetah. For Half Cheetah, we created a modified version called Half Cheetah Discrete. Details can be found in Appendix A. As justified in [CLB+17], only domains should be used for the evaluation of IRL algorithms in which the episodes are always of the same length. This is because early ending of episodes may contain implicit information about the reward. For example, in the 'Mountain Car' domain, the episode ends when the car has successfully driven up the hill. For this reason, we have adjusted all domains so that episodes are always of the same length, with the agent receiving the last observation until the end if the episode ended early.

We first trained an expert for each domain using the reward function of the environment. We then used these experts to create exactly one trajectory for each domain, which consisted only of the expert states and not the expert actions. We then used it to train CB-IRL and GAIFO. GAIFO had access to all expert states, while CB-IRL only had access to every tenth expert state. For example, for Lunar Lander, the expert trajectory was about 150 steps long, so the training set for GAIFO consisted of these 150 expert states, while the training set for CB-IRL consisted of only 15 expert states.

For the hyperparameter search, we tested five hyperparameter sets for each algorithm and domain and selected the best one. Using these hyperparameters, we then trained CB-IRL and GAIFO three times with three different seeds. During training we generated 20 episodes every 10,000 steps for each seed and

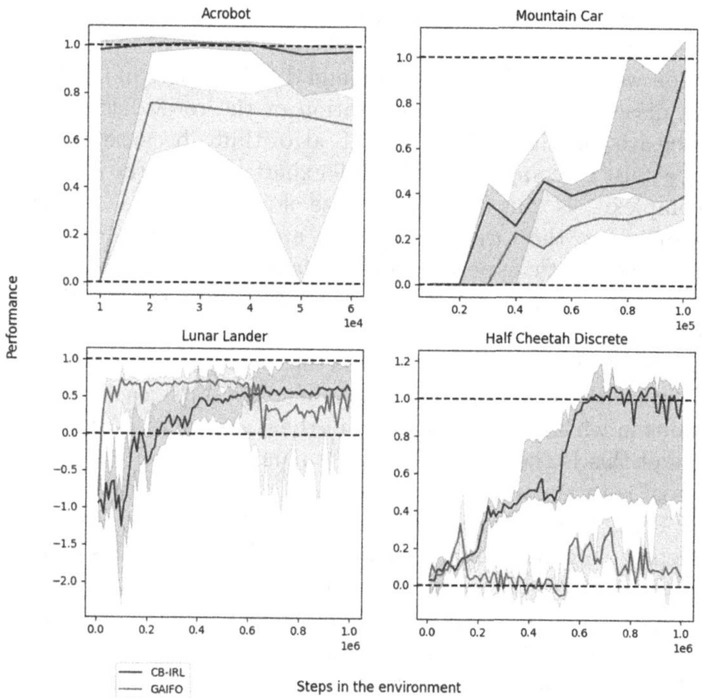

Fig. 4. Scaled performance of CB-IRL and GAIFO on four different domains trained using one expert trajectory, where GAIFO had access to all expert states and CB-IRL had access to only one in ten.

algorithm (for a total of 60 episodes per algorithm every 10,000 steps). For each episode, we calculated the total return using the environment's reward function. The returns were then scaled using the performance of a random agent (representing value 0) and the expert (representing value 1). We then calculated the 0.25, 0.5 (median), and 0.75 quantiles for these 60 return values. For both algorithms, the solid lines represent the median and the shaded areas enclose the 0.25 and 0.75 quantiles.

As can be seen in Fig. 4, CB-IRL mostly performed better than GAIFO in the experiments, even though it had access to only one tenth of GAIFO's training set. Furthermore, CB-IRL showed a more stable learning behavior. The difference was particularly clear in the Half Cheetah Discrete domain. Here, the advantage of CB-IRL became apparent, where the agent did not learn to behave exactly like the expert in every state, but to reach similar states as the expert. CB-IRL has learnt the high-level strategy to "run as far as possible".

A Python implementation of CB-IRL and the code used to create the experiments are available on GitHub [https://github.com/JonasNuesslein/CB-IRL]. For GAIFO we used the implementation of tf2rl [Ota20]. The chosen hyperparameters for the experiments can also be found on GitHub in the file *config.py*.

6 Discussion of the Approach

In this section we discuss the advantages and disadvantages of CB-IRL. Turning first to the disadvantages: The computation of the reward is more computationally intensive than in many other IRL algorithms, because in each step the current state must be compared against all expert states in the case base C. The run-time complexity is thus linear in the size of C. This can be serious for larger case bases, however, the target application areas of CB-IRL are precisely the settings where very little expert data is available. Moreover, the computational intensity can be reduced by calculating a reward only in every k-th step, rather than in every step.

The second drawback of our approach is the specialization of CB-IRL to state-reaching in contrast to state-keeping domains. By state-reaching domains, we mean domains in which certain variables of the state vector have to be changed. An example of this is the OpenAI Gym domain 'Mountain Car' [BCP+16], in which the goal is to maximize the x-position of the car. Another example is the Atari game 'Pong' [MKS+15], in which the goal of the agent is to reach 21 points. By state-keeping domains, we mean domains in which the goal is to leave certain variables of the state vector unchanged. An example of this would be 'Cart-Pole' [BCP+16], where the goal is to keep the angle of the pole at 90° if possible or 'HalfCheetah' [BCP+16], where the goal is to keep a high velocity. Due to the structure of CB-IRL, it is predominantly suitable for state-reaching domains, as the algorithm encourages the agent to reach states from the posterior of the expert trajectory.

The advantages of CB-IRL are that it does not require a reward function, expert actions, or complete expert trajectories. Since the agent can learn with incomplete expert trajectories, it has proven that it imitates the higher-level strategy of the expert and does not imitate the expert on action level.

This allows the agent to learn a near-optimal strategy with little data, which would be insufficient to imitate the expert on action level (as can be seen in the Half Cheetah Discrete domain). The learning behavior also shows a more stable pattern with less "forgetting" of what has already been learned.

A second possible advantage, which we leave as future work to verify, is that the Equality Net is not task-specific and can be reused for other tasks in the same domain, which can enable fast transfer learning.

A third possible advantage also left for future work is that the ability to learn from incomplete trajectories may be beneficial in real-world applications, where state observations may be noisy or delayed.

7 Conclusion

In this paper, we have shown that when very little expert data is available, it is advantageous to imitate the higher-level strategy of the expert, rather than imitating the expert on action level.

To prove that the agent really imitated the strategy and not the expert actions, we considered a special setting of Imitation Learning characterized by incomplete expert trajectories. Moreover, no expert actions were available to the agent (Learning from Observations). The chosen prior for the higher-level strategy was to reach an unknown target state area. But since the expert has demonstrated how to reach it, the agent tries to reach similar states as the expert.

The presented algorithm Case-Based Inverse Reinforcement Learning (CB-IRL) builds on the idea of Temporal Coherence and Case-Based Reasoning. The algorithm trains a neural network to predict whether a state s_2 can be reached from a state s_1 within *windowFrame* time steps (actions). If so, the states can be considered "similar". During inference, the agent uses this network to compare its current state o against expert states $o_e^{(i)}$ from a Case Base. If a similar expert state $o_e^{(j)}$ exists, the position j of this expert state in the expert trajectory serves as a (positive) reward signal for the agent. If no similar expert state exists, the agent receives a penalty. Thus, the agent is trained to reach similar states to the expert states. We tested our approach on four typical domains of Reinforcement Learning, where in every case only one tenth of an expert trajectory was available to the agent. The results show that CB-IRL was able to learn a near-optimal policy, often better than GAIfO, which had access to the full expert trajectory and was trying to imitate the expert at action level.

A Appendix

The OpenAI domain Half Cheetah does not normally contain any absolute position information. To make this domain a state-reaching domain, we additionally added the x-position of the Cheetah to the otherwise 17-dimensional state space. Furthermore, the action space of this domain is originally continuous, which greatly complicates exploration. To facilitate exploration, we created a modified version called "Half Cheetah Discrete". For this, 20 random (continuous) action vectors were sampled from the continuous action space. These 20 action vectors can be seen as basis vectors of the original continuous action space and together they now form a discrete action space (consisting of 20 possible actions). If one of the 20 discrete actions is selected, the corresponding continuous action vector is executed in the background.

References

[AD21] Arora, S., Doshi, P.: A survey of inverse reinforcement learning: challenges, methods and progress. Artif. Intell. **297**, 103500 (2021)

[ADBB17] Arulkumaran, K., Deisenroth, M.P., Brundage, M., Bharath, A.A.: A brief survey of deep reinforcement learning. arXiv preprint arXiv:1708.05866 (2017)

[ALUHMA08] Auslander, B., Lee-Urban, S., Hogg, C., Muñoz-Avila, H.: Recognizing the enemy: combining reinforcement learning with strategy selection using case-based reasoning. In: Althoff, K.-D., Bergmann, R., Minor, M., Hanft, A. (eds.) ECCBR 2008. LNCS (LNAI), vol. 5239, pp. 59–73. Springer, Heidelberg (2008). https://doi.org/10.1007/978-3-540-85502-6_4

[AN04] Abbeel, P., Ng, A.Y.: Apprenticeship learning via inverse reinforcement learning. In: Proceedings of the Twenty-First International Conference on Machine Learning, p. 1 (2004)

[BCP+16] Brockman, G.: OpenAI gym. arXiv preprint arXiv:1606.01540 (2016)

[BRLdM09] Bianchi, R.A.C., Ros, R., Lopez de Mantaras, R.: Improving reinforcement learning by using case based heuristics. In: McGinty, L., Wilson, D.C. (eds.) ICCBR 2009. LNCS (LNAI), vol. 5650, pp. 75–89. Springer, Heidelberg (2009). https://doi.org/10.1007/978-3-642-02998-1_7

[CB16] Choudhury, N., Begum, S.A.: A survey on case-based reasoning in medicine. Int. J. Adv. Comput. Sci. Appl. **7**(8), 136–144 (2016)

[CLB+17] Christiano, P.F., Leike, J., Brown, T., Martic, M., Legg, S., Amodei, D.: Deep reinforcement learning from human preferences. In: Advances in Neural Information Processing Systems 30 (2017)

[DHW21] Dai, S., Hofmann, A., Williams, B.: Automatic curricula via expert demonstrations. arXiv preprint arXiv:2106.09159 (2021)

[DTLS18] DwibediR, D., Tompson, J., LynchR, C., Sermanet, P.: Self-supervised representation learning for continuous control (2018)

[FDH+19] Florensa, C., Degrave, J., Heess, N., Springenberg, J.T., Riedmiller, M.: Self-supervised learning of image embedding for continuous control. arXiv preprint arXiv:1901.00943 (2019)

[FLL17] Fu, J., Luo, K., Levine, S.: Learning robust rewards with adversarial inverse reinforcement learning. arXiv preprint arXiv:1710.11248 (2017)

[GBT+15] Goroshin, R., Bruna, J., Tompson, J., Eigen, D., LeCun, Y.: Unsupervised learning of spatiotemporally coherent metrics. In: Proceedings of the IEEE International Conference on Computer Vision, pp. 4086–4093 (2015)

[HAE+20] Hermann, L., et al.: Adaptive curriculum generation from demonstrations for sim-to-real visuomotor control. In: IEEE International Conference on Robotics and Automation (ICRA), pp. 6498–6505. IEEE (2020)

[HE16] Ho, J., Ermon, S.: Generative adversarial imitation learning. In: Advances in Neural Information Processing Systems 29 (2016)

[KHW+21] Knights, J., Harwood, B., Ward, D., Vanderkop, A., Mackenzie-Ross, O., Moghadam, P.: Temporally coherent embeddings for self-supervised video representation learning. In 25th International Conference on Pattern Recognition (ICPR), pp. 8914–8921. IEEE (2021)

[KK19] Keane, M.T., Kenny, E.M.: How case-based reasoning explains neural networks: a theoretical analysis of XAI using *Post-Hoc* explanation-by-example from a survey of ANN-CBR twin-systems. In: Bach, K., Marling, C. (eds.) ICCBR 2019. LNCS (LNAI), vol. 11680, pp. 155–171. Springer, Cham (2019). https://doi.org/10.1007/978-3-030-29249-2_11

[LHYL19] Lee, Y., Hu, E.S., Yang, Z., Lim, J.J.: To follow or not to follow: selective imitation learning from observations. arXiv preprint arXiv:1912.07670 (2019)

[LLCR18] Li, O., Liu, H., Chen, C., Rudin, C.: Deep learning for case-based reasoning through prototypes: a neural network that explains its predictions. In: Proceedings of the AAAI Conference on Artificial Intelligence, vol. 32 (2018)

[LPS21] Li, W., Paraschiv, F., Sermpinis, G.: A data-driven explainable case-based reasoning approach for financial risk detection. Available at SSRN 3912753 (2021)

[LSSL21] Lee, Y., Szot, A., Sun, S.-H., Lim, J.J.: Generalizable imitation learning from observation via inferring goal proximity. In: Advances in Neural Information Processing Systems 34 (2021)

[MCW09] Mobahi, H., Collobert, R., Weston, J.: Deep learning from temporal coherence in video. In: Proceedings of the 26th Annual International Conference on Machine Learning, pp. 737–744 (2009)

[MKS+15] Mnih, V., et al.: Human-level control through deep reinforcement learning. Nature **518**(7540), 529–533 (2015)

[Ota20] Ota, K.: Tf2rl (2020). https://github.com/keiohta/tf2rl/

[Pom91] Pomerleau, D.A.: Efficient training of artificial neural networks for autonomous navigation. Neural Comput. **3**(1), 88–97 (1991)

[RGB11] Ross, S., Gordon, G., Bagnell, D.: A reduction of imitation learning and structured prediction to no-regret online learning. In: Proceedings of the Fourteenth International Conference on Artificial Intelligence and Statistics, pp. 627–635. JMLR Workshop and Conference Proceedings (2011)

[SLC+18] Sermanet, P., et al.: Time-contrastive networks: self-supervised learning from video. In: 2018 IEEE International Conference on Robotics and Automation (ICRA), pp. 1134–1141. IEEE (2018)

[SRM+18] Savinov, N., et al.: Episodic curiosity through reachability. arXiv preprint arXiv:1810.02274 (2018)

[SXL16] Sermanet, P., Xu, K., Levine, S.: Unsupervised perceptual rewards for imitation learning. arXiv preprint arXiv:1612.06699 (2016)

[TWS18] Torabi, F., Warnell, G., Stone, P.: Generative adversarial imitation from observation. arXiv preprint arXiv:1807.06158 (2018)

[WW14] Wender, S., Watson, I.: Combining case-based reasoning and reinforcement learning for unit navigation in real-time strategy game AI. In: Lamontagne, L., Plaza, E. (eds.) ICCBR 2014. LNCS (LNAI), vol. 8765, pp. 511–525. Springer, Cham (2014). https://doi.org/10.1007/978-3-319-11209-1_36

[YMH+19] Yang, C.: Imitation learning from observations by minimizing inverse dynamics disagreement. In: Advances in Neural Information Processing Systems 32 (2019)

[ZNY11] Zou, W.Y., Ng, A.Y., Yu, K.: Unsupervised learning of visual invariance with temporal coherence. In: NIPS 2011 Workshop on Deep Learning and Unsupervised Feature Learning, vol. 3 (2011)

Analogy-Based Post-treatment of CNN Image Segmentations

Justine Duck[1,2(✉)], Romain Schaller[2], Frédéric Auber[3], Yann Chaussy[3], Julien Henriet[1], Jean Lieber[2], Emmanuel Nauer[2], and Henri Prade[4]

[1] FEMTO-ST DISC, Univ. Bourgogne-Franche-Comté, 25000 Besançon, France
[2] Université de Lorraine, CNRS, Inria, LORIA, 54000 Nancy, France
justine.duck@femto-st.fr
[3] CHU / LNIT UFC, 25000 Besançon, France
[4] IRIT, CNRS, Université de Toulouse, Toulouse, France

Abstract. Convolutional neural networks (CNNs) have proven to be efficient tools for image segmentation when a large number of segmented images are available. However, when the number of segmented images is not so large, the CNN segmentations are less accurate. It is the case for nephroblastoma (kidney cancer) in particular. When a new patient arrives, the expert can only manually segment a sample of scanned images since manual segmentation is a time-consuming process. As a consequence, the question of how to compute accurate segmentations using both the trained CNN and such a sample is raised. A CBR approach based on proportional analogy is proposed in this paper. For a source image segmented by the expert, let a be the CNN segmentation of this image, b be its expert segmentation and c be the CNN segmentation of a target image close to the source image. The proposed approach aims at solving the analogical equation "a is to b as c is to d" with unknown d: the solution d of this equation is proposed as a segmentation of the target image. This approach and some of its improvements are evaluated and show an accuracy increase of the segmentation with respect to the CNN segmentation.

Keywords: Analogical extrapolation · Case-based reasoning · Convolutional neural networks · Medical image segmentation · Kidney cancer

1 Introduction

Convolutional neural networks (CNNs) constitute powerful tools for many tasks, such as image segmentation [9]. However, as many techniques of deep learning, they are demanding in terms of the computing time they require for the learning phase. This is particularly true when the dataset is continuously enriched, as it leads to re-run regularly the learning process. By contrast, case-based reasoning (CBR [14]) is usually less demanding in terms of computing time and also for the volume of resources (including cases) and it is "naturally" fitted to the continuous enrichment of the case base.

M. T. Keane and N. Wiratunga (Eds.): ICCBR 2022, LNAI 13405, pp. 318–332, 2022.
https://doi.org/10.1007/978-3-031-14923-8_21

This article studies the issue of using CBR to improve the results of a CNN when few additional data are available, without having to re-train the CNN. This issue is considered for an application of image segmentation of kidney cancer scans. More specifically, a CNN has been run on images segmented by an expert for 14 patients, with about 100 slices per patient. Given new patient's images, the CNN can propose some segmentations, but with an insufficient precision. To increase this precision, the expert manually segments about 10% of these images and then, the goal is to exploit this 10% to improve the precision of the CNN segmentations of the 90% remaining images. For this purpose, an approach called OV^{2}ASSION based on re-running the CNN with the additional examples (the 10%), has been studied in previous works. In this paper, an alternative approach to OV^{2}ASSION based on CBR methodology and on analogical proportions is studied.

After some necessary preliminaries (Sect. 2), a general approach is presented (Sect. 3) explaining how the CNN image segmentation can be modified by retrieval and adaptation of an image manually segmented. The result is a partial segmentation, meaning that some pixels are *undecided*. Section 4 presents some improvements to the approach, in particular, to make decisions for undecided pixels. Section 5 concludes and describes future directions of work.

2 Preliminaries

This section introduces the notions and notations that are useful for the article. Section 2.1 presents the issue of image segmentation, in the framework of kidney cancer images. Section 2.2 presents two deep-learning approaches for addressing this issue: one based on a CNN and one which is an improvement of this approach in the context of the study, called OV^{2}ASSION. This article proposes another improvement of the approach of the outcome of the CNN that is based on CBR and analogical proportions introduced in Sect. 2.3 and 2.4.

2.1 Image Segmentation and Its Application to Kidney Cancer Management

Nephroblastoma is one of the most frequently abdominal tumor observed in children (generally 1 to 5-year-old boys and girls). This cancer represents 5 to 14% of malignant paediatric tumors. This tumor is developped in the kidney. Most of the time, its initial diagnosis is based on imaging. Generally, ultrasounds are planned first in order to confirm its existence and approximate its position. Then, a CT-scan provides its position, and the healthy tissues and organs are reached with a higher accuracy. Radiologists and surgeons need 3D representation of the tumor and the border organs in order to plan the surgery (e.g. anticipate vascular risks, choose between a total or partial nephrectomy), and also to inform the family.

Image segmentation is a topic of image processing. It consists in associating a single label to each pixel of an image. In the field of health, segmenting a scan consists in defining the anatomical structure to which each pixel belongs. Segmentation is one of the key steps of the construction of 3D representations of all the organs, veins, arteries, cavities and other anatomical elements (such as a tumor). Formally, for an image of $m \times n$ pixels, let $\mathcal{Dom} = \{0, 1, \ldots, m-1\} \times \{0, 1, \ldots, n-1\}$. An image is a mapping associating to each $(i, j) \in \mathcal{Dom}$ the code for the color of the pixel. In this paper, only binary segmentations are considered: there are 2 labels, denoted by the Boolean values 0 and 1. More precisely, the segmentation distinguishes pixels associated to the tumor (label 1) from other pixels (label 0). Formally, a segmentation of a tumor is a mapping $\mathtt{S} : \mathcal{Dom} \to \{0, 1\}$. For $(i, j) \in \mathcal{Dom}$, $\mathtt{S}(i, j)$ is denoted by $\mathtt{S}_{ij}$.

Automatic segmentation is one of the actual key challenges of image processing since most of the time, and in the particular case of the segmentation of nephroblastoma in children, surgeons and radiologists must lead the segmentation process manually. The manual segmentation of the images of a kidney is time consuming (it requires about 6 to 8 hours of medical expert time [2]), hence the usefulness of tools for assisting these experts. The quality of an automatic or semi-automatic segmentation is evaluated comparing it to a reference one given by an expert. In the field of image processing applied to healthcare, the Dice coefficient is usually employed [4]. It gives a similarity value (on $[0, 1]$) between two segmentations $\mathtt{S}^1$ and $\mathtt{S}^2$ defined by

$$\mathtt{DICE}(\mathtt{S}^1, \mathtt{S}^2) = \frac{2 \times \text{number of } (i, j) \in \mathcal{Dom} \text{ such that } \mathtt{S}^1_{ij} = \mathtt{S}^2_{ij} = 1}{\#\mathtt{S}^1 + \#\mathtt{S}^2} \tag{1}$$

where $\#\mathtt{S}$ is the number of $(i, j) \in \mathcal{Dom}$ such that $\mathtt{S}_{ij} = 1$.

If $\mathtt{S}^1$ is the segmentation automatically computed, and $\mathtt{S}^2$ is the desired segmentation (the ground truth, given by the expert), the closest to 1 is $\mathtt{DICE}(\mathtt{S}^1, \mathtt{S}^2)$, the better the segmentation is and the least the expert has additional work to do.

Now, for N images of the same kidney (e.g. N slices as in Fig. 1) providing a 3D representation, a segmentation of this collection of images can be defined as $\mathbf{S} : k \in \{1, 2, \ldots, N\} \mapsto \mathbf{S}(k)$, where $\mathbf{S}(k)$ is a segmentation of the image number k. Now, given $\mathbf{S}^1$ and $\mathbf{S}^2$ two segmentations of the same collection of images, the Dice coefficient of $(\mathbf{S}^1, \mathbf{S}^2)$ can be computed with a definition similar to (1).[1] This is called the *3D Dice coefficient* in the following of the paper and provides a global assessment of a similarity between two collections of segmentations (e.g., for a given patient, the predicted collection of segmentations and the expert collection of segmentations).

The final 3D representations are used by surgeons and radiologists in order to plan the surgery, to have a clear vision of the healthy tissues and also to communicate with the children's families [2].

[1] $(i, j) \in \mathcal{Dom}$ is substituted by $((i, j), k) \in \mathcal{Dom} \times \{1, 2, \ldots, N\}$, $\mathtt{S}^1$ and $\mathtt{S}^2$ are substituted by $\mathbf{S}_1(k)$ and $\mathbf{S}_2(k)$ in the numerator and $\#\mathtt{S}^1 + \#\mathtt{S}^2$ is substituted with $\#\mathbf{S}_1 + \#\mathbf{S}_2$, where $\#\mathbf{S}$ is the number of $((i, j), k)$ such that $\mathbf{S}_{ij}(k)$.

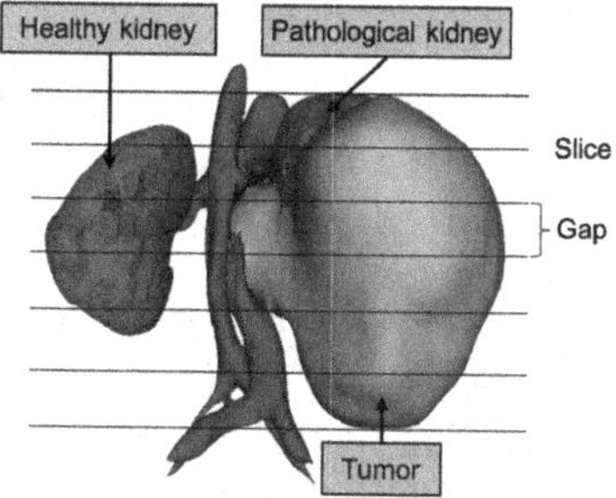

Fig. 1. 3D representation of a kidney with nephroblastoma, with the horizontal slices of the scanner imaging.

2.2 Using a CNN for Kidney Tumor Segmentation

Inside the deep learning paradigm, CNN principles [6] have been implemented in Fully Convolutional Network (FCN) [10], SegNet [1], DeconvNet [12], DeepLab [3], and appear to be high-performance tools for image segmentation.

In medical and biology applications, Thong et al. [16] used CNN to perform segmentation of healthy kidneys. U-Net [15] performed segmentation of cells in microscopy images. Currently, CNNs obtain accurate results on the recognition of the shape of a healthy kidney, because the shapes and areas are more or less the same from one subject to another. However, when the form of the considered structure is complex and varies a lot from one case to another, the segmentation is still a challenge. Neural networks for segmentation also need many heterogeneous data in order to be able to transcribe reliable results. In particular, pathological kidneys deformed by nephroblastoma have very different forms from one patient to another, with unpredictable shapes and situations. This then has led to find another method to segment more complicated structures with limited data.

Having a sufficiently large volume of data representative of all possible data is essential for training a deep neural network. As manual segmentation is expert time-consuming, at the scale of a hospital, the learning set composed of the entire segmented abdomens of patients may be composed of tens of cases only. This may not be large enough for conventional learning since each tumor and pathological kidney is unique and varies greatly from one patient to another. This is the reason why we have designed a new method for training on a small dataset: the OV^{2}ASSION (Overlearning Vector for Valid Sparse SegmentatIONs) [11]. As shown in Fig. 1, the OV^{2}ASSION method is based on the overlearning of some manually segmented slices of the patient, separated by a gap in order to calculate the segmentation of the entire set of unsegmented slices of this patient automatically. Each black line in this figure represents the selected slice for the training of the neural network. The gap between the chosen slices is the same in order to recover information homogeneously at different levels. This method is used in order to train a CNN based on the U-Net architecture.

2.3 Case-Based Reasoning

Let $\mathcal{P}$ (resp. $\mathcal{S}$) be a set. An element $\mathtt{x}$ of $\mathcal{P}$ (resp. $\mathtt{y}$ of $\mathcal{S}$) is called a *problem* (resp. a *solution*). A relation on $\mathcal{P} \times \mathcal{S}$ is assumed to exist, with the meaning "has for solution". A *case* is a pair $(\mathtt{x}, \mathtt{y}) \in \mathcal{P} \times \mathcal{S}$ such that $\mathtt{x}$ has for solution $\mathtt{y}$. This "has for solution" relation is not completely known to the system. However, it is assumed that some cases $(\mathtt{x}^s, \mathtt{y}^s) \in \mathcal{P} \times \mathcal{S}$ are known: they are the *source cases* and constitute the *case base* $\mathtt{CB}$.

CBR aims at solving a problem, called the *target problem* and denoted by $\mathtt{x}^{\mathtt{tgt}}$. A classical process model of CBR consists in (1) selecting k source cases relevant to solve $\mathtt{x}^{\mathtt{tgt}}$ (retrieval step), (2) inferring a solution $\mathtt{y}^{\mathtt{tgt}}$ of $\mathtt{x}^{\mathtt{tgt}}$ by reusing these source cases (adaptation step). If $k = 1$, step (2) is qualified as *single case adaptation*. Other steps, not considered here, follow adaptation.

2.4 Analogical Proportions

Following [13], an *analogical proportion* on a set $\mathcal{U}$ is a quaternary relation on $\mathcal{U}$ denoted, for $(a, b, c, d) \in \mathcal{U}^4$, by $a{:}b{::}c{:}d$ and read "a is to b as c is to d", that satisfies the following postulates:

- $a{:}b{::}a{:}b$ (*reflexivity*);
- if $a{:}b{::}c{:}d$ then $c{:}d{::}a{:}b$ (*symmetry*);
- if $a{:}b{::}c{:}d$ then $a{:}c{::}b{:}d$ (*central permutation*).

On the set $\mathcal{U} = \{0, 1\}$ of the Booleans, the minimal analogical proportion (according to the inclusion of quaternary relations) can be defined by

$$a{:}b{::}c{:}d \quad \text{if} \quad b - a = d - c$$

where the differences take their values in $\{-1, 0, 1\}$. Another analogical proportion, called in the following Sheldon Klein's proportion [5], can be defined by $|b - a| = |d - c|$.

An *analogical equation* is an expression of the form $a{:}b{::}c{:}?$ where ? is the unknown. For the minimal analogical proportion on Booleans, solving this equation consists in computing $b - a + c$: if this value belongs to $\{0, 1\}$ then it is the unique solution. Otherwise, $b - a + c \in \{-1, 2\}$ and the equation has no solution: the triples (a, b, c) such that $a{:}b{::}c{:}?$ has no solution are $(0, 1, 1)$ and $(1, 0, 0)$. By contrast, an equation $a{:}b{::}c{:}?$ based on Sheldon Klein proportional analogy always has a solution. If $(a, b, c) = (0, 1, 1)$ then the unique solution is 0. If $(a, b, c) = (1, 0, 0)$ then the unique solution is 1. Otherwise, the solution is the same as for the minimal analogical proportion, i.e., $b - a + c$.

Analogical proportions and analogical equations have been used in CBR in (at least) two ways. First, when the problem and solution spaces are not the same ($\mathcal{P} \neq \mathcal{S}$), a process called analogical extrapolation is applied (see e.g. [8]): it consists in retrieving $k = 3$ source cases whose problem parts are in analogy with the target problem and then in solving the analogical equation given by their solution parts. Second, when the problem and solution spaces are the same

($\mathcal{P} = \mathcal{S}$), a single case adaptation can be performed by solving an equation $\mathtt{x}^s\mathtt{:y}^s\mathtt{::x}^{\mathtt{tgt}}\mathtt{:?}$ (see [7]). In the following, analogical proportions are used according to this second way.

3 General Approach

This section presents the general approach to propose an alternative to OV²ASSION based on CBR. This approach outputs a *partial segmentation*, that is, a segmentation with some "undecided" pixels, as described in Sect. 3.1. Then, the problem setting is formulated in CBR terms (Sect. 3.2) and a CBR approach is proposed with a straightforward retrieval step (Sect. 3.3) and an adaptation step based on analogical proportions (Sect. 3.4). Finally, the approach is evaluated wrt OV²ASSION, from accuracy and computation time viewpoints (Sect. 3.5).

3.1 Partial Segmentations

A *partial segmentation* is a mapping $\mathtt{PS} : \mathcal{D}om \to \{0, \mathtt{u}, 1\}$ where $\mathtt{PS}_{ij} = 0$ and $\mathtt{PS}_{ij} = 1$ have the same meaning as for segmentations and $\mathtt{PS}_{ij} = \mathtt{u}$ means that PS is *undecided* about the status of the pixel. For some computations in this paper, u is replaced by the value 0.5. A partial segmentation $\mathtt{PS}'$ *extends* a partial segmentation PS means that, for every $(i,j) \in \mathcal{D}om$, if $\mathtt{PS}_{ij} \neq \mathtt{u}$ then $\mathtt{PS}'_{ij} = \mathtt{PS}_{ij}$.

Now, in order to evaluate a partial segmentation $\mathtt{PS}^1$ proposed by the system in comparison to a reference segmentation $\mathtt{S}^2$, the idea is to consider the values $\mathtt{DICE}(\mathtt{S}^1, \mathtt{S}^2)$ for $\mathtt{S}^1$ in the set of segmentations that extend $\mathtt{PS}^1$. Following this idea, the definition of pessimistic, optimistic and average Dice coefficients (the latter being the average of the two formers) can be defined:

$$\mathtt{DICE}^{\mathtt{pessim}}(\mathtt{PS}^1, \mathtt{S}^2) = \min \left\{\mathtt{DICE}(\mathtt{S}^1, \mathtt{S}^2) \mid \mathtt{S}^1 \text{ extends } \mathtt{PS}^1\right\} \tag{2}$$

$$\mathtt{DICE}^{\mathtt{optim}}(\mathtt{PS}^1, \mathtt{S}^2) = \max \left\{\mathtt{DICE}(\mathtt{S}^1, \mathtt{S}^2) \mid \mathtt{S}^1 \text{ extends } \mathtt{PS}^1\right\} \tag{3}$$

$$\mathtt{DICE}^{\mathtt{avg}}(\mathtt{PS}^1, \mathtt{S}^2) = \left(\mathtt{DICE}^{\mathtt{pessim}}(\mathtt{PS}^1, \mathtt{S}^2) + \mathtt{DICE}^{\mathtt{optim}}(\mathtt{PS}^1, \mathtt{S}^2)\right)/2 \tag{4}$$

Pessimistic and optimistic Dice coefficients can be computed as follows. Let $\mathtt{S}^{1,\mathtt{pessim}}$ and $\mathtt{S}^{1,\mathtt{optim}}$ be the segmentations extending $\mathtt{PS}^1$ such that, for $(i,j) \in \mathcal{D}om$:

$$\mathtt{S}^{1,\mathtt{pessim}}_{ij} = \begin{cases} 1 - \mathtt{S}^2_{ij} & \text{if } \mathtt{PS}^1_{ij} = \mathtt{u} \\ \mathtt{PS}^1_{ij} & \text{otherwise} \end{cases} \qquad \mathtt{S}^{1,\mathtt{optim}}_{ij} = \begin{cases} \mathtt{S}^2_{ij} & \text{if } \mathtt{PS}^1_{ij} = \mathtt{u} \\ \mathtt{PS}^1_{ij} & \text{otherwise} \end{cases}$$

It can be shown that the pessimistic and optimistic Dice coefficients can be computed according to the following equalities:

$$\mathtt{DICE}^{\mathtt{pessim}}(\mathtt{PS}^1, \mathtt{S}^2) = \mathtt{DICE}(\mathtt{S}^{1,\mathtt{pessim}}, \mathtt{S}^2) \quad \mathtt{DICE}^{\mathtt{optim}}(\mathtt{PS}^1, \mathtt{S}^2) = \mathtt{DICE}(\mathtt{S}^{1,\mathtt{optim}}, \mathtt{S}^2)$$

3.2 Problem Setting in CBR Terms

It is assumed that a CNN has been trained on the images of a set of patients and that it can be used on a new patient to propose segmentations. This CNN is used in this approach as a black box:

$$\mathtt{CNN} : \text{scanner image of a slice} \mapsto \text{proposed segmentation of this image}$$

Now, let $\{\mathtt{image}^1, \mathtt{image2}, \ldots, \mathtt{image}^N\}$ be the set of scanner images of slices for the new patient, at the level of the kidneys. The image indexes are ordered from the top to the bottom: $\mathtt{image}^i$ is above $\mathtt{image}^{i+1}$ ($i \in \{1, 2, \ldots, N-1\}$). In this application, for the new patient, $N = 136$ (there is a variation of the value of N depending on the size of the kidney which depends in particular on the age of the patient). Only a sample $\{\mathtt{image}^s \mid s \in \mathtt{IIMS}\}$ of images are manually segmented, to lower the required expert time ($\mathtt{IIMS}$ is the set of indexes of the images that are manually segmented). In this application, $\mathtt{IIMS} = \{1+11k \mid k \in \{0, 1, \ldots, 12\}\}$, so the required manual segmentation is about 30 to 45 minutes of expert time. For $s \in \mathtt{IIMS}$, two segmentations are available:

- The segmentation computed by the CNN and denoted in the following $\mathtt{x}^s$: $\mathtt{x}^s = \mathtt{CNN}(\mathtt{image}^s)$;
- The manual segmentation of $\mathtt{image}^s$ given by the expert and denoted in the following $\mathtt{y}^s$.

The pair $(\mathtt{x}^s, \mathtt{y}^s)$ is considered as a source case that encodes the experience of *correcting* the CNN segmentation. So, the case base is $\mathtt{CB} = \{(\mathtt{x}^s, \mathtt{y}^s) \mid s \in \mathtt{IIMS}\}$.

Now, let $\mathtt{IINMS} = \{1, 2, \ldots, N\} \setminus \mathtt{IIMS}$, the set of indexes of images for which no manual segmentation is available. Let $\mathtt{tgt} \in \mathtt{IINMS}$ and $\mathtt{x}^{\mathtt{tgt}} = \mathtt{CNN}(\mathtt{image}^{\mathtt{tgt}})$. The objective is to find a segmentation $\mathtt{y}^{\mathtt{tgt}}$ of $\mathtt{image}^{\mathtt{tgt}}$ by reusing $\mathtt{CB}$, the available experience on CNN to expert corrections in the context of the new patient. For this purpose, a classical CBR approach with the retrieval of a single source case and an adaptation of this case is considered.

3.3 Retrieval

In this application, the implemented case retrieval is straightforward: for a given target problem $\mathtt{x}^{\mathtt{tgt}}$ with $\mathtt{tgt} \in \mathtt{IINMS}$, the source case $(\mathtt{x}^s, \mathtt{y}^s)$ which minimizes $|s - \mathtt{tgt}|$ is chosen. This choice is justified by the fact that the CNN segmentation of the tumor varies rather smoothly according to the slice vertical position.

3.4 Adaptation Using an Analogical Proportion

Given the target problem $\mathtt{x}^{\mathtt{tgt}}$ and the retrieved case $(\mathtt{x}^s, \mathtt{y}^s)$, the adaptation consists in considering that the proposed solution $\mathtt{y}^{\mathtt{tgt}}$ to $\mathtt{x}^{\mathtt{tgt}}$ is such that $\mathtt{x}^s$ is to $\mathtt{y}^s$ as $\mathtt{x}^{\mathtt{tgt}}$ is to $\mathtt{y}^{\mathtt{tgt}}$. In other words, the expert "correction" from $\mathtt{x}^s$ to $\mathtt{y}^s$ is applied on $\mathtt{x}^{\mathtt{tgt}}$. The implemented approach works at the pixel level, meaning that it is based on the analogical equations $\mathtt{x}^s_{ij}{:}\mathtt{y}^s_{ij}{::}\mathtt{x}^{\mathtt{tgt}}_{ij}{:}?$ for each $(i, j) \in \mathcal{D}om$.

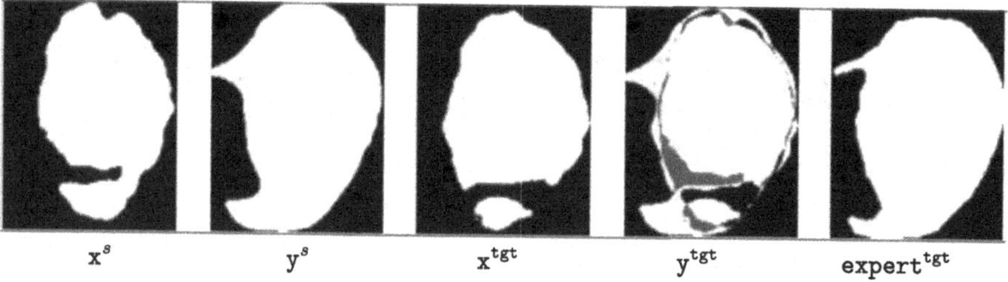

Fig. 2. Example of adaptation based on the proposed approach, with segmentations $\mathtt{x}^s$, $\mathtt{y}^s$ and $\mathtt{x}^{\mathtt{tgt}}$, and partial segmentation $\mathtt{y}^{\mathtt{tgt}}$. In a (partial) segmentation $\mathtt{S}$, $\mathtt{S}_{ij} = 1$ (resp. $\mathtt{S}_{ij} = 0$) is represented by a white (resp. black) pixel. For the partial segmentation $\mathtt{PS} = \mathtt{y}^{\mathtt{tgt}}$, $\mathtt{PS}_{ij} = \mathtt{u}$ is represented by a green pixel. $\mathtt{x}^s$ and $\mathtt{y}^s$ correspond to slice number $s = 90$, $\mathtt{x}^{\mathtt{tgt}}$, $\mathtt{y}^{\mathtt{tgt}}$ and $\mathtt{expert}^{\mathtt{tgt}}$ correspond to slice number $\mathtt{tgt} = 85$, respectively corresponding to what the CNN proposes, how the CBR approach corrects it and what the expert gives.

The minimal analogical equation is chosen, thus such an equation may have no solution. Therefore, the result of this adaptation is only a partial segmentation.

Formally, adaptation is computed this way:

- For each $(i, j) \in \mathcal{D}om$,
  - Solve the analogical equation $\mathtt{x}^s_{ij}{:}\mathtt{y}^s_{ij}{::}\mathtt{x}^{\mathtt{tgt}}_{ij}{:}?$.
  - If it has no solution, then $\mathtt{y}^{\mathtt{tgt}}_{ij} \leftarrow \mathtt{u}$.
  - Otherwise, let d be the solution of this equation.[2] Then $\mathtt{y}^{\mathtt{tgt}}_{ij} \leftarrow d$.
- The partial segmentation $\mathtt{y}^{\mathtt{tgt}}$ is proposed as a (partial) solution to $\mathtt{x}^{\mathtt{tgt}}$.

Figure 2 presents an example of the outcome of such a process.

3.5 Evaluation

The data for this evaluation are constituted by the scanner images of 14 patients with about 100 images per patient and an expert segmentation for each image. A CNN was trained on the images and segmentations of 13 patients. For the 14th patient, the expert segmentations of 1/11 images where kept, with a constant gap between them, which has constituted the case base. The approach was tested on the 10/11 images remaining.

Figure 3 and Table 1 present the results with pessimistic, average and optimistic 3D Dice coefficients, compared to the 3D Dice coefficients for the segmentations provided by the CNN and by OV^{2}ASSION. The figure presents these results slice by slice, for slices number 40 to 100 (for the other slices, the number of pixels for the predicted and expert segmentations that belong to the tumor is very low, making the Dice coefficient of little relevance). The table presents these results with 3D Dice coefficients, comparing predicted and expert segmentations on the tumor as a whole.

[2] With the chosen analogical proportion, the solution, when it exists is unique.

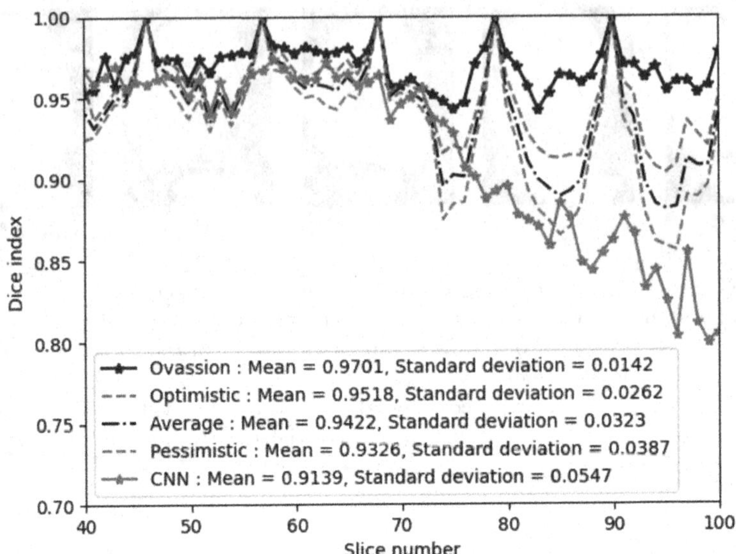

Fig. 3. Evaluation of the approach, slice by slice.

Table 1. Dice evaluation and calculation time of the general approach. For approaches without undecided pixels (CNN and OV^{2}ASSION), the values $\texttt{DICE}^{\texttt{avg}}$ and $\texttt{DICE}$ are equal. The computation time does not include the CNN training.

Approach	$\texttt{DICE}^{\texttt{pessim}}$	$\texttt{DICE}^{\texttt{avg}}$	$\texttt{DICE}^{\texttt{optim}}$	Calculation time (s)
OV^{2}ASSION	—	0.9489	—	$762 + 209 = 971$
Proposed approach	0.8806	0.8974	0.9143	$299 + 473 = 772$
CNN	—	0.8648	—	299

The initial CNN training (with 200 epochs, and with 16 as batch size) took 2 h and 42 min and the segmentation 5 min (this time is common to the three approaches). As indicated in Table 1, the computation on the images of the new patient take 299 sec with the trained CNN, 772 sec with our proposed approach (written in Python), and 971 with OV^{2}ASSION[3].

This shows that the simple case-based approach presented in this section actually improves the output of the CNN thanks to a sample of additional segmentations, but that it is still overcome by the OV^{2}ASSION approach using the same sample (and using a little bit more time). It also shows that the choice of values for undecided pixels could improve the approach, which is studied in the next section.

[3] All these computations have been made on the Mesocenter of computation of Franche-Comté, equiped of processor Intel(R) Xeon(R) Gold 6126 CPU @2.60GHz and Nvidia Volta V100 GPU

4 Improvements of the Approach Based on Post-processing Techniques

This section presents some ways to improve the approach of Sect. 3 and ends with an evaluation.

4.1 Two Local Strategies for Choosing a Value for Undecided Pixels

An analogical equation $a{:}b{::}c{:}?$ on Booleans with minimal analogical proportion has no solution d for $(a, b, c) \in \{(0,1,1),(1,0,0)\}$. Two ways of proposing a solution are considered.

First, considering the Sheldon Klein proportion gives the solution $d = 1 - c$.

Second, considering that the patterns for minimal analogical proportions are (u, u, v, v) and (u, v, u, v) $(u, v \in \{0, 1\})$, the solution requiring the least modifications to these patterns are $d = 1$ for $(a, b, c) = (0, 1, 1)$ and $d = 0$ for $(a, b, c) = (1, 0, 0)$, i.e., $d = c$ for both cases (where the considered modifications are flips of Boolean values). This strategy is called *conservative approach* in the following.

Therefore, these two strategies give the opposite proposition for changing a value $\mathtt{y}_{ij}^{\mathtt{tgt}} = \mathtt{u}$ to $\mathtt{y}_{ij}^{\mathtt{tgt}} \in \{0, 1\}$. These two strategies have been compared, following the same evaluation protocol as in Sect. 3.5, and gives a significant preference for the second one (cf. the evaluation, at the end of this section).

4.2 Use of Convolution Masks

The approaches presented and compared in Sect. 4.1 are limited by the fact that they do not take into account the context, i.e., the segmentations of the pixels that are around an undecided pixel. For example, it seems natural to consider that an undecided pixel surrounded by pixels that are all 0s or all 1s is likely to be associated with the same common value. More generally, the strategy consists in choosing the "main tendancy" of these pixels. For this purpose, a convolution mask is used. By contrast to the CNN approach, the weights of such a mask are not learned but are chosen parameters.

For the sake of simplicity of the presentation, in this section, for a partial segmentation $\mathtt{PS}$, if (i, j) is an "out of bound index" pair (i.e., $(i, j) \notin \mathcal{Dom}$), then $\mathtt{PS}_{ij} = \mathtt{u}$ (the undecided value $\mathtt{u}$ is assimilated to $\mathtt{u} = 0.5$). 3 types of convolution masks were tested, with different values of their weights, knowing that the results (described in§4.4) are poorly sensitive to the choice of the weights.

Use of a 3×3 *Convolution.* A 3×3 convolution mask is a 3×3 matrix $\mathtt{M}$ of real numbers, assumed to be indexed on $\{-1, 0, 1\}$ (i.e., $\mathtt{M}_{kl}$ is defined for $-1 \leq k, \ell \leq 1$). Following a symmetry principle, the masks considered here are of the form $\begin{bmatrix} w_C & w_B & w_C \\ w_B & w_M & w_B \\ w_C & w_B & w_C \end{bmatrix}$, thus are parametrized by w_M (the weight at the middle), w_B (the weight at a border) and w_C (the weight at a corner). Moreover, the mask is assumed to be normalized: the sum of its elements is $w_M + 4w_B + 4w_C = 1$.

Given a partial segmentation PS and a mask M, a new partial segmentation PS′ is defined as follows, for $(i, j) \in \mathcal{D}om$:

$$\text{with } \sigma = \sum_{(k,\ell)\in\{-1,0,1\}^2} \mathtt{M}_{k\ell} \times \mathtt{PS}_{i+k,j+\ell}, \qquad \mathtt{PS}'_{ij} = \begin{cases} 0 & \text{if } \sigma < 0.5 \\ \mathtt{u} & \text{if } \sigma = 0.5 \\ 1 & \text{otherwise} \end{cases}$$

This partial segmentation PS′ is then proposed as a result.

Different values of the parameter triple (w_M, w_B, w_C) were considered. In order to have PS′ extending PS, the choice $w_M > 0.5$ was made: when $\mathtt{PS}_{ij} = \mathtt{u}$, this weight is of no consequence on the decision made and when $\mathtt{PS}_{ij} \neq \mathtt{u}$ then $\mathtt{PS}'_{ij} = \mathtt{PS}_{ij}$. As a consequence, $w_M > 4w_B + 4w_C$: the weight of the middle is greater than the weight of all the other pixels (borders and corners). Moreover, the relation $w_B > w_C$ was made, since the non-corner borders of the mask being closest to the middle that the corners, they have more importance. With these constraints, various values of the parameter triple were chosen, given similar result. The evaluation was made with the triple $(0.6, 0.075, 0.025)$.

Use of a 5×5 *Convolution.* A 5×5 convolution mask was used in a similar way. The convolution mask is based on 6-tuple of weights (because of the symmetry, there are only 6 different values and they are ordered in the tuple by decreasing distance to the center). The evaluation was carried out with the weight tuple $(0.6, 0.05, 0.025, 0.025, 0, 0)$.

Use of a $3 \times 3 \times 3$ *Convolution.* A $3 \times 3 \times 3$ mask is the fusion of three 3×3 masks obtained on the target slice and the slices preceding and following this target slice. This construction supposes beforehand to have obtained the partial segmentations of all the target slices. The $3D$ convolution mask is based on a 4-tuple of weights (because of the symmetry, there are only 4 different values and they are ordered in the tuple by decreasing distance to the center). In the experiment, the chosen tuple was $(0.6, 0.0333, 0.0083, 0.0125)$.

4.3 Use of Closures

The idea has emerged to use convex closures for improving the result and then, more generally, to use other closure functions.

Convex closure and other closures. Given a set X of points of the plane, the *convex closure* (also called convex hull) of X, is the minimal set of points $\mathcal{CC}(X)$ such that for every pair $(P, Q) \in X^2$, the segment $[P, Q]$ is included in X. Formally:

$$\mathcal{CC}(X) = \bigcup \{[P, Q] \mid (P, Q) \in X^2\}$$

The function $\mathcal{CC}$ belongs to the family of closure functions. A *closure function* $\mathcal{C}$ on sets of points X is a function that is extensive ($X \subseteq \mathcal{C}(X)$), non-decreasing (if $X \subseteq Y$ then $\mathcal{C}(X) \subseteq \mathcal{C}(Y)$), and idempotent ($\mathcal{C}(\mathcal{C}(X)) = \mathcal{C}(X)$).

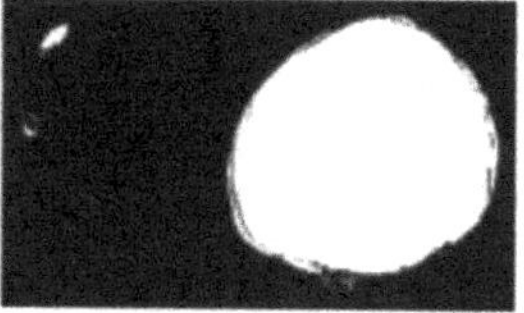 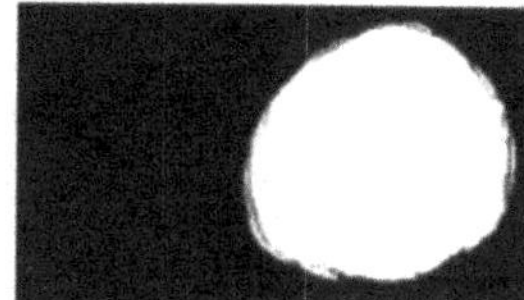 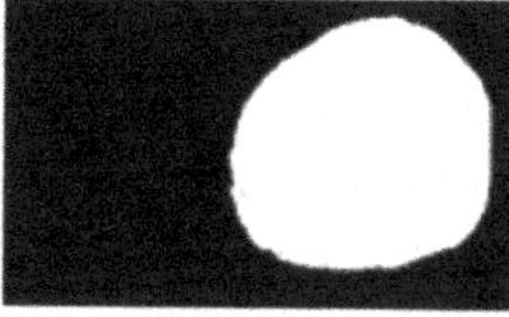

Fig. 4. Example of post-treatment using the rectangular closure. Left: $\mathtt{y}^{\mathtt{tgt}}$ provided by the approach of §3. Center: correction of $\mathtt{y}^{\mathtt{tgt}}$ using rectangular closure. Right: expert segmentation.

Another example of closures on sets of points of the Euclidian plane is $\mathcal{C}_\Delta$, where Δ is a line of the plan: for a set of points X of the plane, $\mathcal{C}_\Delta(X)$ is defined in a similar way as $\mathcal{CC}(X)$, except that the segment $[P, Q]$ has to be parallel to Δ. In particular, given an affine coordinate system Oxy, horizontal closures (resp. vertical closure, rising diagonal closure, and downward diagonal closure) is the closure $\mathcal{C}_\Delta$ where Δ is defined by the equation $y = 0$ (resp. $x = 0$, $y = x$ and $y = -x$). A final example of closure is the rectangular closure, i.e., the smallest rectangle whose edges are parallel to the axis that contains all the values of a set of points X.

How to use closures for the post-treatment. The notions of closures are defined on sets of points of the plane, but are applied on images, making the approximation that a pixel corresponds to a point. Moreover, a segmentation $\mathtt{S}$ is assimilated to the set of pixels (or points) $(i, j) \in \mathcal{D}om$ such that $\mathtt{S}_{ij} = 1$: $\mathtt{S} = \{(i, j) \in \mathcal{D}om \mid \mathtt{S}_{ij} = 1\}$, hence the notion of closure $\mathcal{C}(\mathtt{S})$ of a segmentation $\mathtt{S}$ (given a closure function).

Now, given three segmentations $\mathtt{x}^s$, $\mathtt{y}^s$ and $\mathtt{x}^{\mathtt{tgt}}$ (corresponding to a source case $(\mathtt{x}^s, \mathtt{y}^s)$ and a target problem $\mathtt{x}^{\mathtt{tgt}}$), the approach of Sect. 3 (possibly with some post-treatments of the current section) provides a partial segmentation $\mathtt{y}^{\mathtt{tgt}}$. For each of these three segmentations, a closure can be computed with a closure function $\mathcal{C}$, hence the three segmentations $\mathcal{C}(\mathtt{x}^s)$, $\mathcal{C}(\mathtt{y}^s)$ and $\mathcal{C}(\mathtt{x}^{\mathtt{tgt}})$. Then, a partial segmentation $\mathtt{PS}$ can be found by applying the Sect. 3 approach on these three segmentations: $\mathtt{PS}_{ij}$ is obtained by solving the analogical equations $\mathcal{C}(\mathtt{x}^s)_{ij}{:}\mathcal{C}(\mathtt{y}^s)_{ij}{::}\mathcal{C}(\mathtt{x}^{\mathtt{tgt}})_{ij}{:}?$ (for any $(i, j) \in \mathcal{D}om$). This partial segmentation $\mathtt{PS}$ is used as a prediction of the closure of the desired segmentation. Thus, for $(i, j) \in \mathcal{D}om$, it is expected that $\mathtt{y}^{\mathtt{tgt}}_{ij} \leq \mathtt{PS}_{ij}$. Therefore, the situation $\mathtt{y}^{\mathtt{tgt}}_{ij} > \mathtt{PS}_{ij}$ is considered to be abnormal and, when it occurs, $\mathtt{y}^{\mathtt{tgt}}$ is changed into $\mathtt{PS}_{ij}$. Figure 4 shows that a closure can remove distant noisy pixels. This approach has been tested for horizontal, vertical, rising diagonal, downward diagonal, and rectangular closures.

Table 2. Evaluation of various improvement strategies.

Method	$\mathtt{DICE}^{\mathtt{pessim}}$	$\mathtt{DICE}^{\mathtt{avg}}$	$\mathtt{DICE}^{\mathtt{optim}}$	Computation time (s)
$OV^2ASSION$	—	0.9489	—	$762 + 209$
(b) conservative approach	—	0.9129	—	$299 + 473 + 471$
(c) 5×5 convolution	0.9078	0.9078	0.9078	$299 + 473 + 643$
(c) 3×3 convolution	0.8984	0.9056	0.9128	$299 + 473 + 496$
(c) $3 \times 3 \times 3$ convolution	0.9010	0.9028	0.9045	$299 + 473 + 711$
(a) general approach	0.8806	0.8974	0.9143	$299 + 473$
(d) rectangular closure	0.8713	0.8904	0.9095	$299 + 473 + 1644$
(d) horizontal closure	0.8635	0.8829	0.9024	$299 + 473 + 1626$
(d) vertical closure	0.8630	0.8828	0.9026	$299 + 473 + 1632$
(b) Sheldon Klein	—	0.8820	—	$299 + 473 + 487$
(d) rising diagonal closure	0.8621	0.8815	0.9010	$299 + 473 + 1573$
(d) downward diagonal closure	0.8612	0.8808	0.9005	$299 + 473 + 1385$
CNN	—	0.8648	—	299

(a) General approach, providing a partial segmentation (cf. §3).
(b) Using two local strategies for choosing a value for undecided pixels (cf. §4.1).
(c) Using convolution masks (cf. §4.2).
(d) Using horizontal, vertical, diagonal and rectangular closures (cf. §4.3).

4.4 Evaluation

Table 2 presents an evaluation of the different segmentation approaches: CNN, $OV^2ASSION$, the case-based approach of Sect. 3, and the improvements of this approach proposed in the current section.

The lines are ordered by decreasing 3D $\mathtt{DICE}^{\mathtt{avg}}$. For these data, the best result, according to $\mathtt{DICE}^{\mathtt{avg}}$ is obtained by applying the general approach of Sect. 3 followed by the conservative choice of pixels described in Sect. 4.1. It is noteworthy that (1) for other segmentation problems (e.g. kidneys) this order may be different and (2) some of the other approaches may be improved.

For this first version of our approach, the results are just over the middle between CNN and $OV^2ASSION$ ones, but there is room for improvement, as is detailed in the conclusion of the paper. Every approach considered here uses the CNN computation (that requires 2 h and 42 m of computing time).

The required computing times of our best approach and $OV^2ASSION$ are similar (1243 s for the former and 971 s for the latter, knowing that the former has been programmed in Python and the second uses a highly optimized library). Now, if the expert just want an improvement of the CNN segmentation of one slice (at at time), as a starting point for manual segmentation, our approach needs only about $1243/100 \simeq 12$ s.

5 Conclusion

This article has presented a first case-based approach to improve CNN-based image segmentations given a new sample of expert segmentations from the current context, i.e., in the application, in the context of a new patient suffering from nephroblastoma. This approach improves the result of the CNN but gives still less accurate results than the OV^{2}ASSION approach that consists in re-running the CNN with the additional segmentation sample.

This work gives encouraging results, but has to be improved. Other directions of work follow this study.

First, it can be noticed that the approach presented in this paper relies only on segmentations (given by the CNN and the experts). By contrast, the CNN and the OV^{2}ASSION system use also the images taken from the scanner, with gray levels. A future work aims at using these images for improving the approach. This can be done as an additional post-processing technique for the choice of undecided values for segmentation. This can be done also by using analogical proportions directly on gray levels. More precisely, the idea is as follows. With the current approach, the adaptation consists in solving the analogical equation

$$\mathtt{x}^s{:}\mathtt{y}^s{::}\mathtt{x}^{\mathtt{tgt}}{:}?$$

pixel by pixel. Now, if the mapping of $\mathtt{image}$, an image described by gray levels, into a segmentation $\mathtt{S}$ is denoted by $(\mathtt{image} \mapsto \mathtt{S})$ then, the adaptation would consist in solving the analogical equation

$$(\mathtt{image}^s \mapsto \mathtt{x}^s){:}(\mathtt{image}^s \mapsto \mathtt{y}^s){::}(\mathtt{image}^{\mathtt{tgt}} \mapsto \mathtt{x}^{\mathtt{tgt}}){:}?$$

and obtaining a mapping $(\mathtt{image}^{\mathtt{tgt}} \mapsto \mathtt{y}^{\mathtt{tgt}})$ from which a segmentation would be obtained. How to actually realize this idea is still a challenging question.

A second work consists in studying the use of geometrical moments of a segmentation, i.e. the area of the set of tumor pixels, its centroid and its orientation. The principle is that the geometrical moments can be predicted by analogy (e.g. by solving in $\mathbb{R}$ the analogical equation $\mathtt{area}(\mathtt{x}^s){:}\mathtt{area}(\mathtt{y}^s){::}\mathtt{area}(\mathtt{x}^{\mathtt{tgt}}){:}?$) and to use these predictions to modify $\mathtt{y}^{\mathtt{tgt}}$ (e.g. by making choices for undecided pixels based on the difference between the predicted area and $\mathtt{area}(\mathtt{y}^{\mathtt{tgt}})$).

Third, it is planned to use the interpolation approach presented in [8] to improve the results. This approach is based on the retrieval of two source cases $(\mathtt{x}^r, \mathtt{y}^r)$ and $(\mathtt{x}^s, \mathtt{y}^s)$ such that $\mathtt{x}^{\mathtt{tgt}}$ is *between* $\mathtt{x}^r$ and $\mathtt{x}^s$. Then, it is plausibly inferred that the expected segmentation $\mathtt{y}^{\mathtt{tgt}}$ has to be between $\mathtt{y}^r$ and $\mathtt{y}^s$ (at a pixel by pixel level or globally).

Fourth, the search for a smart combination of these approaches remains to be studied.

Finally, these approaches will be tested for other anatomical structures which still challenge the segmentation using CNN and OV^{2}ASSION: kidneys, veins, arteries, and cavities.

Acknowledgement. The authors would like to thank the European Union for financing this project as part of the SAIAD and SAIAD 2 INTERREG V programs and the SAIAD and SAIAD 2 consortiums partners. Computations have been performed on the supercomputer facilities of the *Franche-Comté Computation Mesocenter*.

References

1. Badrinarayanan, V., Kendall, A., Cipolla, R.: Segnet: a deep convolutional encoder-decoder architecture for image segmentation. IEEE Trans. Pattern Anal. Mach. Intell. **39**(12), 2481–2495 (2017)
2. Chaussy, Y., et al.: 3D reconstruction of Wilms' tumor and kidneys in children: variability, usefulness and constraints. J. Pediatr. Urol. **16**(16), 830.e1-830.e8 (2020)
3. Chen, L.C., Papandreou, G., Kokkinos, I., Murphy, K., Yuille, A.L.: Deeplab: semantic image segmentation with deep convolutional nets, atrous convolution, and fully connected CRFs. IEEE Trans. Pattern Anal. Mach. Intell. **40**(4), 834–848 (2017)
4. Dice, L.R.: Measures of the amount of ecologic association between species. Ecology **26**(3), 297–302 (1945)
5. Klein, S.: Analogy and mysticism and the structure of culture (and Comments & Reply). Curr. Anthropol. **24**(2), 151–180 (1983)
6. LeCun, Y., Bengio, Y., Hinton, G.: Deep learning. Nature **521**(7553), 436 (2015)
7. Lepage, Y., Lieber, J., Mornard, I., Nauer, E., Romary, J., Sies, R.: *The French Correction*: when retrieval is harder to specify than adaptation. In: Watson, I., Weber, R. (eds.) ICCBR 2020. LNCS (LNAI), vol. 12311, pp. 309–324. Springer, Cham (2020). https://doi.org/10.1007/978-3-030-58342-2_20
8. Lieber, J., Nauer, E., Prade, H., Richard, G.: Making the best of cases by approximation, interpolation and extrapolation. In: Cox, M.T., Funk, P., Begum, S. (eds.) ICCBR 2018. LNCS (LNAI), vol. 11156, pp. 580–596. Springer, Cham (2018). https://doi.org/10.1007/978-3-030-01081-2_38
9. Litjens, G., Kooi, T., Bejnordi, B.E., Setio, A.A.A., Ciompi, F., Ghafoorian, M., van der Laak, J.A., van Ginneken, B., Sánchez, C.I.: A survey on deep learning in medical image analysis. Med. Image Anal. **42**, 66–88 (2017)
10. Long, J., Shelhamer, E., Darrell, T.: Fully convolutional networks for semantic segmentation. In: Proceedings of the IEEE conference on computer vision and pattern recognition, pp. 3431–3440 (2015)
11. Marie, F., Corbat, L., Chaussy, Y., Delavelle, T., Henriet, J., Lapayre, J.C.: Segmentation of deformed kidneys and nephroblastoma using case-based reasoning and convolutional neural network. Expert Syst. Appl. **127**, 282–294 (2019)
12. Noh, H., Hong, S., Han, B.: Learning deconvolution network for semantic segmentation. In: Proceedings of the IEEE international conference on computer vision, pp. 1520–1528 (2015)
13. Prade, H., Richard, G.: Analogical proportions: why they are useful in AI. In: Zhou, Z.-H. (ed.) Proceedings 30th International Joint Conference on Artificial Intelligence (IJCAI-21), Virtual Event/Montreal, 19–27 August, pp. 4568–4576 (2021)
14. Riesbeck, C.K., Schank, R.C.: Inside Case-Based Reasoning. Lawrence Erlbaum Associates Inc., Hillsdale, New Jersey (1989)
15. Ronneberger, O., Fischer, P., Brox, T.: U-Net: convolutional networks for biomedical image segmentation. In: Navab, N., Hornegger, J., Wells, W.M., Frangi, A.F. (eds.) MICCAI 2015. LNCS, vol. 9351, pp. 234–241. Springer, Cham (2015). https://doi.org/10.1007/978-3-319-24574-4_28
16. Thong, W., Kadoury, S., Piché, N., Pal, C.J.: Convolutional networks for kidney segmentation in contrast-enhanced CT scans. Comput. Methods Biomech. Biomed. Eng.: Imaging Vis. **6**(3), 277–282 (2018)

Case-Based Applications

An Extended Case-Based Approach to Race-Time Prediction for Recreational Marathon Runners

Ciara Feely[1,2,3(✉)], Brian Caulfield[1,3], Aonghus Lawlor[1,3], and Barry Smyth[1,3]

[1] School of Computer Science, University College Dublin, Dublin, Ireland
ciara.feely@ucdconnect.ie,
{b.caulfield,aonghus.lawlor,barry.smyth}@ucd.ie
[2] SFI Centre for Research Training in Machine Learning, Dublin, Ireland
[3] Insight Centre for Data Analytics, University College Dublin, Dublin, Ireland

Abstract. As running has become an increasingly popular method of personal exercise, more and more recreational runners have been testing themselves by participating in endurance events such as marathons. Even though elite endurance runners have been the subject of considerable research, the training habits and performance potential of recreational runners are not as well-understood. Consequently, recreational runners often have to rely on one-size-fits-all training programmes and race prediction models. As a result, recreational runners frequently suffer from a lack of expert feedback during training and if their race-time prediction is inaccurate this can significantly disrupt their race planning and lead to a sub-optimal race-time after months of hard work. The main contribution of this work is to describe an extended case-based reasoning system for predicting the race-times of recreational runners which, for the first time, uses a combination of training history and past race-times in order to improve prediction accuracy. The work is evaluated using real-world data from more than 150,000 marathon training programmes.

Keywords: Marathon running · CBR for health and fitness · Race-time prediction

1 Introduction

As the number of people participating in endurance events, such as marathons, continues to grow so too does the demand and desire for expert training advice and improved race-time predictions. Yet, most recreational runners cannot benefit from a coach of their own leaving many to fend for themselves when it comes to the cacophony of 'expert' advice, one-size-fits-all training programmes, and must-try race-plans that exist online. This can be overwhelming and demoralising for runners, especially novices and first-timers because it can be difficult to know who to trust and what to pay attention to. At best this can lead to less than perfect training and sub-optimal race-times, at worst it can leave runners injured and heart-broken if they miss their race after months of hard effort.

M. T. Keane and N. Wiratunga (Eds.): ICCBR 2022, LNAI 13405, pp. 335–349, 2022.
https://doi.org/10.1007/978-3-031-14923-8_22

This work builds on previous efforts to help support marathon runners during training and racing, by taking advantage of the wealth of data that is generated from today's wearable sensors, smartphones, and smartwatches – which track every aspect of how we train and recover – and combining it with ideas from machine learning and case-based reasoning to help guide a recreational runner as they train and race. In particular, we focus on race-time prediction – a vital component of pre-race preparation for every marathon runner to help them plan their pacing – and, using feature selection techniques we combine two previous approaches, which separately used training data [1,2] and race history data [3–6], to provide more accurate predictions than either approach alone. Furthermore, we compare this new approach to race-time prediction to previous approaches using a significantly expanded dataset comprising more than 80,000 unique runners, 8,000,000 individual training sessions, and 160,000 races.

2 Related Work

Traditional sports science approaches to marathon performance prediction have resulted in over a hundred equations for estimating marathon finish-time based on anthropological variables, previous race-times and training variables with R^2 values ranging between 0.1–0.99 [7]. About half of the equations require laboratory equipment to measure physiological fitness variables such as VO_{2max}, *critical speed*, and *lactate threshold* making them inaccessible to most runners [8, 9]. Many training determinants of marathon performance have also been studied including the average distance covered per week, average pace, number of runs per week [10]. One common equation is to utilise the past race-time in a previous race and adjust it based on the new distance, however there is not an exact translation in pace from one distance to another [11,12]. Many of these studies have had to rely on small cohorts of elite runners – thus it is unknown whether these equations would translate to the noisier real-world of recreational runners.

The recent rapid adoption of wearable sensors and mobile fitness applications brings new opportunities for studying the training patterns and performance of recreational athletes. Data from such sensors has been harnessed for various sports and fitness reasons thus far including: performance prediction; injury prediction, prevention, and rehabilitation; as well as for developing personalised training and motivation systems [13–23]. For predicting marathon performance for recreational runners, which is a complex task still lacking a clear solution, a case-based reasoning methodology can work well as it oversteps the need for an explicit domain model, and its effectiveness in a variety of applications using time series data has been subject to numerous investigations [24].

The starting point for this work is two previous studies that have used ideas from case-based reasoning to predict marathon race-times using the type of training data captured routinely by wearable sensors. The first study [4,5] explored the role of previous marathon race-times in the development of a CBR system for race prediction with the original work [3,6] on using a single past race extended to include multiple past-races for improved prediction performance. While this work demonstrated the potential for excellent predictive accuracy – under certain conditions it was possible to predict target race-times with an accuracy of 2–3% – it was nevertheless limited by a reliance on past marathon finish-times and therefore not suitable to help novice runners plan their first marathon. The second study [1,2] addressed this short-coming by leveraging marathon training activities rather than past marathon races. Thus, even a novice, first-timer could benefit from a race-prediction at various stages in their training programme. However, this approach could not produce predictions that were as accurate as the previous models based on past races. In the current work, ideas from these two studies will be incorporated into one combined case-based reasoning approach to predicting marathon performance for recreational runners.

3 An Extended Case-Based Reasoning Approach to Race-Time Prediction

As mentioned earlier, previous efforts at marathon race-time prediction have either relied on the runner's past race times [3–6] or their training history [1,2], but not both. In this section we describe an extended case-based reasoning model (Fig. 1) that seeks to combine both types of data for use in race-time prediction.

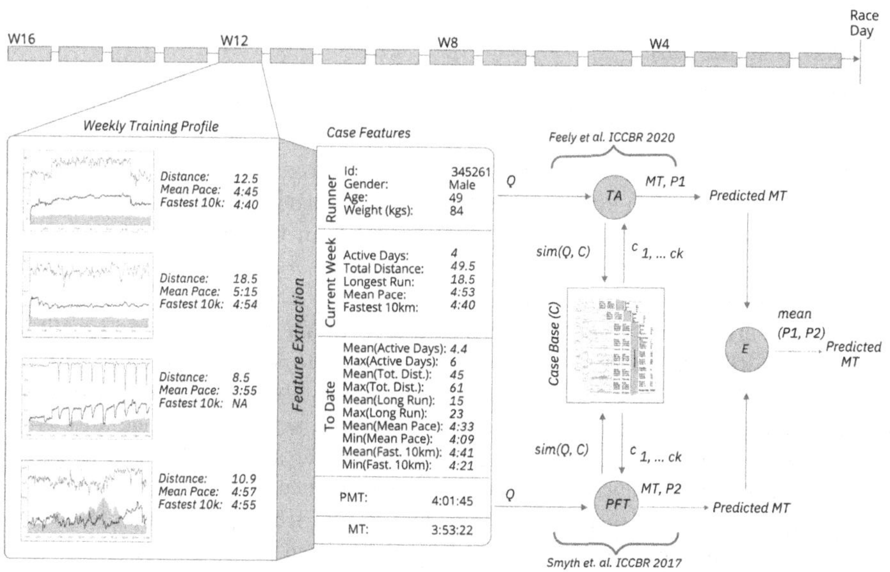

Fig. 1. An overview of a case-based reasoning system

3.1 Training Activity Data

The raw data for the proposed CBR system is based on the type of exercise data (distance, time, speed) that is routinely collected by fitness apps and smart watches, but before it can be used the raw data needs to be converted into a form that can form the basis of a feature-based case description.

When training for a marathon a runner will typically follow a training programme (T) that will prescribe 10–12 weeks of training with 3–6 sessions/activities (A_i) per week. A runner r (with known sex) is associated with a set of training activities $T(r)$ that consists of individual activities $A_1, ...A_n$ with each $A_i = (d, D, T, P)$, where d is the training activity date and D, T, P contain distance (m), time (sec), and pacing (min/km) data generated by their GPS devices. In this study we use raw data collected by the popular Strava app, which is then sampled at 100 m intervals. Thus, D is a set of distances in increments of 100 m for the duration of the activity. T is a set of times, in seconds, corresponding to the time it took the runner to complete a given 100 m segment. And P is the mean grade-adjusted paces (min/km) calculated from D and T for these 100 m segments.

$$T(r) = \{A_1, ...A_n\} \tag{1}$$

Further, from each activity we compute the following key features to serve as a summary of the activity:

1. Total Distance (m)
2. Average Pace (min/km)
3. Fastest 10 km pace (min/km)

Activities with a total distance of 42.195 km ± 5% are designated as *marathons* and for each runner r and marathon activity we identify all of the activities in the 16 weeks prior to the marathon; in this way we can identify marathons and their corresponding training sessions for each runner.

Finally, it is worth noting that in addition to the above preprocessing, additional steps are taken to validate activities as running activities versus walking or cycling; although all of the Strava data used in this study has been labeled as running activities there are occasionally some mislabelled activities. We identify these using a number of simple filters based on activity distance and average speed/pace; for example, mean fastest paces over a given distance must be slower than the current world record for that distance. Additionally, to reduce overlap among training programmes, the fastest marathon per six month season January-June and July-December per year was chosen for each runner.

3.2 Selection of a CBR Model

As demonstrated by the lack of a consistent model from the sports science literature, predicting race-times for recreational runners is complex, and nuanced, and training programmes are highly variable. CBR methodologies lend themselves to such complex domains. To validate this, a linear model and decision tree model were also fitted to the data, and the CBR model outperformed these (RMSE of predicted marathon times compared to actual marathon times for CBR model was between 2–10 min lower) and thus is the focus of this current work.

3.3 Case Representation and Feature Selection

In what follows, we refer to $C(r, w)$ as a *case* for runner r and week w of training before their target race. The *problem description* part of the case is based on a set of features ($F(r, w)$) extracted from the training activities for the given week, and a corresponding set of *cumulative* features up to week w in training. In other words, $F(r, w)$ will include the fastest 10 km pace observed during r's activities in week w and there will be a corresponding feature that captures the (cumulative) fastest 10 km pace so far observed for r in all training weeks up to week w. The *solution* part of the case is the runner's finish-time in their target marathon, (MT). The following basic features are extracted and used in each case:

Table 1. A summary of the training activities feature-set

Feature	Unit	When	Description
Total distance	km	Weekly	Sum of distances covered in sessions
Max (Total distance)	km	Cumulative	Maximum distance covered in a week
Mean (Total distance)	km	Cumulative	Avg. distance covered in a week
Longest run	km	Weekly	Most distance covered in one session
Max (Longest run)	km	Cumulative	Maximum longest run distance
Mean (Longest run)	km	Cumulative	Avg. longest run distance
Training days	unit	Weekly	no. days that a session was tracked
Max (Training days)	unit	Cumulative	Maximum no. sessions in a week
Mean (Training days)	unit	Cumulative	Avg. number of sessions per week
Mean pace	(mins/km)	Weekly	Avg. running pace this week
Min (Mean pace)	(mins/km)	Cumulative	Pace of fastest training week
Mean (Mean pace)	(mins/km)	Cumulative	Average weekly running pace
Fastest 10 km	(mins/km)	Weekly	Pace of the fastest 10 km ran this week
Min (Fastest 10 km)	(mins/km)	Cumulative	Pace of the fastest 10 km ran so far
Mean (Fastest 10 km)	(mins/km)	Cumulative	Average 10 km running pace

In addition to these training features summarised in Table 1, we also extract the previous (fastest) marathon finish-time for each runner; the work of [3,6] have shown that past race times can be effective when it comes to predicting future times. In what follows we will separately compare case representations that use training features only, past race times only, and both.

A case for a query runner r in a given week in training w in the 16-week period leading up to a marathon m consists of the previously described training features $F(r, w)$ and the future marathon time achieved MT; see Eq. 2.

$$C(r, w) = (F(r, w), MT) \tag{2}$$

3.4 Case-Based Prediction Models

Our aim in this work is to compare three different case-based prediction approaches that differ based on the types of features used for race-time prediction. For each version we predict a marathon time for a target runner r_t, at a given training week w, by selecting the k most similar cases to r_t based on a model-dependent subset of features. We use a standard Euclidean distance metric (Manhattan distance also tested but there was little difference in error) to assess similarity and the predicted time is calculated from the mean of the marathon times for these k most similar cases. The steps are summarised in Algorithm 1.

Previous Marathon Time (PMT) Model: The first model is based loosely on the work of [3–6] by using the past marathon time and the sex of the runner to identify a set of similar cases under the constraint that the past marathon time of r_t must be within 5% of the past marathon time for similar cases. Obviously this approach is unaffected by the training week.

Training Activity Model (TA): The next model is inspired by the work of [1] in that it uses the features extracted from the training activities of r in week w (and the cumulative features up to that week) as the basis for case retrieval; as before, cases are filtered based on runner sex due to performance and racing differences among male and female runners [25]. However, unlike the work of [1] in the present study we perform an additional feature selection task by using a stepwise, forward, sequential feature selection process (whereby features are added one at a time to the model based on which feature reduces the error by the greatest amount) to identify a subset of training features to use. We can do this for each week of training so that in principle, each case corresponding to week w can harness a different set of features depending on which features were found to be most useful in predicting marathon times from that point in training.

Combined Model (C): Finally, an obvious extension of the above two methods is to combine past race-times with training features. There are two options to achieve this. One is to simply to combined the previous race-time feature with the training activities and proceed with a unified case representation. A second is to maintain the separation between the previous race-time and training features and combine (average) the predictions coming from each. For the purpose of this study we evaluate both options.

Algorithm 1. Predicting marathon performance

Input: **q**, the query case for runner **r** in week **w**; **CB** the case base; **k** the number of similar cases to retrieve during prediction.

1: $C \leftarrow filter(CB, week = w, sex = r.sex)$
2: $C' \leftarrow sort(C, sim(q, c))$
3: $C_k \leftarrow C'.head(k)$
4: $p \leftarrow mean(C_k.MT)$
5: **return** p

4 Evaluation

4.1 Setup

The dataset used for this evaluation is an anonymised collection of (running) training sessions uploaded to Strava between 2014 and 2017, shared with the authors as part of a data sharing agreement with Strava. The authors do not own the data and thus are not in a position to make the data publicly available. As discussed earlier, marathon races were identified along with sessions from the prior 16 weeks of training. In total there were just over 160,000 training 16-week programmes from 85,000 unique runners, comprising a total of over 8,000,000 individual training sessions/activities; see Table 2 for a brief summary.

Table 2. A summary of the dataset utilised in this work

Sex	No. runners	No. programmes	Age	MT	Dist/Wk	No. days/Wk
F	14198	24538	38.51	239	45.08	3.5
M	71685	136214	40.22	227	45.4	3.3

A standard 10-fold cross-validation is used to evaluate the marathon time predictions for the various techniques under investigation using the percentage error – mean of the absolute error divided by actual marathon time – as a performance metric: See Eq. 3. Specifically, we use the previous race time to predict future marathon time – as a simplification of the approach of [3,4] – in addition to the training features model – which corresponds to [1] – and compare these to the combined features and ensemble approaches which combine previous race times and training histories. Case retrieval is performed in real-time and the time taken to retrieve 20 nearest neighbours from the training set for a given test runner is 1.9 s for females and 6.5 s for males.

$$error = \frac{abs(predicted - actual)}{actual} \tag{3}$$

4.2 Error vs. k Nearest Neighbours

Figure 2 shows the error for different values of k (the number of nearest neighbours retrieved) in the previous race-time model (in black) and the baseline training features model (including all features) for different points in training for males (a) and females (b). As expected, prediction error improves (reduces) for larger values of k up to approximately 15, after which there are diminishing error improvements and thus k was set to 15 for the remainder of this evaluation.

Notice too how prediction error improves as we get closer to race-day (decreasing weeks from race-day). This is to be expected, because more is known about the runner as training progresses. Generally speaking we also see that the approach based on training sessions outperforms the use of a previous race-time. In other words, a runner's current training is more predictive of their next marathon time than a previous marathon time. This of course makes sense as a runner's current training is likely to be a better approximation of their current fitness and ability than a past marathon.

The error associated with female runners tends to be lower, on a like-for-like bases, than the error for male runners. This is consistent with research that female runners tend to be more predictable in their pacing (on race-day) [25] than male runners, which explains why the previous race-time errors are better for females than for males. Interestingly, the same is true for the training features models too, which may indicate that female runners are also in some sense more consistent in their training practices.

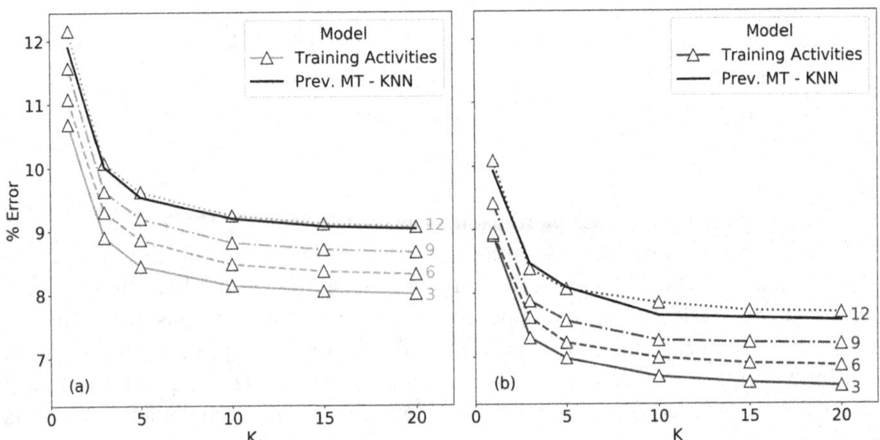

Fig. 2. Percentage error of the training activities model and previous races model (in black) for different values of K = 1...20, at points 3, 6, 9 and 12 weeks from race-day for males (a) and females (b)

4.3 Feature Selection

The results of the stepwise forward sequential feature selection were reasonably consistent for males and females, and for different points in training. Thus for simplicity, one reduced feature-set was selected which excluded the three features related to the number of days spent training per week, the current week's total distance, as well as the cumulative average longest run.

To give a sense of the relative importance of each feature, the relative error of the model without versus with each feature was calculated and the results depicted in Fig. 3 whereby a positive value indicates that the model performs better with the feature, and a negative value indicates that the model performs better without the feature. Note that due to some interactions among features these do not align exactly with the final features chosen.

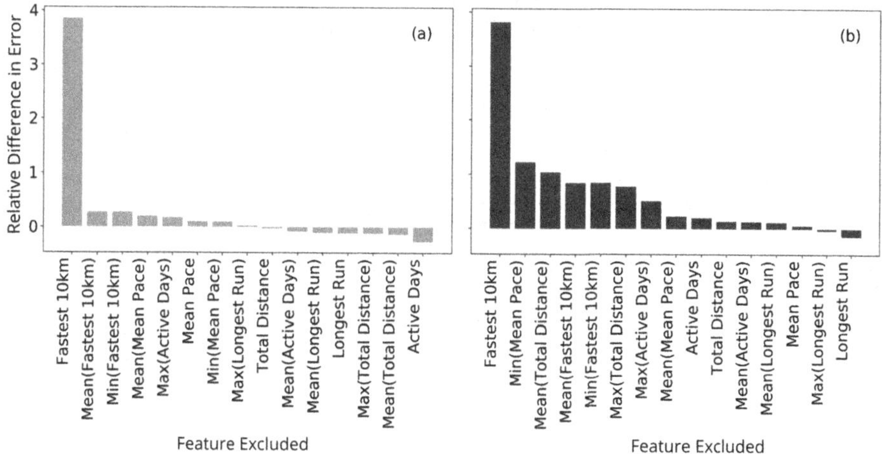

Fig. 3. Relative importance of training features for males (a) and females (b) comparing the relative error increase when each feature is removed from the model

4.4 Performance vs. Training Week

Figure 4 shows the prediction performance of all 4 models by training week, for males (a) and females (b). It also includes the *actual* previous race-time of a runner as a further baseline prediction.

Surprisingly, we can see that using the actual previous race-time of a runner beats the corresponding kNN approach which uses the previous time to identify similar runners and produces a predicted time based on their average finish-times. This is surprising because is suggests that there may be little benefit in using the previous race-time on its own as the basis for a kNN prediction, but in fact we will see that this is not true in the next section. Note too that both of these baselines do not depend on week of training and so they are presented as flat-lines in Fig. 4.

In Fig. 4 we also see that the training features (and combination models) offer improved prediction performance about 10 weeks out from race-day, for males and females; once again the prediction performance is better for females than for males. Moreover, the combination models perform better than either the training features model or the previous race-time model on their own. In general, the *combined model*, which combines training features and previous race-times into a single feature representation, performs best overall, beating the ensemble alternative for each week of training; the error reduces to 7.6% for males and 6.2% for females in the weeks directly before race-day.

Notice however that there is a slight dis-improvement in prediction accuracy in the final week before race-day. A similar effect was found by [1] and it is due to the so called *marathon taper* [26] which sees runners dramatically reducing their training effort in order to recover before race-day. In future, it may be useful to incorporate taper-specific features to further improve race-time prediction based on the work of [26], which shows that how certain types of taper are associated with improved race-times all other things being equal.

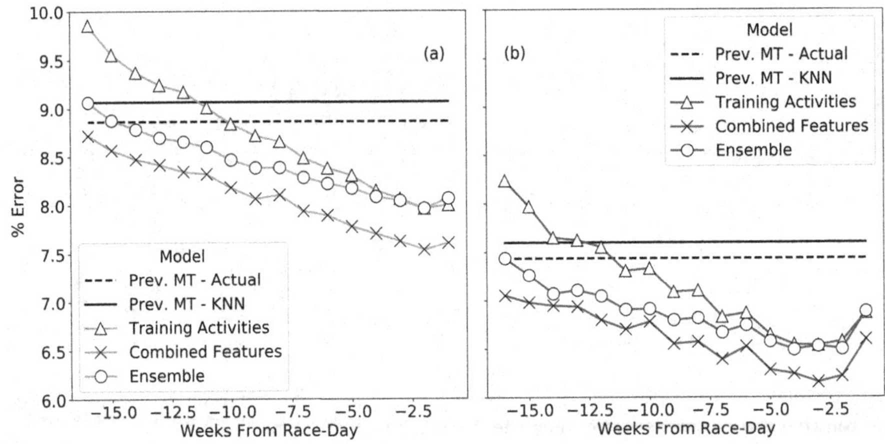

Fig. 4. Percentage error for different weeks in training for each of the previous race-time, training activities, and combined models for males (a) and females (b)

4.5 Performance vs. Ability

We have already seen how prediction performance varies significantly between male and female runners. Another important factor is the ability of runners and to test this we examine prediction performance based on finish-times to evaluate whether faster marathoners are more or less predictable than slower marathoners for example. The results, shown in Fig. 5 for each model and in Fig. 6, demonstrate some important effects due to finish-time.

Notice all of the prediction models tested tend to be less predictable for faster runners – runners completing the marathon in less than 3.5 h – at least compared to the baseline of using their actual previous race-time. One likely reason for this is that these fast runners tend to perform in a very predictable way from race to race, either improving their time by a small degree or dis-improving depending on their training and race conditions. Among such a fast cohort of runners it is difficult to do better than use their previous race-time, which is a useful result in and of itself. In contrast, for the more "recreational runners" previous race times are far less reliable indicators of future performance, at least when used on their own, and so we find that our case-based approaches perform better; once again the combined models outperform just the training features or past race times. And it is useful that the prediction sweet-spot – where the case-based approaches do better – is for runners completing the marathon in between 3.5–4.5 h. These are likely to be runners who are most focused on achieving improvements in their finish-times, especially those targeting the iconic sub-4-h marathon, and so it is particularly useful that this is the type of runner who stands to gain the most from this approach.

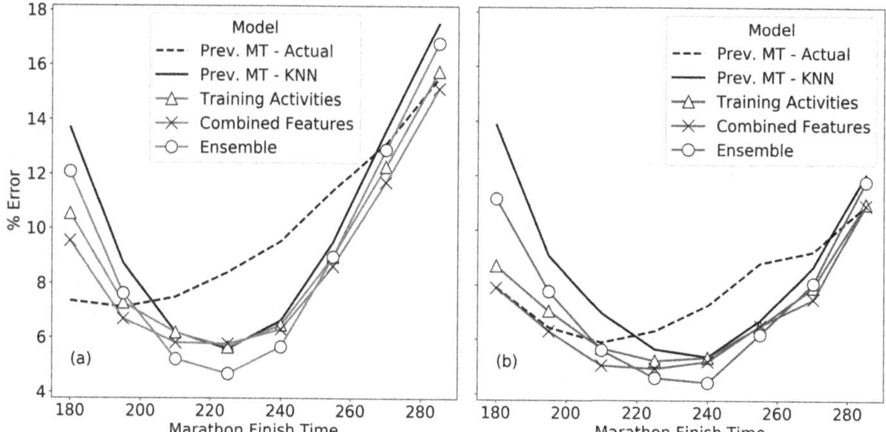

Fig. 5. Percentage error of the models for different values of marathon finish time for males (a) and females (b)

5 From Prediction to Explanation

So far we have focused on helping marathon runners by predicting their race-times at different points in training. There are several reasons why this is useful. Obviously, it is important for marathon runners to have reasonably accurate race-time expectations so that they can calibrate their own race-day pacing and ensure that they achieve the best time possible after their months of training.

A second advantage of having access to race-time predictions during training is to provide runners with feedback about how their training is progressing. For example, if race-time predictions are improving over the weeks then it should be a

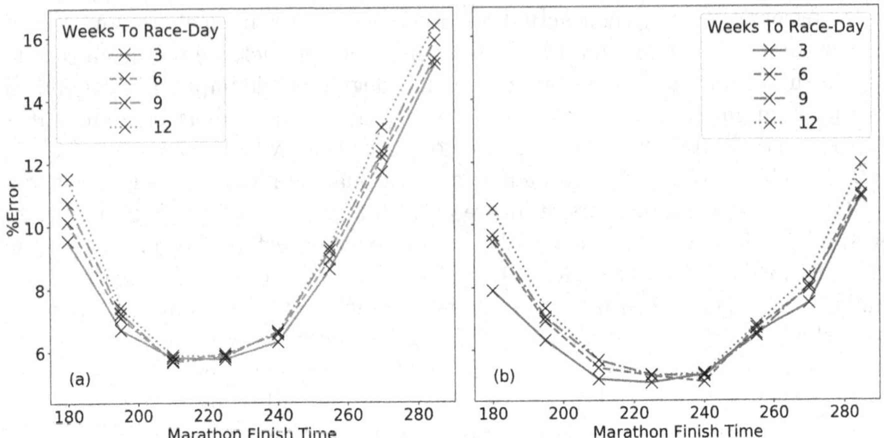

Fig. 6. Percentage error of the combined-features model for different values of marathon finish time for males (a) and females (b) at points 3, 6, 9 and 12 weeks from race-day

sign that their training is progressing well. But if they are dis-improving it might be a sign that their training is not as effective as it might be. This is especially important for relatively inexperienced recreational runners, and predicted race-times are straightforward to understand and compare.

But it may be possible to go even further and take advantage of the approach to provide users with additional explanatory information as the basis for a peer-analysis. For example, Fig. 7 shows a mock-up for just such an analysis by presenting a visual explanation to a runner of how their current training compares to their nearest neighbours in terms of key features such as weekly volume (i.e. total weekly distance), current long-run distance, their current fastest 10 km pace, and the predicted marathon time. Each element of the explanation positions the runner with respect to their peers (nearest neighbours) by showing the minimum and maximum values for these features among their peers and how this relates to predicted race-time. This can help the runner to understand where their current training positions them but also allows them to get a sense of how changes in training (e.g. a longer long-run or a greater weekly training volume) might help to improve their predicted race-time. It is this unique advantage of explainability that contributes to a case-based reasoning approach being preferable over less opaque prediction techniques.

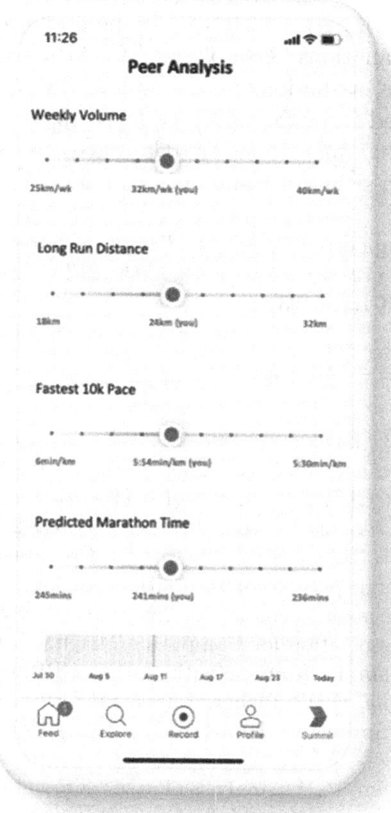

Fig. 7. An example mock-up of the type of peer-analysis that can be used for the purpose of explanation to help runners better understand where they are in their training and performance relative to their peers, that is their k nearest neighbours.

6 Conclusion

The main contribution of this work is an extended case-based reasoning system for predicting the race-time of marathon runners based on a combination of previous race-times and training histories. By combining both types of information it is possible to produce more accurate predictions than is possible using part race times or training histories on their own. Moreover, the prediction benefits are especially well suited for recreational runners. We also demonstrated the explainability of this system in the form of a mock-up description of the nearest neighbors driving a given runner's predicted-race time.

The case-based reasoning methodology was evaluated offline with a dataset of approximately 8 million training sessions across 160,000 training programmes of 85,000 unique runners, and the results are promising. However, a live-use study would be required to rigorously test this system (and such an evaluation is planned as future work), particularly to test the user's response to the accompanying prediction explanations. Also planned for future work is an exploration of additional models for prediction, for example a deep learning model. These models could be extended through additional features, and applied to other running distances such as ultra-marathons or 10 km races, as well as other endurance sports including cycling, swimming and even skiing.

Acknowledgements. Supported by Science Foundation Ireland through the Insight Centre for Data Analytics (12/RC/2289_P2) and the SFI Centre for Research Training in Machine Learning (18/CRT/6183).

References

1. Feely, C., Caulfield, B., Lawlor, A., Smyth, B.: Using case-based reasoning to predict marathon performance and recommend tailored training plans. In: Watson, I., Weber, R. (eds.) ICCBR 2020. LNCS (LNAI), vol. 12311, pp. 67–81. Springer, Cham (2020). https://doi.org/10.1007/978-3-030-58342-2_5
2. Feely, C., Caulfield, B., Lawlor, A., Smyth, B.: Providing explainable race-time predictions and training plan recommendations to marathon runners, In: Fourteenth ACM Conference on Recommender Systems, RecSys 2020, New York, NY, USA, pp. 539–544. Association for Computing Machinery (2020)
3. Smyth, B., Cunningham, P.: Running with cases: a CBR approach to running your best marathon. In: Aha, D.W., Lieber, J. (eds.) ICCBR 2017. LNCS (LNAI), vol. 10339, pp. 360–374. Springer, Cham (2017). https://doi.org/10.1007/978-3-319-61030-6_25
4. Smyth, B., Cunningham, P.: An analysis of case representations for marathon race prediction and planning. In: Cox, M.T., Funk, P., Begum, S. (eds.) ICCBR 2018. LNCS (LNAI), vol. 11156, pp. 369–384. Springer, Cham (2018). https://doi.org/10.1007/978-3-030-01081-2_25
5. Smyth, B., Cunningham, P.: Marathon race planning: a case-based reasoning approach. In: Proceedings of the Twenty-Seventh International Joint Conference on Artificial Intelligence, IJCAI 2018, 13–19 July 2018, Stockholm, Sweden, pp. 5364–5368 (2018)
6. Smyth, B., Cunningham, P.: A novel recommender system for helping marathoners to achieve a new personal-best. In: Proceedings of the Eleventh ACM Conference on Recommender Systems, RecSys 2017, Como, Italy, 27–31 August 2017, pp. 116–120 (2017)
7. Keogh, A., Smyth, B., Caulfield, B., Lawlor, A., Berndsen, J., Doherty, C.: Prediction equations for marathon performance: a systematic review. Int. J. Sports Physiol. Perform. **14**(9), 1159–1169 (2019)
8. Costill, D.: Physiology of marathon running. JAMA **221**, 1024–1029 (1972)
9. Faude, O., Kindermann, W., Meyer, T.: Lactate threshold concepts. Sports Med. **39**(6), 469–490 (2009)
10. Doherty, C., Keogh, A., Davenport, J., Lawlor, A., Smyth, B., Caulfield, B.: An evaluation of the training determinants of marathon performance: a meta-analysis with meta-regression. J. Sci. Med. Sport **23**(2), 182–188 (2020)
11. Riegel, P.S.: Athletic records and human endurance: a time-vs.-distance equation describing world-record performances may be used to compare the relative endurance capabilities of various groups of people. Am. Sci. **69**(3), 285–290 (1981)

12. Slovic, P.: Empirical study of training and performance in the marathon. Res. Q. Am. Alliance Health Phys. Educ. Recreat. **48**(4), 769–777 (1977)
13. Gasparetti, F., Aiello, L.M., Quercia, D.: Evaluating the efficacy of traditional fitness tracker recommendations. In: Proceedings of the 24th International Conference on Intelligent User Interfaces: Companion, IUI 2019, New York, NY, USA, pp. 15–16. ACM (2019)
14. Schneider, O.S., MacLean, K.E., Altun, K., Karuei, I., Wu, M.M.: Real-time gait classification for persuasive smartphone apps: structuring the literature and pushing the limits. In: Proceedings of the 2013 International Conference on Intelligent User Interfaces, IUI 2013, New York, NY, USA, pp. 161–172. ACM (2013)
15. Mulas, F., Pilloni, P., Manca, M., Boratto, L., Carta, S.: Using new communication technologies and social media interaction to improve the motivation of users to exercise,. In: Second International Conference on Future Generation Communication Technologies FGCT 2013, London, United Kingdom, 12–14 November 2013, pp. 87–92 (2013)
16. Berndsen, J., Lawlor, A., Smyth, B.: Running with recommendation. In: HealthRecSys@ RecSys, pp. 18–21 (2017)
17. Berndsen, J., Smyth, B., Lawlor, A.: Pace my race: recommendations for marathon running. In: Proceedings of the 13th ACM Conference on Recommender Systems, pp. 246–250. ACM (2019)
18. Boratto, L., Carta, S., Fenu, G., Manca, M., Mulas, F., Pilloni, P.: The role of social interaction on users motivation to exercise: a persuasive web framework to enhance the self-management of a healthy lifestyle. Pervasive Mob. Comput. **36**, 98–114 (2017)
19. Pilloni, P., Piras, L., Carta, S., Fenu, G., Mulas, F., Boratto, L.: Recommender system lets coaches identify and help athletes who begin losing motivation. IEEE Comput. **51**(3), 36–42 (2018)
20. Buttussi, F., Chittaro, L., Nadalutti, D.: Bringing mobile guides and fitness activities together: a solution based on an embodied virtual trainer. In: Proceedings of the 8th Conference on Human-Computer Interaction with Mobile Devices and Services, MobileHCI 2006, New York, NY, USA, pp. 29–36. ACM (2006)
21. Hosseinpour, M., Terlutter, R.: Your personal motivator is with you: a systematic review of mobile phone applications aiming at increasing physical activity. Sports Med. **49**, 1425–1447 (2019)
22. Mulas, F., Carta, S., Pilloni, P., Manca, M.: Everywhere run: a virtual personal trainer for supporting people in their running activity. In: Proceedings of the 8th International Conference on Advances in Computer Entertainment Technology, ACE 2011, Lisbon, Portugal, 8–11 November 2011, p. 70 (2011)
23. Feely, C., Caulfield, B., Lawlor, A., Smyth, B.: A case-based reasoning approach to predicting and explaining running related injuries. In: Sánchez-Ruiz, A.A., Floyd, M.W. (eds.) ICCBR 2021. LNCS (LNAI), vol. 12877, pp. 79–93. Springer, Cham (2021). https://doi.org/10.1007/978-3-030-86957-1_6
24. Kurbalija, V.: Time series analysis and prediction using case based reasoning technology. Ph.D. thesis, University of Novi Sad, Serbia (2009)
25. Smyth, B.: Fast starters and slow finishers: a large-scale data analysis of pacing at the beginning and end of the marathon for recreational runners. J. Sports Anal. **4**, 229–242 (2018)
26. Smyth, B., Lawlor, A.: Longer disciplined tapers improve marathon performance for recreational runners. Front. Sports Act. Living 275 (2021)

A Case-Based Reasoning Approach to Plugin Parameter Selection in Vocal Audio Production

Michael Clemens(✉), Nancy N. Blackburn, Rushit Sanghrajka, Monthir Ali, M. Gardone, Shilpa Thomas, Hunter Finney, and Rogelio E. Cardona-Rivera

University of Utah, Salt Lake City, UT 84105, USA
michael.clemens@utah.edu

Abstract. The field of intelligent systems for music production aims to produce co-creative tools to aid and support musicians' decision-making while targeting a specific aesthetic in their musical artifact . While case-based reasoning (CBR) approaches have been used to assist music generation and recommendation, music production has not yet been explored. This paper proposes using CBR within a co-creative agent to assist musicians in their aesthetic goals through a vocal audio plugin. Results show that although participants were interested in using a co-creative agent throughout the production process, they acted against the vocal plugin parameter recommendations set by the agent. Participants showed frustration when the co-creative agent acted in a way that deviated from set expectations. From this research, we posit that explainability is an essential aspect of effective CBR models within co-creative agents.

Keywords: Computational creativity · Co-creative agents · Cased-based reasoning

1 Introduction

Audio production is the manipulation and design of audio for consumer media [1]. It is a general term encompassing audio manipulation, design tasks in music production, sound recording, audio post-production, audio mixing, mastering, live sound, and sound design (e.g., for music, film, theater, games). From initial musical ideation to the final release of the artifact, musicians (i.e., instrumentalists, engineers, producers) operate complex audio tools to achieve their desired audio artifact. For example, audio engineers may select appropriate microphones, amplifiers, and digital effects based on music genres, target audience, and creative purpose [2].

Skeuomorphism, when digital implementations of instruments and effects are made to appear as their real-world counterparts, is common amongst audio

M. T. Keane and N. Wiratunga (Eds.): ICCBR 2022, LNAI 13405, pp. 350–364, 2022.
https://doi.org/10.1007/978-3-031-14923-8_23

processing and effects tools' interfaces. Novice users of audio processing tools, however, are likely to have never used hardware equipment such as analog mixing consoles or analog synthesizers. They are thus likely to be unfamiliar with the interaction metaphors of hardware tools [1]. Further, considerable audio-specific technical and theoretical understanding is needed to properly transfer a desired audio concept to the software via the specific tools afforded in these interfaces [3].

To assist musicians and alleviate these technological cognitive burdens, the field of intelligent systems for music production aims to propose and produce automatic tools to aid and support music actors' decision-making [4]. While case-based reasoning (CBR) has been used to study creativity quantitatively [5–7], there has been no support for qualitative metrics of CBR effectiveness within the field of musical aesthetics. Our two research questions are:

- **RQ1**: *How does CBR within a co-creative agent affect music producers' musical artifacts when evaluated on aesthetics?*
- **RQ2**: *How do music producers use adaptive plugins in a vocal production chain?*

We evaluated these research questions through a CBR implementation using an adaptive audio plugin to produce vocal samples. We also explored some music producers' apprehension regarding co-creating with an intelligent agent in the studio. The main contribution of this application paper concerns the latter exploration through an experiment and semi-structured interviews with music producers.

2 Related Works

Within intelligent audio plugin literature, two main tasks have been targeted: *parameter tuning* and recommendation. Plugin recommendation deals mainly with the selection and the arrangement of plugins within a particular audio chain. Stasis et al. [8] used Markov chains to describe plugin sequences based on timbrel descriptive phrases, intended audio effects and music genre for plugin suggestion. Despite the promising results, recommendations are only provided by four separate plugins. Their work investigates how machine learning approaches may be used to recommend audio plugin arrangements.

Moura da Silva et al. [2] address the problem of selecting audio plugins, i.e., effect implementations, as a recommendation task and employ two different methodologies: supervised learning and collaborative filtering. Parameter tuning seeks to identify the most appropriate parameter settings (e.g., gain, treble level) of a specific plugin. The approaches for selecting default parameter values (factory presets) have been based on music genre [9,10] automatic identification of parameter values based on audio samples [11] and adaptive control of digital audio effects using either linear dynamical transformations [12] or nonlinear approaches [13,14].

However, none of these approaches for *adjusting parameters* or choosing the sequencing of plugins have used CBR within their implementation. The following section reviews the literature in which CBR has been effective in audio domains.

2.1 CBR in Music

As a technology, CBR [6,15,16] works to solve problems by reusing (typically through some form of adaptation) answers to similar, previously solved problems. CBR is based on the idea that similar problems have similar solutions. CBR is suited for problems when (1) there are numerous examples of previously solved similar problems available and (2) a major part of the information involved in problem-solving is tacit, that is, difficult to explain and generalize [17]. An additional advantage of CBR is that each new solved problem can be corrected and recalled, allowing the system to enhance its problem-solving capabilities through experience. CBR has been used in the literature for audio domains in two main applications: **music generation** and **music recommendation**.

Music Generation. Pereira et al. [18] explored computational approaches in music composition based on CBR and planning techniques. Their research focused on developing new solutions by retaining, modifying, and extrapolating knowledge from previously expert-created music analysis. This research was pivotal in that it sparked interest in creating musical agents using CBR.

Lopez de Mantaras et al. [19] developed SaxEx, an intelligent musical system based on CBR techniques capable of producing emotive, monophonic music resembling human performance. Their research demonstrated that user interaction within the CBR process is necessary to engage the agent and musician in a co-creative process. TempoExpress [20] is another musical CBR system that automatically performs musically acceptable tempo transformations. The research in music generation using CBR has waned as much of the work now uses neural networks, deep learning models, and ensemble techniques [21]. However, CBR for recommendation systems in music saw a later surge of interest.

Music Recommendation. Since music recommender systems are based on both recommendation systems and music information retrieval (MIR), they must cope with the constraints of both domains [22]. Traditional MIR techniques employ content-based audio-related techniques, which, in addition to the general constraints of content-based systems such as overspecialization and limited diversity, necessitate a deeper understanding of the application domain [23,24].

Gatzioura et al. [25] used a hybrid approach that employed CBR after a contextual pre-filtering process, allowing them to find the most similar previously recommended lists [26]. They found that adding contextual pre-filtering increased the recommenders' accuracy and computational performance as compared to commonly used methods in the field. Lee et al. [27] also found that their system, *C_Music*, increased in performance as well using a context-aware system that employed CBR.

Although it has not been explored in the literature, we believe CBR has the potential to be effective in tailoring the aesthetic decisions of artists producing music for a specific genre. We experimented with a Max for Live plugin using CBR and evaluated our tool through quantitative and qualitative measures to test our hypothesis.

3 Our Co-creative Audio CBR Plugin

We developed a system to explore the potential that a CBR-powered co-creative plugin holds for audio vocal production. Rather than creating an entirely new tool, our intended users were music producers familiar with *Live*[1], a popular Digital Audio Workstation (DAW) published by Ableton. We relied on *Max for Live*—a connector that affords using the Max/MSP graphical programming language[2] within Live, as illustrated in Figs. 1 and 2.

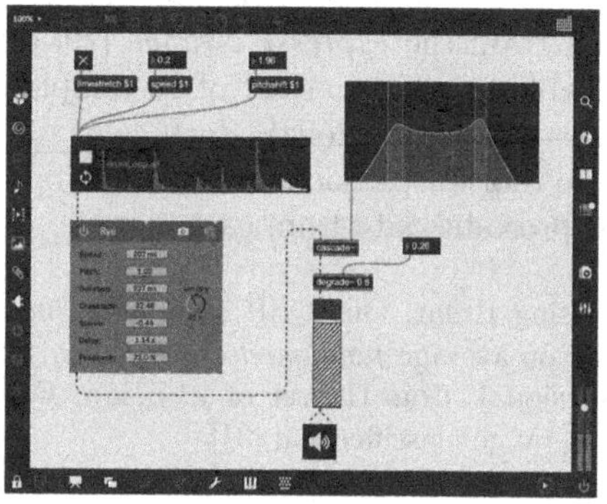

Fig. 1. Max for live allows a user to use the Max/MSP graphical programming language to manipulate audio.

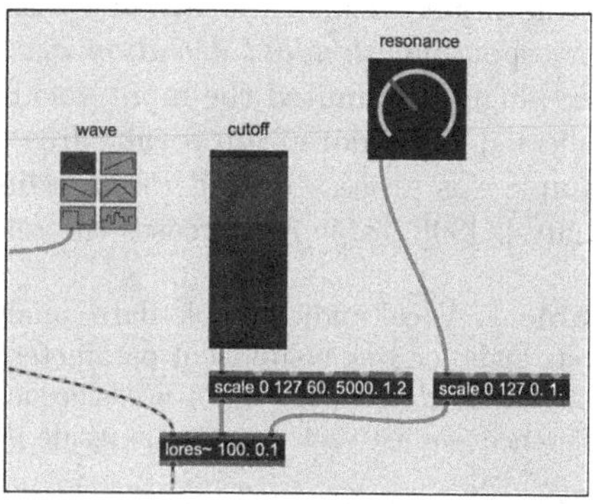

Fig. 2. Through max for live, users can connect audio to effects controlled via dials and sliders.

We configured our system to support the following four audio editing components published by Ableton and independent artists. The **Poundcake Compressor**[3] by artist *artsux* replicates a low-pass gate compressor that manipulates the amplitude and timbre of an input signal. The **Color Limiter**[4] by *Amazing Noises* and the *Ableton Team* manipulates loudness, ceiling, saturation, and color of an input signal. The **GMaudio Dynamic EQ**[5] by artist *groovmekanik* supports attenuating/accentuating unwanted/wanted signal frequencies. Finally, the **Convolution Reverb**[6] by the *Ableton Team* supports manipulating spatial effects of an input signal (e.g., rendering within a cathedral hall, nightclub).

3.1 Our CBR: Parameter Tuning over Audio Components

We arranged our supported audio editing components in series, as listed above—i.e. an input vocal audio signal would always flow from Compressor to Limiter,

[1] https://www.ableton.com/en/live/.
[2] https://cycling74.com/products/max.
[3] https://www.maxforlive.com/library/device/6346/poundcake-compressor.
[4] https://www.ableton.com/en/packs/creative-extensions/.
[5] https://maxforlive.com/library/device/5768/gmaudio-dynamic-eq.
[6] https://www.ableton.com/en/packs/convolution-reverb/.

then to Dynamic EQ, and finally to Reverb. Each component has a unique set of parameters that modulate its performance over the input signal to produce an output one. We designed our CBR algorithm around *few-shot learning* [28] to suggest individual component *parameter values* based on the input *vocal audio signal properties* recorded over several *trials* (i.e. audio editing sessions). The algorithm learns over three trials to produce parameter value suggestions for the next two. That is, the CBR algorithm uses trials 1–3 to identify values for trials 4 and 5; it uses trials 6–8 to identify values for trials 9 and 10.

Our CBR algorithm produces suggestions based on two key prosodic elements of the input vocal audio: its measured average *fundamental frequency* f_0 and corresponding *standard deviation* σ_0. To constrain the *expressive range* [29] of our plugin, we limited the input vocals available to users to a set of 10 samples collected at random from royalty-free libraries offered by Noiiz[7]. Each collected sample was processed with *Praat*, a linguistic tool for prosodic and verbal trait analysis [30]. Table 1 showcases the relevant prosodic data from each sample.

Table 1. Vocal audio sample data, analyzed using Praat. Our CBR algorithm suggests audio editing component parameters based on average *fundamental frequency* f_0 and *standard deviation* σ_0 of user-chosen input signals from the set of 10 below. For reference, we list each sample alongside its vocal range classification [31].

Sample id	Vocal range	Length (s)	$f_0 \pm \sigma_0$ (Hz)
1	Mezzo-Soprano	3.692	247.58 ± 35.76
2	Soprano	2.75	358.39 ± 29.98
3	Soprano	7.742	484.88 ± 48.99
4	Soprano	3.552	370.94 ± 47.33
5	Soprano	5.178	358.65 ± 41.44
6	Tenor	5.365	311.52 ± 54.65
7	Baritone	7.253	251.37 ± 26.95
8	Tenor	4.085	285.82 ± 33.74
9	Baritone	5.461	259.17 ± 18.54
10	Tenor	5.547	311.35 ± 20.29

3.2 Our CBR 4-Phase Cycle

As mentioned, our system learns over three trials and performs CBR for the subsequent two. During the three learning trials, the system offers CBR-based parameter recommendations *as if* the user had selected (the same) three input cases corresponding to the highest, lowest, and a (random) middle vocal audio fundamental frequency from the set in Table 1. During the subsequent two non-learning trials, the system offers CBR-based parameter recommendations based on *actual* inputs selected by the user. We describe our co-creative system's operation below in terms of the four canonical, ordered CBR phases [15].

[7] https://www.noiiz.com.

Retrieve Phase. Based on the fundamental frequency (f_0) of the current vocal sample, our system finds the two closest cases (i.e., trials) and interpolates the user's selected parameter values from those values. Although the standard deviation is used in the subsequent phase, only the fundamental frequency was used during the retrieval process.

Reuse Phase. Our system takes these data and uses Eq. 1 below to compute new parameter values for audio components, which are directly set by the agent as soon as the user starts the trial.

$$p = \left(p_1 + (f - f_1) \cdot \frac{p_2 - p_1}{f_2 - f_1}\right) \cdot random\left(0.1 \cdot \frac{\sigma}{\sigma_{max}}\right) \tag{1}$$

Above, p is the new parameter value, p_1 and p_2 are parameters values from the two closest cases, f is the f_0 of the current voice sample, and f_1 and f_2 are the f_0 from the two closest cases. Further, the final term in Eq. 1 is meant to use the standard deviation of the vocal audio to generate some random noise such that the reused case does not reflect a direct interpolation (represented by the preceding terms). The *random* function uses the random object in Max/MSP that can output a -1 or 1 *randomly.* The noise manifests as a positive or negative update, whose absolute value does not exceed 10% of the standard deviation for all the voice samples used. Equation 1 offers much greater salience to f_0 than to σ on the resulting vocal characteristics to be reused.

Revise Phase. The user can revise recommended parameter values based on their own aesthetic goals while producing the audio.

Retain Phase. The system stores the final result of the trial in its corresponding case library, which can now be used by the system in subsequent trials.

4 Co-creative CBR Utility and Usability Study

We conducted an Institutional Review Board-approved user study, which offered $10.00 to individual participants who were asked to use our plugin in order to produce 10 music tracks for two individual genres. We later assessed their experience via a semi-structured interview. After data collection, we evaluated the plugin via a mixed-methods analysis designed to assess the usability of our co-creative audio CBR plugin, as well as the plugin's utility for targeting a particular musical genre during vocal audio production.

4.1 Recruitment and Duration

We recruited ten music producers ($N = 10$) through convenience sampling via a local Ableton Live User Group, the Ableton Live Users Facebook Group, the Max for Live Users Facebook Group, and emails. The first author (A1) conducted the experiment and interviews remotely via Zoom. The experiment setup and trials lasted between 30 min to 1 h. The semi-structured interviews lasted between 15 and 30 min. The interviews were audio-recorded and transcribed verbatim for later analysis.

Most participants self-identified as male ($N = 8$), live in the United Stated ($N = 9$), with the majority living in the Midwest ($N = 5$). As summarized in Table 2, all but one participant have at least one year of active music production experience, and all but two have used Ableton Live. Although not all participants were familiar with Live *for* vocal production (i.e. some use it for musical scenes, or as a non-production experimental workspace), all participants were familiar with common DAWs and their interaction patterns.

Table 2. Summary of experiment/interview participant demographics. We refer to each participant by a randomly assigned Id(entification) number prefixed with "P-".

Id	Experience (years)	Role	Technologies used
P-1	10	Guitarist	Ableton Live, Soft Tube VSTs, Super8 (Reaper)
P-2	2/12	Composer	Ableton Live, FL Studio, Little Altar Boy. Logic Pro X, Novation Launchpad,
P-3	19	Guitarist	Ableton Live, Archetype: Tim Henson, Cubase, EZ Drummer, Novation Launchkey, Pitch Proof, Soldano Amp
P-4	6	Composer	Ableton Live, Cecilia, Max/MSP, Reaper
P-5	10	Singer	Ableton, Apple Drummer, FL Studio, Logic Pro X, Pro Tools
P-6	8	Producer	Ableton Live, Neutron, Ozone, Valhalla Reverbs, Waves Compressors
P-7	10	Producer	Ableton Live, EQ Eight, Max, Reaper, RX
P-8	10	Bassist	Audacity, EZ Drummer, Sonar Cakewalk
P-9	2	Guitarist	Ableton Live, FL Studio, Isotope, Logic Pro X, Ozone
P-10	1	Composer	GarageBand, Sibelius

4.2 Study Procedure

Participants were instructed to produce tracks for two dichotomous genres: acoustic for soprano-leaning vocals (tracks 1–5), and R&B for the tenor-leaning vocals (tracks 6–10). Producers had a maximum of three minutes to produce each track; therefore, the total time for the experiment was 30 min. Five participants were assigned to group one: producing soprano-leaning vocals followed by tenor-leaning vocals. The remaining five were assigned to group two: producing tenor-leaning vocals followed by soprano-leaning vocals. This grouping was implemented to alleviate any potential ordering effects from the different vocal ranges. Each trial's starting and ending parameter values were recorded to evaluate the effectiveness of the case-based reasoning algorithm implemented in the plugin.

4.3 Data Collection

Parameter Telemetry. Telemetry data was collected to determine the effectiveness of using the co-creative agent (Table 3). One participant's data were excluded since it was corrupted and not recoverable. Another participant's data were excluded due to the file missing most of its data. We developed a python script to extract data from JSON files and print them into a CSV file. Participants adjusted a total of 35 parameters across the plugin's four audio editing components.

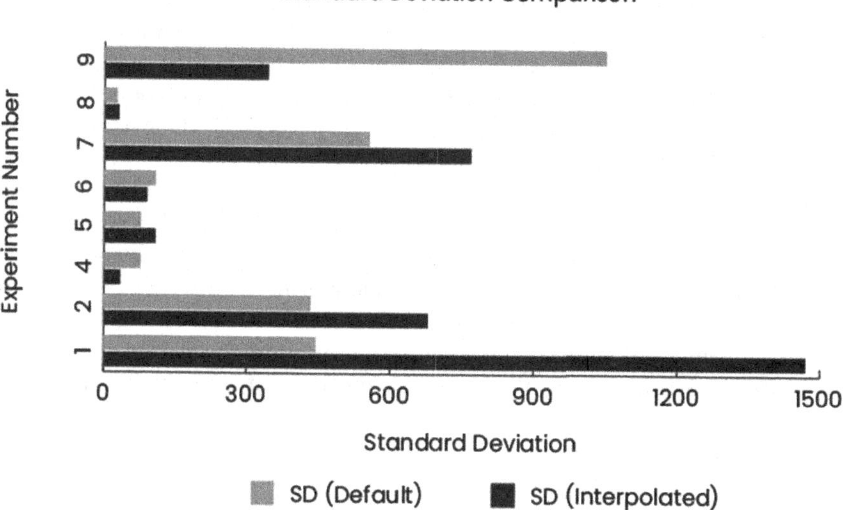

Fig. 3. Standard deviation comparison of audio component parameters for 9 participants, whom each completed 10 trials. Figure 3 shows the standard deviation of data when participants start from default values (blue bar) versus when they start from interpolated values generated by the co-creative agent (orange bar). The results show that while some participants adjusted the parameters less when starting from interpolated values, others adjusted them more. There is thus no clear trend in the data. (Color figure online)

Interviews. The interviewer used a preset question guide (Appendix) to conduct the semi-structured interview. The guide was organized as follows:

1. Broad overview to gain insights about their overall experience and receive the plugin data.
2. Specific questions about their creative flow aimed at understanding their process of editing the tracks and the qualities of the sound they attempted to adjust.
3. Specific questions about the plugin and then about the co-creative agent: specifically asking participants whether they noticed the changes the co-creative agent made to their default settings, how they felt about the updates, and how they would have received the input if they had been aware of the co-creative agent's purpose upfront.

4. Demographics to understand their familiarity with producing music tracks, expertise with various tools, and experience with co-creative agents outside of the experiment
5. Final questions were asked to allow participants to share anything else and ensure they received their remediation.

Interview questions asked were initially vague to get a baseline: asking participants to describe their process and workflow in editing the music tracks provided to them and recording their experience. These were followed by questions asking them if they noticed any changes in some of the experiments and letting them express what they thought. In some cases, if participants seemed not to mention the updated parameters, the interviewer directly asked about it, asking them if they noticed that the default values of the parameters were different. The interviewer then let the participants talk about it: their surprise, their response as to how they handled the changed parameters, and what they thought of the default values.

The penultimate segment of the interview involved discussing what the co-creative agent actually did, and hearing feedback from the participants on their openness and thoughts on working in a music editing task where a co-creative agent would assist in the process by setting some default values for certain parameters. The final part of the interview was about collecting demographics, and their experience with various music editing software, environments and plug-ins.

Transcription. The transcription of the interviews was done with the help of Otter.ai[8], which uses machine learning for their speech-to-text operations. Files were then corrected by hand to ensure that what was transcribed reflected what was said by the speakers. If either the interviewer or interviewee was unintelligible, the transcribers made a note of that by marking the speech as "[*unintelligible*]" or something similar. Names and other personally-identifiable information in the transcriptions were redacted for the anonymity and privacy of the participants. Three transcribers worked on the interviews before being sent to the coding team.

4.4 Quantitative Analysis

Range of Adjustment (RoA). Adjustments ranged from negative and positive values for each parameter. Hence, we took the absolute value of the difference between each parameter's value at the start and end of each trial to determine the range of adjustment.

We studied the RoA for the 35 parameters in each trial before the participant was satisfied with the results and ended the trial. We recorded an average RoA value of 87.21 for soprano tracks (SD = 120.20) and 69.70 for tenor tracks (SD = 57.80). When participants started from interpolated values generated by

[8] https://otter.ai.

the co-creative agent, we recorded an average RoA value of 76.24 (SD = 59.25). These values suggest two things: First, regardless of whether participants started their trials from the default values or the interpolated values generated by the co-creative agent, the difference in RoA was insignificant. Also, the range these parameter adjustments occurred within was substantial, as indicated by the large standard deviation values shown in Fig. 3.

Inter-rater Reliability of Coding. The transcripts from the semi-structured interviews were thematically coded using *iterative open coding* [32]. Three of the authors generated codes iteratively and then used the final set of codes to re-code previous interviews [33]. Three of the interviews were coded by all three authors to test for inter-rater reliability as reported in Table 3. Fleiss' Kappa score was calculated at 0.499, which represents significant agreement based on McHugh's deductions on Cohen's Kappa [34].

Table 3. Fleiss' kappa for observed and expected inter-rater agreement among coders.

Fleiss' kappa	Observed agreement	Expected agreement
0.499	0.77	0.541

4.5 Qualitative Analysis

The qualitative analysis was aimed at understanding the participants' response to the co-creative agent, helping them with the task of producing music in the context of the plug-in that was developed in Ableton Live. Specifically, while the quantitative data collection techniques collected the metrics of how much the participants were interacting with the parameters, the interviews aimed at understanding the reasoning behind the quantitative results.

This section describes a few insights that were extrapolated from analyzing the interviews. Each interview was coded for the presence of a theme, i.e., the reported numbers signify that the participant expressed a given theme at least once over the span of the interview.

Most of the participants who were acting against the parameters were surprised when told about the co-creative agent changing the parameters (3 out of 4).

> **P-3**: "*Like so when I would hit start trial, all of a sudden it would seem like it would be louder. Um, and I think maybe the initial ones when I hit start trial were kind of the same, almost or not quite as much of a jump*".
> **P-6**: "*Okay, I mean, because that I did notice that it was kind of, like, around the same area I was putting stuff*".

When participants acted against the parameters, the interview process revealed that the reason for acting against the changed parameters was that they thought that the CBR agent's suggested parameters were due to a bug in the system, and they reset it or changed it due to that. Consequently, when they were told that the updated parameters were actually from a co-creative agent, most of them expressed surprise. They mentioned that they were unaware that this was intentional. Some of the participants even suggested that having the plug-in inform them explicitly about this would have been helpful in knowing that it was by design.

All participants that used the updated parameters as default values were not surprised when they were told that these parameters were set by the co-creative agent (N=4).

> **P-7**: "*Yeah, yeah, I noticed it*".
> **P-8**: "*I'd be looking for the dry/wet [parameter] to be down, and then it was already up. It's like, 'Wait a minute'. Yeah. So and that was yeah, I noticed that was different*".

The participants that actually used the default values of the updated parameters did not express surprise. Some of them expressed that they were aware that the plug-in set the parameters for them, while some of them did not realize that but used the default values as-is in the editing process.

Majority of participants were using the default parameters or were open to using a co-creative agent that helped set parameters for them in the editing process (N=7). When told about what the co-creative agent was doing, most participants expressed openness to the idea of a co-creative agent setting parameters for them in editing tools of the future. This information was interesting to note because it correlates to our predictions that, in theory, people would be open to working with co-creative agents in a music production setting.

> **P-1**: "*I think it would be helpful if you had a lot of tracks to go through. And you were like, you know, they could all sound the same...*"
> **P-6**: "*I think over time, like I could see it being helpful and being a good starting point*".
> **P-7**: "*I think it's a great way to move forward and save time*".

Majority of participants reported at least one instance where they had a negative experience during the experiment (N=9) **Roughly half the participants had issues where they were unclear about how to perform an action that they needed to perform in the editing process.** (N=6) **Most participants had opinions on the expected behavior of a sound editing plug-in with a co-creative agent in it.** (N=9) When asked how they would expect a tool to work, all participants had ideas on how they would expect the co-creative agent to work and help them in the editing process.

> **P-4**: "*You know, I really like, um, the idea of experimenting with that, and seeing where it could lead, but I think it would not be, it wouldn't be a regular part of what I do, but would be a curious circumstance that is yet another experiment, um, in a long list*".
> **P-6**: "*I'd still want to like A/B back and forth with the raw sound and that, just make sure*".

P-6: "*I think it's definitely something like I can't say for sure if I like if ever use it or not, to be honest, but it's definitely something I would like to mess around with a little bit*".
P-10: "*...but I also feel like that could hinder like creativity to... to an extent because then I feel like it's kind of boxing you more into just kind of what you are drawn towards, I guess that's how it seems...*"

Users experienced frustration when the co-creative agent acted in a manner disparate from their set expectations. Most users had a set expectation that was unique to them for how a co-creative agent should behave during the creation process. Although some producers were satisfied with the recommended parameter settings, others acted against the agent. These data help demonstrate that explainable models within co-creative agents are essential for fostering effective bi-directional communication between the agent and the artist. Without a level of explainability, artists were often confused by the recommended parameter settings. Some producers were encouraged by having a co-creative agent learn from them. However, many were trepidatious of being boxed into a creative corner. Although it seemed helpful that the agent learned from an individual's style, the worry is that total mimicry would stifle the artist's ability to create unique productions.

5 Conclusion and Future Works

In this work, we evaluated a case-based reasoning approach to vocal audio production using a Max for Live plugin in Ableton Live. The implemented system recommends parameter values tailored towards the producer's musical aesthetic choices for producing vocals within a particular genre. This work provides evidence to suggest that while producers are interested in working with co-creative agents in the studio setting, they act negatively towards an agent's recommendations without sufficient explanation from the co-creative agent for those creative choices. These negative actions occurred most frequently when the agent acted in a manner that deviated from expectations held by the music producers. Without a way for the agent to communicate with the producer during the co-creative process, producers relied solely on held expectations and interpreted recommended parameters from that standpoint. From these data, we posit that explainability is essential to effective co-creative agents. The agent must articulate and provide sufficient rationale for its creative choices to be valuable to music producers.

A potential limitation of this work was the number of cases the CBR agent had access to when recommending audio plugin parameter values. Although few-shot learning can be effective in many domains, this assumption may have been detrimental to the results of our research. Another potential limitation of this work may be the lack of inquiry regarding the agent's solution. Did the producers reject a solution based on the interpretability of the solution or the solution's quality? Future work could explore the explainable co-creative space to make agents better suited for co-creation by exposing the agent's creative process.

6 Appendix: Interview Questions Guide

6.1 Overall Experience

- Please upload your output file (download and test this, please)
- Would you describe your workflow while completing the experiment?
- How was your overall experience with the plugin?

6.2 Experiment Questions (Plugin/Co-creative Agent)

- How did you feel about the different tracks you worked with?
- Were you aware of the updated presets that occurred after the third track? (IF NOT: explain the process, then ask these questions:)
- How did it affect your workflow? (easier, quicker, recommendation, co-creative)
- In what ways did you find the plugin helpful?
- In what ways was the plugin a hindrance?
- What was your favorite part about the plugin's design?
- What was your least favorite part about the plugin's design?
- What would you change about the plugin design if you could? (optional)
- Would you add or remove any pieces of the plugin for producing a vocal mix? If yes, why?

6.3 Demographics

- How long have you been producing music?
- What is your favorite Digital Audio Workstation (DAW) to produce with?
- How familiar are you with Ableton Live? How long have you used it?
- Have you used AI-based mastering tools such as Landr, Dolby.io, or SoundCloud before in your mixing/mastering process?
- Have you used machine learning (ML) tools such as Magenta in your creative process?
- Do you have any plugins that you use regularly and why?
- Do you tend to use stock presets when using plugins, or do you modify them and create your own?
- Have you used an adaptive plugin before? If so, which one(s)?
- How was your experience with them?

6.4 Wrap-Up

- Is there anything I covered that you would like to revisit or anything that I missed that you would like to add?
- What is your address for your gift card?
- Those are all the questions we have for you. Thanks for your participation.

References

1. Cartwright, M.: Supporting novice communication of audio concepts for audio production tools. Ph.D. dissertation, Northwestern University (2016)
2. da Silva, P.M.M., Mattos, C.L.C., de Souza Júnior, A.H.: Audio plugin recommendation systems for music production. In: 2019 8th Brazilian Conference on Intelligent Systems (BRACIS). IEEE, pp. 854–859 (2019)
3. Théberge, P., et al.: Any sound you can imagine: making music/consuming technology. Wesleyan University Press (1997)
4. Reiss, J.D.: Intelligent systems for mixing multichannel audio. In: 2011 17th International Conference on Digital Signal Processing (DSP). IEEE, pp. 1–6 (2011)
5. Turner, S.R.: A case-based model of creativity. In: Proceedings of the Thirteenth Annual Conference of the Cognitive Science Society, pp. 933–937 (1991)
6. Kolodner, J.L.: Understanding creativity: a case-based approach. In: Wess, S., Althoff, K.-D., Richter, M.M. (eds.) EWCBR 1993. LNCS, vol. 837, pp. 1–20. Springer, Heidelberg (1994). https://doi.org/10.1007/3-540-58330-0_73
7. Wills, L.M., Kolodner, J.L.: Towards more creative case-based design systems. In AAAI, vol. 94, pp. 50–55 (1994)
8. Stasis, S., Jillings, N., Enderby, S., Stables, R.: Audio processing chain recommendation. In: Proceedings of the 20th International Conference on Digital Audio Effects, (Edinburgh, UK) (2017)
9. Goudard, V., Muller, R.: Real-time audio plugin architectures. Comparative study. IRCAM-Centre Pompidou, France (2003)
10. Robillard, D.: Lv2 atoms: a data model for real-time audio plugins. In: Proceedings of the Linux Audio Conference (LAC-2014) (2014)
11. Peters, N., Choi, J., Lei, H.: Matching artificial reverb settings to unknown room recordings: a recommendation system for reverb plugins. In: Audio Engineering Society Convention 133. Audio Engineering Society (2012)
12. Stark, A.M., Davies, M.E., Plumbley, M.D.: Rhythmic analysis for real-time audio effects. In: International Computer Music Conference, ICMC 2008. University of Surrey (2008)
13. Chourdakis, E.T., Reiss, J.D.: A machine-learning approach to application of intelligent artificial reverberation. J. Audio Eng. Soc. **65**(1/2), 56–65 (2017)
14. Ramírez, M.A.M., Reiss, J.D.: End-to-end equalization with convolutional neural networks. In: 21st International Conference on Digital Audio Effects (DAFx-18) (2018)
15. Aamodt, A., Plaza, E.: Case-based reasoning: foundational issues, methodological variations, and system approaches. AI Commun. **7**(1), 39–59 (1994)
16. Leake, D.B.: Case-based reasoning: experiences, lessons, and future directions (1996)
17. De Mantaras, R.L., Arcos, J.L.: AI and music: from composition to expressive performance. AI Mag. **23**(3), 43–43 (2002)
18. Pereira, F.C., Grilo, C.F.A., Macedo, L., Cardoso, F.A.B.: Composing music with case-based reasoning. In: International Conference on Computational Models of Creative Cognition (1997)
19. Arcos, J.L., De Mántaras, R.L., Serra, X.: Saxex: a case-based reasoning system for generating expressive musical performances. J. New Music Res. **27**(3), 194–210 (1998)
20. Grachten, M., Arcos, J.L., López de Mántaras, R.: *TempoExpress*, a CBR approach to musical tempo transformations. In: Funk, P., González Calero, P.A. (eds.)

ECCBR 2004. LNCS (LNAI), vol. 3155, pp. 601–615. Springer, Heidelberg (2004). https://doi.org/10.1007/978-3-540-28631-8_44
21. Bodily, P.M., Ventura, D.: Musical metacreation: past, present, and future. In: Proceedings of the Sixth International Workshop on Musical Metacreation (2018)
22. Kim, Y.E., et al.: Music emotion recognition: a state of the art review. Proc. ISMIR **86**, 937–952 (2010)
23. Casey, M.A., Veltkamp, R., Goto, M., Leman, M., Rhodes, C., Slaney, M.: Content-based music information retrieval: current directions and future challenges. Proc. IEEE **96**(4), 668–696 (2008)
24. Shao, B., Wang, D., Li, T., Ogihara, M.: Music recommendation based on acoustic features and user access patterns. IEEE Trans. Audio Speech Lang. Process. **17**(8), 1602–1611 (2009)
25. Gatzioura, A., Sànchez-Marrè, M., et al.: Using contextual information in music playlist recommendations. In: CCIA, pp. 239–244 2017
26. De Mantaras, R.L., Plaza, E.: Case-based reasoning: an overview. AI Commun. **10**(1), 21–29 (1997)
27. Lee, J.S., Lee, J.C.: Context awareness by case-based reasoning in a music recommendation system. In: Ichikawa, H., Cho, W.-D., Satoh, I., Youn, H.Y. (eds.) UCS 2007. LNCS, vol. 4836, pp. 45–58. Springer, Heidelberg (2007). https://doi.org/10.1007/978-3-540-76772-5_4
28. Wang, Y., Yao, Q., Kwok, J.T., Ni, L.M.: Generalizing from a few examples: a survey on few-shot learning. ACM Comput. Surv. **53**(3), 1–34 (2020)
29. Smith, G., Whitehead, J.: Analyzing the expressive range of a level generator. In: Proceedings of the 2010 Workshop on Procedural Content Generation in Games, pp. 1–7 (2010)
30. Boersma, P., Weenink, D.: Praat: doing phonetics by computer (6.0.18) [computer software] (2019)
31. McKinney, J.C.: The Diagnosis and Correction of Vocal Faults: A Manual for Teachers of Singing and for Choir Directors. Waveland Press (2005)
32. Strauss, A., Corbin, J.: Basics of qualitative research techniques (1998)
33. Votipka, D., Stevens, R., Redmiles, E., Hu, J., Mazurek, M.: Hackers vs. testers: a comparison of software vulnerability discovery processes. In: 2018 IEEE Symposium on Security and Privacy (SP), pp. 374–391 (2018)
34. McHugh, M.L.: Interrater reliability: the kappa statistic. Biochemia Med. **22**(3), 276–282 (2012)

Forecasting for Sustainable Dairy Produce: Enhanced Long-Term, Milk-Supply Forecasting Using *k*-NN for Data Augmentation, with Prefactual Explanations for XAI

Eoin Delaney[1,2,3](✉), Derek Greene[1,2,3], Laurence Shalloo[3,4], Michael Lynch[5], and Mark T. Keane[1,2,3]

[1] School of Computer Science, University College Dublin, Dublin, Ireland
{eoin.delaney,derek.greene,mark.keane}@insight-centre.org
[2] Insight Centre for Data Analytics, University College Dublin, Dublin, Ireland
[3] VistaMilk SFI Research Centre, Cork, Ireland
laurence.shalloo@teagasc.ie
[4] Teagasc, Animal and Grassland Research Centre, Cork, Ireland
[5] ICBF, Cork, Ireland
mlynch@icbf.com

Abstract. Accurate milk supply forecasting for the dairy sector, covering 1000 s of farms with low resolution data, is a key challenge in achieving a sustainable, precision agriculture that can improve farm management, balancing costs, energy use and environmental protection. We show that case-based reasoning (CBR) can meet this sustainability challenge, by supplementing a time series prediction model on a full-year-forecasting task. Using a dataset of three years of milk supply from Irish dairy farms (N = 2,479), we produce accurate full-year forecasts for each individual farm, by augmenting that farm's data with data from nearest-neighboring farms, based on the similarity of their time series profiles (using Dynamic Time Warping). A study comparing four methods (Seasonal Naïve, LSTM, *Prophet*, $Prophet^{NN}$) showed that the method using CBR data-augmentation ($Prophet^{NN}$) outperformed the other evaluated methods. We also demonstrate the utility of CBR in providing farmers with novel *prefactual* explanations for forecasting that could help them to realize actions that could boost future milk yields and profitability.

Keywords: Smart agriculture · Dairy production · Time series · Prefactual explanation · CBR · Data augmentation

1 Introduction

While SmartAg was originally predicated on delivering enhanced agriculture yields and productivity, increasingly it is becoming more about delivering a sustainable and efficient agriculture that minimally pollutes, delivers

M. T. Keane and N. Wiratunga (Eds.): ICCBR 2022, LNAI 13405, pp. 365–379, 2022.
https://doi.org/10.1007/978-3-031-14923-8_24

equivalent/better production levels from fewer inputs, aiming for a zero-carbon impact on the environment in accordance with the UN's sustainability goals and the promise of "AI for Good" [16,42]. In the dairy sector, this challenge translates into producing the same or higher volumes of milk from fewer animals (e.g., genetically selecting cows that efficiently process what grass they eat), on pastures that make minimal use of artificial fertilizers (e.g., through using clover/grass mixes) and where carbon impacts are offset or balanced (e.g., using locally-grown grass rather than imported feed). Ultimately, meeting these challenges relies on understanding the relationships between a complex array of inputs (from animal genetics, to farm management to pollution measurement) and the volume of produce output by this sector, namely milk. Accurate long-term milk-supply forecasting plays a fundamental role in driving on-farm decision-making and processing capacity. Previous time series research has argued that *"combining of CBR with other approaches, seems promising and can improve the quality of forecasting"* [33]. CBR systems have also been successfully applied in oceanographic forecasting tasks [11]. More generally, in the agriculture domain, CBR solutions have enjoyed success in a variety of prediction tasks including grass growth prediction [24,25,40] and rangeland grasshopper infestation prediction [4,15]. In this paper, we show the promise of AI techniques, in particular how time series analyses can be improved by data-augmentation techniques, using k-nearest neighbor methods from CBR [1], to accurately forecast long-term milk supply. In addition, we show how CBR can be used to generate *prefactual* explanations to help farmers realize actions that could be taken to boost milk yield in future years (Sect. 3), before concluding and discussing promising avenues for future research (Sect. 4).

1.1 Why Milk-Supply Forecasting is Important for Sustainability

In any given year, milk supply forecasting is a fundamental driver for the dairy sector. Dairy companies use their forecasts to establish pricing, contracts with farms, and the production requirements for their factories. As such, proper forecasting strongly influences on-farm management (e.g., in under/over production and manner of production), the consumption of resources in the sector (e.g., fertilizer use, tanker-transport use for milk collections) and the processing efficiency of factories (e.g., avoiding waste from surplus milk supplies) [36,41]. Dairy processors can drive sustainability changes through accurate and precise forecasting. However, forecasting in this sector faces significant challenges. Milk-supply forecasts (i) must be made for 1000 s of farms which differ from one another in their herd-profiles, the land farmed and their farm-management practices, (ii) have to be made in advance for the *full year*, for planning purposes, not incrementally as the year unfolds, (iii) can encounter disruption from climate-change and disease outbreaks (e.g., a hot summer can stop grass growth).

1.2 Predicting Milk Supply with Low-Resolution Data at Scale

Several models exist in the literature that can forecast milk supply accurately, but typically only for experimental farms, which have extensive and carefully-recorded data (e.g., on individual cows, farm management practices; see [45] for a review). In this single-farm prediction context, the most successful models are the surface-fitting model and the NARX (Nonlinear autoregressive model with exogenous inputs; which has a RMSE = 75.5 kg for a 365 day horizon [44]). These models use features such as Days-In-Milk (number of days a cow has been lactating) and the NCM (number of cows milked) in the herd. Some studies have used as many as 12 features, including genetics, feed, and grazing management information of the individual cows. However, such high-resolution data is rarely available for most commercial farms [45]. So, it is unclear how these forecasting methods can commercially scale to 1000 s of farms.

In the present work, we attempt to forecast using low-resolution data where we have little information on individual cows and on-farm practices. In our time series model, we forecast for a given farm using the following minimal case-features: DATE (dd-mm-yyyy), WEEK (no. in year), MONTH (no. in year), HERD-DIM (Mean Days-in-Milk for the herd), CALVINGS (cumulative no. of calving's) to predict the target variable SUPPLY-QUANTITY (no. of litres in a given bulk-tanker collection). The DIM (Days-In-Milk) feature records the number of days a cow has been milking for and is important because a cow's milk yield varies over the season with a predictable profile (i.e., the so-called lactation curve that increases to Day-60 and then trails off (see [18]), The CALVINGS (cumulative no. of calving's) feature captures the number of offspring in the herd and is important because a cow only commences milking when it has given birth. Forecasting from these low-resolution inputs is quite hard because many key factors are missing (e.g., individual cow characteristics, amount and quality of feed used, calving management, etc.). Furthermore, the target variable, SUPPLY-QUANTITY, is not as informative as it could be, because it does not necessarily reflect one complete milking of the herd on a given day. It is a measure of the milk collected in a bulk tank on the farm (see Fig. 1) by a tanker truck, and can reflect several milkings of the whole herd; specifically, as tanker collection times can vary between 1–3 days, a single collection could contain 1–5 complete milkings of the herd. Figure 2 shows the variability that can occur in these weekly milk-supply figures from one farm over the three-year period.

Fig. 1. An on-farm, bulk tank where cooled milk is stored, before being collected by a tanker truck by the milk processor.

1.3 How CBR Might Improve Milk Forecasting

Previous unpublished work on this milk forecasting problem, using low resolution data, has shown that deep learning methods can make better predictions than traditional auto-regressive methods. However, the absolute error-levels from these models were unacceptably high. The standard data-analytics approach to this problem uses historical milk-supply, time series data to predict on a farm-by-farm basis and then aggregates these predictions to get the forecast for all the farms supplying a single milk-processing company. Our conjecture was that the error found in previous models was due to one or other of three factors: (i) having insufficient data for a given farm, (ii) disruptive events in a farm's history that undermined generalizations across years (e.g., a once-off disease outbreak), (iii) changes in the tanker-collection schedule for a given farm. Hence, we hypothesised that, if the data for a single farm were supplemented with data from similar farms during the prediction step, then these sources of error might be reduced. This hypothesis invites a CBR solution, where we use k-NN to find a small number of nearest-neighbor farms based on some similarity metric (i.e., not necessarily spatially-proximate farms) and then use their data to augment the dataset for the time series predictions. A key question for this solution is how to

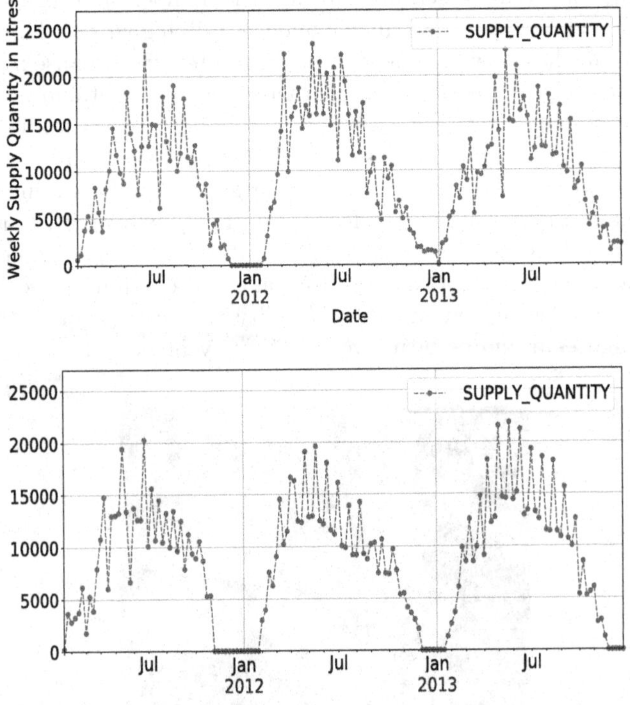

Fig. 2. Example of (a) 3-year milk supply profile of one farm, and (b) its nearest neighbor, retrieved using a dynamic time warping distance

determine the similarity between farms. Our solution bases this similarity on the multi-year profile of milk-supply between farms. One problem with this profile-similarity approach is that two farms may have very similar supply profiles but they may not align to one another in the time axis [2,31], because one farm may have started milking slightly earlier/later in the year compared to the other. To solve this problem, we retrieve farms with a k-NN using a dynamic time warping (DTW) distance measure, which has previously been used in CBR systems for both classification and regression tasks [28]. DTW allows the matching of profiles irrespective of temporal-offsets that might occur in the year. Figure 2 shows one farm-profile over a three year period and its nearest neighbor when DTW is used.

2 A Study on Forecasting Milk Supply

Dataset. The data considered in this work covers dairy herds/farms (N = 3,104) across 14 Irish counties for one dairy company (Glanbia) over four consecutive years. Cases describe the number of cows and calves in a herd at each milk collection and milk collected (target variable). On removing farms with missing data, the dataset had N = 2,479 farms. Specific dates are anonymised throughout this paper on request from the industry partner furnishing the data.

Forecasting Methods. Four different forecasting methods were used. First, as a simple benchmark [19], a Seasonal Naïve Forecasting method was used; it assumes that every week of the prediction-year's milk supply will be exactly the same as that of last year. While this is a popular benchmark in the forecasting space [19], it has surprisingly not been evaluated in previous milk supply prediction to the best of our knowledge (e.g., see review from [45]). Second, the *Long Short Term Memory (LSTM)* deep learning model was used as previously unpublished work found it to work best on this problem; LSTM stores sequences in long and short term states and then reuses them for prediction [17]. However, this has been shown to underperform basic statistical models on long-term forecasting and its processing overheads are an issue to be considered [29]. Third, the *Prophet* forecasting method, a generative additive model regularized with Bayesian techniques [38] was also used; it has been shown to work best for time series with strong seasonal effects and several seasons of historical data and in its simplest form is expressed as follows:

$$y(t) = g(t) + s(t) + \epsilon_t \tag{1}$$

Here the trend component, $g(t)$, automatically selects change points based on historic data by imposing a Laplacian prior. The seasonal component $s(t)$ is approximated with a Fourier series and a smoothing prior is imposed (see Eq. 2). For yearly seasonality we set the regular period $P = 365.25$ and we set $N = 10$ allowing one to calculate the Fourier coefficients, a_n and b_n, as recommended by [38].

$$s(t) = \sum_{n=1}^{N} (a_n cos(\frac{2\pi nt}{P}) + b_n sin(\frac{2\pi nt}{P})) \tag{2}$$

The error term ϵ_t represents unusual changes that are not accommodated by the model but do contribute to the final forecast. An optional holiday term $h(t)$ can be included which accommodates strange but regular occurrences in a time series (e.g., a jump in activity around Christmas time when forecasting retail sales). Unlike many traditional forecasting techniques (e.g., ARIMA), *Prophet* automatically provides uncertainty estimates on its forecasts and does not require measurements to be regularly spaced in the time axis.

This technique has many useful *analyst-in-the-loop* characteristics that could be exploited in practical applications (e.g., specifying the maximum capacity of a farm, unusual events such as disease-outbreaks or seasonal-changes can be set in advance of prediction). Fourth and finally, our own $Prophet^{NN}$ was used; it extends the *Prophet* model by adding the k-nearest-neighboring farms (using DTW as a distance metric) to augment the training data prior to prediction (in the reported results $k = 3$ was used in this model). Specifically, the historic and predicted supply from the 3-NN herds are added as additional features in the model.

Evaluation Metrics. Measures used included absolute error (AE) and mean absolute error (MAE), both measured in terms of litres-of-milk. We also considered MASE (Mean absolute scaled error), since it is the preferred evaluation technique in the forecasting literature, having many benefits over traditional measures [20]. When the MASE score is <1 it means that the proposed method is outperforming the Seasonal Naïve forecast, whereas a MASE score >1 means the opposite (i.e., smaller value better). Kullback-Leibler Divergence scores were used to compare model distributions to the ground truth.

Setup and Evaluation. The first three years were used as training data and the final year as test data. Holdout strategies are preferred for real-world non-stationary time series data [6], where we want to maximize the ability of the models to learn seasonal effects from the full three years of training data. For each week of the test year we have a predicted value and the actual value. Forecasts were generated for each farm and then aggregated. For the LSTM implementation, the Adam optimizer was used with 100 epochs, a batch size of 4, and a learning rate of 0.001. The Keras API was used [7]. Dropout layers were implemented to prevent overfitting. The *Prophet* model was implemented using the month, week, herd average DIM, and cumulative calving number features, with milk supply quantity as the target variable. No additional hyperparameters were implemented. In $Prophet^{NN}$, $k = 3$ for retrieving nearest neighbors for each farm when the forecasts were being made. All other $Prophet^{NN}$ parameters were identical to those used in *Prophet*.

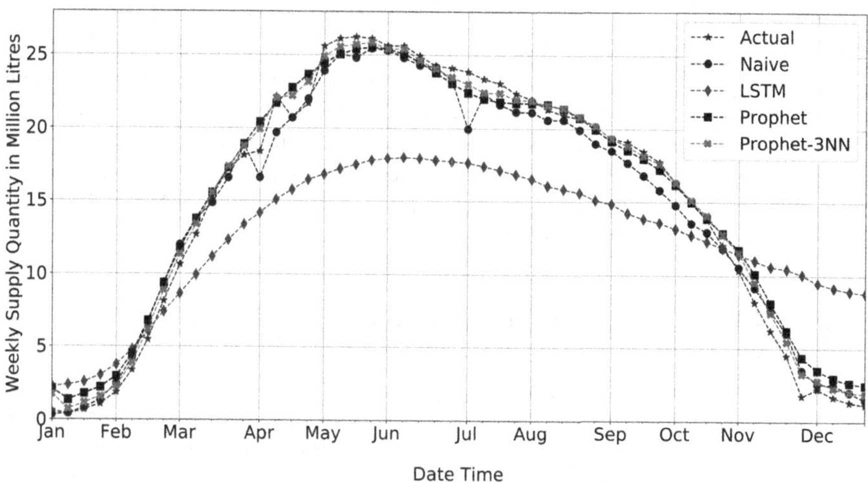

Fig. 3. A comparison of forecasts from the four methods relative to actual milk supply, as calculated on the final test year.

Table 1. Annual supply forecasts and error measures for each milk supply forecasting model. The ground truth value for actual production was 774.5 M ltrs.

Evaluation	Unit	S-Naïve	LSTM	*Prophet*	$Prophet^{NN}$
Predicted amount	Ltrs	755.8 M	652.6 M	796.1 M	789.6 M
Absolute error	Ltrs	18.7 M	129.1 M	21.6 M	15.1 M
MAE (Weekly)	Ltrs	0.97 M	4.8 M	0.95 M	0.58 M
MASE	N/A	1	4.96	0.976	0.595

Results and Discussion. The $Prophet^{NN}$ model performs reliably better (MASE = 0.595) than both the original *Prophet* model (MASE = 0.976) and the Naïve forecast (MASE = 1.00; see Table 1). In terms of the absolute error over the whole year, the $Prophet^{NN}$ prediction (789.6 M ltrs) is closest to the actual value (774.5 M ltrs), with a commercially acceptable error-margin (at 15.1 M ltrs). It is 3.6 M litres more accurate than the next best model (the Naïve model). This ordering of models by accuracy is mirrored by Kullback-Leibler Divergence scores, $D_{KL}(P||Q)$, comparing each model's distribution (Q) to the 2014 ground-truth distribution (P): $Prophet^{NN}$ (0.003), Naïve (0.004), *Prophet* (0.008), LSTM (0.068). Notably, in milk supply prediction, small differences in error measures result in large differences in real-world, commercial outcomes (i.e., in millions of litres). In this respect, the Naïve model really does quite well, whereas the LSTM model is notably bad, confirming its under-performance in long-term forecasting [29]; however, it might improve with farm-by-farm hyper-parameter tuning. All models tend to underpredict the peak milk-supply occurring in the summer months (see Fig. 3). This is a common theme in milk supply forecasting [32,45]. However, $Prophet^{NN}$ performs best during this three-month period, (MAE = 0.38 M). Both *Prophet* models overpredict milk supply at the start and end of the year, when supply is lowest, as farms begin and end milking for the year, when the Naïve model performs best (MAE = 0.37 M). This result suggests that an ensemble approach may be useful in future work, where different models are used for different parts of the year. To summarize, the $Prophet^{NN}$ compares better than the other models evaluated in terms of MASE, MAE, AE and Kullback-Leibler Divergence score.

3 Providing Explainable Insights to Farmers

While providing forecasts on future milk supply from historical data can significantly enhance planning and resource allocation, the forecasts themselves do not provide any information on how a farm could increase its future output and boost profitability. One motivating reason for providing explanations to end-user farmers is to aid them in improving their current practice [23]. In the context of dairy farming this could translate into providing insights or recommendations that will help farmers to boost future milk output from the farm. Our focus in providing explanations to farmers is not on why a certain forecast is made based on historic data, but instead it is on realizing steps that could be taken to improve future yields.

3.1 Prefactual Explanations

A *prefactual explanation* describes a conditional (if-then) proposition about an, as yet not undertaken, action and the corresponding outcome that may (or may not) take place in the future [5,10]. While counterfactuals focus on past events, prefactuals center on the future and capture the idea of something that is not yet a fact, but could well become a fact [10].

In terms of goal planning, prefactual explanations can help individuals to determine how and whether a certain goal may be achieved in the future, and plan subsequent actions accordingly [10]. While counterfactual explanations have enjoyed success in providing explanations for past events (most commonly in classification systems [8,9,21,22,43]), prefactual explanations are relatively untapped, yet extremely promising for eXplainable AI (XAI) in forecasting scenarios. Perhaps the most relevant work here is in the area of goal-based recommendation, where CBR has been successfully applied to predict realistic new personal best race times for athletes and to recommend a suitable training plan to achieve their goals [12,37]. Similarly, in predicting forage-loss estimates due to grasshopper infestation, treatment recommendations have been provided that can help to minimize future economic loss [4]. These prefactual explanations could be used to provide insights to farmers that could help them to increase their milk output in future years. In the next sub-section, we describe a novel framework to formulate prefactual explanations, which is based on contrasting low-performing herds with high-performing *exemplar cases*.

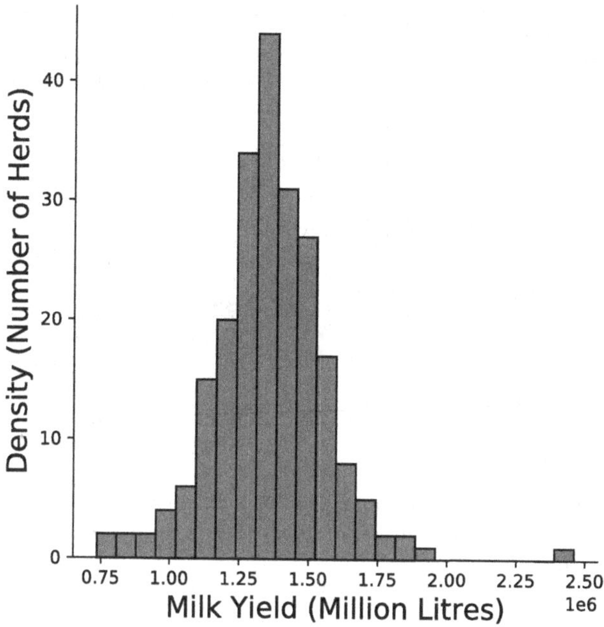

Fig. 4. The distribution of total milk output from medium size dairy farms (75–85 Cows, N = 233 cases) over a four year period.

3.2 Using Prototypes in Prefactual Explanations

Prototypes are instances that are maximally representative of a class (typically retrieved using class centroids [30]) and have been used in several problem domains successfully to generate global explanations [13,26,30]. While there are no specific class labels in our problem, one observation from the case-base is that farms with a similar herd size (e.g., medium sized herds of ≈80 cows [39,41]) tend to vary greatly in terms of their milk output over the four-year period covered in the dataset (see Fig. 4). So, for a fixed herd-size, there are both high performing herds with high milk yield, and low performing herds at the lower end of the distribution. By leveraging information from the high performing *exemplar cases* at the upper end of the distribution, lower-performing farms could modify their management practices with a view to enhancing future returns (e.g., an increased yield in the next year). More simply, prefactual explanations that use high-performing farms as exemplars should provide a basis for informing farmers on best practice. In the following sub-sections, we discuss the aspects of farm-management that could be the subject of these prefactual recommendations, with a view to identifying those that improve sustainability.

(I) Increasing Herd Size: As one might expect, there is a strong correlation between the number of animals on a farm and milk yield across the whole case-base (Pearson's $r = 0.947$). But, Fig. 4 shows us that that many farms can

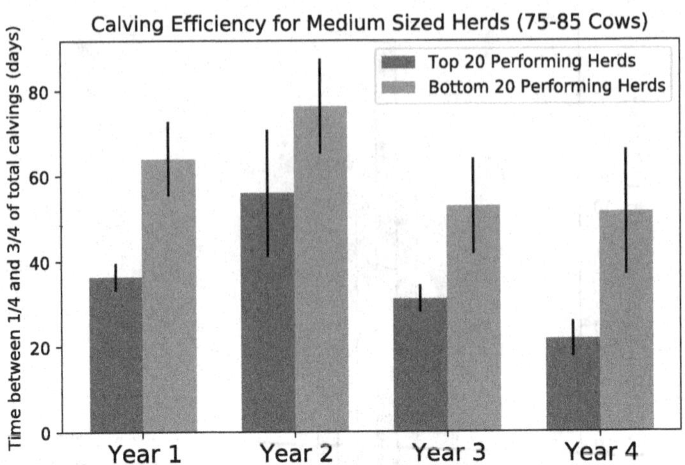

Fig. 5. Comparing both the most and the least efficient farms (at the tails of the distribution). The most efficient farms, in terms of milk output, calve much faster than the least efficient farms.

increase their yield without increasing the size of their herd. There are several reasons why increasing herd size is not a good strategy for a farmer to take; (i) it requires new investment to buy more animals, (ii) it increases running costs of the herd (e.g., feed, fertilizer for grass, shelter, veterinary costs), estimated to be €1516 per animal on an Irish farm in 2022 [14,35], (iii) it increases the likelihood of disease being introduced into a "closed" herd [35]. However, perhaps the biggest issue is that it is not a sustainable strategy. A prefactual could tell a farmer *"You could boost your yield by 10% next year if you increase your herd size by 10%"*, but such advice will also increase the carbon-costs of the farm and the potential for environmental damage and pollution (e.g., more cows equals more methane). As such, a more sustainable strategy would be to improve management practices without expanding the herd-size.

(II) Constraining Calving: Dairy farmers using sustainable pasture-based systems where cows are mainly fed on grass in fields, are now strongly advised to control the timing of calving in their herds. Research has shown that constraining calving to a 6-week window in spring can greatly improve milk yield and herd fertility in pasture based-systems [35]. These benefits arise because after calving, cows begin milk production just as grass growth starts to peak; so, the animals ability to produce milk synchronises with the availability of sustainable feed (i.e., grass as opposed to bought-in, carbon-heavy supplementary feeds, such as soya or corn). Extended calving intervals result in the breakdown of the synchrony between feed supply and feed demand and often result in reduced fertility, over-fat cows and an increased likelihood of disease in the herd [35]. All of these factors negatively impact milk yield and often lead to increases in artificial insemination, veterinary and hormonal costs [3,35]. Indeed, this proposed relationship between calving-periods and milk yield is supported by analyses of our dataset. We estimated on-farm calving efficiency by analysing the mean amount of time taken between the calving of the 1/4 and 3/4 of calves born on farms across the four year period. Using a fixed herd size for (i) the top 20 performing *exemplar* herds, and (ii) the worst 20 performing herds (see e.g., Fig. 5), it was found that the best or *exemplary* herds calve significantly faster than herds with lower milk yields (one sided t-test, $p < 0.001$). Therefore, one useful prefactual explanation for farmers hoping to boost subsequent yield could be of the form; *"If you constrain calving to a shorter period than last year, your future milk supply is likely to increase"*.

(III) Optimizing the Supply Profile: To gain insights into the optimal supply profile for a herd, we compare the prototypical supply profile for both high-performing herds and herds with the lowest supply for a fixed herd-size. Prototypical herds are created using centroids from: (i) k-medoids clustering with a DTW distance measure as it retrieves realistic instances that are already part of the case-base [30], and (ii) k-means clustering with dynamic barycenter averaging as suggested by [34]. This analysis showed that *exemplary* herds have a much shorter drying-off period compared to the weaker performing herds (See Fig. 6). This "drying-off" period (which usually lasts 6–8 weeks) typically occurs at the end of the year, when cows are not milked, to allow them to recover health-wise before the next calving season [27]. Although this period plays a critical role in rejuvenating an animal's health, too long a dry period can result in over-fat cows and reduced fertility. So, an extended dry period can reduce milk yield on a given farm. While research suggests that drying off decisions should be made on an individual cow basis [27], we found that lower performing herds tend to have over-extended periods of no-milkings, hurting their yields. The prototypical supply curves for *exemplar* herds, unlike low-yielding herds, quickly grow to reach their peak yield in early summer and slowly taper off towards the dry period in late November/early-December. Indeed, their milk-supply curves track the grass growth curves observed on farms during these periods (see Kenny et al., [25]), where grass growth typically peaks in early May before tapering off into Autumn. Therefore, one useful prefactual explanation for farmers hoping to boost subsequent yield could be of the form; *"If you slightly reduce the drying off period, (i) your future milk supply is likely to increase as you will have longer milking periods, (ii) you could be less reliant on purchasing feed as the supply curve is more likely to track the grass growth curve"*.

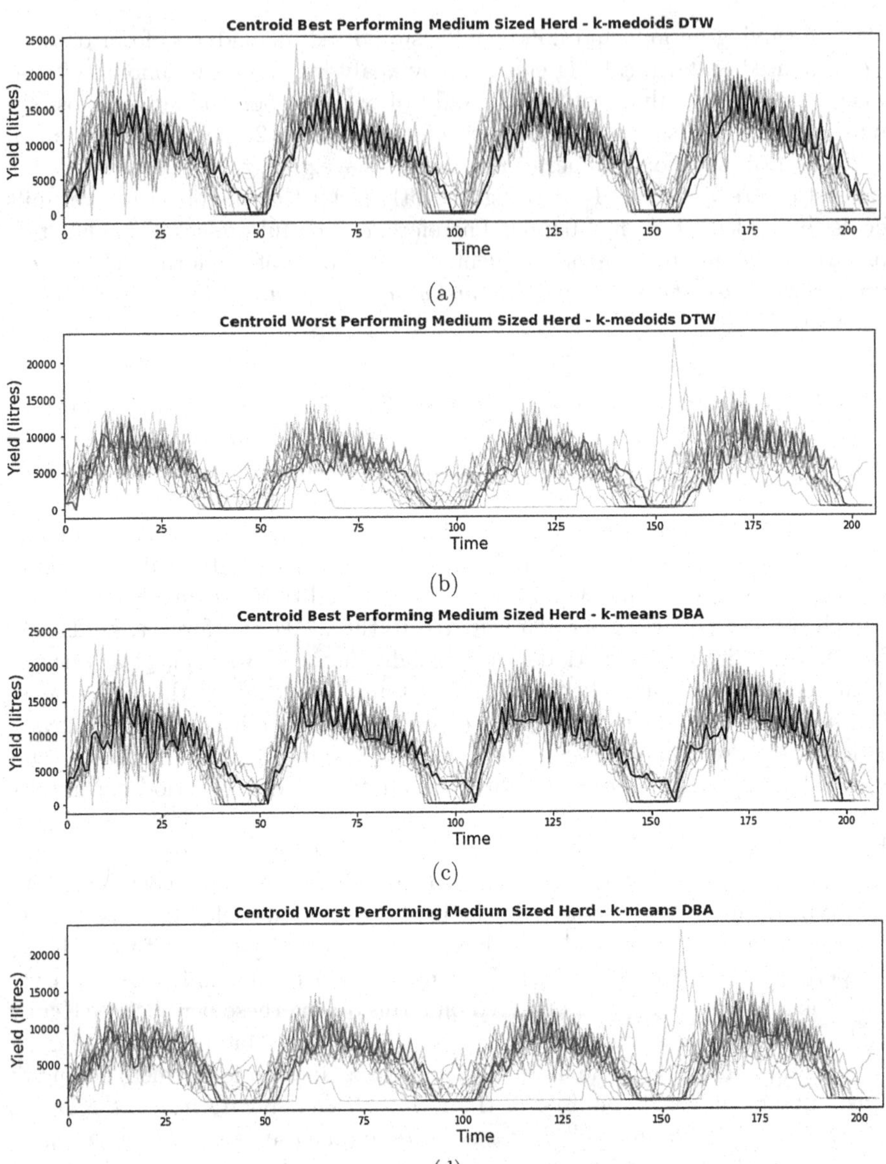

(a)

(b)

(c)

(d)

Fig. 6. Prototypical milk yield supply profiles over a four year period for high (in blue) and low (in red) performing medium-sized herds according to prototypes retrieved using the centroid from: (i) k-medoids DTW shown in (a) & (b), and (ii) k-means DBA in (c) & (d). (Color figure online)

4 Conclusion and Future Directions

Facing the challenge of developing a precision agriculture that can support sustainability, we have demonstrated a promising CBR data-augmentation technique, using nearest neighboring farms with similar production profiles, which makes acceptably accurate long-term forecasts for milk supply based on low resolution data. As milk-supply forecasting drives significant aspects of the agricultural sector, better forecasting can play a critical role in reducing resource waste from farm to factory and in budgeting-on farm. An immediate avenue for future work is to investigate hyperparamater tuning on a validation set in an attempt to boost predictive performance. We also explored the utility of CBR in providing novel goal-oriented *prefactual* explanations to farmers to help them realize actions that could boost milk yield in future years. A core novelty of this work is in generating *prefactual* explanations through leveraging high performing *exemplar* cases, and in future work we would like to develop alternative algorithmic approaches to generate such explanations and to explore their utility in domains beyond agriculture. All of the current work, demonstrates how CBR and AI has the potential to improve farm-management practices in ways that deliver a more efficient, less polluting and more sustainable agriculture.

Acknowledgements. This publication has emanated from research conducted with the financial support of (i) Science Foundation Ireland (SFI) to the Insight Centre for Data Analytics under Grant Number 12/RC/2289_P2 and (ii) SFI and the Department of Agriculture, Food and Marine on behalf of the Government of Ireland under Grant Number 16/RC/3835 (VistaMilk).

References

1. Aha, D.W., Kibler, D., Albert, M.K.: Instance-based learning algorithms. Mach. Learn. **6**(1), 37–66 (1991). https://doi.org/10.1007/BF00153759
2. Berndt, D.J., Clifford, J.: Using dynamic time warping to find patterns in time series. In: KDD Workshop, vol. 10, pp. 359–370. Seattle, WA, USA (1994)
3. Boichard, D.: Estimation of the economic value of conception rate in dairy cattle. Livest. Prod. Sci. **24**(3), 187–204 (1990)
4. Branting, K., Hastings, J.D., Lockwood, J.A.: Carma: a case-based range management advisor. In: IAAI, pp. 3–10 (2001)
5. Byrne, R.M., Egan, S.M.: Counterfactual and prefactual conditionals. Can. J. Exp. Psychol./Revue Can. de Psychol. Expérimentale **58**(2), 113 (2004)
6. Cerqueira, V., Torgo, L., Mozetič, I.: Evaluating time series forecasting models: an empirical study on performance estimation methods. Mach. Learn. **109**(11), 1997–2028 (2020). https://doi.org/10.1007/s10994-020-05910-7
7. Chollet, F., et al.: Keras (2015). https://github.com/fchollet/keras
8. Dai, X., Keane, M.T., Shalloo, L., Ruelle, E., Byrne, R.M.: Counterfactual explanations for prediction and diagnosis in xai. In: To appear in AIES 2022 (2022)
9. Delaney, E., Greene, D., Keane, M.T.: Instance-based counterfactual explanations for time series classification. In: Sánchez-Ruiz, A.A., Floyd, M.W. (eds.) ICCBR 2021. LNCS (LNAI), vol. 12877, pp. 32–47. Springer, Cham (2021). https://doi.org/10.1007/978-3-030-86957-1_3

10. Epstude, K., Scholl, A., Roese, N.J.: Prefactual thoughts: mental simulations about what might happen. Rev. Gen. Psychol. **20**(1), 48–56 (2016)
11. Fdez-Riverola, F., Corchado, J.M.: Fsfrt: forecasting system for red tides. Appl. Intell. **21**(3), 251–264 (2004). https://doi.org/10.1023/B:APIN.0000043558.52701.b1
12. Feely, C., Caulfield, B., Lawlor, A., Smyth, B.: Using case-based reasoning to predict marathon performance and recommend tailored training plans. In: Watson, I., Weber, R. (eds.) ICCBR 2020. LNCS (LNAI), vol. 12311, pp. 67–81. Springer, Cham (2020). https://doi.org/10.1007/978-3-030-58342-2_5
13. Gee, A.H., Garcia-Olano, D., Ghosh, J., Paydarfar, D.: Explaining deep classification of time-series data with learned prototypes. CEUR Workshop Proc. **2429**, 15–22 (2019)
14. Gowing, P., Dunne, J.: Cost control for 2022 (2022). https://www.teagasc.ie/news--events/daily/dairy/cost-control-for-2022.php
15. Hastings, J., Branting, K., Lockwood, J.: Carma: a case-based rangeland management adviser. AI Mag. **23**(2), 49–49 (2002)
16. Herweijer, C., Combes, B., Gillham, J.: How AI can enable a sustainable future. PwC report (2018)
17. Hochreiter, S., Schmidhuber, J.: Long short-term memory. Neural Comput. **9**(8), 1735–1780 (1997)
18. Horan, B., Dillon, P., Berry, D., O'Connor, P., Rath, M.: The effect of strain of holstein-friesian, feeding system and parity on lactation curves characteristics of spring-calving dairy cows. Livest. Prod. Sci. **95**(3), 231–241 (2005)
19. Hyndman, R.J., Athanasopoulos, G.: Forecasting: principles and practice. OTexts (2018)
20. Hyndman, R.J., Koehler, A.B.: Another look at measures of forecast accuracy. Int. J. Forecast. **22**(4), 679–688 (2006)
21. Keane, M.T., Kenny, E.M., Delaney, E., Smyth, B.: If only we had better counterfactual explanations: five key deficits to rectify in the evaluation of counterfactual xai techniques. In: IJCAI-21 (2021)
22. Keane, M.T., Smyth, B.: Good Counterfactuals and where to find them: a case-based technique for generating counterfactuals for explainable AI (XAI). In: Watson, I., Weber, R. (eds.) ICCBR 2020. LNCS (LNAI), vol. 12311, pp. 163–178. Springer, Cham (2020). https://doi.org/10.1007/978-3-030-58342-2_11
23. Kenny, E.M., Ford, C., Quinn, M., Keane, M.T.: Explaining black-box classifiers using post-hoc explanations-by-example: the effect of explanations and error-rates in xai user studies. Artif. Intell. **294**, 103459 (2021)
24. Kenny, E.M., et al.: Bayesian case-exclusion and personalized explanations for sustainable dairy farming. In: IJCAI, pp. 4740–4744 (2021)
25. Kenny, E.M., Ruelle, E., Geoghegan, A., Shalloo, L., O'Leary, M., O'Donovan, M., Keane, M.T.: Predicting grass growth for sustainable dairy farming: a CBR system using bayesian case-exclusion and *Post-Hoc*, personalized explanation-by-example (XAI). In: Bach, K., Marling, C. (eds.) ICCBR 2019. LNCS (LNAI), vol. 11680, pp. 172–187. Springer, Cham (2019). https://doi.org/10.1007/978-3-030-29249-2_12
26. Kim, B., Khanna, R., Koyejo, O.O.: Examples are not enough, learn to criticize! criticism for interpretability. In: Advances in Neural Information Processing Systems, pp. 2280–2288 (2016)
27. Kok, A., Chen, J., Kemp, B., Van Knegsel, A.: Dry period length in dairy cows and consequences for metabolism and welfare and customised management strategies. Animal **13**(S1), s42–s51 (2019)

28. Mahato, V., O'Reilly, M., Cunningham, P.: A comparison of k-nn methods for time series classification and regression. In: AICS, pp. 102–113 (2018)
29. Makridakis, S., Spiliotis, E., Assimakopoulos, V.: Statistical and machine learning forecasting methods: concerns and ways forward. PLoS One **13**(3), e0194889 (2018)
30. Molnar, C.: Interpretable machine learning. Lulu.com (2020)
31. Mueen, A., Keogh, E.: Extracting optimal performance from dynamic time warping. In: Proceedings of the 22nd ACM SIGKDD International Conference on Knowledge Discovery and Data Mining, pp. 2129–2130 (2016)
32. Murphy, M.D., O'Mahony, M.J., Shalloo, L., French, P., Upton, J.: Comparison of modelling techniques for milk-production forecasting. J. Dairy Sci. **97**(6), 3352–3363 (2014)
33. Nakhaeizadeh, G.: Learning prediction of time series. A theoretical and empirical comparison of CBR with some other approaches. In: Wess, S., Althoff, K.-D., Richter, M.M. (eds.) EWCBR 1993. LNCS, vol. 837, pp. 65–76. Springer, Heidelberg (1994). https://doi.org/10.1007/3-540-58330-0_77
34. Petitjean, F., Forestier, G., Webb, G.I., Nicholson, A.E., Chen, Y., Keogh, E.: Dynamic time warping averaging of time series allows faster and more accurate classification. In: 2014 IEEE international conference on data mining, pp. 470–479. IEEE (2014)
35. Shalloo, L., Cromie, A., McHugh, N.: Effect of fertility on the economics of pasture-based dairy systems. Animal **8**(s1), 222–231 (2014)
36. Shalloo, L., Creighton, P., O'Donovan, M.: The economics of reseeding on a dairy farm. Irish J. Agric. Food Res. **50**(1), 113–122 (2011)
37. Smyth, B., Cunningham, P.: A novel recommender system for helping marathoners to achieve a new personal-best. In: Proceedings of the Eleventh ACM Conference on Recommender Systems, pp. 116–120 (2017)
38. Taylor, S.J., Letham, B.: Forecasting at scale. Am. Stat. **72**(1), 37–45 (2018)
39. Teagasc: Teagasc national farm survey 2020 - dairy enterprise fact-sheet (2020). https://www.teagasc.ie/media/website/publications/2021/NFS_Dairy_Factsheet 2020.pdf
40. Temraz, M., Kenny, E.M., Ruelle, E., Shalloo, L., Smyth, B., Keane, M.T.: Handling climate change using counterfactuals: using counterfactuals in data augmentation to predict crop growth in an uncertain climate future. In: Sánchez-Ruiz, A.A., Floyd, M.W. (eds.) ICCBR 2021. LNCS (LNAI), vol. 12877, pp. 216–231. Springer, Cham (2021). https://doi.org/10.1007/978-3-030-86957-1_15
41. Upton, J., Murphy, M., De Boer, I., Koerkamp, P.G., Berentsen, P., Shalloo, L.: Investment appraisal of technology innovations on dairy farm electricity consumption. J. Dairy Sci. **98**(2), 898–909 (2015)
42. Vinuesa, R., et al.: The role of artificial intelligence in achieving the sustainable development goals. Nat. Commun. **11**(1), 1–10 (2020)
43. Wiratunga, N., Wijekoon, A., Nkisi-Orji, I., Martin, K., Palihawadana, C., Corsar, D.: Actionable feature discovery in counterfactuals using feature relevance explainers. Case-based reasoning for the explanation of intelligent systems, Third Workshop on XCBR (2021)
44. Zhang, F., Murphy, M.D., Shalloo, L., Ruelle, E., Upton, J.: An automatic model configuration and optimization system for milk production forecasting. Comput. Electron. Agric. **128**, 100–111 (2016)
45. Zhang, F., Shine, P., Upton, J., Shaloo, L., Murphy, M.D.: A review of milk production forecasting models: past & future methods (2020)

A Case-Based Approach for Content Planning in Data-to-Text Generation

Ashish Upadhyay(✉) and Stewart Massie

Robert Gordon University, Aberdeen, UK
{a.upadhyay,s.massie}@rgu.ac.uk

Abstract. The problem of Data-to-Text Generation (D2T) is usually solved using a modular approach by breaking the generation process into some variant of planning and realisation phases. Traditional methods have been very good at producing high quality texts but are difficult to build for complex domains and also lack diversity. On the other hand, current neural systems offer scalability and diversity but at the expense of being inaccurate. Case-Based approaches try to mitigate the accuracy and diversity trade-off by providing better accuracy than neural systems and better diversity than traditional systems. However, they still fare poorly against neural systems when measured on the dimensions of content selection and diversity. In this work, a Case-Based approach for content-planning in D2T, called CBR-Plan, is proposed which selects and organises the key components required for producing a summary, based on similar previous examples. Extensive experiments are performed to demonstrate the effectiveness of the proposed method against a variety of benchmark and baseline systems, ranging from template-based, to case-based and neural systems. The experimental results indicate that CBR-Plan is able to select more relevant and diverse content than other systems.

Keywords: Data-to-Text Generation · Case-based planning · Content planning

1 Introduction

Data-to-Text Generation (D2T) is the process of summarising insights and information extracted from non-linguistic structured data in a textual format [3,15]. With business processes often generating a huge amount of domain-specific data, which is not easily understandable by humans, there is a growing need to synthesise this data by converting it into textual summaries that are more accessible. There are many real-world applications, from weather or financial reporting [5,7,16] to medical support and sports journalism [9,23]. There are two main problems that should be addressed in a D2T problem: **content planning**, selecting and ordering important content from the input data (implicit or explicit), as in *what to say?*; and **surface realisation**, conveying the selected content in a textual summary, as in *how to say?*. Content planning is the focus of this work.

M. T. Keane and N. Wiratunga (Eds.): ICCBR 2022, LNAI 13405, pp. 380–394, 2022.
https://doi.org/10.1007/978-3-031-14923-8_25

There are different types of systems that can be used to solve the D2T problem. Traditional methods, that use a modular approach with hand-crafted rules and templates acquired from domain knowledge, are very good at producing high-quality textual summaries with accurate information [7,15,16]. However, they lack diversity and generate monotonous texts. Also, in complex domains, it is difficult to hand-craft the rules for every possible situation, making these systems difficult to scale. Current state-of-the-art neural systems usually take an end-to-end approach and are capable of producing diverse and fluent summaries while offering better scalability across domains [13,23]. However, they are prone to errors and often generate inaccurate texts not supported by the input. There have been some attempts to utilise neural systems in a modular way by breaking them into separate planning and realisation phases [2,12]. Whilst offering better performance than the end-to-end counterparts they tend to be more conservative and achieve better accuracy at the cost of diversity.

Case-Based approaches, also by taking a somewhat modular approach, try to mitigate the accuracy and diversity trade-off by retrieving similar problems from the case-base and reusing them to dynamically generate a custom template for the new problem [1,22]. They offer better accuracy than neural systems while better diversity than traditional systems. Nonetheless, the case-based approaches still perform below par with neural systems when evaluated for content selection and diversity in generations. Thus, missing out on much relevant information that may be important for the summary and would have been selected by a human author.

In this work, we propose a Case-Based Reasoning (CBR) approach for content-planning in D2T problems that selects the main components for a summary and organises them to create a plan by reusing solutions of previous similar problems. In this process, first, several key components are identified that contribute to writing a D2T summary, and then a CBR method is used to create a content-plan by selecting and organising a subset of those components. The main contributions of this work are as follows:

1. develop a new CBR-based model for the content-planning task in D2T[1];
2. introduction of a new concept identification process to support evaluation of D2T approaches; and
3. demonstrating the performance of the proposed method at content selection effectiveness and diversity on a standard D2T evaluation data set.

The rest of the paper is organised as follows: in the next section we discuss relevant related works from the literature; then in Sect. 3, we provide an in-depth background of the problem and provide insight on where this work fits into a bigger picture; which is followed with the description of our proposed method in Sect. 4; and the experimental setup in Sect. 5. We then discuss the results obtained from the experiments in Sect. 6; and finally conclude the paper with some key takeaways and future directions in Sect. 7.

---

[1] code-base is available at https://github.com/ashishu007/data2text-cbr-plan.

2 Related Works

Data-to-Text Generation (D2T) is a sub-field of Natural Language Generation (NLG) aiming to summarise structured non-linguistic data as opposed to Text-to-Text Generation (T2T) which aims to summarise linguistic data in textual summaries [3]. D2T has been studied for decades, one of the very first systems proposed in the 1980s, generated textual summaries of financial data [7]. There have been several other traditional systems in multiple domains ranging from weather forecasting to medical support documentation [5,9,16]. They have followed a modular approach by breaking the problem into several smaller ones and solving them separately with different modules designed with carefully crafted rules [14]. Recent advancements in neural techniques have given rise to learning based neural systems that initially tried to model the whole task into a single end-to-end process [13,23]. But recent trends have seen the resurgence of modular approaches even in neural systems demonstrating better performance than their end-to-end counterparts [2,10,12]. However, the planning-based neural systems tend to be more conservative by generating easier and less diverse summaries in order to become more accurate.

Traditional D2T systems are capable of producing high-quality texts but come with the challenge of scalability across domains and lesser diversity in the text generated. On the other hand, neural systems offer better scalability and diversity than traditional systems, but at the expense of accurate generations. Case-Based systems also take a modular approach and aim to mitigate this accuracy and diversity trade-off by generating a custom template for a new problem using solutions from similar past experiences [1,21,22]. Although the idea of CBR systems being more accurate than neural and more diverse than traditional counterparts appears sound, typical performance is poorer than neural systems in terms of content selection and diversity.

Case-Based Planning has also been studied for a long time with initial methods being applied in several domains ranging from holiday and logistics to story planning [4,17,20]. In this work, the focus is to build a CBR-based content-planning module for D2T problems that generates better content-plans with respect to content selection and diversity.

3 Problem Description and Representation

Each case in a D2T case-base is an event which consists of the event's data on the problem side and its textual summary on the solution side. The textual summary of each event aims to describe the important insights and information extracted from the event's data. In easier domains, the event summary contains information from only the single event but in more complex domains, the summary may contain information from its neighbouring cases as well [22].

The problem side of each case in the case-base is represented by multiple entities. Each of these entities is further represented with several features that aim to describe the entities. Each feature is assigned a value, which in most cases,

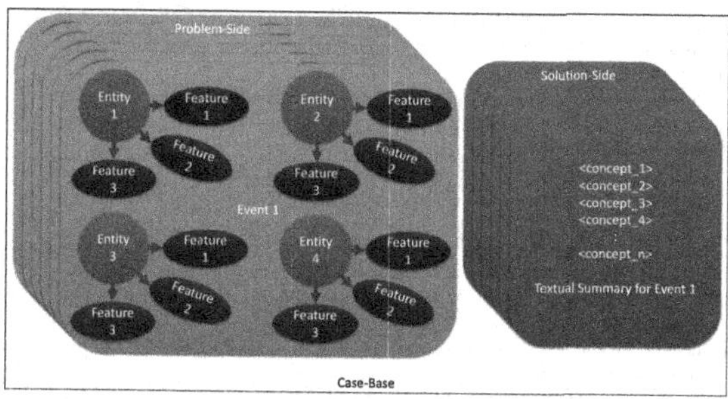

Fig. 1. Case-base in a Data-to-Text Generation problem

is numerical but may also be either categorical or textual. Solutions-side of the event summaries is a combination of multiple concepts each describing single or multiple entities with some type of information. Each concept is essentially a sentence from the textual summary. An example case-base with its problem and solution sides is shown in Fig. 1.

Taking the sports domain datasets [19,23] as an example, an event can be seen as a match between two teams for which a summary is written. Each event is represented by its entities which are the players and teams that play in the game. Furthermore, each entity is represented with several features which are the stat categories that are recorded for each player or team. The textual summary is a set of concepts each describing an entity (or combination of entities) from the event.

To build a D2T system, the following points should be taken in account:

- first, identify all the relevant concepts that may be interesting for any event and can be included in the summaries;
- second, select important concepts with respect to a given event that is interesting and should be included in the event's summary;
- third, decide which entities (or a combination of entities) should be described using each selected concept; and
- finally, generates a semantically accurate sentence for each concept describing an entity and pragmatically orders them to generate the final summary.

In this work, we will focus on the first three steps of this process. We will use information gathered from some corpus analysis to identify several possible concepts. Then we will use a CBR method to select the relevant concepts for a target case, and finally, another data-driven method will be used to identify the entities that will be described by each selected concept. This is analogous to the **Content Planning** phase of a standard D2T system [2,12].

4 Content Planning Methodology

In this work, we focus on building a method for generating a content-plan that will be used by a text-generator model to produce an event's summary. As discussed earlier, a summary is a set of concepts each describing an entity (or a

S01	The Philadelphia 76ers (16-52) defeated the Detroit Pistons (24-44) 94-83 on Wednesday in Philadelphia .
S02	The 76ers were able to pull off the win despite Nerlens Noel leaving the game with a right foot contusion after playing just 22 minutes .
S03	He had 11 points on 5-of-10 shooting , four rebounds and three blocks in that time and did not return .
S04	It was Ish Smith who led the way for Philadelphia , as he was moved into the starting point guard role while Isaiah Canaan was moved to the bench .
S05	Smith thrived in the role , recording 15 points on 6-of-12 shooting , eight assists and three steals in 26 minutes .
S06	Canaan struggled coming off the bench , putting up just nine points on 2-of-10 shooting and four assists in 22 minutes .
S07	Jason Richardson shot his way out of a slump , scoring 15 points on 4-of-7 shooting in 25 minutes , as it was just the first time in five games that Richardson scored in double figures .
S08	Conversely , Robert Covington struggled , as he shot just 1-of-6 from the field on his way to three points in 22 minutes off the bench .
S09	It was a quick fall back to reality for the Pistons , as just a day after upsetting the Grizzlies and ending a 10 - game losing streak , they lost to one of the NBA 's worst teams .
S10	They were without Greg Monroe , who sat out his second consecutive game with a strained knee .
S11	Despite the loss , Detroit did have some strong performances .
S12	Reggie Jackson followed up Tuesday night 's big game with a triple-double , putting up 11 points on just 4-of-17 shooting , 11 rebounds and 10 assists in 32 minutes .
S13	Kentavious Caldwell-Pope also followed up his 24-point performance on Tuesday in a strong way , scoring 20 points on 7-of-16 shooting and grabbing eight rebounds in 36 minutes .
S14	Up next , the 76ers will take on the Knicks at home Friday , while the Pistons head home Saturday to take on the Bulls .

Fig. 2. An example summary from SportSett dataset

combination of entities) from the event. Thus a content-plan is a set of concepts, ordered in a sequence, each aligned with one or more entities. To build the content-plan, the first step is to identify all the possible concepts that may be relevant to any event's summary. Then, for a given target event (new problem), a subset of identified concepts and associated entities corresponding to each concept should be selected and ordered. The final stage would be to select a suitable template for each selected concept and populate it with the corresponding entity's values. But this final step of generating the text by selecting and populating templates is out of the scope of this work.

4.1 Concept Identification

The summaries in a typical D2T domain contain information of different complexities. A summary is written with multiple sentences, where each sentence can have several information elements of different types. For example, in Fig. 2, S12 identifies that player 'Reggie Jackson' scored a triple-double[2] with 11 points, rebounds and 10 assists in the game, continuing his good performance from the previous game. Firstly, the straightforward information, such as he scored 11 points and rebounds, can be directly copied from the input data (problem side representation) into the output summary. Secondly, the information that the player scored a triple-double is not explicitly stated in the input data, rather it needs to be derived from several features from the single event, which in this case would be from the player's stats, such as points, rebounds, etc. This kind of information will be more difficult for a system to generate, as it requires the system to be capable of performing inference and arithmetic operations. Lastly, the fact that it was the player's continuation from the previous game can only be derived by taking the data from several events into account. This will be even

[2] https://en.wikipedia.org/wiki/Double-double#Triple-double.

harder as the amount of data that needs to be considered for inference will grow massively. Thus, an event's summary can have three types of information:

- **Intra-Event Basic (Basic; B)** information that can be directly copied from an event's input data into the output summary;
- **Intra-Event Complex (Within; W)** information that needs to be implicitly derived from given information in an event's data; and
- **Inter-Event (Across; A)** the information that can be only derived from taking the data of multiple events into account.

Sentences in a summary can be classified based on the type of information it contains into one of the seven categories: just Basic, **B**; just Within, **W**; just Across, **A**; both Basic and Within, **B&W**; both Basic and Across, **B&A**; both Within and Across **W&A**; and finally, all Basic, Within and Across, **B&W&A**. In addition to different types of information in the summary, each sentence can describe different types of entities: a **Player (P)**; and a **Team (T)**. Taking another example from Fig. 2, S01 describes two teams' information whereas sentence S02 describes a team's and a player's information, while S03 describes a player's information. Thus, a sentence, based on the entity it describes, can be classified into the following five categories: just one Player, **P**; just one Team, **T**; more than one Players, **P&P**; more than one Teams, **T&T**; and finally, both Players and Teams, **P&T**.

An event summary from the SportSett dataset, based on the information and entities a sentence describes, can be classified into a total of 35 categories (7 types of information times 5 types of entities). We term each of these 35 categories as different concepts that can be used to write a summary of an event. We show the proportion of these concepts in our case-base in Fig. 3. On $x - axis$, we see all possible concepts, and on $y - axis$, we show the number of sentences categorised as that concept. These statistics are calculated using an automated system that extracts the entities mentioned in a sentence and classifies the sentence into its information-type category. This system consists of two modules: first, an entity extraction module, the same as the method used in building train data for IE models in [23]; and second, an information-type classifier, which is a Roberta model [8] fine-tuned with a multi-label classifier head trained on 600 samples and tested on 250 manually annotated samples. The classifier achieves 91% of the Macro-F1 score.

It is noted that although the examples used here for demonstration are specific to a dataset, the same approach can be applied to other datasets or domains with similar settings such as MLB D2T [11].

4.2 Concept Selection

After we have identified all possible concepts, the next step in writing a D2T summary is to select a subset of concepts that may be important and interesting for the target event's summary. Since the event summaries in D2T domains follow the principle of '*similar problems have similar solutions*', we can employ

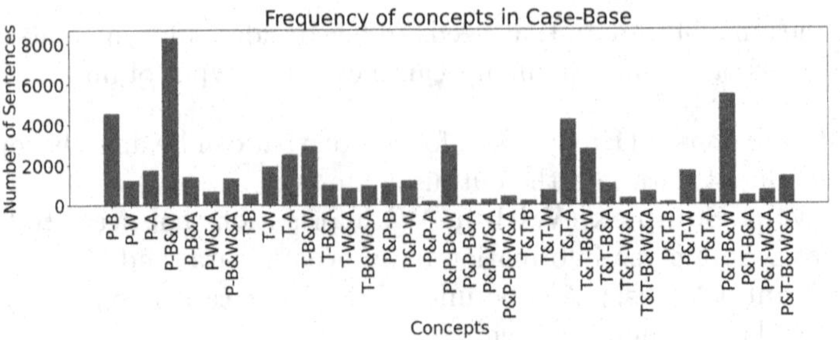

Fig. 3. Frequency of concepts in the case-base

a standard CBR approach to select a subset of concepts by retrieving similar events from previous examples and then reusing their solution to propose the solution for the new problem. To build a CBR model for this concept selection stage, we first need to build our case-base which will consist of events with their entity-based representation on the problem-side and their list of concepts used in the summary on the solution-side.

The problem-side representation of an event can be built by combining the representation of the different entities an event contains. Each entity in an event is represented with several features, all of which are assigned a value, effectively representing an entity with a vector of length the same as the number of features. An event can have multiple entities, making the initial representation of an event two-dimensional. In this work, the entity representation is simplified by taking its arithmetic mean to build a one-dimensional representation of an event. The solution-side's concept list of an event can be extracted using the same technique used for calculating the proportion of concepts described in the previous section. An example problem-side representation and solution-side concept list of an event from the SportSett dataset is shown in Fig. 4.

With the case-base developed, when a new problem arrives, its problem representation is built using its entities and then the most similar problem is retrieved from the case-base using Euclidean distance. The retrieved case is reused as the solution to the new problem. It is noted that a more sophisticated approach for retrieval can be developed by exploring alternative similarity measures and considering the top-k most similar cases when proposing the new solution. But these are left to the future work and here the focus is on utilising a simple approach for building the content-planning module of a data-to-text generation pipeline.

4.3 Entity Selection

The next step in content selection and planning is to select the entities (or combination of entities) that should be described in each of the selected concepts in the previous stage. This is achieved by ranking all the different types of entities in a stack where the highest-ranked entity will be described using the first concept of its type, the second-highest ranked entity will be described with

Entities	$Repr_{ENT}$						$avg(Repr_{ENT})$
$Player_1$	f_{1p1}	f_{2p1}	f_{3p1}	f_{4p1}	$\cdots$	f_{ip1}	$<P_1>$
$Player_2$	f_{1p2}	f_{2p2}	f_{3p2}	f_{4p2}	$\cdots$	f_{ip2}	$<P_2>$
$\vdots$	$\vdots$	$\vdots$	$\vdots$	$\vdots$	$\vdots$	$\vdots$	$\vdots$
$Player_n$	f_{1pn}	f_{2pn}	f_{3pn}	f_{4pn}	$\cdots$	f_{ipn}	$<P_n>$
$Team_1$	f_{1t1}	f_{2t1}	f_{3t1}	f_{4t1}	$\cdots$	f_{jt1}	$<T_1>$
$Team_2$	f_{1t2}	f_{2t2}	f_{3t2}	f_{4t2}	$\cdots$	f_{jt2}	$<T_2>$

$Repr_{EVENT}$	$<P_1>$	$<P_2>$	$\cdots$	$<P_n>$	$<T_1>$	$<T_2>$

(a) Problem-side representation

Sentence	Entity Type	Content Type	Concepts
Sixers came out in domination mode in the third and outscored **Bulls** , 37 - 18 , to take a 102 - 76 lead heading into the fourth .	Team & Team	Within	T&T-W
Bulls put up a fight in the fourth but the **Sixers** were able to cruise to their first win of the season without a problem .	Team & Team	Within & Across	T&T-W&A
Joel Embiid led the **Sixers** with 30 points on 9 - of - 14 shooting , in 33 minutes of action .	Player & Team	Basic & Within	P&T-B&W
⋮	⋮	⋮	⋮
Bobby Portis followed up with 20 points , 10 rebounds , two assists and two steals , while **Antonio Blakeney** added 15 points , five rebounds and two assists .	Player & Player	Basic	P&P-B

Concpet List	$\langle T\&T-W\rangle, \langle T\&T-W\&A\rangle, \langle P\&T-B\&W\rangle, \cdots, \langle P\&P-B\rangle$

(b) Solution-side concept-list

Fig. 4. (a) Problem-side and (b) Solution-side of an event

the second concept of its type, and so on. Thus, an algorithm is needed to rank the entities of an event. This can be achieved by learning the feature weights of the entity's representation, which can be used to score the entities and rank them based on the scores. To formalise:

$$Repr_{ENT} = [f_1, f_2, f_3, \cdots, f_n]$$
$$W = [w_1, w_2, w_3, \cdots, w_n], \forall w \in (-1, 1)$$
$$Score_{ENT} = \sum_{i=1}^{n} f_i \cdot w_i$$

The feature weights W are calculated using a PSO algorithm [6] optimised on a classification dataset for both the entity types (players and teams). For team entities, the classification data is prepared by subtracting the losing team's representation from winning team's representation and assigning it the label 1 (or win), and vice-versa for label 0 (or lost).

$$(Rep_{clf})^i = [(f_{1W} - f_{1L}), (f_{2W} - f_{2L}), \cdots, (f_{nW} - f_{nL})]$$
$$(Rep_{clf})^j = [(f_{1L} - f_{1W}), (f_{2L} - f_{2W}), \cdots, (f_{nL} - f_{nW})]$$
$$Lab^i = 1 \& Lab^j = 0$$

Similarly, win-loss data can be created for player entities as well where a player mentioned in the respective event summary will be considered a winner compared to a player from the event not mentioned in the summary.

5 Experimental Setup

This experiment aims to evaluate our new CBR planning-based algorithm, which we call CBR-Plan. At this stage, we are not interested in the text itself but rather the plan for the text solution. Hence, we measure the effectiveness of CBR-Plan by measuring its ability to select the same concepts and associated entities as chosen by a journalist who has already written solutions for the problems. A basketball dataset forms the case base and CBR-Plan is compared to both benchmark and state-of-the-art systems.

5.1 Dataset

The SportSett dataset [19] of NBA matches is used to generate an evaluation case base[3] in which a match becomes a case. Each match contains a textual summary as the output and the associated match statistics, with the box- and line-scores, as the problem input. There is a temporal aspect involved here, as future matches should not be available to the learner. Hence the training set contains the earlier matches from the 2014, 2015 and 2016 seasons (total of 4775, some matches from the 2016 season have more than one summary) while the dev and test sets contain matches from the 2017 and 2018 seasons (1230 matches each) respectively.

The training set is used to create the case-base following the method described in Sect. 4.2. There are total 4775 cases in the case-base for concept selection. For the entity ranking method, we again use the instances from the train set for preparing the PSO train data. We collect 66,738 instances for the players' feature weighting task while 7,380 instances are available for the teams' feature weighting task.

5.2 Benchmarks and Baselines

CBR-Plan is compared with four existing models, as follows:

- **Template-Based (Template)**: the baseline model proposed in [23] which contains a few handcrafted templates to verbalise the data of a few entities from an event. In this work, an updated version of this model [22] is used which adds a few more templates for generating extra information (next-game information of a team).

[3] We have used the GEM version of the dataset from https://huggingface.co/datasets/GEM/sportsett_basketball.

- **Case-Based Model (CBR)**: a case-based approach to Data-to-Text generation [22] which breaks down the summaries into several components. Then a case-base for each component is built which consists of the entity's feature values as problem representation while templates verbalising that entity's features as the solution. To generate an event summary, a standard case-based approach is used to retrieve the best template for different entities in each component.
- **Entity Model (Ent)**: an entity-focused approach [11] uses a sequence-to-sequence model consisting of an MLP encoder and LSTM decoder with copy mechanism. An added module updates the input record's representation during the generation process. At each decoding step, a GRU is used to decide the record that needs to be updated and then update its value.
- **Macro-Plan Model (MP)**: a neural pipeline model for data-to-text generation proposed in [12]. It consists of two separate modules: first, a micro-planning module, which takes all the entities as input and selects and orders the important entities (or combination of entities) using a Pointer network to build a micro-plan. The second module is a text generator which makes use of a standard LSTM based sequence-to-sequence model with a copy mechanism to generate a summary from the micro-plan.

Both the neural models are trained using the same hyper-parameters as described by the authors in their works.

5.3 Evaluation Metrics

Performance is measured on two important dimensions of data-to-text generation: content selection and diversity. Content selection is evaluated by comparing each method's output with the human reference summaries. Two measures are calculated, first for the proposed concepts and then for the entities selected.

Each method outputs a list of concepts for each new problem in the test set using the approach described in Sect. 4.2. They also produce a list of entities with the same length as the concept list, where the planned text to be generated for each concept would include the entity of the same index from the entity list, using the approach described in Sect. 4.3. The concept and entity list is extracted from human reference and generated summaries by first splitting the summaries into sentences and then extracting the entities from each sentence using the approach employed for calculating extractive evaluation metrics in [23]. This gives an entity list for the current problem. Finally, the sentence can be classified into its content-type, which when combined with entity-type in the sentence will give the concept list for the case's text summary. For each method, concept and entity lists are compared with the human reference (**Gold**) lists by calculating **F2**, **precision** and **recall** scores to evaluate the **content selection** capability of the systems. Since the system generations are expected to be of similar length as gold summaries, a system achieving higher precision with smaller generations is not good. So F2 becomes a better measure to evaluate these systems which give more weight to recall than precision. For **diversity**, we measure the **proportion of different concepts** used by each method compared to the gold summaries.

Table 1. Content selection scores and average concept length

	Concepts			Entities			#Concept
System	F2	Prec	Rec	F2	Prec	Rec	Avg
Gold	–	–	–	–	–	–	12.76
Template	25.52	37.81	23.6	48.24	89.39	43.26	7.97
CBR	32.15	47.3	29.76	60.09	90.91	55.39	8.03
Ent	25.38	24.05	25.73	54.05	60.27	52.7	13.66
MP	26.47	33.13	25.2	49.9	78.98	45.7	9.71
CBR – Plan	36.75	33.32	37.72	61.97	61.12	62.19	14.45

6 Results and Discussion

The results are discussed in two parts: first, for content selection; and second, for diversity compared to the human reference summaries.

6.1 Content Selection

F2, precision and recall scores are shown in Table 1 for both entities and concepts selected by the five evaluated models. With concept selection, Template achieves the second-worst F2, second-highest precision, and worst recall score. CBR has the highest precision while second-best F2 and recall. For the two neural systems, Ent has the worst F2 and precision with second-worst recall; while MP has third-best F2, second-worst precision and recall. Our proposed algorithm, **CBR-Plan**, achieves the highest F2 and recall score with third best precision score. Similar patterns can be seen in the entity selection scores as well.

In both cases, (**CBR-Plan**) achieves the highest F2 and recall scores. This suggests that the proposed method can select more relevant concepts and entities, similar to human reference summaries when compared to the other systems. However, it is also selecting most concepts and entities that are not present in Gold summaries (note these selections may still be relevant). Looking at the average number of concepts selected (see the last col. of Table 1) gives a deeper insight into the precision and recall scores. We can observe that most systems that have higher precision scores are generating smaller summaries. By doing so, the systems can achieve higher precision but miss many relevant concepts that are interesting and should be included in the summary. Similar behaviours have been observed with neural models in other relevant works as well [18]. By generating a solution based on the number of concepts present in similar human-generated solutions, CBR-Plan is producing a more realistic solution aligned with the human summaries than most of the comparative algorithms.

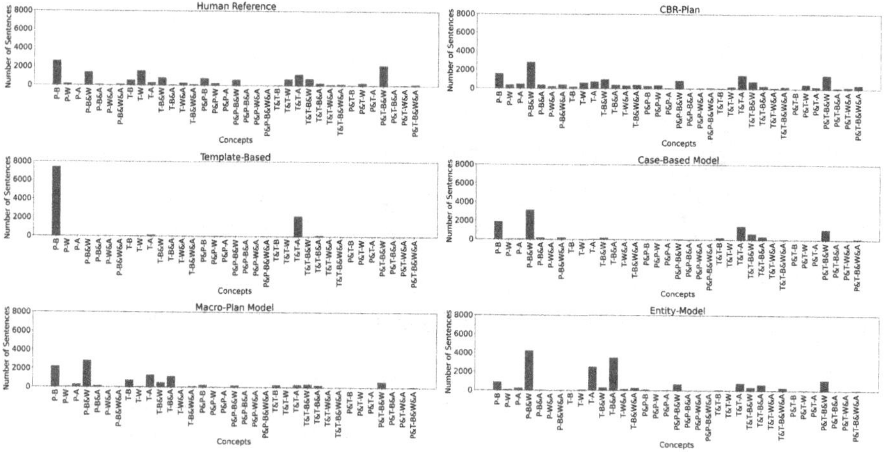

Fig. 5. Proportion of different concepts in different systems

Table 2. Correlation between concept frequency of different systems versus gold

System	CBR-Plan	Template	CBR	MP	Ent
Correlation	0.7571	0.6288	0.6973	0.5954	0.3105

6.2 Diversity

In this section, we investigate the ability of different systems to select different concepts in their summary generations. In Fig. 5, the frequency of different concepts being selected is shown for the human reference summaries and each evaluated model. The human reference summary has a relatively even distribution over all concepts. Intuitively, we would expect a well-automated system to generate summaries with a similar distribution over the concepts as the human-generated solution.

If we look at the distribution of the different systems, we can observe that Template and CBR are only selecting a few popular concepts and completely ignoring the others. With the neural systems, while MP does select across many concepts there is still a popularity bias by heavily selecting the most popular concepts. For example, it is selecting mostly P-B, P-B&W, T-B, and T-B&W, which seem to be the most popular ones, but is missing many other important concepts. Similarly, Ent has a popularity bias in selecting high numbers of a few popular concepts.

CBR-Plan can select a broad range of concepts that is most similar to the distribution seen with human reference summaries. Along with selecting the most popular ones, CBR-Plan is also able to select non-popular but important concepts. We show Pearson's correlation coefficient of concept distribution in system generation versus human reference summaries in Table 2. CBR-Plan has the highest correlation with human reference summaries followed by CBR, MP,

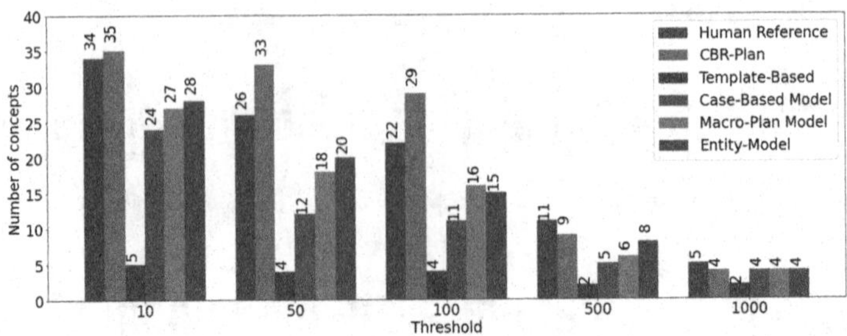

Fig. 6. Concept frequency of different systems after a threshold

Template and Ent. It is also surprising to see the Ent model performing so poorly on this measure, which appears to be due to the model selecting higher numbers of some rare concepts, e.g. T-B&A, and T-A.

Figure 6 shows the number of total concepts that have been selected by each model above a threshold figure. With the increase in the threshold, the number of concepts will decrease. It can be seen that the steep drop in CBR, MP and Ent is higher than for the human reference which is indicative of popularity bias, whereas CBR-Plan is more similar to the human reference and sometimes selects even higher numbers.

6.3 Qualitative Analysis

In Fig. 7, we show an example of concepts and entities selected in the human reference summary as well as in the different systems' generation. For example, the human summary starts with a 'T-W' concept associated with entity Chicago


```
{
  "Gold": [
    "Chicago Bulls|T-W", "Philadelphia 76ers & Chicago Bulls|T&T-W", "Philadelphia 76ers & Chicago Bulls|T&T-W",
    "Philadelphia 76ers & Chicago Bulls|T&T-W&A", "Joel Embiid & Philadelphia 76ers|P&T-B&W", "Ben Simmons|P-B&W", "Robert Covington|P-B",
    "Philadelphia 76ers|T-B", "Zach LaVine & Chicago Bulls|P&T-B&W","Bobby Portis & Antonio Blakeney|P&P-B", "Chicago Bulls|T-B", "Chicago Bulls|T-A",
    "Philadelphia 76ers|T-A"
  ],
  "CBR-Plan": [
    "Philadelphia 76ers & Chicago Bulls|T&T-B&W", "Ben Simmons & Philadelphia 76ers|P&T-B&W&A", "Philadelphia 76ers|T-W", "Chicago Bulls|T-W",
    "Philadelphia 76ers|T-B&W", "Ben Simmons & Joel Embiid|P&P-B&W", "Dario \u0160ari\u0107 & Philadelphia 76ers|P&T-B&A", "Philadelphia 76ers|T-W",
    "Philadelphia 76ers & Chicago Bulls|T&T-B&W&A", "Joel Embiid & Philadelphia 76ers|P&T-B&W", "Ben Simmons & Landry Shamet|P&P-B",
    "Joel Embiid|P-B&W&A"
  ],
  "Template": [
    "Joel Embiid|P-B", "Zach LaVine|P-B", "Robert Covington|P-B", "Bobby Portis|P-B", "Antonio Blakeney|P-B", "Jabari Parker|P-B",
    "Philadelphia 76ers|T-A", "Philadelphia 76ers|T-A"
  ],
  "CBR": [
    "Philadelphia 76ers & Chicago Bulls|T&T-B&W", "Ben Simmons|P-B&W", "Joel Embiid & Philadelphia 76ers|P&T-B&W",
    "Robert Covington & Philadelphia 76ers|P&T-B&W", "Bobby Portis|P-B&W", "Zach LaVine|P-B&W", "Philadelphia 76ers & Chicago Bulls|T&T-A"
  ],
  "Macro-Plan": [
    "Philadelphia 76ers & Chicago Bulls|T&T-W", "Philadelphia 76ers & Chicago Bulls|T&T-B", "Ben Simmons|P-B&W", "Philadelphia 76ers|T-A",
    "Philadelphia 76ers & Chicago Bulls|T&T-W&A", "Zach LaVine|P-B&W", "Jabari Parker|P-B", "Bobby Portis|P-B", "Jabari Parker|P-B",
    "Chicago Bulls|T-A", "Philadelphia 76ers|T-A"
  ],
  "Entity-Model": [
    "Philadelphia 76ers|T-B&A", "Philadelphia 76ers & Chicago Bulls|T&T-B&W", "Joel Embiid & Philadelphia 76ers|P&T-B&W", "Zach LaVine|P-B&W",
    "Dario \u0160ari\u0107|P-B&W", "Amir Johnson & Bobby Portis|P&P-B&W", "Ben Simmons & T.J. McConnell|P&P-B", "Justin Holiday|P-B&W",
    "Joel Embiid & Justin Holiday|P&P-B&W", "Zach LaVine|P-B&W", "Dario \u0160ari\u0107|P-B&W", "Ben Simmons & T.J. McConnell|P&P-B&W",
    "Antonio Blakeney|P-A"
  ]
}
```


Fig. 7. Concepts and entities selected in different systems

Bulls. That means, the first sentence talks about Chicago Bulls with Intra-Complex (Within) type information. We can observe that Template is mostly selecting concepts that includes a player with their Intra-Basic type information. CBR is selecting concepts of different types, some with combinations of different entities as well, but is still smaller in size. Both neural models are selecting different types of concepts but are either smaller (MP) or selecting easier (Ent, which rarely selects Inter-Event content). In contrast CBR-Plan is able to select different concept types of reasonable length with different content-types as well.

7 Conclusion and Future Works

In this work, a Case-Based planning approach is introduced for content planning in D2T problems. The proposed method first identifies important components for an event's summary known as concepts and then uses a CBR approach to select a subset of those concepts important and relevant for the event. In the final step, a ranking method is used to rank the entities of an event and align them to the concepts selected in previous step. Extensive experimentation is conducted to demonstrate the effectiveness of proposed methodology by comparing it against several benchmark and baseline systems of different types, ranging from template-based to case-based and neural approaches. Experiments demonstrate that the proposed method is able to achieve best recall in terms of selecting relevant content and provides most diversity by selecting different concepts more aligned with human reference summaries than the other systems.

In future, the aim is to utilise the selected concepts from this work in surface realisation and generating the final event summary. The next process will be inspired by previous CBR D2T systems [22] where the most suitable templates will be extracted for transforming the concepts with their respective entities into text. We also plan to enrich the entities' representation by adding across-event information in order to improve the retrieval process. A richer representation will help in the next iteration of surface realisation, ultimately improving the quality of the generated summaries.

References

1. Adeyanju, I., Wiratunga, N., Lothian, R.: Learning to author text with textual CBR. In: European Conference on Artificial Intelligence (2010)
2. Castro Ferreira, T., van der Lee, C., van Miltenburg, E., Krahmer, E.: Neural data-to-text generation: a comparison between pipeline and end-to-end architectures. In: Proceedings of the 2019 Conference on Empirical Methods in Natural Language Processing and the 9th International Joint Conference on Natural Language Processing (EMNLP-IJCNLP), pp. 552–562 (2019)
3. Gatt, A., Krahmer, E.: Survey of the state of the art in natural language generation: core tasks, applications and evaluation. J. Artif. Intell. Res. **61**, 65–170 (2018)
4. Gervás, P., Díaz-Agudo, B., Peinado, F., Hervás, R.: Story plot generation based on CBR. Knowl. Based Syst. **18**, 235–242 (2005)

5. Goldberg, E., Driedger, N., Kittredge, R.: Using natural-language processing to produce weather forecasts. IEEE Expert **9**(2), 45–53 (1994)
6. Kennedy, J.: Particle Swarm Optimization, pp. 760–766. Springer, US (2010)
7. Kukich, K.: Design of a knowledge-based report generator. In: 21st Annual Meeting of the Association for Computational Linguistics, pp. 145–150. Association for Computational Linguistics (1983)
8. Liu, Y., et al.: Roberta: a robustly optimized bert pretraining approach. arXiv preprint. arXiv:1907.11692 (2019)
9. Portet, F., et al.: Automatic generation of textual summaries from neonatal intensive care data. Artif. Intell. **173**(7–8), 789–816 (2009)
10. Puduppully, R., Dong, L., Lapata, M.: Data-to-text generation with content selection and planning. In: The Thirty-Third AAAI Conference on Artificial Intelligence, pp. 6908–6915. AAAI (2019)
11. Puduppully, R., Dong, L., Lapata, M.: Data-to-text generation with entity modeling. In: Proceedings of the 57th Annual Meeting of the Association for Computational Linguistics. pp. 2023–2035 (2019)
12. Puduppully, R., Lapata, M.: Data-to-text generation with macro planning. Trans. Assoc. Comput. Linguis. **9**, 510–527 (2021)
13. Rebuffel, C., Soulier, L., Scoutheeten, G., Gallinari, P.: A hierarchical model for data-to-text generation. In: Jose, J.M., et al. (eds.) ECIR 2020. LNCS, vol. 12035, pp. 65–80. Springer, Cham (2020). https://doi.org/10.1007/978-3-030-45439-5_5
14. Reiter, E.: An architecture for data-to-text systems. In: Proceedings of the 11th European Workshop on Natural Language Generation, pp. 97–104 (2007)
15. Reiter, E., Dale, R.: Building Natural Language Generation Systems. Cambridge University Press, Cambridge (2000)
16. Sripada, S., Reiter, E., Davy, I.: Sumtime-mousam: configurable marine weather forecast generator. Expert Update **6**(3), 4–10 (2003)
17. Stewart, S.I., Vogt, C.A.: A case-based approach to understanding vacation planning. Leisure Sci. **21**(2), 79–95 (1999)
18. Thomson, C., Reiter, E.: Generation challenges: results of the accuracy evaluation shared task. In: Proceedings of the 14th International Conference on Natural Language Generation, pp. 240–248. Aberdeen, Scotland (2021)
19. Thomson, C., Reiter, E., Sripada, S.: SportSett:basketball - a robust and maintainable data-set for natural language generation. In: Proceedings of the Workshop on Intelligent Information Processing and Natural Language Generation (2020)
20. Thomson, R., Massie, S., Craw, S., Ahriz, H., Mills, I.: Plan recommendation for well engineering. In: Mehrotra, K.G., Mohan, C.K., Oh, J.C., Varshney, P.K., Ali, M. (eds.) IEA/AIE 2011. LNCS (LNAI), vol. 6704, pp. 436–445. Springer, Heidelberg (2011). https://doi.org/10.1007/978-3-642-21827-9_45
21. Upadhyay, A., Massie, S., Clogher, S.: Case-based approach to automated natural language generation for obituaries. In: Watson, I., Weber, R. (eds.) ICCBR 2020. LNCS (LNAI), vol. 12311, pp. 279–294. Springer, Cham (2020). https://doi.org/10.1007/978-3-030-58342-2_18
22. Upadhyay, A., Massie, S., Singh, R.K., Gupta, G., Ojha, M.: A case-based approach to data-to-text generation. In: Sánchez-Ruiz, A.A., Floyd, M.W. (eds.) ICCBR 2021. LNCS (LNAI), vol. 12877, pp. 232–247. Springer, Cham (2021). https://doi.org/10.1007/978-3-030-86957-1_16
23. Wiseman, S., Shieber, S., Rush, A.: Challenges in data-to-document generation. In: Proceedings of the 2017 Conference on Empirical Methods in Natural Language Processing, pp. 2253–2263 (2017)

The Use of Computer-Assisted Case-Based Reasoning to Support Clinical Decision-Making – A Scoping Review

Richard Noll(✉), Jannik Schaaf, and Holger Storf

Institute of Medical Informatics, Goethe University Frankfurt, University Hospital Frankfurt, 60590 Frankfurt, Germany
{Richard.Noll,Jannik.Schaaf,Holger.Storf}@kgu.de

Abstract. Clinical decision-making in healthcare is often difficult because of the increasing number of diagnostic findings and the overlap of disease characteristics. Information systems can be applied to support decision-making. Case-Based Reasoning (CBR) is used to solve a current case using similar past cases in the hospital's database. By assisting with diagnosis or treatment, CBR could improve the overall quality of healthcare for patients. However, the impact of CBR in clinical decision support has not yet been reviewed in depth in the literature. This scoping review highlights the properties of systems already in use, focusing on clinical applications, validation, interoperability, and case retrieval. A search query was performed in PubMed and Web of Science, and the results were selected for eligibility by title, abstract and full text screening. The following data items were observed: 'Publication year', 'Country of study', 'Disease group', 'Medical application', 'Patient number', 'Type of clinical data', 'Data interoperability', 'Type of similarity measure' and 'Expert validation'. The results showed that cancer and neoplasms are by far the most treated diseases, and demographic as well as historical data from patient or family records are frequently used as input. Most CBR systems were applied for therapy and diagnosis. More than 50% of all studies use data sets with > 100 records. About 24% of all systems were validated by experts, and 14% addressed data interoperability. CBR can be a useful approach to support clinical decision-making but needs further research to be used in clinical routine.

Keywords: Case-Based Reasoning · Clinical Decision-Making · Clinical Decision Support System

1 Background

When presenting a new patient to a clinical facility, the physician has the task of making several decisions, e.g., regarding the correct diagnosis and appropriate treatment. Clinical decision-making comprises three integrated phases: diagnosis, severity assessment, and management. The physician makes the decision considering various factors, such as medical history, physical examinations, and his own experience [1]. However, decision-making for an individual patient has become more challenging due to the increasing

M. T. Keane and N. Wiratunga (Eds.): ICCBR 2022, LNAI 13405, pp. 395–409, 2022.
https://doi.org/10.1007/978-3-031-14923-8_26

amount of data from genetics, proteomics, and diagnostic imaging on Electronical Health Records (EHRs) [2]. In addition, many diseases have overlapping conditions. A single disorder can result in a wide range of signs and symptoms, and many disorders can result in similar signs and symptoms [1]. In case of rare diseases, there is also the additional challenge of lack of expertise and resources, which leads to delayed or even incorrect diagnoses and treatment [3]. Human cognitive abilities are limited, and this increasing complexity of decision-making requires validated decision support systems and computerised support at different levels and stages of the treatment process [2].

While technical processes and information systems are used in a variety of forms and in a wide range of healthcare settings, a particular focus lies on the decision support for medical professionals [4]. An application that assists in healthcare decision-making is often referred to as Clinical Decision Support System (CDSS). The term CDSS is used repeatedly in this review and includes other clinical systems used for decision-making that are not explicitly referred to as CDSS. Significantly, the main purpose of a CDSS is not to completely take the decision away from the medical professional. The system is only intended to assist during the decision-making process. Using both his own knowledge and the system's information, the professional could make a better analysis of the patient's data than either the human or the CDSS could do alone. The CDSS should therefore have a positive impact on the quality of clinical decisions in hospitals, general practice, and other healthcare settings [5].

Computer-assisted Case-based Reasoning (CBR) is a form of technical assistance which solves problems of a current target case with a methodology based on solutions of similar problems from the past [6]. CBR is applied in medical but also in various non-medical settings [5]. CBR can assist in the process of detecting a disease and help the medical professional make an appropriate decision. It is a problem-solving methodology inspired by the decision-making procedure of the human brain and is defined as a four step-process: Retrieve, Reuse, Revise, Retain [7].

In a CDSS based on CBR, an individual patient's medical file is first matched against a computerised clinical knowledge database (Retrieve). The user of the software then receives patient-specific assessments and recommendations to support decisions regarding, for example, diagnosis or treatment (Reuse). Based on the output of the system, the medical professional decides which information and recommendations are relevant and which are irrelevant to the target case (Revise). After revision, the target case is included into the original case base (Retain). This is the learning phase of CBR, as new knowledge about the target case and its possible diagnosis and treatment is acquired after each cycle. In practice, CBR systems are in many cases limited exclusively to the retrieve step [8].

Although it could enhance the overall healthcare quality of patients [9, 10], the impact of CBR in the domain of clinical decision support has not been reviewed in depth in the literature. So far, there are only reviews that roughly outline this topic or only deal with it in a very general manner. For instance, Narindrarangkura et al. focused on the larger topic of Artificial Intelligence (AI) in CDSS [11]. Kong et al. examined knowledge representations and inferences in CDSS without addressing the specifics of CBR [12]. El-Sappagh et al. examines CBR frameworks with a focus on applications for diabetes mellitus and compares medical with non-medical uses [13]. Therefore, a more comprehensive overview of CBR for clinical decision support is necessary in order to map research performed in this area, to reveal knowledge gaps and give clinicians and researchers an overview of developments and current systems regarding this topic. The scoping review presented here will focus on disease groups, application areas, data scope, similarity metrics, data interoperability (interaction of heterogeneous systems for efficient data exchange), development status and expert validation of medical CBR systems. Possible future research approaches and limitations will also be considered.

The objective of this scoping review is to answer the following five research questions: (1) How has the research on "CBR in CDSS" evolved in recent years, compared to the general research on "AI in CDSS"?, (2) Which disease groups are dominantly addressed by CBR systems and for what purpose?, (3) What type and volume of data is collected and in what form is data exchanged within the CDSS?, (4) Which similarity metrics are used to retrieve past cases?, (5) Are the systems validated by human expertise?

2 Methods

The reporting of this scoping review follows the Transparent Reporting of Systematic Reviews and Meta-Analyses (PRISMA) guideline for scoping reviews, which is a common guideline in medical research to report scoping reviews. Accordingly, this review was designed using the PRISMA-ScR 2018 Checklist (AF1 PRISMA Checklist: https://osf.io/2xwcv) [14]. We considered 20 out of 22 checklist items.

After the identification of the objectives, the following five steps are applied in this scoping review: (2.1) identification of relevant keywords, (2.2) conducting the search query, (2.3) selection of eligible studies, (2.4) collection of data, and (2.5) compilation and summary of results.

In the preparation of this paper, a review protocol was created and uploaded to Open Science (https://osf.io/xauvt) [15]. The author RN prepared the protocol in March 2022, which was approved by all other authors on April 25, 2022. The protocol was published on April 27, 2022. The five-step process of the applied methodology is presented below.

2.1 Identifying Relevant Keywords

To identify keywords relevant to the search query in Sect. 2.2, the procedure described below was proposed by author RN and approved by all authors. An initial search was performed via PubMed, a database for medical publications of the National Library of Medicine (NLM). In PubMed the term "case-based reasoning [Text Word]" was generally searched for. The suffix *Text Word* defines the search scope for the preceding string, including titles, abstracts, Medical Subject Headings (MeSH), and other terms. MeSH belong to the NLM's controlled vocabulary and are used for indexing articles in PubMed [16]. This initial search, conducted in February 2022, yielded 179 results for the years between 2011 and 2021. These articles were exported from PubMed and imported into an online review tool named *Rayyan* [17], where a filter option was used to automatically identify the most frequently occurring topics and keywords that were indexed with the publications. Terms based on the broader topic of decision or diagnostic support were selected. This also included terms of MeSH indexed in PubMed.

2.2 Conducting the Search Query

The search strings are determined from the pre-identified frequent terms and the search query for PubMed was defined with Boolean operators "AND" and "OR", as shown in Fig. 1.

```
(Case-Based Reasoning[Text Word] AND Decision Support Systems, Clinical[MeSH Terms])
OR
(Case-Based Reasoning[Text Word] AND Decision Making[MeSH Terms])
OR
(Case-Based Reasoning[Text Word] AND Diagnosis, Computer-Assisted[MeSH Terms])
OR
(Case-Based Reasoning[Text Word] AND Decision Support Techniques[MeSH Terms])
OR
(Case-Based Reasoning[Text Word] AND Clinical Decision-Making[MeSH Terms])
OR
(Case-Based Reasoning[Text Word] AND Diagnosis[MeSH Terms])
OR
(Case-Based Reasoning[Text Word] AND Decision Support[Text Word])
```

Fig. 1. Search query for the PubMed database

The search query was also performed on Web of Science (WoS). However, since MeSH terms are not used in WoS, the suffixes in the square brackets of the search terms were removed for the search. The field tag "TS" was used for the search terms, which searches the terms in title, abstract, author keywords and KeyWords Plus (Interdisciplinary search for all articles that have common citations) [18]. The category of "medical informatics" was selected to filter out non-medical and non-technical content. The rest of the search was carried out the same way as in PubMed.

Published articles from the period January 01, 2001 to February 28, 2022 were considered in the search. The results of the PubMed and WoS queries were subsequently merged in *Rayyan* and analysed for duplicates, which were removed accordingly.

Another search query for "AI in CDSS" was conducted on March 11, 2022 to compare research development in this general area with the research on "CBR in CDSS". This search was done via PubMed and WoS for the years 2011–2021. For this purpose, the two terms "Artificial Intelligence" and "Clinical Decision Support" were combined with the Boolean operator "AND".

2.3 Screening of Identified Publications

In order to check the eligibility of articles resulting from the search query, two rounds of screening were conducted to select the publications: A screening based on bibliographic data and a full text screening. The eligibility criteria for the title and abstract screening, consisting of five questions, were listed in a screening form, as shown in Table 1. All authors approved the form.

Table 1. Five step screening form for title and abstract screening with 'Inclusion' and 'Exclusion' criteria

No.	Question	Inclusion	Exclusion
1	What type of publication is the article?	• Conference Paper • Journal Paper	• Literature Review • Study Protocol • Commentary • Editorial • Other
2	Is an abstract available?	Yes, an abstract is available	No, an abstract is not available
3	Is the publication written in English?	Yes, the publication is written in English	No, the publication is not written in English
4	Does the publication contain primary research or report of a Clinical Decision Support System?	Yes, the publication contains primary research or report of a Clinical Decision Support System	No, the publication contains any other description of software and not a Clinical Decision Support System
5	Does the publication contain primary research or report of a system based on Case-Based Reasoning?	Yes, the publication contains primary research or report of a system based on Case-Based Reasoning	No, the publication contains any other description of a model and not Case-Based Reasoning

The title and abstract screening was performed by RN and JS via *Rayyan*. In *Rayyan*, the authors involved in this screening can decide whether to "include" or "exclude" a publication. There is the additional option of selecting "maybe" and taking the decision later and/or in cooperation with the other author. The decisions for the consideration of a publication made by the others are not visible to one another during the joint review process to avoid influence of any kind. At the end, the decisions of the authors are evaluated together and any conflicts that arise are discussed and resolved by all authors.

The publications qualified for full text screening were exported from the *Rayyan* tool and inserted into the literature management system *Citavi* (citavi.com).

Full text screening was carried out via *Citavi* by the author RN in a similar way to the title and abstract screening. This process was reviewed by JS. The eligibility criteria for the full text screening consisting of three questions are listed in Table 2. The result of the full text screening was discussed with all authors and after general agreement, the data items were extracted.

2.4 Data Extraction

The data extraction was first carried out for 20 publications by the author RN. The result was then agreed and discussed with the author JS. After successful consultation, the data extraction was continued by RN and the list of data items shown in Table 3 was continuously updated and adjusted (AF2 Data extraction sheet: https://osf.io/2xwcv).

Table 2. Three step screening form for full text screening with 'Inclusion' and 'Exclusion' criteria

No.	Question	Inclusion	Exclusion
1	Is a full text available?	Yes, a full text is available	No, a full text is not available
2	Does the publication describe a Clinical Decision Support System for a specific medical application?	Yes, the publication describes a Clinical Decision Support System for a specific medical application	No, the publication describes any other Clinical Decision Support System for deployment in an unspecified or more general context
3	Is one of the focal points of the described Clinical Decision Support System the presentation of a Case-Based Reasoning approach?	Yes, one of the focal points of the described Clinical Decision Support System is the presentation of a Case-Based Reasoning approach	No, none of the focal points of the described Clinical Decision Support System is the presentation of a Case-Based Reasoning approach

Table 3. Data extraction sheet with specified variables and their definition. The suffix '(Y/N)' denotes results separated in a 'Yes' (is described) and 'No' (is not described) category. The categorisation into disease groups is based on the 21 health categories of the UKCRC Health Research Classification System [19].

Variable	Definition
Publication year	Year of the publication date of the article
*Country of study	Countries that were part of the research and conduct of the article
*Disease group	Categorisation of disease groups identified in the studies
*Medical application	Type of application: Diagnosis, Treatment, Basic Research, or other decision support
Patient number	Number of patients included in the study
*Type of clinical data	Data used as input parameters of the system
Data interoperability (Y/N)	Description of data interoperability and standards for exchange of data
*Type of similarity measure	Equations, such as Euclidean distance or other measures
Expert validation (Y/N)	Performance/Output of the system validated by human domain experts

*For these variables, a study could be assigned to more than one category.

2.5 Visualisation and Summarisation of Results

At the completion of the data extraction, the gathered data items (see Table 3) were summarised and visualised to present the results in this publication. A flow chart according to

PRISMA-ScR was chosen to illustrate the selection of studies. To display the extracted data items, timelines (Publication year), bar charts (Disease Group, Type of clinical data, Type of similarity measure) and pie charts (Medical application, Patient number, Data Interoperability, Expert validation) were created.

3 Results

The process of literature selection is shown in Fig. 2 in form of a flowchart. For the years between 2011 – February 2022, 101 publications in PubMed and 62 publications in WoS were identified. After removing the duplicates, 125 records remained. These records were thereupon checked for eligibility. A further 24 articles were excluded because either no full text was available or no medical context or CBR process was described. At the end of the screening, 66 studies remained that were eligible for data charting. A list of all included articles and extracted data items can be accessed on Open Science (AF3 Included articles: https://osf.io/2xwcv).

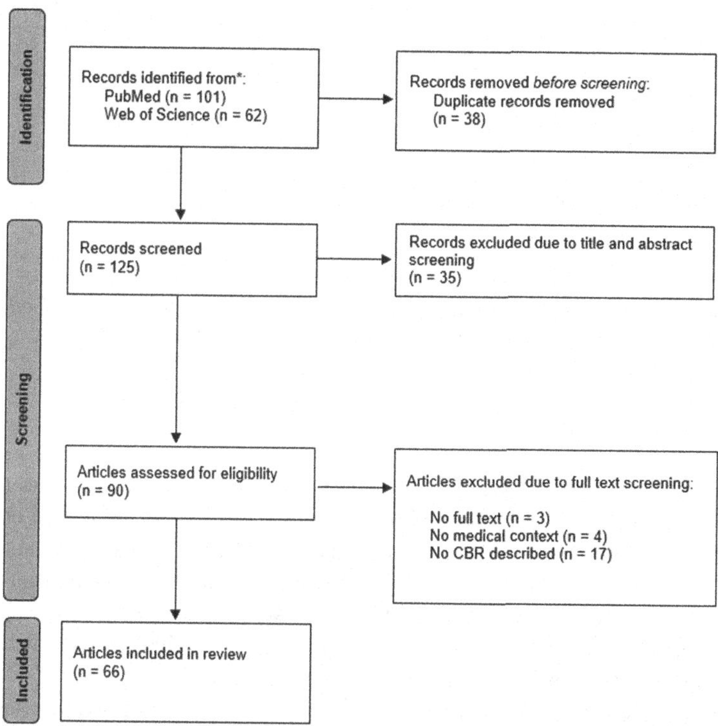

Fig. 2. Literature flow diagram describing records identification and screening

3.1 Countries and Years of Publications

Most studies were conducted in whole or partially in China ($n = 10$), France ($n = 7$), Germany ($n = 9$), Spain ($n = 10$), United Kingdom ($n = 13$), and the USA ($n = 6$). The timeline of publications, see Fig. 3, (i), shows the years in which the articles were published. Research on "CBR in CDSS" has stagnated somewhat in recent years. A negative trend in research papers can be observed from 2011 to 2013. The number of publications increased again in 2014 and 2015. In the following years until 2021, the number of publications decreases slightly and fluctuates slightly from one year to another. For the beginning of 2022 (till February 28, 2022) there was no relevant paper yet, therefore the diagram has no data node at this point. For comparison, Chart section (ii) shows a search query for "AI in CDSS" conducted on March 11, 2022.

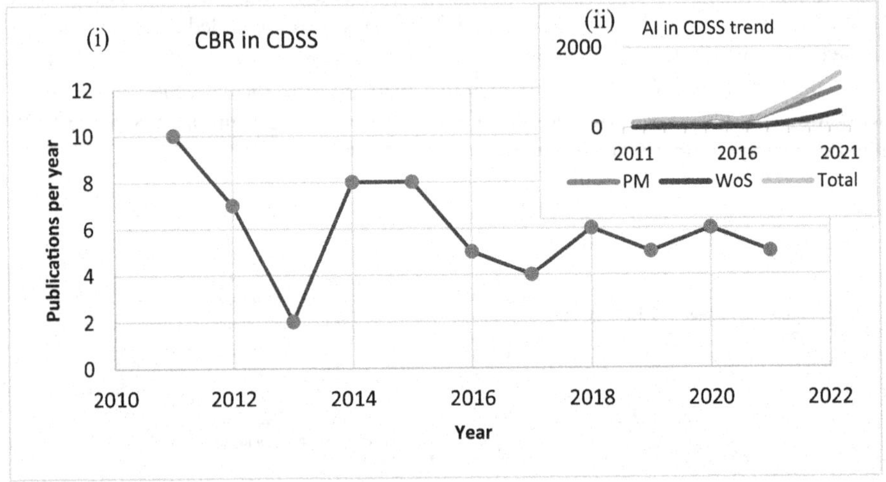

Fig. 3. Publication timeline representing the number of publications for (i) research on "CBR in CDSS" and (ii) research on "AI in CDSS" over the period 2011–2021

3.2 Disease Categories

In terms of disease groups – see Fig. 4 – cancer, and neoplasm (n = 25) are the most frequently targeted diseases treated with CBR applications. Metabolic and endocrine (e.g., Diabetes mellitus) (n = 13) are the second most addressed diseases. Generic health relevance (e.g., elder health) (n = 8), oral and gastrointestinal (e.g., Hepatitis) (n = 7), and cardiovascular conditions (e.g., high blood pressure) (n = 7) rank below them with similar frequencies. The categories musculoskeletal, reproductive health and childbirth, neurological, infection and blood are rarely examined (n = 1).

There are some articles in which the same authors have conducted several consecutive studies. For example, in the field of insulin bolus advice (metabolic and endocrine), five papers, and in the area of breast cancer (cancer and neoplasm), three papers have been published consecutively. The rest of the data set consists of either individual articles or papers with only one subsequent publication.

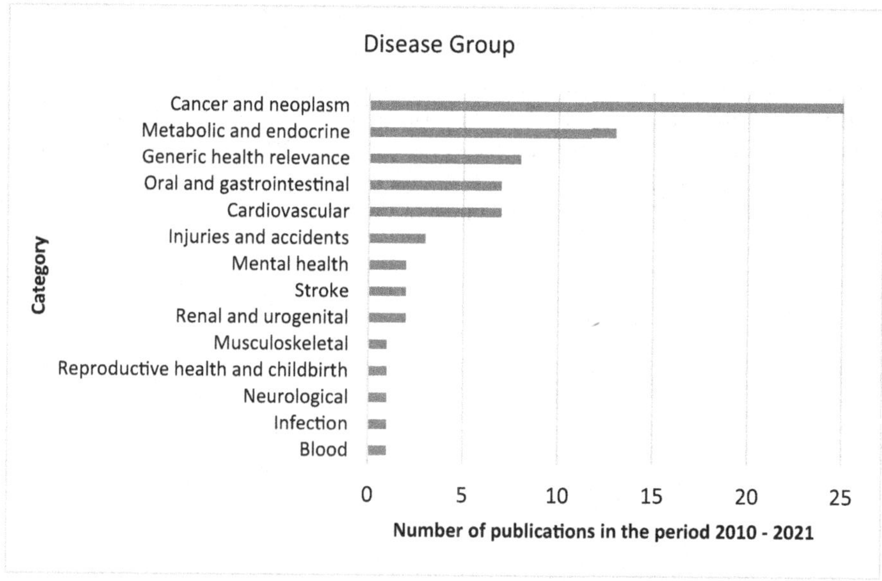

Fig. 4. Different disease categories identified in the studies and ranked by frequency of occurrence in these studies

3.3 Clinical Data, Application, and Patient Number

CBR systems often use demographic (n = 29) and historical data from the patient or family record (n = 30) as input. However, this information is often part of an extended data stream, e.g., demographic data combined with image and test data. Figure 5 shows the remaining clinical data input used in the identified 66 publications.

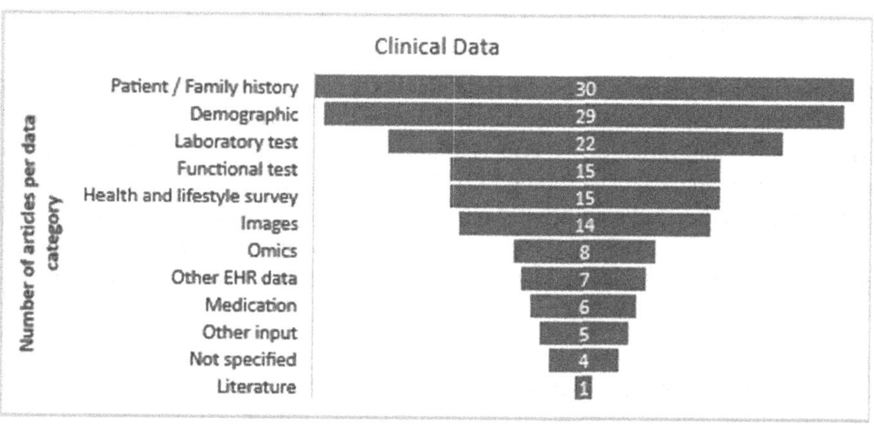

Fig. 5. Different types and frequencies of clinical data used as input to the CBR systems described in the studies. When interpreting the frequencies of the disease groups considered, successive publications by the same group of researchers must be taken into account.

Regarding medical applications, 90% (n = 61) of the CBR systems were designed for therapeutic/treatment or diagnostic purposes. Only a small percentage (n = 7) was devoted to basic research and other decision support, as shown in Fig. 6 (i).

More than 50% (n = 40) of all studies use data sets with more than 100 patient records. In most studies (n = 24) the size of the data set is between 100–1000 records. Less than 20 patient records are used in 12% of the studies. Between 20 and 99 patient records occur in 18% of the studies, as shown in Fig. 6 (ii).

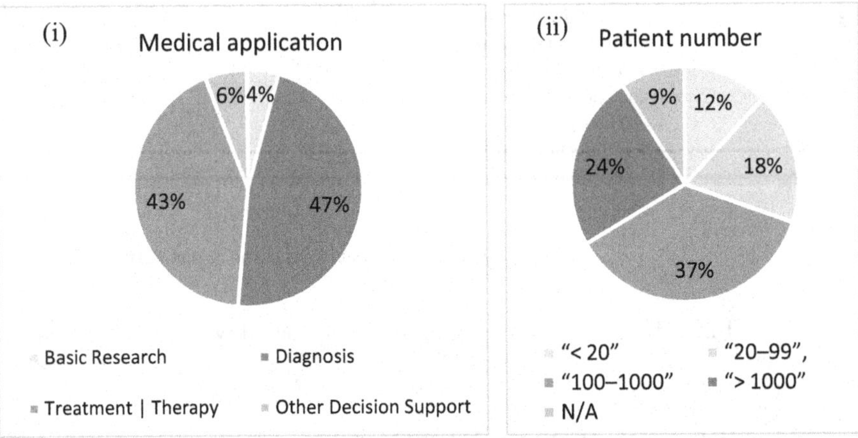

Fig. 6. Pie chart of (i) the percentage of the medical application and (ii) the different database sizes in the studies

3.4 Similarity Metric

Among the similarity metrics used for analogy search in the retrieve step of CBR, the Euclidean distance appears frequently in the articles with 25 occurrences. In many cases, publications design a similarity function that is not specified or labelled, but often resembles the similarity and distance metrics listed in Fig. 7. In addition, weights are often assigned to the input variables, as certain parameters have a higher influence on the target variable than others [20]. The setting of weights must be considered when calculating the distances, as they can significantly impact the result of the similarity measurement. Weights are typically selected by experts [21] or determined by other methods such as equal weight techniques [22] or Machine Learning algorithms including decision trees and genetic algorithms [20, 23].

3.5 System Properties and Validation

Figure 8 visualises expert validation (i), and data interoperability (ii) of the 66 studies identified.

About 24% (n = 16) of the systems designed in the studies were validated by experts. A share of 14% (n = 9) deal with data interoperability. Five of the studies dealing with interoperability focus on international standards for the exchanging of data such as Health Level 7 (HL7) or Fast Healthcare Interoperability Resources (FHIR).

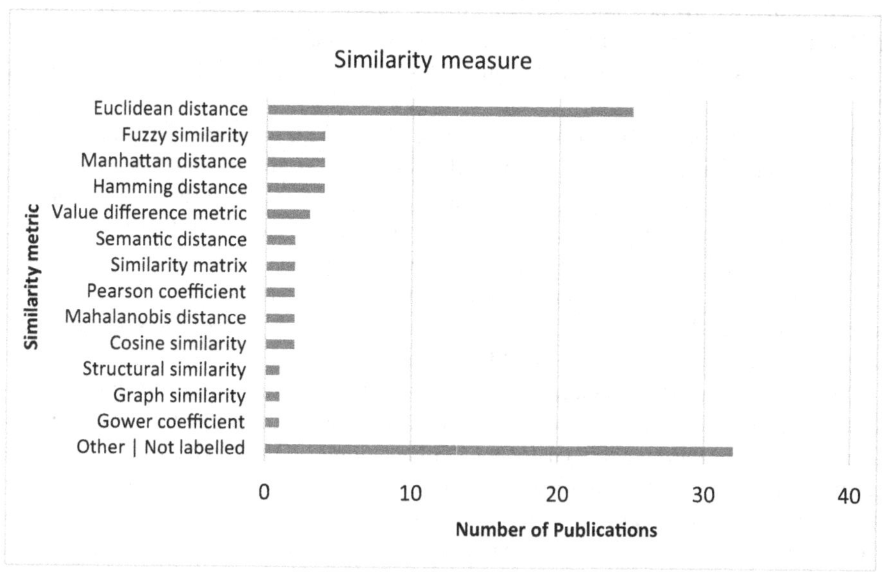

Fig. 7. Frequencies of similarity metrics used in the studies to measure analogies in the retrieval step of CBR processes

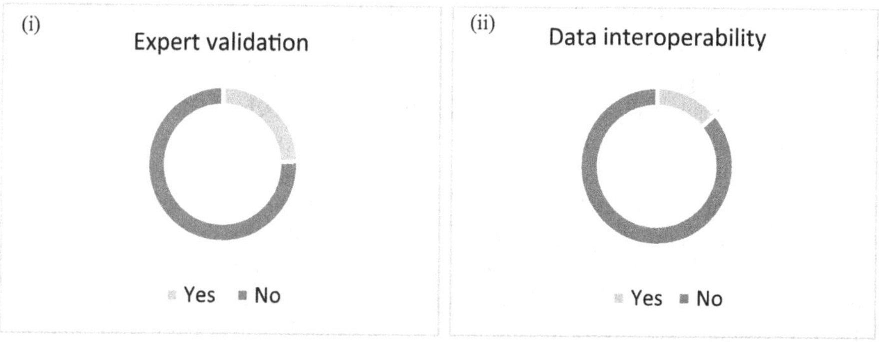

Fig. 8. (i) Expert validation and (ii) data interoperability plotted as pie charts to illustrate the relative shares. The exact values are stated in the corresponding text section.

4 Discussion

The scoping review presented here aims to provide an overview of the current and past development of CBR systems in clinical decision-making. The different systems in the eligible 66 publications of the years 2011–2021 were reviewed and analysed.

The described CDSS are predominantly used for diagnostic, therapeutic and treatment applications in the cancer and neoplasm domain and are most researched in China, Germany, Spain, and the United Kingdom. The studies mainly take large data sets (>100), which mostly contain demographic and patient data. A large prevalence allows the CBR algorithms to be trained sufficiently and to capture enough feature characteristics, just as physicians benefit from different attributes in differential diagnoses [24].

To measure the similarity between past case data and the current case, systems often use Euclidean distance. However, many studies introduce similarity and distance metrics that are not further labelled. Similarity metrics can also be used for different purposes, for example, to measure the similarity of numerical (e.g., Euclidean distance) or categorical data (e.g., Hamming distance) [25]. Feature weighting is not to be neglected and is of decisive importance in distance measurement [20]. Furthermore, a validation by experts and medical professionals has been conducted for only 16 of the systems. Data interoperability is discussed in 14% of the studies.

Not all selected 66 publications and the systems they contain can be discussed in detail within the scope of this review. However, this review shows clinicians and software developers what is known about CBR for CDSS and points to knowledge gaps in previous research that can be considered for future investigations. One gap is the lack of expert validation or the difficulty of carrying out such validation due to the associated enormous effort for larger data sets. However, expert validation can determine the usefulness and comprehensibility of decision support systems for users and health professionals [26]. Another point that has been poorly addressed in the studies is the interoperability of data. By integrating data exchange standards such as HL7, the autonomy of a software module from the overall system can be achieved and it can therefore be deployed and expanded as required without the need for special adaptations [27]. Merging CDSS and clinical information systems that interact with the EHR can build a virtual health record (VHR) and a homogeneous framework for modelling clinical concepts [28].

Most studies also mention issues and limitations for research and development in the clinical CBR domain. One limitation that is highlighted in some studies is the issue of incomplete data sets as databases grow larger. This affects the stability of the similarity ranking. Löw et al. deal with the handling of missing values in data, which is of critical importance when integrating training data into the CBR algorithm [8]. A further topic to be considered is the efficient retrieval of similar cases in the database to avoid long-running times, where the use of cloud computing is a possible workaround [29]. The method of assigning weights for the similarity metrics should also be carefully evaluated. When it comes to selection of weights by experts, it should be noted that this can be very subjective [30]. The genetic algorithm approach has been proven in many studies for the development of a weighted similarity function, for example in El-Sappagh et al. [23] and Yin et al. [31]. While most of these limitations are interesting for software developers, they are less pervasive on the physician and user side. However, as this review is also intended to address medical practitioners, these limitations were not investigated across all papers, but should not be neglected when developing such systems.

While general research on the use of AI in the field of medical decision support has increased significantly in recent years (especially in the past 5 years from 2016–2021), research in the field of CBR for CDSS has stagnated, cf. Fig. 3. However, CBR has a decisive advantage over other AI algorithms due to its explanatory and customisable character [13, 24]. Many AI systems developed today, especially neural networks, are "black boxes" where the user of the system cannot reconstruct how the decision was obtained [32]. This makes it difficult or impossible for the user to follow the system's decisions and thus diminishes the system's credibility.

CBR systems on the other hand not only output simple diagnostic suggestions, but also allow the user to view local and global similarity searches and set weights, metrics, and parameters to optimise retrieval [30]. A key point is the output of therapy and treatment recommendations of past cases, which is useful as additional input for further proceeding with a patient [33]. Furthermore, the system can learn by the user's continuous evaluation of the proposed solutions [13]. In future healthcare applications, all the above factors could turn CBR into a reliable tool for clinical decision-making.

5 Conclusion

This scoping review discusses in detail the research and findings of the literature on CBR in clinical decision-making since 2011. Computer-assisted CBR is used to support medical practitioners in diagnosis and treatment for different diseases. The choice of input data, similarity metric and patient cohort is critical to the reliability of the application. In future research, the consideration of data interoperability and expert validation could be a crucial sticking point to make such case-based support systems operational for day-to-day clinical practice. Through a user-oriented approach, CBR could become an effective tool in the ever-increasing digitalisation of healthcare.

Acknowledgements and Competing Interests. The author was assisted by the Institute of Medical Informatics in Frankfurt in developing this protocol. The authors declare that they have no competing interests.

Funding. This review is part of the SATURN project at the University Hospital of the Goethe University Frankfurt and is funded by the Federal Ministry of Health in Germany (Reference: 2520DAT02B).

References

1. Berman, S.: Clinical decision making. In: Berman's Pediatric Decision Making, 5th edn., pp. 1–6. Elsevier/Mosby, Philadelphia (2011)
2. Minsky, B.D., Rödel, C.M., Valentini, V.: Rectal cancer. In: Tepper, J.E., Bogart, J.A., Gunderson, L.L. (eds.) Clinical Radiation Oncology, pp. 992–1018.e6. Elsevier, Philadelphia (2016)
3. Walkowiak, D., Domaradzki, J.: Are rare diseases overlooked by medical education? Awareness of rare diseases among physicians in Poland: an explanatory study. Orphanet J. Rare Dis. **16**(400), 1–12 (2021)
4. Teufel, A., Binder, H.: Clinical decision support systems. Visc. Med. **37**(6), 491–498 (2021)
5. Berner, E.S. (ed.): Clinical Decision Support Systems. Theory and Practice. SpringerLink Bücher. Springer, New York (2007). https://doi.org/10.1007/978-0-387-38319-4

6. Roy, D.P., Chakraborty, B.: Case-based reasoning and some typical applications. In: Information Resources Management Association (ed.) Leadership and Personnel Management. Concepts, Methodologies, Tools, and Applications. Premier Reference Source, pp. 1090–1126. Business Science Reference, Hershey (2016)
7. Khan, M.J., Hayat, H., Awan, I.: Hybrid case-base maintenance approach for modeling large scale case-based reasoning systems. HCIS **9**(1), 1–25 (2019). https://doi.org/10.1186/s13673-019-0171-z
8. Löw, N., Hesser, J., Blessing, M.: Multiple retrieval case-based reasoning for incomplete datasets. J. Biomed. Inform. **92**, 1–15 (2019)
9. Ali, S.I., et al.: Clinical decision support system based on hybrid knowledge modeling: a case study of chronic kidney disease-mineral and bone disorder treatment. Int. J. Environ. Res. Public Health **19**(1), 226 (2021)
10. Shen, Y., Colloc, J., Jacquet-Andrieu, A., Lei, K.: Emerging medical informatics with case-based reasoning for aiding clinical decision in multi-agent system. J. Biomed. Inform. **56**, 307–317 (2015)
11. Narindrarangkura, P., Kim, M.S., Boren, S.A.: A scoping review of artificial intelligence algorithms in clinical decision support systems for internal medicine subspecialties. ACI Open **5**(2), 67–79 (2021)
12. Kong, G., Xu, D., Yang, J.: Clinical decision support systems: a review of knowledge representation and inference under uncertainties. IJCIS **1**(2), 159–167 (2008)
13. El-Sappagh, S., Elmogy, M.M.: Medical case based reasoning frameworks. Int. J. Decis. Supp. Syst. Technol. **8**(3), 31–62 (2016)
14. Tricco, A.C., et al.: PRISMA extension for scoping reviews (PRISMA-ScR): checklist and explanation. Ann. Intern. Med. **169**(7), 467–473 (2018)
15. Moher, D., et al.: Preferred reporting items for systematic review and meta-analysis protocols (PRISMA-P) 2015 statement. Syst. Rev. **4**(1), 1–9 (2015)
16. Jenuwine, E.S., Floyd, J.A.: Comparison of Medical Subject Headings and text-word searches in MEDLINE to retrieve studies on sleep in healthy individuals. J. Med. Libr. Assoc.: JMLA **92**(3), 349–353 (2004)
17. Ouzzani, M., Hammady, H., Fedorowicz, Z., Elmagarmid, A.: Rayyan-a web and mobile app for systematic reviews. Syst. Rev. **5**(210), 1–10 (2016)
18. Clarivate: KeyWords Plus generation, creation, and change. https://support.clarivate.com/ScientificandAcademicResearch/s/article/KeyWords-Plus-generation-creation-and-changes?language=en_US. Accessed 10 Mar 2022
19. HRCS Online: Health Categories - HRCS Online. https://hrcsonline.net/health-categories/. Accessed 28 Mar 2022
20. Chang, P.C., Lin, J.J., Liu, C.H.: An attribute weight assignment and particle swarm optimization algorithm for medical database classifications. Comput. Methods Programs Biomed. **107**(3), 382–392 (2012)
21. Saraiva, R.M., Bezerra, J., Perkusich, M., Almeida, H., Siebra, C.: A hybrid approach using case-based reasoning and rule-based reasoning to support cancer diagnosis: a pilot study. Stud. Health Technol. Inform. **216**, 862–866 (2015)
22. McSherry, D.: Conversational case-based reasoning in medical decision making. Artif. Intell. Med. **52**(2), 59–66 (2011)
23. El-Sappagh, S., Elmogy, M., Riad, A.M.: A fuzzy-ontology-oriented case-based reasoning framework for semantic diabetes diagnosis. Artif. Intell. Med. **65**(3), 179–208 (2015)
24. Ehtesham, H., Safdari, R., Mansourian, A., Tahmasebian, S., Mohammadzadeh, N., Pourshahidi, S.: Developing a new intelligent system for the diagnosis of oral medicine with case-based reasoning approach. Oral Dis. **25**(6), 1555–1563 (2019)

25. López, B., Pous, C., Gay, P., Pla, A., Sanz, J., Brunet, J.: eXiT*CBR: a framework for case-based medical diagnosis development and experimentation. Artif. Intell. Med. **51**(2), 81–91 (2011)
26. Ahmed, M.U., Begum, S., Funk, P., Xiong, N., von Scheele, B.: A multi-module case-based biofeedback system for stress treatment. Artif. Intell. Med. **51**(2), 107–115 (2011)
27. Joyia, G.J., Akram, M.U., Akbar, C.N., Maqsood, M.F.: Evolution of health level-7. In: Proceedings of the 2018 International, pp. 118–123 (2018)
28. Marcos, M., Maldonado, J.A., Martínez-Salvador, B., Boscá, D., Robles, M.: Interoperability of clinical decision-support systems and electronic health records using archetypes: a case study in clinical trial eligibility. J. Biomed. Inform. **46**(4), 676–689 (2013)
29. Barigou, B.N., Barigou, F., Benchehida, C., Atmani, B., Belalem, G.: The design of a cloud-based clinical decision support system prototype: management of drugs intoxications in childhood. Int. J. Healthc. Inf. Syst. Inform. **13**(4), 28–48 (2018)
30. Gu, D., Liang, C., Zhao, H.: A case-based reasoning system based on weighted heterogeneous value distance metric for breast cancer diagnosis. Artif. Intell. Med. **77**, 31–47 (2017)
31. Yin, Z., Dong, Z., Lu, X., Yu, S., Chen, X., Duan, H.: A clinical decision support system for the diagnosis of probable migraine and probable tension-type headache based on case-based reasoning. J. Headache Pain **16**(1), 1–9 (2015). https://doi.org/10.1186/s10194-015-0512-x
32. Lamy, J.B., Sekar, B., Guezennec, G., Bouaud, J., Seroussi, B.: Explainable artificial intelligence for breast cancer: a visual case-based reasoning approach. Artif. Intell. Med. **94**, 42–53 (2019)
33. Brown, D., Aldea, A., Harrison, R., Martin, C., Bayley, I.: Temporal case-based reasoning for type 1 diabetes mellitus bolus insulin decision support. Artif. Intell. Med. **85**, 28–42 (2018)

Author Index

Printed in the United States
by Baker & Taylor Publisher Services